IMPORTANT

HERE IS YOUR REGISTRATION CODE TO AC

YOUR PREMIUM McGRAW-HILL ONLINE R

D1302766

For key premium online resources you need THIS CODE to gain access. Once the code is entered, you will be able to use the Web resources for the length of your course.

If your course is using **WebCT** or **Blackboard**, you'll be able to use this code to access the McGraw-Hill content within your instructor's online course.

Access is provided if you have purchased a new book. If the registration code is missing from this book, the registration screen on our Website, and within your WebCT or Blackboard course, will tell you how to obtain your new code.

Registering for McGraw-Hill Online Resources

TO gain access to your McGraw-Hill web resources simply follow the steps below:

1. USE YOUR WEB BROWSER TO GO TO: **www.mhhe.com/seyler**
2. CLICK ON **FIRST TIME USER**.
3. ENTER THE REGISTRATION CODE* PRINTED ON THE TEAR-OFF BOOKMARK ON THE RIGHT.
4. AFTER YOU HAVE ENTERED YOUR REGISTRATION CODE, CLICK **REGISTER**.
5. FOLLOW THE INSTRUCTIONS TO SET-UP YOUR PERSONAL UserID AND PASSWORD.
6. WRITE YOUR UserID AND PASSWORD DOWN FOR FUTURE REFERENCE. KEEP IT IN A SAFE PLACE.

TO GAIN ACCESS to the McGraw-Hill content in your instructor's **WebCT** or **Blackboard** course simply log in to the course with the UserID and Password provided by your instructor. Enter the registration code exactly as it appears in the box to the right when prompted by the system. You will only need to use the code the first time you click on McGraw-Hill content.

Thank you, and welcome to your McGraw-Hill online Resources!

* YOUR REGISTRATION CODE CAN BE USED ONLY ONCE TO ESTABLISH ACCESS. IT IS NOT TRANSFERABLE.

0-07-297876-7 T/A SEYLER: READ, REASON, WRITE, 7E

· REGISTRATION CODE ·

8WAP-90MB-ZJ5G-502S-8LLT

READ
Reason
Write

AN ARGUMENT TEXT AND READER

SEVENTH EDITION

Dorothy U. Seyler

Boston   Burr Ridge, IL   Dubuque, IA   Madison, WI   New York   San Francisco   St. Louis
Bangkok   Bogotá   Caracas   Kuala Lumpur   Lisbon   London   Madrid   Mexico City
Milan   Montreal   New Delhi   Santiago   Seoul   Singapore   Sydney   Taipei   Toronto

The McGraw·Hill Companies

Higher Education

READ, REASON, WRITE

Published by McGraw-Hill, a business unit of The McGraw-Hill Companies, Inc. 1221 Avenue of the Americas, New York, NY, 10020. Copyright © 2005, 2002, 1999, 1995, 1991, 1987, 1984 by The McGraw-Hill Companies, Inc. All rights reserved. No part of this publication may be reproduced or distributed in any form or by any means, or stored in a database or retrieval system, without the prior written consent of The McGraw-Hill Companies, Inc., including, but not limited to, any network or other electronic storage or transmission, or broadcast for distance learning.

Some ancillaries, including electronic and print components, may not be available to customers outside the United States.

1 2 3 4 5 6 7 8 9 0 DOC/DOC 0 9 8 7 6 5 4

ISBN 0-07-287372-8

Editor-in-chief: Emily Barrosse
Publisher and executive editor: Lisa Moore
Developmental editor: Joshua Feldman
Marketing manager: Lori DeShazo
Senior media producer: Todd Vaccaro
Production editor: Leslie LaDow
Production supervisor: Tandra Jorgensen
Cover designer: Cassandra Chu
Interior designer: Maureen McCutcheon
Photo research coordinator: Natalia Peschiera
Art editor: Katherine McNab

Cover image: Mario Carreno, "Geometrico, Azules, Rojos, Negros y Blancos," 1974.
Collection of Emilio Ellena/Kactus Foto/Superstock.

This book was set in 10/12 Palatino, PMS Color 307, by Carlisle Communications, Ltd. and printed on acid-free 45# New Era Matte by R.R. Donnelley and Sons, Inc.

Library of Congress Cataloging-in-Publication Data
Seyler, Dorothy U.
 Read, reason, write / Dorothy U. Seyler.--7th ed.
   p. cm.
 Includes bibliographical references and index.
 ISBN 0-07-287372-8 (pbk.)
  1. English language—Rhetoric. 2. Persuasion (Rhetoric) 3. College readers. 4. Report writing. I. Title.
PE1408.S464 2004
808'.0427—dc22
                                                            2004049980

www.mhhe.com

About the Author

DOROTHY U. SEYLER is Professor of English at Northern Virginia Community College. A Phi Beta Kappa graduate of the College of William and Mary, Dr. Seyler holds advanced degrees from Columbia University and the State University of New York at Albany. She taught at Ohio State University, the University of Kentucky, and Nassau Community College before moving with her family to Northern Virginia.

She has coauthored *Introduction to Literature* in its second edition. She is the author of *Understanding Argument*, of *Doing Research* (second edition), of *The Reading Context* and *Steps to College Reading*, both in their third editions, and of *Patterns of Reflection*, now in its fifth edition. In addition, Professor Seyler has published articles in professional journals and popular magazines. She enjoys tennis and golf, traveling, and writing about both sports and travel.

Contents

Preface

I have written in previous prefaces to *Read, Reason, Write* that being asked to prepare a new edition is much like being asked back to a friend's house: although you count on it, you are still delighted when the invitation comes. Well, the sixth edition kept old friendships and made new ones as well, so here I am, writing a preface to the seventh edition, twenty years after first presenting this text to college students and their instructors. Over these twenty years, *Read, Reason, Write* has grown in size—most books have—but also in stature within the teaching community and in its value to students. Of course, neither this text nor I am getting older, only better, as this seventh edition demonstrates!

Although some important new material strengthens the seventh edition, the essential character of *Read, Reason, Write* remains the same. This text still combines instruction in critical reading and analysis, argument, and research strategies with a rich collection of readings providing practice for these skills and new ideas and insights for readers. A key purpose of *Read, Reason, and Write* remains to help students develop into better writers of the kinds of papers they are most often required to write, both in college and in the workplace: summaries, analyses, reports, arguments, and documented essays. To fulfill this key purpose, the text must do more than provide instruction and opportunities for practice; the text must demonstrate to student writers that these seemingly disparate skills connect in important ways. *Read, Reason, Write* remains a new kind of text because it shows students the interrelatedness of reading, analytic, argumentative, and research skills and seeks, in connecting these skills, always to extend each student's critical thinking ability.

FEATURES OF *READ, REASON, WRITE*

- An emphasis on good reading skills for effective arguing and writing.
- Instruction, models, and practice in understanding reading context and analyzing elements of style.
- Instruction, models, and practice in writing summaries and book reviews.
- Focus on argument as contextual: written (or spoken) to a specific audience with the expectation of counterarguments.
- Explanations and models of various types of arguments that bridge the gap between an understanding of logical structures and the ways we actually write arguments.

- Presentation of Aristotelian, Toulmin, and Rogerian models of argument as useful guides to analyzing the arguments of others and organizing one's own arguments.
- In-depth discussion of logical argument, including extensive coverage of induction and deduction.
- Guidelines and revision boxes throughout the text that provide an easy reference for students.
- Instruction, models, and practice in researching and evaluating sources and in composing and documenting researched papers.
- A rich collection of readings, both timely and classic, that provide examples of the varied uses of language and strategies for argument.
- A brief but comprehensive introduction to reading and analyzing literature, found in the Appendix.

NEW FEATURES IN THE SEVENTH EDITION

This new edition keeps the key features of the previous editions while making some important changes that will make this seventh edition even more helpful to both students and instructors. The significant changes include:

- A new, more inviting design to provide ease of use for instructors and students.
- A new chapter devoted to visual argument.
- Two readings at the end of each of the first eight chapters that provide the opportunity for (1) analysis of style, argument strategies and logic, or visuals and statistics or (2) debate of an issue. Issues for debate include teen drinking, euthanasia, animal rights, and "who earns what and why."
- A reorganization of Section II to provide greater coverage of argument. Section II now features six chapters: an introduction to the nature of argument, ending in a debate on the teen drinking age; instruction in writing arguments that moves through the writing process with students; more information on argument with a close look at induction, deduction, and logical fallcies; instruction and practice in reading, analyzing, and writing definition arguments and position papers; instruction and practice in reading, analyzing, and writing with statistics and visuals; and instruction and practice in reading, analyzing, and writing causal and problem/solution arguments.
- Step-by-step guides to writing various kinds of arguments and models of those arguments to help students complete their assignments in argument.
- An updated guide to writing documented essays, complete with documentation models based on the latest edition of the *MLA Handbook*.
- Eleven new or significantly changed and updated chapters of readings. There are new chapter topics such as bioethics, sports controversies, and the post-9/11 American landscape; of the 68 readings 50 are new, giving all chapters a new and more current focus.

- The addition of prereading questions to initiate student involvement in the reading to come.
- A streamlining and refocusing of questions following the readings that guide students through (1) reading for understanding, (2) analyzing and thinking critically about the reading, and then (3) reflecting and writing on the reading. Often questions for reflection and possible writing encourage students to seek additional information, perhaps through an online search.

Our times demand that we understand what we read, that we think critically about others' ideas and argue effectively in support of our own, and that we can sort through the wealth of available information and ideas, rejecting what is unreliable and synthesizing the useful with what we already understand. We live in an information society, a society in which many people make their livings by collecting, sorting, transmitting, and reacting to a constant flow of pictures, numbers, and words. In this new century, those who learn to read, reason, and write effectively will be successful in their work. Those who enjoy exercising these skills will be happy in that work.

ACKNOWLEDGMENT

No book of value is written alone. I am pleased to acknowledge the contributions of others in shaping this text. My thanks are due—as always—to the library staff at the Annandale Campus of Northern Virginia Community College, especially to Marian Delmore, Ruth Stanton, Ellen Westman, and Carol Simwell, who have helped me locate needed information and have kept me current with the new technology. Mary Atkins, our department secretary, has my gratitude for her patient help with technology issues. I would also like to thank students Ian Habel, Monica Becker, Chris Brown, Laura Mullins, Alan Peterson, Monica Mitchell, and Connie Childress, whose essays grace this text. They should be proud of the skill and effort they put into their writing. My thanks as well to Jimmie Killingsworth and Joanna Gibson of Texas A&M University, organizers of highly successful focus groups on the previous edition of this text. I would also like to thank the participants in these focus groups: Ruth Alfred; Kathryn Julia Bedard; Abby Bowers; Joel Buenaflor; Margaret Douglas Carstarphen; Nina Casetra; Dragana Djordjevic; Kate Everett; Nina French; Noelle M. Howland; Nick Lawrence; Samantha Marsh; Ana Martinez; Nicole Eve McDaniel; Gina E. Opdycke; Jungsik Park; Sarah Peters; Anthony Rintela; Ryan Sanders; Sarah C. Spring; Brad Thomas; Alina Walker; and Dong Shin Yi.

I appreciate as well the many good suggestions of the following reviewers of the seventh edition:

Ann L. Alderman
Holy Names College

Valerie Auer
University of Texas at Dallas

Martin Behr
California State University, Northridge

Paul Birznieks
Montgomery College

Geoffrey A. Cross
University of Louisville

Jo Ann Dadisman
West Virginia University

Tracy Druckart
Humboldt State University

Ruth R. Haber
Worcester State College

Kathleen Lawson
Oakland University

Paul W. Lundburg
Fergus Falls Community College

Jennifer Nelson
*Community College of Southern
   Nevada*

Samuel B. Olorounto
New River Community College

Nelson Sager
Sul Ross State

Amy Jo Swing
Lake Superior College

Grace Talusan
Tufts University

Patricia Teel
Victor Valley Community College

Virginia Wagner
Mendocino College

My former editor Steve Pensinger needs to be remembered for steering me, with good sense and good humor, through four editions of this book. I am also grateful to Tim Julet and Alexis Walker for guidance through the fifth edition and to Chris Narozny, developmental editor of the sixth edition. My hat's off to Lisa Moore, executive editor for the sixth and now the seventh edition, and to Joshua Feldman, developmental editor for the seventh edition. I have been blessed with a chorus of voices enriching this text over its lifetime.

I'll close once again by dedicating this book to my daughter Ruth who, in spite of a demanding career and busy social life, continues to give generously of her time reading drafts and possible essays for each new edition. It is my wish for students that they come to understand what she now realizes: that it is the liberal education that makes continued growth of the human spirit both possible and pleasurable.

Dorothy U. Seyler

Critical Reading and Analysis

SECTION

1

Writers and Their Sources

WRITING, READING, AND THE CONTEXTS OF ARGUMENT

Arguments are everywhere! Do you agree? Well, what about textbooks, you counter. They are designed to inform, not to present an argument. True—to a degree. On the other hand, the author makes choices about what's important to include and how students should go about the business of learning the material of a particular course. Even writing primarily designed to inform says to readers: Do it my way! Think about these ideas as I would! Well, what about novels or personal essays, you "argue." Surely they are not arguments. A good point—to a degree. The ideas about human life and experience that appear in works we can label "expressive" are more subtle, more indirect, than the points we meet head-on in an argument. Still, expressive writing gives us ideas or ways of seeing the world. Perhaps we need to recognize that writing strategies and purposes spread along a continuum; they do not fit into neat categories.

You can accept the larger scope of argument and still be wise to expect that in your current course on argument—or critical thinking—you probably will not be asked to write a short story or a personal essay. You might, though, be asked to write a summary or a style analysis, so you will need to think about how those writing tasks connect to the world of argument. Count on this: You will be asked to write! Why work on your writing skills? Here are some good answers to this question:

- Communication skills are the single most important skill sought by employers.
- The better a writer you become, the better reader you will become—of the many books you will be assigned throughout your college experience.
- The more confident a writer you become, the more efficiently you will handle written assignments in all your courses.
- Because writing is an act of discovery, the more you write, the more you will learn about who you are and what really matters to you.

You will probably be given a variety of writing assignments in your course. Pay close attention to each assignment so that you will know what sort of writing you will be expected to present. To help you learn the conventions of different types of writing for different audiences, this text includes a variety of articles: informative essays, editorials, articles from scholarly journals, book reviews. When faced with writing, think about what role each assignment calls for. Are you expected to be a student demonstrating knowledge, a citizen arguing for tougher drunk-driving laws, or a scholar presenting the results of research? Understand that any writer, including you, can take on different roles, writing for different audiences, using different strategies to reach each audience.

RESPONSES TO SOURCES

If this is a text about *writing* arguments, why does it contain so many readings, you may wonder. There are good reasons for the collection of readings you find here:

- College and the workplace will demand that you learn complex information and ideas through reading. This text will give you practice in reading more challenging works.
- You may need to learn to read somewhat differently than the way you are used to. You will need to read to learn. You will need to think critically about what you read. Skimming will not give you the knowledge you will be tested on; skipping sections because you don't feel like reading is not a success strategy in college or the workplace.
- You will use your reading as a basis for writing. In other writing classes, you may have based your essays on your interests, pet peeves, or career goals. Now you will be writing based in some way on a source or sources you have been assigned or have selected in response to an assignment. The focus of attention shifts from you to your subject, a subject others have debated before you. You will need to understand the issue, to think carefully about the view of others on the issue, and then to develop your own thinking.

To explore further a writer's responses to sources, let's begin by examining "The Gettysburg Address," Abraham Lincoln's famous speech dedicating the Civil War battlefield. We can use this document to see the various ways writers respond—in writing—to the writing of others.

THE GETTYSBURG ADDRESS | ABRAHAM LINCOLN

Fourscore and seven years ago our fathers brought forth on this continent a new nation, conceived in liberty and dedicated to the proposition that all men are created equal. Now we are engaged in a great civil war, testing whether that nation, or any nation so conceived and so dedicated, can long endure. We are met on a great battlefield of that war. We have come to dedicate a portion of that field as a final resting place for those who here gave their lives that that nation might live. It is altogether fitting and proper that we should do this. But, in a larger sense, we cannot dedicate—we cannot consecrate—we cannot hallow—this ground. The brave men, living and dead, who struggled here have consecrated it far above our poor power to add or to detract. The world will little note nor long remember what we say here, but it can never forget what they did here. It is for us, the living, rather to be dedicated here to the unfinished work which they who fought here have thus far so nobly advanced. It is rather for us to be here dedicated to the great task remaining before us—that from these honored dead we take increased devotion to that cause for which they gave the last full measure of devotion; that we here highly resolve that these dead shall not have died in vain; that this nation, under God, shall have a new birth of freedom; and that government of the people, by the people, for the people shall not perish from the earth.

Do You Like It?
What Did You Gain from It?   THE PERSONAL RESPONSE

The English instructor teaching a collection of famous speeches might ask her class to write a paragraph in response to one of these questions. Both questions ask students to express their personal values, tastes, and interests. Here, for example, is one young student's response to Lincoln's speech:

> I liked it. "The Gettysburg Address" helped me to understand what it's like to care about something and fight for it. I wonder, though, how many people today care enough about their country or some principle to go to war to protect it.

Personal response writing should not be offered when the assignment calls for analysis or argument.

What Does It Say? How Could It
Be Summarized or Paraphrased?   THE RESPONSE TO CONTENT

Instructors often ask students to *summarize* or *paraphrase* their reading of a complex chapter, a supplementary text, a difficult poem, or a series of journal articles on library reserve. Frequently, book report assignments specify that summary and evaluation be combined. Your purpose in writing a summary is to show your understanding of the work's main ideas and of the relationships among those ideas. If you can put what you have read into your own words and focus on the text's chief points, then you have command of that material. Here is a sample restatement of Lincoln's "Address":

> Our nation was initially built on a belief in liberty and equality, but its future is now being tested by civil war. It is appropriate for us to dedicate this battlefield, but those who fought here have dedicated it better than we. We should dedicate ourselves to continue the fight to maintain this nation and its principles of government.

Sometimes it is easier to recite or quote famous or difficult works than to state, more simply and in your own words, what has been written. The ability to summarize or paraphrase reflects both reading and writing skills. For more coverage of writing summaries, see pages 13–16; for more coverage of paraphrases, see pages 16–17.

How Is It Written?
How Does It Compare with Another Work? THE ANALYTIC RESPONSE

You will find that summary requirements are often combined with analysis or evaluation, as in a book report. Most of the time you will be expected to *do something* with what you have read, and to summarize or paraphrase will be insufficient. Frequently you will be asked to analyze a work—that is, to explain the elements of structure and style that a writer has chosen. You will want to examine sentence patterns, organization, metaphors, and other techniques selected by the writer to convey attitude and give force to ideas. Developing your skills in analysis will make you both a better reader and a better writer.

Many writers have examined Lincoln's word choice, sentence structure, and choice of metaphors to make clear the sources of power in this speech.[*] If you were to analyze Lincoln's style, you would want to emphasize, among other elements, his effective use of *tricolon:* the threefold repetition of a grammatical structure, with the three points placed in ascending order of significance.

> Lincoln uses two effective tricolons in his brief address. The first focuses on the occasion for his speech, the dedication of the battlefield: "we cannot dedicate—we cannot consecrate—we cannot hallow. . . ." The best that the living can do is formally dedicate; only those who died there for the principle of liberty are capable of making the battlefield "hallow." The second tricolon presents Lincoln's concept of democratic government, a government "of the people, by the people, for the people." The purpose of government—"for the people"—resides in the position of greatest significance.

---

[*]See, for example, Gilbert Highet's essay, "The Gettysburg Address," in *The Clerk of Oxenford: Essays on Literature and Life* (New York: Oxford UP, 1954), to which I am indebted in the following analysis.

A second type of analysis, a comparison of styles of two writers, is a frequent variation of the analytic assignment. By focusing on similarities and differences in writing styles, you can see more clearly the role of choice in writing and may also examine the issue of the degree to which differences in purpose affect style. One student, for example, produced a thoughtful and interesting study of Lincoln's style in contrast to that of Martin Luther King, Jr., as revealed in his "I Have a Dream" speech (see pages 675–77):

> Although Lincoln's sentence structure is tighter than King's and King likes the rhythms created by repetition, both men reflect their familiarity with the King James Bible in their use of its cadences and expressions. Instead of saying eighty-seven years ago, Lincoln, seeking solemnity, selects the Biblical expression "Fourscore and seven years ago." Similarly, King borrows from the Bible and echoes Lincoln when he writes "Five score years ago."

Is It Logical?
Is It Adequately Developed?
Does It Achieve Its Purpose? THE JUDGMENT OR EVALUATION RESPONSE

Even when the stated purpose of an essay is "pure" analysis, the analysis implies a judgment. We analyze Lincoln's style because we recognize that "The Gettysburg Address" is a great piece of writing and we want to see how it achieves its power. On other occasions, judgment is the stated purpose for close reading and analysis. The columnist who challenges a previously published editorial has analyzed the editorial and has found it flawed. The columnist may fault the editor's logic or lack of adequate or relevant support for the editorial's main idea. In each case the columnist makes a negative judgment about the editorial, but that judgment is an informed one based on the columnist's knowledge of language and the principles of good argument.

Part of the ability to judge wisely lies in recognizing each writer's purpose. It would be inappropriate to assert that Lincoln's address is weakened by its lack of facts about the battle. The historian's purpose is to record the number killed or to analyze the generals' military tactics. Lincoln's purpose was different.

> As Lincoln reflected upon this young country's being torn apart by civil strife, he saw the dedication of the Gettysburg battlefield as an opportunity to challenge the country to fight for its survival and the principles upon which it was founded. The result was a brief but moving speech that appropriately examines the connection between the life and death of soldiers and the birth and survival of a nation.

These sentences establish a basis for an analysis of Lincoln's train of thought and use of metaphors, but this analysis, and positive judgment, is grounded in an understanding of Lincoln's purpose and the context in which he spoke.

How Does It Help Me to Understand Other Works, Ideas, Events?   THE RESEARCH RESPONSE

Frequently you will read not to analyze or evaluate but rather to use the source as part of learning about a particular subject. Lincoln's address is significant for the Civil War historian both as an event of that war and as an influence on our thinking about that war. "The Gettysburg Address" is also vital to the biographer's study of Lincoln's life or to the literary critic's study either of famous speeches or of the Bible's influence on English writing styles. Thus Lincoln's brief speech is a valuable source for students in a variety of disciplines; it becomes part of their research process. Able researchers study it carefully, analyze it thoroughly, place it in its proper historical, literary, and personal contexts, and use it to develop their own arguments.

To begin practice in reading and responding to sources, study the following article by Mark Steinberg. The exercises that follow will check your reading skills and your understanding of the various responses to reading just discussed. Use the prereading questions to become engaged with each text.

"NUMBED DOWN" IN AMERICA | MARK STEINBERG

A former associate deputy attorney general and director of the Office for National Security in the Department of Justice, Mark Steinberg (b. 1945) is a Los Angeles lawyer with a practice focused on intellectual property, antitrust, and general civil litigation. His article was published on June 17, 2000, in the *Washington Post*.

PREREADING QUESTIONS How does the author introduce his topic in the opening four paragraphs? How does he use this material later in his essay?

1   A college basketball coach who has amassed a phenomenal winning record on the basis of repeated intimidation and physical abuse of young players, officials and college administrators is told he can keep his job so long as he is not caught again doing what he should not have done even once.

2   The former members of a high school academic decathlon team who catapulted their school to glory, then shame, by cheating their way to victory in a national competition say that their biggest mistake was getting caught.

3   In an anonymous Internet posting in a chat room for law firm associates, a young lawyer muses about what to do if one is nearing but might not reach the billed-hour minimum required to qualify for an annual bonus: "I guess it would be easy enough to take on a pro bono case at year end and just pad your hours on that matter."

4   Another contributor to the same chat room, who identifies himself as a law student about to graduate, says: I "found out that all these years everyone—and I mean 80 percent of the class here at my law school—had been cheating. I'm a commuter student who works full-time so I've been a little out of it, but apparently students pay others to write papers for them, ask fellow students

about exam questions before taking them (deliberately lying so they can take the same exam later), use cheat sheets etc."

5   These examples are points on a continuum, manifestations of another kind of crisis of values in America. This one is not about the morality or legality of abortion, the death penalty or birth control; it's about what conduct we should tolerate from those driven by the pursuit of success, whether on the basketball court, in academia or in business.

6   The question is worth discussing because the health of our social environment hinges on the answer. As more and more people come to see their jobs exclusively as vehicles for reaching the pot or medal of gold, our society in countless ways is becoming a less civil, less trustworthy, less pleasant place to be. We have begun to tolerate conduct that not so long ago we thought of—and responded to—as crude, immoral or just plain nasty.

7   The "numbing down" of our collective tolerance for mean, dishonest and abusive behavior is, in a way, a reflection of our own changing choices. Today there is an audience for gross violence, both real ("extreme" boxing) and simulated (professional wrestling). There is also an unparalleled reverence for wealth and those who produce it. Thus, in many of the major accounting, law and investment banking firms of America, the poorly kept secret is that there are "rainmakers"—people who produce disproportionate amounts of the firm's income—who can abuse and harass others without fear of reproach.

8   And finally—as Bobby Knight[1] can attest—today we are willing to pay an unnaturally high price for winning. That price goes well beyond the salary of someone like Knight, and even beyond our own diminished self-respect for continuing to fawn over him and others like him. The price we pay extends to something genuinely, unquestionably important: the values of those who see in these "winners" both the formula for achieving success and the rewards of it. Through abuse and bullying one can rise to the top and, *mirabile dictu*, when one reaches the top, one can abuse and bully to one's heart's content.

9   That the ultimate price has been paid, yet again, is evident from the remark of one of the young people in Bobby Knight's charge. When asked how the debate over Knight's future might be brought to an end, a player said: "I'm pretty sure if we won a lot of games and won a national championship, it would cure all of this."

10   But if there is a cure for all of this, it will not be found in more of the same. Rather, it will come from close, candid examination of whether the values we say we hold are the values we practice. Are money and winning the exclusive measures of our success? Does achieving great victory justify a breach of ethics, civility or humanity? Should we countenance abuse and harassment by powerful people because they are powerful? Do we value ourselves more for whom we stand above than for what we have accomplished in our own estimation? Is loyalty to an institution—whether a team, a partnership or a corporation—an unfashionable and embarrassing relic of the past?

---

[1]Knight, former basketball coach at Indiana University, was fired in the summer of 2000—Ed.

I grew up in a country in which I believed I knew how most of those who   11
lived and worked around me would answer these questions. I like to think that
I still do.

QUESTIONS FOR READING AND REASONING

1. What is the author's main idea? Where does he state it?
2. What are the causes of our "numbed down" condition?
3. What solutions does Steinberg offer?
4. How would you describe the tone of this essay? Is the author angry? Bemused? Analytic? Sad? Something else?
5. In his conclusion, Steinberg asks questions that he does not answer. Do you understand how readers are supposed to answer the questions? Is this strategy an effective conclusion? Why or why not?

QUESTIONS FOR REFLECTING AND WRITING

1. Would you describe the opening examples as revealing conduct that is "crude, immoral, or just plain nasty"? Write a paragraph answer to this question. Then consider: Which one of the different responses to reading is illustrated by your paragraph?
2. Do you agree with the author that we have developed a tolerance for behavior that is inconsistent with what we say we value? If you disagree, explain your position.
3. "The Gettysburg Address" is a valuable document for several kinds of research projects. For what kinds of projects would Steinberg's essay be useful? List several possibilities; be prepared to discuss your list with classmates.

ACTIVE READING: USE YOUR MIND!

Reading is not about looking at black marks on a page—or turning the pages as quickly as we can. Reading means constructing meaning from the marks on the page, getting a message. We read with our brains, not our eyes and hands! This concept is often underscored by the term *active reading.* To help you always achieve active reading, not passive page turning, follow these guidelines.

GUIDELINES for Active Reading

- **Understand your purpose in reading.** Do not just start turning pages to complete an assignment. Think first about your purpose. Are you reading for knowledge on which you will be tested? Focus on your purpose as you read, asking yourself, "What do I need to learn from this work?"

- **Reflect on the title before reading further.** Titles are the first words writers give us. Take time to look for clues in a title that may reveal the work's subject and perhaps the writer's approach or attitude as well. Henry Fairlie's title "The Idiocy of Urban Life," for example, tells you both Fairlie's subject (urban or city living) and his position (urban living is idiotic).

- **Become part of the writer's audience.** Not all writers have you and me in mind when they write. As an active reader, you need to "join" a writer's audience by learning about the writer, about the time in which the piece was written, and about the writer's expected audience. For readings in this text you are aided by introductory notes. These notes give you a *context* for reading; be sure to study them.

- **Predict what is coming.** Look for a writer's main idea or purpose statement. Study the work's organization. Then use this information to anticipate what is coming. When you read "There are three good reasons for requiring a dress code in schools," you know the writer will list *three* reasons.

- **Concentrate.** Slow down and give your full attention to reading. Watch for transition and connecting words that show you how the parts of a text connect. Read an entire article or chapter at one time—or you will need to start over to make sense of the entire piece.

- **Annotate as you read.** The more senses you use, the more active your involvement. That means marking the text as you read (or taking notes if the material is not yours). Underline key sentences, such as the writer's thesis. Then, in the margin, indicate that it is the thesis. With a series of examples (or reasons), label them and number them. When you look up a word's definition, write the definition in the margin next to the word. Draw diagrams to illustrate concepts; draw arrows to connect example to idea. Studies have shown that students who annotate their texts get higher grades. Do what successful students do.

- **Keep a reading journal.** In addition to annotating what you read, you may want to develop the habit of writing regularly in a journal. A reading journal gives you a place to note impressions and reflections on your reading, your initial reactions to assignments, and ideas you may use in your next writing.

EXERCISE: Active Reading

Read the following selection, noting the annotations that have been started for you. As you read, add your own annotations. Then write a journal entry—four to five sentences at least—to capture your reactions to the following column.

POLITICAL ADS AND THE VOTERS THEY ATTRACT | RICHARD MORIN

A journalist with the *Washington Post*, Richard Morin writes a regular Sunday column titled "Unconventional Wisdom" that presents interesting new information from the social sciences. The following column appeared November 23, 2003.

Even though it pains me to report it, those <u>negative political advertise-</u> <u>ments</u> designed to scare the pants off us appear to work quite well. But here's a surprise—so do those positive ads filled with happy children and cascading violins.

What's the connection? Both depend on manipulating the emotions of viewers.

What's more, emotion-drenched political ads are most effective among so-phisticated voters, who probably would be the most chagrined to learn that they're suckers for political mudslinging and cheerleading, claims Ted Brader, a political science professor and researcher at the Institute for Social Research at the University of Michigan.

"Emotions are so central to what makes us tick," Brader said. "Political sci-entists for years have basically ignored them. But if you think about what causes us to do anything in life, political or otherwise, there are always strong emo-tions involved."

His study, which he is expanding into a book, began as research for his PhD at Harvard University. Brader recruited 286 voting-age men and women in 11 Massachusetts communities during the weeks leading up to the 1998 Democ-ratic gubernatorial primary. The race pitted incumbent Attorney General Scott Harshbarger against former state senator Patricia McGovern.

Test subjects were randomly assigned to one of four groups. Each group watched a half-hour local news broadcast that featured one of four seem-ingly genuine 30-second campaign ads that Brader had prepared. Two ads were positive in tone and two were negative. The names of the candidates were alternated so that each one was featured an equal number of times in the ads.

The scripts for the two positive ads were identical. What was different were the accompanying sounds and images. One ad featured uplifting "cues"—symphonic music and warm, colorful images of children intended to inspire an even more enthusiastic reaction to the upbeat message—while the other used bland visual and audio enhancements.

The scripts for the two negative ads also were the same. But one featured tense, discordant music and grainy pictures of crime scenes to create a sense of fear. The other ad lacked the scary special effects.

The test subjects answered a survey before and after the experiment that measured, among other things, interest in the campaign and candidate pref-erence. And yes, after the study the participants were let in on the secret. "They were 'debriefed' after their participation and given a written explana-tion that the political ads they saw were completely fictitious, made by me for the study and not by the candidates, and there was not necessarily any con-nection between what is said in the ads and the candidates' actual positions," Brader said.

It's good that he did eventually 'fess up, because the enhanced ads worked better than Brader or his faculty advisers suspected they would. When enthu-siasm cues were added to a positive script, the test subjects' self-reported likelihood to vote on Election Day was a whopping 29 percentage points

[margin notes:]
1 topic

Note: Both types of ads work—why?

2

3

4

5

6

7

8

9

10

higher than those of subjects who saw the positive ad without the emotion-enhancing cues.

11   The negative ad with fear-inducing cues was particularly effective in persuading viewers to vote for the candidate promoted in the ad. Nearly 10 percent of those who saw the "fear" ad switched allegiance, and 20 to 25 percent were less certain of their choice after seeing their favored candidate dragged through the mud.

12   Those exposed to fear cues also could remember more details of related news stories shown in the broadcast. It also made them more likely to want to obtain more information about the candidates, suggesting one benefit to negative ads: "They may scare people into thinking" about political campaigns, Brader said.

13   Brader also found that better-informed, better-educated voters were more susceptible to fear-inducing and enthusiasm-enhancing ads than less-knowledgeable voters. "That really contradicts the traditional claim that emotional appeals work primarily on the ignorant masses," or those who are otherwise easily led, he said.

14   Why are smarties so susceptible to emotional ads? Brader doesn't know. It could be, he said, that such ads "resonate with people who are already emotional about politics to begin with because they have a vested interest."

15   For political consultants, this is news they can use. "Candidates should aim positive ads at their base of support and fear ads at undecided and opposing voters," Brader advised. "Front-runners, incumbents in times of peace and prosperity, and members of the majority party in a district should rely principally on enthusiasm. Their opponents—trailing candidates, challengers, members of the minority party—should be drawn to the use of fear."

UNDERSTANDING YOUR SOURCES

Readers will always expect accurate, fair, and sensitive uses of sources. An inaccurate summary does not serve its purpose. A passage that is misquoted or quoted out of context makes readers question your credibility. So, after reading and annotating, develop your understanding of a source more fully by doing a preliminary analysis that answers the following questions:

1. *What is the work's primary purpose? Does it combine purposes?* Remember that texts can be classified as expressive (evoking feelings), expository (imparting information), or persuasive (arguing for a position). We can also distinguish between a serious purpose and a humorous one, remembering that humor can be used to advance a serious topic. Remember, too, that these purposes shade into one another. Arguments appeal to emotions, and passionate fiction can teach us about human life and experience. You may assume that a textbook's primary purpose is to give information, but keep in mind that the textbook can take a position on various conflicts within the field.

2. *What is the thesis, the main idea of the work?* At times the best way to under-stand a text's thesis is to first ask, "What is the subject?" Then ask, "What does the author assert about that subject, or want me to understand about that subject?" Stating the thesis as a complete sentence will help you move from subject to assertion. You may find one or two sentences that state the work's thesis, but keep in mind that sometimes the thesis is implied, not stated.

3. *How is the thesis developed and supported?* Consider: Does the writer present a series of examples to illustrate the main idea? Or blend reasons and evi-dence to develop an argument? Does the writer organize chronologically? Set up a contrast pattern or make an analogy? Explain causes? Observing both the type of support and its organization will help you see how the parts fit together. When you "know what it says," you can write a summary or be-gin to analyze or judge the work.

WRITING SUMMARIES

Preparing a good summary is not always as easy as it looks. *A summary briefly restates, in your own words, the main points of a work in a way that does not misrepre-sent or distort the original.* A good summary shows your grasp of main ideas and your ability to express them clearly. You need to condense the original while giv-ing all key ideas appropriate attention. As a student you may be assigned a sum-mary to:

- Show that you have read and understood assigned works ("Prepare a sum-mary of each essay on the reading list").
- Complete a test question ("What kinds of political ads are effective?").
- Have a record of what you have read for future study or to prepare for class discussion.
- Explain the main ideas in a work that you will also examine in some other way, such as in a book review or a refutation essay.

If you are writing summaries of assigned readings in your journal, be sure to separate them from personal responses that you also record. When assigned a summary, pay careful attention to word choice. Avoid judgment words, such as: "Brown then proceeds to develop the *silly* idea that. . . ." Follow these guidelines for writing good summaries.

GUIDELINES for Writing Summaries

1. **Write in a direct, objective style, using your own words.** Use few, if any, direct quotations, probably none in a one-paragraph summary.

2. **Begin with a reference to the writer (full name) and the title of the work and then state the writer's thesis.** (You may also want to include where and when the work was published.)

3. **Complete the summary by providing other key ideas.** Show the reader how the main ideas connect and relate to one another.

4. **Do not include specific examples, illustrations, or background sections.**

5. **Combine main ideas into fewer sentences than were used in the original.**

6. **Keep the parts of your summary in the same balance as you find in the original.** If the author devotes about 30 percent of the essay to one idea, that idea should get about 30 percent of the space in your summary.

7. **Select precise, accurate verbs to show the author's relationship to ideas.** Write Jones *argues*, Jones asserts, Jones *believes*. Do not use vague verbs that provide only a list of disconnected ideas. Do *not* write Jones *talks about*, Jones *goes on to say*.

8. **Do not make any judgments about the writer's style or ideas.** Do *not* include your personal reaction to the work.

EXERCISE: Summary

With these guidelines in mind, read the following two summaries of Mark Steinberg's "'Numbed Down' in America" (see pages 7–9). Then answer the question: What is flawed or weak about each summary? To aid your analysis, (1) underline or highlight all words or phrases that are inappropriate in each summary and (2) put the number of the guideline next to any passage that does not adhere to that guideline.

SUMMARY #1

I really thought that Mark Steinberg's "'Numbed Down' in America" (Washington Post, June 17, 2000) contained some interesting ideas about America's values crisis. Steinberg talks about Bobby Knight and some lawyers who cheated. He seems to think that Americans should not try to make money or win. I don't think he's right about this. But winning and making money aren't the only ways to measure success.

SUMMARY #2

In Mark Steinberg's "'Numbed Down' in America," published June 17, 2000, in the Washington Post, Steinberg talks about a crisis of values in America. He says that the problem is our conduct. He gives examples of Bobby Knight, a high school academic team, and some lawyers. He goes on to say that we are crude or immoral and only want to win and make money. He wonders if we should accept these values. He doesn't answer the questions he raises at the end of his essay.

Although we can agree that the writers of these summaries have read and basically understood most of Steinberg's essay, we can also find weaknesses in each summary. The second summary can be greatly improved by some eliminating, combining, and refocusing of ideas. Here is a much-improved version of summary 2:

REVISED SUMMARY #2
In Mark Steinberg's "'Numbed Down' in America," published June 17, 2000, in the <u>Washington Post</u>, he asserts that America is experiencing a crisis of values. Using several examples from school to sports to professionals, Steinberg shows that Americans have become too accepting of nasty and immoral behavior. We seem to be willing to tolerate this behavior because we have put too much emphasis on winning at any cost and making lots of money, by cheating if necessary. Steinberg hopes that Americans will reject crude and immoral behavior as inconsistent with the values that we say are important to us.

At times you may need to write a summary of a page or two rather than one paragraph. Frequently, long reports are preceded by a one-page summary. A longer summary may become part of an article-length review of an important book. Or instructors may want a longer summary of a lengthy or complicated article or text chapter. The following is an example from *Psychology Today* of a summary, written for nonspecialists, of a recent study in the social sciences.

THE TIES THAT UNBIND | AARON DALTON

Our cultural vocabulary indicates that marriages move one way—downhill. 1 The "honeymoon period" implies post-honeymoon strife; the "seven-year itch" suggests that we tire of our mate at year seven.

Now, Wright State University psychology professor Lawrence Kurdek, Ph. D., 2 confirms that our lexicon is accurate. His surveys of over 500 couples have revealed that most married couples experience a gradual but steady decline in marital quality over the four-year period after they tie the knot. Newlyweds tend to wear rose-colored glasses at first, says Kurdek, but reality kicks in after they see their partner drink from the milk carton or forget to take out the trash one too many times. Though happiness stabilizes after four years, it declines again around year seven. This dip is harder to explain, Kurdek says, but may stem from the tendency to reexamine life as time goes on.

Having kids is another factor: Pairs with biological children had lower mar- 3 ital quality than childless couples or those living with stepchildren, reports Kurdek in a recent issue of *Developmental Psychology*. "Caring for children may result in time taken away from the marriage," he says.

Not all spouses are destined for dissatisfaction, says Kurdek. To prevent 4 disappointment down the road, new couples should temper high expectations with a dose of reality; like any relationship, wedlock has its ups and downs.

Observe the differences between the longer summary of Lawrence Kurdek's work and the paragraph summary of Mark Steinberg's essay:

- Some key terms or ideas may be presented in direct quotation (see paragraph 3).

- When summarizing a report of research, explain the methods used by the researchers and the results of the study in some detail.
- Use appropriate transitional and connecting words ("Having kids is another factor") to show how the parts of the summary connect.
- Repeat the author's name ("says Kurdek") to keep the reader's attention on the work you are summarizing, not on you, the writer of the summary.

WRITING PARAPHRASES

Although the words *summary* and *paraphrase* are sometimes used interchangeably, they are not exact synonyms. Summary and paraphrase are alike in that they are both written responses to sources. They differ in *how* they respond and *why. Like a summary, a paraphrase is an objective restatement of someone's writing, but the purpose of a paraphrase is to clarify a complex passage or to include material from a source in your own writing.*

When using sources for research, you will incorporate some of their information and ideas in your own paper, in your own words, and with proper documentation. Usually each paraphrased passage is fairly brief and is blended in with your own thinking on the topic. When your purpose is to clarify a poem, a complex philosophical passage, or prose filled with figurative language, your paraphrase will be longer, maybe longer than the original. Here is an example: first a passage from British philosopher Bertrand Russell's "A Free Man's Worship," followed by a paraphrase. As you read Russell's passage, underline words or phrases you find confusing. Then, as you read the paraphrase, look back to the original to see how the writer has restated Russell's ideas.

FROM "A FREE MAN'S WORSHIP" | BERTRAND RUSSELL

[F]or Man, condemned to-day to lose his dearest, tomorrow himself to pass through the gate of darkness, it remains only to cherish, ere yet the blow falls, the lofty thoughts that ennoble his little day; disdaining the coward terrors of the slave to Fate, to worship at the shrine that his own hands have built; undismayed by the empire of chance, to preserve a mind free from the wanton tyranny that rules his outward life; proudly defiant of the irresistible forces that tolerate, for a moment, his knowledge and his condemnation, to sustain alone, a weary but unyielding Atlas [someone bearing a heavy load, as Atlas did, holding up the sky on his shoulders], the world that his own ideals have fashioned despite the trampling march of unconscious power.

PARAPHRASE OF THE PASSAGE BY RUSSELL

All that we can do, before we lose our loved ones and then face our own death, is to place value on the important ideas that mark humans as special creatures and give meaning to our lives. We must reject any fear of dying that would make us slaves to Fate and instead be proud of what we have accomplished. We must not be distressed by the powers of chance or blind luck. We must not let their control over much that happens to us keep us from maintaining a mind that is free, a mind that we use to think for ourselves. Keeping our minds free and embracing knowledge are ways to defy the powers of the universe over which we have no control. And so, even though we may at times grow weary of battling the blind forces of the universe, we continue to find strength in the interior world that we have shaped by our ideals.

Note, first, that the paraphrase is longer than the original. The goal is to clarify, not to highlight main ideas only. Second, the paraphrase clarifies the passage by turning Russell's one long sentence into several sentences and using simpler language. When you can state a writer's ideas in your own words, you have really understood the writer's ideas.

When you are asked the question "What does it say?" think about whether you need a summary or a paraphrase. When an instructor asks you to state, in your own words, the meaning of Lincoln's long concluding sentence in "The Gettysburg Address," the instructor wants a paraphrase. When an instructor asks you what an assigned essay is about, the instructor wants a summary.

ACKNOWLEDGING SOURCES INFORMALLY

You must always identify sources you are using and make clear to readers how you are using them. Identify each source by author and title and make clear your relationship to each source. What follows are some of the conventions of writing you need to use when writing about sources.

Referring to People and Sources

Readers in academic, professional, and other serious contexts expect writers to follow specific conventions of style when referring to authors and to various kinds of sources. Study the following guidelines and examples and then mark the next few pages for easy reference—perhaps by turning down a corner of the first and last pages.

References to People
- In a first reference, give the person's full name (both the given name and the surname): *Ellen Goodman, Robert J. Samuelson.* In second and subsequent references, use only the last name (surname): *Goodman, Samuelson.*
- Do not use Mr., Mrs., or Ms. Special titles such as President, Chief Justice, or Doctor may be used in the first reference with the person's full name.
- Never refer to an author by her or his first name. Write *Dickinson,* not *Emily; Whitman,* not *Walt.*

References to Titles of Works

Titles of works must *always* be written as titles. Titles are indicated by capitalization and by either quotation marks or underlining. (In handwritten or typed papers, italic type is represented by underlining. Even with the ease of shifting type fonts when using a computer, nonpublished works, such as your essays for courses, should contain underlining, not italic type.)

Guidelines for Capitalizing Titles

- The first and last words are capitalized.
- The first word of a subtitle is capitalized.
- All other words in titles are capitalized except
  - Articles (*a, an, the*).
  - Coordinating conjunctions (*and, or, but, for, nor, yet, so*).
  - Prepositions (e.g., *in, for, about*).

Titles Requiring Quotation Marks

Titles of works published within other works—within a book, magazine, or newspaper—are indicated by quotation marks.

Essays	"The Real Pregnancy Problem"
Short stories	"The Story of an Hour"
Poems	"To Daffodils"
Articles	"Choose Your Utopia"
Chapters	"Writers and Their Sources"
Lectures	"Crazy Mixed-Up Families"
TV episode	"Resolved: Drug Prohibition Has Failed" (one debate on the television show <u>Firing Line</u>)

Titles Requiring Underlining (Italics *in Print*)

Titles of works that are separate publications and, by extension, titles of items such as works of art and films are underlined.

Plays	<u>A Raisin in the Sun</u>
Novels	<u>War and Peace</u>
Nonfiction books	<u>Read, Reason, Write</u>
Book-length poems	<u>The Odyssey</u>
Magazines	<u>U.S. News & World Report</u>
Journals	<u>The New England Journal of Medicine</u>
Newspapers	<u>New York Times</u>
Films	<u>The Wizard of Oz</u>
Paintings	<u>The Birth of Venus</u>
Recordings	<u>Eine Kleine Nachtmusik</u>
TV programs	<u>Nightline</u>

Read the following article (published October 1, 1999, in the *Washington Post*) and respond by answering the questions that follow. Observe, as you read, how the author refers to the writer and source he uses to develop the article and how he presents material from the source. We will use this article as a guide to handling quotations.

THE REAL PREGNANCY PROBLEM | WILLIAM RASPBERRY

William Raspberry writes both local and syndicated columns each week, usually focusing on urban or race problems or issues regarding the poor.

1   America has been fulminating for years about the problem of teen pregnancy. Me too. A quick computer search turns up 37 columns in which I mention the phrase. Maggie Gallagher wishes we'd give it a rest.

2   She didn't say it quite so directly; she's not that rude. What she did say, in an intriguing new "report to the nation" from the Institute for American Values, is that the problems we lump under the rubric of "teen pregnancy" often are about something quite different.

3   Listen: "The teen birth rate is, and has been for many years, much lower today than it was in the 1950s and early 1960s, when many teens married and began their families young. It is the unwed birthrate that has grown rapidly enough to earn the label 'epidemic.' "

4   In other words, while we've been harping on "teen pregnancy," what really has been happening is a striking decline in the importance we place on marriage.

5   But isn't the problem "children having children"? Surely Gallagher wouldn't want us to encourage child marriages. Listen again to what Gallagher, also a syndicated columnist in addition to being on the institute staff, and her research team have to say in "The Age of Unwed Mothers: Is Teen Pregnancy the Problem?":

6   The bulk of today's teen pregnancy problem is less "children having children" than increasing numbers of young adult women having babies outside of marriage. . . . Unwed teen moms younger than 18 account for only 13 percent of babies born out of wedlock.

7   As a society, we aim a fair amount of public money and many strong words at the problem of 'teen pregnancy,' that is, at the 376,000 births in one recent year to single mothers under the age of 20. Yet we pay comparatively little attention—indeed it often seems that as a society we are stone-cold silent—regarding the 439,000 births that same year to single mothers in their early twenties.

8   Are we against the former but indifferent to the latter? If so, what is our reasoning? Consider the prospects for a typical 20- or 22-year-old single mother and her baby. Are they really that much different, or better, than those facing an 18- or 19-year-old single mother?

9   Gallagher, like the Manhattan-based Institute for American Values for which she led this investigation, is unabashedly pro-marriage. But that in no way diminishes the validity of her insight: We have, in some important respects, stopped being a marriage culture.

10   The trend may have begun with feminist (and other) reaction against the teen marriages of the 1950s as "traps." Increases in the divorce rate sparked talk about marriage for the "wrong" reasons. And then, perhaps along with increased career opportunities for women, marriage was spoken of increasingly as a "bad deal" for women. Teen mothers contend, with great earnestness, that they are terrific mothers but too young for marriage; that will come later, they say (though it frequently does not).

11   Not only has the stigma against single parenthood been greatly reduced (with what unintended consequences?) but, according to Gallagher, professional counselors today frequently advise pregnant young women quite specifically against marrying the fathers of their babies—against falling into the "trap."

12   The advice turns out to be somewhat less liberating than it sounds. As the report notes,

> A young man who gets his girlfriend pregnant, but declines to marry on the grounds that he is too young, will typically enjoy ample opportunities in the coming years, as he "grows up," to enter into a lower-risk marriage with another woman.

13   The same cannot be said for the girlfriend. Entering into single motherhood, as against marriage, is likely to permanently compromise her future prospects for marriage.

14   Gallagher's contribution is not to recount the well-documented economic arguments against single motherhood but to drive home the degree to which young people's separation of parenthood from marriage reflects an attitude shift in the larger society.

15   She ends the 50-page report with 16 public policy proposals, of which these two top the list:

16   "Put an emphasis on marriage, not just age, at the center of all of our efforts and programs in the area of teen sexuality and teen pregnancy," and

17   "Retire the term 'teen pregnancy' from our public discourse. As a popular name for a serious social problem, the term has outlived its usefulness and now obscures more than it reveals. . . . How about 'unwed parenthood' as a substitute?"

QUESTIONS FOR READING AND REASONING

1.   Who is Maggie Gallagher? What did she write?
2.   What is the "real" pregnancy problem, according to Gallagher and Raspberry?
3.   How big a problem is it, in Gallagher's view?
4.   What may be, according to Raspberry, some of the causes of the problem?
5.   What, for women, may be a result of having a child outside of marriage?
6.   What are two of Gallagher's proposals for addressing the problem?
7.   Does Raspberry agree with Gallagher's ideas? How do you know?

8. How does Raspberry first refer to the writer whose work he uses? How does he refer to her after paragraph 1? What other information does he give about the writer?

9. How does Raspberry refer to the source?

PRESENTING DIRECT QUOTATIONS: A GUIDE TO FORM AND STYLE

Although most of your papers will be written in your own words and style, you will sometimes use direct quotations. Just as there is a correct form for references to people and to works, there is a correct form for presenting borrowed material in direct quotation. Study the guidelines and examples and then mark these pages, as you did the others, for easy reference.

Reasons for Using Quotation Marks

We use quotation marks in four ways:

- To indicate dialogue in works of fiction or drama.
- To indicate the titles of some kinds of works.
- To indicate the words that others have spoken or written.
- To separate ourselves from or call into question particular uses of words.

When Raspberry writes: "Listen: 'The teen birth rate is, and has been for many years, much lower today . . .' " we recognize that he is presenting Gallagher's ideas to us in her own words. That is the third use of quotation marks listed above. However, when Raspberry writes: "Increases in the divorce rate sparked talk about marriage for the 'wrong' reasons," Raspberry is not quoting Gallagher. Instead he is questioning the use of the word *wrong*. He also puts the word "traps" in quotation marks for the same reason. Having children without being married may turn out to be the bigger "trap." This is the fourth use of quotation marks. The following guidelines apply to all four uses of quotation marks.

A Brief Guide to Quoting

1. Quote accurately. Do not misrepresent what someone has written. Take time to compare what you have copied with the original, paying particular attention to spelling and punctuation.

2. Put *all* words taken from a source in quotation marks. (To lift words from a source without making it clear that they are not your words is to plagiarize, an action viewed as stealing in academic and professional communities.) Never change words. Never delete words without so indicating with spaced dots (. . .). If you need to add words to make the meaning of a passage clear, place the added words in [square brackets] [ ], not (parentheses) ( ).

ORIGINAL:	"In other words, while we've been harping on 'teen pregnancy,' what really has been happening is a striking decline in the importance we place on marriage."
INCORRECT:	"While Raspberry and other writers have been harping on 'teen pregnancy,' what really has been happening is a striking decline in the importance society places on marriage."
CORRECT:	Raspberry explains that "while we've [columnists and other writers] been harping on 'teen pregnancy,' what really has been happening is a striking decline in the importance we place on marriage." (See 9 below for the use of single quotation marks within quotations.)

3. *Always* make the source of quoted words clear. If you do not indicate the author of quoted words, readers will have to assume that you are calling those words into question. Note that Raspberry introduces the author, on whose report he draws, in paragraph 1 and then repeats her name *five* times so that we are reassured that direct quotations continue to come from Gallagher's report.

4. If you want to quote words from an author (for example, Gallagher) quoted by another author (Raspberry), you must make clear that you are getting Gallagher's words from Raspberry's article, not directly from Gallagher's report:

ORIGINAL QUOTATION:	"Put an emphasis on marriage, not just age, at the center of all of our efforts and programs in the area of teen sexuality and teen pregnancy."
INCORRECT:	Gallagher says that we should "put an emphasis on marriage, not just age, at the center of all of our efforts and programs in the area of teen pregnancy."
CORRECT:	One of Gallagher's proposals, quoted by Raspberry, is to "put an emphasis on marriage, not just age, at the center of all of our efforts and programs in the area of teen pregnancy."

5. Place commas and periods *inside* the closing quotation mark—even when only one word is quoted:

> Raspberry explains that we have encouraged parenting outside of marriage by describing marriage as a "bad deal," a "trap."

6. Place colons and semicolons *outside* the closing quotation mark:

> Raspberry presents information from Gallagher's report "The Age of Unwed Mothers: Is Teen Pregnancy the Problem?": There were "376,000 births in one recent year to single mothers under the age of 20"; however, there were "439,000 births that same year to single mothers in their early twenties."

7. Do not quote unnecessary punctuation. When you place quoted material at the end of a sentence you have written, use only the punctuation needed to complete the sentence:

ORIGINAL: "[A]ccording to Gallagher, professional counselors today frequently advise pregnant young women quite specifically against marrying the fathers of their babies—against falling into the 'trap.' "

INCORRECT: Raspberry quotes Gallagher as observing that "professional counselors today frequently advise pregnant young women quite specifically against marrying the fathers of their babies—."

CORRECT: Raspberry quotes Gallagher as observing that "professional counselors today frequently advise pregnant young women quite specifically against marrying the fathers of their babies."

8. When the words you quote make up only part of your sentence, do not capitalize the first quoted word, even if it was capitalized in the original source. *Exception:* The passage you quote follows an introduction that ends in a colon:

INCORRECT: Raspberry points out that "Not only has the stigma against single parenthood been greatly reduced . . . but, according to Gallagher, professional counselors today frequently advise pregnant young women . . . against marrying the fathers of their babies."

CORRECT: Raspberry points out that "not only has the stigma against single parenthood been greatly reduced . . . but, according to Gallagher, professional counselors today frequently advise pregnant young women . . . against marrying the fathers of their babies."

ALSO
CORRECT: Raspberry examines the impact of the idea that early marriage is a trap: "Not only has the stigma against single parenthood been greatly reduced . . . but, according to Gallagher, professional counselors today frequently advise pregnant young women . . . against marrying the fathers of their babies."

9. Use single quotation marks (the apostrophe key on your keyboard) to identify quoted material within quoted material:

> Raspberry observes that there has been a feminist "reaction against the teen marriages of the 1950s as 'traps.' "

10. Depending on the structure of your sentence, use a colon, a comma, or no punctuation before a quoted passage. A colon provides a formal introduction to quotes. Use it sparingly for emphasis or to introduce a long quotation. Use a comma *only* when your sentence structure requires it. Quoted words presented in a "that" clause are *not* preceded by a comma.

ORIGINAL: "Increases in the divorce rate sparked talk about marriage for the 'wrong' reasons."

CORRECT: Raspberry offers this cause for increased parenting outside of marriage: "Increases in the divorce rate sparked talk about marriage for the 'wrong' reasons."

CORRECT:	"Increases in the divorce rate," Raspberry asserts, "sparked talk about marriage for the 'wrong' reasons."
CORRECT:	Raspberry observes that "increases in the divorce rate sparked talk about marriage for the 'wrong' reasons."

11. To keep direct quotations as brief as possible, omit irrelevant portions. Indicate that you have left out words by putting in ellipsis points (three spaced dots: . . .): Raspberry asserts that "Gallagher . . . is unabashedly pro-marriage." Some instructors want the ellipses placed in square brackets— [. . .]—to indicate that they are your addition to the original material, not ellipses that were part of the original. Modern Language Association (MLA) style does not require the square brackets unless you are quoting a passage that already has ellipses as part of the quoted material. In that case, your brackets would distinguish your omission from an omission in the original material.

12. Think about your reader. When you quote, give enough context to make the quoted material clear. Do not put so many quoted passages into a sentence that your reader gets tired trying to follow the ideas. Also, make certain that your sentences are both complete and correctly constructed. Quoting is not an excuse to write fragments or badly constructed sentences.

AWKWARD:	Raspberry notes causes for the decline in a marriage culture: "increased career opportunities for women" and "counselors . . . advise pregnant young women against . . . marrying the fathers of their babies."

First, running the two ideas together in one sentence can be confusing to readers. Second, the two quoted passages are not in parallel structure. The first is a noun ("opportunities"); the second is a complete sentence ("counselors . . . advise . . . against . . . marrying").

NOT ENOUGH CONTEXT:	Raspberry talks about "marriage for the 'wrong' reasons."
BETTER:	Raspberry observes that "increases in the divorce rate sparked talk about marriage for the 'wrong' reasons."
MISLEADING:	Raspberry notes that columnists have written many columns on "teen pregnancy," and Maggie Gallagher "wishes we'd give it a rest."
BETTER:	Raspberry notes that columnists have written many columns on "teen pregnancy," but Maggie Gallagher thinks that the "term has outlived its usefulness and now obscures more than it reveals."

Gallagher does not argue that we should stop focusing on the problem of teen pregnancy. She argues that the label "teen pregnancy" takes the public's attention away from the larger issue of women having children without being married.

> **NOTE:** All examples of quoting given above are in the present tense. We write that "Raspberry notes," "Raspberry believes," "Raspberry asserts." Even though his article was written in the past, we use the present tense to describe his ongoing ideas. (See p. 336 in "Other Styles of Documentation" for a variation of this convention.)

FOR DEBATE

As you read the following article, practice active reading, including annotating the essay. Concentrate first on what the author has to say but also observe the structure or organization of the essay and the author's use of quotations and references to authors and works.

CENTURY OF FREEDOM | ROBERT J. SAMUELSON

A graduate of Harvard University, Robert Samuelson (b. 1945) began his career as a reporter and is now a columnist whose articles are syndicated in many newspapers each week and biweekly in *Newsweek* magazine. Although he often writes about economics, Samuelson also examines political and cultural issues, especially those that have a connection to economic issues, as he does in the following column published December 22, 1999.

PREREADING QUESTIONS Why is the fate of freedom in this century "fragile"? What are some of the problems we may face trying to meet new ideas of freedom?

1　　What 20th-century development most altered the human condition? There is no shortage of candidates: the automobile, antibiotics, the airplane, computers, contraceptives, radio and television, to name a few. But surely the largest advance in human well-being involves the explosion of freedom. In a century scarred by gulags, concentration camps and secret-police terror, freedom is now spreading to an expanding swath of humanity. It is not only growing but also changing—becoming more ambitious and ambiguous—in ways that might, perversely, spawn disappointment and disorder in the new century.

2　　In 1900 this was unimaginable. "Freedom in the modern sense [then] existed only for the upper crust," says political sociologist Seymour Martin Lipset of George Mason University. There were exceptions—America certainly, but even its freedom was curtailed. In 1900 women could vote in only four western states. Not until the ratification of the 19th Amendment in 1920 could all women vote. In the South, a web of laws prevented black Americans from voting. It took the Voting Rights Act of 1965 to change that.

3　　Elsewhere the picture was bleaker. In 1900 empires dotted the world. The British Empire contained roughly 400 million people, about a quarter of the world's population. Lesser empires were still enormous: the Austro-Hungarian, the Ottoman, the French and others. Human subjugation was the rule, not the exception.

4   Consider the situation now. In 1999 Freedom House—a watchdog group based in Washington—classified as "free" 88 of the world's 191 countries, with 2.4 billion people or about 40 percent of the total. These nations enjoyed free elections and traditional civil rights of speech, religion and assembly. Of course, there are shades of gray. In this twilight zone Freedom House placed 53 countries with 1.6 billion people, because either elections or civil liberties were compromised. Russia was "partially free"; China was "not free."

5   Still, the world's frame of reference has fundamentally altered. Even in societies where freedoms are abused, their absence usually becomes an issue. But freedom has not simply spread. It's also evolved, especially in the United States. The freedom that Americans expect as they enter the 21st century is not the same as the freedom they expected as they entered the 20th.

6   Traditional freedom historically meant liberation from oppression. But now freedom increasingly involves "self-realization." People need, it's argued, to be freed from whatever prevents them from becoming whoever they want to be. There's a drift toward "positive liberty" that emphasizes "the things that government ought to do for us," says sociologist Alan Wolfe of Boston College. This newer freedom blends into individual "rights" (for women, minorities, the disabled) and "entitlements" (for health care, education and income support) deemed essential for self-realization.

7   The broader freedom is not just American. In a new book, *Development as Freedom,* the Nobel-Prize-winning economist Amartya Sen argues that "the expansion of freedom is both the primary end and . . . principal means of development" in poorer countries. But Sen's freedom eclipses the classic political and economic freedoms. It includes "social opportunities" (expanded education and health care), "transparency guarantees" (a lack of corruption) and more "entitlements" (to ensure basic decency and prevent "abject misery"). Indeed, it seems to include almost anything that might advance human well-being.

8   In some ways, freedom's explosion connects the century's two great constants: war and economic progress. Deaths in World War I and World War II are crudely reckoned at 10 million and as many as 60 million, respectively. But these vast tragedies ultimately paid some dividends for common people, because they doomed colonial empires. Also, the nature of the wars emphasized freedom. They were too destructive to be mere contests of nations. They had to be about ideals. The Cold War—an ideological conflict—conveyed the same message.

9   If war expanded freedom, prosperity embellished it. Since 1900 the world's population has roughly quadrupled, from almost 1.6 billion to 6 billion. Meanwhile, the global production of goods and services—from food and steel to air travel and health care—has risen 14 to 15 times, estimates economist Angus Maddison for the Organization for Economic Cooperation and Development in Paris. As nations grew wealthier, traditional freedom wasn't enough. People ascended what psychologist Abraham Maslow called the human hierarchy of needs—from food and shelter to self-esteem and spiritual needs, such as jus-

tice and beauty. People could not (it was said) be "free" without realizing these larger yearnings.

Freedom's fate in the next century is fragile, in part because the very no- 10 tion is now so ill-defined. Classic freedom—coupling the opportunity for success with the danger of failure—hardly ensures personal fulfillment or social order. "On the one hand, you're told you're free," says Lipset. "But on the other, you're a potential loser. And if you lose, you don't feel free." The traditional freedoms of belief and lifestyle also require, if they are not to foster anarchy, tolerance and self-restraint.

But at least traditional freedom is universal. Everyone can, in theory, enjoy 11 the freedoms of speech, religion, assembly and property. This sort of freedom promises the absence of coercion. By contrast, the new freedoms of individual "rights" and "entitlements" are increasingly exclusive, can involve social competition for benefits and may mean the subtle (or not so subtle) coercion of one group by another—all tending to weaken a sense of community. The "rights" of women, gays and the disabled cannot be directly enjoyed by men, straights or the nondisabled. Financing entitlements means taxes—a form of collective coercion—by which taxpayers subsidize beneficiaries.

Freedom, always a combustible concept, promises to become more so, be- 12 cause in a world of television and the Internet, ideas glide almost spontaneously across cultural and political boundaries. The eagerness of the West to export its ideals may increasingly collide with the willingness and capacity of others to abandon or modify their own. What we value, they may fear or mishandle. Freedom is a great blessing. But it has never been easy—and never will be.

QUESTIONS FOR READING

1. What is Samuelson's subject? What is his thesis? Is there one sentence that you think works as the essay's thesis? If so, did you underline it when annotating?

2. Look again at paragraph 1. There is more than one sentence that could be a thesis statement. Which one is the better choice for the author's main idea? Why?

3. How did the century's wars contribute to freedom?

4. What is the traditional idea of freedom? What is the newer concept of freedom all about?

QUESTIONS FOR REASONING AND ANALYSIS

1. What kind of support does Samuelson provide for the idea of the "century of freedom"? What general plan or organization does the author use?

2. In paragraph 11, Samuelson puts the words *rights* and *entitlements* in quotation marks. Why? What point does he want to make with that strategy?

3. This essay was written before September 11, 2001. How might the author have written the final paragraph after that date? Explain your suggested revision.

QUESTIONS FOR REFLECTING AND WRITING

1. Which of the problems mentioned in paragraphs 10, 11, and 12 most threaten freedom in the twenty-first century, in your view? Why?

2. Do you agree with Samuelson that freedom is the most significant development in the twentieth century? If so, why? If not, what development would you argue for instead? Explain and support your view. If you write, refer correctly to the author and title and present any direct quotations from Samuelson in correct form.

AMERICAN FOREIGN POLICY AND THE KING GEORGE SYNDROME | JOSHUA MITCHELL

Joshua Mitchell is chair of the Government Department at Georgetown University. He is the author of a number of articles and two books, including *The Fragility of Freedom: Tocqueville on Religion, Democracy, and the American Future* (1995). The following essay appeared in the *Washington Post*, August 10, 2003.

PREREADING QUESTIONS What "King George" is the author probably referring to? Who is Alexis de Tocqueville, and what did he write about America?

1   "Peoples always bear some marks of their origin. Circumstances of birth and growth affect their entire career." So Alexis de Tocqueville tells us. And in the United States our origin involves the tale—somewhat fanciful but nevertheless salutary—of local citizens and great leaders declaring their freedom from King George III in the late 18th century. Nearly 250 years later, American foreign policy in Afghanistan and in Iraq is driven by an idea so inscribed into the American psyche that it amounts to a syndrome: Cast off the tyrannical leader, then citizens and leaders alike will band together to bring about the freedom that a tyrant's presence alone precluded. It happened in America; surely it will happen everywhere else. Thus our war of liberation, to free Iraq of its King George III.

2   In both Afghanistan and in Iraq we have won the war, but we stand in danger of losing what we won because our foreign policy suffers from the King George Syndrome. Freedom is neither a spontaneous nor a universal aspiration. Other goods captivate the minds of peoples from other lands; order, honor and tribal loyalties being the most obvious. And because these other goods orient these people no less powerfully than freedom orients us, we are apt to be sorely surprised when peoples who are liberated turn to new tyrants who can ensure order; to terrorists who die for the honor of their country or of Islam; and to tribal warlords whose winner-take-all mentality is corrosive to the pluralism and toleration that are the very hallmarks of modern democracy.

3   The problem is far more profound than critics of various policies realize, and it is appropriate now for us to move beyond our verbal sparrings, accusations and conspiracy theories in order to clarify an issue that unpleasantly confronts us here at the beginning of the 21st century.

At the end of the 20th century we were told that we had reached "the end 4 of history," that freedom was on the verge of captivating the hearts and minds of citizens around the globe. And in light of the heady experience of 1989, when the edifice of the Soviet Union began to collapse, it seemed evident that the question of how freedom was to be understood was settled for the entire world. In the global politics of the 20th century, the question was never whether freedom was the universal good but rather how it might best be understood.

Notwithstanding the perils that are now behind us, the 20th century did 5 bring about something that we in the 21st century will probably look back upon with loving affection: the temporary masking of those darker aspirations in the human heart: order, honor, and tribal affiliation. Ah, to live again engrossed by the ghastly clarity of the Cold War world, with its easy opposition between the free-market economies of the West and the command economies of the East, as if freedom from scarcity were the singular motivation in the human heart.

Not so. The end of the bipolar world has meant the renewed visibility of 6 these other motivations, especially in the Middle East, where the legacy of colonialism and Islam's perceived inability to reconcile itself with modernity have rendered the peoples of the region deeply suspicious of liberation and the freedom it purports to herald. The peoples of the Middle East know nothing of the final victory of freedom and of the end of history. That myth is ours, not theirs. The 21st century is upon us, and it is time to put away our 20th-century fancies. They once served us well, but we have entered a new world, with landmarks as unfamiliar as the parts of the globe whose suffering we witness and whose hostility we receive.

What is to be done? Above all, we must not let our foreign policy succumb 7 to the King George Syndrome. Freedom will not emerge spontaneously in other parts of the globe.

Tocqueville himself knew this. In his words, "nothing is so perilous as free- 8 dom's apprenticeship." Our wars of liberation will liberate illiberal aspirations, and rather than standing back with incredulity when this happens, we had better give plenty of thought beforehand to the fact that the tyrants we depose will be preferable to the chaos a liberated people will initially endure; that honor is still the currency of value in the Middle East, more so than goods and services; and that the affiliations of blood are immensely more meaningful there than the sovereignty of the individual citizen.

Statesmanship is surely the art of taking the next step. If freedom does 9 come to prevail in the Middle East, or in any other region of the globe without a long experience with it, it will be because prudent policies will have been developed that take full cognizance of the importance of order, honor, and tribal affiliation—and that thoughtfully work through these cultural categories rather than pretend that they are irrelevant. The King George Syndrome makes sense in America, but nowhere else.

QUESTIONS FOR READING

1. What point does Mitchell seek to establish by quoting Tocqueville?
2. What does Mitchell mean by the "King George Syndrome"?
3. What problems has this syndrome created for the United States in Afghanistan and Iraq?
4. What values other than freedom influence the behavior of many people in the world?
5. What political dynamic of the twentieth century seemed to hide the appeal of these other values?
6. What advice does Mitchell give for U.S. foreign policy in the twenty-first century?

QUESTIONS FOR REASONING AND ANALYSIS

1. What is Mitchell's thesis, the claim of his argument? Where does he state it?
2. What does Mitchell mean by "the bipolar world" that he refers to in paragraph 6? What does he mean by "the ghastly clarity of the Cold War world"? Why was it ghastly? How did it have clarity? Why might we want to return to this time rather than have to deal with our own time?
3. Explain his statement: "Our wars of liberation will liberate illiberal aspirations."
4. Does Mitchell say that we should not have sought to liberate Afghanistan or Iraq? Does he imply that we should not have? Or does he have another purpose? What does he want readers to understand from reading his essay?

QUESTIONS FOR REFLECTING AND WRITING

1. Do you agree that our problems in this young twenty-first century reveal that some groups of people are more moved by order, honor, and tribal loyalties than by freedom and material values? Are you surprised by these differences in values? Explain.
2. Look again at Robert Samuelson's "Century of Freedom." Over what points do Mitchell and Samuelson agree? How does Mitchell add to the discussion started by Samuelson? Given what Samuelson sees as possible problems with the development of freedom, do you think that he would agree or disagree with the key points of Mitchell's argument? Explain.

SUGGESTIONS FOR DISCUSSION AND WRITING

1. Bill Gates has argued that e-books will replace paper books in the not-too-distant future. What are the advantages of e-books? What are the advantages of paper books? Are there any disadvantages to either type of book? Which would you prefer? How would you argue for your preference?

2. Write a one-paragraph summary of either Joshua Mitchell's or Robert Samuelson's essay. Be sure that your summary clearly states the author's main idea, the claim of his argument. Take your time and polish your word choice.

3. Read actively and then prepare a one-and-a-half-page summary of either Brandon Centerwall's "Television and Violent Crime" (pages 390–400) or Linda J. Waite's "Social Science Finds: 'Marriage Matters' " (pages 569–76). Your readers want an accurate and balanced but much shorter version of the original because they will not be reading the original article. Explain not only what the writer's main ideas are but also how the writer develops his or her essay. That is, what kind of research supports the article's thesis? Pay close attention to your word choice.

GOING ONLINE

Robert Samuelson refers to the organization Freedom House. Check out its website (www.freedomhouse.org). For what kinds of projects might material at this website be useful? Select either an essay or a chart from the site, read it, and then write a brief summary.

CHAPTER 2

Responding Critically to Sources

In some contexts, the word *critical* carries the idea of harsh judgment: "The manager was critical of her secretary's long phone conversations." In other contexts, though, the term means to evaluate carefully. When we speak of the critical reader or critical thinker, we have in mind someone who reads actively, who thinks about issues, and who makes informed judgments. Here is a profile of the critical reader or thinker:

TRAITS OF THE CRITICAL READER/THINKER

- **Focused on the facts.**
  Give me the facts and show me that they are relevant to the issue.
- **Analytic.**
  What strategies has the writer/speaker used to develop the argument?
- **Open-minded.**
  Prepared to listen to different points of view, to learn from others.

- **Questioning/skeptical.**

  What other conclusions could be supported by the evidence presented?

  How thorough has the writer/speaker been?

  What persuasive strategies are being used?

- **Creative.**

  What are some entirely different ways of looking at the issue or problem?

- **Intellectually active, not passive.**

  Willing to analyze logic and evidence.

  Willing to consider many possibilities.

  Willing, after careful evaluation, to reach a judgment, to take a stand on issues.

EXAMINING THE CONTEXT

Reading critically requires preparation. Instead of "jumping into reading," begin by asking questions about the work's total context. You need to be able to answer the following four questions before—or while—you read.

Who Is the Author?

Key questions to answer include:

- *Does the author have a reputation for honesty, thoroughness, and fairness?* Read the biographical note, if there is one; ask your instructor about the author; learn about the author in a biographical dictionary or online; try *Book Review Digest* (in your library or online) for reviews of the author's books.

- *Is the author writing within his or her area of expertise?* People can voice opinions on any subject, but they cannot transfer expertise from one subject area to another. A football player endorsing a political candidate is a citizen with an opinion, not an expert on politics.

- *Is the author identified with a particular group or set of beliefs? Does the biography place the writer in a particular institution or organization?* For example, a member of a Republican administration may be expected to favor a Republican president's policies. A Roman Catholic priest may be expected to take a stand against abortion. These kinds of details provide hints, but you should not decide, absolutely, what a writer's bias will be until you have read the work with care. Be alert to reasonable expectations, but avoid stereotyping a writer.

What Kind of Audience Is Being Addressed?

Understanding the intended audience can help you answer two questions: the depth and sophistication of the work and a possible bias or slant.

- *Does the writer expect a popular audience, a general but educated audience, or a specialized audience that will share professional expertise or cultural, political, or religious preferences?* Often you can judge the expected audience by noting the kind of publication in which an article appears or the publisher of the book. For example, *Reader's Digest* is written for a mass audience; *Psychology Today, Science,* or *Newsweek,* for example, aim for a general but more knowledgeable reader. By contrast, articles in the *New England Journal of Medicine* are written by medical doctors and research scientists for a specialized audience.

- *Does the writer expect readers who are likely to be favorable to the writer's views?* Some newspapers are fairly consistently liberal, whereas others are usually politically conservative. (Do you know the political leanings of your local paper?) The particular interests of the *Christian Science Monitor* and *Ms.* should be considered when you read articles from these sources. Remember: All arguments are "slanted" or "biased"—that is, they take a stand. That's okay. You just need to read with an awareness of a writer's particular background and interests.

What Is the Author's Purpose in Writing?

Is the piece informative or persuasive in intent? Designed to entertain or to be inspiring? Think about the title; read a book's preface to learn of the author's goals; pay attention to tone as you read.

What Are the Writer's Sources of Information?

Some questions to ask about sources include: Where was the information obtained? Is it still valid? Are sources clearly identified? Be suspicious of writers who want us to believe that their unnamed "sources" are "reliable." Pay close attention to dates. A biography of King George III published in 1940 may still be the best source. An article urging the curtailing of county growth based on population statistics from the 1980s is no longer reliable.

EXERCISES: Examining the Context

1. What can you judge about the reliability or bias of the following? Consider author, audience, and purpose.
    a. An article on the Republican administration, written by a former campaign worker for a Democratic presidential candidate.
    b. A discussion, published in the *Boston Globe,* of the Patriots' hope for the next Super Bowl.
    c. A letter to the editor about conservation, written by a member of the Sierra Club. (What is the Sierra Club? Study some of its publications or check out its website to respond to this topic.)
    d. A column in *Newsweek* on economics. (Look at the business section of *Newsweek.* Your library has the magazine.)
    e. A 1948 article in *Nutrition Today* on the best diets.

    f.   A biography of Benjamin Franklin published by Oxford University Press.

    g.   A *Family Circle* article about a special vegetarian diet written by a doctor. (Who is the audience for this magazine? Where is it sold?)

    h.   A pamphlet by Jerry Lewis urging you to contribute to a fund to combat muscular dystrophy.

    i.   A discussion of abortion in *Ms.* magazine.

    j.   An editorial in your local newspaper entitled "Stop the Highway Killing."

2.   Analyze an issue of your favorite magazine. Look first at the editorial pages and articles written by the staff, then at articles contributed by other writers. Answer these questions for both staff writers and contributors:

    a.   Who is their audience?

    b.   What is the purpose of the articles and of the entire magazine?

    c.   What type of article dominates the issue?

    d.   Describe their style and tone. How appropriate are the style and tone?

3.   Select one environmental website and study what is offered. The EnviroLink Network (www.envirolink.org) will lead you to many sites. Another possibility is the Nature Conservancy (www.tnc.org). Write down the name of the site you chose and its uniform resource locator (URL). Then answer these questions:

    a.   Who is the intended audience?

    b.   What seems to be the primary purpose or goal of the site?

    c.   What type of material seems to dominate the site?

    d.   For what kinds of writing assignments might you use material from the site?

UNDERSTANDING ATTITUDE

Critical readers read for implication and are alert to tone or nuance. When you read, think about not just *what* is said but *how* it is said. Consider the following excerpt:

> What happened to the War on Drugs? Did Bush—the old man, not the son— think that we actually *won* that war? Or did he confuse the War on Drugs with the stupid Gulf War he's so proud of winning? Well, he never did understand "the vision thing."

First, we recognize that the writer's subject is the War on Drugs, an expression used in the past to emphasize the government's programs to reduce drug use in the United States. Second, we understand that the writer does not believe that the war has been won; rather, we still have a drug problem that we need to address. We know this from the second sentence, the rhetorical question that we answer by thinking that maybe Bush thought the drug problem had been solved but the writer—and we—know better. What else do you observe in this passage? What is the writer's attitude toward George Bush? Note the writer's language. The former president is "the old man." He is proud of winning a "stupid" war. He, by implication, is stupid to think that he helped win the War on Drugs. And, finally, we are reminded of Bush's own words that he didn't have a vision of what he wanted to do as president.

How would you rewrite the passage to make it more favorable to Bush? Here is one version that students wrote to give the passage a positive attitude toward Bush:

> What has happened to the War on Drugs? Did some members of President George Bush's administration think that government policies had been successful in reducing drug use? Or did the administration change its focus to concentrate on winning the Gulf War? Perhaps, in retrospect, President Bush should have put more emphasis on the war against drugs.

The writers have not changed their position that the War on Drugs has not been won—yet they have greatly altered our outlook on the subject. This version suggests that the failure to win the drug war was the fault of Bush's administration, not of Bush himself, and that perhaps the failure is understandable given the need to focus attention on the Gulf War. In addition, references to the former president treat him with dignity. What is the difference in the two passages? Only the word choice.

Denotative and Connotative Word Choice

The students' ability to rewrite the passage on the War on Drugs to give it a positive attitude tells us that, although some words may have similar meanings, they cannot always be substituted for one another without changing the message. Words with similar meanings have similar *denotations.* Often, though, words with similar denotations do not have the same connotations. A word's *connotation* is what the word suggests, what we associate the word with. The words *house* and *home,* for example, both refer to a building in which people live. They have the same denotation. But the word *home* suggests ideas—and feelings—of family and security. Thus the word *home* has a strong positive connotation. *House* by contrast brings to mind a picture of a physical structure but little else because the word doesn't carry any "emotional baggage."

We learn the connotations of words the same way we learn their denotations—in context. Most of us, living in the same culture, share the same connotative associations of words. At times, the context in which a word is used will affect the word's connotation. For example, the word *buddy* usually has positive connotations. We may think of an old or trusted friend. But when an unfriendly person who thinks a man may have pushed in front of him says, "Better watch it, *buddy,*" the word has a negative connotation. Social, physical, and language contexts control the connotative significance of words. Become more alert to the connotative power of words by asking what words the writers could have used instead.

> **NOTE:** Writers make choices; their choices reflect and convey their attitudes.
>
> *Studying the context in which a writer uses emotionally charged words is the only way to be sure that we understand the writer's attitude.*

EXERCISES: Connotation

1.   For each of the following words or phrases, list at least two synonyms that have a more negative connotation than the given word:
     a.   child   e.   scholarly
     b.   persistent   f.   trusting
     c.   thin   g.   underachiever
     d.   a large group   h.   quiet
2.   For each of the following words, list at least two synonyms that have a more positive connotation than the given word:
     a.   notorious   e.   fanatic
     b.   fat   f.   reckless
     c.   politician   g.   sot
     d.   old (people)   h.   cheap
3.   Read the following paragraph and decide how the writer feels about the activity described. Note the choice of details and the connotative language that make you aware of the writer's attitude.

     Needing to complete a missed assignment for my physical education class, I dragged myself down to the tennis courts on a gloomy afternoon. My task was to serve five balls in a row into the service box. Although I thought I had learned the correct service movements, I couldn't seem to translate that knowledge into a decent serve. I tossed up the first ball, jerked back my racket, swung up on the ball—clunk—I hit the ball on the frame. I threw up the second ball, brought back my racket, swung up on the ball—ping—I made contact with the strings, but the ball dribbled down on my side of the net. I trudged around the court, collecting my tennis balls; I had only two of them.

4.   Write a paragraph describing an activity that you liked or disliked without saying how you felt. From your choice of details and use of connotative language, convey your attitude toward the activity. (The paragraph in exercise 3 is your model.)
5.   Select one of the words listed below and explain, in a paragraph, what the word connotes to you personally. Be precise; illustrate your thoughts with details and examples.
     a.   nature   d.   nerd
     b.   mother   e.   playboy
     c.   romantic   f.   artist

COLLABORATIVE EXERCISES: On Connotation

1.   List all of the words you know for *human female* and for *human male.* Then classify them by connotation (positive, negative, neutral) and by level of usage (formal, informal, slang). Is there any connection between type of connotation and level of usage? Why are some words more appropriate in some social contexts than in others? Can you easily list more negative words used for one sex than for the other? Why?

2.   Some words can be given a different connotation in different contexts. First, for each of the following words, label its connotation as positive, negative, or neutral. Then, for each word with a positive connotation, write a sentence in which the word would convey a more negative connotation. For each word with a negative connotation, write a sentence in which the word would suggest a more positive connotation.

   a.   natural   d.   free
   b.   old   e.   chemical
   c.   committed   f.   lazy

3.   Each of the following groups of words might appear together in a thesaurus, but the words actually vary in connotation. After looking up any words whose connotation you are unsure of, write a sentence in which each word is used correctly. Briefly explain why one of the other words in the group should not be substituted.

   a.   brittle, hard, fragile   d.   strange, remarkable, bizarre
   b.   quiet, withdrawn, glum   e.   thrifty, miserly, economical
   c.   shrewd, clever, cunning

Recognizing Tone

Closely related to a writer's attitude is the writer's tone. We can describe a writer's attitude toward the subject as positive, negative, or (rarely) neutral. Attitude is the writer's position on, or feelings about, his or her subject. The way that attitude is expressed—the voice we hear and the feelings conveyed through that voice—is the writer's *tone*. Writers can choose to express attitude through a wide variety of tones. We may reinforce a negative attitude through an angry, somber, sad, mocking, peevish, sarcastic, or scornful tone. A positive attitude may be revealed through an enthusiastic, serious, sympathetic, jovial, light, or admiring tone. We cannot be sure that just because a writer selects a light tone, for example, the attitude must be positive. Humor columnists such as Dave Barry often choose a light tone to examine serious social and political issues. Given their subjects, we recognize that the light and amusing tone actually conveys a negative attitude toward the topic.

COLLABORATIVE EXERCISE: On Tone

With your class partner or in small groups, examine the following three paragraphs, which are different responses to the same event. First, decide on each writer's attitude. Then describe, as precisely as possible, the tone of each paragraph.

1.   It is tragically inexcusable that this young athlete was not examined fully before he was allowed to join the varsity team. The physical examinations given were unbelievably sloppy. What were the coach and trainer thinking of not to insist that each youngster be examined while undergoing physical stress? Apparently they were not thinking about our boys at all. We can no longer trust our sons and our daughters to this inhumane system so bent on victory that it ignores the health—indeed the very lives—of our children.

2. It was learned last night, following the death of varsity fullback Jim Bresnick, that none of the players was given a stress test as part of his physical examination. The oversight was attributed to laxness by the coach and trainer, who are described today as being "distraught." It is the judgment of many that the entire physical education program must be reexamined with an eye to the safety and health of all students.

3. How can I express the loss I feel over the death of my son? I want to blame someone, but who is to blame? The coaches, for not administering more rigorous physical checkups? Why should they have done more than other coaches have done before or than other coaches are doing at other schools? My son, for not telling me that he felt funny after practice? His teammates, for not telling the coaches that my son said he did not feel well? Myself, for not knowing that something was wrong with my only child? Who is to blame? All of us and none of us. But placing blame will not return my son to me; I can only pray that other parents will not have to suffer so. Jimmy, we loved you.

ANALYZING STYLE

We have begun the process of understanding attitude by becoming more aware of context and connotation and more alert to tone. Tone is created and attitude conveyed primarily through word choice and sentence structure but also through several other techniques.

Word Choice

In addition to responding to a writer's choice of connotative language, observe the kinds of words that are chosen, the *level of diction* used. Are the writer's words primarily typical of conversational language, or of a more formal style? Does the writer use slang words or technical words? Is the word choice concrete and vivid or abstract and intellectual? These differences help to shape tone and affect our response to what we read. Lincoln's word choice in "The Gettysburg Address" (see p. 4) is formal and abstract. Lincoln writes: "on this continent" rather than "in this land," "we take increased devotion" rather than "we become more committed." Another style, the technical, will be found in some articles in this text. The social scientist may write that "the child . . . is subjected to extremely punitive discipline," whereas a nonspecialist, more informally, might write that "the child is controlled by beatings or other forms of punishment."

One way to create an informal style is to choose simple words: "land" instead of "continent." To create greater informality, a writer can use contractions: "we'll" for "we will." There are no contractions in "The Gettysburg Address." Contractions are one of the chief marks of a highly informal style. In your academic and professional writing, you should aim for a style informal enough to be inviting to readers but one that, in most cases, avoids contractions or slang words.

Sentence Structure

The eighteenth-century satirist Jonathan Swift once said that writing well was a simple matter of putting "proper words in proper places." Writers need to think not just about the words they choose but also about their arrangement into sentence patterns. Studying a writer's sentence patterns will reveal how they affect style and tone. When analyzing these features, consider the following questions:

1. *Are the sentences generally long or short, or varied in length?*
Are the structures primarily:

- *Simple* (one independent clause)
  In 1900 empires dotted the world.
- *Compound* (two or more independent clauses)
  Women make up only 37 percent of television characters, yet women make up more than half of the population.
- *Complex* (at least one independent and one dependent clause)
  As nations grew wealthier, traditional freedom wasn't enough.

Sentences that are both long and complex in structure create a more formal style. Long compound sentences joined by *and* do not increase formality much because such sentences are really only two or more short, simple patterns hooked together. On the other hand, a long "simple" sentence with many modifiers will create a more formal style. The following example, from an essay on leadership by Michael Korda, is more complicated than the sample compound sentence above:

- *Expanded simple sentence*
  [A] leader is like a mirror, reflecting back to us our own sense of purpose, putting into words our own dreams and hopes, transforming our needs and fears into coherent policies and programs.

In "The Gettysburg Address" three sentences range from 10 to 16 words, six sentences from 21 to 29 words, and the final sentence is an incredible 82 words. All but two of Lincoln's sentences are either complex or compound-complex sentences. By contrast, in "Century of Freedom," Robert Samuelson, who does have a number of longish sentences, especially when he is quoting others, includes a paragraph (#5) with five sentences. These five sentences are composed of 9, 13, 6, 8, and 25 words. The second and fifth sentences are complex in structure—note the greater number of words as well—but the other three are all simple sentences.

2. *Does the writer use sentence fragments (incomplete sentences)?*
Although many instructors struggle to rid student writing of fragments, professional writers know that the occasional fragment can be used effectively for emphasis. Science-fiction writer Bruce Sterling, thinking about the "melancholic beauty" of a gadget no longer serving any purpose, writes:

- Like Duchamp's bottle-rack, it becomes a found objet d'art. A metallic fossil of some lost human desire. A kind of involuntary poem.

The second and third sentences are, technically, fragments, but because they build on the structure of the first sentence, readers can add the missing words "It becomes" to complete the sentences. The brevity, repetition of structure, and involvement of the reader to "complete" the fragments all contribute to a strong conclusion to Sterling's paragraph.

3. *Does the writer seem to be using an overly simplistic style? If so, why?*

Overly simplistic sentence patterns, just like an overly simplistic choice of words, can be used to show that the writer thinks the subject is silly or childish or insulting. In one of her columns, Ellen Goodman objects to society's over-simplifying of addictions and its need to believe in quick and lasting cures. She makes her point with reference to two well-known examples—but notice her technique:

- Hi, my name is Jane and I was once bulimic but now I am an exercise guru . . .
- Hi, my name is Oprah and I was a food addict but now I am a size 10.

4. *Does the writer use parallelism (coordination) or antithesis (contrast)?*

When two phrases or clauses are parallel in structure, the message is that they are equally important. Look back at Korda's expanded simple sentence. He coordinates three phrases, asserting that a leader is like a mirror in these three ways:

- Reflects back our purpose
- Puts into words our dreams
- Transforms our needs and fears

Antithesis creates tension. A sentence using this structure says "not this" but "that." Lincoln uses both parallelism and antithesis in one striking sentence:

- The world will little note nor long remember
    <u>what</u> we say here,
  but it [the world] can never forget
    <u>what</u> they did here.

Metaphors

When Korda writes that a leader is like a mirror, he is using a *simile.* When Lincoln writes that the world will not remember, he is using a *metaphor*—actually *personification.* Metaphors, whatever their form, all make a comparison between two items that are not really alike. The writer is making a *figurative comparison,* not a literal one. The writer wants us to think about some ways in which the items are similar. Metaphors state directly or imply the comparison; similes express the comparison using a connecting word; personification always compares a nonhuman item to humans. The exact label for a metaphor is not as important as:

- Recognizing the use of a figure of speech
- Identifying the two items being compared
- Understanding the point of the comparison
- Grasping the emotional impact of the figurative comparison.

> **REMEMBER:** We need to pay attention to writers' choices of metaphors. They reveal much about their feelings and perceptions of life. And, like connotative words, they affect us emotionally even if we are not aware of their use. Become aware. Be able to "open up"—explain—metaphors you find in your reading.

EXERCISE: Opening Up Metaphors

During World War II, E. B. White, the essayist and writer of children's books, defined the word *democracy* in one of his *New Yorker* columns. His definition contains a series of metaphors. One is: democracy "is the hole in the stuffed shirt through which the sawdust slowly trickles." We can open up or explain the metaphor this way:

> Just as one can punch a hole in a scarecrow's shirt and discover that there is only sawdust inside, nothing to be impressed by, so the idea of equality in a democracy "punches" a hole in the notion of an aristocratic ruling class and reveals that aristocrats, underneath, are ordinary people, just like you and me.

Here are two more of White's metaphors on democracy. Open up each one in a few sentences.

> Democracy is "the dent in the high hat."
> Democracy is "the score at the beginning of the ninth."

Organization and Examples

Two other elements of writing, organization and choice of examples, also reveal attitude and help to shape the reader's response. When you study a work's organization, ask yourself questions about both placement and volume. Where are these ideas placed? At the beginning or end—the places of greatest emphasis—or in the middle, suggesting that they are less important? With regard to volume, ask yourself, "What parts of the discussion are developed at length? What points are treated only briefly? *Note:* Sometimes simply counting the number of paragraphs devoted to the different parts of the writer's subject will guide you to a better understanding of the writer's main idea and purpose in writing.

Repetition

Well-written, unified essays will contain some repetition of key words and phrases. Some writers go beyond this basic strategy for coherent writing and use repetition to produce an effective cadence, like a drum beating in the background, keeping time to the speaker's fist pounding the lectern for emphasis. In his repetition of the now-famous phrase "I have a dream," Martin Luther King, Jr., gives emphasis to his vision of an ideal America (see pp. 675–77). In the following paragraph a student tried her hand at repetition to give emphasis to her definition of liberty:

> Liberty is having the right to vote and not having other laws which restrict that right; it is having the right to apply to the university of your choice without being rejected because of race. Liberty exists when a gay man has the right to a teaching position and is not released from the position when the news of his orientation is disclosed. Liberty exists when a woman who has been offered a job does not have to decline for lack of access to day care for her children, or when a 16-year-old boy from a ghetto can get an education and is not instead compelled to go to work to support his needy family.

These examples suggest that repetition generally gives weight and seriousness to writing and thus is appropriate when serious issues are being discussed in a forceful style.

Hyperbole, Understatement, and Irony

Grace Lichtenstein chose as the title of her book on college sports: *Playing for Money.* Now, college athletes do play, but presumably not for money. The title emphasizes that these "games" are serious business, not "play," for the athletes, coaches, and colleges. The bringing together of words that presumably do not go together—"play" and "money"—ironically underscores the problems in college athletics that Lichtenstein examines.

Quotation Marks, Italics, and Capital Letters

Several visual techniques can also be used to give special attention to certain words. A writer can place a word or phrase in quotation marks and thereby question its validity or meaning in that context. Ellen Goodman, writes, for example:

- I wonder about this when I hear the word "family" added to some politician's speech.

Goodman does not agree with the politician's meaning of the word *family,* as she reveals in her essay, but we know this immediately from her use of quotation marks. The expression *so-called* has the same effect:

- There has been a crackdown on the Chinese people's *so-called* liberty.

Italicizing (underscoring when typing) a key word or phrase also gives added emphasis. Dave Barry, in his essay printed below, uses italics for emphasis:

- Do you want appliances that are smarter than you? Of course not. Your appliances should be *dumber* than you, just like your furniture, your pets and your representative in Congress.

Capitalizing words not normally capitalized has the same effect of giving emphasis. As with exclamation points, writers need to use italics or capitalization sparingly, or the emphasis sought through contrast will be lost.

EXERCISES: Recognizing Elements of Style

1. Name the technique or techniques used in each of the following passages. Then briefly explain the idea of each passage.
   a. We are becoming the tools of our tools. (Henry David Thoreau)
   b. The bias and therefore the business of television is to *move* information, not collect it. (Neil Postman)
   c. If guns are outlawed, only the government will have guns. Only the police, the secret police, the military. The hired servants of our rulers. Only the government—and a few outlaws. (Edward Abbey)
   d. Having read all the advice on how to live 900 years, what I think is that eating a tasty meal once again will surely doom me long before I reach 900 while not eating that same meal could very well kill me. It's enough to make you reach for a cigarette! (Russell Baker)
   e. If you are desperate for a quick fix, either legalize drugs or repress the user. If you want a civilized approach, mount a propaganda campaign against drugs. (Charles Krauthammer)
   f. Oddly enough, the greatest scoffers at the traditions of American etiquette, who scorn the rituals of their own society as stupid and stultifying, voice respect for the custom and folklore of Native Americans, less industrialized people, and other societies they find more "authentic" than their own. (Judith Martin)
   g. Text is story. Text is event, performance, special effect. Subtext is ideas. It's motive, suggestions, visual implications, subtle comparisons. (Stephen Hunter)
   h. This flashy vehicle [the school bus] was as punctual as death: seeing us waiting at the cold curb, it would sweep to a halt, open its mouth, suck the boy in, and spring away with an angry growl. (E. B. White)
2. Read the following essay by Dave Barry. Use the questions that precede and follow the essay to help you determine Barry's attitude toward his subject and to characterize his style.

REMOTE CONTROL | DAVE BARRY

A humor columnist for the *Miami Herald* since 1983, Dave Barry (b. 1947) is now syndicated in more than 150 newspapers. A Pulitzer Prize winner in 1988, Barry has written several books, including *Dave Barry Slept Here* (1989). The following column appeared in March 2000.

PREREADING QUESTIONS What is Barry's purpose in writing? What does he want to accomplish in this column—besides being funny?

Recently the *Washington Post* printed an article explaining how the appli- 1
ance manufacturers plan to drive consumers insane.

Of course they don't *say* they want to drive us insane. What they *say* they 2
want to do is have us live in homes where "all appliances are on the Internet,
sharing information" and appliances will be "smarter than most of their owners." For example, the article states, you could have a home where the dishwasher "can be turned on from the office" and the refrigerator "knows when
it's out of milk" and the bathroom scale "transmits your weight to the gym."

I frankly wonder whether the appliance manufacturers, with all due respect, 3
have been smoking crack. I mean, did they ever stop to ask themselves *why* a
consumer, after loading a dishwasher, would go to the office to start it? Would
there be some kind of career benefit?

YOUR BOSS: What are you doing?   4

YOU (tapping computer keyboard): I'm starting my dishwasher!   5

YOUR BOSS: That's the kind of productivity we need around here!   6

YOU: Now I'm flushing the upstairs toilet!   7

Listen, appliance manufacturers: We don't *need* a dishwasher that we can 8
communicate with from afar. If you want to improve our dishwashers, give us
one that senses when people leave dirty dishes on the kitchen counter, and
shouts at them: *"Put those dishes in the dishwasher right now or I'll leak all over
your shoes!"*

Likewise, we don't need a refrigerator that knows when it's out of milk. We 9
already have a foolproof system for determining if we're out of milk: We ask
our wife. What we could use is a refrigerator that refuses to let us open its door
when it senses that we are about to consume our fourth Jell-O Pudding Snack
in two hours.

As for a scale that transmits our weight to the gym: Are they *nuts?* We don't 10
want our weight transmitted to our own *eyeballs!* What if the gym decided to
transmit our weight to all these other appliances on the Internet? What if, God
forbid, our refrigerator found out what our weight was? We'd never get the
door open again!

But here is what really concerns me about these new "smart" appliances: 11
Even if we like the features, we won't be able to use them. We can't use the
appliance features we have *now.* I have a feature-packed telephone with 43
buttons, at least 20 of which I am afraid to touch. This phone probably can
communicate with the dead, but I don't know how to operate it, just as I don't
know how to operate my TV, which has features out the wazooty and requires
three remote controls. One control (44 buttons) came with the TV; a second (39
buttons) came with the VCR; the third (37 buttons) was brought here by the ca-
ble man, who apparently felt that I did not have enough buttons.

So when I want to watch TV, I'm confronted with a total of 120 buttons, 12
identified by such helpful labels as PIP, MTS, DBS, F2, JUMP and BLANK. There are
three buttons labeled power, but there are times—especially if my son and his
friends, who are not afraid of features, have changed the settings—when I honestly cannot figure out how to turn the TV on. I stand there, holding three remote controls, pressing buttons at random, until eventually I give up and go

turn on the dishwasher. It has been, literally, years since I have successfully recorded a TV show. That is how "smart" my appliances have become.

13   And now the appliance manufacturers want to give us even *more* features. Do you know what this means? It means that some night you'll open the door of your "smart" refrigerator, looking for a beer, and you'll hear a pleasant, cheerful voice—recorded by the same woman who informs you that Your Call Is Important when you call a business that does not wish to speak with you personally—telling you: "Your celery is limp." You will not know how your refrigerator knows this, and, what is worse, you will not know who else your refrigerator is telling about it ("Hey, Bob! I hear your celery is limp!"). And if you want to try to make the refrigerator *stop*, you'll have to decipher Owner's Manual instructions written by and for nuclear physicists ("To disable the Produce Crispness Monitoring feature, enter the Command Mode, then select the Edit function, then select Change Vegetable Defaults, then assume that Train A leaves Chicago traveling westbound at 47 mph, while Train B . . .").

14   Is this the kind of future you want, consumers? Do you want appliances that are smarter than you? Of course not. Your appliances should be *dumber* than you, just like your furniture, your pets and your representatives in Congress. So I am urging you to let the appliance industry know, by phone, letter, fax and e-mail, that when it comes to "smart" appliances, you vote no. You need to act quickly. Because while you're reading this, your microwave oven is voting YES.

QUESTIONS FOR READING AND REASONING

1. After thinking about Barry's subject and purpose, what do you conclude to be his thesis? Does he have more than one main idea?

2. How would you describe the essay's tone? Serious? Humorous? Ironic? Angry? Something else? Does a nonserious tone exclude the possibility of a degree of serious purpose? Explain your answer.

QUESTIONS FOR REFLECTING AND WRITING

1. What passages in the article do you find funniest? Why?

2. What strategies does Barry use to create tone and convey attitude? List, with examples, as many as you can.

WRITING ABOUT STYLE

What does it mean to "do a style analysis"? A style analysis answers the question "How is it written?" Let's think through the steps in preparing a study of a writer's choice and arrangement of language.

Purpose

We can think about purpose in part by excluding what would be inappropriate. A style analysis is not the place for challenging the ideas of the writer. A style analysis requires the discipline to see how a work has been put together *even if you disagree with the writer's views.* You do not have to agree with a writer to appreciate his or her skill in writing. A style analysis may imply, or even briefly express, a positive evaluation of the author's writing—but that is not the same as agreeing or disagreeing with the author's ideas.

Audience

If you think about audience in the context of your purpose, you should conclude that a summary of content does not belong in a style analysis. Why? Because we write style analyses for people who have already read the work. Remember, though, that your reader may not know the work in the detail that you know it, so you will need to give examples to illustrate the points of your analysis.

Establishing a General Plan

First, keep in mind that your analysis should be organized according to elements of style, not according to the organization of the work you are examining. Scrap any thoughts of "hacking" your way through the essay, commenting on the work paragraph by paragraph. This approach invites summary rather than analysis. It also means that you have not selected an organization that supports your purpose in writing. Think of an essay as like the pie in Figure 2.1. We could divide the pie according to key ideas—if we were summarizing. But we can also, as the diagram shows, carve the pie according to elements of style, the techniques we have discussed in this chapter. This is the general plan you want to follow for your essay.

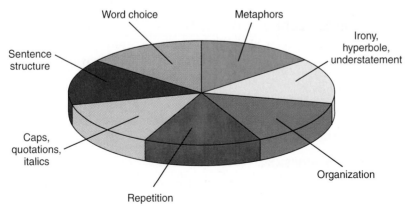

FIGURE 2.1 Analyzing Style

So, your task is to study the work and then select those techniques you think are most important in creating the writer's attitude and to discuss them one at a time. Do not try to include the entire pie; instead, select three or four elements to examine in some detail. If you were asked to write an analysis of the Dave Barry column, for example, you might select his use of italics and quotation marks, his use of hyperbole, and his use of irony. These are three techniques that stand out in Barry's writing.

Drafting the Style Analysis

If you were to select three elements of style, as in the Dave Barry example above, your essay might look something like this:

Paragraph 1: Introduction	1. Attention-getter 2. Author, title, publication information of article/book 3. Brief explanation of author's subject 4. Your thesis—that you will be looking at style
Paragraph 2: First body paragraph	Analysis of italics and quotation marks. (See below for more details on body paragraphs.)
Paragraph 3: Second body paragraph	1. Topic sentence that introduces analysis of hyperbole 2. Three or more examples of hyperbole 3. Explanation of how each example connects to the author's thesis—that is, how the example of hyperbole works to convey attitude. This is your analysis; don't forget it!
Paragraph 4: Third body paragraph	Analysis of irony—with same three part as illustrated above.
Paragraph 5: Conclusion	Restate your thesis: We can understand Barry's point through a study of these three elements of his style.

A CHECKLIST FOR REVISION

When revising and polishing your draft, use these questions to complete your essay.

☐ Have I handled all titles correctly?

☐ Have I correctly referred to the author?

☐ Have I used quotation marks correctly when presenting examples of style? (Use the guidelines in Chapter 1 for these first three questions.)

☐ Do I have an accurate, clear presentation of the author's subject and thesis?

☐ Do I have enough examples of each element of style to show my readers that these elements are important?

☐ Have I connected examples to the author's thesis? That is, have I shown my readers how these techniques work to develop the author's attitude?

To reinforce your understanding of style analysis, read the following essay by Ellen Goodman, answer the questions that follow, and then study the student essay that analyzes Goodman's style.

CHOOSING FAMILIES | ELLEN GOODMAN

Author of *Close to Home* (1979), *At Large* (1981), and *Keeping Touch* (1985), collections of her essays, Ellen Goodman (b. 1941) has been a feature writer for the *Boston Globe* since 1967 and a syndicated columnist since 1976. She has won a Pulitzer Prize for distinguished commentary. In addition to appearing in the *Globe*, the following column was printed in many newspapers across the country, including the *Washington Post*, on November 24, 1988.

PREREADING QUESTIONS What is Goodman's subject? Why is it incorrect to say that her subject is Thanksgiving?

BOSTON—They will celebrate Thanksgiving the way they always do, in the Oral Tradition. Equal parts of food and conversation. A cornucopia of family. 1

These are not restrained people who choose their words and pick at their stuffing. These are people who have most of their meals in small chicken-sized households. But when they come together, they feast on the sounds as well as tastes of a turkey-sized family. 2

Indeed, their Thanksgiving celebrations are as crowded with stories as their tables are with chairs. Arms reach indelicately across each other for second helpings, voices interrupt to add relish to a story. And there are always leftovers too enormous to complete, that have to be wrapped up and preserved. 3

But what is it that makes this collection of people a family? How do we make a family these days? With blood? With marriage? With affection? I wonder about this when I hear the word "family" added to some politician's speech like gravy poured over the entire plate. The meaning is supposed to be obvious, self-evident. It is assumed that when we talk about family we are all talking about the same thing. That families are the same. But it's not that simple. 4

For the past eight years, the chief defender of the American family has lived in the White House. But Reagan's own family has always looked more like our contemporary reality than his traditional image. There has been marriage and divorce among the Reagans, adoption and blending, and more than one estrangement. There is a mother, this holiday season, who hasn't talked to her daughter for more than a year. 5

6   The man who will take his place as head of this family ideology has wrapped himself in a grandfatherly image. Yet Bush's family is also extended in ways that are common but not always comforting to other Americans.

7   As young people, George and Barbara Bush left home again and again, setting up temporary quarters in 17 cities. Now they have five children scattered in an equal number of states: Texas and Florida, Colorado, Virginia and Connecticut. Theirs, like many of ours, do not live at home, but come home, for the holidays.

8   We hold onto a particular primal image of families—human beings created from the same genetic code, living in the same area code. We hold onto an image of *the* family as something rooted and stable. But that has always been rare in a country where freedom is another word for mobility, both emotional and physical.

9   In America, families are spliced and recombined in as many ways as DNA. Every year our Thanksgiving tables expand and contract, place settings are removed and added. A guest last year is a member this year. A member last year may be an awkward outsider this year. How many of our children travel between alienated halves of their heritage, between two sets of people who share custody of their holidays?

10   Even among those families we call stable or intact, the ride to the airport has become a holiday ritual as common as pumpkin pie. Many parents come from retirement homes, many children from college, many cousins from jobs in other Zip Codes. We retrieve these people, as if from a memory hole, for reunions.

11   What then makes a family, in the face of all this "freedom"? It is said that people don't choose their parents. Or their aunts and uncles. But in a sense Americans do choose to *make* a family out of these people. We make room for them in our lives, choose to be with them and preserve that choice through a ritual as simple as passing seconds at a table.

12   All real families are made over time and through tradition. The Oral Tradition. We create a shared treasure trove of history, memories, conversation. Equal parts of food and conversation. And a generous serving of pleasure in each other's company.

QUESTIONS FOR READING, REASONING, AND WRITING

1. What is Goodman's attitude toward families; that is, what does she assert about families in this column? Is there one sentence that states her thesis? If so, which one? If not, write a thesis for the essay.

2. Characterize Goodman's style. Analyze her word choice, metaphors, sentence structure, organization, and use of the Reagan and Bush families as examples. How does each contribute to our understanding of her point?

3. Why are Goodman's metaphors especially notable? Open up—or explain—three of her metaphors.

STUDENT ESSAY

GOODMAN'S FEAST OF STYLE

Alan Peterson

Thanksgiving is a time for "families" to come together, eat a big meal, share their experiences and each other's company. In her November 24, 1988, article "Choosing Families," which appeared on Thanksgiving Day in the Washington Post, Ellen Goodman asks the question: "Who makes up these families?" By her definition, a family does not consist of just "blood" relatives; a family contains acquaintances, friends, relatives, people who are "chosen" to be in this year's "family." An examination of Goodman's essay reveals some of the elements of style she uses to effectively ask and answer her question.

Goodman's clever organization compels the reader to read on. She begins by focusing on a Thanksgiving dinner scene, referring to families and households in terms of food. After setting the table by evoking the reader's memories of Thanksgivings past, Goodman asks the central question of her essay: "[W]hat is it that makes this collection of people a family?" (49) Goodman argues that the modern meaning of family has evolved so much that the traditional definition of family is no longer the standard. To clarify modern definitions, she provides examples of famous families: First Families. After suggesting that the Reagans have been the "chief defender of the American family" (49) for the last eight years, she points out that the Reagans, with their divorces, their adoptions, their estrangements, are anything but the traditional family they wish to portray. Rather, the Reagans represent the human traits that define the "contemporary reality" (49) of today's families. Next, President Bush's family is examined. Goodman points out that the Bushes' five children live in five different states, and that Barbara and George Bush, as young people,

Introduction includes author, title, and date of article.

Student's thesis

Analysis of Goodman's organization.

Page reference given, according to MLA style.*

---

*This essay illustrates formal documentation according to the Modern Language Association (MLA).

set up "temporary quarters in 17 cities" (50). She develops an answer to her question in the ensuing paragraphs. She observes that families today are disjointed, nontraditional, different from one another. She refers to families that are considered "stable or intact" (50) and shows how even those families can be spread out all over the country. In her closing paragraphs she repeats the question "What makes a family?" Then, after another reference to Thanksgiving dinner, she concludes the article by stating her main point: "All real families are made over time and through tradition" (50). Goodman's organization—a question, some examples, several answers, and strong confirmation—powerfully frames her thesis.

In an essay written about a theme as homespun as family and Thanksgiving celebrations, a reader would not expect the language to be too formal. Choosing her words carefully, Goodman cultivates a familiar and descriptive, yet not overly informal style. Early in the essay, Goodman uses simple language to portray the Thanksgiving meal. She refers to voices interrupting, arms reaching, leftovers that have to be wrapped up. Another effective technique of diction Goodman employs is the repetition of words and sounds. She points out that the Bushes, as young people, "left home again and again" (50). She defines the image we have of families as that of people created from the same "genetic code, living in the same area code," and of cousins in "other Zip Codes" (50). Then, characterizing the reality of the configuration of today's American families, Goodman states: "A guest last year is a member this year," while a "member last year may be an awkward outsider this year" (50). An additional example of repetition appears in the first and last paragraphs. Goodman repeats the sentence fragment "Equal parts of food and conversation" (50). This informal choice of words opens and closes her essay, cleverly setting the tone in the beginning and reiterating the theme at the end.

Perhaps the most prevalent element of style present in Goodman's piece, and a dominant characteristic of her essay style, is her use of metaphors. From the opening sentences all the way through to the end, this article is full of

Analysis of Goodman's word choice and repetition.

Analysis of Goodman's metaphors.

metaphors. Keeping with the general focus of the piece (the essay appeared on Thanksgiving Day), many of the metaphors liken food to family. Her references include "a cornucopia of family," "chicken-sized households" and a "turkey-sized family," people who "feast on the sounds as well as the tastes," and voices that "add relish to a story" (49). She imparts that a politician can use the word "family" like "gravy poured over the entire plate" (49). Going to the airport to pick up family members of these disjointed American families has become "a holiday ritual as common as pumpkin pie" (50). Goodman draws parallels between the process of "choosing" people to be with and the simple ritual of passing seconds at the table. Indeed, the essay's mood emphasizes the comparison of and inextricable bond between food and family.

    Ellen Goodman's "Choosing Families" is a thought-provoking essay on the American family. She organizes the article so that readers are reminded of their own Thanksgiving experiences and consider who is included in their "families." After asking "What is it that makes this collection of people a family?" Goodman provides election-year examples of prominent American families, then an explanation of "family" that furnishes her with an answer. Her word choice and particularly the repetition of words and sounds make reading her essay a pleasure. The metaphors Goodman uses link in readers' minds the images of Thanksgiving food and the people with whom they spend the holiday. Her metaphors underscore the importance she places on having meals with the family, which is the one truly enduring tradition for all people. Perhaps the most important food-and-family metaphor comes in the last sentence: "a generous serving of pleasure in each other's company" (50).

Conclusion restates Goodman's position and student's thesis.

Work Cited

Goodman, Ellen. "Choosing Families." Washington Post. 24 Nov. 1988. Rpt. in
    Read, Reason, Write: An Argument Text and Reader. 7th ed. Ed. Dorothy
    U. Seyler. New York: McGraw-Hill, 2005. 49–50.

COMBINING SUMMARY, ANALYSIS, AND EVALUATION: WRITING THE REVIEW

Writing a good review requires combining skills you have been working on: critical reading, accurate summary, analysis of style, and evaluation of the work—book or film—in the context of the writer or director's subject, intended audience, and comparative success. Let's look again at steps in the writing process as they apply to writing a review.

Audience

Try to imagine writing your review for your classmates, not just your instructor. Try not to focus on this assignment as writing to be graded. Rather, think about why we turn to reviews: What do readers want to learn? They want to know if they should read the book or see the film. Your job is to help readers make that decision.

Purpose

Your purpose, then, is to provide clear, accurate information and a fair evaluation of both the material covered (or not covered) and the presentation of that material. Balance is important. You do not want most of your review to be summary, with just a few sentences of evaluation "stuck on" at the end. You also do not want a detailed summary of the work's beginning followed by skimpy coverage of the rest. This lack of balance may suggest to readers that you have not read or seen the entire work. Just remember: when reviewing a novel or movie, do not explain the entire plot. You do not want to give away the ending!

Establishing a General Plan

First, study the work carefully. Be sure that you can write a complete and accurate summary, even if you need to leave some of the plot details out of your review. Second, the analysis part of your review needs two elements: comment on the work's structure and special features plus discussion of the writer's (or director's) style. How is the work put together? For a nonfiction book, how many chapters or sections are there, and what does each cover? Does the book contain visuals? An index? For a film, how does the story unfold? What actors are in the lead roles? What special effects are used? These are the kinds of questions readers expect a review to answer.

Your analysis of style needs to be connected to the work's intended audience. For example, is the biography informally written or heavily documented with notes and references? What is the level of formality of the book? What is the age level or knowledge level of the author's expected audience? Films are rated for age groups. Books can also be rated for age and level of knowledge of the subject.

Your summary and analysis can point the way to a fair and sensible evaluation. If, for example, you have many problems understanding a book aimed at a general audience, then it is fair to say that the author has not successfully reached his or her audience. If, on the other hand, you selected a book to review that was designed for specialists, then your reading challenge is not relevant to a fair judgment. All it allows you to do is point out that the book is tough going for a nonspecialist (or a movie sequel, for example, is hard to follow in spots for those who did not see the original film). Your evaluation should include an assessment of content and presentation. Did the book or film fulfill its intended purpose? Was it as thorough as you expected in the light of other works on the same or a similar topic? (A study of American literature in the 1920s, for instance, that fails to mention Ernest Hemingway would surely be evaluated as incomplete and thus flawed.)

Drafting the Review

There is no simple formula for combining summary, analysis, and evaluation in a review. Some instructors simplify the task by requiring a two-part review: summary first and then analysis and evaluation. If you are not so directed, then some blending of the three elements will be expected. Often reviews begin with an opening that is both an attention-getter and a broad statement of the work's subject or subject category. (This is a *biography* of Franklin; this is a *female action-hero* flick.) An evaluation in general terms follows to complete the opening paragraph. Then the reviewer uses a "summary–analysis–evaluation" pattern, providing details of content and presentation and then assessing the work.

To get some good ideas about how to proceed with your review, study the short, annotated review by Lynda Ransdell and the longer review by student Ian Habel. You may also want to look at other reviews in newspapers and magazines to expand your understanding of strategies for writing reviews.

ANNOTATED REVIEW

Dr. Cynthia Pemberton's new book, *More Than a Game: One Woman's Fight for Gender Equity in Sport*, is destined to become a classic in sport sociology, sport history, and women's studies. The author chronicles the trials and tribulations of Dr. Pemberton's Title IX battle at Linfield College, a small liberal arts college in Oregon. She uses an effective writing style to tell a painful and fascinating story that begins with her naivete about the potential impact of questioning gender equity at her college, and ends with her decision to move on to a different career as an educator and administrator in higher education. Throughout the book, Pemberton describes the different types of roadblocks encountered—and how she dealt with those roadblocks. The subtle discrimination is shocking. The strength of her character in dealing with these roadblocks is impressive. One of my favorite parts of the book is how she effectively disarms the myth that men's minor sports are being dropped because women's

Opening includes author, title, and general evaluation.

Summary with evaluation of style.

Reviewer's comment on the book's subject.

sports are being added—due to Title IX. In reality, women's sports are much less powerful than men's major sports, yet we continue to receive the blame for dropping men's athletic teams. In reality, excesses in major men's sports such as football and basketball contribute to belt-tightening in high school and college athletics.

Evaluation

The book made me laugh and cry—always a good sign when searching for the ultimate book to read—or, when searching for the ultimate book to make an impact on students who are unfamiliar with Title IX. Mostly, I could relate to her stories—given my background as a former small college coach and faculty member.

Analysis— Book's target audience—plus evaluation.

The target audience for this book includes educators, coaches, athletes, and administrators at any level. Additionally, anyone interested in studying women's sports or pursuing a Title IX case will love this book. It is a "must read" for students studying the humanistic, realistic, and not so glamorous side of Title IX. It should help educate those preparing to file a Title IX grievance, or those who have not had to fight a battle in women's athletics. It will dramatically open the eyes of those who take women's contemporary participation opportunities, training facilities, and coaching for granted.

Ends with strong evaluation.

The passion, courage, and knowledge used to write this book solidify Dr. Cynthia Pemberton's status as one of the premier experts on Title IX in the U.S.

STUDENT REVIEW

WINCHESTER'S ALCHEMY: TWO MEN AND A BOOK

Ian Habel

One can hardly imagine a tale promising less excitement for a general audience than that of the making of the Oxford English Dictionary (OED). The sensationalism of murder and insanity would have to labor intensely against the burden of lexicography in crafting a genuine page-turner on the subject. Much to my surprise, Simon Winchester, in writing The Professor and the Madman: A Tale of Murder, Insanity, and the Making of The Oxford English Dictionary, has succeeded in producing so compelling a story that I was forced to devour it completely in a single afternoon, an unprecedented personal feat.

The Professor and the Madman is the story of the lives of two apparently very different men and the work that brought them together. Winchester begins by recounting the circumstances that led to the incarceration of Dr. W. C. Minor, a well-born, well-educated, and quite insane American ex-Army surgeon. Minor, in a fit of delusion, had murdered a man whom he believed to have crept into his Lambeth hotel room to torment him in his sleep. The doctor is tried and whisked off to the Asylum for the Criminally Insane, Broadmoor.

The author then introduces readers to the other two main characters: the OED itself and its editor James Murray, a low-born, self-educated Scottish philologist. The shift in narrative focus is used to dramatic effect. The natural assumption on the part of the reader that these two seemingly unrelated plots must eventually meet urges us to read on in anticipation of that connection. As each chapter switches focus from one man to the other, it is introduced by a citation from the OED, reminding us that the story is ultimately about the dictionary. The citations also serve to foreshadow and provide a theme for the chapter. For example, the OED definition of *murder* heads the first chapter, relating to the details of Minor's crime.

Winchester acquaints us with the shortcomings of seventeenth- and eighteenth-century attempts at compiling a comprehensive dictionary of the English language. He takes us inside the meetings of the Philological Society, whose members proposed the compilation of the dictionary to end all dictionaries. The OED was to include examples of usage illustrating every shade of meaning for every word in the English language. Such a mammoth feat would require enlisting thousands of volunteer readers to comb the corpus of English literature in search of illustrative quotations to be submitted on myriad slips of paper. These slips of paper on each word would in turn be studied by a small army of editors preparing the definitions.

It is not surprising that our Dr. Minor, comfortably tucked away at Broadmoor, possessing both a large library and seemingly infinite free time, should become one of those volunteer readers. After all, we are still rightfully assuming some connection of the book's two plot lines. Yet what sets Dr. Minor apart from his fellow volunteers (aside from the details of his incarceration) is the remarkable efficiency with which he approached his task. Not content merely to fill out slips of paper for submission, Minor methodically indexed every possibly useful mention of any word appearing in his personal library. He then asked to be kept informed of the progress of the work, submitting quotations that would be immediately useful to editors. In this way he managed to "escape" his cell and plunge himself into the work of contemporaries, to become a part of a major event of his time.

Minor's work proved invaluable to the OED's staff of editors, led by James Murray. With the two plot lines now intertwined, readers face such questions as "Will they find out that Minor is insane?" "Will Minor and Murray ever meet?" and "How long will they take to complete the dictionary?" The author builds suspense regarding a meeting of Minor and Murray by providing a false account of their first encounter, as reported by the American press, only to shatter us with the fact that this romantic version did not happen. I'll let Winchester give you the answers to these questions, while working his magic on you, drawing you into this fascinating tale of the making of the world's most famous dictionary.

ANALYZING TWO OR MORE SOURCES

Newswriters and analysts, influenced by their particular ways of seeing the world, view events differently. Scientists examining the same set of facts do not always draw the same conclusions; neither do historians and biographers agree on the significance of the same documents. How do we recognize and cope with these disparities? As critical readers we analyze what we read, pose questions, and refuse to believe everything we find in print or hear on television. To develop these skills in recognizing differences, instructors frequently ask students to contrast the views of two or more writers. In psychology class, for example, you may be asked to contrast the views of Sigmund Freud and John B. Watson on child development. In a communications course, you may be asked to contrast the moderator styles of two talk-show hosts. We can examine differences in content or presentation, or both. Here are guidelines for preparing a contrast of sources.

GUIDELINES for Preparing a Contrast of Sources

1. **Work with sources that have something in common.** Think about the context for each, that is, each source's subject and purpose. (It would not make much sense to contrast a textbook chapter, for example, with a TV talk show because their contexts are so different.)

2. **Read actively to understand the content of the two sources.** Tape films, radio, or TV shows so that you can listen/view them several times, just as you would read a written source more than once.

3. **Analyze for differences, focusing on your purpose in contrasting.** If you are contrasting the ideas of two writers, for example, then your analysis will focus on ideas, not on writing style. To explore differences in two news accounts, you may want to consider all of the following: the impact of placement in the newspaper/magazine, accompanying photographs or graphics, length of each article, what is covered in each article, and writing styles. Prepare a list of specific differences.

4. **Organize your contrast.** It is usually best to organize by points of difference. If you write first about one source and then about the other, the ways that the sources differ may not be clear for readers. Take the time to plan an organization that clearly reveals your contrast purpose in writing. To illustrate, a paper contrasting the writing styles of two authors can be organized according to the following pattern:

   Introduction: Introduce your topic and make clear your purpose to contrast styles of writer A and writer B.

   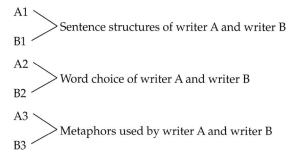

   Conclusion: Explain the effect of the differences in style of the writers.

5. **Illustrate and discuss each of the points of difference for each of the sources.** Provide examples and explain the impact of the differences in level of formality or connotation.

6. **Always write for an audience who may be familiar with your general topic but not with the specific sources you are discussing.** Be sure to provide adequate context (names, titles of works, etc.).

EXERCISE: Analyzing Two Sources

The news is supposed to be objective and balanced. Analysis, however, is part of presenting the news, journalists would argue. And, whenever two people choose to write on the same topic, there are bound to be differences in choice of specifics and emphasis—and that's before there are differences in political perspective. So, we are wise to use more than one news source for our information.

The following two articles are front-page reports of President Bush's televised speech on Iraq delivered September 7, 2003. Read and annotate each article. Think about differences in content, attitude, and judgment. What details of the speech get the most attention from each writer? Is there a difference in tone? Prepare a list of points of difference you would include in a comparative analysis. Discuss differences with your class partner or in small groups and decide on one list. Organize your selected points of difference and list details you would use to develop each point as if you were planning to draft an essay. Be prepared to explain and defend your choice of outline.

BUSH PUSHES FOR U.N. IN IRAQ | BILL SAMMON

This article, published September 8, 2003, in the *Washington Times* begins on page A1, on the top left of the paper, and then is completed on page A11. It is one column wide with only a moderately-sized headline. On page A11, the rest of the article is accompanied by one photograph—of Bush facing the camera, behind the lectern, looking quite serious.

1   President Bush last night called on the Untied Nations to take greater control of postwar Iraq, which he said has degenerated into the central battleground in the global war against terrorism.

2   "Members of the United Nations now have an opportunity, and the responsibility, to assume a broader role in assuring that Iraq becomes a free and democratic nation," Mr. Bush said in a rare, primetime address to the nation.

3   For the first time, the president said it would cost $87 billion to continue peacekeeping operations in Iraq and Afghanistan, with the bulk of that money—$52 billion—going directly to the Pentagon. Another $20 billion would go toward Iraq's reconstruction, including the establishment of police and military forces.

4   The speech came amid growing doubts about America's ability to single-handedly restore order in Iraq, the site of almost daily attacks against GIs and three major bombings in recent weeks. More Americans have died in Iraq since May 1, when the president declared an end to major combat operations, than during the three-week war itself.

5   Although the United Nations balked at backing the war, Mr. Bush recently has resigned himself to asking the world body for help in winning the peace. He said "enlisting the support of other nations" is now a primary component of the administration's Iraq strategy.

By taking his case directly to the American people, the president sought to counter the daily drumbeat of negative headlines from Iraq. He implored Americans to take the long view of the war on terror, which he said will require patience and resolve.   6

"Two years ago, I told the Congress and the country that the war on terror would be a lengthy war, a different kind of war, fought on many fronts in many places," he said from the White House.   7

"Iraq is now the central front. Enemies of freedom are making a desperate stand there—and there they must be defeated. This will take time and require sacrifice."   8

The president's speech did little to quell mounting criticism from Democratic presidential contenders, such as Howard Dean, who waited just 10 minutes after Mr. Bush stopped speaking to critique the performance during a conference call with reporters.   9

Other Democrats lashed out even before the president spoke. Rep. Jane Harman, ranking Democrat on the House Intelligence Committee, said yesterday that postwar planning for Iraq is "a shambles. I want the president to tell us what's really in store for Americans," she said on CNN's "Late Edition With Wolf Blitzer."   10

"How much are we going to pay? What is the possible loss of life going forward?" she added. "And how is he going to repair the damage to our relationship with international organizations, so that they step up and bear a reasonable share of this?"   11

Mr. Bush touched on some of those issues, although not with a level of specificity that is likely to satisfy his Democratic detractors.   12

Aside from disclosing a specific price tag for peacekeeping operations, he spoke in mostly broad terms about the overarching strategy of the global war on terrorism.   13

"The Middle East will either become a place of progress and peace, or it will be an exporter of violence and terror that takes more lives in America and in other free nations," he said. "The triumph of democracy and tolerance in Iraq, in Afghanistan, and beyond, would be a grave setback for international terrorism."   14

Mr. Bush also addressed the recent bombings in Iraq, which killed scores at a U.N. headquarters, the Jordanian embassy and a Shi'ite mosque.   15

"There is more at work in these attacks than blind rage," he said. "The terrorists have a strategic goal. They want us to leave Iraq before our work is done."   16

Critics of the president said he gave the speech to reverse a slide in his popularity. A recent Zogby poll showed Mr. Bush's job approval rating at 45 percent, although the latest Gallup poll has it much higher at 59 percent.   17

White House aides said Mr. Bush was merely updating the nation on the ongoing war effort. The president used lofty rhetoric to stir emotions on the eve of the two-year anniversary of the September 11 terrorist attacks.   18

"We have been tested these past 24 months, and the dangers have not passed," he said. "Yet, Americans are responding with courage and confidence."   19

PRESIDENT SIDESTEPS
EXIT STRATEGY ISSUE

MICHAEL TACKETT

Senior correspondent Michael Tackett published this analysis on page 1 of the *Chicago Tribune* on September 8, 2003.

1   President Bush's challenge Sunday night was to explain why America won the war but keeps losing the battles.

2   Needing to reassure an increasingly skeptical public about the cost of the conflict in Iraq—in both lives and treasure—the president fell back on recycled themes, trying again to stitch together a pattern of evidence that connected the terrorist threat of Osama bin Laden's Al Qaeda network to the regime of Saddam Hussein in Iraq.

3   His evidence was no more powerful than before, when critics dismissed it as shaky. It is only in a post facto sense that a link has emerged, in that terrorist-style attacks within Iraq's borders are bringing a general sense of disorder after the swift capitulation of the Iraqi army.

4   The president offered thematic sustenance about the hows and whys of the U.S. presence and mission in Iraq, though none of it rang particularly new. He did offer a much-needed specific about the cost, an additional $87 billion. But he left out any attempt to answer a pressing question on so many minds: What is the exit strategy?

5   He also returned to a place where he was before the war started, imploring other nations to join the coalition, to send troops and to contribute financially. His rationale seemed to be that more nations had a direct stake in Iraq after terrorists bombed a temporary United Nations headquarters in Baghdad. Secretary of State Colin Powell is working to draft another UN Security Council resolution for assistance. The early returns on him succeeding this time are not promising.

6   The president did not use the moment to acknowledge any shortcomings in his administration's approach. Rather, he seemed to suggest that what is needed was more of the same, and in the case of the funding, a stunning amount more.

7   He asked for more elusive support in the form of patience and resolve.

8   Bush's speech came at the start of a week in which there will be intense focus on the second anniversary of the Sept. 11, 2001, attacks. It was on that tragic day, and especially in the weeks that followed, that Bush developed a strong bond of trust with many Americans. So it was a timely moment to start the week off with his view that the two—the terrorist attacks and the war in Iraq—are inextricably related.

CALL FOR SACRIFICE VAGUE

9   "Two years ago, I told the Congress and the country that the war on terror would be a lengthy war, a different kind of war, fought on many fronts in many places," Bush said. "Iraq is now the central front. Enemies of freedom are making a desperate stand there, and they must be defeated. This will require time and require sacrifice."

A call for sacrifice has been largely missing from the president's exhorta- 10
tions to the country in fighting the war on terror. And he did little to flesh out
that notion in his address from the Cabinet Room. What kind of sacrifice? How
do Americans buy in? By putting up with extra security at airports? Or is it just
meant for the soldiers?

"I thought that he was going to stand up there and say, 'Look, this is what's 11
happened since we defeated the regime. I know there have been doubts. So I
wanted to tell you what we are doing,' " said Rep. Rahm Emanuel (D-Ill.).
"Rather than straighten the ship, I think it's still in choppy waters. I thought he
could have leveled with the American people."

Bush tried to make the mission in Iraq sound orderly and well-thought-out, 12
employing the speechwriter's device for clarity, the triplet: destroying the terrorists, enlisting the support of other nations and helping Iraqis prepare for a
day when they will defend and govern themselves.

Each item on his checklist is problematic. There are reports of dozens of ji- 13
hadis flooding into Iraq—would-be martyrs who can be as lethally effective as
terrorists elsewhere in the Middle East. Other nations are balking at supporting
the United States, a kind of diplomatic payback for the U.S. decision to essentially go it alone on war. Self-governance remains a noble but distant prospect.

QUESTIONING THE COST
Each of those items also carries an extraordinary price tag. Before the speech, 14
some Republicans had begun to question the cost. Some Democrats were
even questioning the motive and making it personal. Rep. David Obey (D-Wis.)
called directly for the resignation of Defense Secretary Donald Rumsfeld and
his top deputy, Paul Wolfowitz.

Presidents normally husband the moments when they ask for prime time 15
on television to address the country. For the president, one of the more recent
was when he landed on an aircraft carrier off Southern California in May to declare the end of "major combat operations."

Bush's cinematic landing on the carrier in May now appears increasingly 16
awkward. For Democrats, it has become a ready punch line.

"The big mistake in Iraq was, don't ever spike the ball on the 40-yard line," 17
Emanuel said.

For much of the post-Sept. 11 portion of his presidency, Bush has had lit- 18
tle concerted opposition. That is changing as the intensity rises in the fight for
the Democratic presidential nomination. And Democrats provided a ready preview of what Bush can expect in their debate last week in New Mexico, when
he was the target of their most pointed rhetorical fire and not each other.

In the early days of his presidency, Bush had an uneasy grasp of the bully 19
pulpit. Since Sept. 11, he has used it repeatedly and largely effectively at urgent national moments, such as when the nation was attacked or when he was
ordering the military into action.

This was a different kind of moment. He was speaking not about the clar- 20
ity of war but about the ambiguity of occupation and peacemaking. This president doesn't do ambiguity nearly so well.

FOR ANALYSIS

Now read, analyze, and be prepared to discuss the following two essays.

THE FAT ENVIRONMENT | ELLEN GOODMAN

See page 49 for biographical details about Ellen Goodman. The following column was published July 26, 2003.

PREREADING QUESTIONS How do you read Goodman's title? That is, what do you expect her essay to be about? How often do you eat at fast-food restaurants such as McDonald's? How many sodas do you drink, on average, each day?

1   BOSTON—I work in a danger zone. Across the street from my office is a restaurant that sells bagels larger than my hand. Around the corner is a Ben and Jerry's that scoops an ice cream flavor that is "Phish food" for the whale-sized. This morning the local pizza place put up a sign announcing "all you can eat" night.

2   Life on this Boulevard of Broken Diets is not easy. After all, like most Americans I subscribe to the "just say no" school of weight control. This is a school that promotes theorists like Will and Power. It offers a school motto of Personal Responsibility.

3   Even as the ideal body has gotten slimmer and the real body has gotten wider, students of this philosophy react like our Puritan ancestors. We assume that what separates the saved from the damned is virtue.

4   Well, fat chance for virtue. The only part of our economy that seems to be expanding is the waistline. Sixty percent of Americans are overweight. Twice as many kids are overweight as a generation ago. And in the past few weeks we've had health warnings about fat that range from diabetes to Alzheimer's.

5   The only good news is that we are beginning to shift from describing obesity as a moral failing to describing it as a public health epidemic. We are beginning to shift at least some attention from self-control to environment-out-of-control.

6   This change is partly due to the collective, um, weight of scientific studies. Yale's Kelly Brownell, who coined the phrase "toxic environment," sums them up this way: "When the environment changes, weight changes." When, for example, immigrants from thinner countries come to America they gain weight, while their cousins back home stay lean. When you give moviegoers a big box of popcorn instead of a small one, they eat about 50 percent more.

7   The change also comes from the discovery that there really were business plans for the fattening of America. We don't actually have much less will power than we used to. In *Fat Land*, Greg Critser details the deliberate supersizing of servings from the Big Mac to the Big Gulp. Instead of expanding the number of customers, they expanded the existing customers.

At the same time, we have learned something from the campaigns against 8
smoking. Yes, it's up to the smoker to stub out the last Marlboro. But personal
responsibility is not a free pass for corporate irresponsibility. It's easier to just
say no when you aren't being manipulated and marketed to say yes. Willpower
is influenced by price, advertising and even lawsuits.

It's not an accident that Kraft, maker of Oreo cookies and macaroni and 9
cheese, became the first Big Foodie to pledge to help the fight against obesity. The company is, after all, a subsidiary of the much-sued Philip Morris before it changed its name and image to Altria.

As Margo Wootan of the Center for Science in the Public Interest says, 10
"Kraft belongs to a tobacco company that knows what the inside of a courtroom looks like." It didn't take a PhD, she adds, to realize that everyone would
figure out that cookies and cheese contribute to obesity.

One of Kraft's pledges it to stop marketing in schools. Indeed, the public 11
seems most willing to acknowledge the weight of the environment in the
weight of kids.

The first step in downsizing Americans may be in the schools. Over the past 12
decade, schools have said yes to soft drinks and junk food in hallway vending
machines. Now some large school districts from Los Angeles to New York have
banned the sale of sodas. There are bills in Massachusetts and Maine to get rid
of junk food in those same machines.

But it's likely to be a long haul to get smaller portions, labeling in fast-food 13
restaurants and to slim down advertising to kids. Wootan says, "People still
haven't made the connection about how industry practices shape and influence their choices. Your child begs you for junk food, begs you to go to Mc-
Donald's and you think, 'That's kids.' You don't think, "Shame on that food
company.' " Food is one part of a complex obesity problem that includes Game
Boys instead of ballgames and TV instead of track. Moreover, it's still tricky to
attack fat as a health issue without attacking fat people, and we've had a big
enough portion of that, thank you. But Brownell believes, "We are at a place
where it no longer makes sense to blame people for a problem their environment is causing."

What do we need to change the environment? How about Will and Power? 14

QUESTIONS FOR READING

1. What is Goodman's subject?

2. In the past, how have we explained excess weight? What current shift in thinking does Goodman see?

3. What are the reasons for the shift in thinking? Be able to state all of them in your
   own words.

4. Where might the focus for change begin?

QUESTIONS FOR REASONING AND ANALYSIS

1. Analyze Goodman's organization, completing this pattern with needed specifics:
   - opening:
   - establishing the issue:
   - 2nd subtopic of the issue:
   - 3rd subtopic of the issue:
   - conclusion:

2. Analyze Goodman's word choice, sentence patterns, and metaphors. What is effective about her uses of these strategies? How would you describe her style and tone?

3. What important qualifiers does the author include in paragraph 13? Why? State her thesis.

QUESTIONS FOR REFLECTING AND WRITING

1. How did you answer the second prereading question? After reading this essay, do you think that you should answer differently? Why or why not?

2. Do you agree with Goodman that environment may be a source of causes for American obesity? If you disagree, how would you challenge her argument?

3. What, if anything, should the government do about the problem?

LET THE GOING GET TOUGH—WE HAVE OUR SUVS | RONALD R. FRASER

A former transportation specialist, Ronald Fraser holds a Ph.D. in public policy from George Mason University and is president and senior editor of the Cheshire Company, an organization that provides research, writing, and editorial services to business and government.

PREREADING QUESTIONS Do you own or would you like to own an SUV? Can you explain the current appeal of SUVs?

1   At first glance, America's SUV craze seems illogical. Only when it is viewed as part of an emerging grass-roots highway policy does it make sense. After all, why would millions of Americans trade in comfortable two-wheel-drive vehicles for rugged, four-wheel-drive Broncos, Pathfinders and Cherokees—vehicles capable of handling adverse road conditions seldom found anywhere in the United States? The only explanation that makes any sense is that Americans dearly want a more challenging driving experience.

2   Starting in the 1950s, U.S. highway policies focused on constructing the 41,000-mile Interstate system, a smooth, high-speed network designed for two-wheel-drive vehicles. Perhaps the grandest public works project in history,

the Interstate, completed in 1991 at a cost of $129 billion, is a symbol of the auto's golden age.

Much of this aging roadway system needs a face lift, though, and we are looking at skyrocketing maintenance costs over the coming decades. But is that what American motorists really want?

Because so many people now are eager to spend their own money to equip their vehicles for a roadless environment, perhaps it makes little sense for the federal government to continue overspending on our highway infrastructure.

If Americans want the frontier experience promised by their Broncos and Durangos, why should out-of-date highway policies stand in their way? Why should taxpayers who drive conventional cars spend billions to maintain smooth roads when millions of American drivers are ready for the off-road experience?

Here's a highway plan for the new century.

First, Interstate maintenance spending should reflect the growing number of SUVs. As their numbers go up, Interstate maintenance spending should go down. Once four-wheel drive SUVs top 50 percent, we can cease maintaining half of all Interstate lanes and allow them to revert to the mud-and-rut conditions of the 19th century trails from which they are descended.

Next, because the SUV people will drive readily in the more challenging un-maintained Interstate lanes, they will be spared paying federal gas taxes at the pump. Conventional automobiles, on the other hand, will continue to enjoy the smooth ride found in the lanes that are well maintained and will continue to pay the federal gas taxes.

Finally, while the gas-sucking SUV set might boost our national fuel consumption, this cost will be offset by the huge savings associated with lower road repair costs. On balance, the environment will benefit from a new policy that no longer attempts to pave America. The new policy promises to return thousands of miles of highway to their earlier condition. SUV drivers, accused of fouling the environment through their wasteful use of fossil fuels, can represent themselves as dedicated conservationists.

With the passage of time, the Interstate system will take on a frontier look and feel, but Americans are ready for it. A rugged John Wayne frontier spirit already rules on most city and suburban roadways. All we need is a national highway policy to match it.

QUESTIONS FOR READING

1. What is Fraser's subject?
2. What are the details of Fraser's "highway plan"? Are we to embrace this highway plan?

QUESTIONS FOR REASONING AND ANALYSIS

1. What is the author's primary strategy for conveying attitude? What is Fraser's attitude toward SUVs? What word choice helps you answer this question?

2. What, then, is Fraser's thesis? What key ideas does he want us to understand and accept?

QUESTIONS FOR REFLECTION AND WRITING

1. Do you enjoy and appreciate the strategy that Fraser uses, or are you bothered by it in some way? If you appreciate it, what makes it clever? If you are bothered, why?

2. Which problem with SUVs does Fraser refer to? What are two other problems with the vehicle?

3. Should SUVs be held to the same emissions standards as cars? Should the government require more fuel-efficient cars and trucks? Explain your position.

SUGGESTIONS FOR DISCUSSION AND WRITING

1. Analyze the style of one of the essays from Section 4 of this text. Do not comment on every element of style; select several elements that seem to characterize the writer's style and examine them in detail. Remember that style analyses are written for an audience familiar with the work, so summary is not necessary.

2. Many of the authors included in this text have written books that you will find in your library. Select one that interests you, read it, and prepare a review of it that synthesizes summary, analysis, and evaluation. Prepare a review of about 300 words; assume that the book has just been published.

3. Choose two newspaper and/or magazine articles that differ in their discussion of the same person, event, or product. You may select two different articles on a person in the news, two different accounts of a news event, an advertisement and a *Consumer Reports* analysis of the same product, or two reviews of a book or movie. Analyze differences in both content and presentation and then consider why the two accounts differ. Organize by points of difference and write to an audience not necessarily familiar with the articles.

4. Choose a recently scheduled public event (the Super Bowl, the Olympics, a presidential election, the Academy Award presentations, the premiere of a new television series) and find several articles written before and several after the event. First compare articles written after the event to see if they agree factually. If not, decide which article appears to be more accurate and why. Then examine the earlier material and decide which was the most and which the least accurate. Write an essay in which you explain the differences in speculation before the event and why you think these differences exist. Your audience will be aware of the event but not necessarily aware of the articles you are studying.

The World of Argument

CHAPTER 3

Understanding the Basics of Argument

In this section we will explore the processes of thinking logically and analyzing issues to reach informed judgments. Remember: mature people do not need to agree on all issues to respect one another's good sense, but they do have little patience with uninformed or illogical statements masquerading as argument.

CHARACTERISTICS OF ARGUMENT

Argument Is Conversation with a Goal

When you enter into an argument (as speaker, writer, or reader), you become a participant in an ongoing debate about an issue. Since you are probably not the first to address the issue, you need to be aware of the ways that the issue has been debated by others and then seek to advance the conversation, just as you would if you were having a more casual conversation with friends. If the time of the movie is set, the discussion now turns to whose car to take or where to meet. If you were to just repeat the time of the movie, you would add nothing useful to the conversation. Also, if you were to change the subject to a movie you saw last week, you would annoy your friends by not offering useful information or showing that you valued the current conversation. Just as with your conversation about the movie, you want your argument to stay focused on the issue, to respect what others have already contributed, and to make a useful addition to our understanding of the issue.

Argument Takes a Stand on an Arguable Issue

A meaningful argument concentrates on a debatable issue. We usually do not argue about facts. "Professor Jones's American literature class meets at 10:00 on Mondays" is not arguable. It is either true or false. We can check the schedule of classes to find out. (Sometimes the facts change; new facts replace old ones.) We also do not debate personal preferences for the simple reason that they are just that—personal. If the debate is about the appropriateness of boxing as a sport, for you to declare that you would rather play tennis is to fail to advance the conversation. You have expressed a personal preference, interesting perhaps, but not relevant to the debate.

Argument Uses Reasons and Evidence

Some arguments merely "look right." That is, conclusions are drawn from facts, but the facts are not those that actually support the assertion, or the conclusion is not the only or the best explanation of those facts. To shape convincing arguments, we need more than an array of facts. We need to think critically, to analyze the issue, to see relationships, to weigh evidence. We need to avoid the temptation to "argue" from emotion only, or to believe that just stating our opinion is the same thing as building a sound argument.

Argument Incorporates Values

Arguments are based not just on reason and evidence but also on the beliefs and values we hold and think that our audience may hold as well. In a reasoned debate, you want to make clear the values that you consider relevant to the argument. In an editorial defending the sport of boxing, one editor wrote that boxing "is a sport because the world has not yet become a place in which the qualities that go into excellence in boxing [endurance, agility, courage] have no value" (*Washington Post,* February 5, 1983). But James J. Kilpatrick also appeals to values when he argues, in an editorial critical of boxing, that we should not want to live in a society "in which deliberate brutality is legally authorized and publicly applauded" (*Washington Post,* December 7, 1982). Observe, however, the high level of seriousness in the appeal to values. Neither writer settles for a simplistic personal preference: "boxing is exciting" or "boxing is too violent."

Argument Recognizes the Topic's Complexity

Much false reasoning (the logical fallacies discussed in Chapter 5) results from a writer's oversimplifying an issue. A sound argument begins with an understanding that most issues are terribly complicated. The wise person approaches such ethical concerns as abortion or euthanasia or such public policy issues as tax cuts or trade agreements with the understanding that there are many philosophical, moral, and political issues that complicate discussions of these topics. Recognizing an argument's complexity may also lead us to an understanding that there can be more than one "right" position. The thoughtful arguer respects the views of others and avoids ridiculing opposing points of view.

THE SHAPE OF ARGUMENT: THE ARISTOTELIAN MODEL

Still one of the best ways to understand the basics of argument is to reflect on what the Greek philosopher Aristotle describes as the three "players" in any argument: the *writer* (or *speaker*), the *argument itself*, and the *reader* (or *audience*). Aristotle calls the argument itself the *logos*—the assertion and support for that assertion. A successful argument needs a logical and convincing *logos*. An argument also implies an audience, those whose views on our topic we want to influence. Aristotle calls this part of argument *pathos*. Good arguers need to be alert to the values and attitudes of their audience and to appeal effectively to the emotions of that audience. However, Aristotle also explains that part of our appeal to an audience rests in the *logos,* our logic and evidence. An "argument" that is all emotional appeal will not move thoughtful audiences.

Finally (and for Aristotle the most important of the three players) is the writer/speaker, or *ethos.* No argument, Aristotle asserts, no matter how logical seeming, no matter how appealing emotionally, will succeed if the audience rejects the arguer's credibility, the writer's "ethical" qualities. As members of the audience we need to believe that the arguer is a person of knowledge, honesty, and goodwill.

As Figure 3.1 illustrates, we argue in a specific context of three interrelated parts. We present support for a concrete assertion, thesis, or claim to a specific audience whose demands and expectations and character we have given thought to when shaping our argument. And we present ourselves as informed, competent, and reliable so that our audience will give serious attention to our

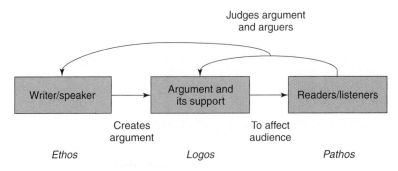

FIGURE 3.1 Aristotelian Structure of Argument

argument. Remember: your audience evaluates *you* as a part of their evaluation of your argument. Lose your credibility and you lose your argument.

THE SHAPE OF ARGUMENT: THE TOULMIN MODEL

British philosopher Stephen Toulmin adds to what we have learned from Aristotle by focusing our attention on the basics of the argument itself. First, consider this definition of argument: *An argument consists of evidence and/or reasons presented in support of an assertion or claim that is either stated or implied.* For example:

CLAIM:	We should not go skiing today
EVIDENCE:	because it is too cold.
EVIDENCE:	Because some laws are unjust,
CLAIM:	civil disobedience is sometimes justified.
EVIDENCE:	It's only fair and right for academic institutions to
CLAIM:	accept students only on academic merit.

The basics of a complete argument, Toulmin asserts, are actually a bit more complex than these examples suggest. Each argument has a third part that is not stated in the preceding examples. This third part is the "glue" that connects the support—the evidence and reasons—to the argument's claim and thus fulfills the logic of the argument. Toulmin calls this glue an argument's *warrants.* These are the principles or assumptions that allow us to assert that our evidence or reasons—what Toulmin calls the *grounds*—do indeed support our claim. (Figure 3.2 illustrates these basics of the Toulmin model of argument.)

Look again at the sample arguments to see what warrants must be accepted to make each argument work:

CLAIM:	We should not go skiing today.
EVIDENCE:	It is too cold.
ASSUMPTIONS (WARRANTS):	When it is too cold, skiing is not fun; the activity is not sufficient to keep one from becoming uncomfortable. AND: Too cold is what is too cold for me.
CLAIM:	Civil disobedience is sometimes justified.
EVIDENCE:	Some laws are unjust.
ASSUMPTIONS (WARRANTS):	To get unjust laws changed, people need to be made aware of the injustice. Acts of civil disobedience will get people's attention and make them aware that the laws need changing.
CLAIM:	Academic institutions should accept students only on academic merit.
EVIDENCE:	It is fair and right.
ASSUMPTIONS (WARRANTS):	Fair and right are important values. AND: Academic institutions are only about academics.

CLAIM:	Academic institutions should accept students only on academic merit.
EVIDENCE:	It is only fair and right.
WARRANT:	(1) Fair and right are important values. (2) Academic institutions are only about academics.

FIGURE 3.2 The Toulmin Structure of Argument

Assumptions play an important role in any argument, so we need to be sure to understand what they are. Note, for instance, the second assumption operating in the first argument: the temperature considered uncomfortable for the speaker will also be uncomfortable for her companions—an uncertain assumption. In the second argument, the warrant is less debatable, for acts of civil disobedience usually get media coverage and thus dramatize the issue. The underlying assumptions in the third example stress the need to know one's warrants. Both warrants will need to be defended in the debate over selection by academic merit only.

COLLABORATIVE EXERCISE: Building Arguments

With your class partner or in small groups, examine each of the following claims. Select two, think of one statement that could serve as evidence for each claim, and then think of the underlying assumption(s) that complete each of the arguments.

1. Professor X is not a good instructor.
2. Americans need to reduce the fat in their diets.
3. Tiger Woods is a great golfer.
4. Physical education classes should be graded pass/fail.
5. College newspapers should be free of supervision by faculty or administrators.

THE LANGUAGE OF CLAIMS AND SUPPORT

What kinds of statements function as claims and as support?

- Claims: usually either inferences or judgments, for these are debatable assertions.
- Support: facts, opinions based on facts (inferences, or opinions based on values, beliefs, or ideas (judgments) or some combination of the three.

Let's consider what kinds of statements each of these terms describes.

> **NOTE:** Placing such qualifiers as "I believe," "I think," or "I feel" in an assertion does not free you from the need to support that claim. The statement "I believe that President Clinton was a great president" calls for an argument based on evidence and reasons.

Facts

Facts are statements that are verifiable. Factual statements refer to what can be counted or measured or confirmed by reasonable observers or trusted experts.

> There are 26 desks in Room 110.
>
> In the United States about 400,000 people die each year as a result of smoking.

These are factual statements. We can verify the first by observation—by counting. The second fact comes from medical records. We rely on trusted record-keeping sources and medical experts for verification. By definition, we do not argue about the facts. Usually. Sometimes "facts" change, as we learn more about our world. For example, only in the last 30 years has convincing evidence been gathered to demonstrate the relationship between smoking and various illnesses of the heart and lungs. And sometimes "facts" are false facts. These are statements that sound like facts, but are incorrect. For example: Agassi has won more Wimbledon titles than Sampras. Not so.

Inferences

Inferences are opinions based on facts. Inferences are the conclusions we draw from an analysis of facts.

> There will not be enough desks in Room 110 for upcoming fall-semester classes.
>
> Smoking is a serious health hazard.

Predictions of an increase in student enrollment for the coming fall semester lead to the inference that most English classes scheduled in Room 110 will run with several more students per class than last year. The dean should order new desks. Similarly, we infer from the number of deaths that smoking is a health problem; statistics show more people dying from tobacco than from AIDS, or murder, or car accidents, causes of death that get media coverage but do not produce nearly as many deaths.

Inferences vary in their closeness to the facts supporting them. That the sun will "rise" tomorrow is an inference, but we count on its happening, acting as if it is a fact. However, the first inference stated above is based not just on the fact of 26 desks but on another inference—a projected increase in student enrollment—and two assumptions. The argument looks like this:

FACT:	There are 26 desks in Room 110.
INFERENCE:	There will be more first-year students next year.
ASSUMPTIONS:	1. English will remain a required course.
	2. No additional classrooms are available for English classes.
CLAIM:	There will not be enough desks in Room 110 for upcoming fall-semester classes.

This inference could be challenged by a different analysis of the facts supporting enrollment projections. Or, if additional rooms can be found, the dean will not need to order new desks. Inferences can be part of the support of an argument, or they can be the claim of an argument.

Judgments

Judgments are opinions based on values, beliefs, or philosophical concepts. (Judgments also include opinions based on personal preferences, but we have already excluded these from argument.) Judgments concern right and wrong, good and bad, better or worse, should and should not:

> No more than 26 students should be enrolled in any English class.
>
> Cigarette advertising should be eliminated, and the federal government should develop an antismoking campaign.

To support the first judgment, we need to explain what constitutes overcrowding, or what constitutes the best class size for effective teaching. If we can support our views on effective teaching, we may be able to convince the college president that ordering more desks for Room 110 is not the best solution to an increasing enrollment in English classes. The second judgment also offers a solution to a problem, in this case a national health problem. To reduce the number of deaths, we need to reduce the number of smokers, either by encouraging smokers to quit or not to start. The underlying assumption: Advertising does affect behavior.

EXERCISE: Facts, Inferences, and Judgments

Compile a list of three statements of fact, three inferences, and three judgments. Try to organize them into three related sets, as illustrated here:

- Smoking is prohibited in some restaurants.
- Secondhand smoke is a health hazard.
- Smoking should be prohibited in all restaurants.

We can classify judgments to see better what kind of assertion we are making and, therefore, what kind of support we need to argue effectively.

FUNCTIONAL JUDGMENTS (guidelines for judging how something or someone works or could work):

> Tiger Woods is the best golfer to play the game.
>
> Antismoking advertising will reduce the number of smokers.

AESTHETIC JUDGMENTS (guidelines for judging art, literature, music, or natural scenes):

> The sunrise was beautiful.
>
> *The Great Gatsby*'s structure, characters, and symbols are perfectly wedded to create the novel's vision of the American dream.

ETHICAL JUDGMENTS (guidelines for group or social behavior):

   Lawyers should not advertise.

   It is discourteous to talk during a film or lecture.

MORAL JUDGMENTS (guidelines of right and wrong for judging individuals
and for establishing legal principles):

   Taking another person's life is wrong.

   Equal rights under the law should not be denied on the basis of race or sex.

Functional and aesthetic judgments generally require defining key terms and
establishing criteria for the judging or ranking made by the assertion. How, for
example, do we compare golfers? On the amount of money won? The number
of tournaments won? Or the consistency of winning throughout one's career?
What about the golfer's quality and range of shots? Ethical and moral judgments may be more difficult to support because they depend not just on how
terms are defined and criteria established but on values and beliefs as well. If
taking another person's life is wrong, why isn't it wrong in war? Or is it? These
are difficult questions that require thoughtful responses.

EXERCISES: Understanding Assumptions, Facts, False Facts, Inferences, and Judgments

1.   Categorize the judgments you wrote for the previous exercise (p. 78) as either
     aesthetic, moral, ethical, or functional. Alternatively, compile a list of three
     judgments that you then categorize.
2.   For each judgment listed for exercise 1, generate one statement of support,
     either a fact or an inference or another judgment. Then state the warrant (under-
     lying assumption) required to complete each argument.
3.   Read the following article and then complete the exercise that follows. This
     exercise tests both careful reading and your understanding of the differences
     among facts, inferences, and judgments.

PARADISE LOST | RICHARD MORIN

Richard Morin, a journalist with the *Washington Post*, writes a regular Sunday column
titled "Unconventional Wisdom," a column presenting interesting new information
from the social sciences. The following article was Morin's column for July 9, 2000.

   Here's my fantasy vacation: Travel back in time to the 1700s, to some lan-   1
guid South Pacific island paradise where ripe fruit hangs heavy on the trees and
the native islanders live in peace with nature and with each other.

   Or at least that was my fantasy vacation until I talked to anthropologist   2
Patrick Kirch, one of the country's leading authorities on the South Pacific and

director of the Phoebe Hearst Museum of Anthropology at the University of California at Berkeley.

3   The South Seas islands painted by Paul Gauguin and celebrated by Robert Louis Stevenson were no Gardens of Eden, Kirch writes in his riveting new history of the South Pacific, *On the Road of the Winds.* Many of these islands witnessed episodes of environmental depredation, endemic warfare and bloody ritual long before seafaring Europeans first visited. "Most islands of the Pacific were densely populated by the time of European contact, and the human impact on the natural ecosystem was often disastrous—with wholesale decimation of species and loss of vast tracts of land," he said.

4   Kirch says we can blame the French for all the loose talk about a tropical nirvana. "French philosophers of the Enlightenment saw these islands, especially Tahiti, as the original natural society where people lived in a state of innocence and food fell from the trees," he said. "How wrong they were."

5   French explorer Louis Antoine de Bougainville visited Tahiti for two weeks in 1769 and thought he discovered a paradise awash in social tolerance and carefree sex. Bougainville's breathless description of Tahiti became the basis for Jean Jacques Rousseau's concept of *l'homme naturel*—the noble savage.

6   Savage, indeed. Even as Bougainville poked around their craggy volcanic island, Rousseau's "noble savages" were busy savaging each other. The Tahitians were in the midst of a bitter civil war, complete with ritual sacrifice to their bloodthirsty war god, Oro. On Mangaia in the Cook Islands, Kirch discovered ovens and pits filled with the charred bones of men, women, and even children.

7   And forget that free-love nonsense. Dating, mating and reproduction were tricky business throughout the South Seas several hundred years ago. To keep the population in check, the residents of tiny Tikopia in the Santa Cruz Islands practiced infanticide. Abortion also was common. And to "concentrate" their bloodlines, Kirch said, members of the royal class in Hawaii married their brothers and sisters. If they only knew . . .

8   Not all South Seas islands were little cesspools. On some of the smaller islands, early Polynesians avoided cultural collapse by adopting strict population control measures, including enforced suicide. "Some young men were encouraged to go to sea and not return," he said.

9   Perhaps the best example of the havoc wrought by the indigenous peoples of the South Pacific is found on desolate Easter Island, home of the monolithic stone heads that have gazed out from the front of a thousand travel brochures. Until recently, researchers believed that Easter Island's open, grassy plains and barren knife-point volcanic ridges had always been, well, grassy plains and barren ridges.

10   Not true, says Kirch. The island was once covered with dense palm and hardwood forests. But by the 1700s, when the first Europeans arrived, these forests had been burned by the islanders to clear land for agriculture, transforming lush groves into semi-tropical tundra. "On Easter Island, the ultimate

extinction of the palm and other woody plants had a further consequence: the inability to move or erect the large stone statues" because there were no logs to use as rollers to move the giant heads from the quarries, Kirch writes.

The stone carvers' society collapsed, as did Easter Island culture. By the 11 time Dutch explorer Jacob Roggeveen arrived on Easter Sunday in 1722, residents had taken to living in underground caves for protection from the social chaos that had enveloped their island home.

When viewed today, Kirch says, the monoliths remain an "imposing stone 12 text that suggests a thousand human sagas." They also carry a lesson to our age, he argues—warning us "to achieve a sustainable relationship with our planet"—or else.

Label each of the following sentences as F (fact), FF (false fact), I (inference), or J (judgment).

_____ 1. In the 1700s native South Pacific islanders lived in peace and harmony.

_____ 2. It is foolish to romanticize life on South Sea islands.

_____ 3. French philosopher Rousseau based his idea of the noble savage on the Tahitians.

_____ 4. The stone statues on Easter Island suggest many stories.

_____ 5. In the past, noble Hawaiians married within their families.

_____ 6. Tahitians were savage people.

_____ 7. Some South Pacific islanders used to practice abortion and infanticide.

_____ 8. Easter Island has always had grassy plains and barren ridges.

_____ 9. Finding and using "sustainable" strategies will help preserve the environment.

_____ 10. People should not marry family members.

MORE ON TOULMIN'S ANALYSIS OF ARGUMENT

Philosopher Stephen Toulmin was particularly interested in stressing the great range in the strength or probability of various arguments. Some kinds of arguments are stronger than others because of the language or logic they use. Other arguments must, necessarily, be heavily qualified for the claim to be supportable. Toulmin developed his language for the structure of arguments to provide a strategy for analyzing the degree of probability in a given argument and to remind us of the need to qualify some kinds of claims. You have already seen how the idea of warrants, or assumptions, helps us think about the "glue" that presumably makes a given argument work. Additional Toulmin terms and concepts can help us analyze the arguments of others and prepare more convincing arguments of our own.

Claims

A claim is what the argument asserts or seeks to prove. It answers the question "What is your point?" In an argumentative speech or essay, the claim is the speaker or writer's main idea or thesis. Although an argument's claim "follows" from reasons and evidence, we often present an argument—whether written or spoken—with the claim stated near the beginning of the presentation. We can be aided in recognizing an argument's claim by recognizing that we can have claims of fact, claims of value, and claims of policy.

Claims of Fact

Although facts usually support claims, we do argue over some facts. Historians and biographers may argue over what happened in the past, although they are more likely to argue over the significance of what happened. Scientists also argue over the facts, over how to classify an unearthed fossil, for example, or whether the fossil indicates that the animal had feathers. For example:

CLAIM: The small, predatory dinosaur *Deinonychus* hunted its prey in packs.

This claim is supported by the discovery of several fossils of *Deinonychus* close together and with the fossil bones of a much larger dinosaur. Their teeth have also been found in or near the bones of dinosaurs that have died in a struggle.

Assertions about what will happen are sometimes classified as claims of fact, but they can also be labeled as inferences supported by facts. Predictions about a future event may be classified as claims of fact:

CLAIM: The United States will win the most gold medals at the 2004 Olympics.

CLAIM: I will get an A on tomorrow's psychology test.

What evidence would you use today to support each of these claims? (And, did the first one turn out to be correct?)

Claims of Value

These include moral, ethical, and aesthetic judgments. Assertions that use such words as *good* or *bad*, *better* or *worse*, and *right* or *wrong* will be claims of value. The following are all claims of value:

CLAIM: Pete Sampras is a better tennis player than Andre Agassi.

CLAIM: *Adventures of Huckleberry Finn* is one of the most significant American novels.

CLAIM: Cheating hurts others and the cheater too.

CLAIM: Abortion is wrong.

Arguments in support of judgments demand relevant evidence, careful reasoning, and an awareness of the assumptions one is making. Support for claims of value often include other value statements. For example, to support the claim that censorship is bad, arguers often assert that the free exchange of ideas is good and necessary in a democracy. The support is itself a value statement. The arguer may believe, probably correctly, that most people will more readily agree to the support (the free exchange of ideas is good) than to the claim (censorship is bad).

Claims of Policy

Finally, claims of policy are assertions about what should or should not happen, what the government ought or ought not to do, how to best solve social problems. Claims of policy debate, for example, college rules, state gun laws, or federal aid to Africans suffering from AIDS. The following are claims of policy:

CLAIM: College newspapers should not be controlled in any way by college authorities.

CLAIM: States should not have laws allowing people to carry concealed weapons.

CLAIM: The United States must provide more aid to African countries where 25 percent or more of the citizens have tested positive for HIV.

Claims of policy are often closely tied to judgments of morality or political philosophy, but they also need to be grounded in feasibility. That is, your claim needs to be doable, to be based on a thoughtful consideration of the real world and the complexities of public policy issues.

Grounds (or Data or Evidence)

The term *grounds* refers to the reasons and evidence provided in support of a claim. Although the words *data* and *evidence* can also be used, note that *grounds* is the more general term because it includes reasons or logic as well as examples or statistics. We determine the grounds of an argument by asking the question "Why do you think that?" or "How do you know that?" When writing your own arguments, you can ask yourself these questions and answer by using a *because* clause:

CLAIM: Smoking should be banned in restaurants
            because
GROUNDS: secondhand smoke is a serious health hazard.
CLAIM: Pete Sampras is a better tennis player than Andre Agassi
            because
GROUNDS: 1. he has been ranked number one longer than Agassi,
            2. he has won more tournaments than Agassi, and
            3. he has won more major tournaments than Agassi.

Warrants

Why should we believe that your grounds do indeed support your claim? Your argument's warrants answer this question. They explain why your evidence really is evidence. Sometimes warrants reside in language itself, in the meanings of the words we are using. If I am *younger* than my brother, then my brother must be *older* than I am. In a court case attempting to prove that Jones murdered Smith, the relation of evidence to claim is less assured. If the police investigation has been properly managed and the physical evidence is substantial, then Smith may be Jones's murderer. The prosecution has—presumably beyond a reasonable doubt—established motive, means, and opportunity for Smith to commit the murder. In many arguments based on statistical data, the argument's warrant rests on complex analyses of the statistics—and on the conviction that the statistics have been developed without error. In some philosophical arguments, the warrants are the logical structures (often shown mathematically) connecting a sequence of reasons. Still, without taking courses in statistics and logic, you can develop an alertness to the "good sense" of some arguments and the "dubious sense" of others. You know, for example, that good SAT scores are a predictor of success in college. Can you argue that you will do well in college because you have good SATs? No. We can determine only a statistical probability. We cannot turn probabilities about a group of people into a warrant about one person in the group. (In addition, SAT scores are only one predictor, one variable. Another key variable is motivation.)

What is the warrant for the Sampras claim?

CLAIM: Pete Sampras is a better tennis player than Andre Agassi.

GROUNDS: The three facts listed above.

WARRANT: It is appropriate to judge and rank tennis players on these kinds of statistics. That is, the better player is one who has held the number one ranking for the longest time, has won the most tournaments, and also has won the most major tournaments.

Backing

Standing behind an argument's warrant may be additional *backing*. Backing answers the question "How do we know that your evidence is good evidence?" You may answer this question by providing authoritative sources for the data used (for example, the Census Bureau or the U.S. Tennis Association). Or, you may explain in detail the methodology of the experiments performed or the surveys taken. When scientists and social scientists present the results of their research, they anticipate the question of backing and automatically provide a detailed explanation of the process by which they acquired their evidence. In criminal trials, defense attorneys challenge the backing of the prosecution's argument. They question the handling of blood samples sent to labs for DNA testing, for instance. The defense attorneys want jury members to doubt the *quality* of the evidence, perhaps even to doubt the reliability of DNA testing altogether.

This discussion of backing returns us to the point that one part of any argument is the audience, those whom we want to convince. To create an effective argument, you need to assess the potential for acceptance of your warrants and backing. Is your audience likely to share your values, your religious beliefs, or your scientific approach to issues? If you are speaking to a group at your church, then backing based on the religious beliefs of that church may be effective. If you are preparing an argument for a general audience, then using specific religious assertions as warrants or backing probably will not result in an effective argument.

Qualifiers

Some arguments are absolute; they can be stated without qualification. *If I am younger than my brother, then he must be older than I am.* Most arguments need some qualification; many need precise limitations. If, when playing bridge, I am dealt eight spades, then my opponents and partner together must have five spade cards—because there are thirteen cards of each suit in a deck. My partner *probably* has one spade but *could be* void of spades. My partner *possibly* has two or more spades, but I would be foolish to count on it. When bidding my hand, I must be controlled by the laws of probability. Look again at the smoking ban claim. Observe the absolute nature of both the claim and its support. If second-hand smoke is indeed a health hazard, it will be that in *all* restaurants, not just in some. With each argument we need to assess the need and the degree of qualification that is appropriate to a successful argument.

Sweeping generalizations often come to us in the heat of a debate or when we first start to think about an issue. For example: *Gun control is wrong because it restricts individual rights.* But on reflection surely you would not want to argue against all forms of gun control. (Remember: an unqualified assertion is understood by your audience to be absolute.) Would you sell guns to felons in jail or to children on the way to school? Obviously not. So, let's try the claim again, this time with two important qualifiers:

> QUALIFIED   Adults without a criminal record should not be restricted in the
> CLAIM: purchase of guns.

Others may want this claim further qualified to eliminate particular types of guns or to control the number purchased or the process for purchasing. The gun-control debate is not about absolutes; it is all about which qualified claim is best.

Rebuttals

Arguments can be challenged. Smart debaters assume that there are people who will disagree with them. They anticipate the ways that opponents can challenge their arguments. When you are planning an argument, you need to think about how you can counter or rebut the challenges you anticipate. Think of yourself as an attorney in a court case preparing your argument *and* a defense of the other attorney's challenges to your argument. If you ignore the important role of rebuttals, you may not win the jury to your side.

USING TOULMIN'S TERMS TO ANALYZE ARGUMENTS

Terms are never an end in themselves; we learn them when we recognize that they help us to organize our thinking about a subject. Toulmin's terms can aid your reading of the arguments of others. You can "see what's going on" in an argument if you analyze it, applying Toulmin's language to its parts. Not all terms will be useful for every analysis because, for example, some arguments will not have qualifiers or rebuttals. But to recognize that an argument is *without qualifiers* is to learn something important about that argument.

First, here is a simple argument broken down into its parts using Toulmin's terms:

GROUNDS:	Because Dr. Bradshaw has an attendance policy,
CLAIM:	students who miss more than seven classes will
QUALIFIER:	most likely (last year, Dr. Bradshaw did allow one student, in unusual circumstances, to continue in the class) be dropped from the course.
WARRANT:	Dr. Bradshaw's syllabus explains her attendance policy, a
BACKING:	policy consistent with the concept of a discussion class that depends on student participation and consistent with the attendance policies of most of her colleagues.
REBUTTAL:	Although some students complain about an attendance policy of any kind, Dr. Bradshaw does explain her policy and her reasons for it the first day of class. She then reminds students that the syllabus is a contract between them; if they choose to stay, they agree to abide by the guidelines explained on the syllabus.

This argument is brief and fairly simple. Let's see how Toulmin's terms can help us analyze a longer, more complex argument. Read actively and annotate the following essay while at the same time noting the existing annotations using Toulmin's terms. Then answer the questions that follow the article.

INURED TO INEQUALITY | STEVEN RATTNER

The author is a managing principal at the private investment firm Quadrangle Group. His essay was published in the *Washington Post* on June 16, 2003.

PREREADING QUESTIONS What does the word "inured" mean? (If you are unsure, look it up before reading the essay.) How unequal, economically, is American society?

Toulmin's terms

1   The litany of well-founded complaints about the latest tax legislation seems endless. More complications for a tax code both parties profess to want to simplify. New frontiers in using gimmickry to

Student Annotations opening strategy:

hide the true cost of the legislation. Questionable usefulness in sparking our economy. And another enormous hit to our horrifying long-term fiscal outlook.

2   Add to this list one more pernicious aspect of the U.S. economy   def: now made worse: the huge gap in income among Americans, the widest of any major country and not getting noticeably better.

claim

3   Americans have become familiar with the headline-grabbing escalation of CEO pay packages. But after a frisson of worrying in the mid-'90s, we seem to have become inured to the record dispar-   def: ity of income across nearly all professions and income levels.

qualifier

4   According to a Federal Reserve study this year, pre-tax family incomes of the top 10 percent grew by 19.3 percent between 1998 and 2001 after inflation, compared with 11.9 percent for the rest of Americans. Last fall the Census Bureau found that by any of five sophisticated measures, the gap in incomes has continued to widen.

backing
grounds

backing

5   Most discussions of income inequality properly center on pretax statistics, in search of a true measure of how the labor markets and the economy are functioning. Considering pre-tax income is also proper because we should not legislate or redistribute our way to income equality. But neither should tax policy worsen the disparity between rich and poor.

warrant

rebuttal

6   Widening that gap is what we've just done. According to analysis by the Tax Policy Center of the Brookings Institution and the Urban Institute, the new tax provisions will raise the after-tax income of Americans making more than $1 million by 4.4 percent while raising the average American's income by only 1.8 percent. More than 70 percent of households will receive $500 or less. For 8 million lower-income Americans who pay taxes, the news is truly dispiriting: no tax cut at all.

backing
grounds

7   That's because the bulk of the cut will be used to reduce capital gains and dividend taxes, and even though ownership of stocks has broadened in the past decade, the highest-income Americans still have a disproportionate share of the wealth. In fact, distribution of wealth is even more unequal than the distribution of income. In 1998, 47.3 percent of households' "net financial assets" resided with the top 1 percent of Americans, according to an analysis of consumer finance data by Edward Wolff.

8   Proponents of the tax bill decry such talk as class warfare. But is it class warfare to talk about fairness? And if fairness isn't enough, how about the social tensions and economic inefficiencies that can result from such an enormous rich-poor divide? We have had a progressive income tax for many years; why would we choose to make it less progressive at this moment, when natural economic forces are already driving us toward more inequality?

rebuttal

warrant
(States values.)

9   Those forces include many of the same winds that have given us high productivity, low inflation and unprecedented prosperity over

the past decade, notwithstanding the current bump in the road. The technological revolution and growth in the service sector increased the need for skilled employees, while the downsizing of American corporations as they became more efficient reduced the need for unskilled workers. Classic labor market economics at work led us to greater income inequality.

10   This year, *BusinessWeek* labeled economists who worry about income inequality "declinists," meaning that they believe the American economy isn't going to grow much so we should focus on how to divide the pie rather than how to grow it.

11   That's disingenuous. Of course we shouldn't hold back eco- def: nomic growth just to keep the rich from getting richer. And many of us believe that our economy remains the most efficient and competitive in the world, fully capable of resuming very satisfying growth after the indigestion of the late '90s passes.

12   But achieving that growth potential and lessening income inequality are not inconsistent. For example, investing in education and training—a concept given short shrift by the Bush administration—improves the quality of our workforce, which leads to higher productivity, which leads to more economic growth. Along the way, labor market economics work in our favor by shifting the supply of workers from unskilled to skilled.

13   The massive tax cuts of the past two years mean no money for these kinds of initiatives or for other kinds of public investments. Indeed, the Bush administration has repeatedly proposed cuts in a variety of antipoverty programs.

14   We shouldn't dismiss all tax cuts simply because they benefit the wealthy. Double taxation of dividends is a source of economic inefficiency, and eliminating it would be a laudable goal. But we need balance, not a tax bill whose benefits are sharply tilted in one direction.

15   Policies that promote income inequality might also be tolerable if they represented the best way to encourage economic growth. But this tax cut hardly addresses today's need for more spending. It is aimed primarily at the wealthiest Americans, who are already spending all they want to, rather than putting money in the pockets of the Americans most likely to spend it. With interest rates at record lows, a lack of incentives is hardly what's holding back business investment; it's anemic demand.

16   Some argue that income mobility obviates the unpleasant consequences of income inequality. First, a number of studies have shown that income mobility affects a minority of the population and that there is little evidence it is increasing. But what's really significant is that CEO John Smith (whose average pay went up 14 percent in 2002) is making a far higher multiple of the income of waitress Mary Jones than was the case in the past—not the slim possibility that Mary Jones can somehow move into a higher income bracket.

(Even if it's not getting any worse, it is still too great a gap.)	17 Some sketchy recent data suggest that income inequality may have stopped worsening or perhaps gotten a little better as fierce efforts by companies to cut costs reach higher-paid workers. Not only is it too soon to reach that judgment but, even if it's true, the level of inequality is so great that we certainly shouldn't be tinkering with tax and spending policies in a way that makes it worse.
grounds ⟶	18 In 1971 the top 5 percent of Americans made about 6.3 times what the bottom 20 percent made. In 2001, after 30 years of relentless widening, that same group made 8.4 times what the bottom 20 percent did. Income inequality in the United Sates is now not only at a record level and not only the greatest since we began measuring it—it is also on a par with that of a Third World country. Is that the American dream? _concluding strategy:_

QUESTIONS FOR READING

1. What is Rattner's subject? State his claim in your own words.
2. What is the evidence that American society has become more unequal in income?
3. Does the author want total equality in incomes?

QUESTIONS FOR REASONING AND ANALYSIS

1. What type of evidence does Rattner provide to support his claim? How does he provide backing for his grounds?
2. What are the primary counterarguments that Rattner anticipates? (Read his rebuttal statements and then work back to stating each of his expected counterarguments.)
3. What values does the author state as his warrant? Do you find his stating of values an effective strategy in his argument? Explain.
4. Analyze his opening and conclusion. What are his strategies? What may make them effective strategies?
5. Evaluate Rattner's argument. Has he provided all the "parts" in an effective blend?

QUESTIONS FOR REFLECTING AND WRITING

1. Are you surprised by any of the facts in this essay? If so, which ones and why? If not, where has your knowledge of these economic issues come from? (You might want to share your sources of knowledge with classmates.)
2. Do you agree with Rattner that we ought not to widen the income gap? Or do you believe that widening the gap is okay? Explain your position.

USING TOULMIN'S TERMS AS A GUIDE TO STRUCTURING ARGUMENTS

You have seen how Toulmin's terms can help you to analyze and see what writers are actually "doing" in their arguments. You have also observed from both the short and the longer argument that writers do not usually follow the terms in precise order. Indeed, you can find both grounds and backing in the same sentence, or claim and qualifiers in the same paragraph, and so on. Still, the terms can help you to sort out your thinking about a claim you want to support. The following exercises will provide practice in your use of these terms to plan an argument.

EXERCISES: Using Toulmin's Terms to Plan Arguments

1. In groups or on your own, build an outline for the claim: "It is foolish to romanticize life on South Sea islands." Use information from Richard Morin's article "Paradise Lost" (pp. 79–81) for some of your grounds. Set up your plan on a page (or more) with each of Toulmin's terms listed down the left margin and your plan for the parts of the argument opposite each appropriate term. (Be sure to refer to Morin and his article when you use information from "Paradise Lost"; the references are your *backing*.)

2. Select one of the following claims, or one of your own if your instructor approves, and plan an argument, listing as many grounds as you can and paying attention to possible rebuttals of counterarguments. Use the same format as described in the previous exercise. Expect your outline to be 1–2 pages.
   a. Professor X is (or is not) a good teacher.
   b. Colleges should (or should not) admit students only on the basis of academic merit.
   c. Americans need (or do not need) to reduce the fat in their diets.
   d. Physical education classes should (or should not) be graded pass/fail.
   e. Public schools should (or should not) have dress codes.
   f. Helmets for bicyclists should (or should not) be mandatory.
   g. Sales taxes on cigarettes should (or should not) be increased.
   h. All cigarette advertising should (or should not) be prohibited.

FOR DEBATE

LET MY TEENAGER DRINK | T. R. REID

A former Tokyo correspondent and London Bureau Chief for the *Washington Post*, T. R. Reid is now the *Post's* Rocky Mountain correspondent. He is also the author of several books on Japan, including *Ski Japan* (1994) and *Confucius Lives Next Door: What Living in the East Teaches Us about Living in the West* (2000). His argument for teen drinking was published May 4, 2003.

PREREADING QUESTIONS Do you or did you drink "underage"? If so, did this lead to any problems? Do you think the drinking age should be lowered in the United States?

1   My 16-year-old called me from a bar. She said my 17-year-old was there, too, along with the rest of the gang from high school: "Everything's fine, Dad. We'll be home after last call."

2   I breathed a quiet sigh of relief. Like many other parents, I knew my teenagers were out drinking that Saturday night. Unlike most American kids,

though, my daughters were drinking safely, legally and under close adult supervision—in the friendly neighborhood pub two blocks from our London
home.

My kids could do that because Britain, like almost every other developed 3
nation, has decided that teenagers are going to drink whether it's legal or
not—and that attempts at prohibition inevitably make things worse.

Some countries have no minimum drinking age—a conservative approach 4
that leaves the issue up to families rather than government bureaucrats. In
most Western democracies, drinking becomes legal in the late teens. In Britain,
a 16-year-old can have a beer in a pub if the drink accompanies a meal. Most
publicans we knew were willing to call a single bag of potato chips—sorry,
"crisps"—a full meal for purposes of that law.

And yet teen drinking tends to be a far more dangerous problem in the 5
prohibitionist United States than in those more tolerant countries. The reason lies in the law itself. Because of our nationwide ban on drinking before
the age of 21, American teenagers tend to do their drinking secretly, in the
worse possible places—in a dark corner of the park, at the one house in the
neighborhood where the adults have left for the weekend, or, most commonly, in the car.

Amid a national outcry over an epidemic of "binge drinking," the politi- 6
cians don't like to admit that this problem is largely a product of the liquor laws.
Kids know they have to do all their drinking before they get to the dance or the
concert, where adults will be present.

On campus, this binge of fast and furious drinking is known as "pre- 7
gaming." Any college student will tell you that the pre-game goal is to get
good and drunk—in the dorm room or in the car—before the social event begins. It would be smarter, and more pleasant for all concerned, to stretch out
whatever alcohol there is over the course of an evening. But Congress in its
wisdom has made this safer approach illegal.

Our family currently has kids at three U.S. universities. The deans of all 8
three schools have sent us firm letters promising zero tolerance for underage
drinking. In conversation, though, the same deans concede readily that their
teenage students drink every weekend—as undergraduates always have.

The situation would be vastly easier to manage, these educators say, if they 9
could allow the kids to drink in public—thus obviating the "pre-game" binge—
and provide some kind of adult presence at the parties.

But those obvious steps would make a school complicit in violating the pro- 10
hibition laws—and potentially liable for civil lawsuits.

The deans lament that there is no political will to change the national drink- 11
ing age—or even to hand the issue back to the states. Politicians, after all, garner support and contributions from the interest groups by promising to "stop
teen drinking."

But, of course, the law doesn't stop teens from drinking. "Most college 12
students drink . . . regardless of the legal drinking age, without harming themselves or anyone else," writes Richard Keeling, editor of the *Journal of American College Health*.

13   As a wandering *Post* correspondent, I have raised teenagers in three places: Tokyo, London and Colorado. No parent will be surprised to read that high school and college students had easy access to alcohol in all three places. In all three countries, kids sometimes got drunk. But overseas, they did their drinking at a bar, a concert or a party. There were adults—and, often, police—around to supervise. As a result, most teenagers learned to use alcohol socially and responsibly. And they didn't have to hide it from their parents.

14   In the United States, our kids learn that drinking is something to be done in the dark, and quickly. Is that the lesson we want to teach them about alcohol use? It makes me glad my teenagers had the legal right to go down the street to that pub.

QUESTIONS FOR READING

1.   What is Reid's claim?
2.   Explain the term "pre-gaming."
3.   What do college administrators say is their position on underage drinking on campus? What do they say actually happens on their campuses?

QUESTIONS FOR REASONING AND ANALYSIS

1.   Analyze Reid's argument, using Toulmin's terms. What passages contain his evidence (grounds)? Does he qualify his claim? (Study his word choice throughout.)
2.   Evaluate Reid's argument. What kind of evidence does he use? Is it convincing? With what audience(s) might his argument be most successful?

QUESTIONS FOR REFLECTING AND WRITING

1.   Do you agree with Reid? If so, is that because you want to drink legally or because you think he has a convincing argument?
2.   If you disagree, what are your counterarguments? Organize a rebuttal for class debate or for an essay.

DON'T MAKE TEEN DRINKING EASIER | JOSEPH A. CALIFANO, JR.

Joseph Califano is a lawyer and former secretary of Health, Education, and Welfare (1977–1979). The author of nine books, he is founder and currently president of the National Center on Addiction and Substance Abuse at Columbia University. His rebuttal to T. R. Reid's article was published in the *Washington Post* on May 11, 2003.

PREREADING QUESTIONS If you were going to rebut Reid's argument, how would you challenge him? Given what you know about Joseph Califano, how do you expect him to challenge Reid?

1   T. R. Reid's May 4 op-ed piece, "Let My Teenager Drink," is a dangerous example of what happens if we let anecdote trump facts. Reid jumps from the

comfort he derives from his 16- and 17-year-old daughters "out drinking Saturday night" at a neighborhood pub in London, where it is legal, to the conclusion that the English and Europeans have far fewer problems with teen drinking than we do in the United States, where the age to legally buy alcohol is 21.

Let's start with the facts. In 2001 the Justice Department released an analysis comparing drinking rates in Europe and the United States. The conclusion: American 10th-graders are less likely to use and abuse alcohol than people of the same age in almost all European countries, including Britain. British 15- and 16-year-olds were more than twice as likely as Americans to binge drink (50 percent vs. 24 percent) and to have been intoxicated within the past 30 days (48 percent vs. 21 percent). Of Western European nations, only Portugal had a lower proportion of young people binge drinking, which is defined as having five or more drinks in a row.

That same year, in a study of 29 nations, including Eastern and Western Europe, the World Health Organization found that American 15-year-olds were less likely than those in 18 other nations to have been intoxicated twice or more. British girls and boys were far likelier than their U.S. counterparts to have been drunk that often (52 and 51 percent vs. 28 and 34 percent).

Then there are the consequences of teen drinking. This month a Rand study that followed 3,400 people from seventh grade through age 23 reported that those who had three or more drinks within the past year, or any drink in the past month, were likelier to use nicotine and illegal drugs, to have stolen items within the past year and to have problems in school. In a report issued last December, the American Medical Association found that teen drinking—not bingeing, just drinking—can seriously damage growth processes of the brain and that such damage "can be long term and irreversible." The AMA warned that "short term or moderate drinking impairs learning and memory far more in youth than in adults" and that "adolescents need only drink half as much to suffer the same negative effects." This exhaustive study concluded that teen drinkers "perform worse in school, are more likely to fall behind and have an increased risk of social problems, depression, suicidal thoughts and violence."

Alcohol is a major contributing factor in the three leading causes of teen death—accidents, homicide and suicide—and increases the chances of juvenile delinquency and crime. Studies at the National Center on Addiction and Substance Abuse at Columbia University have found that teenagers who drink are more likely than those who do not to have sex and have it at an earlier age and with multiple partners.

There are many reasons why teens drink, but I doubt that states setting the drinking age at 21 is one of them. Focus groups of young women suggest that the increase in their binge drinking is related to their wanting to "be one of the boys" and to reduce inhibition, particularly because of the pressure many feel to have sex. Few understand that, on average, one drink has the impact on a woman that it takes two drinks to have on a man. Adolescents of both sexes who have low self-esteem or learning disabilities, or who suffer eating disorders, are at higher risk of drinking.

7   As for the alcohol industry's role: The Center on Alcohol Marketing and Youth at Georgetown University recently revealed that during the past two years, those under 21 heard more beer and liquor commercials on the radio than did adults. The Kaiser Family Foundation Teen Media Monitor, released in February, identified Coors Light and Budweiser beers as two of the five largest advertisers on the most popular television shows for teen boys. For the alcohol industry, it's a good long-term investment, because underage drinkers are likelier to become heavy adult drinkers and grow up to become that 9 percent of adult drinkers who consume 46.3 percent of the alcohol sold in the Untied States. If Mr. Reid thinks that politicians are hanging tough on the drinking age of 21 in order to "garner support and contributions from interest groups," I suggest he take a look at the political contributions from the alcohol industry to keep the price down by killing tax increases (and in this Congress to roll taxes back) and to prevent content and caloric labeling of its products.

8   Fortunately, overwhelming majorities of teens in the United States (84 percent) and adults (83 percent) favor keeping the legal drinking age of 21. Rather than paint rosy but unrealistic pictures of life in countries where teens can legally buy alcohol, we need to get serious about preventing underage drinking. We need to address the many factors that influence teens to drink: genetics, family situation, peer pressure, schools, access to alcohol, alcohol advertising targeting teens. The best place to start is to help parents understand the consequences of their teens drinking.

QUESTIONS FOR READING

1. What is Califano's purpose in writing? What is the claim of his argument?
2. How do American teens compare with Europeans teens in terms of alcohol consumption, binge drinking, and intoxication?
3. What are the consequences of teen drinking?
4. What are some of the causes of teen drinking?
5. How do American adults and teens feel about this country's drinking age?

QUESTIONS FOR REASONING AND ANALYSIS

1. Analyze Califano's argument using Toulmin's terms.
2. Analyze the author's organization. What does he do first? Second? And so on? How does his organization help his rebuttal?
3. Evaluate Califano's argument. What kind of evidence (grounds) does he use? Is it effective?

QUESTIONS FOR REFLECTING AND WRITING

1. Do you agree with Califano? If so, then presumably you accept the legal drinking age of 21—right? If you disagree with Califano, what are your counterarguments?
2. Usually, what kind of argument works best with you, one based on personal experience and anecdote or one based on statistics?

1. What are some problems caused by college students' drinking? You may be able to offer some answers to this question based on your knowledge and experience. You may also want to go **online** for some statistics about college drinking and health and safety risks. Drawing on both experience and data, what claim can you support?

2. Compare the style and tone in Reid's and Califano's essays. Has each one written in a way that works for the author's approach to this issue? Be prepared to explain your views or develop them into a comparative analysis of style.

3. Steven Rattner (pp. 86–89) raises issues of economic inequality in American society. Should we (or should we not) develop policies that would help to shrink the income gap? Plan an argument, using Toulmin's terms to help sort out the parts, in support of one side or the other.

GOING ONLINE

A good starting place for online research about college drinking and health and safety risks is at **www.collegedrinkingprevention.gov**, or conduct your own search.

CHAPTER 4

Writing Effective Arguments

The basics of good writing remain much the same for works as seemingly different as the personal essay, the argument, and the researched essay. Good writing is focused, organized, and concrete. Effective essays are written in a style and tone that are suited to both the audience and the writer's purpose. These are sound principles, all well known to you. But how, exactly, do you achieve them when writing argument? This chapter will help you answer that question.

KNOW YOUR AUDIENCE

Too often students plunge into writing without thinking much about audience, for, after all, their "audience" is only the instructor who has given the assignment, just as their purpose in writing is to complete the assignment and get a grade. These views of audience and purpose are likely to lead to badly written arguments. First, if you are not thinking about readers who may disagree with you, you may not develop the best defense of your claim—which may need a rebuttal to possible counterarguments. Second, you may ignore your essay's needed introductory material on the assumption that the instructor, knowing the assignment, has a context for understanding your writing. To avoid these pitfalls, use the following questions to sharpen your understanding of audience.

Who Is My Audience?

If you are writing an essay for the student newspaper, your audience consists—primarily—of students, but do not forget that faculty and administrators also read the student newspaper. If you are preparing a letter-to-the-editor refutation of a recent column in your town's newspaper, your audience will be the readers of that newspaper—that is, adults in your town. Some instructors give assignments that create an audience such as those just described so that you will practice writing with a specific audience in mind.

   If you are not assigned a specific audience, imagine your classmates, as well as your instructor, as part of your audience. In other words, you are writing to many readers in the academic community. These readers are intelligent and thoughtful, expecting sound reasoning and convincing evidence. These readers also represent varied values and beliefs, as they are from diverse cultures and experiences. Do not confuse the shared expectations of writing conventions, sound reasoning, and accuracy in presenting data with shared beliefs.

What Will My Audience Know about My Topic?

What can you expect a diverse group of readers to know? Whether you are writing on a current issue or a centuries-old debate, you must expect most readers to have some knowledge of the issues. Their knowledge does not free you from the responsibility of developing your support fully, though. In fact, their knowledge creates further demands. For example, most readers know the main arguments on both sides of the abortion issue. For you to write as if they do not—and thus to ignore the arguments of the opposition—is to produce an argument that probably adds little to the debate on the subject.

   On the other hand, what some readers "know" may be little more than an overview of the issues from TV news—or the emotional outbursts of a family member. Some readers may be misinformed or prejudiced, but they embrace their views enthusiastically nonetheless. So, as you think about the ways to develop and support your argument, you will have to assess your readers' knowledge and sophistication on your chosen topic. This assessment will help you decide how much background information to provide or what false facts need to be revealed and dismissed.

Where Does My Audience Stand on the Issue?

Expect readers to hold a range of views, even if you are writing to students on your campus or to an organization of which you are a member. It is not true, for instance, that all students want coed dorms or pass/fail grading. And, if everyone already agrees with you, you have no reason to write. An argument needs to be about a topic that is open to debate. So:

- Assume that some of your audience will probably never agree with you but may offer you grudging respect if you compose an effective argument.
- Assume that some readers do not hold strong views on your topic and may be open to convincing, if you present a good case.
- Assume that those who share your views will still be looking for a strong argument in support of their position.
- Assume that if you know you hold an unpopular view on your topic your best strategy will be a conciliatory approach.

How Should I Speak to My Audience?

Your audience will form an opinion of you based on how you write and how you reason. The image of argument—and the arguer—that we have been creating in this text's discussion is of thoughtful claims defended with logic and evidence. However, the heated debate at yesterday's lunch does not resemble this image of argument. Sometimes the word *persuasion* is used to separate the emotionally charged debate from the calm, intellectual tone of the academic argument. Unfortunately, this neat division between argument and persuasion does not describe the real world of debate. The thoughtful arguer also wants to be persuasive, to win over the audience. And highly emotional presentations can contain relevant facts in support of a sound idea. Instead of thinking of two separate categories—argument and persuasion—think instead of a continuum from the most rigorous logic at one end to extreme flights of fantasy on the other. Figure 4.1 suggests this continuum with some kinds of arguments placed along it.

Where should you place yourself along the continuum in the language you choose and the tone you create? You will have to answer this question with each specific writing context. Much of the time you will choose "thoughtful, re-

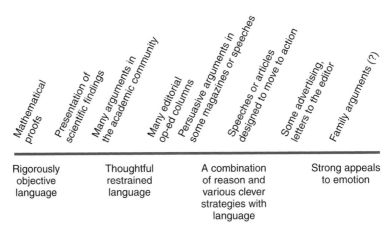

FIGURE 4.1 A Continuum of Argumentative Language

strained language" as expected by the academic community, but there may be times that you will use various persuasive strategies. Probably you will not select "strong appeals to emotion" for your college or workplace writing. Remember that you have different roles in your life, and you use different *voices* as appropriate to each role. You (presumably) speak with courtesy and intelligence to instructors and employers but use slang with friends; you speak condescendingly (surely not often!) to a younger brother or sister. Most of the time, for most of your arguments, you will want to use the serious voice you normally select for serious conversations with other adults. This is the voice that will help you establish your credibility, your *ethos*.

Irony or Sarcasm?

As you learned in Chapter 2, irony is a useful rhetorical strategy for giving one's words greater emphasis by actually writing the opposite of what you mean. Many writers use irony effectively to give punch to their arguments. Irony catches our attention, makes us think, and engages us with the text. Sarcasm is not quite the same as irony. Irony can cleverly focus reader attention on life's complexities. Sarcasm is more often vicious than insightful, relying on harsh, negative word choice. Probably in most of your academic work, you will want to avoid sarcasm, and you will want to think carefully about the effect of any strongly worded appeal to your reader's emotions. Better to persuade your audience with the force of your reasons and evidence than to lose them because of the static of nasty language. But the key, always, is to know your audience and understand how best to present a convincing argument to that specific group.

UNDERSTAND YOUR WRITING PURPOSE

There are many kinds of arguments. As you consider possible topics for an essay, think about what you actually want to *do* with each topic—beyond wanting to write convincingly in defense of your claim. Different types of arguments require different approaches, or different kinds of evidence. It helps to be able to recognize what kind of argument you are contemplating. Here are some useful ways to classify arguments:

- **Inductive argument or investigative paper similar to those in the social sciences.** If you are given an assignment to collect evidence in an organized way to support a claim about advertising strategies or violence in children's programming, then you will be writing an investigative paper, presenting evidence that you have gathered and analyzed to support your claim.
- **Claim of values, or position paper.** If you are given the assignment to argue for your position on euthanasia, trying juveniles as adults, or national identification cards, you need to recognize that this assignment calls for a claim of values. You will be writing a rather philosophical argument, presenting reasons in support of a complex, controversial issue. You will need to pay close attention to your warrants or assumptions.

- **A definition argument.** If you are asked to consider the qualities or traits we should look for in a president or professor, you are really being asked to define "a good president" or "a good professor." Some of your points may seem quite concrete—practical—to you, but your specifics are really tied to an ideal you imagine, and that ideal is best understood as a definition.
- **A problem/solution argument, or claim of policy.** If you are given the broad subject: "What should we do about _____?" and you have to fill in the blank, you are being asked to recommend solutions to a current problem. What should we do about students' disruptive behavior? About gridlock on your town's streets? These kinds of questions ask for different types of answers than do questions about what traits make a good president or who are the greatest athletes.
- **A refutation or rebuttal of someone else's argument.** If you are given the assignment to find a letter to the editor, newspaper editorial, or essay in your textbook with which you disagree, you are being asked to prepare a refutation essay, a specific challenge to a specific argument. You know, then, that you will repeatedly refer to the work you are rebutting, so you will need to know that work thoroughly.

You will keep your focus and argue more convincingly if you understand at the beginning of your thinking about a topic just what will be required to build a successful argument.

MOVE FROM TOPIC TO CLAIM TO POSSIBLE SUPPORT

When you write a letter to the editor of a newspaper, you have chosen to respond to a particular issue, to someone else's argument that has bothered you. In this writing context, you already know your topic and, probably, your claim as well. You also know that your purpose will be to refute the article you have read. In composition classes, the context is not always so clearly established, but you will usually be given some guidelines with which to get started.

Selecting a Topic

Suppose that you are asked to write an argument that is in some way connected to First Amendment rights. Your instructor has limited and focused your topic choice and purpose. Start thinking about possible topics that relate to freedom-of-speech and censorship issues. To aid your topic search and selection, use one or more invention strategies:

- Brainstorm (make a list).
- Freewrite (write without stopping for 10 minutes).
- Map or cluster (connect ideas to the general topic in various spokes, a kind of visual brainstorming).
- Read (in this case, look through the text for ideas).

Your invention strategies lead, let us suppose, to the following list of possible topics:

Administrative restrictions on the college newspaper
Hate speech restrictions or codes
Deleting certain books from high school reading lists
Controls and limits on alcohol and cigarette advertising
Restrictions on violent TV programming
Dress codes/uniforms

Looking over your list, you realize that the last item, dress codes/uniforms, may be about freedom but not freedom of speech, so you drop it from consideration. All of the other topics have promise. Which one do you select? Two considerations should guide you: interest and knowledge. First, your argument is likely to be more thoughtful and lively if you choose an issue that matters to you. But you can also appreciate the usefulness of information and ideas on the topic. Unless you have time for the necessary study to become informed, you are wise to choose a topic about which you have given some thought and thus feel comfortable exploring. To continue the example, let's suppose that you decide to write about television violence because you are concerned about violence in American society and you have given this issue some thought. It is time to phrase your topic as a tentative thesis or claim.

Drafting a Claim

Good claim statements will keep you focused in your writing—in addition to establishing your main idea for readers. Give thought, then, both to your position on the issue and to the wording of your claim. Here are some problem claim statements to avoid:

- Claims using vague words such as *good* or *bad*.

  VAGUE: TV violence is bad for us.
  BETTER: We need more restrictions on violent TV programming.

- Claims in loosely worded "two-part" sentences.

  UNFOCUSED: Campus rape is a serious problem, and we need to do something about it.
  BETTER: College administrators and students need to work together to reduce both the number of campus rapes and the fear of rape.

- Claims that are not appropriately qualified.

  OVERSTATED: Violence on television is making us a violent society.
  BETTER: TV violence is contributing to viewers' increased fear of violence and insensitivity to violence.

- Claims that do not help you focus on your purpose in writing.

UNCLEAR: Not everyone agrees on what is meant by violent TV
PURPOSE: programming.

(Perhaps this is true, but more important, this claim suggests that you will define violent programming. Such an approach would not keep you focused on a First Amendment issue.)

BETTER: Restrictions on violent TV programs can be justified.

(Now your claim directs you to the debate over restrictions of content.)

Listing Possible Grounds

As you learned in Chapter 3, you can generate grounds to support a claim by adding a "because" clause after a claim statement. We can start a list of grounds for the topic on violent TV programming in this way:

We need more restrictions on violent television programming *because*

- Many people, including children and teens, watch many hours of TV.
- People are affected by the dominant activities/experiences in their lives.
- There is a connection between violent programming and desensitizing and fear of violence and possibly more aggressive behavior in heavy viewers.
- Society needs to protect young people.

You have four good points to work on, a combination of reasons and inferences drawn from evidence.

Listing Grounds for the Other Side or Another Perspective

Remember that arguments generate counterarguments and that there are other Toulmin terms you should use to help you look at all parts of your argument. Continue your exploration of this topic by considering possible rebuttals to your proposed grounds. How might someone who does not want to see restrictions placed on television programming possibly respond to each of your points? Let's think about them one at a time:

We need more restrictions on violent television programming because

1. *Many people, including children and teens, watch many hours of TV.*

Your opposition cannot really challenge your first point on the facts, only its relevance to restricting programming. The opposition might argue that if parents think their children are watching too much TV, they should turn it off. The restriction needs to be a family decision.

2. *People are affected by the dominant activities/experiences in their lives.*

It seems common sense to expect people to be influenced by dominant forces in their lives. Your opposition might argue, though, that first, many people have the TV on for many hours but often are not watching it intently for all of that time. The more dominant forces in our lives are parents and teachers and peers, not the TV. The opposition might argue, second, that people seem to be influenced to such different degrees by television that it is not fair or logical to restrict everyone when perhaps only a few are truly influenced by their TV viewing to a harmful degree.

3. *There is a connection between violent programming and desensitizing and fear of violence and possibly more aggressive behavior in heavy viewers.*

Some people are entirely convinced by studies showing these negative effects of violent TV programming, but others point to the less convincing studies or make the argument that if violence on TV were really so powerful an influence, most people would be violent or fearful or desensitized.

4. *Society needs to protect young people.*

Your opposition might choose to agree with you in theory on this point—and then turn again to the argument that parents should be doing the protecting. Government controls on programming restrict adults, as well as children, whereas it may only be some children who should watch fewer hours of TV and not watch adult "cop" shows at all.

Working through this process of considering opposing views can help you see where you may want to do some research for facts—results of studies, for example—to provide backing for your grounds and how you can best develop your reasons to take account of typical counterarguments. This process may also lead to a decision to qualify your claim in some ways.

Planning Your Approach

Now that you have thought about arguments on the other side, you decide that you want to argue for this point:

> To protect young viewers, we need restrictions on violence in children's
> programs and ratings for prime-time adult shows that clearly establish the
> degree of violence in those shows.

Notice how this qualified claim is in response to two points of the rebuttals, that adults would be greatly restricted in order to protect children and that parents should be controlling what their own children watch. Our student hasn't given in to the other side but has chosen to narrow the argument to emphasize the protection of children.

Next, it's time to check some of the articles in this text or go online to get some data to develop points 1 and 3. You need to know that 99 percent of homes have at least one TV; you need to know that by the time young people graduate from high school they have spent more time in front of the TV than in the classroom. Also, you can find the average number of violent acts by hour of TV in children's programs. Then, too, there are the various studies of fearfulness and aggressive behavior that will give you some statistics to use to develop the third point. Be sure to select reliable sources and then cite the sources you use. Citing sources is not only required and right; it is also part of the process of establishing your credibility and thus strengthening your argument.

Finally, how are you going to answer the point about parents controlling their children? You might counter that in theory this is the way it should be—but in fact not all parents are at home watching what their children are watching, and not all parents care enough to pay attention. However, all of us suffer from the consequences of those children who are influenced by their TV watching to become more aggressive or fearful or desensitized. These children grow up to become the adults the rest of us have to interact with, so the problem becomes one for the society as a whole to solve, not individual parents. If you had not disciplined yourself to go through the process of listing possible rebuttals, you may not have thought through this part of the debate.

DRAFT YOUR ARGUMENT

Although it is certainly true that some writers are highly intuitive, discovering what they want to say only as they actually write, many of us can benefit from a step-by-step process of invention—such as we have been exploring in the last few pages. In addition, the more detailed your planning, the more notes you have from working through the Toulmin structure, the easier it will be to get started on your draft. Many students report that they can control their writing anxiety when they generate detailed notes. A page or two of notes that also suggest an organizational strategy can remove that awful feeling of staring at a blank page—whether that "blank page" is your notebook or computer screen.

In the following chapters on argument, you will find specific suggestions for organizing the various kinds of arguments we listed in the section on understanding your writing purpose. But you can always rely on one of the following two basic organizations for argument, regardless of the specific type of argument:

PLAN 1: ORGANIZING AN ARGUMENT

Attention-getting opening (why the issue is important, or current, etc.)

Claim statement

Reasons and evidence in order from least important to most important

Challenge to potential rebuttals or counterarguments

Conclusion that reemphasizes claim

PLAN 2: ORGANIZING AN ARGUMENT

Attention-getting opening

Claim statement (or possibly leave to the conclusion)

Order by arguments of opposing position, with your challenge to each

Conclusion that reemphasizes (or states for the first time) your claim

GUIDELINES for Drafting

HERE ARE A FEW WORDS OF ADVICE ON THE DRAFTING STAGE:

- **Try to get a complete draft of an essay in one sitting, so that you can "see" the whole piece.**
- **If you can't think of a clever opening, state your claim and move on to the body of your essay.** After you draft your reasons and evidence, a good opening may occur to you.
- **If you find that you need something more in some parts of your essay, leave space there as a reminder that you will need to return to that paragraph later.**
- **Try to avoid using either a dictionary or thesaurus while drafting.** Your goal is to get the ideas down. You will polish later.
- **Learn to draft at your computer.** Revising is so much easier that you will be more willing to make significant changes if you work at your PC. If you are handwriting your draft, leave plenty of margin space for additions or for directions to shift parts around.

REVISING YOUR DRAFT

If you have drafted at the computer, begin revising by making a print copy of your draft. Most of us cannot do an adequate job of revision by looking at a computer screen. Then remind yourself that revision is a three-step process: rewriting, editing, and proofreading.

Rewriting

You are not ready to polish the writing until you are satisfied with the argument. Look first at the total piece. Do you have all the necessary parts: a claim, support, some response to possible counterarguments? Examine the order of your reasons and evidence. Do some of your points belong, logically, in a different place? Does the order make the most powerful defense of your claim? Be willing to move whole paragraphs around to test the best organization. Also reflect on the argument itself. Have you avoided logical fallacies? Have you qualified statements when appropriate? Do you have enough support? The best support for your argument?

Consider development: Is your essay long enough to meet assignment requirements? Are points fully developed to satisfy the demands of readers? One key to development is the length of your paragraphs. If most of your paragraphs are only two or three sentences, you have not developed the point of each paragraph satisfactorily. It is possible that some paragraphs need to be combined because they are really on the same subtopic. More typically, short paragraphs need further explanation of ideas or examples to illustrate ideas. Compare the following paragraphs for effectiveness through development:

First Draft of a Paragraph from an Essay on Gun Control

> One popular argument used against the regulation of gun ownership is the need of citizens, especially in urban areas where the crime rate is higher, to possess a handgun for personal protection, either carried or kept in the home. Some citizens may not be aware of the dangers to themselves or their families when they purchase a gun. Others, more aware, may embrace the myth that "bad things only happen to other people."

Revised Version of the Paragraph with Statistics Added

> One popular argument used against the regulation of gun ownership is the need of citizens, especially in urban areas where the crime rate is higher, to possess a handgun for personal protection, whether it is carried or kept in the home. Although some citizens may not be aware of the dangers to themselves or their families when they purchase a gun, they should be. According to the Center to Prevent Handgun Violence, from their Web page "Firearm Facts," "guns that are kept in the home for self-protection are 22 times more likely to kill a family member or friend than to kill in self-defense." The Center also reports that guns in the home make homicide three times more likely and suicide five times more likely. We are not thinking straight if we believe that these dangers only apply to others.

A quick trip to the Internet has provided this student with some facts to support his argument. Observe how he has referred informally but fully to the source of his information. (If your instructor requires formal MLA documentation in all essays, then you will need to add a Works Cited page and give a full reference to the website. See pp. 287–302.)

Editing

When you have added to or deleted from your draft or moved parts of the draft around to shape a more effective argument, make your changes, print another copy, and begin the second phase of revision: editing. As you read through this time, pay close attention to unity and coherence, to sentence patterns, and to word choice. Read each paragraph as a separate unit to be certain that everything is on the same subtopic. Then look at your use of transition and connecting words, both within and between paragraphs. Ask yourself: Have you guided the reader through the argument? Have you shown how the parts connect by using appropriate transitions, connectors such as *therefore, in addition, as a consequence, also,* and so forth?

Read again, focusing on each sentence, checking to see that you have varied sentence patterns and length. Read sentences aloud to let your ear help you find awkward constructions or unfinished thoughts. Strive as well for word choice that is concrete and specific, avoiding wordiness, clichés, trite expressions, or incorrect use of specialized terms. Observe how Samantha edited one paragraph in her essay "Balancing Work and Family":

Draft Version of Paragraph

Women have come a long way in equalizing themselves, but inequality within marriages do exist. One reason for this can be found in the media. Just last week America turned on their televisions to watch a grotesque dramatization of skewed priorities. On Who Wants to Marry a Millionaire, a panel of women vied for the affections of a millionaire who would choose one of them to be his wife. This show said that women can be purchased. Also that men must provide and that money is worth the sacrifice of one's individuality. The show also suggests that physical attraction is more important than the building of a complete relationship. Finally, the show says that women's true value lies in their appearance. This is a dangerous message to send to both men and women viewers.

Margin notes:
- ? agr
- vague reference agreement
- wordy
- short sentences
- vague reference

Edited Version of Paragraph

Although women have come a long way toward equality in the workplace, inequality within marriages can still be found. The media may be partly to blame for this continued inequality. Just last week Americans watched a grotesque dramatization of skewed priorities. On Who Wants to Marry a Millionaire, a panel of women vied for the affections of a millionaire who would choose one of them to be his wife. Such displays teach us that women can be purchased, that men must be the providers, that the desire for money is worth the sacrifice of one's individuality, that physical attraction is more important than a complete relationship, and that women's true value lies in their appearance. These messages discourage marriages based on equality and mutual support.

Samantha's editing has eliminated wordiness and vague references and has combined ideas into one forceful sentence. If you have a good argument, you do not want to lose readers because you have not taken the time to polish your writing.

A Few Words about Words and Tone

You have just been advised to check your word choice to eliminate wordiness, vagueness, clichés, and so on. Here is a specific checklist of problems often found in student papers and some ways to fix the problems.

- *Eliminate clichés.* Do not write about "the fast-paced world we live in today" or the "rat race." First, do you know for sure that the pace of life for someone who has a demanding job is any faster than it was in the past? Travel is faster, but on the job using time effectively has always mattered. Also, using clichés suggests that you are too lazy to find your own words.

- *Avoid jargon.* In the negative sense of this word. Specialists in any group have their own "language." That's one meaning of jargon. The negative meaning refers to nonspecialists who fill their writing with "heavy-sounding terms" to give the appearance of significance. Watch for any overuse of "scientific" terms such as *factor* or *aspect,* or other vague, awkward language.

- *Avoid language that is too informal for most of your writing contexts.* What do you mean when you write: *"Kids* today watch too much TV"? Alternatives include *children, teens, adolescents.* These words are both less slangy and more precise.

- *Avoid nasty attacks on the opposition.* Change "those jerks who are foolish enough to believe that TV violence has no impact on children" to language that explains your counterargument without attacking those who may disagree with you. After all, you want to change the thinking of your audience, not make them resent you for name calling.

- *Avoid all discriminatory language.* In the academic community and the adult workplace, most people are bothered by language that belittles any one group. This includes language that is racist or sexist or reflects negatively on the elderly or disabled or those who do not share your sexual orientation or religious beliefs. Just don't do it!

Proofreading

You also do not want to lose the respect of readers because you submit a paper filled with "little" errors, errors in punctuation, mechanics, and incorrect word choice. Most readers will forgive one or two little errors but will become annoyed if they begin to pile up. So, after you are finished rewriting and editing, print a copy of your paper and read it slowly, looking specifically at punctuation, at the handling of quotations and references to writers and to titles, and at those pesky words that come in two or more "versions": *to, too,* and *two; here* and *hear; their, there,* and *they're;* and so forth. If instructors have found any of these kinds of errors in your papers over the years, then focus your attention on the kinds of errors you have been known to make. Refer to Chapter 1 for handling references to authors and titles and for handling direct quotations. Use a glossary of usage in a handbook for homonyms (the words that sound alike but have different meanings), and check a handbook for punctuation rules. Take pride in your work and present a paper that will be treated with respect. What follows is a checklist of the key points for writing good arguments that we have just examined.

A CHECKLIST FOR REVISION ■·■

- [ ] Have I selected an issue and purpose consistent with assignment guidelines?
- [ ] Have I stated a claim that is focused, appropriately qualified, and precise?
- [ ] Have I developed sound reasons and evidence in support of my claim?
- [ ] Have I used Toulmin terms to help me study the parts of my argument, including rebuttals to counterarguments?

- [ ] Have I found a clear and effective organization for presenting my argument?
- [ ] Have I edited my draft thoughtfully, concentrating on producing unified and coherent paragraphs and polished sentences?
- [ ] Have I eliminated wordiness, clichés, jargon?
- [ ] Have I selected an appropriate tone for my purpose and audience?
- [ ] Have I considered a conciliatory approach and emphasized common ground with those who might disagree with me?
- [ ] Have I used my word processor's spell check and proofread a printed copy with great care?

FOR DEBATE AND ANALYSIS

IN DEFENSE OF VOLUNTARY EUTHANASIA | SIDNEY HOOK

A philosopher, educator, and author, Sidney Hook (1902–1989) taught philosophy at New York University and was a senior research fellow at the Hoover Institution. He published numerous articles and books on philosophy throughout his busy career, and his autobiography, *Out of Step: An Unquiet Life in the Twentieth Century*, appeared in 1987. The following argument for euthanasia, incorporating his personal experience with grave illness, was published in the *New York Times* in 1987.

PREREADING QUESTIONS Have you lost a loved one who suffered at the end of his or her life? If so, how has that experience shaped your thinking on the issue? Do you have a position on doctor-assisted suicide? If so, what is your view?

A few short years ago, I lay at the point of death. A congestive heart fail- 1
ure was treated for diagnostic purposes by an angiogram that triggered a stroke. Violent and painful hiccups, uninterrupted for several days and nights, prevented the ingestion of food. My left side and one of my vocal cords became paralyzed. Some form of pleurisy set in, and I felt I was drowning in a sea of slime. At one point, my heart stopped beating; just as I lost consciousness, it was thumped back into action again. In one of my lucid intervals during those days of agony, I asked my physician to discontinue all life-supporting services or show me how to do it. He refused and predicted that someday I would appreciate the unwisdom of my request.

A month later, I was discharged from the hospital. In six months, I regained 2
the use of my limbs, and although my voice still lacks its old resonance and carrying power I no longer croak like a frog. There remain some minor disabilities and I am restricted to a rigorous, low sodium diet. I have resumed my writing and research.

My experience can be and has been cited as an argument against honor- 3
ing requests of stricken patients to be gently eased out of their pain and life. I cannot agree. There are two main reasons. As an octogenarian, there is a reasonable likelihood that I may suffer another "cardiovascular accident" or worse. I may not even be in a position to ask for the surcease of pain. It seems

to me that I have already paid my dues to death—indeed, although time has softened my memories they are vivid enough to justify my saying that I suffered enough to warrant dying several times over. Why run the risk of more?

4   Secondly, I dread imposing on my family and friends another grim round of misery similar to the one my first attack occasioned.

5   My wife and children endured enough for one lifetime. I know that for them the long days and nights of waiting, the disruption of their professional duties and their own familial responsibilities counted for nothing in their anxiety for me. In their joy at my recovery they have been forgotten. Nonetheless, to visit another prolonged spell of helpless suffering on them as my life ebbs away, or even worse, if I linger on into a comatose senility, seems altogether gratuitous.

6   But what, it may be asked, of the joy and satisfaction of living, of basking in the sunshine, listening to music, watching one's grandchildren growing into adolescence, following the news about the fate of freedom in a troubled world, playing with ideas, writing one's testament of wisdom and folly for posterity? Is not all that one endured, together with the risk of its recurrence, an acceptable price for the multiple satisfactions that are still open even to a person of advanced years?

7   Apparently those who cling to life no matter what, think so. I do not.

8   The zest and intensity of these experiences are no longer what they used to be. I am not vain enough to delude myself that I can in the few remaining years make an important discovery useful for mankind or can lead a social movement or do anything that will be historically eventful, nor less event-making. My autobiography, which describes a record of intellectual and political experiences of some historical value, already much too long, could be posthumously published. I have had my fill of joys and sorrows and am not greedy for more life. I have always thought that a test of whether one had found happiness in one's life is whether one would be willing to relive it— whether, if it were possible, one would accept the opportunity to be born again.

9   Having lived a full and relatively happy life, I would cheerfully accept the chance to be reborn, but certainly not to be reborn again as an infirm octogenarian. To some extent, my views reflect what I have seen happen to the aged and stricken who have been so unfortunate as to survive crippling paralysis. They suffer, and impose suffering on others, unable even to make a request that their torment be ended.

10   I am mindful too of the burdens placed upon the community, with its rapidly diminishing resources, to provide the adequate and costly services necessary to sustain the lives of those whose days and nights are spent on mattress graves of pain. A better use could be made of these resources to increase the opportunities and qualities of life for the young. I am not denying the moral obligation the community has to look after its disabled and aged. There are times, however, when an individual may find it pointless to insist on the fulfillment of a legal and moral right.

What is required is no great revolution in morals but an enlargement of   11
imagination and an intelligent evaluation of alternative uses of community resources.

Long ago, Seneca observed that "the wise man will live as long as he   12
ought, not as long as he can." One can envisage hypothetical circumstances in
which one has a duty to prolong one's life despite its costs for the sake of others, but such circumstances are far removed from the ordinary prospects we are
considering. If wisdom is rooted in knowledge or the alternatives of choice, it
must be reliably informed of the state one is in and its likely outcome. Scientific medicine is not infallible, but it is the best we have. Should a rational person be willing to endure acute suffering merely on the chance that a miraculous
cure might presently be at hand? Each one should be permitted to make his
own choice—especially when no one else is harmed by it.

The responsibility for the decision, whether deemed wise or foolish, must   13
be with the chooser.

QUESTIONS FOR READING

1. What subject is introduced in Hook's opening two paragraphs? What strategy
    does he use as an introduction?

2. What have some people seen in his experience? For what two reasons does Hook
    disagree with them?

3. When others observe the pleasures of life the author can still experience, what
    are Hook's responses? Summarize his reasons for not wanting to continue to live
    on in his eighties.

QUESTIONS FOR REASONING AND ANALYSIS

1. What is Hook's position on euthanasia? Where does he state his claim?

2. Analyze the nature of the author's argument. What kind of evidence does he
    provide?

3. Hook writes of "intelligent evaluation," of "wisdom," "knowledge," and "a ra-
    tional person." How would you describe his philosophy? What does he value
    as essential to being human?

QUESTIONS FOR REFLECTION AND WRITING

1. Hook argues that he should be free to make choices about his life—or death—
    as long as he does not harm others. Do you agree with this philosophy, in gen-
    eral? Do you agree that it applies to the choice of euthanasia? Why or why not?

2. What is your position on euthanasia? What are your reasons?

EUTHANASIA—A CRITIQUE | PETER A. SINGER AND MARK SIEGLER

A graduate of the University of Toronto Medical School and holding a master's in public health from Yale University, Dr. Peter A. Singer (b. 1960) is assistant professor of medicine and associate director of the Center for Bioethics at the University of Toronto. He is the author of many articles on bioethics, end-of-life care, and euthanasia. Dr. Mark Siegler (b. 1941) obtained his medical degree from the University of Chicago, where he is director of the Center of Clinical Medical Ethics. Dr. Siegler is a recognized authority in the field of clinical medical ethics, having written more than 100 articles, six books, and the chapters on clinical ethics in two standard texts on internal medicine. In the following article, published in the *New England Journal of Medicine* on June 20, 1990, the authors provide a good review of the issues that are central to the debate on euthanasia and present their views on this issue.

PREREADING QUESTIONS   Do you have a current position on doctor-assisted suicide? If so, what is your view? If not, do you think the issue deserves more thought on your part? Why or why not? If you have a position, what are the main sources of influence: family, friends, religious beliefs?

1   A vigorous medical and political debate has begun again on euthanasia, a practice proscribed 2500 years ago in the Hippocratic oath.[1-4] The issue has been publicized recently in three widely divergent settings: a journal article, a legislative initiative in California, and public policy in the Netherlands.

2   The case of "Debbie" shows that euthanasia can be discussed openly in a respected medical journal. "It's Over, Debbie" was an anonymous, first-person account of euthanasia, published on January 8, 1988, in the *Journal of the American Medical Association*,[5-8] that stimulated widespread discussion and elicited spirited replies. Later in 1988, perhaps as a result, the Council on Ethical and Judicial Affairs of the American Medical Association reaffirmed its opposition to euthanasia.[9]

3   In California, a legislative initiative[10,11] has shown that in the near future euthanasia may be legalized in certain U.S. jurisdictions. A bill proposing a California Humane and Dignified Death Act was an attempt to legalize euthanasia through the referendum process, which allows California voters to approve controversial issues directly. Public-opinion polls reported that up to 70 percent of the electorate favored the initiative, and many commentators flatly predicted that the initiative would succeed. Nevertheless, the signature drive failed, collecting only 130,000 of the 450,000 required signatures. Attributing the failure to organizational problems, the proponents vowed to introduce the legislation again in California and in other states in 1990.

4   Experience in the Netherlands has shown that a liberal democratic government can tolerate and defend the practice of euthanasia. Although euthanasia is technically illegal in the Netherlands, in fact it is part of Dutch public policy today.[1,12-16] There is agreement at all levels of the judicial system, in-

cluding the Supreme Court, that if physicians follow the procedural guidelines issued by a state commission, they will not be prosecuted for performing euthanasia.[16] The Dutch guidelines emphasize five requirements: an explicit, repeated request by the patient that leaves no doubt about the patient's desire to die; very severe mental or physical suffering, with no prospect of relief; an informed, free, and consistent decision by the patient; the lack of other treatment options, those available having been exhausted or refused by the patient; and consultation by the doctor with another medical practitioner (and perhaps also with nurses, pastors, or others).[13] The usual method of performing euthanasia is to induce sleep with a barbiturate, followed by a lethal injection of curare.[1] An estimated 5000 to 10,000 patients receive euthanasia each year in the Netherlands.[16]

In view of these developments, we urge physicians to consider some reasons for resisting the move toward euthanasia. This article criticizes the main arguments offered by proponents and presents opposing arguments. The case for euthanasia is described in detail elsewhere.[10,17]   5

CRITIQUE OF THE CASE FOR EUTHANASIA

In the debate about euthanasia, imprecision of language abounds. For the purposes of this article, euthanasia is defined as the deliberate action by a physician to terminate the life of a patient. The clearest example is the act of lethal injection. We distinguish euthanasia from such other acts as the decision to forgo life-sustaining treatment (including the use of ventilators, cardiopulmonary resuscitation, dialysis, or tube feeding—the issue raised in the Cruzan case[18]); the administration of analgesic agents to relieve pain; "assisted suicide," in which the doctor prescribes but does not administer a lethal dose of medication; and "mercy killing" performed by a patient's family or friends. The Dutch guidelines described above and the terms proposed in the California initiative represent two versions of euthanasia.   6

The case for euthanasia is based on two central claims.[10,17] First, proponents argue that patients whose illnesses cause them unbearable suffering should be permitted to end their distress by having a physician perform euthanasia. Second, proponents assert that the well-recognized right of patients to control their medical treatment includes the right to request and receive euthanasia.   7

Relief of Suffering

We agree that the relief of pain and suffering is a crucial goal of medicine.[19] We question, however, whether the care of dying patients cannot be improved without resorting to the drastic measure of euthanasia. Most physical pain can be relieved with the appropriate use of analgesic agents.[20] Unfortunately, despite widespread agreement that dying patients must be provided with necessary analgesia,[21] physicians continue to underuse analgesia in the care of dying patients because of concern about depressing respiratory drive or creating addiction. Such situations demand better management of pain, not euthanasia.   8

9   Another component of suffering is the frightening prospect of dying shackled to a modern-day Procrustean bed, surrounded by the latest forms of high technology. Proponents of euthanasia often cite horror stories of patients treated against their will. In the past, when modern forms of life-saving technology were new and physicians were just learning how to use them appropriately, such cases occurred often; we have begun to move beyond that era. The law, public policy, and medical ethics now acknowledge the right of patients to refuse life-sustaining medical treatment, and a large number of patients avail themselves of this new policy.[22-24] These days, competent patients may freely exercise their right to choose or refuse life-sustaining treatment; to carry out their preferences, they do not require the option of euthanasia.

10   We acknowledge that some elements of human suffering and mental anguish—not necessarily related to physical pain—cannot be eliminated completely from the dying process. These include the anticipated loss of important human relationships and membership in the human community, the loss of personal independence, the feeling of helplessness, and the raw fear of death. Euthanasia can shorten the duration of these emotional and psychological hardships. It can also eliminate fears about how and when death will occur. Finally, euthanasia returns to the patient a measure of control over the process of dying. These are the benefits of euthanasia, against which its potential harms must be balanced.

Individual Rights

11   The second argument in favor of euthanasia is based on the rights of the individual. Proponents contend that the right of patients to forgo life-sustaining medical treatment should include a right to euthanasia. This would extend the notion of the right to die to embrace the concept that patients have a right to be killed by physicians. But rights are not absolute. They must be balanced against the rights of other people and the values of society. The claim of a right to be killed by a physician must be balanced against the legal, political, and religious prohibitions against killing that have always existed in society generally and in medicine particularly. As the President's Commission for the Study of Ethical Problems in Medicine and Biomedical and Behavioral Research has observed, "Policies prohibiting direct killing may also conflict with the important value of patient self-determination. . . . The Commission finds this limitation on individual self-determination to be an acceptable cost of securing the general protection of human life afforded by the prohibition of direct killing."[22] We agree. In our view, the public good served by the prohibition of euthanasia outweighs the private interests of the persons requesting it.

THE CASE AGAINST EUTHANASIA

12   The arguments against euthanasia are made from two perspectives: public policy and the ethical norms of medicine.

Euthanasia Is Perilous Public Policy

13   Proponents of euthanasia use the concept of individual rights to support their claim, but this same concept can be used for the opposite purpose. The argument against euthanasia on grounds of civil rights involves a consideration

of the rights not just of those who would want euthanasia themselves but of all citizens. As public policy, euthanasia is unacceptable because of the likelihood, or even the inevitability, of involuntary euthanasia—persons being euthanized without their consent or against their wishes.

There are four ways in which the policy of voluntary euthanasia could lead   14
to involuntary euthanasia. The first is "crypthanasia" (literally, "secret euthanasia").[15] In the Netherlands, for instance, it is alleged that vulnerable patients are euthanized without their consent. Dutch proponents of euthanasia disavow these reports and claim that they are unrelated to the toleration of voluntary euthanasia. We suggest, however, that a political milieu in which voluntary euthanasia is tolerated may also foster involuntary euthanasia and lead to the killing of patients without consent. The second way in which involuntary euthanasia may occur is through "encouraged" euthanasia, whereby chronically ill or dying patients may be pressured to choose euthanasia to spare their families financial or emotional strain.[25] The third way is "surrogate" euthanasia. If voluntary euthanasia were permissible in the United States, the constitutional guarantees of due process, which tend to extend the same rights to incompetent as to competent patients, might permit euthanizing incompetent patients on the basis of "substituted judgment" or nebulous tests of "burdens and benefits." Finally, there is the risk of "discriminatory" euthanasia. Patients belonging to vulnerable groups in American society might be subtly coerced into "requesting" euthanasia. In the United States today, many groups are disempowered, disenfranchised, or otherwise vulnerable: the poor, the elderly, the disabled, members of racial minorities, the physically handicapped, the mentally impaired, alcoholics, drug addicts, and patients with the acquired immunodeficiency syndrome. In a society in which discrimination is common and many citizens do not have access even to basic health care, the legalization of euthanasia would create another powerful tool with which to discriminate against groups whose "consent" is already susceptible to coercion and whose rights are already in jeopardy.

The proponents of euthanasia contend that procedural safeguards, such   15
as the five provisions of the Dutch guidelines noted above, will prevent involuntary euthanasia. They claim further that society permits many dangerous activities if adequate procedural safeguards are provided to reduce risk and protect the public. We agree that safeguards would reduce the risk of involuntary euthanasia, but they would not eliminate it entirely. In the case of euthanasia, safeguards have not been adequately tested and shown to be effective. Even in their presence, we are concerned that patients could be euthanized without their consent or even against their wishes. Even one case of involuntary euthanasia would represent a great harm. In the current era of cost containment, social injustice, and ethical relativism, this risk is one our society should not accept.

Euthanasia Violates the Norms of Medicine

In addition to being perilous as public policy, euthanasia violates three   16
fundamental norms and standards of medicine. First, as noted above, it diverts attention from the real issues in the care of dying patients—among

them, improved pain control, better communication between doctors and patients, heightened respect for the patient's right to choose whether to accept life-sustaining treatment, and improved management of the dying process, as in hospice care. The hospice movement has demonstrated that managing pain appropriately and allowing patients control over the use of life-sustaining treatments reduce the need for euthanasia.

17　　Second, euthanasia subverts the social role of the physician as healer. Historically, physicians have scrupulously avoided participating in activities that might taint their healing role, such as capital punishment or torture. Physicians should distance themselves from euthanasia to maintain public confidence and trust in medicine as a healing profession.

18　　Third, euthanasia strikes at the heart of what it means to be a physician.[26] Since the time of Hippocrates, the prohibition against it has been fundamental to the medical profession and has served as a moral absolute for both patients and physicians. This prohibition has freed physicians from a potential conflict of interest between healing and killing and in turn has enabled patients to entrust physicians with their lives. It has enabled physicians to devote themselves singlemindedly to helping patients achieve their own medical goals. This prohibition may even have encouraged medical research and scientific progress, because physicians, with the consent of patients, are motivated to perform risky, innovative procedures that are aggressive and sometimes painful, with a total commitment to benefit the patient.

CONCLUSIONS

19　　Pressure to legalize euthanasia will surely increase in an era of spiraling health care costs, but it must be resisted. Euthanasia represents a development that is dangerous for many vulnerable patients and that threatens the moral integrity of the medical profession. Physicians must become more responsive to the concerns of patients that underlie the movement for euthanasia and must provide better pain management, more compassionate terminal care, and more appropriate use of life-sustaining treatments. But physicians need to draw the line at euthanasia. They and their professional associations should defend the integrity of medicine by speaking out against the practice. Finally, even if euthanasia is legalized in some jurisdictions, physicians should refuse to participate in it, and professional organizations should censure any of their members who perform euthanasia.

REFERENCES

[1]Angell M. Euthanasia. N Engl J Med 1988; 319:1348–50.

[2]Singer PA. Should doctors kill patients? Can Med Assoc J 1988; 138: 1000–1.

[3]Kinsella TD, Singer PA, Siegler M. Legalized active euthanasia: an Aesculapian tragedy. Bull Am Coll Surg 1989; 74(12):6–9.

[4]Wanzer SH, Federmann DD, Adelstein SJ, et al. The Physician's responsibility toward hopelessly ill patients: A second look. N Engl J Med 1989; 320:844–9.

[5]It's over, Debbie. JAMA 1988; 259:272.

[6]Vaux KL. Debbie's dying: mercy killing and the good death. JAMA 1988; 259:2140–1.

[7]Gaylin W, Kass LR, Pellegrino ED, Siegler M. 'Doctors must not kill.' JAMA 1988; 259:2139–40.

[8]Lundberg GD. 'It's over, Debbie' and the euthanasia debate. JAMA 1988; 259:2142–3.

[9]The Council on Ethical and Judicial Affairs of the American Medical Association. Euthanasia. Report: C (A-88). AMA council report. Chicago: American Medical Association, 1988:1.

[10]Risley RL. A humane and dignified death: a new law permitting physician aid-in-dying. Glendale, Calif.: Americans Against Human Suffering, 1987.

[11]Parachini A. Mercy, murder, & mortality: perspectives on euthanasia: the California Humane and Dignified Death Initiative. Hastings Cent Rep 1989; 19(1):Suppl:10–2.

[12]Pence GE. Do not go slowly into that dark night: mercy killing in Holland. Am J Med 1988; 84:139–41.

[13]Rigter H, Borst-Eilers E, Leenen HJJ. Euthanasia across the North Sea. BMJ 1988; 297:1593–5.

[14]Rigter H. Mercy, murder, & morality: euthanasia in the Netherlands: distinguishing facts from fiction. Hastings Cent Rep 1989; 191(1):Suppl:31–2.

[15]Fenigsen R. Mercy, murder & morality: perspectives on euthanasia: a case against Dutch euthanasia. Hastings Cent Rep 1989; 19(1):Suppl:22–30.

[16]de Wachter MAM. Active euthanasia in the Netherlands. JAMA 1989; 262:3316–9.

[17]Humphry D. Wickett A. The right to die: understanding euthanasia. New York: Harper & Row, 1986.

[18]Angell M. Prisoners of technology: the case of Nancy Cruzan. N Eng J Med 1990; 322:1226–8.

[19]Cassell EJ. The nature of suffering and the goals of medicine. N Engl J Med 1982; 306:639–45.

[20]Foley KM. The treatment of cancer pain. N Engl J Med 1985; 313:84–95.

[21]Angell M. The quality of mercy. N Engl J Med 1982; 306:98–9.

[22]President's Commission for the Study of Ethical Problems in Medicine and Biomedical and Behavioral Research. Deciding to forgo life-sustaining treatment: a report on the ethical, medical, and legal issues in treatment decisions. Washington, D.C.: Government Printing Office, 1983.

[23]The Hastings Center. Guidelines on the termination of life-sustaining treatment and the care of the dying: a report. Briarcliff Manor, N.Y.: Hastings Center, 1987.

[24]Emanuel EJ. A review of the ethical and legal aspects of terminating medical care. Am J Med 1988; 84:291–301.

[25]Kamisar Y. Some non-religious views against proposed "mercy-killing" legislation. Minn Law Rev 1958; 42:969–1042.

[26]Kass LR. Neither for love nor money: why doctors must not kill. Public Interest 1989; 94(winter):25–46.

QUESTIONS FOR READING

1. What debate do the authors join in with their essay?
2. How many people in the Netherlands apparently employ euthanasia each year? Summarize the required guidelines physicians must follow to use euthanasia there without prosecution.
3. How do Singer and Siegler define *euthanasia*? What is not included in their definition?
4. What are the two reasons of those who argue for euthanasia? Summarize the authors' rebuttal of each reason.
5. What two approaches do the authors take in arguing against euthanasia?
6. Why is euthanasia bad public policy? What could voluntary euthanasia lead to? What characteristics of modern society make, in the authors' view, legalizing euthanasia too risky?
7. What do the authors want physicians to do?

QUESTIONS FOR REASONING AND ANALYSIS

1. What do the authors want to accomplish in their opening references to the article on "Debbie," the California initiative, and the practice of euthanasia in the Netherlands?
2. Analyze the essay's organization, indicating the paragraphs that belong in each part.
3. What do the authors accomplish in paragraph 10?
4. What is Singer and Siegler's claim?

QUESTIONS FOR REFLECTING AND WRITING

1. Do you agree that interest in euthanasia is increasing? What evidence would you cite to support your answer?
2. Which of the two arguments supporting euthanasia is the most convincing, in your view? Which of the arguments against euthanasia is the most convincing? Why?
3. Where do you stand on the issue of legalizing euthanasia? Be prepared to defend your position.

SUGGESTIONS FOR DISCUSSION AND WRITING

1. Do you agree with Singer and Siegler that we live in an "era of cost containment, social injustice, and ethical relativism"? Why or why not? The authors do not cite evidence for this assertion. Develop an argument either in support of this claim or to challenge it.

2. These two articles on euthanasia make for interesting comparisons beyond their differing positions on the issue. Do a comparative analysis of the style, format, and choice of evidence in the two essays. Consider: How is each essay effective in its context of audience and purpose? Why would neither essay be effective with the other one's audience?

3. Where do you stand on the issue of euthanasia? Be prepared to defend your position.

GOING ONLINE

You may want to go online to find information beyond what is available in the chapter's essays. You can start your search at these sites: www.religioustolerance.org/euthanas.htm; www.finalexit.org; www.euthanasia.com.

CHAPTER 5

Learning More about Argument: Induction, Deduction, and Logical Fallacies

You can build on your knowledge of the basics of argument, examined in Chapter 3, by understanding some traditional forms of argument: induction, deduction, and analogy. It is also important to recognize arguments that do not work.

INDUCTION

Induction is the process by which we reach inferences—opinions based on facts, or on a combination of facts and less debatable inferences. The inductive process moves from particular to general, from support to assertion. We base our inferences on the facts we have gathered and studied. In general, the more evidence, the more convincing the argument. No one wants to debate tomorrow's sunrise; the evidence for counting on it is too convincing. Most inferences, though, are drawn from less evidence, so we need to examine inductive arguments closely to judge their reasonableness.

The pattern of induction looks like this:

EVIDENCE: There is the dead body of Smith. Smith was shot in his bedroom between the hours of 11:00 P.M. and 2:00 A.M., according to the coroner. Smith was shot by a .32-caliber pistol. The pistol left in the bedroom contains Jones's fingerprints. Jones was seen, by a neighbor, entering the Smith home at around 11:00 the night of Smith's death. A coworker heard Smith and Jones arguing in Smith's office the morning of the day Smith died.

CLAIM: Jones killed Smith.

The facts are presented. The jury infers that Jones is a murderer. Unless there is a confession or a trustworthy eyewitness, the conclusion is an inference, not a fact. This is the most logical explanation; that is, the conclusion meets the standards of simplicity and frequency while accounting for all of the known evidence.

The following paragraph illustrates the process of induction. In their book *Discovering Dinosaurs,* authors Mark Norell, Eugene Gaffney, and Lowell Dingus answer the question "Did dinosaurs really rule the world?"

> For almost 170 million years, from the Late Triassic to the end of the Cretaceous, there existed dinosaurs of almost every body form imaginable: small carnivores, such as *Compsognathus* and *Ornitholestes,* ecologically equivalent to today's foxes and coyotes; medium-sized carnivores, such as *Velociraptor* and the troodontids, analogous to lions and tigers; and the monstrous carnivores with no living analogs, such as *Tyrannosaurus* and *Allosaurus.* Included among the ornithischians and the elephantine sauropods are terrestrial herbivores of diverse body form. By the end of the Jurassic, dinosaurs had even taken to the skies. The only habitats that dinosaurs did not dominate during the Mesozoic were aquatic. Yet, there were marine representatives, such as the primitive toothed bird *Hesperornis.* Like penguins, these birds were flightless, specialized for diving, and probably had to return to land to reproduce. In light of this broad morphologic diversity [number of body forms], dinosaurs did "rule the planet" as the dominant life form on Earth during most of the Mesozoic [era that includes the Triassic, Jurassic, and Cretaceous Periods, 248 to 65 million years ago].

Observe that the writers organize evidence by type of dinosaur to demonstrate the range and diversity of these animals. A good inductive argument is based on a sufficient volume of *relevant* evidence. The basic shape of this inductive argument is illustrated in Figure 5.1.

CLAIM:	Dinosaurs were the dominant life form during the Mesozoic Era.
GROUNDS:	The facts presented in the paragraph.
ASSUMPTION (WARRANT):	The facts are representative, revealing dinosaur diversity.

FIGURE 5.1 The Shape of an Inductive Argument

Observe the inductive process in the following section from David Norman's *Dinosaur!*

HADROSAUR NESTS | DAVID NORMAN

1   During 1978 a remarkable dinosaur find was made, not in the field during an expedition but in a rock shop at Bynum in Montana, by two paleontologists, Dr. Robert Makela and John Horner. They found the bones of baby hadrosaurs which had been excavated nearby. The find started a sequence of events that was to attract worldwide attention to the rock formations in this part of Montana.

2   Makela and Horner traced the baby dinosaur bones back to their original location in the Late Cretaceous rocks of a range of low hills southwest of Bynum. Investigation of the site soon resulted in the discovery of not just baby dinosaur bones, but egg shell fragments, and finally a complete nest containing the jumbled remains of baby hadrosaurs and crushed egg shell. The nest was a shallow, basin-like depression which had clearly been scooped out in the ground, and there seemed to be some trace of vegetation associated with, or perhaps lining the nest. This remarkable discovery set off fieldwork in the area which continues unabated to the present day. It was the first discovery of a nest with babies still inside, and was to lead to surprising insights into the social life of hadrosaurs and the other creatures which lived in this area of the world during the Late Cretaceous.

3   In the following year, 1979, a proper field crew travelled out to Montana to collect from the same area. They found more nest sites of hadrosaurs, and in a nearby rocky hill—later to become known as "Egg Mountain"—large numbers of eggs of a different ornithopod dinosaur—a hypsilophodontid later named *Orodomeus makeli*. As if that was not enough, the field crews also discovered a bone bed—a layer of rock on which were preserved the scattered remains of a huge herd of hadrosaurs numbering perhaps tens of thousands. Further sites have been discovered since which have made this area one of the world's richest for the remains of dinosaurs and eggs.

4   The hadrosaur which had laid the eggs at the sites in Montana was new to science and was named *Maiasaura*, for an old Roman mother goddess also known as the Bona Dea or "good goddess." The name was chosen deliberately because of what they found when they examined the nests. These were clearly

carefully made, having been scooped out of the earth to make a large bowl-shaped depression. This was apparently lined with soft vegetation within which the eggs were laid. The nests were notable for two features. First, the egg shells were broken into small pieces, which suggested that they had been trampled by the hatchlings. Second, the baby hadrosaurs had worn teeth, which suggested that the young hatchlings had either been fed while in the nest, or had made forays out of the nest and then returned later. This is strong evidence that the parents looked after their young, which had never before been recognized in dinosaurs.

The final proof, if any were needed, that this was the likely nesting behav- 5 ior of these dinosaurs comes from the nests themselves. The young had in some cases perished in the nest. How otherwise could the presence of their small bones be explained? It became clear that the instinct for the young to stay in the nest was extremely powerful. Perhaps in this case the parent had been killed while searching for fresh food for its young, leaving its young abandoned to die of starvation as they waited patiently for the parent to return.

As work continued at the Montana sites it gradually became apparent that 6 many of the nests which were found together were actually at the same geological level—in fact, they had been made at the same time. This brought with it the further realization that the crews had discovered not just a few odd nests, but a complete dinosaur nesting colony. Dinosaurs seemed to have returned to this area from season to season to lay their eggs in much the same way as birds return to nest sites year after year.

Add to this the discovery of the bone bed indicating the presence of huge 7 herds of hadrosaurs in the vicinity, and it becomes tempting to believe that these dinosaurs migrated in huge herds across North America during the Late Cretaceous. It seems quite possible that vast herds would have followed rich pastures through the year, returning each season to their nesting grounds to rest, lay their eggs, and rear their young. Herding, nesting in colonies, and parental care of the young imply considerable social interaction between these dinosaurs.

QUESTIONS FOR ANALYSIS

1. What, specifically, is Norman's subject?
2. Underline all statements that are inferences, number them, and then find the evidence presented for each of the inferences.
3. What is the most general—most significant—inference that Norman draws from the blend of evidence and other inferences? Where is it stated?

COLLABORATIVE EXERCISE: Induction

With your class partner or in small groups, make a list of facts that could be used to support each of the following inferences:

1. Whole-wheat bread is nutritious.
2. Fido must have escaped under the fence during the night.
3. Sue must be planning to go away for the weekend.
4. Students who do not hand in all essay assignments fail Dr. Bradshaw's English class.
5. The price of Florida oranges will go up in grocery stores next year.

DEDUCTION

Although induction can be described as an argument that moves from particular to general, from facts to inference, deduction cannot accurately be described as the reverse. Deductive arguments are more complex than suggested by such a description. *Deduction is the reasoning process that draws a conclusion from the logical relationship of two assertions, usually one broad judgment or definition and one more specific assertion, often an inference.* Suppose on the way out of American history class, you say, "Abraham Lincoln certainly was a great leader." Someone responds with the expected question "Why do you think so?" You explain: "He was great because he performed with courage and a clear purpose in a time of crisis." Your explanation contains a conclusion and an assertion about Lincoln (an inference) in support. But behind your explanation rests an idea about leadership, in the terms of deduction, a *premise.* The argument's basic shape is illustrated in Figure 5.2.

Traditionally, the deductive argument is arranged somewhat differently from these sentences about Lincoln. The two reasons are called *premises*; the broader one, called the *major premise,* is written first and the more specific one, the *minor premise,* comes next. The premises and conclusion are expressed to make clear that assertions are being made about categories or classes. To illustrate:

MAJOR PREMISE: All people who perform with courage and a clear purpose in a crisis are great leaders.

MINOR PREMISE: Lincoln was a person who performed with courage and a clear purpose in a crisis.

CONCLUSION: Lincoln was a great leader.

CLAIM:	Lincoln was a great leader.
GROUNDS:	1. People who perform with courage and clear purpose in a crisis are great leaders.
	2. Lincoln was a person who performed with courage and a clear purpose in a crisis.
ASSUMPTION (WARRANT):	The relationship of the two reasons leads, logically, to the conclusion.

FIGURE 5.2 The Shape of a Deductive Argument

If these two premises are correctly, that is, logically, constructed, then the conclusion follows logically, and the deductive argument is *valid*. This does not mean that the conclusion is necessarily *true*. It does mean that if you accept the truth of the premises, then you must accept the truth of the conclusion, because in a valid argument the conclusion follows logically, necessarily. How do we know that the conclusion must follow if the argument is logically constructed? Let's think about what each premise is saying and then diagram each premise to represent each assertion visually. The first premise says that all people who act a particular way are people who fit into the category called "great leaders":

The second premise says that Lincoln, a category of one, belongs in the category of people who act in the same particular way that the first premise describes:

If we put the two diagrams together, we have the following set of circles, demonstrating that what the conclusion asserts follows from the premises:

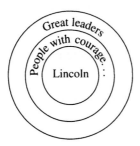

We can also make negative and qualified assertions in a deductive argument. For example:

PREMISE: No cowards can be great leaders.

PREMISE: Falstaff was a coward.

CONCLUSION: Falstaff was not a great leader.

Or, to reword the conclusion to make the deductive pattern clearer: No Falstaff (no member of this class) is a great leader. Diagramming to test for validity, we find that the first premise says no A's are B's:

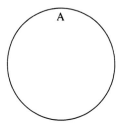 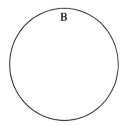

The second premise asserts all C's are A's:

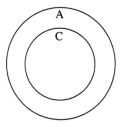

Put together, we see that the conclusion follows necessarily from the premises: No C's can possibly be members of class B.

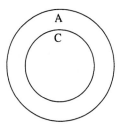 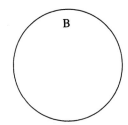

We can, in addition, shape a deductive argument with a qualified premise and conclusion.

PREMISE: All boys in my class are seniors.

PREMISE: Some boys in my class are football players.

CONCLUSION: Some seniors are football players

or

Some football players are seniors.

Diagramming to test the argument's validity, we observe that, indeed, the conclusion follows from the premises:

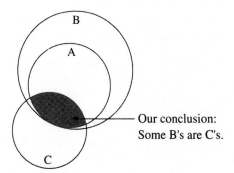

Our conclusion:
Some B's are C's.

Some deductive arguments merely look right, but the two premises do not lead logically to the conclusion that is asserted. We must read each argument carefully or diagram each one to make certain that the conclusion follows from the premises. Consider the following argument: *Unions must be communistic because they want to control wages.* The sentence contains a conclusion and one reason, or premise. From these two parts of a deductive argument we can also determine the unstated premise, just as we could with the Lincoln argument: *Communists want to control wages.* If we use circles to represent the three categories of people in the argument and diagram the argument, we see a different result from the Lincoln argument:

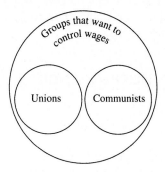

Diagramming the argument reveals that it is invalid; that is, it is not logically constructed because the statements do not require that the union circle be placed inside the communist circle. We cannot draw the conclusion we want from just any two premises, only from those that provide a logical basis from which a conclusion can be reached.

We must first make certain that deductive arguments are properly constructed or valid. But suppose the logic works and yet you do not agree with the claim? Your complaint, then, must be with one of the premises, a judgment or inference that you do not accept as true. Consider, as an example, the following argument:

MAJOR PREMISE:	(All) dogs make good pets.
MINOR PREMISE:	Fido is a dog.
CONCLUSION:	Fido will make a good pet.

This argument is valid. (Diagram it; your circles will fit into one another just as with the Lincoln argument.) However, you are not prepared to agree, necessarily, that Fido will make a good pet. The problem is with the major premise. For the argument to work, the assertion must be about *all* dogs, but we know that not all dogs will be good pets.

When composing a deductive argument, your task will be to defend the truth of your premises. Then, if your argument is valid (logically constructed), readers will have no alternative but to agree with your conclusion. If you disagree with someone else's logically constructed argument, then you must show why one of the premises is not true. Your counterargument will seek to discredit one (or both) of the premises. The Fido argument can be discredited by your producing examples of dogs that have not made good pets.

A deductive argument can serve as the core of an essay, an essay that supports the argument's claim by developing support for each of the premises. Since the major premise is either a broad judgment or a definition, it will need to be defended on the basis of an appeal to values or beliefs that the writer expects the reader to share. The minor premise, usually an inference about a particular situation (or person), would be supported by relevant evidence, as with any inductive argument. You can see this process at work in the Declaration of Independence. Questions follow the Declaration to guide your analysis of this famous example of the deductive process.

THE DECLARATION OF INDEPENDENCE |

In Congress, July 4, 1776
The unanimous declaration of the thirteen
United States of America

1   When in the course of human events, it becomes necessary for one people to dissolve the political bands which have connected them with another, and to assume among the powers of the earth, the separate and equal station to which the Laws of Nature and of Nature's God entitle them, a decent respect to the opinions of mankind requires that they should declare the causes which impel them to the separation.

2   We hold these truths to be self-evident, that all men are created equal, that they are endowed by their Creator with certain unalienable rights, that among these are life, liberty and the pursuit of happiness. That to secure these rights,

governments are instituted among men, deriving their just powers from the consent of the governed. That whenever any form of government becomes destructive of these ends, it is the right of the people to alter or to abolish it, and to institute new government, laying its foundation on such principles and organizing its powers in such form, as to them shall seem most likely to effect their safety and happiness. Prudence, indeed, will dictate that governments long established should not be changed for light and transient causes; and accordingly all experience hath shown, that mankind are more disposed to suffer, while evils are sufferable, than to right themselves by abolishing the forms to which they are accustomed. But when a long train of abuses and usurpations, pursuing invariably the same object evinces a design to reduce them under absolute despotism, it is their right, it is their duty, to throw off such government, and to provide new guards for their future security. Such has been the patient sufferance of these Colonies; and such is now the necessity which constrains them to alter their former systems of government. The history of the present King of Great Britain is a history of repeated injuries and usurpations, all having in direct object the establishment of an absolute tyranny over these States. To prove this, let facts be submitted to a candid world.

He has refused his assent to laws, the most wholesome and necessary for 3 the public good.

He has forbidden his Governors to pass laws of immediate and pressing im- 4 portance, unless suspended in their operation till his assent should be obtained; and when so suspended, he has utterly neglected to attend to them.

He has refused to pass other laws for the accommodation of large districts 5 of people, unless those people would relinquish the right of representation in the Legislature, a right inestimable to them and formidable to tyrants only.

He has called together legislative bodies at places unusual, uncomfortable, 6 and distant from the depository of their public records, for the sole purpose of fatiguing them into compliance with his measures.

He has dissolved representative houses repeatedly, for opposing with 7 manly firmness his invasions on the rights of the people.

He has refused for a long time, after such dissolutions, to cause others to 8 be elected; whereby the legislative powers, incapable of annihilation, have returned to the people at large for their exercise; the State remaining in the meantime exposed to all the dangers of invasion from without and convulsions within.

He has endeavoured to prevent the population of these States; for that 9 purpose obstructing the laws of naturalization of foreigners; refusing to pass others to encourage their migration hither, and raising the conditions of new appropriations of lands.

He has obstructed the administration of justice, by refusing his assent to 10 laws for establishing judiciary powers.

He has made judges dependent on his will alone, for the tenure of their of- 11 fices, and the amount and payment of their salaries.

He has erected a multitude of new offices, and sent hither swarms of offi- 12 cers to harass our people, and eat out their substance.

13   He has kept among us, in times of peace, standing armies without the consent of our legislatures.

14   He has affected to render the military independent of and superior to the civil power.

15   He has combined with others to subject us to a jurisdiction foreign to our constitution, and unacknowledged by our laws; giving his assent to their acts of pretended legislation:

16   For quartering large bodies of armed troops among us:

17   For protecting them, by a mock trial, from punishment for any murders which they should commit on the inhabitants of these States:

18   For cutting off our trade with all parts of the world:

19   For imposing taxes on us without our consent:

20   For depriving us, in many cases, of the benefits of trial by jury:

21   For transporting us beyond seas to be tried for pretended offences:

22   For abolishing the free system of English laws in a neighbouring Province, establishing therein an arbitrary government, and enlarging its boundaries so as to render it at once an example and fit instrument for introducing the same absolute rule into these Colonies:

23   For taking away our Charters, abolishing our most valuable laws, and altering fundamentally the forms of our governments:

24   For suspending our own Legislatures, and declaring themselves invested with power to legislate for us in all cases whatsoever.

25   He has abdicated government here, by declaring us out of his protection and waging war against us.

26   He has plundered our seas, ravaged our coasts, burnt our towns, and destroyed the lives of our people.

27   He is at this time transporting large armies of foreign mercenaries to complete the works of death, desolation and tyranny, already begun with circumstances of cruelty and perfidy scarcely paralleled in the most barbarous ages, and totally unworthy the head of a civilized nation.

28   He has constrained our fellow citizens taken captive on the high seas to bear arms against their country, to become the executioners of their friends and brethren, or to fall themselves by their hands.

29   He has excited domestic insurrections amongst us, and has endeavoured to bring on the inhabitants of our frontiers, the merciless Indian savages, whose known rule of warfare, is an undistinguished destruction of all ages, sexes, and conditions.

30   In every stage of these oppressions we have petitioned for redress in the most humble terms; our repeated petitions have been answered only by repeated injury. A prince whose character is thus marked by every act which may define a tyrant is unfit to be the ruler of a free people.

31   Nor have we been wanting in attention to our British brethren. We have warned them from time to time of attempts by their legislature to extend an unwarrantable jurisdiction over us. We have reminded them of the circumstances of our emigration and settlement here. We have appealed to their native justice and magnanimity, and we have conjured them by the ties of our

common kindred to disavow these usurpations, which would inevitably interrupt our connections and correspondence. They too have been deaf to the voice of justice and of consanguinity. We must, therefore, acquiesce in the necessity, which denounces our separation, and hold them, as we hold the rest of mankind, enemies in war, in peace friends.

We, therefore, the Representatives of the United States of America, in 32 General Congress assembled, appealing to the Supreme Judge of the world for the rectitude of our intentions, do, in the name, and by the authority of the good people of these Colonies, solemnly publish and declare, That these United Colonies are, and of right ought to be Free and Independent States; that they are absolved from all allegiance to the British Crown, and that all political connection between them and the State of Great Britain, is and ought to be totally dissolved; and that as Free and Independent States, they have full power to levy war, conclude peace, contract alliances, establish commerce, and to do all other acts and things which Independent States may of right do. And for the support of this declaration, with a firm reliance on the protection of Divine Providence, we mutually pledge to each other our lives, our fortunes, and our sacred honor.

QUESTIONS FOR ANALYSIS

1. What is the Declaration's central deductive argument? State the argument in the shape illustrated above: major premise, minor premise, conclusion. Construct a valid argument. If necessary, draw circles representing each of the three terms in the argument to check for validity. (*Hint:* Start with the claim "George III's government should be overthrown.")

2. Which paragraphs are devoted to supporting the major premise? What kind of support has been given?

3. Which paragraphs are devoted to supporting the minor premise? What kind of support has been given?

4. Why has more support been given for one premise than the other?

EXERCISES: Completing and Evaluating Deductive Arguments

Turn each of the following statements into valid deductive arguments. (You have the conclusion and one premise, so you will have to determine the missing premise that would complete the argument. Draw circles if necessary to test for validity.) Then decide which arguments have premises that could be supported by noting the kind of support that might be provided. Explain why you think some arguments have insupportable premises. Here is an example:

PREMISE:	All Jesuits are priests.
PREMISE:	No women are priests.
CONCLUSION:	No women are Jesuits.

Since the circle for women must be placed outside the circle for priests, it must also be outside the circle for Jesuits. Hence the argument is valid. The first premise is true by definition; the term *Jesuit* refers to an order of Roman Catholic priests. The second premise is true for the Roman Catholic Church, so if the term priest is used only to refer to people with a religious vocation in the Roman Catholic Church, then the second premise is also true by definition.

1. Mrs. Ferguson is a good teacher because she can explain the subject matter clearly.
2. Segregated schools are unconstitutional because they are unequal.
3. Michael must be a good driver because he drives fast.
4. The media clearly have a liberal bias because they make fun of religious fundamentalists.

ANALOGY

The argument from analogy is an argument based on comparison. Analogies assert that since A and B are alike in several ways, they must be alike in another way as well. The argument from analogy concludes with an inference, an assertion of a significant similarity in the two items being compared. The other similarities serve as evidence in support of the inference. The shape of an argument by analogy is illustrated in Figure 5.3.

Although analogy is sometimes an effective approach to an issue because clever, imaginative comparisons are often moving, analogy is not as rigorously logical as either induction or deduction. Frequently an analogy is based on only two or three points of comparison, whereas a sound inductive argument presents many examples to support its conclusion. Further, to be convincing, the points of comparison must be fundamental to the two items being compared. An argument for a county leash law for cats developed by analogy with dogs may cite the following similarities:

- Cats are pets, just like dogs.
- Cats live in residential communities, just like dogs.
- Cats can mess up other people's yards, just like dogs.
- Cats, if allowed to run free, can disturb the peace (fighting, howling at night), just like dogs.

GROUNDS:	A has characteristics 1, 2, 3, and 4.
	B has characteristics 1, 2, and 3.
CLAIM:	B has characteristic 4 (as well).
ASSUMPTION (WARRANT):	If B has three characteristics in common with A, it must have the key fourth characteristic as well.

FIGURE 5.3 The Shape of an Argument by Analogy

Does it follow that cats should be required to walk on a leash, just like dogs? If such a county ordinance were passed, would it be enforceable? Have you ever tried to walk a cat on a leash? In spite of legitimate similarities brought out by the analogy, the conclusion does not logically follow because the arguer is over-looking a fundamental difference in the two animals' personalities. Dogs can be trained to a leash; most cats (Siamese are one exception) cannot be so trained. Such thinking will produce sulking cats and scratched owners. But the analogy, delivered passionately to the right audience, could lead community activists to lobby for a new law.

Observe that the problem with the cat-leash-law analogy is not in the similarities asserted about the items being compared but rather in the underlying assumption that the similarities logically support the argument's conclusion. A good analogy asserts many points of comparison and finds likenesses that are essential parts of the nature or purpose of the two items being compared. The best way to challenge another's analogy is to point out a fundamental difference in the nature or purpose of the compared items. For all of their similarities, when it comes to walking on a leash, cats are *not* like dogs.

EXERCISES: Analogy

1. Analyze the following analogies. List the stated and/or implied points of comparison and the conclusion in the pattern illustrated on p. 132. Then judge each argument's logic and effectiveness as a persuasive technique. If the argument is not logical, state the fundamental difference in the two compared items. If the argument could be persuasive, describe the kind of audience that might be moved by it.

    a. College newspapers should not be under the supervision or control of a faculty sponsor. Fortunately, no governmental sponsor controls the *New York Times,* or we would no longer have a free press in this country. We need a free college press, too, one that can attack college policies when they are wrong.

    b. Let's recognize that college athletes are really professional and start paying them properly. College athletes get a free education, and spending money from boosters. They are required to attend practices and games, and—if they play football or basketball—they bring in huge revenues for their "organization." College coaches are also paid enormous salaries, just like professional coaches, and often college coaches are tapped to coach professional teams. The only difference: the poor college athletes don't get those big salaries and huge signing bonuses.

    c. Just like any business, the federal government must be made to balance its budget. No company could continue to operate in the red as the government does and expect to be successful. A constitutional amendment requiring a balanced federal budget is long overdue.

2. Read and analyze the following analogy by Zbigniew Brzezinski. The questions that follow his article will aid your analysis.

WAR AND FOOTBALL | ZBIGNIEW BRZEZINSKI

Former national security advisor to President Jimmy Carter, Dr. Brzezinski (b. 1928) is an expert on politics and foreign affairs. He has published many books and articles, including *The Grand Chessboard: American Primacy and Its Geostrategic Imperative* (1997), and currently works at the Center for Strategic and International Studies. His article on football was published in the *Washington Post* on January 7, 2000.

1   I discovered American football late in life. Initially, I thought the game was a bore. When I saw my first football match after coming to America as a child reared on soccer, I was even appalled. Why are all these men, helmeted and wearing protective gear, bending over and then piling on top of one another? I was mystified by their conspiratorial huddling. And when I first heard the referee announce "penalty declined," I remember turning to my American guide and naively noting that it was chivalrous of the rewarded team to have done so.

2   After my appointment to the White House in the mid-'70s, I was favored by invitations to sit in the Redskins' owner's box—and the Washington thing to do, of course, was to go. Before long it dawned on me: The game is unique in the manner it translates into sport all the main ingredients of real warfare. Henceforth I was hooked.

3   Consider the following parallels:

4   • The owners of the teams are like heads of state. Some are nasty dictators, some merely preside like monarchs. Some posture and are loudmouths, but all are treated with a deference worthy of kings. The senior Cooke—my occasional and very regal host—both reigned and ruled; his son merely reigned. The new, post-Cooke owner conveys an intelligent passion for football, reminiscent of President Nixon, that will probably benefit the team.

5   • The coaches are the CinCs, to use Washington jargon. They set the overall strategy and supervise its tactical implementation in the course of combat. In constant wireless contact with their forces as well as with their scouting experts (a k a intelligence), examining instant play photos (a k a overhead imagery) and consulting their deputies for offensive and defensive operations, they are clearly the commanders in chief. Some are like Gen. Eisenhower; others remind you of Gen. MacArthur. The truly victorious ones (e.g., Gibbs or Parcells) reflect the needed ability to simultaneously inspire, intimidate and innovate.

6   • The quarterbacks, as is often noted, are the field commanders. They make last-minute tactical decisions on the basis of direct observation of hostile deployments, and they're expected, when necessary, to improvise tactically, though in the context of their CinCs' overall strategy. Some hustle and take risks; some stay put and just grind away. Again, shades of Gen. Patton or of Gen. Westmoreland.

7   • The teams engage in offensive and defensive maneuvers, as in real war. They rely either on a concentration of power (especially in ground attacks), on flanking attacks or on sudden deployment behind enemy

lines (passing). Deception, speed and force are the required ingredients for success. Skill, precision and iron discipline are instilled by intense training.

- Good intelligence is also essential. Hence much effort is spent on the 8
constant monitoring of the enemy's tactics, with specialists (high in the stands, equipped with long-distance observation equipment) seeking to spot potential weaknesses while identifying also the special strengths of the opponent. Timely strategic as well as tactical adjustments (especially during halftime) are often a key to the successful completion of the campaign (a k a game).
- As in real combat, teams suffer casualties, and these can cripple even a 9
strong team. It is especially important to protect the field commander-quarterbacks; they are a key target of enemy action since their loss can be especially disruptive.
- Last but not least, the home front also plays a role. Systematic motiva- 10
tion of the morale of civilians (the spectators) can play an important role in stirring the combatants into greater passion while demoralizing the enemy. The home-field advantage is thus the equivalent to fighting in the defense of your own homeland.

Once I understood the above, the mindless piles of bodies, the strange 11
posturing of grown men and the armored uniforms all came to make sense to me. A great game. Like a war.

QUESTIONS FOR READING

1. What were Brzezinski's initial views of American football?
2. What are the points of comparison between football and war? State these in summary form in your own words.

QUESTIONS FOR REASONING AND ANALYSIS

1. The author's subject is clear, as is his use of analogy as a strategy. But, what is his purpose in writing? What does he want readers to conclude from his analogy? (Consider: How do you read the last two sentences? What are most people's attitudes toward war?)
2. What, then, is Brzezinski's thesis, the claim of his argument?
3. What elements of style add to the analogy's effectiveness? How would you describe the essay's tone?

QUESTIONS FOR REFLECTING AND WRITING

1. What kinds of readers are least likely to be moved by the author's analogy? Why?
2. If you do not accept Brzezinski's analogy, how would you counter it?

ARGUMENTS THAT DO NOT WORK: LOGICAL FALLACIES

A thorough study of argument needs to include a study of logical fallacies because so many "arguments" fail to meet standards of sound logic and good sense. Before examining specific types of arguments that do not work, let's consider briefly why people offer arguments that aren't sensible.

Causes of Illogic

Ignorance

One frequent cause for illogical debate is simply a lack of knowledge of the subject. Some people have more information than others, either from formal study or from wide-ranging experiences. The younger you are, the less you can be expected to know about or understand complex issues. On the other hand, if you want to debate a complex or technical issue, then you cannot use ignorance as an excuse for producing a weak argument. To illustrate: Following the 1992 riots in Los Angeles, then press secretary Marlin Fitzwater asserted that welfare programs of the 1960s and 1970s caused the riots. When reporters asked which programs, Fitzwater responded that he did not have a list with him! Instead of ducking the need for evidence, you want to read as much as you can, listen carefully to discussions, ask questions, and, when called on to write, select topics about which you have knowledge or which you are willing to study before writing.

Egos

Ego problems are another cause of weak arguments. Those with low self-esteem often have difficulty in debates because they attach themselves to their ideas and then feel personally attacked when someone disagrees with them. Usually the next step is a defense of their views with even greater emotion and irrationality, even though self-esteem is enhanced when others applaud our knowledge and thoughtfulness, not our irrationality.

Prejudices

A third cause of irrationality is the collection of prejudices and biases that we carry around, having absorbed them "ages ago" from family and community. Prejudices range from the worst ethnic, religious, or sexist stereotypes to political views we have adopted uncritically (Democrats are all bleeding hearts; Republicans are all rich snobs), to perhaps less serious but equally insupportable notions (if it's in print, it must be right; if it's not meat and potatoes, it is not really dinner). People who see the world through distorted lenses cannot possibly assess facts intelligently and reason logically from them.

A Need for Answers

Finally, many bad arguments stem from a human need for answers—any answers—to the questions that deeply concern us. We want to control our world because that makes us feel secure, and having answers makes us feel in control. This need can lead to illogic from oversimplifying problems, from refusing to settle for qualified answers to questions.

The causes of illogic lead us to a twofold classification of bad arguments: logical fallacies that result from (1) oversimplifying the issue or from (2) ignoring the issue by substituting emotion for reason.

Fallacies That Result from Oversimplifying

Errors in Generalizing

Errors in generalizing include overstatement and hasty or faulty generalization. All have in common an error in the inductive pattern of argument. In each fallacy, the inference drawn from the evidence is unwarranted, either because too broad a generalization is made or because the generalization is drawn from incomplete or incorrect evidence. *Overstatement* occurs when the argument's assertion is an unqualified generalization—that is, it refers to all members of a category or class, although the evidence justifies an assertion about only some of the class. Overstatements often result from stereotyping, giving the same traits to everyone in a group. Overstatements are frequently signaled by words such as *all, every, always, never,* and *none.* But remember that assertions such as "children love clowns" are understood to refer to "all children," even though the word *all* does not appear in the sentence. It is the writer's task to qualify statements appropriately, using words such as *some, many,* or *frequently,* as appropriate. Overstatements are discredited by finding only one exception to disprove the assertion. One frightened child who starts to cry when the clown approaches will destroy the argument. Here is another example:

- Lawyers are only interested in making money.

  (What about lawyers who work to protect consumers, or public defenders, who take care of those unable to pay for a lawyer?)

  Hasty or faulty generalizations may be qualified assertions, but they still oversimplify by arguing from insufficient evidence or by ignoring some relevant evidence. For example:

- Political life must lead many to excessive drinking. In the last six months the paper has written about five members of Congress who have either confessed to alcoholism or have been arrested on DUI charges.

  (Five is not a large enough sample from which to generalize about *many* politicians. Also, the five in the newspaper are not a representative sample; they have made the news because of their drinking.)

Forced Hypothesis

The *forced hypothesis* is also an error in inductive reasoning. The explanation (hypothesis) offered to account for a particular situation is "forced," or illogical, because either (1) sufficient evidence does not exist to draw any conclusion or (2) the evidence can be explained more simply or more sensibly by a different hypothesis. This logical fallacy often results from failure to consider other possible explanations. You discredit a forced hypothesis by providing alternative conclusions that are more sensible or just as sensible as the one offered. Consider the following example:

- Professor Redding's students received either A's or B's last semester. He must be an excellent teacher.

  (The grades alone cannot support the conclusion. Professor Redding could be an excellent teacher; he could have started with excellent students; he could be an easy grader.)

Non Sequitur

The term *non sequitur,* meaning literally "it does not follow," could apply to all arguments that do not work, but the term is usually reserved for those arguments in which the conclusions are not logically connected to the reasons, those arguments with the "glue" missing. In a hasty generalization, for example, there is a connection between support (five politicians in the news) and conclusion (many politicians with drinking problems), just not a convincing connection. With the *non sequitur* there is no recognizable connection, either because (1) whatever connection the arguer sees is not made clear to others or because (2) the evidence or reasons offered are irrelevant to the conclusion. For example:

- Donna will surely get a good grade in physics; she earned an A in her biology class.

  (Doing well in one course, even one science course, does not support the conclusion that the student will get a good grade in another course. If Donna is not good at math, she definitely will not do well in physics.)

Slippery Slope

The *slippery slope* argument asserts that we should not proceed with or permit A because, if we do, the terrible consequences X, Y, and Z will occur. This type of argument oversimplifies by assuming, without evidence and usually by ignoring historical examples, existing laws, or any reasonableness in people, that X, Y, and Z will follow inevitably from A. This kind of argument rests on the belief that most people will not want the final, awful Z to occur. The belief, however accurate, does not provide a sufficiently good reason for avoiding A. One of the best-known examples of slippery slope reasoning can be found in the gun-control debate:

- If we allow the government to register handguns, next it will register hunting rifles; then it will prohibit all citizen ownership of guns, thereby creating a police state or a world in which only outlaws have guns.

  (Surely no one wants the final dire consequences predicted in this argument. However, handgun registration does not mean that these consequences will follow. The United States has never been a police state, and its system of free elections guards against such a future. Also, citizens have registered cars, boats, and planes for years without any threat of these belongings being confiscated.)

False Dilemma

The *false dilemma* oversimplifies an issue by asserting only two alternatives when there are more than two. The either–or thinking of this kind of argument can be an effective tactic if undetected. If the arguer gives us only two choices and one of those is clearly unacceptable, then the arguer can push us toward the preferred choice. For example:

- The Federal Reserve System must lower interest rates, or we will never pull out of the recession.

  (Clearly, staying in a recession is not much of a choice, but the alternative may not be the only or the best course of action to achieve a healthy economy. If interest rates go too low, inflation can be triggered. Other options include the government's creating new jobs and patiently letting market forces play themselves out.)

False Analogy

When examining the shape of analogy, we also considered the problems with this type of argument. (See p. 133.) Remember that you challenge a false analogy by noting many differences in the two items being compared or by noting a significant difference that has been ignored.

Post Hoc Fallacy

The term *post hoc*, from the Latin *post hoc, ergo propter hoc* (literally, "after this, therefore because of it") refers to a common error in arguments about cause. One oversimplifies causation by confusing a time relationship with cause. Reveal the illogic of *post hoc* arguments by pointing to other possible causes:

- We should throw out the entire city council. Since the members were elected, the city has gone into deficit spending.

  (Assuming that deficit spending in this situation is bad, was it caused by the current city council? Or did the current council inherit debts? Or is the entire region suffering from a recession?)

EXERCISES: Fallacies That Result from Oversimplifying

1. Here is a list of the fallacies we have examined so far. Make up or collect from your reading at least one example of each fallacy.
   a. Overstatement
   b. Stereotyping
   c. Hasty generalization
   d. Forced hypothesis
   e. *Non sequitur*
   f. Slippery slope
   g. False dilemma
   h. False analogy
   i. *Post hoc* fallacy

2. Explain what is illogical about each of the following arguments. Then name the fallacy represented. (Sometimes an argument will fit into more than one category. In that case name all appropriate terms.)
   a. Everybody agrees that we need stronger drunk-driving laws.
   b. The upsurge in crime on Sundays is the result of the reduced rate of church attendance in recent years.
   c. The government must create new jobs. A factory in Illinois has laid off half its workers.
   d. Steve has joined the country club. Golf must be one of his favorite sports.
   e. Blondes have more fun.
   f. You'll enjoy your Volvo; foreign cars never break down.
   g. Gary loves jokes. He would make a great comedian.
   h. The economy is in bad shape because of the Federal Reserve Board. Ever since they expanded the money supply, the stock market has been declining.
   i. Either we improve the city's street lighting, or we will fail to reduce crime.
   j. DNA research today is just like the study of nuclear fission. It seems important, but it's just another bomb that will one day explode on us. When will we learn that government must control research?
   k. To prohibit prayer in public schools is to limit religious practice solely to internal belief. The result is that an American is religiously "free" only in his own mind.
   l. Professor Johnson teaches in the political science department. I'll bet she's another socialist.
   m. Coming to the aid of any country engaged in civil war is a bad idea. Next we'll be sending American troops, and soon we'll be involved in another Vietnam.
   n. We must reject affirmative action in hiring or we'll have to settle for incompetent employees.

3. Examine the logic in this famous passage from Lewis Carroll's *Alice in Wonderland*. What logical fallacy does the King commit?

   The King turned pale, and shut his note-book hastily. "Consider your verdict," he said to the jury, in a low trembling voice.

   "There's more evidence to come yet, please your Majesty," said the White Rabbit, jumping up in a great hurry: "this paper has just been picked up."

   "What's in it?" said the Queen.

"I haven't opened it yet," said the White Rabbit; "but it seems to be a letter, written by the prisoner to—to somebody."

"It must have been that," said the King, "unless it was written to nobody, which isn't usual, you know."

"Who is it directed to?" said one of the jurymen.

"It isn't directed at all," said the White Rabbit; "in fact, there's nothing written on the *outside.*" He unfolded the paper as he spoke, and added, "It isn't a letter, after all: it's a set of verses."

"Are they in the prisoner's handwriting?" asked another of the jurymen.

"No, they're not," said the White Rabbit, "and that's the queerest thing about it." (The jury all looked puzzled.)

"He must have imitated somebody else's hand," said the King. (The jury all brightened up again.)

"Please, your Majesty," said the Knave, "I didn't write it, and they can't prove that I did: there's no name signed at the end."

"If you didn't sign it," said the King, "that only makes the matter worse. You *must* have meant some mischief, or else you'd have signed your name like an honest man."

There was a general clapping of hands at this: it was the first really clever thing the King had said that day.

"That *proves* his guilt, of course," said the Queen, "so, off with—"

"It doesn't prove anything of the sort!" said Alice. "Why, you don't even know what they're about!"

Fallacies That Result from Ignoring the Issue

There are many arguments that divert attention from the issue under debate. Of the six discussed here, the first three try to divert attention by introducing a separate issue or "sliding by" the actual issue; the following three seek diversion by appealing to the audience's emotions or prejudices. In the first three the arguer tries to give the impression of presenting an argument; in the last four the arguer charges forward on emotional manipulation alone.

Begging the Question

To assume that part of your argument is true without supporting it is to *beg the question.* Arguments seeking to pass off as proof statements that must themselves be supported are often introduced with such phrases as "the fact is" (to introduce opinion), "obviously," and "as we can see." For example:

- Clearly, lowering grading standards would be bad for students, so a pass/fail system should not be adopted.

    (Does a pass/fail system lower standards? No evidence has been given. If so, is that necessarily bad for students?)

Red Herring

The *red herring* is a foul-smelling argument indeed. The debater introduces a side issue, some point that is not relevant to the debate:

- The senator is an honest woman; she loves her children and gives to charities.

  (The children and charities are side issues; they do not demonstrate honesty.)

Straw Man

The *straw man* argument attributes to opponents erroneous and usually ridiculous views that they do not hold so that their position can be easily attacked. We can challenge this illogic by demonstrating that the arguer's opponents do not hold those views or by demanding that the arguer provide some evidence that they do:

- Those who favor gun control just want to take all guns away from responsible citizens and put them in the hands of criminals.

  (The position attributed to proponents of gun control is not only inaccurate but actually the opposite of what is sought by gun-control proponents.)

Ad Hominem

One of the most frequent of all appeals to emotion masquerading as argument is the *ad hominem* argument (literally, argument "to the man"). Sometimes the debate turns to an attack of a supporter of the issue; other times, the illogic is found in name calling. When someone says that "those crazy liberals at the ACLU just want all criminals to go free," or a pro-choice demonstrator screams at those "self-righteous fascists" on the other side, the best retort may be silence, or the calm assertion that such statements do not contribute to meaningful debate.

Common Practice or Bandwagon

To argue that an action should be taken or a position accepted because "everyone is doing it" is illogical. The majority is not always right. Frequently when someone is defending an action as ethical on the ground that everyone does it, the action isn't ethical and the defender knows it isn't. The bandwagon argument is a desperate one. For example:

- There's nothing wrong with fudging a bit on your income taxes. After all, the superrich don't pay any taxes and the government expects everyone to cheat a little.

  (First, not everyone cheats on taxes; many pay to have their taxes done correctly. And if it is wrong, it is wrong regardless of the number who do it.)

Ad Populum

Another technique for arousing an audience's emotions and ignoring the issue is to appeal *ad populum,* "to the people," to the audience's presumed shared values and beliefs. Every Fourth of July, politicians employ this tactic, appealing to God, mother, apple pie, and "traditional family values." As with all emotional gimmicks, we need to reject the argument as illogical.

- Good, law-abiding Americans must be sick of the violent crimes occurring in our once godly society. But we won't tolerate it anymore; put the criminals in jail and throw away the key.

  (This does not contribute to a thoughtful debate on criminal justice issues.)

EXERCISES: Fallacies That Result from Ignoring the Issue

1. Here is a list of fallacies that result from ignoring the issue. Make up or collect from your reading at least one example of each fallacy.
    a. Begging the question
    b. Red herring
    c. Straw man
    d. *Ad hominem*
    e. Common practice or bandwagon
    f. *Ad populum*

2. Explain what is illogical about each of the following arguments. Then name the fallacy represented.
    a. Gold's book doesn't deserve a Pulitzer Prize. She has been married four times.
    b. I wouldn't vote for him; many of his programs are basically socialist.
    c. Eight out of 10 headache sufferers use Bayer to relieve headache pain. It will work for you, too.
    d. We shouldn't listen to Colman McCarthy's argument against liquor ads in college newspapers because he obviously thinks young people are ignorant and need guidance in everything.
    e. My roommate Joe does the craziest things; he must be neurotic.
    f. Since so many people obviously cheat the welfare system, it should be abolished.
    g. She isn't pretty enough to win the contest, and besides she had her nose "fixed" two years ago.
    h. Professors should chill out; everybody cheats on exams from time to time.
    i. The fact is that bilingual education is a mistake because it encourages students to use only their native language and that gives them an advantage over other students.
    j. Don't join those crazy liberals in support of the American Civil Liberties Union. They want all criminals to go free.
    k. Real Americans understand that free trade agreements are evil. Let your representatives know that we want American goods protected.

3. Examine the following letter to the editor by Christian Brahmstedt that appeared in the *Washington Post* on January 2, 1989. If you think it contains logical fallacies, identify the passages and explain the fallacies.

HELP THOSE WHO HELP, NOT HURT, THEMSELVES

1   In the past year, and repeatedly throughout the holiday season, the Post has devoted an abnormally large share of newsprint to the "plight" of the vagrants who wander throughout the city in search of free handouts: i.e., the "homeless."

2   As certain as taxes, the poor shall remain with civilization forever. Yet these "homeless" are certainly not in the same category as the poor. The poor of civilization, of which we have all been a part at one time in our lives, are proud and work hard until a financial independence frees them from the category. The "homeless" do not seek work or pride. They are satisfied to beg and survive on others' generosity.

3   The best correlation to the "homeless" I have witnessed are the gray squirrels on Capitol Hill. After feeding several a heavy dose of nuts one afternoon, I returned the next day to see the same squirrels patiently waiting for a return feeding. In the same fashion, the "homeless" are trained by Washington's guilt-ridden society to continue begging a sustenance rather than learning independence.

4   The Post has preached that these vagrants be supported from the personal and federal coffers—in the same manner as the squirrels on Capitol Hill. This support is not helping the homeless; it is only teaching them to rely on it. All of our parents struggled through the depression as homeless of a sort, to arise and build financial independence through hard work.

5   The "homeless" problem will go away when, and only when, Washingtonians refuse to feed them. They will learn to support themselves and learn that society demands honest work for an honest dollar.

6   It would be better for Washington citizens to field their guilt donations to the poor, those folks who are holding down two or more jobs just to make ends meet, rather than throwing their tribute to the vagrants on the sewer grates. The phrase "help those who help themselves" has no more certain relevance than to the "homeless" issue.

EXERCISES: Analyzing Arguments

1. Analyze the following letter to the editor titled "Beer Commercials Do No Harm," published on January 28, 1989, and written by James C. Sanders, president of the Beer Institute. How effectively does Sanders make his case? How convincing is the evidence that he presents? Do

you accept his warrant that his evidence is authoritative? If not, what do you think he should have included in the letter? Try to answer these questions in detail to be prepared for class discussion.

BEER COMMERCIALS DO NOT HARM

1   With respect to the letter to the editor of Jan. 13 concerning the banning of beer commercials, we believe it is appropriate to respond. While the tragedy of drunk driving and other abuses of alcohol beverages is of concern to us all, there are much broader problems and solutions that must be addressed.

2   First, we must consider the empirical evidence on the effect or lack of effect of alcohol beverage advertising and its impact on abuse. There exists a substantial body of evidence that suggests that the only impact of alcohol beverage advertising is that of brand preference, shifting those who choose to drink to a particular beverage or brand name.

3   There exists no sound evidence that alcohol beverage advertising has an adverse impact on abuse. Alcohol beverage advertising does not promote excessive consumption, influence nondrinkers to become drinkers or induce young people to drink.

4   In fact, studies show that parents and peers, respectively, are the major contributors to a young person's decision to consume or not to consume. Furthermore, studies have shown that "the best controlled studies show no overall effect of alcohol advertising on consumption."

5   Another related issue is the right to commercial free speech. The alcohol beverage industry—specifically, the beer and wine industries—advertises on television legal products whose responsible, moderate consumption is enjoyed by the majority of our population. This is not to disregard a certain percentage of citizens who should not consume our product—specifically, underage persons and alcoholics.

6   The alcohol beverage industry is concerned and involved in programs that educate, inform and support positive, realistic solutions to alcohol abuse. We are working with many organizations whose goals are to reduce the problems associated with the misuse of our products. Radical or empirically unsound approaches to alcohol problems serve only to divert us from sound, positive solutions.

2.   Analyze the logical fallacies in the following student essay. Make notes of specific problems to be prepared for class discussion.

DEATH

In the editorial section of the *Washington Post* I came across an article titled "New York on the Brink." The article is about New York thinking and trying to impose the death penalty. The editors are against the death sentence, and I disagree with them.

The death sentence is obviously a moral and political issue. But is it right to let killers just serve time and be released back into society after taking someone's life? The death penalty has been around as long as man. It is needed to get rid of the murderers and keep the innocent safe and secure.

The article says that President George Bush's speech in New York urging a mandatory federal death penalty for the killing of law enforcement officers is unfair. Why is that unfair? The police are out to protect the innocent. It is unfair not to serve justice on those individuals. If a criminal goes around killing the protectors of law and peace, who knows what they can and will do to the common citizens.

Another thing to think about is the overcrowding of prisons. There is very little room for prisoners these days. The author didn't even think of that. By ridding society of the killers, it will make room for other criminals to serve time. I wonder if the author is willing to pay extra taxes to build new prisons.

The author also argues that the death penalty doesn't prevent murders from happening. There have always been murderers throughout history, and there will always be murders. But I think that I would think twice about killing someone if I knew that I would die as well. But there will always be people who take the chance. The death penalty would just get rid of those who do them.

The author's final argument is that sanctioned killing is as abhorrent as murder. I think the author would have a change of heart if someone close to him or her was murdered. It is only fair that the murderer pay the same price as the victim.

It is time that people start to open their eyes and realize that it is a life and death world out there. And the only way to change the suffering of the law abiders is to get rid of the law breakers. The death penalty is the price a free society pays to stay free.

THE REFUTATION ESSAY: EVALUATING THE ARGUMENTS OF OTHERS

When your primary purpose in writing is to challenge someone's argument rather than to present your own argument, you are writing a *refutation*. A good refutation does not merely point an accusing finger at another's argument. Rather, it demonstrates, in an orderly and logical way, the weaknesses of logic or evidence in the argument, or it both analyzes weaknesses and builds a counterargument. Refutations can challenge a specific, written argument, but they can also challenge a prevailing attitude or belief that is, in the writer's view, contrary to the evidence. The sample refutation that follows shows the first purpose. It is annotated to show you how the author puts together his refutation. But first, study the following guidelines to prepare a good refutation essay:

GUIDELINES for Preparing a Refutation Essay

1. **Read accurately.** Make certain that you have understood your opponent's argument. If you assume views not expressed by the writer and accuse the writer of holding those illogical views, you are guilty of the straw man fallacy, of attributing and then attacking a position that the person does not hold. Look up terms and references you do not know and examine the logic and evidence thoroughly.

2. **Pinpoint the weaknesses in the original argument.** Analyze the argument to determine, specifically, what flaws the argument contains. If the argument contains logical fallacies, make a list of the ones you plan to discredit. Examine the evidence presented. Is it insufficient, unreliable, or irrelevant? Decide, before drafting your refutation, exactly what elements of the argument you intend to challenge.

3. **Write your thesis.** After analyzing the argument and deciding on the weaknesses to be challenged, write a thesis which establishes that your disagreement is with the writer's logic, assumptions, or evidence, or a combination of these.

4. **Draft your essay, using the following three-part organization:**

   a. *The opponent's argument.* Usually you should not assume that your reader has read or remembered the argument you are refuting. Thus at the beginning of your essay, you need to state, accurately and fairly, the main points of the argument to be refuted.

   b. *Your thesis.* Next make clear the nature of your disagreement with the argument you are refuting.

   c. *Your refutation.* The specifics of your counterargument will depend upon the nature of your disagreement. If you are challenging the writer's evidence, then you must present the more recent evidence to explain why the evidence used is unreliable or misleading. If you are challenging assumptions, then you must explain why they do not hold up. If your thesis is that the piece is filled with logical fallacies, then you must present and explain each fallacy.

GENDER GAMES | DAVID SADKER

A professor of education at American University, David Sadker has written extensively on educational issues, especially on the treatment of girls in the classroom. He is the author of *Failing at Fairness: How Our Schools Cheat Girls* (1995). "Gender Games" appeared in the *Washington Post* on July 31, 2000. Read, study the annotations, and then answer the questions that follow.

Attention-getting opening.

1   Remember when your elementary school teacher would announce the teams for the weekly spelling bee? "Boys against the girls!" There was nothing like a gender showdown to liven things up. Apparently, some writers never left this elementary level of intrigue. A spate of recent books and articles takes us back to the "boys versus girls" fray but this time, with much higher stakes.

Claim to be refuted.

2   May's *Atlantic Monthly* cover story, "Girls Rule," is a case in point. The magazine published an excerpt from *The War Against Boys* by Christina Hoff Sommers, a book advancing the notion that boys are the real victims of gender bias while girls are soaring in school.

What's right about the opponent's argument.

3   Sommers and her supporters are correct in saying that girls and women have made significant educational progress in the past two decades. Females today make up more than 40 percent of medical and law school students, and more than half of college students. Girls continue to read sooner and write better than boys. And for as long as anyone can remember, girls have received higher grades than boys.

1st point of refutation

4   But there is more to these selected statistics than meets the eye. Although girls continue to receive higher report card grades than boys, their grades do not translate into higher test scores. The same girls who beat boys in the spelling bees score below boys on the tests that matter: the PSATs crucial for scholarships, the SATs and the ACTs needed for college acceptances, the GREs for graduate school and even the admission tests for law, business and medical schools.

2nd point of refutation

5   Many believe that girls' higher grades may be more a reflection of their manageable classroom behavior than their intellectual accomplishment. Test scores are not influenced by quieter classroom behavior. Girls may in fact be trading their initiative and independence for peer approval and good grades, a trade-off that can have costly personal and economic consequences.

3rd point of refutation

6   The increase in female college enrollment catches headlines because it heralds the first time that females have outnumbered males on college campuses. But even these enrollment figures are misleading. The female presence increases as the status of the college decreases. Female students are more likely to dominate two-year schools than the Ivy League. And wherever they are, they find themselves segregated and channeled into the least prestigious and least costly majors.

7   In today's world of e-success, more than 60 percent of computer science and business majors are male, about 70 percent of physics majors are males, and more than 80 percent of engineering students are male. But peek into language, psychology, nursing and humanities classrooms, and you will find a sea of female faces.

Higher female enrollment figures mask the "glass walls" that separate the 8
sexes and channel females and males into very different careers, with very different paychecks. Today, despite all the progress, the five leading occupations of employed women are secretary, receptionist, bookkeeper, registered nurse and hairdresser/cosmetologist.

Add this to the "glass ceiling" (about 3 percent of Fortune 500 top man- 9
agers are women) and the persistence of a gender wage gap (women with advanced degrees still lag well behind their less-educated male counterparts) and the crippling impact of workplace and college stereotyping becomes evident.

Even within schools, where female teachers greatly outnumber male 10
teachers, school management figures remind us that if there is a war on boys, women are not the generals. More than 85 percent of junior and senior high school principals are male, while 88 percent of school superintendents are male.

Despite sparkling advances of females on the athletic fields, two-thirds of 11
athletic scholarships still go to males. In some areas, women have actually lost ground. When Title IX was enacted in 1972, women coached more than 90 percent of intercollegiate women's teams. Today women coach only 48 percent of women's teams and only 1 percent of men's teams.

> 4th point of refutation

If some adults are persuaded by the rhetoric in such books as *The War* 12
Against Boys, be assured that children know the score. When more than 1,000 Michigan elementary school students were asked to describe what life would be like if they were born a member of the opposite sex, more than 40 percent of the girls saw positive advantages to being a boy: better jobs, more money and definitely more respect. Ninety-five percent of the boys saw no advantage to being a female.

> 5th point of refutation

The War Against Boys attempts to persuade the public to abandon sup- 13
port for educational initiatives designed to help girls and boys avoid crippling stereotypes. I hope the public and Congress will not be taken in by the book's misrepresentations. We have no time to wage a war on either our boys or our girls.

> Author concludes by stating his claim.

QUESTIONS FOR READING

1. What work, specifically, is Sadker refuting? What is the claim presented by this work?
2. What facts about girls does Sadker grant to Sommers?
3. What facts about girls create a different story, according to Sadker?

QUESTIONS FOR REASONING AND ANALYSIS

1. What is Sadker's claim? What is he asserting about girls?
2. What does Sadker think about the whole idea of books such as Sommers's?

QUESTIONS FOR REFLECTING AND WRITING

1. What statistic is most startling to you? Why?

2. Do you agree that Sadker's statistics are more significant in telling us how women are doing in school, sports, and work? If you disagree with Sadker, how would you counter his argument?

3. Think about your high school experiences. Do you think that teachers are waging a war against boys? What evidence do you have to support your views?

EXERCISE: Analyzing an Argument

Read the following article by Robert Bork and analyze his evidence and logic. As a part of your analysis, answer these questions:

1. What kind of argument is this?
2. What is Bork's claim?
3. What kinds of grounds does he present?
4. What is the tone of his argument? (Do you think that he expects readers to agree with him?)
5. Has he supported his claim to your satisfaction or not?
6. Do you find any logical fallacies in his argument? If so, how would you challenge them?

ADDICTED TO HEALTH | ROBERT H. BORK

A conservative legal scholar currently at the American Enterprise Institute for Policy Research, Robert Bork (b. 1927) has been acting attorney general and solicitor general of the U.S. Court of Appeals. His appointment to the Supreme Court, rejected by the Congress, has led to a book by Bork on the whole affair and to other books and articles on legal and public-policy issues. The following appeared in the *National Review* on July 28, 1997.

1   Government efforts to deal with tobacco companies betray an ultimate ambition to control Americans' lives.

2   When moral self-righteousness, greed for money, and political ambition work hand in hand they produce irrational, but almost irresistible, policies. The latest example is the war on cigarettes and cigarette smokers. A proposed settlement has been negotiated among politicians, plaintiffs' lawyers, and the tobacco industry. The only interests left out of the negotiations were smokers, who will be ordered to pay enormous sums with no return other than the deprivation of their own choices and pleasures.

3   It is a myth that today's Americans are a sturdy, self-reliant folk who will fight any officious interference with their liberties. That has not been true at least since the New Deal. If you doubt that, walk the streets of any American city and see the forlorn men and women cupping their hands against the wind to light cigarettes so that they can get through a few more smokeless hours in

their offices. Twenty-five percent of Americans smoke. Why can't they demand and get a compromise rather than accepting docilely the exile that employers and building managers impose upon them?

The answer is that they have been made to feel guilty by self-righteous 4 non-smokers. A few years back, hardly anyone claimed to be seriously troubled by tobacco smoke. Now, an entire class of the morally superior claim to be able to detect, and be offended by, tobacco smoke several offices away from their own. These people must possess the sense of smell of a deer or an Indian guide. Yet they will happily walk through suffocating exhaust smoke from buses rather than wait a minute or two to cross the street.

No one should assume that peace will be restored when the last cigarette 5 smoker has been banished to the Alaskan tundra. Other products will be pressed into service as morally reprehensible. If you would know the future, look at California—the national leader in health fanaticism. After a long day in Los Angeles flagging a book I had written, my wife and I sought relaxation with a drink at our hotel's outdoor bar. Our anticipation of pleasure was considerably diminished by a sign: "Warning! Toxic Substances Served Here." They were talking about my martini!

And martinis are a toxic substance, taken in any quantity sufficient to in- 6 duce a sense of well-being. Why not, then, ban alcohol or at least require a death's head on every martini glass? Well, we did once outlaw alcohol; it was called Prohibition. The myth is that Prohibition increased the amount of drinking in this country; the truth is that it reduced it. There were, of course, some unfortunate side effects, like Al Capone and Dutch Schultz. But by and large the mobsters inflicted rigor mortis upon one another.

Why is it, then, that the end of Prohibition was welcomed joyously by the 7 population? Not because alcohol is not dangerous. Not because the consumption of alcohol was not lessened. And not in order to save the lives of people with names like Big Jim and Ice Pick Phil. Prohibition came to an end because most Americans wanted to have a drink when and where they felt like it. If you insist on sounding like a law-and-economics professor, it ended because we thought the benefits of alcohol outweighed the costs.

That is the sort of calculation by which we lead our lives. Automobiles kill 8 tens of thousands of people every year and disable perhaps that many again. We could easily stop the slaughter. Cars could be made with a top speed of ten miles an hour and with exteriors the consistency of marshmallows. Nobody would die, nobody would be disabled, and nobody would bother with cars very much.

There are, of course less draconian measures available. On most highways, 9 it is almost impossible to find anyone who observes the speed limits. On the theory of the tobacco precedent, car manufacturers should be liable for deaths caused by speeding; after all, they could build automobiles incapable of exceeding legal speed limits.

The reason we are willing to offer up lives and limbs to automobiles is, 10 quite simply, that they make life more pleasant (for those who remain intact)— among other things, by speeding commuting to work, by making possible family vacations a thousand miles from home, and by lowering the costs of products shipped from a distance. The case for regulating automobiles far more severely than we do is not essentially different from the case for heavy regulation of cigarettes or, soon, alcohol.

11   But choices concerning driving, smoking, and drinking are the sort of things that ought to be left to the individual unless there are clear, serious harms to others.

12   The opening salvo in the drive to make smoking a criminal act is the proposed settlement among the cigarette companies, plaintiffs' lawyers, and the states' attorneys general. We are told that the object is to protect teenagers and children (children being the last refuge of the sanctimonious). But many restrictions will necessarily affect adults, and the tobacco pact contains provisions that can only be explained as punishment for selling to adults.

13   The terms of the settlement plainly reveal an intense hatred of smoking. Opposition to the pact comes primarily from those who think it is not severe enough. For example, critics say the settlement is defective in not restricting the marketing of cigarettes overseas by American tobacco companies. Connecticut's attorney general, Richard Blumenthal, defended the absence of such a provision: "Given our druthers we would have brought them to their knees all over the world, but there is a limit to our leverage." So much for the sovereignty of nations.

14   What the settlement does contain is bad enough. The pact would require the companies to pony up $60 billion; $25 billion of this would be used for public-health issues to be identified by a presidential panel and the rest for children's health insurance. Though the purpose of the entire agreement is punitive, this slice is most obviously so.

15   The industry is also required to pay $308 billion over 25 years, in part to repay states for the cost of treating sick smokers. There are no grounds for this provision. The tobacco companies have regularly won litigation against plaintiffs claiming injury on the grounds that everybody has known for the past forty years that smoking can cause health problems. This $308 billion, which takes from the companies what they have won in litigation, says, in effect, that no one assumed the risk of his own behavior.

16   The provision is groundless for additional reasons. The notion that the states have lost money because of cigarettes ignores the federal and state taxes smokers have paid, which cover any amount the states could claim to have lost. Furthermore, a percentage of the population dies early from smoking. Had these people lived longer, the drain on Medicare and Medicaid would have been greater. When lowered pension and Social Security costs are figured in, it seems certain that government is better off financially with smoking than without it. If we must reduce the issue to one of dollars, as the attorneys general have done, states have profited financially from smoking. If this seems a gruesome and heartless calculation, it is. But don't blame me. The state governments advanced the financial argument and ought to live with its consequences, however distasteful.

17   Other provisions of the settlement fare no better under the application of common sense. The industry is to reduce smoking by teenagers by 30 percent in

five years, 50 percent in seven years, and 60 percent in ten years. No one knows how the industry is to perform this trick. But if those goals are not met, the industry will be amerced $80 million a year for each percentage point it falls short.

The settlement assumes teenage smoking can be reduced dramatically by 18 requiring the industry to conduct an expensive anti-smoking advertising campaign, banning the use of people and cartoon characters to promote cigarettes, and similar tactics. It is entirely predictable that this will not work. Other countries have banned cigarette advertising, only to watch smoking increase. Apparently the young, feeling themselves invulnerable, relish the risk of smoking. Studies have shown, moreover, that teenagers are drawn to smoking not because of advertising but because their parents smoke or because of peer pressure. Companies advertise to gain or maintain market share among those who already smoke.

To lessen the heat on politicians, the pact increases the powers of the Food 19 and Drug Administration to regulate tobacco as an addictive drug, with the caveat that it may not prohibit cigarette smoking altogether before the year 2009. The implicit promise is that the complete prohibition of cigarettes will be seriously contemplated at that time. In the meantime, the FDA will subject cigarettes to stricter and stricter controls on the theory that tobacco is a drug.

Another rationale for prohibiting or sharply limiting smoking is the sup- 20 posed need to protect non-smokers from secondhand smoke. The difficulty is that evidence of causation is weak. What we see is a possible small increase in an already small risk which, as some researchers have pointed out, may well be caused by other variables such as misclassification of former smokers as non-smokers or such lifestyle factors as diet.

But the tobacco companies should take little or no comfort from that. 21 Given today's product-liability craze, scientific support, much less probability, is unnecessary to successful lawsuits against large corporations.

The pact is of dubious constitutionality as well. It outlaws the advertising 22 of a product it is legal to sell, which raises the problem of commercial speech protected by the First Amendment. The settlement also requires the industry to disband its lobbying organization, the Tobacco Institute. Lobbying has traditionally been thought to fall within the First Amendment's guarantee of the right to petition the government for the redress of grievances.

And who is to pay for making smoking more difficult? Smokers will have the 23 price of cigarettes raised by new taxes and by the tobacco companies' costs of complying with the settlement. It is a brilliant strategy: Smokers will pay billions to have their pleasure taken away. But if the tobacco settlement makes little sense as public policy, what can be driving it to completion? The motivations are diverse. Members of the plaintiff's bar, who have signally failed in litigation against tobacco to date, are to be guaranteed billions of dollars annually. The states' attorneys general have a different set of incentives. They are members of the National Association of Attorneys General, NAAG, which is commonly, and accurately, rendered as the National Association of Aspiring Governors.

So far they have got what they wanted. There they are, on the front pages 24 of newspapers all over the country, looking out at us, jaws firm, conveying

images of sobriety, courage, and righteousness. They have, after all, done battle with the forces of evil, and won—at least temporarily.

25   Tobacco executives and their lawyers are said to be wily folk, however.
They may find ways of defeating the strictures laid upon them. It may be too
soon to tell, therefore, whether the tobacco settlement is a major defeat or a
victory for the industry. In any case, we can live with it. But whenever individual responsibility is denied, government control of our behavior follows. After
cigarettes it will be something else, and so on *ad infinitum.* One would think
we would have learned that lesson many times over and that we would have
had enough of it.

FOR READING AND ANALYSIS

FEDS VS. FIRST AMENDMENT | MICHAEL GREBB

Michael Grebb (b. 1970) holds a degree in journalism from Ohio University and is a
senior editor at *Cablevision* magazine. The following article was published in
Cablevision on June 28, 1999.

PREREADING QUESTIONS   What does the title suggest that the article will be about?
Who are "Feds"? What are "First Amendment" issues?

1   Forget V-chips. More draconian measures may be on the way.

2   Now that everyone agrees that violent movies and television shows are the
previously unreported Eighth Sign that will hasten the Apocalypse, the feds
have decided to move into publicity mode. This is the time when Washington
power brokers start trying to get their names in the papers and news shows
with promises to clamp down on the evil media.

3   The latest chapter in this saga is all about checking IDs. Really. The Clinton
Administration has convinced the National Association of Theater Owners to
require photo identification for young people trying to get into "R" rated
movies. In addition, the theater owners have agreed to support a national
study on the causes of violence and help out with a planned educational campaign to teach parents about the movie-ratings system. Despite the fact that
movie ratings have been around for decades, "I think people don't really know
the ratings system entirely," insists Tom Freedman, special assistant to the
President and senior director of public policy.

4   Then there's the V-chip. The Federal Communications Commission held a
self-congratulatory seance on June 9 to announce that new TV sets will indeed
contain the V-chip as promised. FCC Commissioner Gloria Tristani, who heads
the FCC's internal V-chip task force, quipped that in Washington, "when someone does what they're supposed to do when they say they're going to do it,
that's news." FCC Chairman Bill Kennard made the most salient observation at
the event when he noted, "We can't hope to be the national censor for everything that's going out over the airwaves and via satellite."

Interestingly, just as the V-chip gets ready to hit the streets, Sens. John 5
McCain (R-Ariz.) and Joseph Lieberman (D-Conn.) have introduced the "21st
Century Media Responsibility Act" pushing the makers of video games, TV
shows, movies and music to come up with a uniform ratings system. How that
will affect V-chips, which were made for today's rating system, is anyone's
guess.

Of course, movie theaters were already supposed to be checking IDs. The 6
V-chip rollout schedule is the same it always was. There are already ratings for
video games, movies, TV shows and music. So why all the announcements?
Well, Washington just loves window dressing. But that doesn't mean that more
draconian measures—with real teeth—won't come in the future.

Luckily for us, the First Amendment—like those newly vigilant theater 7
owners—always cards at the door. True, the feds usually figure out a way to
sneak in the back service entrance, which is often left unlatched by incidents
like the tragedy in Littleton, Colo. But once inside, they seldom take a drink.
Rest assured that if no one is watching them closely, before long they will start
drinking and the First Amendment could be too late to bounce them onto the
street.

So far, nothing appears to be on the horizon that would amount to gov- 8
ernment censorship or coercion, but it's clear that a growing culture of potential demagoguery is taking shape. In the coming months, more pressure will
come to bear on the industry as the government floats countless trial balloons.
Food for thought as the feds snoop around the bar, waiting to grab a drink
when one of us isn't looking.

QUESTIONS FOR READING

1. What is Grebb's subject?
2. Grebb says that checking IDs at the movies and V-chips for TV are not new. Why, then, is he writing about these issues?
3. What is the author's view of a bill to extend V-chip ratings to video games and music?

QUESTIONS FOR REASONING AND ANALYSIS

1. What is Grebb's claim?
2. What evidence does the author provide? What is the primary support for his claim?
3. Study Grebb's word choice. What are "draconian measures"? What image does he use in the last two paragraphs? How would you describe the essay's tone?
4. Think about the author's writing context. Does he expect his readers to share his views on govememt ratings and other controls? How do you know?

QUESTIONS FOR REFLECTING AND WRITING

1. Evaluate the argument. Does Grebb provide convincing support for his claim? Why or why not? If you were going to refute this argument, how would you proceed?

2. Are ratings a good idea for movies? TV shows? Music? Should there be one rating system or different ones for the different art forms, as we now have? Be prepared to explain and defend your views on this issue.

MONGREL AMERICA | GREGORY RODRIGUEZ

A senior fellow at New America Foundation, Gregory Rodriguez (b. 1967) is currently working on a book on America's changing views on race as a result of Mexican immigration. His essay, published in the January/February 2003 issue of *Atlantic Monthly,* was one of several written by New America Foundation scholars examining "the state of the union."

PREREADING QUESTIONS What does Rodriguez mean by *mongrel* America? What are some of the ways in which immigrants of the last thirty years have changed this country?

1   Are racial categories still an important—or even a valid—tool of government policy? In recent years the debate in America has been between those who think that race is paramount and those who think it is increasingly irrelevant, and in the next election cycle this debate will surely intensify around a California ballot initiative that would all but prohibit the state from asking its citizens what their racial backgrounds are. But the ensuing polemics will only obscure the more fundamental question: What, when each generation is more racially and ethnically mixed than its predecessor, does race even mean anymore? If your mother is Asian and your father is African-American, what, racially speaking, are you? (And if your spouse is half Mexican and half Russian Jewish, what are your children?)

2   Five decades after the end of legal segregation, and only thirty-six years after the Supreme Court struck down anti-miscegenation laws, young African-Americans are considerably more likely than their elders to claim mixed heritage. A study by the Population Research Center, in Portland, Oregon, projects that the black intermarriage rate will climb dramatically in this century, to a point at which 37 percent of African-Americans will claim mixed ancestry by 2100. By then more than 40 percent of Asian-Americans will be mixed. Most remarkable, however, by century's end the number of Latinos claiming mixed ancestry will be more than two times the number claiming a single background.

3   Not surprisingly, intermarriage rates for all groups are highest in the states that serve as immigration gateways. By 1990 Los Angeles County had an intermarriage rate five times the national average. Latinos and Asians, the groups that have made up three quarters of immigrants over the past forty years, have helped to create a climate in which ethnic or racial intermarriage is more accepted today than ever before. Nationally, whereas only eight percent of for-

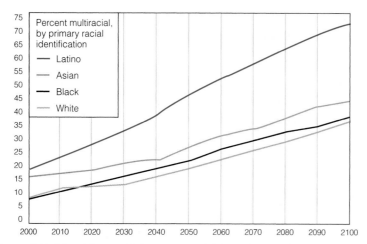

Projected Multiracial Population, 2000–2100 Led by Latinos, Americans are intermarrying and producing mixed-race children at a rapid rate

eign-born Latinos marry non-Latinos, 32 percent of second-generation and 57 percent of third-generation Latinos marry outside their ethnic group. Similarly, whereas only 13 percent of foreign-born Asians marry non-Asians, 34 percent of second-generation and 54 percent of third-generation Asian-Americans do.

Meanwhile, as everyone knows, Latinos are now the largest minority group 4 in the nation. Two thirds of Latinos, in turn, are of Mexican heritage. This is significant in itself, because their sheer numbers have helped Mexican-Americans do more than any other group to alter the country's old racial thinking. For instance, Texas and California, where Mexican-Americans are the largest minority, were the first two states to abolish affirmative action: when the collective "minority" populations in those states began to outnumber whites, the racial balance that had made affirmative action politically viable was subverted.

Many Mexican-Americans now live in cities or regions where they are a ma- 5 jority, changing the very idea of what it means to be a member of a "minority" group. Because of such demographic changes, a number of the policies designed to integrate nonwhites into the mainstream—affirmative action in college admissions, racial set-asides in government contracting—have been rendered more complicated or even counterproductive in recent years. In California cities where whites have become a minority, it is no longer clear what "diversity" means or what the goals of integration policies should be. The selective magnet-school program of the Los Angeles Unified School District, for example, was originally developed as an alternative to forced busing—a way to integrate ethnic-minority students by encouraging them to look beyond their neighborhoods. Today, however, the school district is 71 percent Latino, and Latinos' majority status actually puts them at a disadvantage when applying to magnet schools.

But it is not merely their growing numbers (they will soon be the majority 6 in both California and Texas, and they are already the single largest contemporary immigrant group nationwide) that make Mexican-Americans a leading indicator of the country's racial future; rather, it's what they represent. They have always been a complicating element in the American racial system, which depends on an oversimplified classification scheme. Under the pre-civil-rights formulation, for example, if you had "one drop" of African blood, you were fully black. The scheme couldn't accommodate people who were part one thing and part another. Mexicans, who are a product of intermingling—both cultural and genetic—between the Spanish and the many indigenous peoples of North and Central America, have a history of tolerating and even reveling in such ambiguity. Since the conquest of Mexico, in the sixteenth century, they have practiced mestizaje—racial and cultural synthesis—both in their own country and as they came north. Unlike the English-speaking settlers of the western frontier, the Spaniards were willing everywhere they went to allow racial and cultural mixing to blur the lines between themselves and the natives. The fact that Latin America is far more heavily populated by people of mixed ancestry than Anglo America is the clearest sign of the difference between the two outlooks on race.

7   Nativists once deplored the Mexican tendency toward hybridity. In the mid nineteenth century, at the time of the conquest of the Southwest, Secretary of State James Buchanan feared granting citizenship to a "mongrel race." And in the late 1920s Representative John C. Box, of Texas, warned his colleagues on the House Immigration and Naturalization Committee that the continued influx of Mexican immigrants could lead to the "distressing process of mongreliza-tion" in America. He argued that because Mexicans were the products of mix-ing, they harbored a relaxed attitude toward interracial unions and were likely to mingle freely with other races in the United States.

8   Box was right. The typical cultural isolation of immigrants notwithstanding, those immigrants' children and grandchildren are strongly oriented toward the American melting pot. Today two thirds of multiracial and multiethnic births in California involve a Latino parent. Mexicanidad, or "Mexicanness" is becoming the catalyst for a new American cultural synthesis.

9   In the same way that the rise in the number of multiracial Americans muddles U.S. racial statistics, the growth of the Mexican-American mestizo population has begun to challenge the Anglo-American binary view of race. In the 1920 census Mexicans were counted as whites. Ten years later they were reassigned to a sep-arate Mexican "racial" category. In 1940 they were officially reclassified as white. Today almost half the Latinos in California, which is home to a third of the nation's Latinos (most of them of Mexican descent), check "other" as their race. In the first half of the twentieth century Mexican-American advocates fought hard for the privileges that came with being white in America. But since the 1960s activists have sought to reap the benefits of being nonwhite minorities. Having spent so long trying to fit into one side or the other of the binary system, Mexican-Ameri-cans have become numerous and confident enough to simply claim their brown-ness—their mixture. This is a harbinger of America's future.

10   The original melting-pot concept was incomplete: it applied only to white ethnics (Irish, Italians, Poles, and so forth), not to blacks and other nonwhites. Israel Zangwill, the playwright whose 1908 drama *The Melting Pot* popularized

the concept, even wrote that whites were justified in avoiding intermarriage with blacks. In fact, multiculturalism—the ideology that promotes the permanent coexistence of separate but equal, cultures in one place—can be seen as a by-product of America's exclusion of African-Americans from the melting pot; those whom assimilation rejected came to reject assimilation. Although the multicultural movement has always encompassed other groups, blacks gave it its moral impetus.

But the immigrants of recent decades are helping to forge a new American 11 identity, something more complex than either a melting pot or a confederation of separate but equal groups. And this identity is emerging not as a result of politics or any specific public policies but because of powerful underlying cultural forces. To be sure, the civil-rights movement was instrumental in the initial assault on racial barriers. And immigration policies since 1965 have tended to favor those immigrant groups—Asians and Latinos—who are most open to intermarriage. But in recent years the government's major contribution to the country's growing multiracialism has been—as it should continue to be—a retreat from dictating limits on interracial intimacy and from exalting (through such policies as racial set-asides and affirmative action) race as the most important American category of being. As a result, Americans cross racial lines more often than ever before in choosing whom to sleep with, marry, or raise children with.

Unlike the advances of the civil-rights movement, the future of racial iden- 12 tity in America is unlikely to be determined by politics or the courts or public policy. Indeed, at this point perhaps the best thing the government can do is to acknowledge changes in the meaning of race in America and then get out of the way. The Census Bureau's decision to allow Americans to check more than one box in the "race" section of the 2000 Census was an important step in this direction. No longer forced to choose a single racial identity, Americans are now free to identify themselves as mestizos—and with this newfound freedom we may begin to endow racial issues with the complexity and nuance they deserve.

QUESTIONS FOR READING

1. What are the projected numbers of mixed ancestry for African Americans, Asian Americans, and Latinos?
2. Where are intermarriage rates the highest currently?
3. What is America's largest minority?
4. Where will Mexican Americans soon be the majority group?
5. What kinds of programs have these demographic changes affected?
6. What has long been the attitude of Mexicans toward racial mixing?
7. What is the difference between the melting pot and multiculturalism?
8. What is the new racial identity, and what are emerging attitudes toward the identifying of race in America?

QUESTIONS FOR REASONING AND ANALYSIS

1. What is Rodriguez's subject? What is his claim—what is changing, what is causing the change, and what is Rodriguez's attitude toward the changes?

2. What *type* of argument is this? That is, what kind of evidence does Rodriguez use to support his claim?

3. Why should the changes in demographics that Rodriguez examines change government policies? How does the author support his view on these changes?

4. Evaluate Rodriguez's argument. Do his predictions seem credible? Are the changes he describes consistent with your experiences?

QUESTIONS FOR REFLECTING AND WRITING

1. What group is least likely to agree with the authors' conclusions about policy change? Has Rodriguez convinced you of the appropriateness of eliminating such policies as affirmative action and racial set-asides? Why or why not?

2. Is the ongoing blending of cultures good for families? Good for the country? Why or why not? Be prepared to defend your position—with good evidence and good reasons, not with emotion and illogic.

1. a. Develop one of the following analogies, listing as many similarities as you can and thinking as you write about a conclusion your analogy reasonably leads to.

    Life is like a ride on the starship *Enterprise.*
    Students are like the early explorers to the North Pole.
    Humans are like spiders in a web.
    The mind is like a vast ocean.
    Modern science is like magic.

    b. Exchange your list with a classmate and check each other's analogies to see if there is a fundamental difference that negates the argument. Some comparisons or a conclusion may need revision.

    c. Develop your analogy (revised if necessary) into a short essay. The conclusion of your analogy is your essay's claim.

2. Think of your own analogy to develop an argument on student needs, student rights, or student responsibilities. Follow the guidelines for the first assignment above.

3. Select an editorial, op-ed column, a letter to the editor, or one of the essays in this text as an argument with which you disagree. Prepare a refutation of your opponent's logic or evidence or both. Follow the guidelines for writing a refutation found on page 147.

CHAPTER 6

Reading, Evaluating, and Writing Definition Arguments and Position Papers

This chapter focuses on two forms of argument, definition and the position paper, that may seem more abstract than the forms we've discussed previously. But let's remember what we've learned about argument: we enter into an ongoing conversation with others—and with the views already expressed on the issue. So even the seemingly more abstract and general definition arguments and claims of value in position papers need to be grounded in what has already been expressed "out there." For nearly any form of argument, presenting your stance within the proper context is essential.

THE DEFINITION ARGUMENT: DEBATING THE MEANING OF WORDS

"Define your terms!" someone yells in the middle of a heated debate. Although yelling may not be the best strategy, the advice is sound for writers of argument. People disagree more than we may think over the meaning of words. We cannot let words mean whatever we want and still communicate, but we do need to realize that many words have multiple meanings. Words also differ in their connotations, in the emotional associations we attach to them. For some, civil disobedience is illegal behavior; for others, it's patriotism in action.

When to Define

There are two occasions for defining words as a *part* of your argument. First, you need to define any technical terms that may not be familiar to your readers—or that readers may not understand as fully as they think they do. David Norman, early in his book on dinosaurs, writes:

> Nearly everyone knows what some dinosaurs look like, such as *Tyrannosaurus, Triceratops,* and *Stegosaurus.* But they may be much more vague about the lesser known ones, and may have difficulty in distinguishing between dinosaurs and other types of prehistoric creatures. It is not at all unusual to overhear an adult, taking a group of children around a museum display, being reprimanded sharply by the youngsters for failing to realize that a woolly mammoth was not a dinosaur, or—more forgivably—that a giant flying reptile such as *Pteranodon,* which lived at the time of the dinosaurs, was not a dinosaur either.
>
> So what exactly is a dinosaur? And how do paleontologists decide on the groups they belong to?

Norman answers his questions by explaining the four elements that all dinosaurs have, by constructing a definition of *dinosaur.*

Second, you need to define any word you are using in a special way. If you were to write: "We need to teach discrimination at an early age," you should add: "by *discrimination* I do not mean prejudice. I mean discernment, the ability to see differences." (*Sesame Street* has been teaching children this good kind of discrimination for many years.) The argument about Lincoln's leadership, used in Chapter 4, turns on a definition of leadership. To support that argument successfully, you need to explain and defend a definition of leadership as well as to demonstrate that Lincoln meets the specifics of your definition.

Sometimes we turn to definition because we believe that a word is being used incorrectly. Columnist George Will once argued that we should forget *values* and use instead the word *virtues*—that we should seek and admire virtues, not values. Some writers bemoan the current loss of *community,* but Annette Fuentes (see Chapter 7) thinks that communities are being redefined—they are not lost, just changing. At some point in these discussions, our purpose shifts. Instead of using definition as one step in the argument, definition becomes the central purpose of the argument. This is the third use of definition: an extended definition *is* the argument.

GUIDELINES for Evaluating Definition Arguments

When reading definition arguments, what should you look for? The basics of good argument apply to all arguments: a clear statement of claim, qualified if appropriate, a clear explanation of reasons and evidence, and enough relevant evidence to support the claim. How do we recognize these qualities in a definition argument? Use the following points as guides to evaluating:

- **Why is the word being defined?** Has the writer convinced you of the need to understand the word's meaning or change the way the word is commonly used?

- **How is the word defined?** Has the writer established his or her definition, clearly distinguishing it from what the writer perceives to be objectionable definitions? It is hard to judge the usefulness of the writer's position if the differences in meaning remain fuzzy. If George Will is going to argue for using *virtues* instead of *values*, he needs to be sure that readers understand the differences he sees in the two words.

- **What strategies are used to develop the definition?** Can you recognize the different types of evidence presented and see what the writer is doing in his or her argument? This kind of analysis can aid your evaluation of a definition argument.

- **What are the implications in accepting the author's definition?** Why does George Will want readers to embrace *virtues* rather than *values*? Will's argument is not just about subtle points of language; his argument is about attitudes that affect public-policy issues. Part of any evaluation of a definition argument must include our recognition of—and assessment of—the author's definition.

- **Is the definition argument convincing?** Do the reasons and evidence lead you to agree with the author, to accept the idea of the definition and its implications as well?

Preparing a Definition Argument

In addition to the guidelines for writing arguments presented in Chapter 4, you can use the following advice specific to writing definition arguments.

Planning

1. **Think:** Why do you want to define your term? To add to our understanding of a complex term? To challenge the use of the word by others? Know your purpose.

2. **Think:** How are you defining the word? What are the elements/parts/steps in your definition? Some brainstorming notes are probably helpful to keep your definition concrete and focused.

3. **Think:** What strategies will you use to develop and support your definition? Defining gives you a purpose, but it does not automatically suggest

ways to develop your argument. Consider using several of these possible strategies for development:

- *Word origin or history of usage.* The word's original meaning can be instructive. If the word has changed meaning over time, explore these changes as clues to how the word can (or should) be used, especially if you are going to object to the term's current use.
- *Descriptive details.* Illustrate with specifics. List the traits of a leader or patriot or courageous person. Explain the behaviors that make a wise or courteous person. Describe the situations that show the existence of liberty. Use negative traits as well as positive ones. That is, show what is *not* covered by the word.
- *Comparison and/or contrast.* Clarify and limit your definition by contrasting it with words of similar meanings. For example, what are the differences between courtesy and manners or knowledge and wisdom or neighborhoods and communities?
- *Examples.* Illustrate your definition with actual or hypothetical examples. Churchill, Lincoln, and Franklin D. Roosevelt could all be used as examples of leaders. You can also create a hypothetical ideal candidate for Congress or for student government president.
- *Function or use.* A frequent strategy for defining is explaining an item's use or function: A pencil is a writing instrument. A similar approach can give insight into more general or abstract terms as well. For example, what do we have—or gain—by emphasizing virtues instead of values? What does a community *do* that a neighborhood does not do?
- *Metaphors.* Consider using figurative comparisons. When fresh—not clichés—they add vividness and punch to your writing.

Drafting

1. Begin with an opening paragraph or two that introduces your subject in an interesting way. Possibilities include the occasion that has led to your writing—explain for instance, a misunderstanding about your term's meaning that you want to correct.

2. Do *not* begin by quoting or paraphrasing a dictionary definition of the term. "According to Webster . . ." is a tired approach lacking reader interest. If the dictionary definition were sufficient, you would have no reason to write an entire essay to define the term.

3. State your thesis—your definition of the term—early in your essay, if you can do so in a sentence or two. If you do not state a brief thesis—the claim of your argument—then establish your purpose in writing early in your essay. (You may find that there are too many parts to your definition to combine into one or two sentences.)

4. Use several specific strategies for developing your definition. Select several strategies from the list you contemplated during your planning stage and

organize your approach around these strategies. That is, you can develop one paragraph of descriptive details, another of examples, another of contrast with words that are similar but not exactly the same in meaning.

5. Consider specifically refuting the error in word use that led to your decision to write your own definition. If you are motivated to write based on what you have read, then make a rebuttal part of your definition argument.

6. Consider discussing the implications of your definition. You can give weight and value to your argument by defending the larger significance of readers' embracing your definition.

A CHECKLIST FOR REVISION

☐ Do I have a good understanding of my purpose? Have I made this clear to readers?

☐ Have I clearly stated my definition? Or clearly established the various parts of the definition that I discuss in separate paragraphs?

☐ Have I organized my argument, building the parts of my definition into a logical, coherent structure?

☐ Have I used specifics to clarify and support my definition?

☐ Have I used the basic checklist for revision in Chapter 4 (see pp. 108–9)?

STUDENT ESSAY

PARAGON OR PARASITE?

Laura Mullins

Attention-getting introduction.

Do you recognize this creature? He is low maintenance and often unnoticeable, a favorite companion of many. Requiring no special attention, he grows from the soil of pride and rejection, feeding regularly on a diet of ignorance and insecurity, scavenging for hurt feelings and defensiveness, gobbling up dainty morsels of lust and scandal. Like a cult leader clothed in a gay veneer,

Clever extended metaphor.

disguising himself as blameless, he wields power. Bewitching unsuspecting but devoted groupies, distracting them from honest self-examination, deceiving them into believing illusions of grandeur or, on the other extreme, unredeemable

Subject introduced.

worthlessness, he breeds jealousy, hate, and fear; thus, he thrives. He is Gossip.

One of my dearest friends is a gossip. She is an educated, honorable, compassionate, loving woman whose character and judgment I deeply admire and respect. After sacrificially raising six children, she went on to study medicine and become a doctor who graciously volunteers her expertise. How, you may be wondering, could a gossip deserve such praise? Then you do not understand the word. My friend is my daughter's godmother; she is my gossip, or *god-sib*, meaning sister-in-god. Derived from Middle English words *god*, meaning spiritual, and *sip/sib/syp*, meaning kinsman, this term was used to refer to a familiar acquaintance, close family friend, or intimate relation, according to the *Oxford English Dictionary*. As a male, he would have joined in fellowship and celebration with the father of the newly born; if a female, she would have been a trusted friend, a birth-attendant or midwife to the mother of the baby. The term grew to include references to the type of easy, unrestrained conversation shared by these folks.

Etymology of gossip and early meanings.

As is often the case with words, the term's meaning has certainly evolved, maybe eroded from its original idea. Is it harmless, idle chat, innocuous sharing of others' personal news, or back-biting, rumor-spreading, and manipulation? Is it a beneficial activity worthy of pursuit, or a deplorable danger to be avoided?

Current meanings.

In her article "Evolution, Alienation, and Gossip" (for the Social Issues Research Centre in Oxford, England), Kate Fox writes that "gossip is not a trivial pastime; it is essential to human social, psychological, and even physical well-being." Many echo her view that gossip is a worthy activity, claiming that engaging in gossip produces endorphins, reduces stress, and aids in building intimate relationships. Gossip, seen at worst as a harmless outlet, is encouraged in the workplace. Since much of its content is not inherently critical or malicious, it is viewed as a positive activity. However, this view does nothing to encourage those speaking or listening to evaluate or examine motive or purpose; instead, it seems to reflect the "anything goes" thinking so prevalent today.

Good use of sources to develop definition.

Conversely, writer and high school English and geography teacher Lennox V. Farrell of Toronto, Canada, in his essay titled "Gossip: An Urban Form of Sorcery," presents gossip as a kind of "witchcraft . . . based on using unsubstantiated accusations by those who make them, and on uncritically accepting these by those enticed into listening." Farrell uses gossip in its more widely understood definition, encompassing the breaking of confidences, inappropriate sharing of indiscretions, destructive tale-bearing, and malicious slander.

What, then, is gossip? We no longer use the term to refer to our children's godparents. Its current definition usually comes with derogatory implications. Imagine a backyard garden: you see a variety of greenery, recognizing at a glance that you are looking at different kinds of plants. Taking a closer look, you will find the gossip vine; inconspicuously blending in, it doesn't appear threatening, but ultimately it destroys. If left in the garden it will choke and then suck out life from its host. Zoom in on the garden scene and follow the creeping vine up trees and along a fence where two neighbors visit. You can overhear one woman saying to the other, "I know I should be the last to tell you, but your husband is being unfaithful to me." (Caption from a cartoon by Alan De la Nougerede.)

The current popular movement to legitimize gossip seems an excuse to condone the human tendency to puff-up oneself. Compared in legal terms, gossip is to conversation as hearsay is to eyewitness testimony; it's not credible. Various religious doctrines abhor the idea and practice of gossip. An old Turkish proverb says, "He who gossips to you will gossip of you." From the Babylonian Talmud, which calls gossip the three-pronged tongue, destroying the one talking, the one listening, and the one being spoken of, to the Upanishads, to the Bible, we can conclude that no good fruit is born from gossip. Let's tend our gardens and check our motives when we have the urge to gossip. Surely we can find more noble pursuits than the self-aggrandizement we have come to know as gossip.

Good use of metaphor to depict gossip as negative.

Conclusion states view that gossip is to be avoided—the writer's thesis.

THE POSITION PAPER: EXAMINING CLAIMS OF VALUES

We studied the refutation argument in Chapter 5 and the definition argument earlier in this chapter. A third type of argument to understand is the claim of value that we frequently label the position paper.

Characteristics of the Position Paper

The position paper or claim of value may be the most difficult of argument assignments simply because it is often perceived to be the easiest. Let's think about this kind of argument:

- The claim of value is more general or abstract or philosophical than other types of arguments.
- It makes a claim about what is right or wrong, good or bad, for us as individuals or as a society. Topics can vary from capital punishment to pornography to endangered species.
- A claim of value is developed in large part by a logical sequencing of reasons. But a support of principles also depends on relevant facts. Remember the long list of specific abuses listed in the Declaration of Independence (pp. 128–31).
- A successful claim of value argument requires more than a forceful statement of personal beliefs.

GUIDELINES for Evaluating a Claim of Value

When reading position papers, what should you look for? Again, the basics of good argument apply here as well as with definition arguments. To evaluate claims of values specifically, use the following questions as guides:

- **What is the writer's claim?** Is it clear?
- **Is the claim qualified if necessary?** Some claims of value are broad philosophical assertions ("Capital punishment is immoral and bad public policy"). Others are qualified ("Capital punishment is acceptable only in crimes of treason").
- **What facts are presented?** Are they credible? Are they relevant to the claim's support?
- **What reasons are given in support of the claim?** What assumptions are necessary to tie reasons to claim? Make a list of reasons and assumptions and analyze the writer's logic. Do you find any fallacies?
- **What are the implications of the claim?** For example, if you argue for the legalization of all recreational drugs, you eliminate all "drug problems" by definition. But what new problems may be created by this approach? Consider more car accidents and reduced productivity for openers.
- **Is the argument convincing?** Does the evidence provide strong support for the claim? Are you prepared to agree with the writer, in whole or in part?

Supporting a Claim of Value

In addition to the guidelines for writing arguments presented in Chapter 4, you can use the following advice specific to writing position papers or claims of value.

Planning

1. **Think:** What claim, exactly, do you want to support? Should you qualify your first attempt at a claim statement?

2. **Think:** What grounds (evidence) do you have to support your claim? You may want to make a list of the reasons and facts you would consider using to defend your claim.

3. **Think:** Study your list of possible grounds and recognize the assumptions (warrants) and backing for your grounds.

4. **Think:** Now make a list of the grounds most often used by those holding views that oppose your claim. This second list will help you prepare counterarguments to possible rebuttals, but first it will help you test your commitment to your position. If you find the opposition's arguments persuasive and cannot think how you would rebut them, you may need to rethink your position. Ideally, your two lists will confirm your views but also increase your respect for opposing views.

5. **Consider:** Should I use a conciliatory approach? With an emotion-laden or highly controversial issue, the conciliatory approach can be an effective strategy. Conciliatory arguments include:
   - The use of nonthreatening language
   - The fair expression of opposing views
   - A statement of the common ground shared by opposing sides.

   You may want to use a conciliatory approach when: (1) you know your views will be unpopular with at least some members of your audience; (2) the issue is highly emotional and has sides that are "entrenched" so that you are seeking some accommodations rather than dramatic changes of position; (3) you need to interact with members of your audience and want to keep a respectful relationship going.

Drafting

1. Begin with an opening paragraph or two that introduces your topic in an interesting way. Possibilities include a statement of the issue's seriousness or reasons why the issue is currently being debated—or why we should go back to reexamine it. Some writers are spurred by a recent event that receives media coverage; recounting such an event can produce an effective opening. You can also briefly summarize points of the opposition that you will challenge in supporting your claim.

2. Decide where to place your claim statement. Your best choices are either early in your essay or at the end of your essay, after you have made your case. The second approach can be an effective alternative to the more common pattern of stating one's claim early.

3. Organize evidence in an effective way. One plan is to move from the least important to the most important reasons, followed by rebuttals to potential counterarguments. Another possibility is to organize by the arguments of the opposition, explaining why each of their reasons fails to hold up. A third approach is to organize logically. That is, if some reasons build on the accepting of other reasons, you want to begin with the necessary underpinnings and then move forward from those.

4. Provide a logical defense of or specifics in support of each reason. You have not finished your task by simply asserting several reasons for your claim. You also need to present facts or examples for or a logical explanation of each reason. For example, you have not defended your views on capital punishment by asserting that it is right or just to take the life of a murderer. Why is it right or just? Executing the murderer will not bring the victim back to life. Do two wrongs make a right? These are some of the thoughts your skeptical reader may have unless you explain and justify your reasoning. *Remember:* Quoting another writer's opinion on your topic does not provide proof for your reasons. It merely shows that someone else agrees with you.

5. Maintain an appropriate level of seriousness for an argument of principle. Of course, word choice must be appropriate to a serious discussion, but in addition be sure to present reasons that are also appropriately serious. For example, if you are defending the claim that music CDs should not be subject to content labeling because such censorship is inconsistent with First Amendment rights, do not trivialize your argument by including the point that young people are tired of adults controlling their lives. (This is another issue for another paper.)

A CHECKLIST FOR REVISION ■·■

☐ Do I have a clear statement of my claim? Is it qualified, if appropriate?

☐ Have I organized my argument, building the parts of my support into a clear and logical structure that readers can follow?

☐ Have I avoided logical fallacies?

☐ Have I found relevant facts and examples to support and develop my reasons?

☐ Have I paid attention to appropriate word choice, including using a conciliatory approach if that is a wise strategy?

☐ Have I used the basic checklist for revision in Chapter 4 (see pp. 108–9)?

STUDENT ESSAY

EXAMINING THE ISSUE OF GUN CONTROL

Chris Brown

Introduction connects ambivalence in American character to conflict over gun control.

The United States has a long history of compromise. Issues such as representation in government have been resolved because of compromise, forming some of the bases of American life. Americans, however, like to feel that they are uncompromising, never willing to surrender an argument. This attitude has led to a number of issues in modern America that are unresolved, including the issue of gun control. Bickering over the issue has slowed progress toward legislation that will solve the serious problem of gun violence in America, while keeping recreational use of firearms available to responsible people. To resolve the conflict over guns, the arguments of both sides must be examined, with an eye to finding the flaws in both. Then perhaps we can reach some meaningful compromises.

Student organizes by arguments for no gun control.

Gun advocates have used many arguments for the continued availability of firearms to the public. The strongest of these defenses points to the many legitimate uses for guns. One use is protection against violence, a concern of some people in today's society. There are many problems with the use of guns for protection, however, and these problems make the continued use of firearms for protection dangerous. One such problem is that gun owners are not always able to use guns responsibly. When placed in a situation in which personal injury or loss is imminent, people often do not think intelligently. Adrenaline surges through the body, and fear takes over much of the thinking

1. Guns for protection

process. This causes gun owners to use their weapons, firing at whatever threatens them. Injuries and deaths of innocent people, including family members of the gun owner, result. Removing guns from the house seems to be the only solution to these sad consequences.

Responding to this argument, gun advocates ask how they are to defend themselves without guns. But guns are needed for protection from other guns. If there are no guns, people need only to protect themselves from criminals using knives, baseball bats, and other weapons. Obviously the odds of surviving a knife attack are greater than the odds of surviving a gun attack. One reason is that a gun is an impersonal weapon. Firing at someone from 50 feet away requires much less commitment than charging someone with a knife and stabbing repeatedly. Also, bullet wounds are, generally, more severe than knife wounds. Guns are also more likely to be misused when a dark figure is in one's house. To kill with the gun requires only to point and shoot; no recognition of the figure is needed. To kill with a knife, by contrast, requires getting within arm's reach of the figure.

There are other uses of guns, including recreation. Hunting and target shooting are valid, responsible uses of guns. How do we keep guns available for recreation? The answer is in the form of gun clubs and hunting clubs. Many are already established; more can be constructed. These clubs can provide recreational use of guns for responsible people while keeping guns off the streets and out of the house.

2. Recreational uses

The last argument widely used by gun advocates is the constitutional right to bear arms. The fallacies in this argument are that the Constitution was written in a vastly different time. This different time had different uses for guns, and a different type of gun. Firearms were defended in the Constitution because of their many valid uses and fewer problems. Guns were mostly muskets, guns that were not very accurate beyond close range. Also, guns took more than 30 seconds to load in the eighteenth century and could fire only one shot before reloading. These differences with today's guns affect the relative safety of guns then and now. In addition, those who did not live in the city at the time used hunting for food as well as for recreation; hunting was a necessary component of life. That is not true today. Another use of guns in the eighteenth century was as protection from animals. Wild animals such as bears and cougars were much more common. Settlers, explorers, and hunters needed protection from these animals in ways not comparable with modern life.

3. Second Amendment rights

Finally, Revolutionary America had no standing army. Defense of the nation and of one's home from other nations relied on local militia. The right to bear arms granted in the Constitution was inspired by the need for national protection as well as by the other outdated needs previously discussed. Today America has a standing army with enough weaponry to adequately defend itself from outside aggressors. There is no need for every citizen to carry a musket, or an AK-47, for the protection of the nation. It would seem, then, that the Second Amendment does not apply to modern society.

Student establishes a compromise position.

To reach a compromise, we also have to examine the other side of the issue. Some gun-control advocates argue that all guns are unnecessary and should be outlawed. The problem with this argument is that guns will still be available to those who do not mind breaking the law. Until an economically sound and feasible way of controlling illegal guns in America is found, guns cannot be totally removed, no matter how much legislation is passed. This means that if guns are to be outlawed for uses other than recreational uses, a way must be found to combat the illegal gun trade that will evolve. Tough criminal laws and a large security force are all that can be offered to stop illegal uses of guns until better technology is available. This means that, perhaps, a good resolution would involve gradual restrictions on guns, until eventually guns were restricted only to recreational uses in a controlled setting for citizens not in the police or military.

Conclusion restates student's claim.

Both sides on this issue have valid points. Any middle ground needs to offer something to each side. It must address the reasons people feel that they need guns for protection, allow for valid recreational use, and keep guns out of the hands of the public, except for properly trained police officers. Time and money will be needed to move toward the removal of America's huge handgun arsenal. But, sooner or later a compromise on the issue of gun control must be made to make America a safer, better place to live.

FOR DEBATE
THE NEXT RIGHTS REVOLUTION? | RICHARD A. EPSTEIN

A professor of law at the University of Chicago, Richard Epstein (b. 1943) has published widely—and produced controversy—on a number of legal topics, including issues of private property and labor law. Two of his recent books are *Simple Rules for a Complex World* (1995) and *Private and Common Property* (2000). His contribution to the animal-rights debate appeared in the *National Review* on November 8, 1999.

PREREADING QUESTIONS   Do you already have a position on animal-rights issues? If so, what might you gain from reading the following articles? If not, do you think you should have a position on this issue? Why or why not?

"Fur is murder!" is a slogan you didn't hear very much until recently. In part, it is because the world used to face other forms of outrage, in which human beings lost their lives because of their religious beliefs or, closer to home, were kept out of public places because of their skin color. Against this grim background, the advocates of civil rights and civil liberties had a proper mission: to ensure that all human beings enjoy the full and equal protection of the laws.

Now come the animal-rights advocates, who ask the following provocative question: Has the civil-rights revolution gone far enough by attacking invidious distinctions based on race, color, or religious beliefs? Or should it be regarded as backward and incomplete because it fails to recognize legal rights in (non-human) animals? Is discrimination against animals, as many animal-rights advocates repeatedly insist, like discrimination against blacks? That the law was so wrong, for so long, on the scope of its protection in the prior case raises challenges that we cannot ignore in the second. In what way, exactly, is the law justified in preferring the status of human beings to that of lower animals?

Both sides must be heard on this critical debate. It is unfortunate, therefore, that many of the law courses that address this issue are courses in animal "rights," taught by advocates on one side of the issue, as opposed to animal "law," which offers a more fruitful and historically grounded approach.

The treatment of animals did not suddenly pop onto the social agenda. Rather, it has been with us from the beginning of human society. In ancient times, animals were already crucial to the survival of society. Domesticated animals were the source of food, clothing, agricultural muscle-power, and even (through cavalry) military and strategic strength. Animals were treated as an animate type of property. People acquired ownership of wild animals by capturing them; once acquired, these animals ceased to be free and became the property of owners, to use, breed, consume, or sell. The Romans, for example, reserved their most solemn form of conveyance for certain key draft animals, which they recognized as critical capital assets. Only land rivaled them in value.

In the 19th and 20th centuries, one weakness of this system of animal law became apparent. Its property-based rules provided no mechanism to prevent the systematic extinction of wild animals through over-hunting and over-fishing. To counter this risk, legal systems instituted, with varying degrees of success, statutes that limited the catch of whales, fish, and wild game in order to counteract the "tragedy of the commons" that results when a hunter keeps his entire quarry, but suffers only a tiny fraction of the losses caused by the eventual extinction of the herd. More recently, stringent protections afforded to endangered species have generated controversy, as farmers have claimed—rightly in my view—that they have been unfairly forced to stand aside while protected animals decimate their sheep and cattle, for which they receive not a dime in compensation from the government.

6   Behind these traditional debates lies one key assumption: *The animal itself cannot be recognized as a holder of property rights valid against human beings.* Today's vocal defenders of animal rights brand this assumption "species-ist." Sometimes the classical view made animals property; at other times, they were the object of public regulation. In both cases, the legal rules were imposed largely for the benefit of human beings, either as owners of animals or as part of the public at large that benefited from their preservation.

7   Today's animal-rights activists want to overturn this "species-ist" consensus; they call for a declaration of independence of animals from their owners. While this clarion call generates tremendous emotional resonance, it is intellectually dangerous. Last August, I asked in the *New York Times:* "Would even bacteria have rights? There would be nothing left of human society if we treated animals not as property but as independent holders of rights."

8   The animal-rights activists were unhappy with that comment, but they are philosophically misguided on several grounds. First, they claim that our understanding of the complex behavior of animals has been revolutionized in such a way that the status of animals must be changed. But although the field of animal behavior has made enormous strides in recent years, the basic understanding has not changed. The law has understood for a long time that animals have extensive powers of anticipation and rationalization; they can form, and break, alliances; they can show anger, annoyance, and remorse; they can store food for later use; they respond to courtship and aggression; they can engage in acts of rape and acts of love; they respect, and violate, territories. In many ways, their repertory of emotions is quite broad, rivaling that of human beings. But the fact remains that they do not have the higher capacity for language and thought that characterizes human beings as a species.

9   We should never pretend that the case against recognizing animal rights is easier than it really is; by the same token, we cannot accept the facile argument that our new understanding of animals must lead to a new appreciation of their rights. The fundamentals of animal behavior were well known to the men who fashioned the old legal order.

10   Second, animal-rights activists claim that because people today do not need to rely on animal labor in order to survive, greater animal rights must be recognized. They tend to phrase this claim in a universalistic way, as if it were true uniformly of all societies, when, in fact, less fortunate societies would suffer greatly from the loss of animal-based food and clothing. There would be serious harm even in the prosperous lands that could survive without using animals for consumption or labor, because the demands of the activists cut far

deeper. For them, the mere ownership of animals is a sin: no pets, no circuses, no milk, no cheese, no horses to ride, no dogs, cats, birds, or fish around the house. These relationships are based on an inequality of power and are thus condemned; the animals who seem to like being cared for suffer from, as it were, a form of false consciousness!

An even more ominous consequence would forbid the use of animals for medical science. The argument here is moral, for no one would dispute the proposition that animals should not be used in research if the same results could be achieved at the same cost by test tubes or computer simulations alone. Nor would many people want future surgeons to try out new techniques on animals if they could be performed, without risk, on human beings. Sadly, however, these animal tests are necessary. We have a dreadful shortage today of human organs for transplantation, and unless we are prepared to do studies on pigs and perhaps chimpanzees, we shall never develop an understanding of how to overcome the problem of organ rejection. And unless we are prepared to harvest animal organs, then all research done in this area will prove idle.

I think any delay in this testing would be undesirable. If that be species-ism, I plead guilty—because, while I do care about the welfare of animals, I consider the welfare of humans a higher concern.

If parity between animal rights and human rights is ever acknowledged, more than medical research will suffer. Our entire system of property allows owners to transform the soil and to exclude others. Now, if the first human being on the scene may exclude subsequent arrivals, what happens when animals are given similar rights? Their dens, burrows, nests, and hives long antedate human arrival. The principle of first possession might therefore block us from clearing the land for farms, homes, and factories—unless we can find a way to make just compensation to each animal for its losses. But I fail to see how this system would work, for to transfer animals from one habitat to another only impermissibly displaces animals at the second location.

The blunt truth is that the arrival of human beings necessarily results in the death of some earlier animal occupants, even if it increases the welfare of others. So if prior in time is higher in right, then we should fold up our tents right now and let the animals fight it out for territory, just as if we had never arrived on the face of the globe.

The defenders of animal rights shrink, at least publicly, from the stark implications of their position, and choose to dwell instead on their victories in court. But the legal arguments the activists make in these court cases are credible precisely because they have nothing whatsoever to do with their broader claims. Animal owners have recovered large awards for the malpractice of veterinarians. The damages paid are meant to cover not only the market value of the animal, but the loss of companionship to the owner. This is good law and solid economics, because it recognizes that when these non-monetary elements are included, the *actual* losses to the owner exceed the market value. It is commonplace today to allow one spouse to sue for the damages that result from the loss of companionship when the other spouse is injured or dies. But, whether for human beings or pets, the interests vindicated are those of the party who suffers the emotional loss and the loss of companionship, not the interests of the person or animal who has died or been injured. These cases derive their power from a property-rights conception. It is hard, then, to see how they augur a new judicial age in which animals will have rights of their own against owners. It is not as though offspring of the deceased animal have an action for wrongful death.

16   A similar logic applies to a recent federal-court decision in Washington, D.C., in which a zoo visitor was held to have "standing" to sue under a federal law requiring that zookeepers confine primates in such a way that the animals' "psychological well-being" is assured. That objective is certainly laudable in simple human terms. But the recognition of the zoo visitor's standing to sue makes it crystal clear that the rights vindicated by the action were those of the individual plaintiff, and not those of the animal.

17   No one can deny the enormous political waves created by animal rights activists. It is also easy to understand how their anti-property theme gains adherents among those who, for other reasons, don't like private property. But even though it's understandable, we have to recognize that the results of a victory by animal-rights extremists would be pernicious. Rules that prevent gratuitous cruelty to animals should be supported, because animals suffer. But it is one thing to raise social consciousness about the plight of animals and another to raise their status to an asserted parity with human beings. That move, if systematically implemented, would pose a mortal threat to society that few human beings will, or should, accept.

18   We have quite enough difficulty in persuading or coercing human beings to respect the rights of their fellows, so that all can live in peace. By treating animals as our moral equals, we would undermine the liberty and dignity of human beings—making the slaughters of Hitler, Stalin, or Pol Pot seem no worse than the daily activity of preparing cattle for market. That is one kind of moral equivalence we must never allow. Animals are properly property. To misunderstand the rights of animals is to cheapen the rights of human beings.

QUESTIONS FOR READING

1.   In his introductory two paragraphs, Epstein presents his topic—the animal-rights debate. Although he does not state his position, can you tell by his introduction what his position may be? If so, by what clues?

2.   What distinction does Epstein make between courses in animal rights and courses in animal law? What is important about this difference in language?

3.   What has animal law established in the past? What are animals unable to do under current laws?

4.   What is Epstein's position on using animals for research? How does he support his position?

5.   How would human life be altered if all animals were given rights under our laws?

QUESTIONS FOR REASONING AND ANALYSIS

1. What is Epstein's claim?
2. What is the author's reaction to changes in animal law desired by animal-rights activists? How does he rebut two of their arguments?
3. Locate several places where Epstein seeks a conciliatory approach. Are these passages successful in finding a middle ground, given the rest of Epstein's argument? Why or why not?
4. Examine the author's word choice when he refers to the opposition. What do his language and tone suggest to you about his perception of his audience? That is, does he expect most of his readers to agree or disagree with him?

QUESTIONS FOR REFLECTING AND WRITING

1. Epstein concludes by asserting that if we treat animals as our equals, we "undermine the liberty and dignity of human beings" and make no distinction between the slaughters of tyrants and the slaughter of the cattle farmer. Do you agree with these assertions? Why or why not?
2. Do you agree with Epstein's argument? In whole? In part? Explain your position and think about how you would rebut any parts of his argument with which you disagree.

ANIMAL RIGHTS V. ANIMAL RESEARCH: A MODEST PROPOSAL | JOSEPH BERNSTEIN

Dr. Joseph Bernstein is an assistant professor of orthopedics at the University of Pennsylvania's hospital and a senior fellow at the Leonard Davis Institute of Health Economics, also at the University of Pennsylvania. Bernstein's "modest proposal" for animal research appeared in the *Journal of Medical Ethics* in 1996 along with Timothy Sprigge's response.

PREREADING QUESTIONS What is the source of Bernstein's title? (Hint: Check Chapter 23.) Does the demand for advances in medicine justify the use of animals in research? Is the use of animals ethical so long as they are not abused? What constitutes abuse?

Many people love animals. Some animal lovers, though, in the name of their love, oppose the use of any animals in any medical research, regardless of the care given, regardless of the cause. Of course, many other animal lovers acknowledge the need for animal subjects in some medical studies, as long as no alternatives exist, and provided that care, respect and dignity are applied at all times. Unhappily, between the opponents of animal research and the researchers themselves lies no common ground, no place for an agreement to disagree: the opponents are not satisfied merely to abstain from animal experimentation themselves—they want everyone else to stop too.

Despite that, I would argue that in this case (to a far greater extent than, say, in the case of abortion) the animal rights question can be answered by exactly that tactic: the abstention of the opposition. Of course, I do not advocate abstention from debate; and, of course, abstention from performing research by those who are not researchers is not meaningful. Rather, I propose that the protesters—and every citizen they can enlist—abstain from the benefits of animal research. I say let the proponents of animal rights boycott the products of animal research. Let them place fair market-place pressure on ending activities they find reprehensible. Let them mobilise the tacit support they claim. Let the market for therapies derived from animal research evaporate, and with it much of the funding for such work. Let the animal lovers attain their desired goal without clamour, and without violence.

3   To assist them, I offer a modest proposal.

4   I suggest that we adopt a legal release form, readily available to all patients, which will enable them to indicate precisely which benefits of animal research they oppose—and from which, accordingly, they refuse to benefit. This form could be sent to all hospitals and physicians, and would be included in the patient's chart, much like operative consent forms, or Do Not Resuscitate instructions. It should resolve the issue once and for all.

5   This "Animal Research Advance Directive" would look something like this:

6   Dear Doctor:

Animals deserve the basic freedom from serving as experiment subjects against their will. Today, we who are committed to seeing the world's scientific laboratories free from unwilling and innocent animals, hereby refuse to benefit from research performed on these victims.

7   Accordingly, I ask that you care for me to the best of your abilities, but request that:

(CHECK ALL THAT APPLY)

8   ☐ You do not perform on me a coronary bypass operation, or fix any heart defect my child may be born with, as these operations and the heart lung machine used during the procedures were developed using dogs. In fact, since the entire field of cardiology has been polluted by animal research for nearly a century, I cannot in good conscience accept any cardiological care.

9   ☐ You treat my child for any disease she may develop, but do not give her a vaccine that was tried first on a blameless animal. As I am not aware of any vaccines that were not animal-tested, please skip them all.

10   ☐ You avoid offering any suggestions regarding my diet and habits, when that information was derived from animal studies. This includes salt and fat intake, tobacco smoke, and various cancer-causing food additives. Do not bother to test my cholesterol levels, as the association between high cholesterol and heart disease is knowledge stolen from the suffering of the innocent.

11   ☐ Should I develop a malignancy, you do not give me chemotherapy, as those drugs were administered first to animals. I must also decline surgical treatment as well, since modern surgical technique and equipment owes its existence to sinful animal research. Finally, do not treat my disease with radiation, since that field, too, was contaminated by dog studies.

☐ You amputate my leg or arm should I break it in such fashion that it requires surgery. Fracture fixation devices were designed through the suffering of dogs, so I must refuse repair of the bone. That probably will hurt a lot, but since I must refuse all pain medicine studied on rats (and that includes just about all of them), it is best if you just remove the damaged limb.   12

Needless to say, I will not accept an AIDS vaccine should one be developed, as unwilling Rhesus monkeys have been used in AIDS research.   13

Thank you for considering my wishes. Only through the concerted avoidance of these ill-gotten technologies can we halt the barbaric practice of animal research. Of course, I have no objection to studying disease on humans. To that end, I pledge my body to science upon my death. It probably will occur a lot sooner than I'd like.   14

QUESTIONS FOR READING

1.   What is Bernstein "proposing"?
2.   Why does he include such a long checklist? What does he want to make clear to readers?

QUESTIONS FOR REASONING AND ANALYSIS

1.   Does Bernstein seriously expect to see the use of an "Animal Research Advance Directive"? How do you know the answer to this question?
2.   What is the tone of this essay? What language and strategies help to create the tone?

QUESTIONS FOR REFLECTING AND WRITING

1.   Has Bernstein presented a convincing argument? Are his persuasive strategies effective? Explain your response.
2.   If you wanted to refute Bernstein's argument, how would you proceed?

A REPLY TO JOSEPH BERNSTEIN | TIMOTHY SPRIGGE

Endowment fellow in philosophy at the University of Edinburgh, Timothy Sprigge (b. 1932) has contributed articles to scholarly journals of philosophy and published several books of philosophy, including *Theories of Existence* (1985) and *Rational Foundations of Ethics* (1990). His argument on the animal-rights debate, a response to Joseph Bernstein's argument, also appeared in the *Journal of Medical Ethics* in 1996.

PREREADING QUESTIONS Does the demand for advances in medicine justify the use of animals in research? Is the use of animals ethical so long as they are not abused? What constitutes abuse?

1   Dr Bernstein's "A modest proposal" lays down a witty challenge to opponents of animal experimentation. However, matters are rather less clear cut than he evidently realises and there are various reasons, which I list below, why an anti-vivisectionist may feel no obligation to sign such directives under present conditions. Things would be different if (1) adequately funded facilities on the National Health Service were introduced which would make no use of further medical advances based on painful animal experimentation; (2) public funding for (painful) animal research and "alternative" research henceforth reflected the proportion of those who would not, and those who would, opt for these facilities.

2   (1) A first point is that Dr Bernstein does not distinguish between the use of animals in research which does, and that which does not, involve serious suffering for them (including that imposed by their housing, such as the extremes of boredom, but obviously not including being painlessly killed). The original anti-vivisection societies were, as their names imply, opposed to the cutting up of conscious live animals rather than to human use of animals in general (as may be the case with many animal rightists nowadays) and it seems to me reasonable to use "vivisection" today in a broader sense to cover all research which involves serious animal suffering (something worse, for example, than we feel when we receive an injection). Opponents of this are not necessarily opponents of all use of animals in medical research and it is not clear how many of the medical procedures Dr Bernstein lists were developed through work involving such serious suffering (as opposed, for example, to painless killing). It would facilitate rational debate if both defenders and critics of animal research were clearer on this point than they usually are.

3   (2) Even if, in practice, most of these procedures have been developed in ways which did involve serious animal suffering, it is another question whether they could have been developed without this. The anti-vivisectionist who believes that they could have been, or even probably could have been, developed (by now) by other means has no reason to avoid them because of their unfortunate and, as he thinks, (probably) unnecessary history. In fact, I suggest, no one really knows how far medicine could have advanced had work of a kind which most anti-vivisectionists would condemn, been avoided.[1] If this is so, there is no bad faith in the anti-vivisectionist making use of advances in medicine which he/she guesses would probably have been gained in other ways had the ethics of the past been more like theirs now.

4   The autobahnen in Germany were originally developed for their utility in transporting troops for aggressive war. Should those against aggressive war therefore not use those built in the Hitler period? Likewise Volkswagen cars were developed as cars for the people in the Third Reich as part of a plan to encourage love of that regime. Is one wrong to drive or travel in one today?

5   Many nations established their present borders in wars which involved all manner of what we would now regard as atrocities. Should its decent citizens refuse loyalty to any country with such a past?

6   Few people would answer these questions affirmatively, doubtless believing that, since we cannot change past history, refusing to benefit from its evils,

especially where similar benefits could probably have been won otherwise, would be a pointless sacrifice.

In short, one may avail oneself of knowledge and techniques which exist now, however first acquired, with a clear conscience even if they were developed in ways which fall below what one would like to be the moral standards of today. Where procedures rely on very recent research he/she should perhaps avoid benefiting from it, if he/she can, because this is likely to be part of a current research programme which he/she should be attempting to discourage. But even here if one believes that similarly useful developments in medicine could have occurred without such pain for animals it is not unreasonable or inconsistent to avail oneself of it, in the absence of alternatives (either of procedures or research) which might have been developed instead in a society less ready to base itself on animal suffering.

(3) If our society had long been based on a culture which outlawed the causing of serious pain to animals for human benefit it would have been so different through and through that no one can tell whether humans would have been better off or worse off now than they are. After all, we are the product of a history which, in innumerable ways, depended on behaviour which we would now dub immoral, and we just have to accept that for better or for worse. The moral question now is whether these practices can be justified in the light of the moral ideals to which we now aspire and the knowledge we now possess. So there is no more call on those of us who argue for the cessation of such animal experimentation as involves serious suffering to reject what was acquired in the past by means of it than there is for us to distance ourselves from most of our institutions with their morally mixed past.

(4) Judgments about whether people in the past are to be morally condemned for what they did are highly problematic. People act in a historical context and cannot be expected to live by standards which have been developed since. The anti-vivisectionist thinks that we are now ready for higher standards, in our relations with animals. For one thing the technologies of discovery are more sophisticated and need not be so physically intrusive or painful as perhaps they were bound to be in the past. For another thing, surgery was so dreadful for everyone until the development of anaesthetics, that perhaps people could not be expected to be too sensitive about animals amidst so much inevitable pain for themselves. But, with medical advances meaning so much less pain for us humans of today (when the groups to which we belong behave themselves, as admittedly too few do), it is surely time to be more sensitive about the suffering of animals for our advantage.

It would clarify the whole debate enormously if the following were sharply distinguished: animal-based research which 1) must involve serious animal suffering; 2) does involve it but which could be replaced by research (whether using animals or not) which does not; 3) does not involve it. All sides might then agree that 2) is wrong (inasmuch as the suffering would be uncontentiously unnecessary) and attention could then be paid to how much falls into the first category and whether the benefits it may bring justify the harm both to animals and those who must render themselves callous to their suffering. As for category 3) that divides into various types the morality of which is, indeed, important but much less urgent. At any rate, I see no reason why an anti-vivisectionist should feel the need to avoid the benefits of research other than what he/she is sure is of the first type.

REFERENCE

[1] Balls M. Recent progress towards reducing the use of animal experimentation in biomedical research. In: Garratini S, van Bekkum DW, eds. *The importance of animal experimentation for safety and biomedical research.* Dordrecht: Kluwer Academic Publishers, 1990: 228–9.

QUESTIONS FOR READING

1. In replying to Bernstein's argument, Sprigge makes several distinctions. What distinctions does he make regarding use of animals in research? What distinction does he make with regard to the past and the present?

2. What does the author assert regarding the behavior of people in the past? Have we opposed the use of animals for human advantages in the past?

3. What distinctions does he recommend for the present use of animals in medical research? How will these distinctions clarify the debate?

QUESTIONS FOR REASONING AND ANALYSIS

1. What is Sprigge's position with regard to the use of medical science based on animal research in the past?

2. To support his argument, Sprigge makes several analogies. Do they provide effective reasoning in support of his argument?

QUESTIONS FOR REFLECTING AND WRITING

1. Does Sprigge make a convincing argument for animal-rights activists benefiting from medical science based on animal experiments in the past? Do you agree with him on this point? Why or why not?

2. Is Sprigge effective in establishing some common ground for both sides? If so, what is that common ground? If you think that he has failed to do this, explain why.

3. What are your responses to Sprigge's three categories of current animal-based research? Do you agree that number 2 is wrong? Do you agree that number 3 is not as urgent for debate as number 1? What is your position on number 1? Why?

SUGGESTIONS FOR DISCUSSION AND WRITING

1. Analyze the differences in approach of Bernstein and Sprigge. What strategies of debate does each use? Which do you find the most effective? Why?

2. In many states there are no laws regarding the private ownership of wild animals. You can, if you wish, keep a tiger in a cage in your backyard. Should individuals be allowed to own wild animals? If so, why? If not, why not?

3. Is it possible to oppose the abuse of animals and still justify the existence of zoos? If so, why? If not, why not?

CHAPTER 7

Reading, Evaluating, and Using Visuals and Statistics in Argument

We live in a visual age. Many of us go to movies to appreciate and judge the film's visual effects. The Internet is awash in pictures and colorful icons. Perhaps the best symbol of our visual age is *USA Today*, a paper filled with pictures in color and many tables and other graphics as a primary way of presenting information. *USA Today* has forced the more traditional papers to add color photos to their front pages to compete. We also live in a numerical age. Lisa Mundy, writing in "A Date to Remember," observes that using the expression 9/11 to refer to the events of September 11, 2001, says something about our times: "We are all digital thinkers now, accustomed to looking at our calendars, our watches, and seeing numerals." This chapter brings together these markers of our times as they are used in argument—and as argument—for we find statistics and visuals used as part of argumentative books and essays, but we also need to remember that cartoons and advertisements are arguments in and of themselves.

READING GRAPHICS

Graphics—photographs, diagrams, tables, charts, and graphs—present a good bit of information in a condensed but also visually engaging format. Graphics are everywhere: in textbooks, magazines, newspapers. It's a rare training session or board meeting that is conducted without the use of graphics to display information. So, you want to be able to read graphics and create them, when appropriate, in your own writing. Here are general guidelines for reading all types of graphics. The guidelines will use Figure 7.1 to illustrate points; study the figure repeatedly as you read through the guidelines.

GUIDELINES for Reading Graphics

1. **Locate the particular graphic referred to in the text and study it at that point in your reading.** Graphics may not always be placed on the same page as the text reference. Stop your reading to find and study the graphic; that's what the writer wants you to do. Find Figure 7.1 on this page.

2. **Read the title or heading of the graphic.** Every graphic, except photographs, is given a title. What is the subject of the graphic? What kind of information is provided? Figure 7.1 shows differences in suicide rates by race, gender, and age.

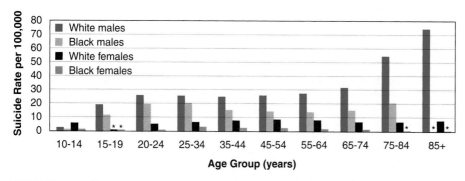

FIGURE 7.1 Differences in Suicide Rate According to Race, Gender, and Age
(Source: Data from the U.S. Bureau of the Census, 1994).

3. **Read any notes, description, and the source information at the bottom of the graphic.** Figure 7.1 came from the U.S. Bureau of the Census for 1994. Critical questions: What is this figure showing me? Is the information coming from a reliable source? Is it current enough to still be meaningful?

4. **Study the labels—and other words—***that appear as part of the graphic.* You cannot draw useful conclusions unless you understand exactly what is being shown. Observe in Figure 7.1 that the four bars for each age group (shown along the horizontal axis) represent white males, black males, white females, and black females, in that order, for each age category.

5. **Study the information, making certain that you understand what the numbers represent.** Are the numerals whole numbers, numbers in hundreds or thousands, or percentages? In Figure 7.1 we are looking at suicide *rates per 100,000 people* for four identified groups of people at different ages. So, to know exactly how many white males between 15 and 19 commit suicide, we need to know how many white males between 15 and 19 there are (or were in 1994) in the United States population. The chart does not give us this information. It gives us *comparative rates* per 100,000 people in each category and tells us that almost 20 in every 100,000 of white males between 15 and 19 commit suicide.

6. **Draw conclusions.** Think about the information in different ways. Critical questions: What does the author want to accomplish by including these figures? How are they significant? What significant conclusions can you draw from Figure 7.1? Answer the following questions to guide your thinking.

   a. Which of the four compared groups faces the greatest risk from suicide over his or her lifetime? Would you have guessed this group? Why or why not? What might be some of the causes for the greatest risk to this group?
   b. What is the greatest risk factor for increased suicide rate—race, gender, age, or a combination? Does this surprise you? Would you have guessed a different factor? Why?
   c. Which group, as young teens, is at greatest risk? Are you surprised? Why or why not? What might be some of the causes for this?

Graphics provide information, raise questions, explain processes, engage us emotionally, make us think. Study the various graphics in the exercise that follows to become more expert in reading and responding critically to visuals.

EXERCISES: Reading and Analyzing Graphics

1. Study the pie charts in Figure 7.2 and then answer the following questions.
   a. What is the subject of the charts?
   b. In addition to the information within the pie charts, what other information is provided?
   c. Which group increases by the greatest relative amount? How would you account for that increase?
   d. Which figure surprises you the most? Why?

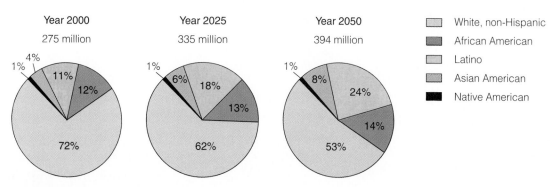

FIGURE 7.2 The Shifting of U.S. Racial-Ethnic Mix (Sources: U.S. Bureau of the Census. *Current Population Reports* P25:1130, 1996 James Henslin. *Sociology: A Down-to-Earth Approach,* 5th ed.).

2. Study the line graph in Figure 7.3 and then answer the following questions.
   a. What two subjects are treated by the graph?
   b. In 2000 what percentage of men's income did women earn?
   c. During which five-year period did men's incomes increase by the greatest amount?
   d. Does the author's prediction for the year 2005 suggest that income equality for women will have taken place?
   e. Are you bothered by the facts on this graph? Why or why not?
3. Study the table in Figure 7.4 and then answer the following questions.
   a. What is being presented and compared in this table?
   b. What, exactly, do the numerals in the second line represent? What, exactly, do the numerals in the third line represent? (Be sure that you understand what these numbers mean.)
   c. For the information given in lines 2, 3, 4, and 5, in which category have women made the greatest gains on men?
   d. See if you can complete the missing information in the last line. Where will you look to find out how many men and women are single parents in 2000?
   e. Which figure surprises you the most? Why?
4. Maps, as you can see from color plate 1, can be used to show all kinds of information, not just the locations of cities, rivers, or mountains. Study the map and then answer the questions that follow.
   a. What, exactly, does the map show? Why does it not "look right"?
   b. How many electoral votes did each candidate win?
   c. How are the winning states for each candidate clustered? What conclusions can you draw from observing this clustering?
   d. What advice would you give to each party to ensure that party's presidential win in 2004?
5. Study the photograph on page 191 and then answer these questions.
   a. This famous photograph was frequently reprinted and even referred to during debates in Congress on the Civil Rights Act of 1964. What is its subject?
   b. What details make it dramatic? What message does it send?
   c. What is your response to the photo? How does it make you feel? What does it lead you to think about?

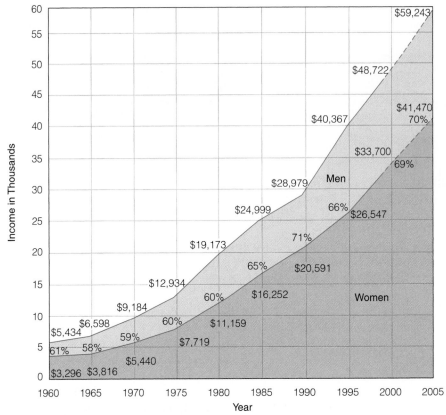

FIGURE 7.3 What Percentage of Men's Income Do Women Earn? The Gender Gap Over Time. (Source: James M. Henslin, *Sociology*, 5th ed.).

Note: The income jump from 1990 to 1995 is probably due to a statistical procedure. The 1995 source (for 1990 income) uses "median income," while the 1997 source (for 1995 income) merely says "average earnings." How the "average" is computed is not stated. For a review of this distinction, see Table 5.2. Broken lines indicate the author's estimates.

	1970		2000	
	MEN	**WOMEN**	**MEN**	**WOMEN**
Estimated life expectancy	67.1	74.1	74.24	79.9
% high school graduates	53	52	87	88
% of BAs awarded	57	43	45	55
% of MAs awarded	60	40	45	55
% of PhDs awarded	87	13	61	39
% in legal profession	95	5	70	30
Median earnings	$26,760	$14,232	$35,345	$25,862
Single parents	1.2 million	5.6 million	n/a	n/a

FIGURE 7.4 Men and Women in a Changing Society. (Sources: for 1970: *1996 Statistical Abstract*, U.S. Dept. of Commerce, Economics and Statistics Administration, Bureau of the census. 2000 data: National Center for Education Statistics http://nces.ed.gov/fastfacts).

6. Study color plates 5 and 6 and answer the following questions for each one.

    a. What does each photo show us? What details make each one dramatic?
    b. Both photos appeared in a sociology textbook. What message does each one send to viewers? Why would a sociologist select them for a college text?

THE USES OF AUTHORITY AND STATISTICS

Most of the visuals you have just studied provide a way of presenting statistics—data that many today consider essential to defending a claim. One reason you check the source information accompanying graphics is that you need to know—and evaluate—the authority of that source. When a graphic's numbers have come from the Census Bureau, you know you have a reliable source. When the author writes that "studies have shown . . . ," you want immediately to become suspicious of the authority of the data. All elements of the arguments we read—and write—need to be evaluated. They all contribute to the writer's credibility, or lack thereof.

Judging Authorities

We all know that movie stars and sports figures are not authorities on cereals and soft drinks. But what about *real* authorities? When writers present the opinions or research findings of authorities as support for a claim, they are saying to readers

Photo courtesy: Charles Moore /Black Star

that the authority is trustworthy and the opinions valuable. But what they are asserting is actually an assumption or warrant, part of the glue connecting evidence to claim. Remember: warrants can be challenged. If the "authority" can be shown to lack authority, then the logic of the argument is destroyed. Use this checklist of questions to aid your evaluation of authorities.

☐ *Is the authority actually an authority on the topic under discussion?* When a famous scientist supports a candidate for office, he or she speaks as a citizen, not as an authority.

☐ *Is the work of the authority still current?* Times change; expertise does not always endure. Galileo would be lost in the universe of today's astrophysicists. Be particularly alert to the dates of information in the sciences in general, in genetics and the entire biomedical field, in health and nutrition. It is almost impossible to keep up with the latest findings in these areas of research.

☐ *Does the authority actually have legitimate credentials?* Are the person's publications in respected journals? Is he or she respected by others in the same field? *Just because it's in print does not mean it's a reliable source!*

☐ *Do experts in the field generally agree on the issue?* If there is widespread disagreement, then referring to one authority does not do much to support a claim. This is why you need to understand the many sides of a controversial topic before you write on it, and you need to bring knowledge of controversies and critical thinking skills to your reading of argument. This is also why writers often provide a source's credentials, not just a name, unless the authority is quite famous.

☐ *Is the authority's evidence reliable, so far as you can judge, but the interpretation of that evidence seems odd, or seems to be used to support strongly held beliefs?* Does the evidence actually connect to the claim? A respected authority's work can be stretched or manipulated in an attempt to support a claim that the authority's work simply does not support.

EXERCISES: Judging Authorities

1. Jane Goodall has received worldwide fame for her studies of chimpanzees in Gombe and for her books on those field studies. Goodall is a vegetarian. Should she be used as an authority in support of a claim for a vegetarian diet? Why or why not? Consider:
    a. Why might Goodall have chosen to become a vegetarian?
    b. For what arguments might Goodall be used as an authority?
    c. For what arguments might she be used effectively for emotional appeal?
2. Suppose a respected zoologist prepares a five-year study of U.S. zoos, compiling a complete list of all animals at each zoo. He then updates the list for each of the five years, adding births and deaths. When he examines his data, he finds that deaths are one and one-half times the number of births. He considers this loss alarming and writes a paper arguing for the abolishing of zoos on the grounds

that too many animals are dying. Because of his reputation, his article is published in a popular science magazine. How would you evaluate his authority and his study?

a. Should you trust the data? Why or why not?
b. Should you accept his conclusions? Why or why not?
c. Consider: What might be possible explanations for the birth/death ratio?

Understanding and Evaluating Statistics

There are two useful clichés to keep in mind: "Statistics don't lie, but people lie with statistics" and "There are lies, damned lies, and statistics." The second cliché is perhaps a bit cynical. We don't want to be naïve in our faith in numbers, but neither do we want to become so cynical that we refuse to believe any statistical evidence. What we do need to keep in mind is that when statistics are presented in an argument they are being used by someone interested in winning that argument.

Some writers use numbers without being aware that the numbers are incomplete or not representative. Some present only part of the relevant information. Some may not mean to distort, but they do choose to present the information in language that helps their cause. There are many ways, some more innocent than others, to distort reality with statistics. Use the following guidelines to evaluate the presentation of statistical information.

GUIDELINES for Evaluating Statistics

Make yourself aware of the ways data can be misleading in both the arguments you read and those you write by examining these questions.

1. **Is the information current and therefore still relevant?** Crime rates in your city based on 1990 census data probably are no longer relevant, certainly not current enough to support an argument for increased (or decreased) police-department spending.

2. **If a sample was used, was it randomly selected and large enough to be significant?** Sometimes in medical research, the results of a small study are publicized to guide researchers to important new areas of study. When these results are reported in the press or on TV, however, the small size of the study is not always made clear. Thus one week we learn that coffee is bad for us, the next week that it is okay.

3. **What information, exactly, has been provided?** When you read "Two out of three chose the Merit combination of low tar and good taste," you must ask yourself "Two-thirds of how many altogether?"

4. **How have the numbers been presented?** And what is the effect of that presentation? Numbers can be presented as fractions, whole numbers, or percentages. Writers who want to emphasize budget increases will use whole numbers—billions of dollars. Writers who want to de-emphasize

those increases select percentages. Writers who want their readers to respond to the numbers in a specific way add words to direct their thinking: "*a mere* 3 percent increase" or "the *enormous* $5 billion increase."

EXERCISES: Reading Tables and Charts and Using Statistics

1. Figure 7.5, a table from the *Statistical Abstract of the United States, 2002,* shows U.S. family income data from 1980 to 2000. Percentages and median income are given for all families and then, in turn, for white, black, and Hispanic families. Study the data and then complete the exercises that follow.
   a. In a paper assessing the advantages of a growing economy, you want to include a paragraph on family income growth to show that a booming economy helps everyone, that "a rising tide lifts all boats." Select data from the table that best support your claim. Write a paragraph beginning with a topic sentence and including your data as support. Think about how to present the numbers in the most persuasive form.
   b. Write a second paragraph with the following topic sentence: "Not all Americans have benefited from the boom years" or "a rising tide does not lift all boats." Select data from the table that best support this topic sentence and present the numbers in the most persuasive form.
   c. Exchange paragraphs with a classmate and evaluate each other's selection and presentation of evidence.
2. Go back to Figure 7.1 (p. 187) and reflect again on the information that it depicts. Then consider what conclusions can be drawn from the evidence and what the implications of those conclusions are. Working in small groups or with a class partner, decide how you want to use the data to support a point.
3. Figure 7.6, another table from the *Statistical Abstract,* presents mean earnings by degree earned. First, be sure that you know the difference between mean and median (used in Figure 7.5). Study the data and reflect on the conclusions you can draw from the statistics. Consider: Of the various groups represented, which group most benefits from obtaining a college degree—as opposed to having only a high school diploma?

RESPONDING TO VISUAL ARGUMENTS

Many arguments bombard us today in visual forms. Two such visual arguments are political cartoons and advertising. Most major newspapers have a political cartoonist whose drawings appear regularly on the editorial page. (Some comic strips are also political in nature, at least some of the time.) These cartoons are designed to make a political point in a visually clever and amusing way. (That is why they are both "cartoons" and "political" at the same time.) Their uses of irony and caricatures of known politicians make them among the most emotionally powerful, indeed stinging, of arguments.

YEAR	NUMBER OF HOUSE-HOLDS (1,000)	PERCENT DISTRIBUTION							MEDIAN INCOME (DOLLARS)
		UNDER $15,000	$15,000-$24,999	$25,000-$34,999	$35,000-$49,999	$50,000-$74,999	$75,000-$99,999	$100,000 AND OVER	
ALL HOUSEHOLDS[1]									
1980	82,368	20.2	15.5	14.0	18.9	18.7	7.5	5.2	35,238
1985	88,458	19.6	15.1	13.7	17.7	18.3	8.7	6.8	36,246
1990	94,312	18.4	14.1	13.7	17.2	18.8	9.1	8.7	38,446
1995	99,627	18.3	14.9	13.1	16.4	18.3	9.4	9.6	38,262
1998	103,874	17.1	13.4	13.1	15.5	18.8	10.2	12.0	41,032
1999	104,705	16.0	13.8	12.4	15.8	18.5	10.5	13.2	42,187
2000	106,418	16.0	13.4	12.5	15.5	18.9	10.4	13.4	42,151
WHITE									
1970	57,575	19.4	14.6	16.3	21.8	18.5	5.8	3.7	35,148
1980	71,872	18.1	15.1	14.1	19.5	19.7	8.0	5.6	37,176
1985	76,576	17.6	14.7	13.8	18.2	19.2	9.2	7.4	38,226
1990	80,968	16.0	13.9	13.8	17.6	19.6	9.6	9.3	40,100
1995	84,511	16.4	14.6	13.0	16.7	19.1	9.8	10.4	40,159
1998	87,212	15.2	13.0	13.0	15.7	19.6	10.7	12.9	43,171
1999	87,671	14.2	13.6	12.2	16.0	19.1	11.1	13.8	43,932
2000	88,543	14.4	13.0	12.6	15.4	19.4	11.0	14.2	44,232
BLACK									
1980	8,847	37.6	18.9	13.7	14.4	10.7	3.4	1.3	21,418
1985	9,797	35.9	18.7	13.4	14.1	11.4	4.5	1.9	22,742
1990	10,671	35.4	15.8	13.7	14.6	12.7	4.7	3.1	23,979
1995	11,577	32.3	17.8	13.8	14.5	12.4	6.0	3.1	25,144
1998	12,579	30.5	17.0	13.6	14.5	13.4	6.1	4.9	26,751
1999	12,849	28.1	15.9	13.8	14.6	14.4	6.6	6.7	28,848
2000	13,355	26.0	16.5	12.9	16.8	15.2	6.5	6.1	30,436
HISPANIC[2]									
1980	3,906	26.2	20.1	16.2	17.0	14.0	4.2	2.2	27,161
1985	5,213	28.1	18.8	15.4	16.8	13.1	5.3	2.5	26,803
1990	6,220	26.1	18.2	15.7	16.9	14.1	5.2	3.8	28,671
1995	7,939	28.9	20.3	14.9	14.5	13.1	4.6	3.8	25,668
1998	9,060	24.7	17.1	16.3	15.7	14.6	6.0	5.6	29,894
1999	9,319	21.1	18.4	15.5	16.8	15.1	7.3	5.8	31,761
2000	9,663	18.9	18.3	14.7	17.7	17.4	7.4	5.8	33,455

[1]Includes other races not shown separately.
[2]Persons of Hispanic origin may be of any race.

FIGURE 7.5 Money Income of Households—Percent Distribution by Income Level, Race, and Hispanic Origin, in Constant (2000) Dollars: 1980 to 2000. (Source: U.S. Census Bureau. Statistical Abstract of the United States, 2002).

FIGURE 7.6 Mean Earnings by Highest Degree Earned: 1999. In dollars. For persons 18 years old and over with earnings. Persons as of March the following year. (Source: U.S. Census Bureau. Statistical Abstract of the United States, 2002).

CHARACTERISTIC	TOTAL PERSONS	NOT A HIGH SCHOOL GRADUATE	HIGH SCHOOL GRADUATE ONLY	SOME COLLEGE, NO DEGREE	ASSO-CIATE'S	BACHE-LOR'S	MASTER'S	PROFES-SIONAL	DOCTORATE
All persons[1]	32,356	16,121	24,572	26,958	32,152	45,678	55,641	100,987	86,833
Age:									
25 to 34 years old	29,901	16,916	24,040	26,914	28,088	39,768	46,768	58,043	60,852
35 to 44 years old	36,900	18,894	27,444	34,219	35,370	50,153	56,816	100,240	94,936
45 to 54 years old	41,465	19,707	28,883	36,935	37,508	54,922	62,158	116,327	87,659
55 to 64 years old	38,577	22,212	27,558	32,240	35,703	50,141	57,580	132,326	97,214
65 years old and over	24,263	12,121	18,704	19,052	17,609	30,624	35,639	104,055	78,333
Sex:									
Male	40,257	18,855	30,414	33,614	40,047	57,706	68,367	120,352	97,357
Female	23,551	12,145	18,092	20,241	25,079	32,546	42,378	59,792	61,136
White	33,326	16,623	25,270	27,674	32,686	46,894	55,622	103,450	87,746
Male	41,598	19,320	31,279	34,825	41,010	59,606	68,831	123,086	97,076
Female	23,756	12,405	18,381	20,188	24,928	32,507	41,845	57,314	64,080
Black	24,979	13,569	20,991	24,101	28,772	37,422	48,777	75,509	(B)
Male	28,821	16,391	25,849	27,538	31,885	42,530	54,642	(B)	(B)
Female	21,694	10,734	16,506	21,355	26,787	33,184	44,761	(B)	(B)
Hispanic[2]	22,096	16,106	20,704	23,115	29,329	36,212	50,576	64,029	(B)
Male	24,970	18,020	23,736	27,288	36,740	42,733	60,013	(B)	(B)
Female	18,187	12,684	16,653	18,782	22,695	29,249	41,118	(B)	(B)

B Base figure too small to meet statistical standards for reliability of a derived figure.

[1]Include other races, not shown separately.

[2]Persons of Hispanic origin may be of any race.

Advertisements are among the most creative and powerful forms of argument today. Remember that ads are designed to take your time (for shopping) and your money. Their messages need to be powerful to motivate you to action. With some products (what most of us consider necessities), ads are designed to influence product choice, to get us to buy Brand A instead of Brand B. With other products, ones we really do not need or which may actually be harmful to us, ads need to be especially clever. Some ads do provide some information (car X gets better gas mileage than car Y). Other ads (perfume ads, for example) take us into a fantasy land so that we will spend $50 on a small but pretty bottle. Another type of ad is the "image advertisement," an ad that assures us that a particular company is top-notch. If we admire the company, we will buy its goods or services.

Here are guidelines for reading visual arguments with insight. You can practice these steps with the exercises that follow.

GUIDELINES for Reading Political Cartoons

1. **What scene is depicted?** Identify the situation.
2. **Identify each of the figures in the cartoon.** Are they current politicians, figures from history or literature, the "person in the street," or symbolic representations?
3. **Who speaks the lines in the cartoon?**
4. **What is the cartoon's general subject?** What is the point of the cartoon, the claim of the cartoonist?

GUIDELINES for Reading Advertisements

1. **What product or service is being advertised?**
2. **Who seems to be the targeted audience?**
3. **What is the ad's primary strategy?** To provide information? To reinforce the product's or company's image? To appeal to particular needs or desires? (For example, if an ad shows a group of young people having fun and drinking a particular beer, to what needs/desires is the ad appealing?)
4. **Does the ad use specific rhetorical strategies such as humor, understatement, or irony?**
5. **What is the relation between the visual part of the ad (photo, drawing, typeface, etc.) and the print part (the text, or copy)?** Does the ad use a slogan or catchy phrase? Is there a company logo? Is the slogan or logo clever? Is it well known as a marker of the company? What may be the effect of these strategies on readers?
6. **What is the ad's overall visual impression?** (Consider both images and colors used.)

EXERCISES: Analyzing Cartoons and Ads

1. Analyze the cartoons on pages 198–99 and in the color insert (pp. 4 and 5), using the guidelines listed previously. You may want to jot down your answers to the questions to be well prepared for class discussion.

2. Analyze the ads on pages 200–201 and in the color insert (pp. 6, 7, and 8), again using the guidelines listed previously. After answering the questions listed with the guidelines, consider these as well: Will each ad appeal effectively to its intended audience? If so, why? If not, why not?

(Photo courtesy: Dana Summers/© Tribune Media Services, Inc. All rights Reserved. Reprinted with permission.)

WRITING THE INVESTIGATIVE PAPER

The first step in writing an investigative argument is, of course, to select a topic to study. Composition students, even if not highly skilled in research procedures, can write successful investigative essays on the media, on campus issues, or on various local concerns. Although you begin with a topic—not a claim—since you have to gather evidence before you can see what it means, you should select a topic that holds your interest and that you may have given some thought to before choosing to write. For example, you may have noticed some clever ads for jeans or beer, or perhaps you are bothered by plans for another shopping area along a major street near your home. Either one of these topics can lead to an effective investigative, or inductive, argument.

Gathering and Analyzing Evidence

Let's reflect on strategies you will need to use to gather evidence for a study of magazine ads for a particular kind of product (the topic of the sample student paper that follows).

- Select a time frame and a number of representative magazines.
- Have enough magazines to render at least 25 ads on the product you are studying.
- Once you decide on the magazines and issues to be used, pull *all* ads for your product. Your task is to draw useful conclusions based on adequate data objectively collected. You can't leave some ads out and have a valid study.

THEY'D RATHER BE IN COLORADO.

Taking the same dull vacation can start eating away at you after a while. So why not try Colorado?
The mountains. The magic. The plains. The people. The history. The culture. The fun. The sheer
exhilaration of something new. Something you can't experience anywhere else.
Call us or give our Web site a nibble.

COLORADO
1-800-COLORADO · WWW.COLORADO.COM

Courtesy of the National Federation of Coffee Growers of Columbia

- Study the ads, reflecting on the inferences they allow you to draw. The inferences become the claim of your argument. You may want to take the approach of classifying the ads, that is, grouping them into categories by the various appeals used to sell the product.

More briefly, consider your hunch that your area does not need another shopping mall. What evidence can you gather to support a claim to that effect? You could locate all existing strip or enclosed malls within a 10-mile radius of the proposed new mall site, visit each one, and count the number and types of stores already available. You may discover that there are plenty of malls, but that the area really needs a grocery store or a bookstore. So instead of reading to find evidence to support a claim, you are creating the statistics and doing the analysis to guide you to a claim. Just remember to devise objective procedures for collecting evidence so that you do not bias your results.

Planning and Drafting the Essay

You've done your research and studied the data you've collected; how do you put this kind of argument together? Here are some guidelines to help you draft your essay.

GUIDELINES for Writing an Investigative Argument

1. **Begin with an opening paragraph that introduces your topic in an interesting way.** Possibilities include beginning with a startling statistic or explaining what impact the essay's facts will have on readers.

2. **Devote space early in your paper to explaining your methods or procedures, probably in your second or third paragraph.** For example, if you have obtained information through questionnaires or interviews, recount the process: the questions asked, the number of people involved, the basis for selecting the people, and so on.

3. **Classify the evidence that you present.** Finding a meaningful organization is part of the originality of your study and will make your argument more forceful. It is the way you see the topic and want readers to see it. If you are studying existing malls, you might begin by listing all of the malls and their locations. But then do not go store by store through each mall. Rather, group the stores by type and provide totals.

4. **Consider presenting evidence in several ways, including in charts and tables as well as within paragraphs.** Readers are used to visuals, especially in essays containing statistics.

5. **Analyze evidence to build your argument.** Do not ask your reader to do the thinking that is your job. No data dumps! Explain how your evidence *is* evidence by discussing the connection between facts and the inferences they support.

Analyzing Evidence: The Key to an Effective Argument

This is the thinking part of the process. Anyone can count stores or collect ads. What is your point? How does the evidence you have collected actually support your claim? You must take your readers by the hand and guide them through the evidence. Consider this example:

In a study of selling techniques used in computer ads in business magazines, a student, Brian, found four major selling techniques, one of which he classifies as "corporate emphasis." Brian begins his paragraph on corporate emphasis thus:

> In the technique of corporate emphasis, the advertiser discusses the whole range of products and services that the corporation offers, instead of specific elements. This method relies on the public's positive perception of the company, the company's accomplishments, and its reputation.

Brian then provides several examples of ads in this category, including an IBM ad:

> In one of its eight ads in the study, IBM points to the scientists on its staff who have recently won the Nobel Prize in physics.

But Brian does not stop there. He explains the point of this ad, connecting the ad to the assertion that this technique emphasizes the company's accomplishments:

> The inference we are to draw is that IBM scientists are hard at work right now in their laboratories developing tomorrow's technology to make the world a better place in which to live.

Preparing Graphics

Tables, bar charts, and pie charts are particularly helpful ways to present statistical evidence you have collected for an inductive argument. The sample student paper that follows contains two graphics, one a list of the magazines used in the study of advertising, the second a chart showing the percentage of ads for computer technology found in each of the magazines used. Another possibility: a pie chart showing your classification of ads (or stores or questions on a questionnaire) and the relative amount of each item. For example, suppose you find four selling strategies. You can show in a pie chart the percentage of ads using each of the four strategies.

Today's computers help even the technically unsophisticated prepare simple charts, but even if that seems beyond your skill level, you can always do a simple table. When preparing graphics, keep these points in mind:

- Every graphic must be referred to in the text at the appropriate place—where you are discussing the information in the visual. Graphics are not disconnected attachments to an argument. They give a complete set of data in an easy-to-digest form, but some of that data you must discuss in the essay itself.
- Every graphic (except photographs) needs a label. Use Figure 1, Figure 2, and so forth. Then refer to each graphic by its label.
- Every graphic needs a title. Always place a title after Figure 1 (and so forth), on the same line, at the top of your visual.
- In today's technically sophisticated world, hand-drawn graphics are not acceptable. Underline the graphics' title line, or place the visual within a box. (Check the tool bar at the top of your screen.) Type elements within tables.

Use a ruler or compass to prepare graphics, or learn to use the graphics programs in your computer.

A CHECKLIST FOR REVISION

☐ Have I stated a claim that is precise and appropriate to the data I have collected?

☐ Have I fully explained the methodology I used in collecting my data?

☐ Have I selected a clear and useful organization?

☐ Have I presented and discussed enough specifics to show readers how my data support my conclusions?

☐ Have I used graphics to present the data in an effective summary form?

☐ Have I revised, edited, and proofread my paper?

STUDENT ESSAY

MAGAZINE ADVERTISING FOR COMPUTER PRODUCTS

Monica Becker

Introduction

Subheadings are used to show parts of the study.

The tactics used for advertising computer technology products in popular magazines include the usual strategies of advertising such as the inclusion, placement, and design of ads, as well as more specific tactics intended to target consumers based upon their demographics and psychological profiles. The increasing use of computer technology in all contexts—home, family, education, and business—results in a larger and increasingly diverse target audience for product promotion. Ad specialization, targeting different types of computer users, is becoming a requirement for effective marketing. These realities are reflected in the ads sampled for this study.

Methodology

Student explains process of selecting ads for the study.

The 13 magazines listed in Figure 1 were selected for this study based upon their collective ability to represent a diverse sampling of target audiences. To qualify for inclusion in the study, an advertisement must be for a computer hardware or software product. If an advertisement combined a computer technology product

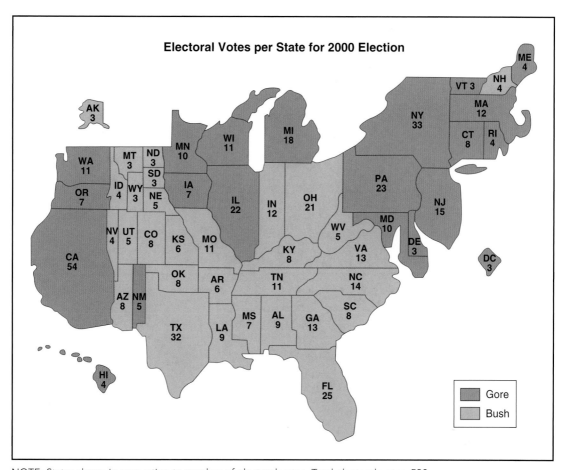

Electoral Votes per State for 2000 Election

Legend: Gore / Bush

NOTE: States drawn in proportion to number of electoral votes. Total electoral votes: 538

[Source: THE NEW YORK TIMES NATIONAL SUNDAY, November 5, 2000. Reprinted by permission of NYT Graphics. From O'Connor and Sabato, American Government, © 2002; published by Allyn and Bacon, Boston, MA. Copyright © 2002 by Pearson Education]

[Source: PhotoEdit]

[Source: Michael Newman/PhotoEdit]

3

[Courtesy Dana Summers/Tribune Media Services, Inc. All rights reserved. Reprinted with permission.]

[DILBERT Reprinted by Permission of United Feature Syndicate INC.]

[HP FTD/Creative i]

[Courtesy of Expedia.com]

PIERCE BROSNAN'S CHOICE

SEAMASTER AQUA TERRA
Co-Axial Escapement
3 year extended warrenty

The name Omega has always been closely associated with quality and reliability. The Seamaster Aqua Terra upholds this pioneering spirit. Its classic design houses the latest in watchmaking technology: the unique Co-Axial Escapement movement, which offers unrivalled long-term accuracy.

Ω
OMEGA

www.omegawatches.com

with another product—for instance, a shared ad for Canon printers and photocopiers— the advertisement was excluded from the sample. Only full-page and multiple full-page display ads were included; half-page, quarter-page, and sidebar-styled ads were omitted from this evaluation. Advertising supplements designed to look like articles, booklet-style, perforated tear-out formats and any ads not included in a magazine's continuous paging were disregarded. Of the selected publications that are released monthly, all are from the month of October 1997. Those publications included in the sample that are published on a weekly basis were selected from a date as close to the middle of October 1997 as possible.

FIGURE 1   PUBLICATIONS INCLUDED IN SAMPLE

Publication	Publication Date
Atlantic Monthly	October 1997
Business Week	October 13, 1997
Forbes	October 6, 1997
GQ	October 1997
Harper's Magazine	October 1997
Mother Jones	October 1997
Newsweek	October 13, 1997
Out	October 1997
Parents	October 1997
Self	October 1997
Time	October 13, 1997
Vanity Fair	October 1997
Working Woman	October 1997

The Strategies

Inclusion within Publications

The most obvious strategy for advertising computer technology products is the decision to place an ad within a publication at all. In Harper's and Mother Jones one finds no ads for hardware or software. These highly intellectual publications, with their socially focused content, do not provide an obvious forum for targeting consumers of computer products. On the other end of the

Student presents
information visually
as well as in
words.

spectrum, businesspeople are likely candidates for purchasing these products; the computer advertising in Business Week, Working Woman, Time, Forbes, and Newsweek comprises between 10 and 25 percent of their total advertising content. (See Figure 2.) The increasing popularity of the Internet as an entertainment medium, new user-friendly operating systems such as Microsoft's Windows95, and the emergence of a younger, more computer-savvy generation to a position of purchasing power have increased the incidence of computer-related advertising in non-business publications. Vanity Fair and Gentlemen's Quarterly, the advertising content of which are typically almost exclusively in fashion merchandise, are beginning to run computer ads. Parents, Out, and Self, which target the parents of young children, the gay community, and young athletic females, respectively, all contain some computer advertising.

Layout

Most advertisements in the sample used conventional full-page bleed and two-page spread formats. Each format has its advantages: the full-page bleed is more affordable and allows the ad to be featured next to articles or other content of interest to the reader, whereas a two-page spread dominates the open-magazine landscape, providing significant impact upon the consumer. The main disadvantage of the two-page spread is the tendency of readers to flip past the ad while in search of reading material; the spread format also isolates the ad from the content of the publication. In response to this "flipping by" tendency, Microsoft has used a novel layout strategy in Time. On pages 55 and 57, an ad for Internet Explorer is staggered in the midst of an article. Page 55, featuring only a picture of a computer and the word "Internet," reveals little about the nature of the product, but its striking graphics are likely to command the reader's attention. Page 57 offers closure to this curiosity by adding copy to clarify the ad's purpose. In Business Week a similar tactic is used for IBM's RS/6000 Supercomputer, except that each of these staggered pages could conceivably stand alone as single-page ads.

FIGURE 2.   Percentage of advertisements for computer technology products in sampled publications

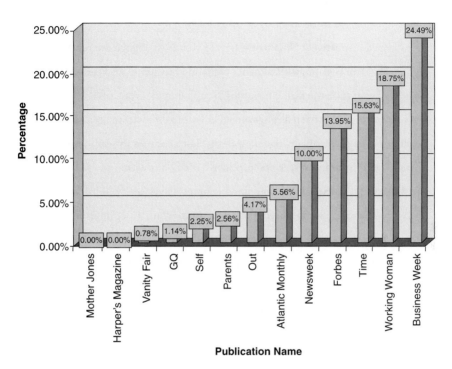

Placement within Publication

Two companies took advantage of outside back-cover placement for their advertisements. Intel placed their Pentium II Processor ads on the back covers of Self and Vanity Fair, and Apple Computer was featured on the back of Business Week. Back-cover placement is costly but effective in that it forces product exposure on the reader, even when the magazine is closed. Intel's purchase of back-cover space in Self and Vanity Fair was likely based on the assumption that a young, computer-smart readership is beginning to purchase these magazines. Technology advertising in health and fashion publications was previously rare or non-existent; the inclusion of these ads for a central processing unit—a rather technical component—is testament to the changing profile of today's computer consumer.

Microsoft, IBM, and Compaq all took advantage of a similar strategy—inside-cover placement. These two-page spreads impact the reader immediately after opening the front cover of October's Time, Business Week, and Newsweek, respectively. This costly strategy tends to engage the reader more effectively than two-page placements embedded within a publication; most readers begin their magazine browsing by opening the front cover.

Ad placement within a magazine in close proximity to related features or columns is an effective arrangement designed to capture the attention of readers with prior interest in the product. Several ads within the sample appeared in locations rich with related content. Newsweek published an article on Esther Dyson, chairwoman of the Electronic Frontier Foundation and a computer expert, activist, writer, and speaker. The article's layout was interrupted by a two-page advertisement for Sony's VAIO line of computers and peripherals. At the closing of the Dyson feature, an ad for Micron Electronics' PC systems appears on the facing page. The regular "Technology" component in Forbes, featuring an article on collaborative software, was appropriately followed by a two-page ad for Silicon Graphics. Also embedded in the Forbes "Technology" section was a two-page spread for Compaq products. Even Parents magazine placed their ad for Gateway2000 following their "Learning" section that contained an article entitled "Essential Software." In The Atlantic Monthly, between pages of the "Near Myth of Our Failing Schools" piece, IBM purchased advertising space for their CD-ROM release of the 1998 World Book Encyclopedia. The ad features photographs of teenagers and the caption "At least now they have a reason to think they know everything." This is a strategic placement that relates to the educational theme of the surrounding article.

Demographics and Psychological Profiles

One realizes that Bill Gates's vision of a "computer on every desk and in every home" is coming true when Parents has determined that computers have become like any other appliance we have in our homes and that the time is right for developing and promoting an Internet site to complement their magazine. Self, Conde Nast's fashion and fitness magazine, targeted at young career women, is also promoting a World Wide Web site, "Phys.com," which complements all of their women's magazines.

Gender-specific tactics in computer advertising are clearly displayed in Working Woman, a magazine devoted to the office experiences of career women. In the October issue, four out of five computer ads featured female models using the products. IBM ran an ad for their Thinkpad line of notebook computers featuring a profile of a successful business woman. The copy begins: "You're a woman. Hispanic. In L.A. And you want to start your own business. Not just any business. A construction business." This strategy is engineered to appeal to women who may still feel outnumbered or disenfranchised in the business world.

Despite—or perhaps because of—changing family roles, companies like Microcom are running copy like that seen in Working Woman: "Finally, a way to spend more time with what's-his-name and the kids." This ad shows family photographs—a husband, children, and family pets—displayed in frames on a desk. The other sampled business magazines did not have a male equivalent to this family-oriented approach. The approach used in Time for Microsoft Office is similar: a businessman is exiting an elevator next to the words, "You could work a twelve-hour day. Why not just do it in eight?" This tactic plays on the motivation to leave work early, but unlike the Microcom ad, it does not introduce family into the theme.

IBM displays a photograph of a baby with the words, "Protects coastlines, ozone levels, blood cells and future generations," in their campaign for the RS/6000 Supercomputer. Their promotion for the "Reinventing Education" program warms us with a photograph of a school teacher "putting names to faces." An NEC ad from Business Week displays the caption, "Perhaps the first instance where computers are being replaced by people." And Compaq tells us that "Something incredible happens when you give people the power to succeed. They succeed." These ads are designed to humanize computers and the companies that manufacture them by taking the focus away from business and placing it on social issues, or by emphasizing people rather than machines.

As with all products, humor is a particularly effective sales tool. Micron uses humor in their ClientPro MRE ad by showing a depressed looking executive begging for change on a park bench. He *didn't* use their products. Sony, showing a baby suspended atop a man's muscular arm, tells us to "Send a crying baby 3,000 miles in under 2 minutes." When shock of this statement wears off, we realize that we can transmit images over long distances by using their VAIO notebooks and peripherals.

The desire to be different is exploited in Lotus's ad for Domino web server software with its rebellious twist on a familiar quotation, "The great invisible guiding hand of capitalism has just smacked the Internet upside the head—now what?" Apple Computer is even more forceful with this tactic in Business Week, accompanying their photograph of Thomas Edison with two words: "Think different."

Conclusion

Student concludes with a reminder of the ever expanding role of technology in our lives.

The strategies used to promote computer technology in popular magazines are as diverse as the uses we find for this technology in our lives. The advent of digital cameras, computerized entertainment equipment, increasingly affordable home office equipment, improved multimedia and the popularization of the Internet will continue to enrich our computing experiences at home, on the job, and in education. As computer products become more affordable and easy to operate, the base of technology consumers will grow and diversify. Ultimately this will result in more innovative and diverse advertising, and perhaps new and exciting promotional strategies that will demand our future study and analysis.

FOR READING AND ANALYSIS

THE GREATNESS GAP | CHARLES KRAUTHAMMER

A graduate of Harvard Medical School and board certified in psychiatry, Charles Krauthammer (b. 1950) is a syndicated columnist and a regular on the political talk show *Inside Washington*. He has won a Pulitzer Prize for political commentary. The following column appeared in *Time* magazine on July 1, 2002.

PREREADING QUESTIONS   What does Krauthammer mean by the greatness gap? Who would you list as among the world's greatest athletes?

There is excellence, and there is greatness—cosmic, transcendent, Einsteinian. We know it when we see it, we think. But how to measure it? Among Tiger Woods' varied contributions to contemporary American life is that he shows us how. 1

As just demonstrated yet again at the U.S. Open, Woods is the greatest golfer who ever lived. How do we know? You could try Method 1: Compare him directly with the former greatest golfer, Jack Nicklaus. For example, take their total scores in their first 22 major championships (of which Nicklaus won seven, Woods eight). Nicklaus was 40 strokes over par; Tiger was 81 under—an astonishing 121 strokes better. 2

But that is not the right way to compare. You cannot compare greatness directly across the ages. There are so many intervening variables: changes in technology, training, terrain, equipment, often rules and customs. 3

How then do we determine who is greatest? Method 2: The Gap. Situate each among his contemporaries. Who towers? Who is, like the U.S. today, a hyperpower with no second in sight? 4

The mark of true transcendence is running alone. Nicklaus was great, but he ran with peers: Palmer, Player, Watson. Tiger has none. Of the past 11 majors, Woods has won seven. That means whenever and wherever the greatest players in the world gather, Woods wins twice and the third trophy is distributed among the next, oh, 150. 5

In 2000–01, Woods won four majors in a row. The *Washington Post*'s Thomas Boswell found that if you take these four and add the 2001 Players Championship (considered the next most important tournament), Tiger shot a cumulative 1,357 strokes—55 strokes better than the next guy. 6

To find true greatness, you must apply the "next guy" test. Then the clouds part and the deities appear. In 1921 Babe Ruth hit 59 home runs. The next four hit 24, 24, 23, and 23. Ruth alone hit more home runs than half the teams in the major leagues. 7

In the 1981–82 season, Wayne Gretzky scored 212 points. The next two guys scored 147 and 139. Not for nothing had he been known as the Great One—since age 9. 8

Gaps like these are rare as the gods that produce them. By 1968, no one had ever long-jumped more than 27 ft. 4¾ in. In the Mexico City Olympics that 9 year, Bob Beamon jumped 29 ft. 2½ in.—this in a sport in which records are broken by increments of a few inches, sometimes fractions. (Yes, the air is thin in Mexico City, but it was a legal jump and the record stood for an astonishing 23 years.)

10   In physics, a quantum leap means jumping to a higher level without ever stopping—indeed, without even traveling through—anywhere in between. In our ordinary understanding of things, that is impossible. In sports, it defines greatness.

11   Not only did Michael Jordan play a game of basketball so beautiful that it defied physics, but he racked up numbers that put him in a league of his own. Jordan has averaged 31 points a game, a huge gap over the (future) Hall of Famers he played against (e.g., Karl Malone, 25.7; Charles Barkley, 22.1).

12   The most striking visual representation of the Gap is the photograph of Secretariat crossing the finish line at the Belmont Stakes, 31(!) lengths ahead of the next horse. You can barely see the others—the fastest horses in the world, mind you—in the distance.

13   In 1971, Bobby Fischer played World Championship elimination rounds against the best players on the planet. These were open-ended matches that finished only when one player had won six games. Such matches could take months, because great chess masters are so evenly matched that 80% of tournament games end in draws. Victories come at rare intervals; six wins can take forever. Not this time. Fischer conducted a campaign unrivaled since Scipio Africanus leveled Carthage. He beat two challengers six games in a row, which combined with wins before and after, produced a streak of 20 straight victories against the very best—something never seen before and likely never to be seen again.

14   That's a Gap. To enter the pantheon—any pantheon—you've got to be so far above and beyond your contemporaries that it is said of you, as Jack Nicklaus once said of Tiger Woods, "He's playing a game I'm not familiar with."

15   The biologist and philosopher Lewis Thomas was asked what record of human achievements he would launch into space to be discovered one day by some transgalactic civilization. A continual broadcast of Bach would do, Thomas suggested, though "that would be boasting."

16   Why not make it a music video? A Bach fugue over Tiger hitting those miraculous irons from the deep rough onto the greens at Bethpage Black. Nah. The aliens will think we did it all with computer graphics.

QUESTIONS FOR READING

1. What, exactly, is Krauthammer's topic?
2. What is Method 1 for judging Tiger Woods's greatness? Why is it not a good method?
3. How is Method 2 applied?
4. Who are Krauthammer's greats, using Method 2?

QUESTIONS FOR REASONING AND ANALYSIS

1. What is the author's primary purpose in writing? To argue for Woods's greatness? Something else?

2. What is the claim of the argument?

3. When Krauthammer concludes that aliens would not believe a music video of a Bach fugue playing while Woods hits irons from the rough, what is his point? What writing strategy is he using? What makes this an effective conclusion?

4. Evaluate Krauthammer's argument. Has he defined and illustrated his Method 2 adequately? Does his evidence support his claim effectively? Why or why not?

QUESTIONS FOR REFLECTING AND WRITING

1. Which of Krauthammer's examples do you admire the most? Why? Select one and see what more you can learn about that person or horse. Write a one-page biography that focuses on the stats that support the "gap" concept.

2. Do you agree that the gap is the best way to define greatness in sports? Why? If you disagree, explain what other elements you would include to measure greatness. If you agree, think about other elements some would include and devise a way to challenge that counterargument.

WON'T YOU BE MY NEIGHBOR? | ANNETTE FUENTES

Currently an adjunct professor at the Columbia University School of Journalism, Annette Fuentes has worked as a reporter, editor, and columnist for various New York City newspapers. She has won several fellowships and awards and usually writes on health and social policy issues as a freelance journalist. She coauthored *Women in the Global Factory* (1983) with Barbara Ehrenreich. The following article was published in *American Demographics* in June 2000.

PREREADING QUESTIONS How have the words *neighborhood* and *community* changed meaning in our "digital age"? Do you think of your neighborhood as a community?

As technology continues to redefine how we live and where we can work,   1
what will this mean for our neighborhoods? The digital age has already transformed our homes, allowing many of us the flexibility to work in our pajamas, while forcing us to bequeath a section of our residence to office gear. Now it's about to change the definition of our neighborhoods and communities.

In some ways, it already has. Once, the words neighborhoods and communities were interchangeable. A community was defined by the bricks-and-mortar region a person chose to occupy. Increasingly, they are being defined separately: A neighborhood is a place where one lives, and a community is the social circle one chooses to inhabit.   2

Chat rooms, online communities, and message boards have allowed like-minded people to connect with one another in the same way neighborhoods   3 once did, argues futurist Ryan Mathews of FirstMatter LLC, a Westport, Connecticut, think tank. "Now you can live in one geographic area and have a community in multiple geographic areas," says Mathews. "And it's quite possible to not know your neighbors."

4   Yet, rather than eliminate the necessity of neighborhoods and communities, the tools of the New Economy may reinforce the need for both. Chat rooms, instant email, and international cell phones have broadened our sense of place—much the same way tools of the Old Economy (airplanes and automobiles) did years ago, by shortening the distances between places and people. And just as the Old Economy's inventions didn't eliminate the need for a sense of community, new technology isn't about to supersede that most human of desires, either. Says futurist Watts Blacker, also of FirstMatter: "The more ether-centric your life becomes, the more you'll want to be part of the physical community. You'll want it even more because it'll be even more apparent to you when it's not there."

5   As a result, communities with a growing number of at-home workers will generate services to supply their needs. People working at home, for example, will be more likely to want to get out of that home office to work out at a local health club than to have exercise equipment in a home gym. Without the social environment of an office workplace, home workers have a need to connect to other people in their neighborhoods, and that's where retailers can play a role, says M. Leanne Lachman, a principal at Lend Lease real estate investments in New York City. "What we may see evolve is more ordering online, but you have to go by Foot Locker to pick up your order, for example," she says. "That gets people out and about, collecting things."

6   That's just the beginning. Technology, combined with changes in demographics, will once again force us to redesign our physical neighborhoods. It took nearly five decades for Americans to become comfortable with the idea that we were moving away from cities, toward life centered in their suburban outer-rings. Now just as we have begun to accept the "burbs" as the predominate way to view communal life, rapid changes are transforming our ideas of both cities and suburbs—making them seem as outdated as an episode of *Leave it to Beaver.* Soon, our cities may look more like our suburbs and our suburbs may take on characteristics of our cities.

7   The two factors why: boomers and immigrants. We've heard time and again how these two demographic groups will reconstruct the face of America. By one estimate, immigrants and their kids will account for more than half of the 50 million people who will be added to the nation's population over the next 25 years. [See Figure 7.7.] Also within that quarter of a century, America's elderly population will rise by almost 80 percent on the strength of aging boomers, according to demographer William H. Frey of the Milken Institute. [See Figure 7.8.]

8   These population shifts are expected to have a profound impact on our sense of place. Some boomers are expected to seek out resort-like living accommodations in Sunbelt locations. Some may stay where they are. And others, particularly the younger and more affluent segment of the aging boomer

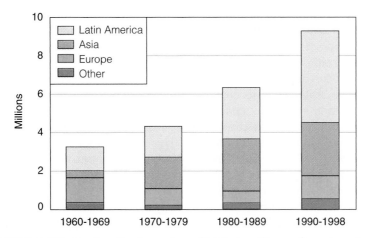

FIGURE 7.7 U.S. immigration by region of birth, in millions of immigrants, 1960s–1990s. (Source: Milken Institute).

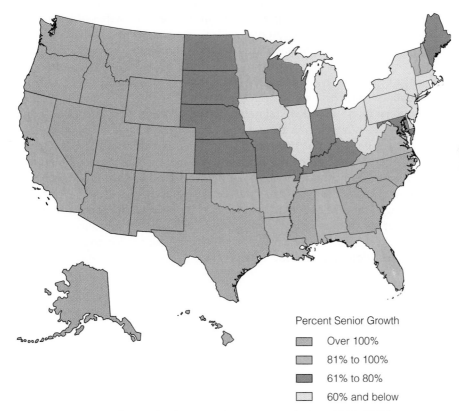

Percent Senior Growth

Over 100%

81% to 100%

61% to 80%

60% and below

FIGURE 7.8 Projected growth of America's senior population, 2000–2025.
(Source: Milken Institute).

population, will give cities an urban facelift. For certain older cities, this changing and evolving aesthetic will fuel astounding growth. A recent Brookings Institute Survey projects downtown residential populations will grow by at least 38 percent in 23 cities between 1998 and 2010.

9   As that shift drives up housing prices, it will force immigrants—folks who typically settle in states such as New York, California, and Texas—to head to the suburbs. In fact, immigrants have already begun to move further out into the greater metropolitan areas, breaking age-old housing patterns and bolstering areas that would otherwise face declining populations or zero-growth rates. From 1990 to 1997, about 3 million people moved into the suburbs. As in the past, young families in search of good schools and a patch of grass continued to lead the march to home ownership.

10   As new families have begun to settle into the older suburbs, the move has raised a host of questions. Across the country, formerly homogeneous and aging communities are suddenly forced to tackle issues ranging from a lack of childcare facilities to the need to support multilingual education in the schools. School districts in New York, California, Texas, and Florida, for example, will face huge teacher shortages over the next few years as the systems try to play catch-up with the shifting demographics. And businesses on suburban main streets are hustling to keep up with the different ethnic tastes of their new local customers. The consumer needs, tastes, and spending habits of new immigrant groups are often somewhat different from native-born groups. Hispanic households, for example, tend to spend more on food, utilities, and shelter, and less on services and healthcare than other demographic groups, even after adjusting for income and family size.

11   It's these types of individual needs that marketers will want to be mindful of over the next 25 years, as the nature of business changes substantively. Marketers have built stores on the assumption of a mobile population, but what do they do when a majority of the population becomes less mobile? Says Mathews: "Businesses in this country have evolved around the mall model: large box, multiple lines. But you can't move those businesses into the city. We've gone through this era of big-box retailing. If these affluent markets move back to the cities, all of these big-box businesses will have to regroup or cease being attractive to their core consumers." Unless they tailor their products to suite the new demands of their consumers.

QUESTIONS FOR READING

1. What is Fuentes's topic? What is her claim? (Is she making more than one point? Think about how you would word this.)
2. How has the "digital age" changed our homes and the way some of us work?
3. What is Fuentes's argument for asserting that the New Economy—and new living patterns—will not eliminate a desire for community?
4. In addition to the New Economy, what two other realities will change living patterns?
5. What changes in living patterns does Fuentes predict? Specifically, what will happen to cities? To older suburbs?

QUESTIONS FOR REASONING AND ANALYSIS

1. Study Figure 7.7. What information does it give you? What are the biggest changes in the sources of immigrants between 1960 and 1998?
2. What does the map in Figure 7.8 tell you? What will be some of the consequences for states with the greatest changes in numbers of seniors?
3. Fuentes does not suggest that all of her demographic predictions are bad news. What potential does she imply and do you see in these projected changes?

QUESTIONS FOR REFLECTING AND WRITING

1. In terms of future need, what kinds of careers would be good choices? If you were a counselor, how would you advise students with regard to job training or career tracks? Defend your position with information from Fuentes.
2. If you want to be a business person—an entrepreneur—what kinds of business opportunities would you seek? Defend your position with information from Fuentes.

SUGGESTIONS FOR DISCUSSION AND WRITING

For all investigative essays—inductive arguments—follow the guidelines in this chapter and use the student essay as your model. Remember that you will need to explain your methods for collecting data, to classify evidence and present it in several formats, and also to explain its significance for readers. Just collecting data does not create an argument. Here are some possible topics to explore:

1. Study print ads for one type of product (e.g., cars, cosmetics, cigarettes) to draw inferences about the dominant techniques used to sell that product. Remember that the more ads you study, the more support you have for your inferences. You should study at least 25 ads.

2. Study print ads for one type of product as advertised in different types of magazines clearly directed to different audiences to see how (or if) selling techniques change with a change in audience. (Remember: To demonstrate no change in techniques can be just as interesting a conclusion as finding changes.) Study at least 25 ads, in a balanced number from the different magazines.

3. Select a major figure currently in the news and conduct a study of bias in one of the news magazines (e.g., *Time, U.S. News & World Report,* or *Newsweek*) or a newspaper. Use at least eight issues of the magazine or newspaper from the last six months and study all articles on your figure in each of those issues. To determine bias, look at the amount of coverage, the location (front pages or back pages), the use of photos (flattering or unflattering), and the language of the articles.

4. Conduct a study of amounts of violence on TV by analyzing, for one week, all prime-time programs that may contain violence. (That is, eliminate sitcoms and decide whether you want to include or exclude news programs.) Devise some classification system for types of violence based on your prior TV viewing experience before beginning your study—but be prepared to alter or add to your categories based on your viewing of shows. Note the number of times each violent act occurs. You may want to consider the total length of time (per program, per night, per type of violent act) of violence during the week you study. Give credit to any authors in this text or other publications for any ideas you borrow from their articles.

5. As an alternative to topic 4, study the number and types of violent acts in children's programs on Saturday mornings. (This and topic 4 are best handled if you have access to a VCR so that you can tape and then replay the programs several times.)

6. Conduct a survey and analyze the results on some campus issue or current public policy issue. Prepare questions that are without bias and include questions to get information about the participants so that you can correlate answers with the demographics of your participants (e.g., age, gender, race, religion, proposed major in college, political affiliation, or whatever else you think is important to the topic studied). Decide whether you want to survey students only or both students and faculty. Plan how you are going to reach each group.

CHAPTER 8

Reading, Evaluating, and Writing Causal and Problem/Solution Arguments

In the last chapter of this section on argument, we examine two more types of arguments, types that can address both philosophical issues and also public policy debates. Arguments about cause and arguments that offer solutions to perceived problems demand our attention as readers and as writers.

ARGUMENTS ABOUT CAUSE

Because we want to know *why* things happen, arguments about cause abound. We want to understand past events (Why was President Kennedy assassinated?); we want to explain current situations (Why do some teens use drugs?); we want to predict the future (Will the economy improve if there is a tax cut?). All three questions ask for a causal explanation, including the last one. To answer the last question with a yes is to assert that a tax cut is a cause of economic improvement.

Characteristics of Causal Arguments

Assigning cause is tricky business. Perhaps that is the first and most important point to make about issues of causation. Here are some other points about causal arguments.

> *Causal arguments are similar in their purpose but can vary considerably in their subject matter and structure.* Some causal arguments are about a particular situation; others seek explanations for a general state of affairs. However, in either case there may be one or there may be several causes, as illustrated here:

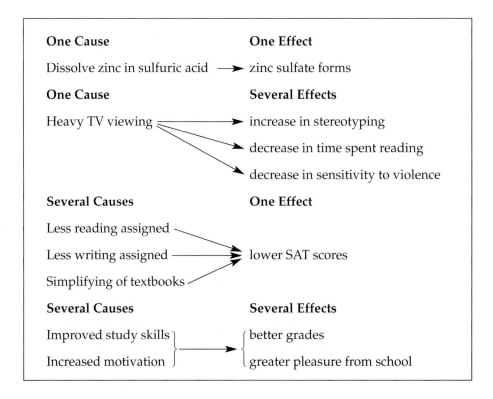

One Cause   **One Effect**

Dissolve zinc in sulfuric acid ——► zinc sulfate forms

One Cause   **Several Effects**

Heavy TV viewing ———► increase in stereotyping

——► decrease in time spent reading

——► decrease in sensitivity to violence

Several Causes   **One Effect**

Less reading assigned

Less writing assigned ———► lower SAT scores

Simplifying of textbooks

Several Causes   **Several Effects**

Improved study skills ⎫   ⎧ better grades

Increased motivation ⎭ ———► ⎨ greater pleasure from school

> *There are specific terms related to the discussion of causation that provide useful distinctions in our thinking about why something has happened (or not happened).* First, when looking for the cause of an event, we look for an *agent*—a person, a situation, another event that caused the event to take place. A lit cigarette dropped in a bed caused a house fire; the lit cigarette is the agent. But why, we ask, did someone drop a lit cigarette on a bed? The person, old and ill, took a sleeping pill and dropped the cigarette when he fell asleep. Where do we stop in this chain of causes? Second, we learn that most events do not occur in a vacuum with a single cause. There are *conditions* surrounding the event, making the assigning of only one cause often difficult. In our example, the man's age and health were conditions. Third, we can also speak of *influences.* The sleeping pill certainly influenced the man to drop the cigarette and cause the fire. Some conditions and influences may qualify as *remote causes. Proximate causes* are more immediate, usually closer in time to the event or situation. The man's dozing off with a lighted cigarette is a proximate cause of the fire. Finally, we come to the *precipitating cause,* the triggering event—in our example, the cigarette's igniting the combustible mattress fabric. Isolating a precipitating cause is usually necessary to prevent events from recurring, but often we need to go further back to determine remote causes or conditions, especially if we are interested in assigning responsibility for what has occurred.

> *Because of the long chains of causes that can be found for some complex situations, arguers about cause need to decide on their focus—based on their purpose in writing.* Suppose, for example, your concern is global warming. Cows contribute to global warming. Factories contribute to global warming. Car emissions contribute to global warming. Are we going to give up cattle farms? Not likely. Are we going to tear down factories? Not likely—but we can get factories to put filters on their smokestacks. Are we going to get rid of cars? Not likely—but we can try to get rid of the harmful emissions from cars. So, you argue for eliminating or controlling those causes that society is most likely to agree to and you ignore other causes that may be less practical to eliminate.

Mill's Methods for Investigating Causes

John Stuart Mill, a nineteenth-century British philosopher, explained in detail some important ways of investigating and demonstrating causal relationships: commonality, difference, and process of elimination. We can benefit in our study of cause by understanding and using his methods.

1. *Commonality.* One way to isolate cause is to demonstrate that one agent is *common* to similar outcomes. For instance, 25 employees attend a company luncheon. Late in the day, 10 report to area hospitals, and another 4 complain the next day of having experienced vomiting the night before. Public health officials will soon want to know what these people ate for lunch.

Different people during the same 12-hour period had similar physical symptoms of food poisoning. The common factor may well have been the tuna salad they ate for lunch.

2. *Difference.* Another way to isolate cause is to recognize one key *difference.* If two situations are alike in every way but one, and the situations result in different outcomes, then the one way they differ must have caused the different outcome. Studies in the social sciences are often based on the single-difference method. To test for the best teaching methods for math, an educator could set up an experiment with two classrooms similar in every way except that one class devotes fifteen minutes three days a week to instruction by drill. If the class receiving the drill scores much higher on a standard test given to both groups of students, the educator could argue that math drills make a measurable difference in learning math. But the educator should be prepared for skeptics to challenge the assertion of only one difference between the two classes. Could the teacher's attitude toward the drills also make a difference in student learning? If the differences in student scores are significant, the educator probably has a good argument, even though a teacher's attitude cannot be controlled in the experiment.

3. *Process of elimination.* One can develop a causal argument around a technique we all use for problem solving: *the process of elimination.* When something happens, we examine all possible causes and eliminate them, one by one, until we are satisfied that we have isolated the actual cause (or causes). When the Federal Aviation Administration has to investigate a plane crash, it uses this process, exploring possible causes such as mechanical failure, weather, human error, or terrorism. Sometimes the process isolates more than one cause or points to a likely cause without providing absolute proof. You will see how Lester Thurow uses the process-of-elimination method in his article at the end of this chapter (pp. 235–37).

EXERCISE: Understanding Causal Patterns

From the following events or situations, select the one you know best and list as many conditions, influences, and causes—remote, proximate, precipitating—as you can think of. You may want to do this exercise with your class partner or in small groups. Be prepared to explain your causal pattern to the class.

1. Teen suicide.
2. Global warming.
3. Increase in the numbers of women elected to public office.
4. High salaries of professional athletes.
5. Increased interest in soccer in the United States.
6. Comparatively low scores by U.S. students on international tests in math and science.

GUIDELINES for Evaluating Causal Arguments

When evaluating causal arguments, what should you look for? The basics of good argument apply to all arguments: a clear statement of claim, qualified if appropriate, a clear explanation of reasons and evidence, and enough relevant evidence to support the claim. How do we recognize these qualities in a causal argument? Use the following points as guides to evaluating:

- **Does the writer carefully distinguish among types of causes?** Word choice is crucial. Is the argument that A and A alone caused B or that A was one of several contributing causes?

- **Does the writer recognize the complexity of causation and not rush to assert only one cause for a complex event or situation?** The credibility of an argument about cause is quickly lost if readers find the argument oversimplified.

- **Is the argument's claim clearly stated, with qualifications as appropriate?** If the writer wants to argue for one cause, not the only cause, of an event or situation, then the claim's wording must make this limited goal clear to readers. For example, one can perhaps build the case for heavy television viewing as *one* cause of stereotyping, loss of sensitivity to violence, and increased fearfulness. But we know that the home environment and neighborhood and school environments also do much to shape attitudes.

- **What reasons and evidence are given to support the argument?** Can you see the writer's pattern of development? Does the reasoning seem logical? Are the data relevant? This kind of analysis of the argument will help you evaluate it.

- **Does the argument demonstrate causality, not just a time relationship or correlation?** A causal argument needs to prove *agency*: A is the cause of B, not just something that happened before B or something that is present when B is present. March precedes April, but March does not cause April to arrive.

- **Does the writer present believable causal agents, agents consistent with our knowledge of human behavior and scientific laws?** Most educated people do not believe that personalities are shaped by astrological signs or that scientific laws are suspended in the Bermuda Triangle, allowing planes and ships to vanish or enter a fourth dimension.

- **What are the implications for accepting the causal argument?** If A and B clearly are the causes of C, and we don't want C to occur, then we presumably must do something about A and B—or at least we must do something about either A or B and see if reducing or eliminating one of the causes significantly reduces the incidence of C to what we consider tolerable.

- **Is the argument convincing?** After analyzing the argument and answering the questions given in the previous points, you need to decide if, finally, the argument works.

Preparing a Causal Argument

In addition to the guidelines for writing arguments presented in Chapter 4, you can use the following advice specific to writing causal arguments.

Planning

1. **Think:** What are the focus and limits of your causal argument? Do you want to argue for one cause of an event or situation? Do you want to argue for several causes leading to an event or situation? Do you want to argue for a cause that others have overlooked? Do you want to show how one cause is common to several situations or events? Diagramming the relationship of cause to effect may help you see what you want to focus on. (See box, p. 220).

2. **Think:** What reasons and evidence do you have to support your tentative claim? Consider what you already know that has led to your choice of topic. A brainstorming list may be helpful.

3. **Think:** How, then, do you want to word your claim? As we have discussed, wording is crucial in causal arguments. Review the discussion of characteristics of causal arguments if necessary.

4. **Think:** What, if any, additional evidence do you need to develop a convincing argument? You may need to do some reading or online searching to obtain data to strengthen your argument. Readers expect relevant, reliable, current statistics in most arguments about cause. Assess what you need and then think about what sources will provide the needed information.

5. **Think:** What assumptions (warrants) are you making in your causal reasoning? Do these assumptions hold up to logical scrutiny? Will readers be likely to agree with your assumptions, or will you need to defend them as part of the development of your argument? For example: One reason to defend the effects of heavy TV watching on viewers is the commonsense argument that what humans devote considerable time to will have a significant effect on their lives. Will your readers be prepared to accept this commonsense reasoning, or will they remain skeptical, looking for stronger evidence of a cause/effect relationship?

Drafting

1. Begin with an opening paragraph or two that introduces your topic in an interesting way. In "Pumps and Pocketbooks," Pietro Nivola begins by stating what someone else has suggested as a cause, a way to achieve a desired effect. He then argues that this strategy will not work. Lester Thurow, in "Why Women Are Paid Less Than Men," writes:

> In the 40 years from 1939 to 1979 white women who work full time have with monotonous regularity made slightly less than 60 percent as much as white men. Why?

This opening establishes the topic and Thurow's purpose in examining causes. The statistics get the reader's attention.

2. Do not begin by announcing your subject. Avoid openers such as: In this essay I will explain the causes of teen vandalism.

3. Decide where to place your claim statement. You can conclude your opening paragraph with it, or you can place it in your conclusion, after you have shown readers how best to understand the causes of the issue you are examining. Thurow uses the second approach effectively in his essay.

4. Present reasons and evidence in an organized way. If you are examining a series of causes, beginning with background conditions and early influences, then your basic plan will be time sequence. Readers need to see the chain of causes unfolding. Use appropriate terms and transitional words to guide readers through each stage in the causal pattern. If you are arguing for an overlooked cause, begin with the causes that have been put forward and show what is flawed in each one. Then present and defend your explanation of cause. This process-of-elimination structure works well when readers are likely to know what other causes have been offered in the past. You can also use one of Mill's other two approaches, if one of them is relevant to your situation. That is, you can present the points of commonality or difference that show your explanation of cause to be valid.

5. Address the issue of correlation rather than cause, if appropriate. After presenting the results of a study of marriage that reveals many benefits (emotional, physical, financial) of marriage, Linda Waite examines the question that she knows skeptical readers may have: does marriage actually *cause* the benefits, or is the relationship one of *correlation* only—that is, the benefits of marriage just happen to come with being married; they are not caused by being married.

6. Conclude by discussing the implications of the causal pattern you have argued for, if appropriate. Lester Thurow ends by asserting that if he is right about the cause of the gender pay gap, then there are two approaches society can take to remove the pay gap. If, in explaining the causes of teen vandalism, you see one cause as "group behavior," a gang looking for something to do, it then follows that you can advise young readers to stay out of gangs. Often with arguments about cause, there are personal or public policy implications in accepting the causal explanation you present.

A CHECKLIST FOR REVISION ■•■•■•□•■•■•□•■•■•□•■•■•□•■•■•□•■•■•□•■•□•■

☐ Do I have a clear statement of my claim? Is it appropriately qualified and focused?

☐ Have I organized my argument so that readers can see my pattern for examining cause?

☐ Have I used the language for discussing causes correctly, distinguishing among conditions and influences and remote and proximate causes? Have I selected the correct word—either *affect* or *effect*—as needed?

☐ Have I avoided the *post hoc* fallacy and the confusing of correlation and cause?

☐ Have I carefully examined my assumptions and convinced myself that they are reasonable and can be defended? Have I defended them when necessary to clarify and thus strengthen my argument?

☐ Have I found relevant facts and examples to support and develop my argument?

☐ Have I used the basic checklist for revision in Chapter 4 (see pp. 108–9)?

Read and study the following annotated argument. Complete your analysis of and response to the essay by answering the questions that follow.

PUMPS AND POCKETBOOKS | PIETRO NIVOLA

A graduate of Harvard University, Pietro Nivola, Ph.D., is a senior fellow in the Governmental Studies Program at the Brookings Institution. He is the author of numerous articles and books in his areas of research, including trade and energy policies and urban problems. His latest book is *Law of the Landscape: How Policies Shape Cities in Europe and America* (1999). The following article appeared in the *Washington Post*, April 24, 2000.

Attention-getting opening.

1   One good way to reduce this country's emissions of carbon dioxide as well as our dependence on foreign oil, suggests an April 17 editorial ["Saving Gas, and the Planet"], is to set tougher standards for the fuel efficiency of motor vehicles.

2   Sorry, but Congress has entertained this notion for almost a quarter-century with disappointing results. Since 1978 the United States has been attempting to do what no other industrial country has tried: reduce the consumption of oil just by imposing regulations—fuel-economy requirements—on new fleets of automobiles. At least two difficulties bedevil this command-and-control approach to energy conservation.

Two reasons for rejecting the existing cause/effect approach.

3   For one, the policy reaches only new vehicles. This means that it takes decades, not just a year or two, to raise the efficiency of the on-road fleet. If, tomorrow morning, federal regulators were to ratchet up the standards for SUVs, minivans and light trucks, most of the existing ones would remain in use, guzzling fuel and spewing greenhouse gases for years to come.

4   Worse, though the vehicular fleet gradually can be forced to record better gas mileage, doing so scarcely dissuades motorists from driving the "improved" vehicles more than ever. The unrelenting increase in vehicle miles traveled vitiates the fuel savings from improvements in mileage per gallon. Indeed, during periods of stable or declining gasoline prices, greater fuel economy of vehicles lowers the marginal cost of driving, actually encouraging motorists to log more miles.

5   The recent surge in nominal gasoline prices has slowed this boomerang, though not for long. Prices will begin to sag in the months ahead. Moreover, adjusting for inflation, even the current price of self-service regular is barely above where it stood in 1996 and well below its peak 18 years ago.

By 1997 Americans were motoring some 2.6 trillion miles a year—the equivalent of 10,715,511 trips to the moon. The federal government's fuel-efficiency rules did nothing to moderate this astronomical amount of motion, at least some of which is extravagant and wasteful.

Naturally, this failure has implications for the nation's thirst for oil and its environmental side effects. Transportation in the United States burns most of the petroleum we buy. It accounts for most of our rising volume of imported oil (which is now up to half our consumption), and for more than half of the damaging chemicals we emit into the atmosphere. While the use of oil dropped in virtually every other sector of the economy between 1973 and 1998, transportation's was up 36 percent. If the aim of government policy is to reverse this trend, reduce the level of oil imports and improve air quality, something other than automotive fuel-economy mandates is necessary.

Like it or not, that something is a higher price at the pump. In an election year, politicians wince at the thought, but if the current spike were permanent, it would likely conserve energy more efficiently over the long haul than does the flawed fuel-economy law. A few years ago, a joint study by the Century Foundation and the Brookings Institution estimated that a 25-cent increase in the federal gasoline tax would have saved more oil than the fuel-economy scheme did from its inception. The reason: economics. Steeper fuel costs affect driving habits, not just the vehicle design, and have an effect on the use of all vehicles, not just new models.

Rather than waste time tweaking the anachronistic 1978 regulatory regime, policymakers might consider these facts: Each year Americans chalk up approximately twice as many vehicle miles per capita as Germans and more than three times as many as the Japanese. This is not because Japanese and German consumers cannot afford cars. Nor is it because Germany and Japan regulate their automobile industries more stringently. Instead, much of the explanation for why people in those countries drive less, ride public transit, walk more and consume far less oil per person is simply that gasoline costs a lot more than it does here.

6

7

Facts leading to need for a new cause/effect strategy.

8

Claim statement and support.

9

Support of claim using Mill's *difference* strategy.

QUESTIONS FOR READING

1. What is the occasion for Nivola's writing; that is, what has led him to write this article?
2. What is Congress's approach to reducing U.S. oil consumption?
3. What two reasons does Nivola offer for rejecting Congress's approach?

QUESTIONS FOR REASONING AND ANALYSIS

1. What is Nivola's claim? That is, what government action will produce the desired result of less oil consumption and less environmental damage?
2. How does the author support his claim?

QUESTIONS FOR REFLECTING AND WRITING

1. Nivola assumes that readers will agree (as apparently does the U.S. Congress) that the extent of our use of oil is a problem. Do you agree that it is a problem? If no, why not?

2. If our oil consumption is a problem, has the author found a viable solution to the problem? Judge the effectiveness of the argument—the reasoning and evidence—regardless of how you may feel about his recommendation. If you do not find the argument convincing, how would you rebut it?

3. How can Nivola and those who share his concerns find ways to convince drivers in this country to "drive less, ride public transit, walk more and consume far less oil per person"?

THE PROBLEM/SOLUTION ARGUMENT: EXPLORING PUBLIC-POLICY ISSUES

Many of the arguments over public policy can be understood as arguments over solutions to problems. Consider the following policy claims.

1. Drunk drivers should receive mandatory six-month suspensions of their licenses.

2. We need to spend whatever is necessary to stop the flow of drugs into this country.

3. The school year in the United States should be extended by at least 30 days.

Each one of these policy claims offers a solution to a problem, as we can see:

1. Fewer people will drink and drive, causing accidents, if they know they will lose their licenses.

2. The way to address the drug problem in this country is to eliminate the supply of drugs.

3. For America to compete in the world, new generations will have to be better educated; to reach that goal a longer school year is necessary.

Let's think about the characteristics of claims of policy as problem/solution arguments.

Characteristics of Problem/Solution Arguments

> *Claims of policy usually focus on the nature of the problem, for how we define a problem has much to do with what kinds of solutions become appropriate.* For example, some people are concerned about our ability to feed a growing world population. But many will argue that the problem is not an agricultural one (how much food we can produce) so much as a political one (to whom will the food be distributed and at what cost). If the problem is agricultural, we need to worry about available farmland, water supply, and

farming technology. If the problem is political, we need to worry about price supports, distribution to poor countries, and grain embargoes imposed for political leverage. To support a policy claim, you first need to define the problem.

> *How the problem is defined also affects what you think are the causes of the problem.* Cause is often a part of the debate and may need to be addressed, particularly if solutions are tied to eliminating what you consider to be the causes.

> *Successful problem/solution arguments present viable solutions, solutions that are connected to what can realistically be accomplished.* Consider Prohibition, for example. This was a solution to problem drinking—except that it didn't work, couldn't be enforced, because the majority of Americans wouldn't accept the law.

> *Claims of policy need to be developed with an understanding of the processes of government, from college administrations to federal structures.*

GUIDELINES for Evaluating Problem/ Solution Arguments

When evaluating problem/solution arguments, what should you look for? In addition to the basics of good argument, use the following points as guides to evaluating:

- **Is the writer's claim not just clear but appropriately qualified and focused?** For example, if the school board in the writer's community is not doing a good job of communicating its goals as a basis for its funding package, the writer needs to focus just on that particular school board, not on school boards in general.

- **Does the writer show an awareness of the complexity of most public-policy issues?** There are many different kinds of problems with American schools and many more causes for those problems. A simple solution—a longer school year, more money spent, vouchers—is not likely to solve the mixed bag of problems. Oversimplified arguments quickly lose credibility.

- **How does the writer define and explain the problem?** Is the way the problem is stated clear? Does it make sense to you? If the problem is being defined differently than most people have defined it, has the writer argued convincingly for looking at the problem in this new way?

- **What reasons and evidence are given to support the writer's solutions?** Can you see how the writer develops the argument? Does the reasoning seem logical? Is the data relevant? This kind of analysis will help you evaluate the proposed solutions.

- **Does the writer address the feasibility of the proposed solutions?** Does the writer make a convincing case for the realistic possibility of achieving the proposed solutions?

- **Is the argument convincing?** Will the solutions solve the problem as it has been defined? Has the problem been defined accurately? Can the solutions be achieved?

Preparing a Problem/Solution Argument

In addition to the guidelines for writing arguments presented in Chapter 4, you can use the following advice specific to defending claims of policy.

Planning

1. **Think:** What should be the focus and limits of your argument? There's a big difference between presenting solutions to the problem of physical abuse of women by men and presenting solutions to the problem of date rape on your college campus. Select a topic that you know something about that you can realistically handle.

2. **Think:** What reasons and evidence do you have to support your tentative claim? Think through what you already know that has led you to select your particular topic. Suppose you want to write on the issue of campus rapes. Is this choice due to a recent event on the campus? Was this event the first in many years, or the last in a trend? Where and when are they occurring? A brainstorming list may be helpful.

3. **Think:** Is there additional evidence that you need to obtain to develop your argument? If so, where can you look for that evidence? Are there past issues of the campus paper in your library? Will the campus police grant you an interview?

4. **Think:** What about the feasibility of each solution you plan to present? Are you thinking in terms of essentially one solution with several parts to it or several separate solutions, perhaps to be implemented by different people? Will coordination be necessary to achieve success? How will this be accomplished? For the problem of campus rape, you may want to consider several solutions as a package to be coordinated by the counseling service or an administrative vice president.

Drafting

1. Begin by either reminding readers of the existing problem you will address or arguing that a current situation should be recognized as a problem. In many cases, you can count on an audience who sees the world as you do and recognizes the problem you will address. But in some cases, your first task will be to convince readers that a problem exists that should worry them. If they are not concerned, they won't be interested in your solutions.

2. Be sure, early in your essay, to define the problem—as you see it—for readers. Do not assume that they will necessarily accept your way of seeing the issue. You may need to defend your assessment of the nature of the problem before moving on to solutions.

3. If appropriate, explain the cause or causes of the problem. If your proposed solution is tied to removing the cause or causes of the problem, then you need to establish cause and prove it early in your argument. If cause is important, argue for it; if it is irrelevant, move to your solution.

4. Explain your solution. If you have several solutions, think about how best to order them. If several need to be developed in a sequence, then present them in that necessary sequence. If you are presenting a package of diverse actions that together will solve the problem, then consider presenting them from the simplest to the more complex. With a problem of campus rape, for example, you may want to suggest better lighting on campus paths at night plus an escort service for women who are afraid to walk home alone plus sensitivity training for male students. Following that order might be the best. Adding more lampposts is much easier than getting students to take sensitivity classes.

5. Explain the process for achieving your solution. If you have not thought through the political or legal steps necessary to implement your solution, then this step cannot be part of your purpose in writing. However, anticipating a skeptical audience that says "How are we going to do that?" you would be wise to have precise steps to offer your reader. You may have obtained an estimate of costs for new lighting on your campus and want to suggest specific paths that need the lights. You may have investigated escort services at other colleges and can spell out how such a service can be implemented on your campus. Showing readers that you have thought ahead to the next steps in the process can be an effective method of persuasion.

6. Support the feasibility of your solution. Be able to estimate costs. Show that you know who would be responsible for implementing. Explain how your solutions can be sold to people who may be unwilling to accommodate your proposals. All of this information will strengthen your argument.

7. Show how your solution is better than others. Anticipate challenges by including in your paper reasons for adopting your program rather than another program. Explain how your solution will be more easily adopted or more effective when implemented than other possibilities. Of course, a less practical but still viable defense is that your solution is the right thing to do. Values also belong in public-policy debates, not just issues of cost and acceptability.

A CHECKLIST FOR REVISION ■•■

☐ Do I have a clear statement of my policy claim? Is it appropriately qualified and focused?

☐ Have I clearly explained how I see the problem to be solved? If necessary, have I argued for seeing the problem that way?

☐ Have I presented my solutions—and argued for them—in a clear and logical structure? Have I explained how these solutions can be implemented and why they are better than other solutions that have been suggested?

☐ Have I used data that are relevant and current?

☐ Have I used the basic checklist for revision in Chapter 4? (See pp. 108–9).

Read and study the following annotated argument. Complete your analysis of and response to the essay by answering the questions that follow.

A NEW STRATEGY
FOR THE WAR ON DRUGS | JAMES Q. WILSON

Author of *The Moral Sense,* James Q. Wilson is a professor of public policy at Pepperdine University. His solution to America's drug problem was published on April 13, 2000, in the *Wall Street Journal.*

Opening presents two solutions that Wilson will challenge.

1   The current Senate deliberation over aid to Colombia aimed at fighting narcotics reminds us that there are two debates over how the government ought to deal with dangerous drugs. The first is about their illegality and the second is about their control. People who wish to legalize drugs and those who wish to curtail their supply believe that their methods will reduce crime. Both these views are mistaken, but there is a third way.

Wilson rebuts first solution.

2   Advocates of legalization think that both buyers and sellers would benefit. People who can buy drugs freely and at something like free-market prices would no longer have to steal to afford cocaine or heroin; dealers would no longer have to use violence and corruption to maintain their market share. Though drugs may harm people, reducing this harm would be a medical problem not a criminal-justice one. Crime would drop sharply.

PRICES WOULD FALL

3   But there is an error in this calculation. Legalizing drugs means letting the price fall to its competitive rate (plus taxes and advertising costs). That market price would probably be somewhere between one-third and 1/20th of the illegal price. And more than the market price would fall. As Harvard's Mark Moore has pointed out, the "risk price"—that is, all the hazards associated with buying drugs, from being arrested to being ripped off—would also fall, and this decline might be more important than the lower purchase price.

4   Under a legal regime, the consumption of low-priced, low-risk drugs would increase dramatically. We do not know by how much, but the little evidence we have suggests a sharp rise. Until 1968 Britain allowed doctors to prescribe heroin. Some doctors cheated, and their medically unnecessary prescriptions helped increase the number of known heroin addicts by a factor of 40. As a result, the government abandoned the prescription policy in favor of administering heroin in clinics and later replacing heroin with methadone.

5   When the Netherlands ceased enforcing laws against the purchase or possession of marijuana, the result was a sharp increase in its use. Cocaine and heroin create much greater dependency, and so the increase in their use would probably be even greater.

6   The average user would probably commit fewer crimes if these drugs were sold legally. But the total number of users would increase sharply. A large fraction of these new users would be unable to keep a steady job. Unless we were prepared to support them with welfare payments, crime would be one of their main sources of income. That is, the number of drug-related crimes *per user* might fall even as the total number of drug-related crimes increased. Add to the list of harms more deaths from overdose, more babies

born to addicted mothers, more accidents by drug-influenced automobile drivers and fewer people able to hold jobs or act as competent parents.

Treating such people would become far more difficult. As psychiatrist Sally Satel has written on this page, many drug users will not enter and stay in treatment unless they are compelled to do so. Phoenix House, the largest national residential drug treatment program, rarely admits patients who admit they have a problem and need help. The great majority are coerced by somebody— a judge, probation officer or school official—into attending. Phoenix House CEO Mitchell Rosenthal opposes legalization, and for good reason. Legalization means less coercion, and that means more addicts and addicts who are harder to treat.   **7**

Douglas Anglin, drawing on experiences in California and elsewhere, has shown that people compelled to stay in treatment do at least as well as those who volunteer for it, and they tend (of necessity) to stay in the program longer. If we legalize drugs, the chances of treatment making a difference are greatly reduced. And as for drug-use prevention, forget it. Try telling your children not to use a legal substance.   **8**

But people who want to keep drugs illegal have problems of their own. The major thrust of government spending has been to reduce the supply of drugs by cutting their production overseas, intercepting their transfer into the U.S. and arresting dealers. Because of severe criminal penalties, especially on handlers of crack cocaine, our prisons have experienced a huge increase in persons sentenced on drug charges. In the early 1980s, about 1/12th of all prison inmates were in for drug convictions; now well over one-third are.   **9**

Wilson rebuts second solution.

No one can be certain how imprisoning drug suppliers affects drug use, but we do know that an arrested drug dealer is easily replaced. Moreover, the government can never seize more than a small fraction of the drugs entering the country, a fraction that is easily replaced.   **10**

Emphasizing supply over treatment is dangerous. Not only do we spend huge sums on it; not only do we drag a reluctant U.S. military into the campaign; we also heighten corruption and violence in countries such as Colombia and Mexico. The essential fact is this: Demand will produce supply.   **11**

We can do much more to reduce demand. Some four million Americans are currently on probation or parole. From tests done on them when they are jailed, we know that half or more had a drug problem when arrested. Though a lot of drug users otherwise obey the law (or at least avoid getting arrested), probationers and parolees constitute the hard core of dangerous addicts. Reducing their demand for drugs ought to be our highest priority.   **12**

Mark Kleiman of UCLA has suggested a program of "testing and control": Probationers and parolees would be required to take frequent drug tests— say, twice weekly—as a condition of remaining on the street. If you failed the test, you would spend more time in jail; if you passed it, you would remain free. This approach would be an inducement for people to enter and stay in treatment.   **13**

Wilson presents his solution.

14   This would require some big changes in how we handle offenders. Police, probation and parole officers would be responsible for conducting these tests, and more officers would have to be hired. Probation and parole authorities would have to be willing to sanction a test failure by immediate incarceration, initially for a short period (possibly a weekend), and then for longer periods if the initial failure were repeated. Treatment programs at little or no cost to the user would have to be available not only in every prison, but for every drug-dependent probationer and parolee.

Challenges of implementing his solution.

15   These things are not easily done. Almost every state claims to have an intensive community supervision program, but few offenders are involved in them, the frequency with which they are contacted is low, and most were released from supervision without undergoing any punishment for violating its conditions.

16   But there is some hope. Our experience with drug courts suggests that the procedural problems can be overcome. In such courts, several hundred of which now exist, special judges oversee drug-dependent offenders, insisting that they work to overcome their habits. While under drug-court supervision, offenders reduce drug consumption and, at least for a while after leaving the court, offenders are less likely to be arrested.

How solution can work.

17   Our goal ought to be to extend meaningful community supervision to all probationers and parolees, especially those who have a serious drug or alcohol problem. Efforts to test Mr. Kleiman's proposals are under way in Connecticut and Maryland.

18   If this demand-reduction strategy works, it can be expanded. Drug tests can be given to people who apply for government benefits, such as welfare and public housing. Some critics will think this is an objectionable intrusion. But giving benefits without conditions weakens the character-building responsibility of society.

PREVENT HARM TO OTHERS

19   John Stuart Mill, the great libertarian thinker, argued that the only justifiable reason for restricting human liberty is to prevent harm to others. Serious drug abuse does harm others. We could, of course, limit government action to remedying those harms without addressing their causes, but that is an uphill struggle, especially when the harms fall on unborn children. Fetal drug syndrome imposes large costs on infants who have had no voice in choosing their fate.

Defense of his solution based on practicality and values.

20   Even Mill was clear that full liberty cannot be given to children or barbarians. By "barbarians" he meant people who are incapable of being improved by free and equal discussion. The life of a serious drug addict—the life of someone driven by drug dependency to prostitution and crime—is the life of a barbarian.

QUESTIONS FOR READING

1. What are the two solutions to the drug problem presented by others?
2. Why, according to Wilson, will legalizing drugs not be a good solution? What are the specific negative consequences of legalization?
3. Government strategies for controlling illegal drugs have included what activities?
4. What percentage of prisoners are now in prison on drug charges?
5. What problems do we face trying to reduce the supply of drugs? What, according to Wilson, drives supply?
6. What is Wilson's proposed solution? Explain the details of his solution.
7. What are some of the difficulties with the author's solution? What does he gain by bringing up possible difficulties?

QUESTIONS FOR REASONING AND ANALYSIS

1. What does Wilson seek to accomplish in his concluding two paragraphs? What potential counterargument does he seek to rebut in his conclusion?
2. On what argument might one agree that Wilson's solution is workable and still object to it? (Think about his concluding comments.)

QUESTIONS FOR REFLECTING AND WRITING

1. Has Wilson convinced you that legalizing drugs will not reduce crime? Why or why not?
2. Is his argument against the supply-reduction approach convincing? Why or why not?
3. Has Wilson's defense of his solution convinced you that it is workable?
4. Do you have a solution to the drug problem?

FOR ANALYSIS AND DEBATE

WHY WOMEN ARE PAID LESS THAN MEN | LESTER C. THUROW

A professor at the MIT Sloan School of Management and consultant to both government and private corporations, Lester C. Thurow (b. 1938) has written extensively on economic and public-policy issues. His books include *Poverty and Discrimination* (1969), *The Political Economy of Income Redistribution Policies* (1977), and *Dangerous Currents* (1983).

"Why Women Are Paid Less Than Men," published in the *New York Times* (March 8, 1981), offers an explanation for the discrepancy between the incomes of men and women.

PREREADING QUESTIONS When he asks "why" at the end of paragraph 1, what kind of analysis or argument does Thurow signal he will develop? Were you aware that women still earn less than men?

1   In the 40 years from 1939 to 1979 white women who work full time have with monotonous regularity made slightly less than 60 percent as much as white men. Why?

2   Over the same time period, minorities have made substantial progress in catching up with whites, with minority women making even more progress than minority men.

3   Black men now earn 72 percent as much as white men (up 16 percentage points since the mid-1950s) but black women earn 92 percent as much as white women. Hispanic men make 71 percent of what their white counterparts do, but Hispanic women make 82 percent as much as white women. As a result of their faster progress, fully employed black women make 75 percent as much as fully employed black men while Hispanic women earn 68 percent as much as Hispanic men.

4   This faster progress may, however, end when minority women finally catch up with white women. In the bible of the New Right, George Gilder's *Wealth and Poverty*, the 60 percent is just one of Mother Nature's constants like the speed of light or the force of gravity.

5   Men are programmed to provide for their families economically while women are programmed to take care of their families emotionally and physically. As a result men put more effort into their jobs than women. The net result is a difference in work intensity that leads to that 40 percent gap in earnings. But there is no discrimination against women—only the biological facts of life.

6   The problem with this assertion is just that. It is an assertion with no evidence for it other than the fact that white women have made 60 percent as much as men for a long period of time.

7   "Discrimination against women" is an easy answer but it also has its problems as an adequate explanation. Why is discrimination against women not declining under the same social forces that are leading to a lessening of discrimination against minorities? In recent years women have made more use of the enforcement provisions of the Equal Employment Opportunities Commission and the courts than minorities. Why do the laws that prohibit discrimination against women and minorities work for minorities but not for women?

8   When men discriminate against women, they run into a problem. To discriminate against women is to discriminate against your own wife and to lower your own family income. To prevent women from working is to force men to work more.

9   When whites discriminate against blacks, they can at least think that they are raising their own incomes. When men discriminate against women they have to know that they are lowering their own family income and increasing their own work effort.

10   While discrimination undoubtedly explains part of the male-female earnings differential, one has to believe that men are monumentally stupid or irrational to explain all of the earnings gap in terms of discrimination. There must be something else going on.

Back in 1939 it was possible to attribute the earnings gap to large differ-   11
ences in educational attainments. But the educational gap between men and
women has been eliminated since World War II. It is no longer possible to use
education as an explanation for the lower earnings of women.

Some observers have argued that women earn less money since they are   12
less reliable workers who are more apt to leave the labor force. But it is difficult to maintain this position since women are less apt to quit one job to take
another and as a result they tend to work as long, or longer, for any one employer. From any employer's perspective they are more reliable, not less reliable, than men.

Part of the answer is visible if you look at the lifetime earnings profile of   13
men. Suppose that you are asked to predict which men in a group of 25-year-
olds would become economically successful. At age 25 it is difficult to tell who
will be economically successful and your predictions are apt to be highly inaccurate.

But suppose that you were asked to predict which men in a group of 35-   14
year-olds would become economically successful. If you are successful at age
35 you are very likely to remain successful for the rest of your life. If you have
not become economically successful by age 35, you are very unlikely to do so
later.

The decade between 25 and 35 is when men either succeed or fail. It is the   15
decade when lawyers become partners in the good firms, when business managers make it onto the "fast track," when academics get tenure at good universities, and when blue-collar workers find the job opportunities that will lead
to training opportunities and the skills that will generate high earnings.

If there is any one decade when it pays to work hard and to be consistently   16
in the labor force, it is the decade between 25 and 35. For those who succeed,
earnings will rise rapidly. For those who fail, earnings will remain flat for the rest
of their lives.

But the decade between 25 and 35 is precisely the decade when women   17
are most apt to leave the labor force or become part-time workers to have children. When they do, the current system of promotion and skill acquisition will
extract an enormous lifetime price.

This leaves essentially two avenues for equalizing male and female earn-   18
ings.

Families where women who wish to have successful careers, compete with   19
men, and achieve the same earnings should alter their family plans and have
their children either before 25 or after 35. Or society can attempt to alter the
existing promotion and skill acquisition system so that there is a longer time
period in which both men and women can attempt to successfully enter the labor force.

Without some combination of these two factors, a substantial fraction of   20
the male-female earnings differentials are apt to persist for the next 40 years,
even if discrimination against women is eliminated.

QUESTIONS FOR READING

1. What situation is the subject of Thurow's argument?
2. Briefly explain why Thurow rejects each of the possible explanations that he covers.
3. What is the author's explanation for the discrepancy between the earnings of white women and white men?

QUESTIONS FOR REASONING AND ANALYSIS

1. What questions should you ask about Thurow's numbers? Do you know the answer to the question?
2. What is Thurow's claim?
3. What evidence does the author provide for his claim? Is it convincing?
4. What strategy for determining cause does Thurow use?

QUESTIONS FOR REFLECTING AND WRITING

1. Do you agree that most people who are going to be successful are so by age thirty-five? Can you think of people who did not become successful until after thirty-five? Is this the kind of assumption that can create its own reality?
2. Evaluate the two solutions Thurow proposes. Do they follow logically from his causal analysis?
3. Thurow's figures are based on the total earnings of workers; they are not comparisons by job category. What are other facts about jobs that men and women hold that may account for some of the discrepancy in pay?

FOUR MYTHS, 30 MILLION POTENTIAL VOTES | BETH SHULMAN

A lawyer, Beth Shulman is vice president, director, and executive board member of the United Food and Commercial Workers Union of the AFL-CIO. She is the author of *The Betrayal of Work: How Low-Wage Jobs Fail 30 Million Americans* (2003). The following article appeared in the *Washington Post* on August 17, 2003.

PREREADING QUESTIONS What meaning of the word "myth" does the author use? What percentage of American families earn $18,000 a year or less? Are you surprised by this figure?

1   As the presidential campaigns seek definition, one pivotal issue remains hidden from view. It is potentially huge, especially for Democrats, because it involves their natural constituents, and it addresses core issues of the economy, social justice and fairness. The issue is low-wage work.

2   Fully 30 million Americans—one in four U.S. workers—earn $8.70 an hour or less, a rate that works out to $18,100 a year, which is the current official poverty level in the United States for a family of four. These low-wage jobs usually lack health care, child care, pensions and vacation benefits. Their working conditions are often grueling, dangerous, even humiliating.

At the same time, more and more middle-class jobs are taking on many of   3
these same characteristics, losing the security and benefits once taken for
granted.

The shameful reality of low-wage work in America should be on every   4
Democrat's cue card as a potential weapon to be used against the Republicans'
rosy economic scenario. But so far it isn't. Why not? One reason may be four
long-standing myths that have for years drowned out a rational discussion of
what should be a national call to conscience:

MYTH #1: LOW-WAGE WORK IS MERELY A TEMPORARY STEP ON THE LADDER TO A BETTER JOB

According to the American dream, if you work hard, apply yourself and   5
play by the rules, you will be able to earn a decent living for yourself and your
family. If you fail to move up, you must be lazy or incompetent.

THE TRUTH

Low-wage job mobility is minimal. Low-wage workers have few career   6
ladders. Those of us lucky enough to have better-paying employment depend on them every day. They are nursing home and home health care workers who care for our parents; they are poultry processors who bone and
package our chicken; they are retail clerks in department stores, grocery
stores and convenience stores; they are housekeepers and janitors who keep
our hotel rooms and offices clean; they are billing and telephone call center
workers who take our complaints and answer our questions; and they are
teaching assistants in our schools and child care workers who free us so that
we can work ourselves.

In a recent study following U.S. adults through their working careers, eco-   7
nomics professors Peter Gottschalk of Boston College and Sheldon Danziger
of the University of Michigan found that about half of those whose earnings
ranked in the bottom 20 percent in 1968 were still in the same group in 1991.
Of those who had moved up, nearly two-thirds remained below the median income. The U.S. economy provides less mobility for low-wage earners, according to an Organization for Economic Cooperation and Development study,
than the economies of France, Italy, the United Kingdom, Germany, Denmark,
Finland or Sweden.

Today's economy is even more rigid. In many industries, such as insurance,   8
retail and financial services, wealthier clients are served by different employees
than lower-status customers. This makes it harder for the lowest wage earners
to move up. Some do, but this happens primarily in the manufacturing sector,
where the number of jobs continues to decline.

MYTH #2: TRAINING AND NEW SKILLS SOLVE THE PROBLEM

Low-wage workers are said to lack the necessary skills for better-paying   9
work in our changing economy. What's needed is retraining and better education for everyone.

THE TRUTH

10   The problem is that there are fewer better jobs to move into. The percentage of low-wage jobs is growing, not shrinking. The growing sectors of our economy are the labor-intensive industries. The two-lowest-paid work categories, retail and service, increased their share of the job market from 30 percent to 48 percent between 1965 and 1998. By the end of the decade, the low end of the job market will account for more than 30 percent of the American workforce. There will be about 1.8 million software engineers and computer support specialists, but more than 3.8 million cashiers.

11   According to the U.S. Bureau of Labor Statistics, half of all new jobs by 2010 will require relatively brief on-the-job training. Only three of every 10 positions currently require more than a high school diploma. Certainly, raising skills and education levels will lead some workers to higher wages and better jobs. But that approach will do little to improve the lives of most of the hard-working women and men in the jobs that will continue to grow as a proportion of our economy.

12   Just as important, those who denigrate low-wage work as "low-skilled" ignore the reality of these jobs. A nursing-home worker must be compassionate, must pay attention to detail and must possess psychological and emotional strength; a call-center worker must have patience and must be able to command enough information to handle questions and complaints; a security guard must be dedicated, alert and conscientious. To say these workers need retraining to earn more lets their employers off the hook for failing to compensate them appropriately for their existing skills and duties.

MYTH #3: GLOBALIZATION STOPS US FROM DOING ANYTHING ABOUT THIS PROBLEM

13   Between 1979 and 1999, 3 million manufacturing jobs vanished as global trade brought in textiles, shoes, cars and steel produced by overseas labor. In June 2003 alone, 56,000 manufacturing jobs were lost. American employers must keep wages and benefits low if they are to compete in the global marketplace.

THE TRUTH

14   Very few low-wage jobs are now in globally competitive industries. It is true that global trade has had a profound impact on our economy and on American workers. But companies in Beijing are not competing with child care providers, nursing homes, restaurants, security guard firms and janitorial services in the United States. Checking out groceries, waiting on tables, servicing office equipment and tending the sick cannot be done from overseas.

15   Employers and politicians use globalization as an excuse to do nothing for low-wage workers, scaring them into accepting lower pay, fewer benefits and less job security. It is invoked to justify reduced social spending and less workplace regulation, and workers believe they are powerless to object. Yet not only does globalization fail to apply to most of America's low-wage jobs, other

industrialized countries facing the same global competition have chosen differently: They provide social safety nets, notably including guaranteed health care. As a result, according to a 1997 study by Timothy Smeeding of Syracuse University, Americans in the lowest income brackets have living standards that are 13 percent below those of low-income Germans and 24 percent below the bottom 20 percent of Swedes.

MYTH #4: LOW-WAGE JOBS ARE MERELY THE RESULT OF AN EFFICIENT MARKET

The economy is a force of nature, and we as a society have little control over whatever difficulties it creates.   16

THE TRUTH

The economic world we live in is the result of our creation, not natural law. America's low-wage workers have little power to change their conditions because of a series of political, economic and corporate decisions over the past quarter-century that undercut the bargaining power of workers, especially those in lower pay grades.   17

Those decisions included the push to increase global trade and open global markets, changes in immigration law, the deregulation of industries that had been highly unionized, Federal Reserve policies focused on reducing inflation threats, and a corporate ideological shift that eliminated America's postwar social contract with workers and emphasized maximizing shareholder value. Those decisions worsened conditions in low-wage jobs and exaggerated disparities in income and wealth.   18

America's most vulnerable workers have also lost many institutions, laws and political allies that could have helped counterbalance these forces. In the 1950s, the number of American workers who were fired, harassed or threatened for trying to organize a union was in the hundreds a year. According to Human Rights Watch, by 1990 that number exceeded 20,000. In 1979, one-fourth of private-sector workers were unionized; only 11 percent are today. At the same time, the purchasing power of the federal minimum wage fell 30 percent during the 1980s. Despite minimal increases in the 1990s, according to calculations by the Economic Policy Institute, the value of the current minimum wage of $5.15 per hour is still 21 percent less than it was in 1979.   19

The richest country in the world should not tolerate such treatment of more than a fourth of its workers. The myths of upward mobility and inevitable market forces blind too many people to the grim reality of low-wage work. A presidential campaign is the right time to begin a conversation on how to change it.   20

QUESTIONS FOR READING

1. What is Shulman's subject?
2. Shulman presents four myths. What are they about—in general—and what problem are they creating?
3. Explain each of the four myths and the author's rebuttal of each one. In particular: What kinds of low-paying jobs are not affected by global competition?

QUESTIONS FOR REASONING AND ANALYSIS

1. What kinds of evidence does Shulman provide? Do the numbers seem logical, their sources credible?
2. The author argues, in response to myth #4, that our economy is one that we have created, not something out of our control. How does she defend this assertion? Is her argument convincing to you?
3. What type of support does Shulman present in her conclusion? Do you find her ending persuasive?

QUESTIONS FOR REFLECTING AND WRITING

1. Have you believed one or more of the myths Shulman lists? If so, has she convinced you that your perceptions have been incorrect? Why or why not?
2. If you are still convinced that one of the myths is accurate, how would you rebut Shulman's argument and defend that myth?

SUGGESTIONS FOR DISCUSSION AND WRITING

1. Think of a problem on your campus or in your community for which you have a workable solution. Organize your argument to include all relevant steps as described in this chapter. Although your primary concern will be to present your solution, depending on your topic you may need to begin by convincing readers of the seriousness of the problem or the causes of the problem—if your solutions involve removing those causes.

2. Think of a problem in education—K–12 or at the college level—that you have a solution for and that you are interested in. You may want to begin by brainstorming to develop a list of possible problems in education about which you could write— or look through Chapter 18 for ideas. Be sure to qualify your claim and limit your focus as necessary to work with a problem that is not so broad and general that your "solutions" become general and vague comments about "getting better teachers." (If one problem is a lack of qualified teachers, then what specific proposals do you have for solving that particular problem?) Include as many steps as are appropriate to develop and support your argument.

3. Think of a situation that you consider serious but that apparently many people do not take seriously enough. Write an argument in which you emphasize, by providing evidence, that the situation is a serious problem. You may conclude by suggesting a solution, but your chief purpose in writing will be to alert readers to a problem.

The Researched and Formally Documented Argument

CHAPTER 9

Getting Started and Locating Sources

(in the Library, Online, in the Field)

We do research all the time. You would not select a college or buy a car without doing research: gathering relevant information, analyzing that information, and drawing conclusions from your study. When you are assigned a research essay for a course, you will need to present the results in an organized way using formal documentation. You may also share your knowledge in a class presentation. Do not let the demands of researching and writing keep you from remembering the important goals of research:

1. New knowledge
   - The biochemical triggers of alcoholism
   - A comparison of shopping habits in urban, suburban, and rural communities
   - The discovery and publication of an artist's drawing notebook
2. New understanding
   - Better methods for preventing and treating alcoholism
   - A shopping-center plan based on the study of shopping habits
   - A reevaluation of the artist's work based on the study of the published notebook

TYPES OF RESEARCH PROJECTS

Not all research projects have the same purpose. Different purposes lead to papers that can be classified as primarily *expository, analytic,* or *argumentative.*

Expository

An expository or informative paper, often called a report, is an account of your study of a specific topic. The purpose is to share information, to explain to readers what the researcher has learned from the study. Market and technical reports are important kinds of informative writing in business. A good report reflects your critical judgment in the selection and arrangement of information. Instructors assign expository research papers when they want students to read widely on a topic, gain greater understanding of complex topics, or learn about the process of research.

Analytic

The analytic paper goes beyond an organized reporting of information to an examination of the implications of that information. A report on problems in education may assemble recent test scores and other data. An analysis will examine possible causes of the problem. Many literary studies are analyses.

Argumentative/Persuasive

The argumentative paper (often called an opinion or thesis paper) uses information and analysis to argue for a claim. In an argumentative paper you cannot just report conflicting positions on your topic. You need to evaluate conflicting positions and refute those at odds with your position. To illustrate, compare the following topics to see how they differ in purpose:

EXPOSITORY: Report of recent literature on infant speech development.

ANALYTIC: Explanation of the process of infant speech development.

ARGUMENTATIVE: Argument for specific actions by parents to aid infant speech development.

Examining types of research projects can help us recognize what will not meet research paper expectations. The following is a cautionary list of kinds of writing to avoid when a research paper has been assigned:

1. A paper that merely strings together quotations from sources.
2. An essay drawn entirely from personal experiences and thoughts.
3. An entirely theoretical paper without any specifics from sources.
4. A paper in which information drawn from sources is not properly documented.

STAGES IN THE RESEARCH PROCESS

Although research writing means *re-searching, re-thinking,* and *re-writing,* a basic process can be described. Having an overview of this process will give you a sense of where you are headed. Note, as you read, how the outline emphasizes the recursive nature of thinking, reading, and writing about a topic.

STAGE **1:** *Select and limit.* Select and limit a topic consistent with assignment guidelines. Review some sources as necessary to aid topic selection. Consider audience, purpose, and required length of paper.

STAGE **2:** *Focus and plan.* Choose an approach or focus for your research. Decide on a tentative thesis, hypothesis, or question to answer. Think, talk, and read to complete this stage. Write a statement of purpose or research proposal.

STAGE **3:** *Gather sources.* In a systematic manner locate potential sources from the library and other appropriate places.

STAGE **4:** *Read and think.* Read and evaluate sources (or study original data). Take notes on relevant information and ideas. Learn about the topic. Re-think what needs to be covered in your study. Re-search as necessary. Make a preliminary outline. Think some more.

STAGE **5:** *Organize and draft.* Plan in detail the structure of your paper. With notes arranged accordingly, write a first draft. Include documentation as you draft.

STAGE **6:** *Revise, edit, and format correctly.* First revise your draft and then edit to remove errors. Prepare the completed paper in an appropriate format with correct documentation of sources.

FINDING A WORKABLE TOPIC

To get started you need to select and limit a topic. One key to success is finding a *workable* topic. No matter how interesting or clever the topic, it is not workable if it does not meet the guidelines of your assignment. Begin with a thorough understanding of the writing context created by the assignment.

What Type of Paper Am I Preparing?

Study your assignment to understand the type of project. Is your purpose expository, analytic, or argumentative? How would you classify each of the following topics?

1. Explain the chief solutions proposed for increasing the Southwest's water supply.
2. Compare the Freudian and behavioral models of mental illness.
3. Find the best solutions to a current environmental problem.
4. Consider: What twentieth-century invention has most dramatically changed our personal lives?

Did you recognize that the first topic calls for a report? The second topic requires an analysis of two schools of psychology, so you cannot report on only one, but you also cannot argue that one model is better than the other. Both topics 3 and 4 require an argumentative paper: you must select and defend a claim.

Who Is My Audience?

If you are writing in a specific discipline, imagine your instructor as a representative of that field, a reader with knowledge of the subject area. If you are learning about the research process in a composition course, your instructor may advise you to write to a general reader, someone who reads newspapers but may not have the exact information and perspective you have. For a general reader, specialized terms and concepts need definition.

> **NOTE:** Consider the expectations of readers of research papers. A research essay is not like a personal essay. A research essay is not about you; it is about a subject, so keep yourself more in the background than you might in a more informal piece of writing.

What Are the Assignment's Time and Length Constraints?

The required length of the paper, the time you have to complete the assignment, and the availability of sources are three constraints you must consider when selecting a research topic. Most instructors will establish guidelines regarding length. Knowing the expected length of the paper is crucial to selecting an appropriate topic, so if an instructor does not specify, be sure to ask.

Suppose, for example, that you must argue for solutions to either an educational or environmental problem. Your paper needs to be about six pages and is due in three weeks. Do you have the space or the time to explore solutions to all the problems caused by overpopulation? Definitely not. Limit your study to one issue such as coping with trash. You could further limit this topic by exploring waste management solutions for your particular city or county.

What Kinds of Topics Should I Avoid?

Here are several kinds of topics that are best avoided because they usually produce disasters, no matter how well the student handles the rest of the research process:

1. *Topics that are irrelevant* to your interests or the course. If you are not interested in your topic, you will not produce a lively, informative paper. If you select a topic far removed from the course content, you may create some hostility in your instructor, who will wonder why you are unwilling to become engaged in the course.

2. *Topics that are broad subject areas.* These result in general surveys that lack appropriate detail and support.

3. *Topics that can be fully researched with only one source.* You will produce a summary, not a research paper.

4. *Biographical studies.* Short undergraduate papers on a person's life usually turn out to be summaries of one or two major biographies.

5. *Topics that produce a strong emotional response in you.* If there is only one "right" answer to the abortion issue and you cannot imagine counterarguments, don't choose to write on abortion. Probably most religious topics are best avoided.

6. *Topics that are too technical for you* at this point in your college work. If you do not understand the complexities of the federal tax code, then arguing for a reduction in the capital gains tax may be an unwise topic choice.

How Can I Select a Good Topic?

Choosing from assigned topics. At times students are unhappy with topic restriction. Looked at another way, your instructor has eliminated a difficult step in the research process and has helped you avoid the problem of selecting an unworkable topic. If topics are assigned, you will still have to choose from the list and develop your own claim and approach.

Finding a course-related topic. This guideline gives you many options and requires more thought about your choice. Working within the guidelines, try to write about what interests you. Here are examples of assignments turned into topics of interest to the student:

1. Trace the influence of any 20th-century event, development, invention.	Music	The influence of the Jazz Age on modern music
2. Support an argument on some issue of pornography and censorship.	Computers	Censorship of pornography on the Internet
3. Demonstrate the popularity of a current myth and then discredit it.	Science fiction	The lack of evidence for the existence of UFOs

When you are able to write on any course-related topic or on any subject at all, you will need to use some strategies for topic selection. You can begin by looking at your text's table of contents or index for subject areas that could be narrowed and focused. Or look through your class notes and think about the subjects already covered that especially interest you. For this course, you can skim through the collection of readings in Section 4 to see what topics attract your attention. If you select an issue discussed in one of the articles in this text, you have already located one source. Don't overlook college-based or local community issues as you search for a topic. The college or local newspapers may provide some sources, but you may also need to visit City Hall or find your own data through a questionnaire. Local topics can be fun and original.

Some people can generate good topics from thinking "in their heads," but others are more productive when they think "on paper." To think on paper, try freewriting, brainstorming, or asking questions. *Freewriting* forces you to get some ideas on paper, because the "rule" is that you write for several minutes. *Brainstorming* is similar except that you make lists of possibilities and play around with that list rather than writing full sentences for a specific length of time. A third strategy is *asking questions*. This strategy works well if you have a broad subject from which you need to create a more limited, focused topic. A student interested in Prohibition might develop these questions:

When was the law passed? When rescinded?

Who wanted Prohibition? Who opposed it?

What forces created the climate for the law's passage?

Where did the temperance movement originate? Where was it most influential?

Who benefited from Prohibition?

Why did people defy the law?

Observe that these questions include the *Who, What, Where, When,* and *Why* questions that reporters ask. For some topics a *How* question may also be appropriate.

You can also try searching an electronic database for topics under a broad subject heading. If, for example, you need a controversial topic in a science field and you recall an early fascination with dinosaurs, type in *dinosaur* to see what subheadings might suggest a research topic. Subheadings under the word will include *dinosaur behavior* and *dinosaur extinction*.

What Is the "Right" Size for a Topic?

Part of selecting a workable topic is making sure that the topic is sufficiently narrowed and focused. Students sometimes have trouble narrowing topics. Somehow it seems easier to write on a broad subject, such as education. You know there will be enough sources, all easy to find. But this line of thinking overlooks your purpose in doing research and what you know about good writing. Consider the following list of increasingly narrower topics about education:

1. Education
2. Problems in education today
3. Problems in K–12 education today
4. Problems with testing students
5. Why standardized tests aren't fair for all students

The first three items are clearly too broad for a short research project. Do you recognize that topic 4 is also too broad? Remember that the more limited and focused your topic, the more concrete and detailed—and thus convincing and engaging—your study will be.

WRITING A TENTATIVE CLAIM OR RESEARCH PROPOSAL

Once you have selected and narrowed a topic, you need to write a tentative claim, research question, or research proposal. Some instructors will ask to see a statement—from a sentence to a paragraph long—to be approved before you proceed. Others may require as much as a one-page proposal that includes a tentative claim, a basic organizational plan, and a description of types of sources to be used. Even if your instructor does not require anything in writing, you need to write something for your benefit—to direct your reading and thinking. Here are three possibilities.

1. **SUBJECT:**   Computers

   TOPIC: The impact of computers on the 20th century

   CLAIM: Computers had the greatest impact of any technological development in the 20th century.

   RESEARCH PROPOSAL: I propose to show that computers had the greatest impact of any technological development in the 20th century. I will show the influence of computers at work, in daily living, and in play to emphasize the breadth of influence. I will argue that other possibilities (such as cars) did not have the same impact as computers. I will check the library's book catalog and databases for sources on technological developments and on computers specifically. I will also interview a family friend who works with computers at the Pentagon.

This example illustrates several key ideas. First, the initial subject is both too broad and unfocused (What about computers?). Second, the claim is more focused than the topic statement because it asserts a position, a claim the student must support. Third, the research proposal is more helpful than the claim only because it includes some thoughts on developing the thesis and finding sources.

2. Less sure of your topic? Then write a research question or a more open-ended research proposal. Take, for example, a history student studying the

effects of Prohibition. She is not ready to write a thesis, but she can write a research proposal that suggests some possible approaches to the topic:

TOPIC:	The effect of Prohibition
RESEARCH QUESTION:	What were the effects of Prohibition on the United States?
RESEARCH PROPOSAL:	I will examine the effects of Prohibition on the United States in the 1920s (and possibly consider some long-term effects, depending on the amount of material on the topic). Specifically, I will look at the varying effects on urban and rural areas and on different classes in society.

3. Asking questions and working with fields of study (think of college departments) offers a third approach. Suppose your assignment is to defend a position on a current social issue. You think you want to do something "on television." Using an electronic database to search for a narrowed topic, you decide on the following:

TOPIC:	Television and violence
RESEARCH PROPOSAL:	I will explore the problem of violence on TV. I will read articles in current magazines and newspapers and see what's on the Internet.

Do you have a focused topic and a proposal that will guide your thinking and research? Not yet. Raise questions by field of study.

LITERARY/ HUMANITIES:	What kinds of violence are found on TV? Children's cartoons? Cop and mystery shows? The news? How are they alike? How different?
SOCIOLOGY:	What are the consequences to our society of a continual and heavy dose of violence on television?
PSYCHOLOGY:	What are the effects of television violence on children? Why are we drawn to violent shows?
POLITICS/ GOVERNMENT:	Should violence on TV be controlled in any way? If so, how?
EDUCATION:	What is the impact on the classroom when children grow up watching a lot of violence on TV? Does it impede social skills? Learning?

Now your thinking is more focused. After reflecting, you choose:

TOPIC:	The negative effects of television violence on children and some solutions
RESEARCH PROPOSAL:	I will demonstrate that children suffer from their exposure to so much violence on TV and propose some solutions. Until I read more, I am not certain of the solutions I will propose; I want to read arguments for and against the V-chip and ratings and other possibilities.

Do not settle for an unfocused topic and vague research proposal. To do so is only to put off the task of thinking about what you want to study and how you will proceed.

PREPARING A WORKING BIBLIOGRAPHY

To begin this next stage of your research, you need to know three things:

1. *Your search strategy.* If you are writing on a course-related topic, your starting place may be your textbook for relevant sections and possible sources (if the text contains a bibliography). For this course, you may find some potential sources among the readings in this text. Think about what you already know or have in hand as you plan your search strategy.

2. *A method for recording bibliographic information.* You have two choices: the always reliable 3 × 5 index cards or a bibliography file in your personal computer.

3. *The documentation format you will be using.* You may be assigned the Modern Language Association (MLA) format, or perhaps given a choice between MLA and the American Psychological Association (APA) documentation styles. Once you select the documentation style, skim the appropriate pages in either Chapter 10 (for MLA) or Chapter 12 (for APA) to get an overview of both content and style.

A list of possible sources is only a *working* bibliography because you do not yet know which sources you will use. (Your final bibliography will include only those sources you cite—actually refer to—in your paper.) A working bibliography will help you see what is available on your topic, note how to locate each source, and contain the information needed to document your paper. Whether you are using cards or computer files, follow these guidelines:

1. Check all reasonable catalogs and indexes for possible sources. (Use more than one reference source even if you locate enough sources there; you are looking for the best sources, not the first ones you find.)

2. Complete a card or prepare an entry for every potentially useful source. You won't know what to reject until you start a close reading of sources.

3. Copy (or download from an online catalog) all information needed to complete a citation and to locate the source. (When using an index that does not give all needed information, leave a space to be filled in when you actually read the source.)

4. Put bibliographic information in the correct format for every possible source; you will save time and make fewer errors. Do not mix or blend styles. When searching for sources, have your text handy and use the model in Chapter 10 or in Chapter 12 as guides.

The following brief guide to correct form will get you started. Illustrations are for cards, but the information and order will be the same in your PC file.

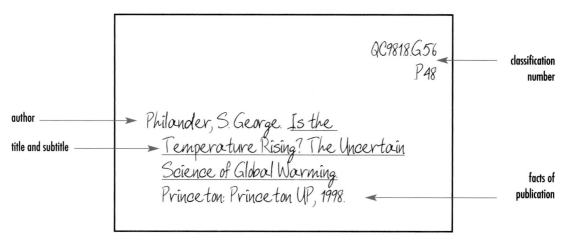

FIGURE 9.1 Bibliography Card for a Book

Guidelines are for MLA style only; use Chapter 12 if you have selected a different style.

Basic Form for Books

As Figure 9.1 shows, the basic MLA form for books includes the following information in this pattern:

1. The author's full name, last name first.
2. The title (and subtitle if there is one) of the book, underlined.
3. The facts of publication: the city of publication (followed by a colon), the publisher (followed by a comma), and the date of publication.

Note that periods are placed after the author's name, after the title, and at the end of the citation. Other information, when appropriate (e.g., the number of volumes), is added to this basic pattern. (See pp. 283–93 for many sample citations.) Include, in your working bibliography, the book's classification number so that you can find it in the library.

Basic Form for Articles

Figure 9.2 shows the simplest form for magazine articles. Include the following information, in this pattern:

1. The author's full name, last name first.
2. The title of the article, in quotation marks.
3. The facts of publication: the title of the periodical (underlined), the volume number (if the article is from a scholarly journal), the date (followed by a colon), and inclusive page numbers.

Morrell, Virginia. "A Cold, Hard
Look at Dinosaurs."
Discover Dec. 1996: 98–108.

FIGURE 9.2 Bibliography Card for a Magazine Article

You will discover that indexes rarely present information in MLA format. Here, for example, is a source on animal rights found in an online database:

Planet of the free apes? Gail Vines.
 New Scientist June 5, 1993 v138 n1876 p39(4)

To turn this information into a correct citation—if you read the article in the journal—you need to:

- Rearrange the information to put the author first.
- Eliminate bold type and place the article title in quotation marks, capitalizing the appropriate words.
- Underline the journal title and present the volume, date, and paging in MLA form.

The correct citation, as it would appear in your PC file, looks this way:

Vines, Gail. "Planet of the Free Apes?" New Scientist 5 June 1993: 39–42.

If you obtain a full-text copy of the article from the online database, your citation requires additional information about the database. (See pp. 300–302 for examples.)

NOTE: A collection of printouts, slips of paper, and backs of envelopes is not a working bibliography! You may have to return to the library for missing information, and you risk making serious errors in documentation. Know the basics of your documentation format and follow that format faithfully.

KNOWING YOUR LIBRARY

All libraries contain books and periodicals, and a system for accessing them. A *book collection* contains the *general collection* (books that circulate), the *reference collection* (books of a general nature essential to research), and the *reserve book collection*. The library's *periodicals collection* consists of popular magazines, scholarly journals, and newspapers. Electronic databases with full texts of articles provide alternatives to the print periodicals collection. (See below.)

The book and periodicals collections are supplemented by audiovisual materials, including works on CD, tape, microfilm or microfiche, and online. Many libraries store back issues of periodicals on microfilm, so learn where the microfilm readers are and how to use them.

Most libraries today provide coin- or card-operated photocopying machines. Using these gives you one way to study noncirculating materials outside the library. In addition, articles from electronic databases and Internet sources can be printed or, in many cases, e-mailed directly to your own PC.

 REMEMBER: All works, regardless of their source or the format in which you obtain them—and this includes online sources—must be fully documented in your paper. Also, there are certain restrictions on copyrighted materials; know the rules to avoid infringing on a copyright.

Locating Books

Your chief guide to the book (and audiovisual) collection is the catalog, probably a computer database.

In a catalog there are at least three entries for each book: the author entry, the title entry, and one or more subject entries. Online catalogs continue to use these same access points plus a keyword option and possibly others, such as the book's International Standard Book Number (ISBN). When you go to your library's home screen and select the catalog, you will come to the search screen. Usually, keyword is the default. If you know the exact title, switch to title, type in the title, and click on "submit search." If instead you want a list of all of the library's books by Hemingway, for example, click on author and type in Hemingway. Keep in mind:

- With a title search, do not type any initial article (a, an, the). Thus, to locate *The Great Gatsby*, type in "Great Gatsby."
- Use correct spelling. If you are unsure of a spelling, use a keyword instead of an author or title search.
- If you are looking for a list of possible books on your subject, do a keyword or subject search.

Reading Entries: Brief and Long View Screens

If you do an author search by last name only, you will get a list of all of the library's books written by writers with that last name. A keyword search will provide a list of all book titles containing your keyword. These "brief view" lists provide enough information to locate a book in the library: author, title, and classification number—the number by which the book is shelved (see Figure 9.3).

For books that look promising for your research, click on *View Record* to obtain the "long view" screen. This screen (see Figure 9.4) provides additional

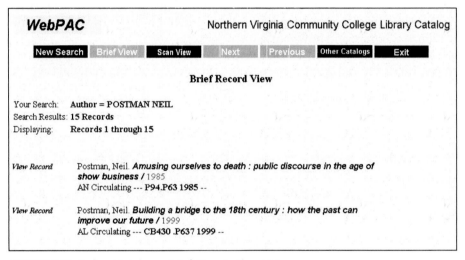

FIGURE 9.3 Online Catalog—Brief View Author List

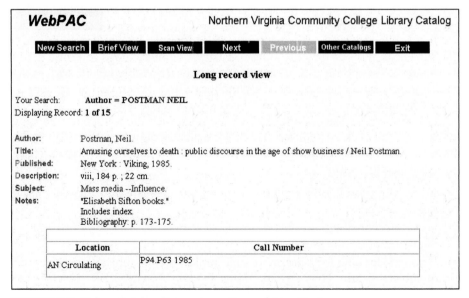

FIGURE 9.4 Online Catalog Entry—Long View of One Book

information, including bibliographic details needed for documentation and one or more subject listings that you can use to find other books on the same subject. For potentially useful books, copy all needed information into your working bibliography.

Classification of Books

Books are shelved according to either the Library of Congress classification system or the Dewey decimal system. You are probably familiar with the Dewey system used by many public libraries, especially small ones. Most colleges, however, use the Library of Congress system, so you will need to familiarize yourself with it.

The LC system classifies with a letter to indicate major subject areas. Subdivisions within each subject category are indicated by a second letter: D for history, DC for French history. Further subdivisions reflecting type, date, author, and specific work are indicated by numerals and the first initial of the author's last name. A specific British history text, George M. Trevelyan's *The English Revolution, 1688–1689,* would have this number:

DA
452
.T7

USING THE REFERENCE COLLECTION

The research process often begins with the reference collection. You will find atlases, dictionaries, encyclopedias, general histories, critical studies, and biographies. In addition, various reference tools such as bibliographies and indexes are part of the reference collection.

Many tools in the reference collection once only in print form are now also online. Some are now only online. Yet online is not always the way to go. Let's consider some of the advantages of each of the formats:

Advantages of the Print Reference Collection

1. The reference tool may be only in print—use it.
2. The print form covers the period you are studying. (Most online indexes and abstracts cover only from 1980 to the present.)
3. In a book, with a little scanning of pages, you can often find what you need without getting spelling or commands exactly right.
4. If you know the best reference source to use and are looking for only a few items, the print source can be faster than the online source.
5. All computer terminals are in use—or down—open a book!

Advantages of Online Reference Materials

1. Online databases are likely to provide the most up-to-date information.
2. You can usually search all years covered at one time.
3. Full texts (with graphics) are sometimes available, as well as indexes with detailed summaries of articles. Both can be printed or e-mailed to your PC.
4. Through links to the Internet, you have access to an amazing amount of material. (Unless you focus your keyword search, however, you may be overwhelmed.)

Before using any reference work, take a few minutes to check its date, purpose, and organization. If you are new to online searching, take a few minutes to learn about each reference tool by working through the online tutorial. (Go to the Help screen.) These strategies can supplement the following brief review of some key reference tools.

Basic Reference Tools

Use your library's reference collection as you need to for facts, for background information, and for indexes to possible sources.

Dictionaries

For the spelling of specialized words not found in your PC's dictionary, consult an appropriate subject dictionary; for foreign words, the appropriate foreign-language dictionary. If you need a word's origin or its definitions from an earlier time, use one of the unabridged dictionaries. Here are two to know:

> *Webster's Encyclopedic Unabridged Dictionary of the English Language.* 1996.
> *The Oxford English Dictionary.* 20 volumes in print. Also online.

General Encyclopedias

Two multi-volume encyclopedias to know are the *Encyclopedia Americana* and the *Encyclopaedia Britannica*. The *Britannica,* the *World Book,* and other encyclopedias are available online as well as in print.

Atlases

Atlases provide much more than simple maps showing capital cities and the names of rivers. Historical atlases show changes in politics, economics, and culture. Topographical atlases support studies in the earth sciences and many environmental issues. Here are just two:

> *Historical Atlas of the United States.* National Geographic Society, 1988.
> *The Times Atlas of the World.* 9th ed. 1992.

Check to see what atlases your library has on CD-ROM.

Quotations, Mythology, and Folklore

Use the following works to understand unfamiliar references:

> *Bartlett's Familiar Quotations.* 16th ed. 1992. In print and online.
> *Funk and Wagnall's Standard Dictionary of Folklore, Mythology, and Legend.*

Almanacs and Yearbooks

The following sources answer all kinds of questions about current events and provide statistical information on just about anything. Many of these works—and others like them—are both in print and online. Check to see which format your library offers.

> *Congressional Record.* 1873 to date. Issued daily during sessions. Online.
> *Facts on File.* 1940 to date. Digest of important news events. Online.
> *Statistical Abstract of the United States.* 1978 to date. Annual publication of the Bureau of the Census. Online.

Biographical Dictionaries

Most libraries have an array of biographical dictionaries, important tools for investigating authors with whom you are unfamiliar.

> *Contemporary Authors.* 1962 to date. A multivolume guide to current fiction and nonfiction writers and their books. Online.
> *International Who's Who.* 1935 to date. Contains brief biographies of important persons from almost every country.
> *American Men and Women of Science.* Provides brief sketches of more than 150,000 scientists. Lists degrees held and fields of specialization. Regularly updated.
> *Who's Who.* 1849 to date. English men and women.
> *Who's Who in America.* 1899 to date.
> *Who's Who in American Women.* 1958 to date.

USING INDEXES TO PERIODICALS: IN PRINT AND ONLINE

Periodicals (magazines, journals, and newspapers) provide good sources for research projects, especially for projects on current issues. The best way to access articles on your topic is to use one or more periodical indexes. To be efficient, you want to select the most useful indexes for your particular study. Your library will maintain some print indexes to popular magazines, some for scholarly journals, and some to newspapers. In addition, your library probably provides many online databases. Online databases are more likely than older print indexes to blend magazines, journals, and newspaper articles, and many online databases include full texts of the articles. Learn which of the indexes provide full texts and which indexes provide only lists of possibly useful articles that you must then locate in your library's paper collection of periodicals.

The Reader's Guide to Periodical Literature

Probably the most-used paper index, *The Reader's Guide to Periodical Literature* (1900 to date) combines author and subject headings that guide users to articles in about 200 popular magazines. As the sample entries in Figure 9.5 show, the information is heavily abbreviated. When using this index, study the explanation provided and check the list of periodicals found in the front of each volume for the complete title of each magazine. Use this index if you want articles written prior to 1980.

The New York Times Index

Newspapers are a good source of information about both contemporary topics and historical events and issues. Because it is one of the most thorough and respected newspapers, the *New York Times* is available in most libraries. So, when your topic warrants it, become familiar with the *New York Times Index,* for it can guide you to articles as far back as the mid-nineteenth century. (Back issues of the newspaper are on microfilm.) The print *NYT Index* is a subject index, cumulated and bound annually, with articles arranged chronologically under each subject heading. The *NYT Index* is also online; your library may have both formats. Articles in the *New York Times* are indexed in other online databases, sometimes with full texts.

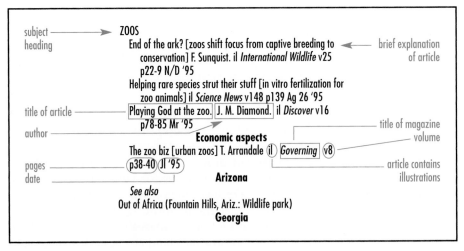

FIGURE 9.5 Entries in *The Reader's Guide to Periodical Literature*

Online Databases

You will probably access online databases by going to your library's home page and then clicking on the appropriate term or icon. (You may have found the book catalog by clicking on "library catalog"; you may find the databases by clicking on "library resources" or some other descriptive label.) You will need to choose a particular database and then type in your keyword for a basic search or select "advanced search" to limit your search by date or periodical or to search for articles by a specific author. Each library will create somewhat different screens, but the basic process of selecting among choices provided and then typing in your search commands remains the same. Figure 9.6 shows a first screen in response to the choice to search for magazine and newspaper articles. Notice that the librarians are suggesting seven databases that are useful for many undergraduate research projects. If you do not want to work in one of these seven, you can click on the alphabetical list of databases or search by subject. (Note: Your library probably has hundreds of databases.) To begin your search for specific articles, select the database that seems most useful for your topic.

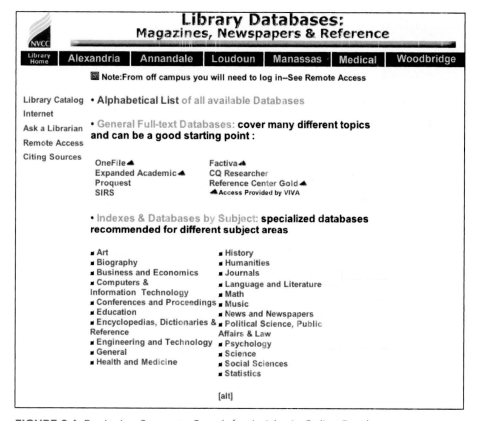

FIGURE 9.6 Beginning Screen to Search for Articles in Online Databases

Suppose you select Expanded Academic. Observe the first screen, shown in Figure 9.7. You can do a basic keyword search or modify your search in a number of ways. The basic keyword search for "zoos and animal rights" yielded 12 articles. Figure 9.8 shows a partial list of those "hits."

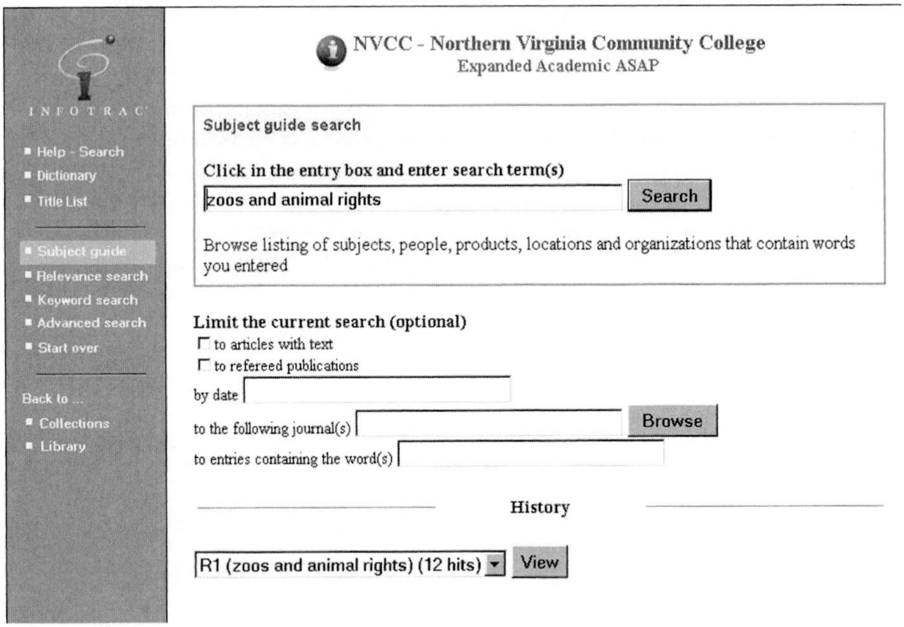

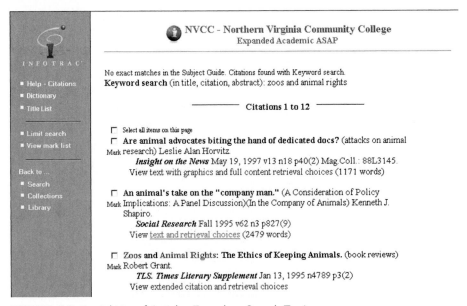

FIGURE 9.7 Search Screen for Online Database

FIGURE 9.8 Partial List of Articles Found on Search Topic

GUIDELINES for Using Online Databases

Keep these points in mind as you use online databases.

1. **Although some online databases provide full texts of all articles, others provide full texts of only some of the articles indexed.** The articles not in full text will have to be located in a print collection of periodicals.

2. **Articles indexed but not available in full text often come with a brief summary or abstract.** This allows you to decide whether the article looks useful for your project. *Do not treat the abstract as the article. Do not use material from it and cite the author. If you want to use the article, find it in your library's print collection or obtain it from another library.*

3. **The information you need for documenting material used from an article is not in correct format for any of the standard documentation styles.** You will have to reorder the information and use the correct style for writing titles. If your instructor wants to see a list of possible sources in MLA format, do not hand in a printout of articles from an online database. (Follow MLA citation guidelines on pp. 300–302.)

4. **Because no one database covers all magazines, you may want to search several databases that seem relevant to your project.**

Indexes to Academic Journals: In Print and Online

The indexes to magazines and journals just reviewed provide many good articles for undergraduate research. At times, though, you may need to use articles exclusively from scholarly journals. Many of the more specialized indexes to journals began as print indexes but are now online as well. The following is a brief list of some of the more academic indexes students frequently use. Your reference librarian can recommend others appropriate to your study.

APPLIED SCIENCE AND TECHNOLOGY INDEX:	An index to periodicals covering engineering, data processing, earth sciences, space science, and more. Online through FirstSearch.
BOOK REVIEW DIGEST:	Begun in 1905, this index is arranged by author of the book reviewed. It contains brief reviews of both fiction and nonfiction works. Online.
ESSAY AND GENERAL LITERATURE INDEX:	From 1900, this author and subject index includes references to both biographical and critical materials. Its chief focus is literary criticism.
EDUCATIONAL RESEARCH INFORMATION CENTER (ERIC):	In its print form, there are two sections, Current Index to Journals in Education and Resources in Education, a collection of unpublished reports on educational issues. ERIC is also online.

THE GPO PUBLICATIONS REFERENCE FILE OR GPO ACCESS (ON THE WEB):	The former has been replaced by the regularly updated index on the Internet. You can reach GPO Access at www.access.gpo.gov/su_docs.
HUMANITIES INDEX:	This index lists articles on art, literature, philosophy, folklore, history, and related topics. Online.
MLA INTERNATIONAL BIBLIOGRAPHY:	The annual listing by the Modern Language Association of books, articles, and dissertations in language and literature. Online.
PUBLIC AFFAIRS INFORMATION SERVICE (PAIS):	This index covers books, pamphlets, reports, and articles on economics, government, social issues, and public affairs. It is international in scope and emphasizes works that are strong on facts and statistics. Online.
SCIENCE CITATION INDEX:	An index of more than 3,000 journals in mathematics and the natural, physical, and behavioral sciences. It includes an index to articles, a subject index based on keywords appearing in titles of articles indexed, and a citation index, arranged by author, that reveals which articles are referred to by other authors in their papers. The online version is SciSearch or through Web of Science.
SOCIAL SCIENCES CITATION INDEX:	Like the Science Citation Index, this index includes a source index, a subject index by keywords, and a citation index. The online version is Social SciSearch or through Web of Science.

SEARCHING THE INTERNET

In addition to using the online databases to find sources, you can search the Internet directly. If you are new to Internet searching, you may want to study online tutorials to be efficient in your search. Also, your college library may conduct workshops on searching—check it out.

Keep in mind these facts about the Internet:

- The Internet is both disorganized and huge, so you can waste time trying to find information that is easily obtained in a reference book in your library.
- The Internet is best at providing current information, such as news and movie reviews. It is also a great source of government information.

- Because anyone can create a website and put anything on it, you will have to especially careful in evaluating Internet sources. Remember that articles in magazines and journals have been selected by editors and are often peer reviewed as well, but no one selects or rejects material for the Web. (More on evaluating sources can be found in Chapter 10.)

Basic Services and Functions of the Internet

When you have access to the Internet, you can obtain information in a variety of ways. The most common are described below.

E-mail

E-mail can be used instead of a printed letter to request information from a government agency or company.

Mailing Lists (Listservs)

You can sign up to receive, via your e-mail, continually updated bulletins on a particular subject. Listservs are essentially organized mailing lists. If you find one relevant to your project, you can subscribe for a while and unsubscribe when you are no longer interested.

Newsgroups

Newsgroups differ from listservs in that the discussions and exchanges are collected for you to retrieve; they are not sent to your e-mail address. Otherwise they are much the same: both are a type of discussion group. To find newsgroups on a specific subject, go to http://groups.google.com, a research tool sponsored by the search engine Google, that surveys all Usenet newsgroups.

World Wide Web

To access the Web from your library terminal or on your own PC through a hookup with your college library, you will, as with the catalog and online databases, start at your library's home page. (If you work from your PC using your Internet service provider's home page, you probably already know something about selecting a search engine or initiating a search.) Usually selecting "search the Internet" will take you to a menu of various search engines and subject directories. Note that not all search engines are the same, and people differ on which are the best, so you may want to get some help selecting the best one for your search. Here are some sites to visit for help in selecting an appropriate search engine:

Librarians' Index to the Internet: http://lii.org
Greg R. Notess's search engine comparison pages: www.notess.com/search
Search Engine Watch: www.searchenginewatch.com

GUIDELINES for Searching the Web

How much information you may find searching for a specific topic, and how useful it is, will vary from one research project to another. Here are some general guidelines to aid your research on the Internet:

1. **Bookmark sites you expect to use often so that you do not have to remember complicated Web addresses, or uniform resource locators (URLs).**

2. **Make your search as precise as possible to avoid getting overwhelmed with hits.**

3. **If you are searching for a specific phrase, put quotation marks around the words.** This will reduce the number of hits and lead to sites more useful to your research. Examples: "Environmental Protection Agency" or "civil disobedience."

4. **Use Boolean connectors to make your search more precise.**

   - AND: This connector limits results to those sites that contain both terms, for example, "zoos AND animal rights."

   - OR: This connector extends the hits to include all sites that contain one or the other search term. So, "zoos OR animal rights" will generate a list of sites containing either term.

   - NOT: This connector limits the search to only the first term, not the second. Thus, "zoos NOT animal rights" will give you sites only about zoo issues not involving animal rights.

5. **If you are not successful with one search engine, try a different one.** Remember that each search engine searches only a part of the Internet.

6. **If you are not successful with a second search engine, check your spelling.** Search engines cannot guess what you mean; spelling must be exact.

7. **To get the best sites for most college research projects, try a directory of evaluated sites or subject guide rather than, say, Yahoo!** (Yahoo! is better for news, people searches, and commercial sites.) Some of the best academic subject guides include:

   - The Argus Clearinghouse (www.clearinghouse.net)

   - The University of California's Infomine (http://infomine.ucr.edu)

   - Internet Scout Project (http://scout.cs.wisc.edu)

8. **Be certain to complete a bibliography card—including the date you accessed the material—for each separate site from which you take information.** Remember: All sources must be documented, including Internet sources. (See pp. 299–302 for documentation guidelines.)

DOING FIELD RESEARCH

Field research can enrich many projects. The following sections give some suggestions.

Federal, State, and Local Government Documents

In addition to federal documents you may obtain through *PAIS* or *GPO Access,* department and agency websites, or the Library of Congress's good legislative site, *Thomas* (http://thomas.loc.gov), consider state and county archives, maps, and other published materials. Instead of selecting a national or global topic, consider examining the debate over a controversial bill introduced in your state legislature. Use online databases to locate articles on the bill and the debate and interview legislators and journalists who participated in or covered the debates or served on committees that worked with the bill.

You can also request specific documents on a topic from appropriate state or county agencies and nonprofit organizations. One student, given the assignment of examining solutions to an ecological problem, decided to study the local problem of preserving the Chesapeake Bay. She obtained issues of the Chesapeake Bay Foundation newsletter and brochures prepared by them advising homeowners about hazardous household waste materials that end up in the Bay. Added to her sources were bulletins on soil conservation and landscaping tips for improving the area's water quality. Local problems can lead to interesting research topics because they are current and relevant to you and because they involve uncovering different kinds of source materials.

Correspondence

Business and government officials are usually willing to respond to written requests for information. Make your letter brief and well written. Either include a self-addressed, stamped envelope for the person's convenience or e-mail your request. If you are not e-mailing, write as soon as you discover the need for information and be prepared to wait several weeks for a reply. It is appropriate to indicate your deadline and ask for a timely response. Three guidelines for either letters or e-mails to keep in mind are:

1. Explain precisely what information you need. Avoid writing a general "please send me anything you have on this topic" kind of letter. Busy professionals are more likely to respond to requests that are specific and reveal a control of the topic.
2. Do not request information that can be found in your library's reference collection.
3. Explain how you plan to use the information. Businesses especially are understandably concerned with their public image and will be disinclined to provide information that you intend to use as a means of attacking them.

Use reference guides to companies and government agencies or their websites to obtain addresses and the person to whom your letter or e-mail should be addressed. For companies, address your request to the public information officer. For e-mail addresses, check the organization's home page.

Interviews

Some experts are available for personal interviews. Call or write for an appointment as soon as you recognize the value of an interview. Remember that interviews are more likely to be scheduled with state and local officials than with the president of General Motors. If you are studying a local problem, also consider leaders of the civic association with an interest in the issue. In many communities, the local historian or a librarian will be a storehouse of information about the community. Former teachers can be interviewed for papers on education. Interviews with doctors or nurses can add a special dimension to papers on medical issues.

If an interview is appropriate for your topic, follow these guidelines:

1. Prepare specific questions in advance.
2. Arrive on time, properly dressed, and behave in a polite, professional manner.
3. Take notes, asking the interviewee to repeat key statements so that your notes are accurate.
4. Take a tape recorder with you but ask permission to use it before taping.
5. If you quote any statements in your paper, quote accurately, eliminating only such minor speech habits as "you know's" and "uhm's." (See Chapter 10 for proper documentation of interviews.)
6. Direct the interview with your prepared questions, but also give the interviewee the chance to approach the topic in his or her own way. You may obtain information or views that had not occurred to you.
7. Do not get into a debate with the interviewee. You are there to learn, not to try to change the interviewee's thinking.

Lectures

Check the appropriate information sources at your school to keep informed of visiting speakers. If you are fortunate enough to attend a lecture relevant to a current project, take careful, detailed notes. Because a lecture is a source, use of information or ideas from it must be presented accurately and then documented. (See Chapter 10 for documentation format.)

Films, Tapes, Television

Your library will have audiovisual materials that provide good sources for some kinds of topics. For example, if you are studying *Death of a Salesman,* view a videotaped version of the play. Also pay attention to documentaries on public television and to the many news and political talk shows on both public and commercial channels. In many cases transcripts of shows can be obtained from the TV station. Alternatively, tape the program while watching it so that you can view it several times. The documentation format for such nonprint sources is illustrated in Chapter 10.

Surveys, Questionnaires, and Original Research

Depending on your paper, you may want to conduct a simple survey or write and administer a questionnaire. Surveys can be used for many campus and local issues, for topics on behavior and attitudes of college students and/or faculty, and for topics on consumer habits. Prepare a brief list of questions with space for answers. Poll faculty through their mailboxes or e-mail and students individually on campus or in your classes. When writing questions, keep these guidelines in mind:

- Use simple, clear language.
- Devise a series of short questions rather than only a few that have several parts to them. (You want to separate information for better analysis.)
- Phrase questions to avoid wording that seeks to control the answer. For example, do *not* ask: How did you survive the *horrors* of the Depression? Do *not* write: Did you perform your civic duty by voting in the last election? These are loaded questions that prejudge the respondent's answers.

In addition to surveys and questionnaires, you can incorporate some original research. As you read sources on your topic, be alert to reports of studies that you could redo and update in part or on a smaller scale. Many topics on advertising and television give opportunities for your own analysis. Local-issue topics may offer good opportunities for gathering information on your own, not just from your reading. One student, examining the controversy over a proposed new shopping mall on part of the Manassas Civil War Battlefield in Virginia, made the argument that the mall served no practical need in the community. He supported his position by describing existing malls, including the number and types of stores each contained and the number of miles each was from the proposed new mall. How did he obtain this information? He drove around the area, counting miles and stores. Sometimes a seemingly unglamorous approach to a topic turns out to be an imaginative one.

CHAPTER 10

Exploring Sources, Selecting Support, and Documenting
(Using MLA)

As you study your sources, keep rethinking your purpose and approach. Test your research proposal or tentative claim against what you are learning. Remember: you can always change the direction and focus of your paper as new approaches occur to you, and you can even change your position as you reflect on what you are learning.

USING SOURCES EFFECTIVELY

You will work with sources more effectively if you keep in mind why you are using them. What you are looking for will vary somewhat, depending on your topic and purpose, but there are several basic approaches:

1. *Acquiring information and viewpoints firsthand.* Suppose that you are concerned about the mistreatment of animals kept in zoos. You do not want to just read what others have to say on this issue. First, visit a zoo, taking notes on what you see. Second, before you go, plan to interview at least one person on the zoo staff, preferably a veterinarian who can explain the zoo's guidelines for animal care. Only after gathering and thinking about these *primary sources* do you want to add to your knowledge by reading articles and books—*secondary sources.* Many kinds of topics require the use of both primary and secondary sources. If you want to study violence in children's TV shows, for example, you should first spend some time watching specific shows and taking notes.

2. *Acquiring new knowledge.* Suppose you are interested in breast cancer research and treatment, but you do not know much about the choices of treatment and, in general, where we are with this medical problem. You will need to turn to sources first to learn about the topic. You should begin with sources that will give you an overview, perhaps a historical perspective of how knowledge and treatment have progressed in the last 30 years. Similarly, if your topic is the effects of Prohibition in the 1920s, you will need to read first for knowledge but also with an eye to ways to focus the topic and organize your paper.

3. *Understanding the issues.* Suppose you think that you know your views on gun control or immigration, so you intend to read only to obtain some useful statistical information to support your argument. Should you scan sources quickly, looking for facts you can use? This approach may be too hasty. As explained in Chapter 3, good arguments are built on a knowledge of counterarguments. You are wise to study sources presenting a variety of attitudes on your issue so that you understand—and can refute—the arguments of others. Remember, too, that with controversial issues often the best argument is a conciliatory one that presents a middle ground and seeks to bring people together. You may also want to consider interviewing an elected official or administering a questionnaire to fellow students.

EVALUATING SOURCES, MAINTAINING CREDIBILITY

When you use facts and opinions from sources, you are saying to readers that the facts are accurate and the ideas credible. If you do not evaluate your sources before using them, you risk losing your credibility as a writer. (Remember Aristotle's idea of *ethos,* how your character is judged.) Just because they are in print does not mean that a writer's "facts" are reliable or ideas worthwhile. Judging the usefulness and reliability of potential sources is an essential part of the research process.

GUIDELINES for Evaluating Sources

Today, with access to so much material on the Internet, the need to evaluate is even more crucial. Here are some strategies for evaluating sources, with special attention to Internet sources:

1. **Locate the author's credentials.** Periodicals often list their writers' degrees, current position, and other publications; books, similarly, contain an "about the author" section. If you do not see this information, check various biographical dictionaries (*Biography Index, Contemporary Authors*) for information about the author. For articles on the Web, look for the author's e-mail address or a link to a home page. *Never use a Web source that does not identify the author or the organization responsible for the material. Critical question:* Is this author qualified to write on this topic? How do I know?

2. **Judge the credibility of the work.** For books, read how reviewers evaluated the book when it was first published. For articles, judge the respectability of the magazine or journal. Study the author's use of documentation as one measure of credibility. Scholarly works cite sources. Well-researched and reliable pieces in quality popular magazines will also make clear the sources of any statistics used or the credentials of any authority who is quoted. One good rule: Never use undocumented statistical information. Another judge of credibility is the quality of writing. Do not use sources filled with grammatical and mechanical errors. For Web sources, find out what institution hosts the site. If you have not heard of the company or organization, find out more about it. *Critical question:* Why should I believe information/ideas from this source?

3. **Select only those sources that are at an appropriate level for your research.** Avoid works that are either too specialized or too elementary for college research. You may not understand the former (and thus could misrepresent them in your paper), and you gain nothing from the latter. *Critical question:* Will this source provide a sophisticated discussion for educated adults?

4. **Understand the writer's purpose.** Consider the writer's intended audience. Be cautious using works designed to reinforce biases already shared by the intended audience. Is the work written to persuade rather than to inform and analyze? Examine the writing for emotionally charged language. For Internet sources, ask yourself why this person or institution decided to have a website or contribute to a newsgroup. *Critical question:* Can I trust the information from this source, given the apparent purpose of the work?

5. **In general, choose current sources.** Some studies published years ago remain classics, but many older works have become outdated. In scientific and technical fields, the "information revolution" has outdated some works published only five years ago. So look at publication dates (When was the website page last updated?) and pass over outdated sources in favor of current studies. *Critical question:* Is this information still accurate?

DOCUMENTING SOURCES TO AVOID PLAGIARISM

Before beginning the process of taking notes, you need to understand why and how to document. The need to document accurately and fully applies to all researchers, regardless of the particular pattern used. Proper documentation shows readers the breadth of your research and distinguishes between the work of others and your understanding of the topic.

Improper documentation of sources—plagiarism—is both unethical and illegal. To fail to document sources is to lose your credibility and reputation. Ideas, new information, and wording belong to their author. To borrow them without acknowledgment is against the law and has led to many celebrated lawsuits. Paying for a paper from a service and submitting a friend's paper are clear examples of plagiarism. More often, though, students plagiarize unintentionally because they do not understand the requirements of documentation. Be certain that you know what constitutes appropriate documentation.

NOTE: MLA documentation requires that precise page references be given for all ideas, opinions, and information taken from sources—except for common knowledge. Author and page references provided in the text are supported by complete bibliographic citations on the Works Cited page.

In sum, you are required to document the following:

- Direct quotations from sources
- Paraphrased ideas and opinions from sources
- Summaries of ideas from sources
- Factual information, except common knowledge, from sources

Understand that putting an author's ideas in your own words in a paraphrase or summary does not eliminate the requirement of documentation. To illustrate, consider the following excerpt from Thomas R. Schueler's report *Controlling Urban Runoff* (Washington Metropolitan Water Resources Planning Board, 1987: 3–4) and a student paragraph based on the report.

SOURCE

The aquatic ecosystems in urban headwater streams are particularly susceptible to the impacts of urbanization . . . Dietemann (1975), Ragan and Dietemann (1976), Klein (1979) and WMCOG (1982) have all tracked trends in fish diversity and abundance over time in local urbanizing streams. Each of the studies has shown that fish communities become less diverse and are composed of more tolerant species after the surrounding watershed is developed. Sensitive fish species either disappear or occur very rarely. In most cases, the total number of fish in urbanizing streams may also decline.

Similar trends have been noted among aquatic insects which are the major food resource for fish . . . Higher post-development sediment and trace metals can interfere in their efforts to gather food. Changes in water temperature, oxygen levels, and substrate composition can further reduce the species diversity and abundance of the aquatic insect community.

STUDENT PARAGRAPH

Studies have shown that fish communities become less diverse as the amount of runoff increases. Sensitive fish species either disappear or occur very rarely, and, in most cases, the total number of fish declines. Aquatic insects, a major source of food for fish, also decline because sediment and trace metals interfere with their food-gathering efforts. Increased water temperature and lower oxygen levels can further reduce the species diversity and abundance of the aquatic insect community.

The student's opening words establish a reader's expectation that the student has taken information from a source, as indeed the student has. But where is the documentation? The student's paraphrase is a good example of plagiarism: an unacknowledged paraphrase of borrowed information that even collapses into copying the source's exact wording in two places. For MLA style, the author's name and the precise page numbers are needed throughout the paragraph. Additionally, most of the first sentence and the final phrase must be put into the student's own words or be placed within quotation marks. The following revised paragraph shows an appropriate acknowledgment of the source used.

REVISED STUDENT PARAGRAPH

In *Controlling Urban Runoff,* Thomas Schueler explains that studies have shown "that fish communities become less diverse as the amount of runoff increases" (3). Sensitive fish species either disappear or occur very rarely and, in most cases, the total number of fish declines. Aquatic insects, a major source of food for fish, also decline because sediment and trace metals interfere with their food-gathering efforts. Increased water temperature and lower oxygen levels, Schueler concludes, "can further reduce the species diversity and abundance of the aquatic insect community" (4).

What Is Common Knowledge?

In general, common knowledge includes:

- Undisputed dates
- Well-known facts
- Generally known facts, terms, and concepts in a field of study when you are writing in that field

So, do not cite a source for the dates of the American Revolution. If you are writing a paper for a psychology class, do not cite your text when using terms such as *ego* or *sublimation*. However, you must cite a historian who analyzes the causes of England's loss to the Colonies or a psychologist who disputes Freud's ideas. *Opinions* about well-known facts must be documented. *Discussions* of debatable dates, terms, or concepts must be documented. When in doubt, defend your integrity and document.

TAKING NOTES ON SOURCES

As you read and learn, expand your research proposal in two ways. First, draft a claim statement that is as clear and focused as you feel comfortable with at this stage. Second, list possible reasons in support of your claim. Keep this list informal but use it to start thinking about the parts your paper will need. Having an informal outline will guide your search for information and your thinking about how and where to use the information.

How are you going to keep track of information and ideas from your study? You have three possibilities: handwritten notes on cards, keyboarded notes in PC files, and annotations of photocopies of sources. How to choose? If your instructor requires you to hand in notes, then you must use the first or second strategy. (Just print out your files and cut pages into separate note "cards.") Here are guidelines for all three methods plus, in Figure 10.1, an example of good note taking.

GUIDELINES for Effective Note Taking

Cards

1. **Use either 4 × 6 cards or half sheets of letter-size paper.**
2. **Write in ink.**
3. **Write only one item on each card.** Each card should contain only one idea, piece of information, or group of related facts. The flexibility of cards is lost if you do not follow this procedure. You want to be able to group cards according to your outline when you are ready to draft the paper.

With a Computer

1. **Make one file titled "notes" or make a separate file for each note.**

2. **Use clear headings and subheadings for notes so that you can find particular notes easily.**

3. **Consider printing copies of your notes and cutting them into separate "cards" for organizing prior to drafting.** (When drafting, do not re-keyboard. Just use your printed notes as a guide to placement in the draft.) Use the "cut and paste" or "move" features of your word processor to rearrange notes into the order you want.

Annotating Photocopies

1. **Do not endlessly highlight your photocopies.** Instead, carefully bracket those passages that contain information you want to use.

2. **Write a note in the margin next to bracketed passages indicating how and where you think you want to use that material.** Use the language of your informal outline to annotate marked passages (e.g., "causes," "effects," "rebuttal to counterargument," "solutions").

3. **Keep in mind that you will have to paraphrase most of the marked passages before using the material in your draft.**

Writing Notes: Cards or Keyboarded

1. **Study first; take notes later.** First, do background reading. Second, skim what appear to be your chief sources. Prepare summary notes and annotate photocopies of sources. Read so that you can develop your preliminary outline. Learn what the writers on your topic consider to be important facts, issues, and arguments. Keep in mind that taking too many useless notes is a frustrating, time-wasting activity.

2. **Before preparing any note, identify the source of the note.** Write or type the author's name, a shortened title if necessary, and the precise page number from which the material comes. *Remember: All borrowed information and ideas must be documented with precise page numbers if you are using MLA style—and for all direct quotations if you are using APA style.*

3. **Type or write an identifying word or phrase for each note.** Identifying words or phrases will help you sort cards or find notes when you are ready to draft. Select words carefully to correspond to the sections of your preliminary outline.

4. **Take down the information itself—accurately and clearly.** Be sure to put all directly quoted passages within quotation marks. To treat a direct quotation as a paraphrase in your paper is to plagiarize.

5. **Distinguish between fact and opinion.** Notes that contain opinion should be indicated with such phrases as "Smith believes that" or "Smith asserts that." Alternatively, label the note "opinion."

6. **Distinguish between information from sources and your own opinions, questions, and reactions to the recorded information.** Write notes to yourself so that you do not forget good ideas that come to you as you are reading. Just be certain to label your notes "my notes"—or draw (or type) a line between information from a source and your response.

Should I Quote or Paraphrase Notes or Use Photocopies of Sources?

Here are the arguments:

- Most of your paper should be in your own words, so most of your notes should be paraphrases or summaries. Putting off paraphrasing means just that—putting it off until you are under the pressure of writing the paper.
- Taking direct-quotation notes will give you the exact wording of passages to think about when you draft your paper. At the drafting stage, you can turn the quoted passages into paraphrases.
- The previous point, along with the valid point of convenience, justifies using copies of sources that you annotate to show what passages you want to use. The potential problem is the same as that for direct-quotation notes.

Probably some combination of strategies is a good choice. Photocopy (or download or e-mail to yourself) key articles so that you have the entire article to work with. Initially tab key passages in books with Post-it notes or slips of paper. Then, as you get close to finishing your study of sources, make at least some paraphrased notes to start the process of moving away from the language of original sources. The more sources you are using, the more convenient and efficient notes will be when you are ready to draft your paper.

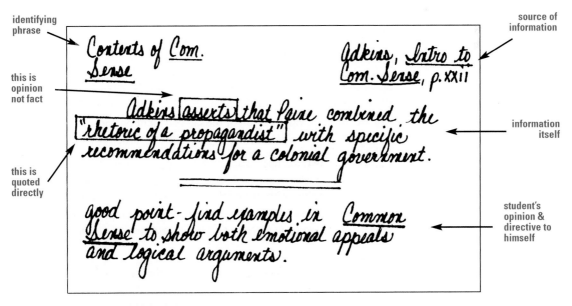

FIGURE 10.1 Sample Note Card

USING "TAGS" TO AVOID MISLEADING DOCUMENTATION

If you are an honest student, you do not want to submit a paper that is plagiarized, even though that plagiarism was unintentional on your part. What leads to unintentional plagiarism?

- A researcher takes careless notes, neglecting to include precise page numbers on the notes, but uses the information anyway, without any documentation.

- A researcher works in material from sources in such a way that, even with page references, readers cannot tell what has been taken from the sources.

Good note-taking strategies will keep you from the first pitfall. Avoiding the second problem means becoming skilled in ways to include source material in your writing while still making your indebtedness to sources absolutely clear to readers. The way to do this: give the author's name in the essay. You can also include, when appropriate, the author's credentials ("According to Dr. Hays, a geologist with the Department of Interior, . . ."). These *introductory tags* give readers a context for the borrowed material, as well as serving as part of the required documentation of sources. *Make sure that each tag clarifies rather than distorts an author's relationship to his or her ideas and your relationship to the source.*

GUIDELINES for Appropriately Using Borrowed Material

Here are three guidelines to follow to avoid misrepresenting borrowed material:

- **Pay attention to verb choice in tags.** When you vary such standard wording as "Smith says" or "Jones states," be careful that you do not select verbs that misrepresent "Smith's" or "Jones's" attitude toward his or her own work. Do not write "Jones wonders" when in fact Jones has strongly asserted her views. (See pages 314–15 for a discussion of varying word choice in tags.)

- **Pay attention to the location of tags.** If you mention Jones after you have presented her views, be sure that your reader can tell precisely which ideas in the passage belong to Jones. If your entire paragraph is a paraphrase of Jones's work, you are plagiarizing to conclude with "This idea is presented by Jones." Which of the several ideas in your paragraph comes from Jones? Your reader will assume that only the last idea comes from Jones.

- **Paraphrase properly.** Be sure that paraphrases are truly *in your own words*. To use Smith's words and sentence style in your writing is to plagiarize.

 NOTE: Putting a parenthetical page reference at the end of a paragraph is not sufficient if you have used the source throughout the paragraph. Use introductory tags to guide the reader through the material.

EXERCISE: Acknowledging Sources

The paragraph below (from Franklin E. Zimring's "Firearms, Violence and Public Policy" [*Scientific American*, Nov. 1991]) provides material for the examples that follow of adequate and inadequate acknowledgment of sources. After reading Zimring's paragraph, study the three examples with these questions in mind: (1) Which example represents adequate acknowledgment? (2) Which examples do not represent adequate acknowledgment? (3) In exactly what ways is each plagiarized paragraph flawed?

SOURCE

Although most citizens support such measures as owner screening, public opinion is sharply divided on laws that would restrict the ownership of handguns to persons with special needs. If the U.S. does not reduce handguns and current trends continue, it faces the prospect that the number of handguns in circulation will grow from 35 million to more than 50 million within 50 years. A national program limiting the availability of handguns would cost many billions of dollars and meet much resistance from citizens. These costs would likely be greatest in the early years of the program. The benefits of supply reduction would emerge slowly because efforts to diminish the availability of handguns would probably have a cumulative impact over time. (page 54)

STUDENT PARAGRAPH 1

One approach to the problem of handgun violence in America is to severely limit handgun ownership. If we don't restrict ownership and start the costly task of removing handguns from our society, we may end up with around 50 million handguns in the country by 2040. The benefits will not be apparent right away but will eventually appear. This idea is emphasized by Franklin Zimring (54).

STUDENT PARAGRAPH 2

One approach to the problem of handgun violence in America is to restrict the ownership of handguns except in special circumstances. If we do not begin to reduce the number of handguns in this country, the number will grow from 35 million to more than 50 million within 50 years. We can agree with Franklin Zimring that a program limiting handguns will cost billions and meet resistance from citizens (54).

STUDENT PARAGRAPH 3

According to law professor Franklin Zimring, the United States needs to severely limit handgun ownership or face the possibility of seeing handgun ownership increase "from 35 million to more than 50 million within 50 years" (54). Zimring points out that Americans disagree significantly on restricting handguns and that enforcing such laws would be very expensive. He concludes that the benefits would not be seen immediately but that the restrictions "would probably have a cumulative impact over time" (54). Although Zimring paints a gloomy picture of high costs and little immediate relief from gun violence, he also presents the shocking possibility of 50 million guns by the year 2040. Can our society survive so much fire power?

Clearly, only the third student paragraph demonstrates adequate acknowledgment of the writer's indebtedness to Zimring. Notice that the placement of the last parenthetical page reference acts as a visual closure to the student's borrowing; then she turns to her response to Zimring and her own views on the problem of handguns.

MLA IN-TEXT (PARENTHETICAL) CITATIONS

The student paragraphs above illustrate the most common form of parenthetical documentation in MLA style: parenthetical references to author and page number, or just to page number if the author has been mentioned in an introductory tag. Because a reference only to author and page number is an incomplete citation (readers could not find the source with such limited information), whatever is cited this way in the essay must refer to a specific source presented fully in a Works Cited list that follows the text of the paper. General guidelines for citing are given below, followed by examples and explanations of the required patterns of documentation.

> **NOTE:** You need a 100 percent correspondence between the sources listed on your Works Cited page(s) and the sources you cite (refer to) in your paper. Do not omit from your Works Cited any sources you refer to in your paper. Do not include in your Works Cited any sources not referred to in your paper.

GUIDELINES for Using Parenthetical Documentation

- **The purpose of documentation is to make clear exactly what material in a passage has been borrowed and from what source the borrowed material has come.**

- **Parenthetical documentation requires specific page references for borrowed material.**
- **Parenthetical documentation is required for both quoted and paraphrased material.**
- **Parenthetical documentation provides as brief a citation as possible consistent with accuracy and clarity.**

The Simplest Patterns of Parenthetical Documentation

The simplest parenthetical reference can be prepared in one of three ways:

1. Give the author's last name (full name in the first reference) in the text of your paper and place the relevant page number(s) in parentheses following the borrowed material.

    Frederick Lewis Allen observes that, during the 1920s, urban tastes spread to

    the country (146).

2. Place the author's last name and the relevant page number(s) in parentheses immediately following the borrowed material.

    During the 1920s, "not only the drinks were mixed, but the company as well"

    (Allen 82).

3. On the rare occasion that you cite an entire work rather than borrowing from a specific passage, give the author's name in the text and omit any page numbers.

    Barbara Tuchman argues that there are significant parallels between the

    fourteenth century and our time.

Each one of these in-text references is complete *only* when the full citation is found in the Works Cited section of your paper.

Allen, Frederick Lewis. Only Yesterday: An Informal History of the Nineteen-

Twenties. New York: Harper, 1931.

Tuchman, Barbara W. A Distant Mirror: The Calamitous 14th Century. New

York: Knopf, 1978.

The three patterns just illustrated should be used in each of the following situations:

1. The work is not anonymous—the author is known.
2. The work is by one author.
3. The work cited is the only work used by that author.
4. No other author in your bibliography has the same last name.

Placement of Parenthetical Documentation

The simplest placing of a parenthetical reference is at the end of the appropriate sentence *before* the period, but, when you are quoting, *after* the quotation mark.

> During the 1920s, "not only the drinks were mixed, but the company as well"
>
> (Allen 82).

Do not put any punctuation between the author's name and the page number.

If the borrowed material ends before the end of your sentence, place the parenthetical reference *after* the borrowed material and before any subsequent punctuation. This placement more accurately shows what is borrowed and what is your own work.

> Sport, Allen observes about the 1920s, had developed into an obsession (66),
>
> another similarity between the 1920s and the 1980s.

If a quoted passage is long enough to require setting off in display form (block quotation), then place the parenthetical reference at the end of the passage, *after* the last period. (Remember that long quotations in display form do not have quotation marks.)

> It is hard to believe that when he writes about the influence of science, Allen is
>
> describing the 1920s, not the 1980s:
>
> > The prestige of science was colossal. The man in the street and the
> >
> > woman in the kitchen, confronted on every hand with new machines and
> >
> > devices which they owed to the laboratory, were ready to believe that
> >
> > science could accomplish almost anything. (164)

And to complete the documentation for all three examples:

Works Cited

Allen, Frederick Lewis. Only Yesterday: An Informal History of the Nineteen-

Twenties. New York: Harper, 1931.

Parenthetical Citations for Complex Sources

Not all sources can be cited in one of the three simplest forms described above, for not all meet the four criteria listed on page 283. Works by two or more authors, for example, will need somewhat fuller references. Each sample form of parenthetical documentation below would be completed with a full Works Cited reference, as illustrated above and in the next section of this chapter.

Two Authors, Mentioned in the Text

Richard Herrnstein and Charles Murray contend that it is "consistently . . .

advantageous to be smart" (25).

Two Authors, Not Mentioned in the Text

The advantaged smart group form a "cognitive elite" in our society

(Herrnstein and Murray 26–27).

A Book in Two or More Volumes

Sewall analyzes the role of Judge Lord in Dickinson's Life (2: 642–47).

OR

Judge Lord was also one of Dickinson's preceptors (Sewall 2: 642–47).

Note: The number before the colon always signifies the volume number: the number(s) after the colon represents the page number(s).

A Book or Article Listed by Title (Author Unknown)

According to the Concise Dictionary of American Biography, William Jennings

Bryan's 1896 campaign stressed social and sectional conflicts (117).

The Times's editors are not pleased with some of the changes in welfare

programs ("Where Welfare Stands" 4:16).

Always cite the title of the article, not the title of the journal, if the author is unknown.

A Work by a Corporate Author

According to the report of the Institute of Ecology's Global Ecological

Problems Workshop, the civilization of the city can lull us into forgetting our

relationship to the total ecological system on which we depend (13).

Although corporate authors may be cited with the page number within the parentheses, your presentation will be more graceful if corporate authors are introduced in the text. Then only page numbers go in parentheses.

Two or More Works by the Same Author

> During the 1920s, "not only the drinks were mixed, but the company as well"
>
> (Allen, Only Yesterday 82).

> According to Frederick Lewis Allen, the early 1900s were a period of
>
> complacency in America (The Big Change 4–5).

> In The Big Change, Allen asserts that the early 1900s were a period of
>
> complacency (4–5).

If your Works Cited list contains two or more works by the same author, the fullest parenthetical citation will include the author's last name, followed by a comma, the work's title, shortened if possible, and the page number(s). If the author's name appears in the text—or the author and title both, as in the third example above—omit these items from the parenthetical citation. When you have to include the title, it is best to simplify the citation by including the author's last name in the text.

Two or More Works in One Parenthetical Reference

> Several writers about the future agree that big changes will take place in work
>
> patterns (Toffler 384–87; Naisbitt 35–36).

Separate each author cited with a semicolon. But if the parenthetical citation would be disruptively long, cite the works in a "See also" note rather than in the text.

Complete Publication Information in Parenthetical Reference

Occasionally you may want to give complete information about a source within parentheses in the text of your paper. Then a Works Cited list is not used. Square brackets are used for parenthetical information within parentheses. This approach may be appropriate when you use only one or two sources, even if many references are made to those sources. Literary analyses are one type of paper for which this approach to citation may be a good choice. For example:

> Edith Wharton establishes the bleakness of her setting, Starkfield, not just
>
> through description of place but also through her main character, Ethan, who
>
> is described as "bleak and unapproachable" (Ethan Frome [New York:
>
> Scribner's, 1911] 3. All subsequent references are to this edition.). Later
>
> Wharton describes winter as "shut[ting] down on Starkfield" and negating life
>
> there (7).

Additional-Information Footnotes or Endnotes

At times you may need to provide additional useful information, explanation, or commentary that is not central to the development of your paper. These additions belong in content footnotes or endnotes. However, use these sparingly and never as a way of advancing your thesis. Many instructors object to content footnotes or endnotes and prefer only parenthetical citations in student papers.

"See Also" Footnotes or Endnotes

More acceptable to most readers is the footnote that refers to other sources of evidence for or against the point to be established. Such footnotes (or endnotes) can be combined with parenthetical documentation. They are usually introduced with "See also" or "Compare," followed by the citation. For example:

Chekhov's debt to Ibsen should be recognized, as should his debt to

Maeterlinck and other playwrights of the 1890s who were concerned with the

inner life of their characters.[1]

[1]See also Eric Bentley, In Search of Theatre (New York: Vintage, 1959) 330; Walter Bruford, Anton Chekhov (New Haven: Yale UP, 1957) 45; and Raymond Williams, Drama from Ibsen to Eliot (New York: Oxford UP, 1953) 126–29.

PREPARING MLA CITATIONS FOR A "WORKS CITED" PAGE

Parenthetical (in-text) citations are completed by a full reference to each source in a list presented at the end of the paper. To prepare your Works Cited page(s), alphabetize, by the author's last name, the sources you have cited and complete each citation according to the forms illustrated and explained in the following pages. The key is to find the appropriate model for each of your sources and then follow the model exactly. (Guidelines for formatting a finished Works Cited page are found on pages 321 and 331.)

Forms for Books: Citing the Complete Book

A Book by a Single Author

Silver, Lee M. Remaking Eden: Cloning and Beyond in a Brave New World.

New York: Avon, 1997.

The subtitle is included, preceded by a colon, even if there is no colon on the book's title page.

A Book by Two or Three Authors

Yergin, Daniel, and Thane Gustafson. Russia 2010: And What It Means for the

World. New York: Random, 1993.

Second (and third) authors' names appear in signature form.

A Book with More Than Three Authors

Baker, Susan P., et al. The Injury Fact Book. Oxford: Oxford UP, 1992.

Use the name of the first author listed on the title page. The English "and others" may be used instead of "et al." Shorten University Press to UP.

Two or More Works by the Same Author

Goodall, Jane. In the Shadow of Man. Boston: Houghton, 1971.

- - -. Through a Window: My Thirty Years with the Chimpanzees of Gombe.

Boston: Houghton, 1990.

Give the author's full name with the first entry. For the second (and additional works), begin the citation with three hyphens followed by a period. Alphabetize the entries by the books' titles.

A Book Written under a Pseudonym with Name Supplied

Wrighter, Carl P. [Paul Stevens]. I Can Sell You Anything. New York:

Ballantine, 1972.

Supply the author's name in square brackets.

An Anonymous Book

Beowulf: A New Verse Translation. Trans. Seamus Heaney. New York: Farrar,

2000.

Do not use "anon." Alphabetize by the book's title.

An Edited Book

Hamilton, Alexander, James Madison, and John Jay. The Federalist Papers. Ed.

Isaac Kramnick. New York: Viking-Penguin, 1987.

Lynn, Kenneth S., ed. Huckleberry Finn: Text, Sources, and Critics. New York:

Harcourt, 1961.

If you cite the author's work, put the author's name first and the editor's name after the title, preceded by "Ed." If you cite the editor's work (an introduction or notes), then place the editor's name first, followed by a comma and "ed."

A Translation

Schulze, Hagen. Germany: A New History. Trans. Deborah Lucas Schneider.

Cambridge: Harvard UP, 1998.

Cornford, Francis MacDonald, trans. The Republic of Plato. New York: Oxford

UP, 1945.

If the author's work is being cited, place the author's name first and the translator's name after the title, preceded by "Trans." If the translator's work is the important element, place the translator's name first, as in the second example above. If the author's name does not appear in the title, give it after the title. For example: By Plato.

A Book in Two or More Volumes

Spielvogel, Jackson J. Western Civilization. 2 vols. Minneapolis: West, 1991.

A Book in Its Second or Subsequent Edition

O'Brien, David M. Storm Center: The Supreme Court and American Politics.

2nd ed. New York: Norton, 1990.

Sundqist, James L. Dynamics of the Party System. Rev. ed. Washington:

Brookings, 1983.

Always include the number of the edition you have used, abbreviated as shown, if it is not the first edition.

A Book in a Series

Maclean, Hugh, ed. Edmund Spencer's Poetry. A Norton Critical Edition. New

York: Norton, 1968.

The series title—and number, if there is one—follows the book's title but is not underlined.

A Reprint of an Earlier Work

Cuppy, Will. How to Become Extinct. 1941. Chicago: U of Chicago P, 1983.

Twain, Mark. Adventures of Huckleberry Finn. 1885. Centennial Facsimile

Edition. Introd. Hamlin Hill. New York: Harper, 1962.

Faulkner, William. As I Lay Dying. 1930. New York: Vintage-Random, 1964.

Since the date of a work is often important, cite the original date of publication as well as the facts of publication for the reprinted version. Indicate any new material that is part of the reprinted book, as in the second example. The third example shows how to cite a book reprinted, by the same publisher, in a paperback version. (Vintage is a paperback imprint of the publisher Random House.)

A Book with Two or More Publishers

Green, Mark J., James M. Fallows, and David R. Zwick. Who Runs Congress? Ralph

Nader Congress Project. New York: Bantam; New York: Grossman, 1972.

If the title page lists two or more publishers, give all as part of the facts of publication, placing a semicolon between them, as illustrated above.

A Corporate or Governmental Author

California State Department of Education. American Indian Education

Handbook. Sacramento: California State Department of Education,

Indian Education Unit, 1991.

Hispanic Market Connections. The National Hispanic Database: A Los

Angeles Preview. Los Altos, CA: Hispanic Market Connections, 1992.

List the institution as the author even when it is also the publisher.

A Book in a Foreign Language

Blanchard, Gerard. Images de la musique au cinéma. Paris: Edilig, 1984.

Capitalize only the first word of titles and subtitles and words normally capitalized in that language (e.g., proper nouns in French, all nouns in German). A translation in square brackets may be provided. Check your work carefully for spelling and accent marks.

The Bible

The Bible. [Always refers to the King James Version.]

The Bible. Revised Standard Version.

The Reader's Bible: A Narrative. Ed. with intro. Roland Mushat Frye.

Princeton: Princeton UP, 1965.

Do not underline the title. Indicate the version if it is not the King James Version. Provide facts of publication for versions not well known.

A Book with a Title in Its Title

Piper, Henry Dan, ed. Fitzgerald's The Great Gatsby: The Novel, the Critics,

the Background. Scribner Research Anthologies. Ed. Martin

Steinmann, Jr. New York: Scribner's, 1970.

Forms for Books: Citing Part of a Book

A Preface, Introduction, Foreword, or Afterword

Sagan, Carl. Introduction. A Brief History of Time: From The Big Bang to

Black Holes. By Stephen W. Hawking. New York: Bantam, 1988. ix–x.

Use this form if you are citing the author of the preface, etc. Provide the appropriate identifying phrase after the author's name and give inclusive page numbers for the part of the book by that author at the end of the citation.

An Encyclopedia Article

Ostrom, John H. "Dinosaurs." McGraw-Hill Encyclopedia of Science and

Technology. 1987 ed.

"Benjamin Franklin." Concise Dictionary of American Biography. Ed. Joseph

G. E. Hopkins. New York: Scribner's, 1964.

When articles are signed or initialed, give the author's name. Complete the name of the author of an initialed article thus: K[enny], E[dward] J. Identify well-known encyclopedias and dictionaries by the year of the edition only. Give the complete facts of publication for less well-known works or those in only one edition.

One or More Volumes in a Multivolume Work

James, Henry. The Portrait of a Lady. Vols. 3 and 4 of The Novels and Tales of

Henry James. 26 vols. New York: Scribner's, 1908.

When using a complete work that makes up one or more volumes of a multivolume work, cite the title and volume number(s) of that work followed by the title, editor (if appropriate), total number of volumes, and facts of publication for the multivolume work.

A Work Within One Volume of a Multivolume Work

> Shaw, Bernard. Pygmalion. New York: Dodd, 1963. Vol 1. of The Complete
>
> Plays with Prefaces. 6 vols.

Cite the author and title of the single work used, the facts of publication for the multivolume work, then the volume number, and title of the complete work. Then give the inclusive publication dates for the work, followed by the total number of volumes.

A Work in an Anthology or Collection

> Hurston, Zora Neale. The First One. Black Female Playwrights: An Anthology
>
> of Plays Before 1950. Ed. Kathy A. Perkins. Bloomington: Indiana UP,
>
> 1989. 80–88.
>
> Comstock, George. "The Medium and the Society: The Role of Television in
>
> American Life." Children and Television: Images in a Changing
>
> Sociocultural World. Ed. Gordon L. Berry and Joy Keiko Asamen.
>
> Newbury Park, CA: Sage, 1993. 117–31.

Cite the author and title of the work you have used. Then give the title, the editor(s), and the facts of publication of the anthology or collection. Conclude by providing inclusive page numbers for the work used.

An Article in a Collection, Casebook, or Sourcebook

> Welsch, Roger. "The Cornstalk Fiddle." Journal of American Folklore 77
>
> (1964): 262–63. Rpt. in Readings in American Folklore. Ed. Jan Harold
>
> Brunvand. New York: Norton, 1979. 106–07.
>
> MacKenzie, James J. "The Decline of Nuclear Power." engage/social April
>
> 1986. Rpt. as "America Does Not Need More Nuclear Power Plants" in
>
> The Environmental Crisis: Opposing Viewpoints. Ed. Julie S. Bach and
>
> Lynn Hall. Opposing Viewpoints Series. St. Paul: Greenhaven, 1986.
>
> 136–41.

Most articles in collections have been previously published, so a complete citation needs to include the original facts of publication (excluding page numbers if they are unavailable) as well as the facts of publication for the collection. End the citation with inclusive page numbers for the article used.

Cross-References

If you are citing several articles from one collection, you can cite the collection and then provide only the author and title of specific articles used, with a cross-reference to the editor(s) of the collection:

> Head, Suzanne, and Robert Heinzman, eds. Lessons of the Rainforest. San
>
> Francisco: Sierra Club, 1990.
>
> Bandyopadhyay, J., and Vandana Shiva. "Asia's Forest, Asia's Cultures." Head
>
> and Heinzman 66–77.
>
> Head, Suzanne. "The Consumer Connection: Psychology and Politics." Head
>
> and Heinzman 156–67.

Forms for Periodicals: Articles in Journals

Article in a Journal with Continuous Paging Throughout the Issues of Each Year

> Truman, Dana M., David M. Tokar, and Ann R. Fischer. "Dimensions of
>
> Masculinity: Relations to Date Rape, Supportive Attitudes, and Sexual
>
> Aggression in Dating Situations." Journal of Counseling and Development
>
> 76 (1996): 555–62.

Give the volume number followed by the year only, in parentheses, followed by a colon and inclusive page numbers.

Article in a Journal with Separate Paging for Each Issue

> Lewis, Kevin. "Superstardom and Transcendence." Arete: The Journal of Sport
>
> Literature 2.2 (1985): 47–54.

When each issue of a journal begins with a new page 1, give the issue number, immediately following the volume number, separated by a period.

Article in a Journal That Uses Issue Numbers Only

> Keen, Ralph. "Thomas More and Geometry." Moreana 86 (1985): 151–66.

If the journal uses only issue numbers, not volume numbers, treat the issue number as a volume number.

Forms for Periodicals: Articles in Magazines

Article in a Monthly Magazine

> Zimring, Franklin E. "Firearms, Violence and Public Policy." Scientific
>
> American Nov. 1991: 48–54.

Do not use volume or issue number. Instead, cite the month(s) and year after the title, followed by a colon and inclusive page numbers. Abbreviate all months except May, June, and July.

Article in a Weekly Magazine

> Sowell, Thomas. "Race, Culture, and Equality." Forbes 5 Oct. 1998: 144–150.

Provide the complete date, using the order of day, month, and year.

An Anonymous Article

> "Death of Perestroika." Economist 2 Feb. 1991: 12–13.

The missing name indicates that the article is anonymous. Alphabetize under D.

A Published Interview

> Angier, Natalie. "Ernst Mayr at 93." Interview. Natural History May 1997: 8–11.

Follow the pattern for a published article, but add the identifying word "Interview" (followed by a period) after the article's title.

A Review

> Bardsley, Tim. "Eliciting Science's Best." Rev. of Frontiers of Illusion: Science,
>
> Technology, and the Politics of Progress, by Daniel Sarewitz. Scientific
>
> American June 1997: 142.
>
> Shales, Tom. "A Chilling Stop in 'Nuremberg.' " Rev. of the movie Nuremberg,
>
> TNT 16 July 2000. Washington Post 16 July 2000: G1.

If the review is signed, begin with the author's name, then the title of the review article. Give the title of the work being reviewed, a comma, and its author, preceded by "Rev. of." Alphabetize unsigned reviews by the title of the review. For reviews of art shows, videos, or computer software, provide place and date or descriptive label to make the citation clear.

Forms for Periodicals: Newspapers

An Article from a Newspaper

> Arguila, John. "What Deep Blue Taught Kasparov—and Us." Christian Science
>
> Monitor 16 May 1997: 18.

A newspaper's title should be cited as it appears on the masthead, excluding any initial article; thus *New York Times,* not *The New York Times.*

An Article from a Newspaper with Lettered Sections

> Fiss, Owen M. "Affirmative Action: Beyond Diversity." Washington Post 7 May
>
> 1997: A21.

Place the section letter immediately before the page number, without any spacing.

An Article from a Newspaper with Numbered Sections

> Roberts, Sam. "Another Kind of Middle-Class Squeeze." New York Times 18
>
> May 1997, sec. 4: 1+.

Place the section number after the date, preceded by a comma and the abbreviation "sec."

An Article from a Newspaper with a Designated Edition

> Pereira, Joseph. "Women Allege Sexist Atmosphere in Offices Constitutes
>
> Harassment." Wall Street Journal 10 Feb. 1988, eastern ed.: 23.

If a newspaper is published in more than one edition each day, the edition used is cited after the date.

An Editorial

> "Japan's Two Nationalisms." Editorial. Washington Post 4 June 2000: B6.

Add the descriptive label "Editorial" after the article title.

A Letter to the Editor

> Wiles, Yoko A. "Thoughts of a New Citizen." Letter. Washington Post 27 Dec.
>
> 1995: A22.

If the letter is titled, use the descriptive word "Letter" after the title. If the letter is untitled, place "Letter" after the author's name.

Citing Other Print and Nonprint Sources

The materials in this section, although often important to research projects, do not always lend themselves to documentation by the forms illustrated above. Follow the basic order of author, title, facts of publication as much as possible and add whatever information is needed to make the citation clear and useful to a reader.

Cartoons and Advertisements

Schulz, Charles M. "Peanuts." Cartoon. Washington Post 10 Dec. 1985: D8.

Give the cartoon title, if there is one; add the descriptive label "Cartoon"; then give the facts of publication. The pattern is similar for advertisements.

Halleyscope. "Halleyscopes Are for Night Owls." Advertisement. Natural

History Dec. 1985: 15.

Computer Software

"Aardvark." The Oxford English Dictionary. 2nd ed. CD-ROM. Oxford:

Oxford UP, 1992.

Give author, title, publication medium (*CD-ROM*, *Diskette*, or *Magnetic Tape*), edition or version, publisher, and year of issue.

Dissertation—Unpublished

Brotton, Joyce D. "Illuminating the Present Through Literary Dialogism: From

the Reformation through Postmodernism." Diss. George Mason U, 2002.

Dissertation—Published

Brotton, Joyce D. Illuminating the Present Through Literary Dialogism: From

the Reformation through Postmodernism. Diss. George Mason U, 2002.

UMI, 2002. ATT3041383.

Sieger, Thomas Martin. "Global Citizenship: A Model for Student Inquiry and

Decision-Making." 1996. Dissertation Abstracts Online Accession No.

AAG9720651. Online. FirstSearch. 1997.

Government Documents

> U.S. President. Public Papers of the Presidents of the United States.
>
>> Washington: Office of the Federal Register, 1961.
>
> United States. Senate. Committee on Energy and Natural Resources.
>
>> Subcommittee on Energy Research and Development. Advanced Reactor
>>
>> Development Program: Hearing, May 24, 1988. Washington: GPO, 1988.
>
> - - -. Environmental Protection Agency. The Challenge of the Environment: A
>
>> Primer on EPA's Statutory Authority. Washington: GPO, 1972.

Observe the pattern illustrated here. If the author of the document is not given, cite the name of the government first followed by the name of the department or agency. If you cite more than one document published by the United States government, do not repeat the name but use the standard three hyphens followed by a period instead. If you cite a second document prepared by the Environmental Protection Agency, use the following pattern:

> United States. Senate . . .
>
> - - -. Environmental Protection Agency . . .
>
> - - -. - - -. [second source from EPA]

If the author is known, follow this pattern:

> Geller, William. Deadly Force. U.S. Dept of Justice National Institute of Justice
>
>> Crime File Study Guide. Washington: U.S. Dept. of Justice, n.d.

If the document contains no date, use the abbreviation "n.d."

> Hays, W. W., ed. Facing Geologic and Hydrologic Hazards. Geological Survey
>
>> Professional Paper 1240-B. Washington: GPO, 1981.

Abbreviate the U.S. Government Printing Office thus: GPO.

An Interview

> Plum, Kenneth. Personal Interview. 5 Mar. 1995.

A Lecture

> Bateson, Mary Catherine. "Crazy Mixed-Up Families." Lecture delivered at
>
>> Northern Virginia Community College, 26 Apr. 1997.

Legal Documents

U.S. Const. Art. 1, sec. 3.

The Constitution is referred to by article and section. Abbreviations are used; do not underline.

Turner v. Arkansas. 407 U.S. 366. 1972.

In citing a court case, give the name of the case (the plaintiff and defendant); the volume, name, and page of the report cited; and the date. The name of a court case is underlined (italicized) in the text but not in the Works Cited.

Federal Highway Act, as amended. 23 U.S. Code 109. 1970. Labor

Management Relations Act (Taft-Hartley Act). Statutes at Large. 61.

1947. 34 U.S. Code. 1952.

Citing laws is complicated, and lawyers use many abbreviations that may not be clear to nonexperts. Bills that become law are published annually in *Statutes at Large* and later in the *U.S. Code*. Provide the title of the bill and the source, volume, and year. References to both *Statutes at Large* and the *U.S. Code* can be given as a convenience to readers.

Unpublished Letter

McCulley, Cecil M. Letter to the author. 5 June 1968.

Treat a published letter as a work in a collection.

Maps and Charts

Hampshire and Dorset. Map. Kent, Eng.: Geographers' A-Z Map, n.d.

The format is similar to that for an anonymous book, but add the appropriate descriptive label.

Plays or Concerts

Mourning Becomes Electra. By Eugene O'Neill. Shakespeare Theater.

Washington DC. 16 May 1997.

Include title, author, theater, city, and date of performance. Principal actors, singers, musicians, and/or the director can be added as appropriate.

Recordings

Stein, Joseph. Fiddler on the Roof. Jerry Bock, composer. Original-Cast

Recording with Zero Mostel. RCA, LSO-1093, 1964.

The conductor and/or performers help identify a specific recording. Also include manufacturer, catalog number, and date of issue.

A Report

Environment and Development: Breaking the Ideological Deadlock. Report of

the Twenty-first United Nations Issues Conference, 23–25 Feb. 1990.

Muscatine, Iowa: Stanley Foundation, n.d.

Television or Radio Program

"Breakthrough: Television's Journal of Science and Medicine." PBS series

hosted by Ron Hendren. 10 June 1997.

Citing Electronic Sources

Remember that the purpose of a citation is to provide readers with the information they need to obtain the source you have used. To locate online sources, more information is usually needed than for standard print works. Think in terms of five basic elements, each of which can be expanded or ignored depending on the specific source:

1. Author (or editor or translator, as appropriate), if there is one
2. "Title" of item, in quotation marks (unless you are citing an entire online book)
3. Information about print publication (if the item also has a print form)
4. Information about the electronic publication (usually including the Title of the site—underlined—the publication date or latest update of the site, and the sponsor's name—possibly a university, a company, an organization—if not mentioned in the title)
5. Access information (including the date you viewed the item and then the electronic address—URL)

If you cannot find all of this information, it may be that not every element applies to the site you are using, but do take time to search the home page for as much information as you can find. AND: Don't forget to put the date you accessed the information in your notes. Study the following two examples of citations to see the information needed and the order of that information.

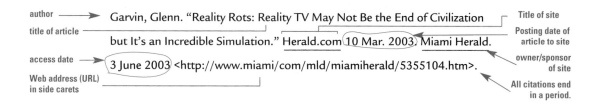

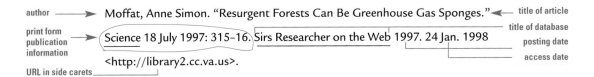

author ⟶ Moffat, Anne Simon. "Resurgent Forests Can Be Greenhouse Gas Sponges." ⟵ title of article

print form publication information ⟶ Science 18 July 1997: 315–16. Sirs Researcher on the Web 1997. 24 Jan. 1998

— title of database
posting date
access date

URL in side carets ⟶ <http://library2.cc.va.us>.

This article appeared in print in *Science* magazine, so the original print facts of publication are supplied after author and title. The researcher accessed the article in an electronic database, so the title of the database and the year of posting in the database are also supplied. Then comes the date of access by the researcher, followed by a URL that shows that the database is owned by a specific library and cannot therefore be accessed by all readers of this book. (The student's instructor, with access to the same library's databases, could, or course, access the database and check the student's work.)

Article from a Database of Previously Published Articles

"Breaking the Glass Ceiling." Editorial. The Economist 10 Aug. 1996: 13.

General Business File ASAP. Jan. 1998. 12 Jan. 1998

<http://sbweb2.med.iacnet.com/infotrac/session/460/259-2012624/

131xrn_39&kbm_13>.

Use the descriptive word "Editorial" just as you would if you were citing the print source. Break the URL only at a backslash.

Abstracts of Articles in Online Databases

For some articles, electronic databases provide only a citation and an abstract, a brief summary of the article. In most cases, the author of the article did not write the abstract. So, *never attribute these abstracts to the author. Never quote from these abstracts. Find and study the complete article.* If you must paraphrase some facts from the abstract, always indicate that you have used the abstract, not the original article. Place the word "Abstract" (followed by a period) after the page numbers for the original facts of publication.

Article from a Reference Database

"Prohibition." Encyclopaedia Britannica Online. 1998. Encyclopaedia

Britannica. 24 Jan. 1998 <http://search.eb.com/>.

Douglas, Susan J. "Radio and Television." HistoryChannel.com. 1996–2003.

History Channel. 31 July 2003 <http://historychannel.com/>.

Path: Television; Radio and Television.

Sometimes URLs are quite long, or the particular document you are citing does not have its own precise URL. You can use the database's search page or its home page followed by "Path" and then the sequence of links that took you to the particular document you are citing.

Online News Source

Associated Press. "Parents: Work Hinders Quality Time with Kids." CNN.com

31 July 2003. 31 July 2003 <http://cnn.com/ Health>.

Article in an Online Magazine

Lithwick, Dahlia. "Rape Nuts: Kobe Bryant's Trial Will Showcase Our Mixed-

up Rape Laws." Slate 30 July 2003. 11 pars. 31 July 2003

<http://slate.msn.com/>.

An Entire Internet Site

Thomas: Legislative Information on the Internet. 30 June 2003. Lib. of

Congress, Washington. 4 August 2003 <http://thomas.loc.gov/>.

Poem from a Scholarly Project

Keats, John. "Ode to a Nightingale." Poetical Works. 1884. Bartleby.com:

Great Books. Ed. Steven van Leeuwen. 5 May 2002

<http://www.bartleby.com/126/41.htm>.

Information from a Government Site

U.S. Department of Health and Human Services. "The HHS Poverty

Guidelines." 21 Jan. 1998. 23 Jan. 1998 <http://aspe.os/

dhhs.gov/poverty/ 7/poverty.htm>.

Information from a Professional Site

"Music Instruction Aids Verbal Memory." APA Press Release. APA Online 27

July 2003. 4 Aug. 2003 <http://www.apa.org/releases/

music_memory.html>.

Use a descriptive label after the title just as you would with an anonymous print source, such as an editorial.

Information from a Professional or Personal Home page

Vachss, Andrew. "How Journalism Abuses Children." The Zero. 2 Aug. 2003

<http://www.andrewvachss.com/av_articles.html>.

For both professional and personal home pages, begin with the name of the person who created the page, and the title of the site (such as The Zero), or if there is no title, use the identifying phrase "Home page" (but not underlined or in quotation marks), the name of any organization associated with the site, access date, and URL.

An Article Published in Print and on CD-ROM (or Diskette, etc.)

Detweiler, Richard A., "Democracy and Decency on the Internet." Chronicle of

Higher Education 28 June 1996: A40. General Periodicals Ondisc.

CD-ROM. UMI-Proquest. April 1997.

A Work or Part of a Work on CD-ROM, Diskette, or Magnetic Tape

"Surrealism." Oxford English Dictionary. 2nd ed. CD-ROM. Oxford: Oxford

UP, 1992.

Eseiolonis, Karyn. "Georgio de Chirico's Mysterious Bathers." A Passion for

Art: Renoir, Cezanne, Matisse and Dr. Barnes. CD-ROM. Corbis

Productions, 1995.

Barclay, Donald. Teaching Electronic Information Literacy. Diskette. New

York: Neal-Schuman, 1995.

EXERCISES: Presenting and Documenting Borrowed Information and Preparing Citations

1. Read the following passage and then the three plagiarized uses of the passage. Explain why each one is plagiarized and how it can be corrected.

    Original Text: Stanley Karnow, *Vietnam, A History. The First Complete Account of Vietnam at War.* New York: Viking, 1983, 319.

Lyndon Baines Johnson, a consummate politician, was a kaleidoscopic personality, forever changing as he sought to dominate or persuade or placate or frighten his friends and foes. A gigantic figure whose extravagant moods matched his size, he could be cruel and kind, violent and gentle, petty, generous, cunning, naïve, crude, candid, and frankly dishonest. He commanded the blind loyalty of his aides, some of whom worshipped him, and he sparked bitter derision or fierce hatred that he never quite fathomed.

a.   LBJ's vibrant and changing personality filled some people with adoration and others with bitter derision that he never quite fathomed (Karnow 319).

b.   LBJ, a supreme politician, had a personality like a kaleidoscope, continually changing as he tried to control, sway, appease, or intimidate his enemies and supporters (Karnow 319).

c.   Often, figures who have had great impact on America's history have been dynamic people with powerful personalities and vibrant physical presence. LBJ, for example, was a huge figure who polarized those who worked for and with him. "He commanded the blind loyalty of his aides, some of whom worshipped him, and he sparked bitter derision or fierce hatred" from many others (Karnow 319).

2.   Read the following passages and then each of the four sample uses of the passage. Judge each of the uses for how well it avoids plagiarism and if it is documented correctly. Make corrections as needed.

Original Text: Stanley Karnow, Vietnam, A History. *The First Complete Account of Vietnam at War.* New York: Viking, 1983, 327.

On July 27, 1965, in a last-ditch attempt to change Johnson's mind, Mansfield and Russell were to press him again to "concentrate on finding a way out" of Vietnam—"a place where we ought not be," and where "the situation is rapidly going out of control." But the next day, Johnson announced his decision to add forty-four American combat battalions to the relatively small U.S. contingents already there. He had not been deaf to Mansfield's pleas, nor had he simply swallowed the Pentagon's plans. He had waffled and agonized during his nineteen months in the White House, but eventually this was his final judgment. As he would later explain: "There are many, many people who can recommend and advise, and a few of them consent. But there is only one who has been chosen by the American people to decide."

a.   Karnow writes that Senators Mansfield and Russell continued to try to convince President Johnson to avoid further involvement in Vietnam, "a place where we ought not to be" they felt. (327).

b.   Though Johnson received advice from many, in particular Senators Mansfield and Russell, he believed the weight of the decision to become further engaged in Vietnam was solely his as the one " 'chosen by the American people to decide' " (Karnow 327).

    c.   On July 28, 1965, Johnson announced his decision to add forty-four battalions to the troops already in Vietnam, ending his waffling and agonizing of the past nineteen months of his presidency. (Karnow 357).

    d.   Karnow explains that LBJ took his responsibility to make decisions about Vietnam seriously (327). Although Johnson knew that many would offer suggestions, only he had " 'been chosen by the American people to decide' " (Karnow 327).

3.   Turn the information printed below into correct bibliographic citations for each of the works. Pay attention to the order of information, the handling of titles, and punctuation. Write each citation on a separate index card, or, if your instructor requests, prepare the citations as an alphabetical listing of works.

    a.   On July 14, 1997, Newsweek magazine printed Robert J. Samuelson's article titled Don't Hold Your Breath on page 40.

    b.   Richard B. Sewell's book The Life of Emily Dickinson was published in 1974. His book was published in two volumes by the New York City publisher Farrar, Straus, & Giroux.

    c.   Richard D. Heffner has edited an abridged version of Democracy in America by Alexis De Tocqueville. This is a Mentor Book paperback, a division of (New York City's) New American Library. The book was published in 1956.

    d.   The Object Stares Back: On the Nature of Seeing by James Elkins is reviewed in an article titled Vision Reviewed by Luciano da F. Costa. The review appeared on pages 124 and 125 in the March 1997 issue of Scientific American.

    e.   Arthur Whimbey wrote the article Something Better Than Binet for the Saturday Review on June 1, 1974. Joseph Rubinstein and Brent D. Slife reprinted the article on pages 102–108 in the third edition of the edited collection Taking Sides. Taking Sides was published in 1984 by the Dushkin Publishing Company located in Guilford, Connecticut.

    f.   The Discovery of Superconductivity appeared in Physics Today on pages 40–42. The author of the article is Jacobus de Nobel. The article appeared in the September 1996 issue, volume 49, number 9.

    g.   You used a biographical article, titled Marc Chagall (1887–1985), from Britannica Online which you found on the Internet September 25, 1999. You used the 1998 version, published by Encyclopaedia Britannica and available at <http://www.eb.com:180>.

    h.   An editorial appeared in the New York Times, on Sunday, September 7, 1997, with the title Protecting Children from Guns. The editorial could be found on page 16 of section 4.

    i.   Anthony Bozza's article "Moby Porn" appeared in the magazine Rolling Stone on June 26, 1977, on page 26. You obtained the text of the article from the September 1997 "edition" of General Periodicals Ondisc. The vendor is UMI-ProQuest.

j.   A Letter to the Editor titled What Can We Do about Global Warming appeared in the Washington Post on July 24, 1997. The letter was written by S. Fred Singer and printed on page A24.

CHAPTER 11

Writing the Researched Essay

As you organize and draft, keep in mind that your argument skills apply to the research paper as well. Do not let documenting of multiple sources distract you from your best use of critical thinking and writing skills.

ORGANIZING THE PAPER

To make decisions about your paper's organization, a good place to begin is with the identifying phrases at the top of your notes or the list of support you developed as you studied sources. They represent subsections of your topic that emerged as you studied sources. They will now help you organize your paper. Here are some guidelines for getting organized to write:

1. *Arrange notes by identifying phrases and read them through.* Read personal notes as well. Work all notes into one possible order as suggested by the identifying phrases. In reading through all notes at one time, you may discover that some now seem irrelevant. Set them aside,

but do not throw them away yet. Some additional note taking may be necessary to fill in gaps that have become apparent. You know your sources well enough by now to be able to find the additional material that you need.

2. *Reexamine your tentative claim or research proposal and the preliminary list that guided your research.* Consider: As a result of reading and reflection, do you need to alter or modify your claim in any way? Or, if you began with a research question, what now is your answer to the question? What, for example, was the impact of Prohibition on the 1920s? Or, is TV violence harmful to children? You need to decide.

3. *Decide on a final claim.* To produce a unified and coherent essay with a clear central idea and a "reason for being," you need a claim that meets the following criteria:

   • *It is a complete sentence, not a topic or statement of purpose.*

TOPIC:	Rape on college campuses.
CLAIM:	There are steps that both students and administrators can take to reduce incidents of campus rape.

   • *It is limited and focused.*

UNFOCUSED:	Prohibition affected the 1920s in many ways.
FOCUSED:	Prohibition was more acceptable to rural than urban areas because of differences in religious values, in patterns of socializing, in cultural backgrounds, and in the economic impact of prohibiting liquor sales.

   • *It can be supported by your research.*

UNSUPPORTABLE:	*Time* magazine does not like George Bush.
SUPPORTABLE:	A study of *Time*'s coverage of President Bush during the 1990–91 winter months reveals a favorable bias during the Persian Gulf War but a negative bias after the war.

   • *It establishes a new or interesting approach to the topic that makes your research worthwhile.*

NOT INVENTIVE:	A regional shopping mall should not be built adjacent to the Manassas Battlefield.
INVENTIVE:	Putting aside an appeal to our national heritage, one can say, simply, that the building of a regional shopping mall adjacent to the Manassas Battlefield has no economic justification.

4. *Write down the organization revealed by the way you have grouped notes and compare this organization with your preliminary plan.* If you have deleted sections or reordered them, justify those changes in your own mind. Consider: Does the new, fuller plan now provide a complete and logical development of your claim?

THE FORMAL OUTLINE

Some instructors expect a formal outline with research essays. Preparing a formal outline requires that you think through the entire structure of your paper and see the relationship of parts. Remember that the more you analyze your topic, the fuller and therefore more useful your outline will be. But do not expect more out of an outline than it can provide. A logical and clear organization does not result from a detailed outline; rather, a detailed outline results from a logical analysis of your topic.

The formal outline uses a combination of numbers and letters to show headings and subheadings. Keep in mind these three points about outlines:

- the parts of the paper indicated by the same *types* of numbers or letters should be equally important;
- headings and subheadings indicated by the same types of numbers or letters should be written in the same format or structure (e.g., A. Obtain*ing* Good Equipment; B. Tak*ing* Lessons; C. Practic*ing*); and
- headings that are subdivided must contain at least *two* subsections (that is, if there is a 1 under A, there has to be a 2). A sample outline accompanies the first research paper at the end of this chapter.

DRAFTING THE PAPER

Plan Your Time

Consider how much time you will need to draft your essay. Working with notes and being careful about documentation make research paper writing more time-consuming than writing undocumented essays. You will probably need two or three afternoons or evenings to complete a draft. You should start writing, then, at least five days before your paper is due to allow time between drafting and revising. Don't throw away weeks of study by trying to draft, revise, and proof your paper in one day.

Handle Documentation As You Draft

Although you may believe that stopping to include parenthetical documentation as you write will cramp your writing, you really cannot wait until you complete your draft to add the documentation. The risk of failing to document accurately is too great to chance. Parenthetical documentation is brief; take the time to include it as you compose. Then, when your paper is finished and you are preparing your list of works cited, go through your paper carefully to make certain that there is a work listed for *every* parenthetical reference.

Choose an Appropriate Writing Style

Specific suggestions for composing the parts of your paper will follow, but first here are some general guidelines for research paper style.

Use the Proper Person

Research papers are written primarily in the third person (*she, he, it, they*) to create objectivity and to direct attention to the content of the paper. You are not likely to use the second person (*you*) at all, for the second person occurs in instructions. The usual question is over the appropriateness of the first person (*I, we*). Although you want to avoid writing "as *you* can see," do not try to skirt around the use of *I* if you need to distinguish your position from the views of others. It is better to write "I" than "it is the opinion of this writer" or "the researcher learned" or "this project analyzed." On the other hand, avoid qualifiers such as "I think." Just state your ideas.

Use the Proper Tense

When you are writing about people, ideas, or events of the past, the appropriate tense is the past tense. When writing about current times, the appropriate tense is the present. Both may occur in the same paragraph, as the following paragraph illustrates:

> Fifteen years ago "personal" computers were all but unheard of. Computers were regarded as unknowable, building-sized mechanized monsters that required a precise 68 degree air-conditioned environment and eggheaded technicians with thick glasses and white lab coats scurrying about to keep the temperamental and fragile egos of the electronic brains mollified. Today's generation of computers is accessible, affordable, commonplace, and much less mysterious. A computer that used to require two rooms to house is now smaller than a briefcase. A computer that cost hundreds of thousands of dollars fifteen years ago now has a price tag in the hundreds. The astonishing progress made in computer technology in the last few years has made computers practical, attainable, and indispensable. Personal computers are here to stay.

In the above example when the student moves from computers in the past to computers in the present, he shifts tenses accurately.

When writing about sources, the convention is to use the present tense *even* for works or authors from the past. The idea is that the source, or the author, *continues* to make the point or use the technique into the present—that is, every time there is a reader. Use of the *historical present tense* requires that you write "Lincoln selects the biblical expression 'Fourscore and seven years ago' " and "King echoes Lincoln when he writes 'five score years ago.' "

Avoid Excessive Quoting

Many students use too many direct quotations. Plan to use your own words most of the time for these good reasons:

- Constantly shifting between your words and the language of your sources (not to mention all those quotation marks) makes reading your essay difficult.

- This is your paper and should sound like you.

- When you take a passage out of its larger context, you face the danger of misrepresenting the writer's views.

- When you quote endlessly, readers may begin to think either that you are lazy or that you don't really understand the issues well enough to put them in your own words. You don't want to present either image to your readers.

- You do not prove any point by quoting another person's opinion. All you indicate is that there is someone else who shares your views. Even if that person is an expert on the topic, your quoted material still represents the view of only one person. You support a claim with reasons and evidence, both of which can usually be presented in your own words.

When you must quote, keep the quotations brief, weave them carefully into your own sentences, and be sure to identify the author in an introductory tag. Study the guidelines for handling quotations on pages 21–24 for models of correct form and style.

Write Effective Beginnings

The best introduction is one that presents your subject in an interesting way to gain the reader's attention, states your claim, and gives the reader an indication of the scope and limits of your paper. In a short research essay, you may be able to combine an attention-getter, a statement of subject, and a thesis in one paragraph. More typically, especially in longer papers, the introduction will expand to two or three paragraphs. In the physical and social sciences, the thesis may be withheld until the conclusion, but the opening introduces the subject and presents the researcher's hypothesis, often posed as a question. Since students sometimes have trouble with research paper introductions in spite of knowing these general guidelines, several specific approaches are illustrated in the following pages:

1. Begin with a brief example or anecdote to dramatize your topic. One student introduced her study of the nightly news with this attention-getter:

When I watched television in the first weeks after moving to the United States, I was delighted by the relaxing display of the news programs. It was different from what I was used to on German television, where one finds a stern-looking man reading the news without any emotion. Here the commentators laugh or show distress; their tone with each other is amiable. Watching the news in this country was a new and entertaining experience for me initially, but as my reading skills improved, I found that I preferred reading newspapers to watching television news. Then, reading Neil Postman's attack on television news shows in "Television News Narcosis" reminded me of my early experience with American TV and led me to investigate the major networks' presentation of the news.

In her second paragraph, the student completed her introduction by explaining the procedures used for analyzing network news programs.

2. In the opening to her study of car advertisements, a student, relating her topic to what readers know, reminds readers of the culture's concern with image:

Many Americans are highly image conscious. Because the "right" look is essential to a prosperous life, no detail is too small to overlook. Clichés about first impressions remind us that "you never get a second chance to make a first impression," so we obsessively watch our weight, firm our muscles, sculpt our hair, select our friends, find the perfect houses, and buy our automobiles. Realizing the importance of image, companies compete to make the "right" products, that is, those that will complete the "right" image. Then advertisers direct specific products to targeted groups of consumers. Although targeting may be labeled as stereotyping, it has been an effective strategy in advertising.

3. Challenging a popular attitude or assumption is an effective attention-getting opening. For a paper on the advantages of solar energy, a student began:

America's energy problems are serious, despite the popular belief that difficulties vanished with the end of the Arab oil embargo in 1974. Our problems remain because the world's supply of fossil fuels is not limitless.

4. Terms and concepts central to your project need defining early in your paper, especially if they are challenged or qualified in some way by your study. The following opening paragraph demonstrates an effective use of definition:

William Faulkner braids a universal theme, the theme of initiation, into the fiber of his novel Intruder in the Dust. From ancient times to the present, a prominent focus of literature, of life, has been rites of passage, particularly those of childhood to adulthood. Joseph Campbell defines rites of passage as "distinguished by formal, and usually very severe, exercises of severance." A "candidate" for initiation into adult society, Campbell explains, experiences a shearing away of the "attitudes, attachments and life patterns" of childhood (9). This severe, painful stripping away of the child and installation of the adult is presented somewhat differently in several works by American writers.

5. Begin with a thought-provoking question. A student, arguing that the media both reflect and shape reality, started with these questions:

    Do the media just reflect reality, or do they also shape our perceptions of reality? The answer to this seemingly "chicken-and-egg" question is: They do both.

6. Beginning with important, perhaps startling, facts, evidence, or statistics is an effective way to introduce a topic, provided the details are relevant to the topic. Observe the following example:

    Teenagers are working again, but not on their homework. Over 40 percent of teenagers have jobs by the time they are juniors (Samuelson A22). And their jobs do not support academic learning since almost two-thirds of teenagers are employed in sales and service jobs that entail mostly carrying, cleaning, and wrapping (Greenberger and Steinberg 62–67), not reading, writing, and computing. Unfortunately, the negative effect on learning is not offset by improved opportunities for future careers.

Avoid Ineffective Openings

Follow these rules for avoiding openings that most readers find ineffective or annoying.

1. *Do not restate the title* or write as if the title were the first sentence in paragraph 1. First, the title of the paper appears at the top of the first page of text. Second, it is a convention of writing to have the first paragraph stand independent of the title.

2. *Do not begin with "clever" visuals* such as artwork or fancy lettering.

3. *Do not begin with humor* unless it is part of your topic.

4. *Do not begin with a question that is just a gimmick, or one that a reader may answer in a way you do not intend.* Asking "What are the advantages of solar energy?" may lead a reader to answer "None that I can think of." A straightforward research question ("Is *Death of a Salesman* a tragedy?") is appropriate.

5. *Do not open with an unnecessary definition quoted from a dictionary.* "According to Webster, solar energy means . . . " is a tired, overworked beginning that does not engage readers.

6. *Do not start with a purpose statement:* "This paper will examine. . . . " Although a statement of purpose is a necessary part of a report of empirical research, a report still needs an interesting introduction.

Compose Solid, Unified Paragraphs

As you compose the body of your paper, keep in mind that you want to (1) maintain unity and coherence, (2) guide readers clearly through source material, and (3) synthesize source material and your own ideas. Do not settle for paragraphs

in which facts from notes are just loosely run together. Review the following discussion and study the examples to see how to craft effective body paragraphs.

Provide Unity and Coherence

You achieve paragraph unity when every sentence in a paragraph relates to and
develops the paragraph's main idea. If you have a logical organization, composing unified paragraphs is not a problem. Unity, however, does not automatically produce coherence; that takes attention to wording. Coherence is achieved
when readers can follow the connection between one sentence and another and
between each sentence and the main idea. Strategies for achieving coherence include repetition of key words, the use of pronouns that clearly refer to those key
words, and the use of transition and connecting words. Observe these strategies
at work in the following paragraph:

> Perhaps the most important differences between the initiations of Robin and
>
> Biff and that experienced by Chick are the facts that Chick's epiphany does
>
> not come all at once and it does not devastate him . Chick learns about
>
> adulthood—and enters adulthood—piecemeal and with support. His first eye-
>
> opening experience occurs as he tries to pay Lucas for dinner and is rebuffed
>
> (15–16). Chick learns , after trying again to buy a clear conscience, the
>
> impropriety and affront of his actions (24). Lucas teaches Chick how he
>
> should resolve his dilemma by setting him "free" (26–27). Later, Chick feels
>
> outrage at the adults crowding into the town, presumably to see a lynching,
>
> then disgrace and shame as they eventually flee (196–97, 210).

Coherence is needed not only within paragraphs but between paragraphs. You
need to guide readers through your paper, connecting paragraphs and showing
relationships by the use of transitions. Transitions can be smooth and still clearly
signal shifts in the paper's subtopics from one paragraph to another. The following opening sentences of four paragraphs from a paper on solutions to rape
on the college campus illustrate smooth transitions:

> ¶ 3 Specialists have provided a number of reasons why men rape .
>
> ¶ 4 Some of the causes of rape on the college campus originate with the
>
> colleges themselves and with how they handle the problem.
>
> ¶ 5 Just as there are a number of causes for campus rapes , there are a
>
> number of ways to help solve the problem of these rapes.
>
> ¶ 6 If these seem like common-sense solutions , why, then, is it so difficult to
>
> significantly reduce the number of campus rapes ?

Without awkwardly writing "Here are some of the causes" and "Here are some of the solutions," the student guides her readers through a discussion of causes for and solutions to the problem of campus rape.

Guide Readers Through Source Material

To understand the importance of guiding readers through source material, consider first the following paragraph from a paper on the British coal strike in the 1970s:

> The social status of the coal miners was far from good. The country blamed them for the dimmed lights and the three-day work week. They had been placed in the position of social outcasts and were beginning to "consider themselves another country." Some businesses and shops had even gone so far as to refuse service to coal miners (Jones 32).

Who has learned that the coal miners felt ostracized or that the country blamed them? As readers we cannot begin to judge the validity of these assertions without some context provided by the writer. Most readers are put off by an unattached direct quotation or some startling observation that is documented correctly but given no context within the paper. Using introductory tags that identify the author of the source and, when useful, the author's credentials helps guide readers through the source material. The following revision of the paragraph above provides not only context but also sentence variety:

> The social acceptance of coal miners, according to Peter Jones, British correspondent for Newsweek , was far from good. From interviews both in London shops and in pubs near Birmingham, Jones concluded that Britishers blamed the miners for the dimmed lights and three-day work week. Several striking miners , in a pub on the outskirts of Birmingham, asserted that some of their friends had been denied service by shopkeepers and that they "consider[ed] themselves another country" (32).

When you use introductory tags, try to vary both the words you use and their place in the sentence. Look, for example, at the first sentence in the sample paragraph above. The tag is placed in the middle of the sentence and is set off by commas. The sentence could have been written two other ways:

> The social acceptance of coal miners was far from good, according to Peter Jones, British correspondent for Newsweek
>
>   *OR*
>
> According to Peter Jones, British correspondent for Newsweek, the social acceptance of coal miners was far from good.

Whenever you provide a name and perhaps credentials for your source, you have these three sentence patterns to choose from. Make a point to use all three options in your paper. Word choice can be varied as well. Instead of writing "Peter Jones says" throughout your paper, consider some of the many options you have:

Jones *asserts*	Jones *contends*	Jones *attests to*
Jones *states*	Jones *thinks*	Jones *points out*
Jones *concludes*	Jones *stresses*	Jones *believes*
Jones *presents*	Jones *emphasizes*	Jones *agrees with*
Jones *argues*	Jones *confirms*	Jones *speculates*

 NOTE: Not all the words in this list are synonyms; you cannot substitute *confirms* for *believes*. First, select the term that most accurately conveys the writer's relationship to his or her material. Then, when appropriate, vary word choice as well as sentence structure.

Readers need to be told how they are to respond to the sources used. They need to know which sources you accept as reliable and which you disagree with, and they need to see you distinguish clearly between fact and opinion. Ideas and opinions from sources need introductory tags and then some discussion from you.

Synthesize Source Material and Your Own Ideas

A smooth synthesis of source material is aided by introductory tags and parenthetical documentation because they mark the beginning and ending of material taken from a source. But a complete synthesis requires something more: your ideas about the source and the topic. To illustrate, consider the problems in another paragraph from the British-coal-strike paper:

> Some critics believed that there was enough coal in Britain to maintain enough power to keep industry at a near-normal level for thirty-five weeks (Jones 30). Prime Minister Heath, on the other hand, had placed the country's usable coal supply at 15.5 million tons (Jones 30). He stated that this would have fallen to a critical 7 million tons within a month had he not declared a three-day work week (Jones 31).

This paragraph is a good example of random details strung together for no apparent purpose. How much coal did exist? Whose figures were right? And what purpose do these figures serve in the paper's development? Note that the entire paragraph is developed with material from one source. Do sources other than Jones offer a different perspective? This paragraph is weak for several reasons: (1) it lacks a controlling idea (topic sentence) to give it purpose and direction; (2) it relies for development entirely on one source; (3) it lacks any discussion or analysis by the writer.

By contrast, the following paragraph demonstrates a successful synthesis:

Of course, the iridium could have come from other extraterrestrial sources besides an asteroid. One theory, put forward by Dale Russell , is that the iridium was produced outside the solar system by an exploding star (500). The theory of a nearby star exploding in a supernova is by far the most fanciful extraterrestrial theory; however, it warrants examination because of its ability to explain the widespread extinctions of the late Cretaceous Period (Colbert 205). Such an explosion, Russell states , could have blown the iridium either off the surface of the moon or directly from the star itself (500–01), while also producing a deadly blast of heat and gamma rays (Krishtalka 19). Even though this theory seems to explain the traces of iridium in the mass extinction, it does not explain why smaller mammals, crocodiles, and birds survived (Wilford 220). As Edwin Colbert explains , the extinctions of the late Cretaceous, although massive, were selective (205). So the supernova theory took a backseat to the other extraterrestrial theories: those of asteroids and comets colliding with the earth. The authors of the book The Great Extinction, Michael Allaby and James Lovelock , subtitled their work The Solution to . . . the Disappearance of the Dinosaurs. Their theory : an asteroid or comet collided with earth around sixty-five million years ago, killing billions of organisms, and thus altering the course of evolution (157). This theory was hardly a new one when they wrote it; the Alvarezes came up with it nearly three years before. However, the fact that the theory of collision with a cosmic body warrants a book describing itself as the solution to the extinction of dinosaurs calls for some thought: is the asteroid or comet theory merely sensationalism, or is it rooted in fact? Paleontologist Leonard Krishtalka declares that few paleontologists have accepted the asteroid theory, himself calling "some catastrophic theories . . . small ideas injected with growth hormone" (22). However, other scientists, such as Allaby and Lovelock, see the cosmic catastrophic theory as a solid one based on more than guesswork (10–11).

This paragraph's synthesis is accomplished by several strategies: (1) the paragraph has a controlling idea; (2) the paragraph combines information from several sources; (3) the information is presented in a blend of paraphrase and short quotations; (4) information from the different sources is clearly indicated to readers; and (5) the student explains and discusses the information.

You might also observe the very different lengths of the two sample paragraphs just presented. Although the second paragraph is quite long, it is not unwieldy because it achieves unity and coherence. By contrast, body paragraphs of only three sentences are probably in trouble.

To sum up, good body paragraphs need:

- a controlling idea
- in most cases, information from more than one source
- analysis and discussion from the student writer

Write Effective Conclusions

Sometimes ending a paper seems even more difficult than beginning one. You know you are not supposed to just stop, but every ending that comes to mind sounds more corny than clever. Perhaps you are trying too hard for a "catchy" ending that really may not be appropriate for a complex and serious research essay. If you have trouble, try one of the following types of endings.

1. Do not just repeat your claim exactly as it was stated in paragraph 1, but expand on the original wording and emphasize the claim's significance. Here is the conclusion of the solar energy paper:

    The idea of using solar energy is not as far-fetched as it seemed years ago. With the continued support of government plus the enthusiasm of research groups, environmentalists, and private industry, solar energy may become a household word quite soon. With the increasing cost of fossil fuel, the time could not be better for exploring this use of the sun.

2. End with a quotation that effectively summarizes and drives home the point of your paper. Researchers are not always lucky enough to find the ideal quotation for ending a paper. If you find a good one, use it. Better yet, present the quotation and then add your comment in a sentence or two. The conclusion to a paper on the dilemma of defective newborns is a good example:

    Dr. Joseph Fletcher is correct when he says that "every advance in medical capabilities is an increase in our moral responsibility" (48). In a world of many gray areas, one point is clear. From an ethical point of view, medicine is a victim of its own success.

3. If you have researched an issue or problem, emphasize your proposed solutions in the concluding paragraph. The student opposing a mall adjacent to the Manassas Battlefield concluded with several solutions:

Whether the proposed mall will be built is clearly in doubt at the moment. What are the solutions to this controversy? One approach is, of course, not to build the mall at all. To accomplish this solution, now, with the rezoning having been approved, probably requires an act of Congress to buy the land and make it part of the National Park. Another solution, one that would please the County and the developer and satisfy citizens objecting to traffic problems, is to build the needed roads before the mall is completed. A third approach is to allow the office park of the original plan to be built, but not the mall. The local preservationists had agreed to this original development proposal, but now that the issue has received national attention, they may no longer be willing to compromise. Whatever the future of the William Center, the present plan for a new regional mall is not acceptable.

Avoid Ineffective Conclusions

Follow these rules to avoid conclusions that most readers consider ineffective and annoying.

1. *Do not introduce a new idea.* If the point belongs in your paper, you should have introduced it earlier.
2. *Do not just stop or trail off,* even if you feel as though you have run out of steam. A simple, clear restatement of the thesis is better than no conclusion.
3. *Do not tell your reader what you have accomplished:* "In this paper I have explained the advantages of solar energy by examining the costs . . ." If you have written well, your reader knows what you have accomplished.
4. *Do not offer apologies or expressions of hope.* "Although I wasn't able to find as much on this topic as I wanted, I have tried to explain the advantages of solar energy, and I hope that you will now understand why we need to use it more" is a disastrous ending.
5. *Do not end with a vague or confusing one- or two-sentence summary of complex ideas.* The following sentences make little sense: "These authors have similar and different attitudes and ideals concerning American desires. Faulkner writes with the concerns of man toward man whereas most of the other writers are more concerned with man toward money."

Choose an Effective Title

Give some thought to your paper's title since that is what your reader sees first and what your work will be known by. A good title provides information and creates interest. Make your title informative by making it specific. If you can create interest through clever wording, so much the better. But do not confuse "cutesiness" with clever wording. Better to be just straightforward than to demean a serious effort with a "cutesy" title. Review the following examples of acceptable and unacceptable titles:

VAGUE:	A Perennial Issue Unsolved
	(There are many; which one is this paper about?)
BETTER:	The Perennial Issue of Press Freedom Versus Press Responsibility
TOO BROAD:	Earthquakes
	(What about earthquakes? This title is not informative.)
BETTER:	The Need for Earthquake Prediction
TOO BROAD:	The Scarlet Letter
	(Never use just the title of the work under discussion; you can use the work's title as a part of a longer title of your own.)
BETTER:	Color Symbolism in The Scarlet Letter
CUTESY:	Babes in Trouble
	(The slang "Babes" makes this title seem insensitive rather than clever.)
BETTER:	The Dilemma of Defective Newborns

REVISING THE PAPER: A GUIDE

After completing a first draft, catch your breath and then gear up for the next step in the writing process: revision. Revision actually involves three separate steps. *Revising*, step 1, means *rewriting*—adding or deleting text, or moving parts of the draft around. Next comes *editing*, a rereading to correct errors from misspellings to incorrect documentation format. Finally, you need to *proofread* the typed copy. If you treat these as separate steps, you will do a more complete job of revision—and get a better grade on the completed paper!

Rewriting

Read your draft through and make changes as a result of answering the following questions:

Purpose and Audience

1. Is my draft long enough to meet assignment requirements and my purpose?
2. Are terms defined and concepts explained appropriately for my audience?

Content

1. Do I have a clearly stated thesis—the claim of my argument?
2. Have I presented sufficient evidence to support my claim?
3. Are there any irrelevant sections that should be deleted?

Structure

1. Are paragraphs ordered to develop my topic logically?
2. Does the content of each paragraph help develop my claim?
3. Is everything in each paragraph on the same subtopic to create paragraph unity?
4. Do body paragraphs have a balance of information and analysis, of source material and my own ideas?
5. Are there any paragraphs that should be combined? Are there any very long paragraphs that should be divided? (Check for unity.)

Editing

Make revisions guided by your responses to the questions, make a clean copy, and read again. This time, pay close attention to sentences, words, and documentation format. Use the following questions to guide revisions.

Coherence

1. Have connecting words been used and key terms repeated to produce paragraph coherence?
2. Have transitions been used to show connections between paragraphs?

Sources

1. Have I paraphrased instead of quoted whenever possible?
2. Have I used introductory tags to create a context for source material?
3. Have I documented all borrowed material, whether quoted or paraphrased?
4. Are parenthetical references properly placed after borrowed material?

Style

1. Have I varied sentence length and structure?
2. Have I used my own words instead of quotations whenever possible?
3. Have I avoided long quotations?
4. Do I have correct form for quotations? For titles?
5. Is my language specific and descriptive?
6. Have I avoided inappropriate shifts in tense or person?
7. Have I removed any wordiness, deadwood, trite expressions, or clichés?
8. Have I used specialized terms correctly?
9. Have I avoided contractions as too informal for most research papers?
10. Have I maintained an appropriate style and tone for academic work?

Proofreading

When your editing is finished, prepare a completed draft of your paper according to the format described and illustrated below. Then proofread the completed copy, making any corrections neatly in ink. If a page has several errors, print a corrected copy. Be sure to make a copy of the paper for yourself before submitting the original to your instructor.

THE COMPLETED PAPER

Your research paper should be double-spaced throughout (including the Works Cited page) with one-inch margins on all sides. Your project will contain the following parts, in this order:

1. *A title page,* with your title, your name, the course name or number, your instructor's name, and the date, neatly centered, if an outline follows. Alternatively, place this information at the top left of the first page, as shown on p. 331.

2. *An outline,* or statement of purpose, if required.

3. *The body or text of your paper.* Number all pages consecutively, including pages of works cited, using Arabic numerals. Place numbers in the upper right-hand corner of each page. Include your last name before each page number.

4. *A list of Works Cited,* placed on a separate page(s) after the text. Title the first page "Works Cited." (Do not use the title "Bibliography.")

SAMPLE RESEARCH ESSAY 1: A DOCUMENTED ARGUMENT

The following paper illustrates MLA style of documentation for an argument that is developed using sources. The paper shows a separate title page and outline, the appropriate pattern if an outline is required. If you do not include an outline, use the second sample research essay as your model for placement of your name and the paper's title. Study the student's blending of information and arguments from sources with her own experience and views on TV to build her argument.

Good example of a title page in a three-part format of title, author, and course information.

Television: The Most Influential Product of the 20th Century

Monica Mitchell

English 112-82

Dr. Dorothy U. Seyler

May 10, 2003

Mitchell 2

Outline

Thesis: The 20th century product with the most widespread, psychological,

and enduring impact is television.

Begin with thesis
statement and use
one standard pattern
consistently.

I. Breadth of Television's Influence

    A. Adaptability to Users

    B. Range of Influence

II. Ways Television Influences Lives

    A. World Coverage

    B. Coverage of Sex and Violence

        1. Scary Nature of Violence for Children

        2. Power to Shape Behavior

    C. Restrictions in Some Countries Because of Its Power

    D. Influence on Elections and Images of Politicians

III. Defense of TV Against Other 20th Century Inventions

    A. Defense Against Computers

    B. Defense Against Flight and Space Travel

Mitchell 3

Television: The Most Influential Product of the 20th Century

"Never before have I witnessed compressed into a single device so much

ingenuity, so much brainpower, so much development, and such phenomenal

results."

(David Sarnoff as qtd. in Fisher and Fisher, xiii)

The 20th century enjoyed—or suffered—more inventions and developments

than all previous centuries combined. Many of these innovations represented

freedom, such as freedom of movement because of cars and airplanes, and

freedom for women as a result of modern birth control. Out of such an

impressive selection, labeling one development of the 1900s the most

influential is at least in part a matter of definition. The inventions of the nuclear

bomb and the space shuttle were certainly tremendously significant. The

Holocaust and the Cold War will forever be remembered as events of historical

magnitude. However, if we are talking about a *product,* a gadget if you will, an

ordinary device in the ordinary person's life, the 20th century development with

the most widespread, psychological, and enduring impact is television.

The Product of the 20th Century is a relatively simple device: once on, it

does nearly all the work for its viewers. There are no inherent physical or

intellectual requirements to enjoy it; in fact, it almost seems as if TV, unlike

other products, will "adapt" to whatever condition viewers are in, making it an

endlessly accommodating appliance. One could be in a full-body cast, unable to

move, yet watching television would still be possible—and perhaps the only

enjoyable activity in such a situation. If one were unable to read, books and

computers would almost be out of the question, but the Product of the 20th

Century wouldn't be, since no typing is required in using it and reading is rare.

If one cannot *see* TV, one can still *hear* it or—the other way around—look at it

without listening. Television can be a news radio, a music stereo, a portable

sports arena. Its top even offers a convenient extra "shelf" to put things on. It

makes a decent dinner companion. It can provide added lighting, baby sit

---

Marginal notes:

Last name and page number in upper right corner.

Repeat title on first page of text.

Student introduces topic with attention-getting quotation.

Double-space throughout.

Student defines key term and ends ¶ 1 with her thesis—her claim.

Student gives examples of adaptability of TV.

children, boost moods, bust moods. Television is the ultimate chameleon product.

Although parts of the "electronic puzzle" of TV were experimented with before 1900, it was, according to David and Jon Marshall Fisher, David Sarnoff who developed TV as we know it today, using electrons to transmit images (278). Television's official U.S. debut took place in 1939, when for the first time a TV camera recorded a presidential speech (Fisher and Fisher 278). The next day, as Fisher and Fisher tell the story, a handful of New York merchants began selling TV sets at the cost of a whopping $1000 (281). Understandably with such a price tag, only eight hundred TVs were sold in the following three months (Fisher and Fisher 281), but with reduced prices and continued marketing, the product gained popularity. As Susan J. Douglas explains in her HistoryChannel.com essay, in 1949 940,000 homes owned TV's. By 1953, 20 million homes could boast a television set. By 1960, the Product of the 20th Century, in black and white or now in color, had firmly established itself in American homes, and by 1978, 97 percent of U.S. homes had at least one set (Douglas). Today, 99 percent of American homes have at least one TV, a higher percentage than those homes with phones.

Sarnoff envisioned that television, in addition to providing entertainment, would offer a new sense of freedom and a deeper global understanding (Fisher and Fisher 200). To a great extent, TV has accomplished this in its relatively short lifespan. In his book Seducing America: How Television Charms the Modern Viewer, Roderick P. Hart confirms that for millions of viewers the names of key places in the world are loaded with implication, even if the viewers themselves have never visited them (5). Berlin, Johannesburg, Tiananmen Square, and Bosnia are just a few examples. The Product of the 20th Century enabled the rest of the world to share—to live—the moments associated with these locations (Hart 5). These places are associated with traumatic events, which we, although outsiders, nonetheless have been part of "virtually," thanks

Student uses brief history only as context for breadth of influence of TV.

¶ blends information from two sources.

Tag makes clear that citation will not include a page number.

Last stat is common knowledge.

to television's instant and realistic delivery. Television's immediacy, in Susan Douglas's view, is both its strength and its weakness. Television powerfully replayed Kennedy's assassination in 1963, Vietnam children burned by napalm, water hoses turned on civil rights marchers, and two more murders before the end of that decade, "providing," Douglas asserts, "some images that unified America and others that reflected, and sometimes exacerbated, the country's deep racial, class, and gender divisions."

Television has massively expanded its program offerings over the years. Now more than ever there is "something for everyone" in terms of interest and taste, another possible dilemma for this gadget. Two controversial elements dominating TV are violence and sex, phenomena that, ironically, might well sum up the 20th century. Some argue that if these two elements are everywhere in our culture, why should showing them on the tube cause such alarm? The counter to this view is that TV presents behaviors that many viewers, especially children, are not psychologically adept to experience. Marie Winn, who specializes in child development issues, cautions that excessive television viewing at a young age interferes with children's practicing their budding language skills (90). Karen Wright notes that typically children view two hours of TV daily and that "children's programs average between 20 and 25 violent acts per hour—four times as many as adult programs" (29). Because of the array of channels and shows offered around the clock at the push of a button— a convenience (curse?) that sets TV apart from other media outlets such as movie theaters—it is difficult for even the most responsible parent to control the images streaming out to children. Whether TV programs are labeled as such, they are all "educational" in one way or another because behavior is learned by watching. Whether we realize it or like it, television, next to parents, is often a child's earliest and most constant teacher. Even with caring parental supervision, children are often troubled by TV images. One ten-year-old (this

Tag placed in middle of quotation for variety.

Student uses personal experience to illustrate her point.

Mitchell 6

writer!) was so frightened by a movie on TV watched at a friend's house that she swore never to visit there again. In theaters the movie (Raiders of the Lost Ark) was restricted for ten-year-olds, but there were no age restrictions for the television broadcast.

Does the Product of the 20th Century also influence viewers to *act* in certain ways? Frequently yes, the studies show. Brandon S. Centerwall provides one telling example in "Television and Violent Crime." He cites a survey of a small Canadian town that two years after having acquired TV for the first time noted a 160 percent increase in aggressive behavior among its children (307). Jerry Mander, author of Four Arguments for the Elimination of Television, is convinced that the medium is inherently corrupt; he insists that TV promotes physical and mental isolation and passivity, disconnects viewers from reality, and facilitates autocracy (27), a scary list if accurate. Wright doesn't state the problem so dramatically, but she does argue that common sense would suggest that we are influenced by activities at which we spend a great deal of time (29). She also reports on a long-term study by Jeffrey G. Johnson, a psychiatric epidemiologist, who followed over 700 youngsters for 17 years. Wright reports these results from Johnson's study:

> Kids who spent more than three hours a day watching television at age 14 were more than four times as likely to have acted aggressively by age 22 than kids who watched TV for less than an hour. The connection held up even after researchers accounted for other possible culprits, including poverty, neglect, and bad neighborhoods. (29)

Finally, if the Product of the 20th Century doesn't affect us to act in certain ways, why would companies pay millions of dollars for commercial time during the Super Bowl, the show that boasts the greatest number of U.S. viewers each year? Clearly advertisers think the high-stakes gamble pays off; otherwise they would not continue year after year.

Student synthesizes three sources and her own commentary.

Introductory tag makes clear that Wright is reporting on Johnson's study.

Note format of block quotation, indented 10 spaces from the left margin.

Television, more than any other product, opens the floodgates of information. In this sense, TV is a box of freedom, as long as the medium is indeed open. Unfortunately, in some countries governments strictly control TV, preventing unwanted influence while indoctrinating citizens with the "appropriate" ideology, strategies that further attest to the apparent power of television. Not surprisingly, those restricting others do not often impose the same limitations on themselves. According to Scott MacCleod in TimeEurope, Crown Prince Abdullah of Saudi Arabia has 33 sets in his office, enabling him to watch all satellite news channels at the same time.

Excessive state control is perhaps caused by fear. Modern history suggests that TV has the power to "make or break" public figures. The Product of the 20th Century brought in a new era, one in which political candidates must develop a love affair with the camera or fail. Walter Mondale, in hindsight, understood this and declared: "Modern politics requires the mastery of television" (qtd. in Fisher and Fisher 5). And, was a presidential election decided by TV image? Mander points out that leading up to the famous 1960 Nixon/Kennedy television debate, Nixon was leading in the polls. But his TV appearance turned a likely victory into loss. A sweaty, haggard-looking Nixon notably contrasted with the younger, handsome Kennedy, images that may have turned the election (33).

Politicians have also learned that television provides the best way to influence the greatest number of voters at one time and that the tube provides an ideal medium to present their "informal selves." Hart reports politicians' chatting on the endless talk shows, playing the saxophone, and answering questions from ordinary folks in town hall meetings inspire some to see this as "returning government to the people" (28). In Hart's opinion, though, such "cozy" atmospheres actually shield politicians from the tough questions of journalists (28). The TV images projecting such "personal sides" (Kennedy

Mitchell 8

tossing a football on the beach, Reagan brushing his horse) do seem to sway public opinion, making television an immensely powerful political tool.

What of other groundbreaking products of the 20th century? Some would argue that the computer ruled the century, but the computer has yet to reach its full potential. More than TV, it is geared towards the educated. This country is still a ways away from 99 percent ownership of a home computer. Both products provide information and entertainment, but, for example, when news broke of the September 11 terror attacks, many people who had access to the Internet instantly reached for the remote to watch the live TV coverage. Why? Could it be that no text or photo rivals "real-time" TV? Some who that day relied on the Internet found major news sites inaccessible—swamped by the number of hits. No such problems with television: Instant, Live, Replay, Slow Motion, Freeze Frame, Sound Clip, Sky-Cam, Ground-Cam, NYFD-Cam.

What about airplanes and space shuttles? The technology is awe-inspiring. Is it "smarter" than TV? Certainly. Does it conquer TV as Product of the 20th Century? No. Although thousands fly every day and aeronautics has expanded in ways the Wright Brothers might never have imagined, the technology has not affected our minds in the same way that TV has. Have planes made us aggressive, passive, Republican, Democrat? What does the average American know about NASA compared to Survivor? Television, the wondrous, monstrous box of information, has in the 20th century revolutionized the way we see and experience the world. It enables a butcher in Bangladesh to tour a Beverly Hills boudoir, a seamstress in Somalia to sled across the Alaskan snow. And, one might question, how would we truly behave—how would we kiss, cry, dress, speak, vote, fight—had we not seen it done on TV?

Transition to comparison with computer.

A strong conclusion with clever word choice.

Mitchell 9

Works Cited

Centerwall, Brandon S. "Television and Violent Crime." Public Interest Spring

1993. Rpt. in Read, Reason, Write. 6th ed. Ed. Dorothy U. Seyler.

New York: McGraw, 2002. 306–15.

Douglas, Susan J. "Radio and Television." HistoryChannel.com. 1996–2003.

History Channel. 5 May 2003 <http://historychannel.com/>. Path:

Television; Radio and Television.

Fisher, David E., and John Marshall Fisher. Tube: The Invention of Television.

New York: Harcourt, 1997.

Hart, Roderick P. Seducing America: How Television Charms the Modern Voter.

Oxford: Oxford UP, 1994.

MacCleod, Scott. "How to Bring Change to the Kingdom." TimeEurope 2002. 4

April 2003 <http://www./time/europe/magazine/

0,13006,901020304-212732-4,00.html>.

Mander, Jerry. Four Arguments for the Elimination of Television. New York:

Morrow, 1978.

Winn, Marie. "A Commitment to Language." The Plug-In Drug. 1997. Rpt. in

Read, Reason, Write. 6th ed. Ed. Dorothy U. Seyler. New York: McGraw,

2002. 89–90.

Wright, Karen. "Guns, Lies, and Video." Discover April 2003: 28–29.

Marginal notes:

Start a new page for the Works Cited. Include only works actually cited. Double-space throughout. Alphabetize and use hanging indentation.

Cites an Internet news source.

Cites a passage from a book reprinted in another book.

SAMPLE RESEARCH ESSAY 2: A LITERARY RESEARCH ESSAY

The following paper, in MLA style, illustrates the use of a few sources but many page references to one literary work. The student's essay was written for a sophomore-level literature course and was based in part on class discussion of *Intruder in the Dust* as an example of an initiation novel. The student demonstrates considerable skill in literary analysis and shows, by his references to Hawthorne and Miller, that he can make connections between other studied works and *Intruder.* Going beyond class discussion and making connections with other works or concepts will be rewarded in any field of study.

Peterson 1

Alan Peterson

American Literature 242

May 5, 1998

Faulkner's Realistic Initiation Theme

William Faulkner braids a universal theme, the theme of initiation, into the fiber of his novel Intruder in the Dust. From ancient times to the present, a prominent focus of literature, of life, has been rites of passage, particularly those of childhood to adulthood. Joseph Campbell defines rites of passage as "distinguished by formal, and usually very severe, exercises of severance." A "candidate" for initiation into adult society, Campbell explains, experiences a shearing away of the "attitudes, attachments and life patterns" of childhood (9). This severe, painful stripping away of the child and installation of the adult is presented somewhat differently in several works by American writers.

One technique of handling this theme of initiation is used by Nathaniel Hawthorne in his story "My Kinsman, Major Molineaux." The story's main character, Robin, is suddenly awakened to the real world, the adult world, when he sees Major Molineaux "in tar-and-feathery dignity" (Hawthorne 528). A terrified and amazed Robin gapes at his kinsman as the large and colorful crowd laughs at and ridicules the Major; then an acquiescent Robin joins with the crowd in the mirthful shouting (Hawthorne 529). This moment is Robin's epiphany, his sudden realization of reality. Robin goes from unsophisticated rube to resigned cynical adult in one quick scene. Hawthorne does hold out hope that Robin will not let this event ruin his life, indeed that he will perhaps prosper from it.

A similar, but decidedly less optimistic, example of an epiphanic initiation occurs in Arthur Miller's play Death of a Salesman. Miller develops an

Peterson 2

initiation theme within a flashback. A teenaged Biff, shockingly confronted with Willy's infidelity and weakness, has his boyhood dreams, ambitions—his vision—shattered, leaving his life in ruins, a truth borne out in scenes in which Biff is an adult during the play (1083–84, 1101). Biff's discovery of the vices and shortcomings of his father overwhelm him. His realization of adult life is a revelation made more piercing when put into the context of his naive and overly hopeful upbringing. A ravaged and defeated Biff has adulthood wantonly thrust upon him. Unlike Hawthorne's Robin, Biff never recovers.

William Faulkner does not follow these examples when dealing with the initiation of his character Chick in Intruder in the Dust. In Robin's and Biff's cases, each character's passage into adulthood was brought about by realization of and disillusionment with the failings and weaknesses of a male adult playing an important role in his life. By contrast, Chick's male role models are vital, moral men with integrity. Chick's awakening develops as he begins to comprehend the mechanisms of the adult society in which he would be a member.

Faulkner uses several techniques for illustrating Chick's growth into a man. Early in the novel, at the end of the scene in which Chick tries to pay for his dinner, Lucas warns Chick to "stay out of that creek" (Faulkner 16).[1] The creek is an effective symbol: it is both a physical creek and a metaphor for the boy's tendency to slide into gaffes that perhaps a man could avoid. The creek's symbolic meaning is more evident when, after receiving the molasses, Chick encounters Lucas in town. Lucas again reminds Chick not to "fall in no more creeks this winter" (24). At the end of the novel, Lucas meets Chick in Gavin's office and states: "you ain't fell in no more creeks lately, have you?" (241). Although Lucas phrases this as a question, the answer is obvious to Lucas, as

---

[1]Subsequent references to Faulkner's novel cite page numbers only.

¶ concludes with emphasis on contrast.

Transition to Faulkner's story by contrast with Hawthorne and Miller.

Footnote first parenthetical reference to inform readers that subsequent citations will exclude the author's name and give only the page number. (See page 286).

well as to the reader, that indeed Chick has not blundered into his naive boyhood quagmire lately. When Lucas asks his question, Chick's actual falling into a creek does not occur to the reader.

Another image Faulkner employs to show Chick growing into a man is the single-file line. After Chick gets out of the creek, he follows Lucas into the house, the group walking in single file. In the face of Lucas's much stronger adult will, Chick is powerless to get out of the line, to go to Edmonds's house (7). Later in the novel, when Miss Habersham, Aleck Sander, and Chick are walking back from digging up the grave, Chick again finds himself in a single-file line with a strong-willed adult in front. Again he protests, then relents, but clearly he feels slighted and wonders to himself "what good that [walking single file] would do" (130). The contrast between these two scenes illustrates Chick's growth, although he is not yet a man.

Faulkner gives the reader other hints of Chick's passage into manhood. As the novel progresses, Chick is referred to (and refers to himself) as a "boy" (24), a "child" (25), a "young man" (46), "almost a man" (190), a "man" (194), and one of two "gentlemen" (241). Other clues crop up from time to time. Chick wrestles with himself about getting on his horse and riding away, far away, until Lucas's lynching is "all over finished done" (41). But his growing sense of responsibility and outrage quell his boyish desire to escape, to bury his head in the sand. Chick looks in the mirror at himself with amazement at his deeds (125). Chick's mother serves him coffee for the first time, despite the agreement she has with his father to withhold coffee until his eighteenth birthday (127). Chick's father looks at him with pride and envy (128–29).

Perhaps the most important differences between the epiphanic initiations of Robin and Biff and that experienced by Chick are the facts that Chick's epiphany does not come all at once and it does not devastate him. Chick learns about adulthood—and enters adulthood—piecemeal and with support. His first eye-opening experience occurs as he tries to pay Lucas for dinner and is

Note transition. (See pages 313–14 on transitions.)

Note interpolation in square brackets.

Good use of brief quotations combined with analysis. (See pages 315–17.)

Characteristics of Chick's gradual and positive initiation explained. Observe coherence techniques. (See pages 313–14.)

rebuffed (15–16). Chick learns, after trying again to buy a clear conscience, the impropriety and affront of his actions (24). Lucas teaches Chick how he should resolve *his* dilemma by setting him "free" (26–27). Later, Chick feels outrage at the adults crowding into the town, presumably to see a lynching, then disgrace and shame as they eventually flee (196–97, 210). As in most lives, Chick's passage into adulthood is a gradual process; he learns a little bit at a time and has support in his growing. Gavin is there for him, to act as a sounding board, to lay a strong intellectual foundation, to confirm his beliefs. Chick's initiation is consistent with Joseph Campbell's explanation: "all rites of passage are intended to touch not only the candidate, but also every member of his circle" (9). Perhaps Gavin is affected the most, but Chick's mother and father, and Lucas as well, are influenced by the change in Chick.

In Intruder in the Dust, William Faulkner has much to say about the role of and the actions of adults in society. He depicts racism, ignorance, resignation, violence, fratricide, citizenship, hope, righteousness, lemming-like aggregation, fear, and a host of other emotions and actions. Chick learns not only right and wrong, but that in order to be a part of society, of his community, he cannot completely forsake those with whom he disagrees or whose ideas he challenges. There is much compromise in growing up; Chick learns to compromise on some issues, but not all. Gavin's appeal to Chick to "just don't stop" (210) directs him to conform enough to be a part of the adult world, but not to lose sight of, indeed instead to embrace, his own values and ideals.

Student concludes by explaining the values Chick develops in growing up.

Peterson 5

Paging is continuous.

Works Cited

Campbell, Joseph. The Hero with a Thousand Faces. Princeton: Princeton UP,

    1949.

Faulkner, William. Intruder in the Dust. New York: Random, 1948.

Hawthorne, Nathaniel. "My Kinsman, Major Molineaux." 1832.

    The Complete Short Stories of Nathaniel Hawthorne. New York:

    Hanover/Doubleday, 1959. 517–30.

Miller, Arthur. Death of a Salesman. 1949. An Introduction to Literature.

    9th ed. Ed. Sylvan Barnet, Morton Berman, and William Burto. Boston:

    Little, 1985. 1025–111.

Place Works Cited on separate page.

Double-space throughout.

Use hanging indentation.

CHAPTER 12

Other Styles

of

Documentation

(APA and More)

Although the research process is much the same regardless of the area of study, documentation varies from one discipline to another. You need to be aware that not all disciplines use MLA. Three common styles of documentation other than MLA are the author/year or APA style, the footnote or endnote style, and the number style. The first two are explained and illustrated in this chapter. The number style, used by some scientists, varies considerably from one group to another. Their style sheets, which you can examine as needed, are listed in the footnote below.[*]

---

[*]*Scientific Style and Format: The CBE Manual for Authors, Editors, and Publishers* (6th ed., 1994), published by the Council of Biology Editors; *ACS Style Guide* (1986), published by the American Chemical Society; *AIP Style Manual* (4th ed., 1990), published by the American Institute of Physics; and *A Manual for Authors of Mathematical Papers* (rev. ed., 1990), published by the American Mathematical Society.

AUTHOR/YEAR OR APA STYLE

The *author/year system* identifies a source by placing the author's last name and the publication year of the source within parentheses at the point in the text where the source is cited. The in-text citations are supported by complete citations in a list of sources at the end of the paper. Most disciplines in the social sciences, biological sciences, and earth sciences use some version of the author/year style. Of the various style manuals presenting this style, the most frequently used is the *Publication Manual of the American Psychological Association* (5th ed., 2002).

APA Style: In-Text Citations

The simplest parenthetical reference can be presented in one of three ways:

1. Place the year of publication within parentheses immediately following the author's name in the text.

    > In a typical study of preference for motherese, Fernald (1985) used an
    >
    > operant auditory preference procedure.

Within the same paragraph, additional references to the source do not need to repeat the year, if the researcher clearly establishes that the same source is being cited.

> Because the speakers were unfamiliar subjects Fernald's work eliminates
>
> the possibility that it is the mother's voice per se that accounts for the
>
> preference.

2. If the author is not mentioned in the text, place the author's last name followed by a comma and the year of publication within parentheses after the borrowed information.

    > The majority of working women are employed in jobs that are at least
    >
    > 75 percent female (Lawrence & Matsuda, 1997).

3. Cite a specific passage by providing the page, chapter, or figure number following the borrowed material. *Always* give specific page references for quoted material.

    - A brief quotation:

    > Deuzen-Smith (1988) believes that counselors must be involved with clients
    >
    > and "deeply interested in piecing the puzzle of life together" (p. 29).

- A quotation in display form:

Bartlett (1932) explains the cyclic process of perception:

> Suppose I am making a stroke in a quick game, such as tennis or cricket.
>
> How I make the stroke depends on the relating of certain new experiences,
>
> most of them visual, to other immediately preceding visual experiences,
>
> and to my posture, or balance of posture, at the moment. (p. 201)

(Indent a block quotation five spaces from the left margin, do not use quotation marks, and double-space throughout. To show a new paragraph within the block quotation, indent the first line of the new paragraph an additional five spaces. Note the placing of the year after the author's name, and the page number at the end of the direct quotation.)

More complicated in-text citations should be handled as follows.

Two Authors, Mentioned in the Text

Kuhl and Meltzoff (1984) tested 4- to 5-month-olds in an experiment . . .

Two Authors, Not Mentioned in the Text

. . . but are unable to show preference in the presence of two mismatched

modalities (e.g., a face and a voice; see Kuhl & Meltzoff, 1984).

Give both authors' last names each time you refer to the source. Connect their names with "and" in the text. Use an ampersand (&) in the parenthetical citation.

More Than Two Authors

For works coauthored by three, four, or five people, provide all last names in the first reference to the source. Thereafter, cite only the first author's name followed by "et al."

As Price-Williams, Gordon, and Ramirez have shown (1969), . . .

or

Studies of these children have shown (Price-Williams, Gordon, & Ramirez,

1969) . . .

then

Price-Williams et al. (1969) also found that . . .

If a source has six or more authors, use only the first author's last name followed by "et al." every time the source is cited.

Corporate Authors

In general, spell out the name of a corporate author each time it is used. If a corporate author has well-known initials, the name can be abbreviated after the first citation.

FIRST IN-TEXT CITATION:	(National Institutes of Health [NIH], 1989)
SUBSEQUENT CITATIONS:	(NIH, 1989)

Two or More Works Within the Same Parentheses

When citing more than one work by the same author in a parenthetical reference, use the author's name only once and arrange the years mentioned in order, thus:

Several studies of ego identity formation (Marcia, 1966, 1983) . . .

When an author, or the same group of coauthors, has more than one work published in the same year, distinguish the works by adding the letters *a, b, c,* and so on, as needed, to the year. Give the last name only once, but repeat the year, each one with its identifying letters; thus:

Several studies (Smith, 1990a, 1990b, 1990c) . . .

When citing several works by different authors within the same parenthesis, list the authors alphabetically; alphabetize by the first author when citing coauthored works. Separate authors or groups of coauthors with semicolons; thus:

Although many researchers (Archer & Waterman, 1983; Grotevant, 1983;

Grotevant & Cooper, 1986; Sabatelli & Mazor, 1985) study identity

formation . . .

APA STYLE: PREPARING A LIST OF REFERENCES

Every source cited parenthetically in your paper needs a complete bibliographic citation. These complete citations are placed on a separate page (or pages) after the text of the paper and before any appendices included in the paper. Sources are arranged alphabetically, and the first page is titled "References." Begin each source flush with the left margin and indent second and subsequent lines five spaces. Double-space throughout the list of references. Follow these rules for alphabetizing:

1. Organize two or more works by the same author, or the same group of coauthors, chronologically.

   Beck, A. T. (1991).

   Beck, A. T. (1993).

2. Place single-author entries before multiple-author entries when the first of the multiple authors is the same as the single author.

    Grotevant, H. D. (1983).

    Grotevant, H. D., & Cooper, C. R. (1986).

3. Organize multiple-author entries that have the same first author but different second or third authors alphabetically by the name of the second author or third and so on.

    Gerbner, G., & Gross, L.

    Gerbner, G., Gross, L., Jackson-Beeck, M., Jeffries-Fox, S., & Signorielli, N.

    Gerbner G., Gross, L., Morgan, M., & Signorielli, N.

4. Organize two or more works by the same author(s) published in the same year alphabetically by title.

Form for Books

A book citation contains these elements in this form:

Seligman, M. E. P. (1991). *Learned optimism.* New York: Knopf.

Weiner, B. (Ed.) (1974). *Achievement motivation and attribution theory.*

Morristown, NJ: General Learning Press.

Authors

Give all authors' names, last name first, and initials. Separate authors with commas, use the ampersand (&) before the last author's name, and end with a period. For edited books, place the abbreviation "Ed." or "Eds." in parentheses following the last editor's name.

Date of Publication

Place the year of publication in parentheses followed by a period.

Title

Capitalize only the first word of the title and of the subtitle, if there is one, and any proper nouns. Italicize the title and end with a period. Place additional information such as number of volumes or an edition in parentheses after the title, before the period.

Butler, R., & Lewis, M. (1982). *Aging and mental health*

(3rd ed.).

Publication Information

Cite the city of publication; add the state (using the Postal Service abbreviation) or country if necessary to avoid confusion; then give the publisher's name, after a colon, eliminating unnecessary terms such as *Publisher, Co.,* and *Inc.* End the citation with a period.

> Newton, D. E. (1996). *Violence and the media.* Santa Barbara: ABC-Clio.
>
> Mitchell, J. V. (Ed.) (1985). *The ninth mental measurements yearbook.* Lincoln:
>
> > University of Nebraska Press.
>
> National Institute of Drug Abuse. (1993, April 13). *Annual national high school*
>
> > *senior survey.* Rockville, MD: Author.

(Give a corporate author's name in full. When the organization is both author and publisher, place the word "Author" after the place of publication.)

Form for Articles

An article citation contains these elements in this form:

> Changeaux, J-P. (1993). Chemical signaling in the brain. *Scientific American,*
>
> > *269,* 58–62.

Date of Publication

Place the year of publication for articles in scholarly journals in parentheses, followed by a period. For articles in newspapers and popular magazines, give the year followed by month and day (if appropriate).

> (1997, March).

(See also example below.)

Title of Article

Capitalize only the title's first word, the first word of any subtitle, and any proper nouns. Place any necessary descriptive information in square brackets immediately after the title.

> Scott, S. S. (1984, December 12). Smokers get a raw deal [Letter to the Editor].

Publication Information

Cite the title of the journal in full, capitalizing according to conventions for titles. Italicize the title and follow it with a comma. Give the volume number, underlined, followed by a comma, and then inclusive page numbers followed by a period. *If* a journal begins each issue with a new page 1, then also cite the issue number in parentheses immediately following the volume number. Do not use "p." or "pp." before page numbers when citing articles from scholarly journals; do use "p." or "pp." in citations to newspaper and magazine articles.

> Martin, C. L., Wood, C. H., & Little, J. K. (1990). The development of gender
>
> stereotype components. *Child Development, 61,* 1891–1904.
>
> Leakey, R. (2000, April–May). Extinctions past and present. *Time,* p. 35.

Form for an Article or Chapter in an Edited Book

> Goodall, J. (1993). Chimpanzees—bridging the gap. In P. Cavalieri & P. Singer
>
> (Eds.) *The great ape project: Equality beyond humanity* (pp. 10–18). New
>
> York: St. Martin's.

Cite the author(s), date, and title of the article or chapter. Then cite the name(s) of the editor(s) in signature order after "In," followed by "Ed." or "Eds." in parentheses; the title of the book; the inclusive page numbers of the article or chapter, in parentheses, followed by a period. End with the place of publication and the publisher of the book.

A Report

> U.S. Merit Systems Protection Board. (1988). *Sexual harassment in the federal*
>
> *workplace: An update.* Washington, DC: U.S. Government Printing Office.

Electronic Sources

Many types of electronic sources are available on the Internet, and the variety can make documenting these sources complex. At a minimum, an APA reference for any type of Internet source should include the following information: a document title or description; dates—the date of publication or latest update and the date of retrieval—use (n.d.) for "no date" when a publication date is not available; an Internet address (the URL) that works; and, whenever possible, an author name.

Do not place URLs within angle brackets (< >). Also do not place a period at the end of a reference when a URL concludes it. However, if you need to break an Internet address across lines, you should break the URL only after a slash. Here are some examples:

Electronic Daily Newspaper Article Available by Search

> Schwartz, J. (2002, September 13). Air pollution con game. *Washington*
>
> *Times.* Retrieved September 14, 2002, from
>
> http://www.washtimes.com

Journal Article available from a Periodical Database

Note that no URL is necessary; just provide the name of the database.

> Dixon, B. (2001, December). Animal emotions. *Ethics & the Environment,*
>
> *6*(2), 22. Retrieved August 26, 2002, from Academic Search Premier
>
> database/EBSCO Host Research Databases.

U.S. Government Report on a Government Web Site

> U.S. General Accounting Office. (2002, March). *Identity theft: Prevalence*
>
> *and cost appear to be growing.* Retrieved September 3, 2002, from
>
> http://www.consumer.gov/idtheft/reports/gao-d02363.pdf

Cite a message posted to a newsgroup or electronic mailing list in the References list. Cite an e-mail from one person to another *only* in the essay, not in the list of References.

SAMPLE PAPER IN APA STYLE

The following paper illustrates APA style. Use one-inch margins and double-space throughout, including any block quotations. Block quotations should be indented *five* spaces from the left margin (in contrast to the 10 spaces required by MLA style). The paper illustrates the following elements of papers in APA style: title page, running head, abstract, author/year in-text citations, subheadings within the text, and a list of references.

Transracial Adoptions 1

Sample title page
for a paper in
APA style.

Adoption: An Issue of Love, Not Race

Connie Childress

Northern Virginia Community College

Transracial Adoptions 2

Abstract

Over 400,000 children are in foster care in the United States. The majority of

these children are non-white. However, the majority of couples wanting to

adopt children are white. While matching race or ethnic background when

arranging adoptions may be the ideal, the mixing of race or ethnic background

should not be avoided, or delayed, when the matching of race is not possible.

Children need homes, and studies of racial adoptees show that they are as

adjusted as adoptees with new parents of their own race or ethnicity.

Legislation should support speedier adoptions of children, regardless of race or

ethnic background.

Adoption: An Issue of Love, Not Race

Nine years ago when my daughter, Ashley, was placed in my arms, it marked the happy ending to a long, exhausting, and, at times, heartbreaking journey through endless fertility treatments and the red tape of adoption procedures. Ironically, she had not been in our home a day before we received a call from another adoption agency that specialized in foreign adoptions. The agency stated that it was ready to begin our home study. As I look at Ashley, with her brown hair, hazel eyes, and fair complexion, I have trouble imagining not having her in my life. I know in my heart that I would have this feeling about my daughter whether she came to us from the domestic agency or the agency bringing us a child from a foreign country. To us the issue was only the child, not his or her race or ethnic background. The issue of race or ethnicity should be considered by adoptive parents along with all the other issues needing thought when they make the decision to adopt. But race or ethnicity alone should not be a roadblock to adoption. It is not society's place to decide for

parents if they are capable of parenting a child of a different race or ethnic background.

Transracial adoptions are those adoptions involving a family and a child of a different race or ethnic background. Cultural differences occur when the family is of one racial or ethnic background and the adoptive child is of

another. Amy Kuebelbeck (1996) reports that, according to the U.S. Department of Health and Human Services, "about 52 percent of children awaiting adoption through state placement services around the country are black." On average, black children wait longer to be adopted than white, Asian, or Hispanic children. Why should it be more difficult for a white family to adopt an African-American child than a child from China or Russia? Or a Hispanic American or mixed-race child? Any of these combinations still results in a mixed-race adoption.

Transracial Adoptions 4

Adoption Issues and Problems

Although interracial adoptions are "statistically rare in the United States," according to Robert S. Bausch and Richard T. Serpe (1997), who cite a 1990 study by Bachrach et al., the issue continues to receive attention from both social workers and the public (p. 137). A *New Republic* editorial (1994) lists several articles, including a cover story in *The Atlantic* in 1992, to illustrate the attention given to transracial adoptions. All of the popular-press articles as well as those in scholarly journals, the editors explain, describe the country's adoption and foster-care problems. While the great majority of families wanting to adopt are white, about half of the children in foster care waiting to be adopted are black. Robert Jackson (1995) estimates that, in 1995, about 440,000 children are being cared for in foster families. The *New Republic* editorial reports on a 1993 study revealing that "a black child in California's foster care system is three times less likely to be adopted than a white child" (p. 6). In some cases minority children have been in a single foster home with parents of a different race their entire life. They have bonded as a family. Yet, often when the foster parents apply to adopt these children, their petitions are denied and the children are removed from their care. For example, Beverly and David Cox, a white couple in Wisconsin, were asked to be foster parents to two young sisters, both African American. The Coxes provided love and nurturing for five years, but when they petitioned to adopt the two girls, not only was their request denied, but the girls were removed from their home. Can removing the children from the only home they have ever known just because of their skin color really be in the best interest of the children? Cole, Drummond, and Epperson (1995) quote Hillary Clinton as saying that "skin color [should] not outweigh the more important gift of love that adoptive parents want to offer" (p. 50).

The argument against transracial adoption has rested on the concern that children adopted by parents of a different race or ethnic background will lose

Page numbers must be given for direct quotations.

Words added to a quotation for clarity are placed in square brackets.

their cultural heritage and racial identity, and that these losses may result in adjustment problems for the children (Bausch & Serpe, 1997). The loudest voice against mixed-race adoptions has been the National Association of Black Social Workers (NABSW), who passed a resolution in 1972 stating their "vehement opposition to the practice of placing Black children with white families" and reaffirmed their position in 1994 (Harnack, 1995, p. 188). Audrey T. Russell (1993), speaking at the 1972 conference, described white adoption of black children as "a practice of genocide" (p. 189). Fortunately, for both children and families wanting to adopt, the NABSW has now reversed its position and concedes that placement in a home of a different race is far more beneficial to the child than keeping the child in foster care (Jackson, 1995). The NABSW's new position may have come in response to the passage of the Multiethnic Placement Act of 1994, legislation designed to facilitate the placement of minority children into adoptive homes. As Randall Kennedy (1995) explains, while this legislation continues to allow agencies to consider "the child's cultural, ethnic and racial background and the capacity of prospective foster or adoptive parents to meet the needs of a child of this background" (p. 44), it prohibits the delaying of an adoption solely for the purpose of racial matching. Kennedy objects to the law's allowing for even some consideration of race matching because he believes that this results in some children never being adopted, as agencies search for a race match. Sandra Haun (1997), a social worker from Fairfax County, Virginia, said in an interview that she does not oppose transracial adoptions but that the best choice for a child is with a family of the same race, if the choice exists. Providing that both adoptive homes could offer the child the same environment in every aspect, then clearly the same-race home may be the best choice. More often than not, however, placing a child in a home of the same race is not an option. How can we worry about a child's cultural identity when the child doesn't have a home to call his or her own? In the cases of minority children who have been with a

Transracial Adoptions 6

foster family of a different race for most of their young lives, the benefits of

remaining in a stable home far outweigh the benefits of moving to a family of

the same race.

The emotional effects of removing a child from a home that he or she has

lived in for an extended period of time is well illustrated in the movie *Losing*

Isaiah. In the film, a black child is adopted by a white social worker and her

husband after the child's birth mother has placed him in the garbage when he is

three days old so that she can be free to search for drugs. When Isaiah is three,

the courts return him to his birth mother, who is now off drugs. Is it fair to

Isaiah for her reward to be at the expense of his emotional health? The attorney

representing the adoptive parents sums up the plight of these children in one

sentence: "The child is then wrenched from the only family they've ever known

and turned over to strangers because of the color of their skin." In the end,

Isaiah's birth mother realizes that this system is unfair to him. She appeals to

his adoptive parents to assist him in his adjustment to his new home.

Some Consequences of Negative Attitudes toward Transracial Adoptions

To protect themselves from heartbreaking situations such as the one

depicted in *Losing Isaiah,* potential adoptive couples in this country are seeking

other alternatives. We know that many couples seeking to adopt often adopt

children from foreign countries. One of the reasons for this is the assumed

shortage of children in the United States available for adoption. What may be

less widely known is that many American children of mixed race or African

American are placed with adoptive families overseas. One of the reasons for this

situation is the continued unwillingness of social workers to place black or

mixed-race children with white couples. The NABSW's years of resistance to

placing black children with white parents has left its mark, although Edmund

Blair Bolles (1984) speculates that the rare placing of black—or American

Indian—children with white couples may reflect racial prejudices rather than a

great concern to preserve black or Indian identities. Whatever the explanation,

Good transition into discussion of movie

Subheadings are often used in papers in the social sciences.

it is ironic that American babies are being "exported" to adoptive homes in other countries while babies from other countries are being "imported" to American adoptive homes. The child social services system needs to be overhauled to remove the stigmas or concerns that keep American children from being adopted in the country of their birth. If one of the arguments against transracial adoptions is the possible loss of cultural identity, how can we tolerate a system which appears to prefer placing African American children outside their own country—their own cultural heritage?

The argument that adopted children may lose their cultural identity is no longer a justifiable objection to transracial adoptions. As Randall Kennedy (1995) asserts, "there exists no credible empirical support that substantiates" the idea that "adults of the same race as the child will be better able to raise that child than adults of a different race" (p. 44). Bausch and Serpe (1997) cite four studies done between 1972 and 1992 that show that "most children of color adopted by white parents appear to be as well adjusted as children of color adopted by same-race parents" (p. 137). Perhaps the most important study is one conducted over twenty years by Rita Simon, American University sociologist. Davis (1995) reports that she studied 204 interracial adoptees over the twenty-year period and found that many of the adoptees supported transracial adoptions. Some did report that they felt isolated from other people of their own race, but we need to remember that those who participated in this study were adopted when adoptions were more secretive (and when races were more separated). At that time, most adoptees, regardless of race, may have felt isolated because of this lack of openness. Simon (1994), in her book (with Howard Alstein and Marygold S. Melli) draws these conclusions:

> Transracial adoptees do not lose their racial identities, they do not appear
> to be racially unaware of who they are, and they do not display negative
> or indifferent racial attitudes about themselves. On the contrary, . . .

Transracial Adoptions 8

transracially placed children and their families have as high a success rate

as all other adoptees and their families. (p. 204)

With open adoptions becoming increasingly popular, more adoptees today are

aware of their adopted state and often have knowledge of one or both of their

birth parents. It is not only possible, but probably easier, to provide

opportunities for today's adoptee to learn about his or her racial and cultural

background. The fact that the child is being raised by a family of a different race

or ethnic background does not condemn that child to a life of ignorance

concerning his or her own racial and cultural identity.

Conclusion

There can be only one logical solution to the issues surrounding mixed-race

adoptions. Children and their adoptive parents should be united as a family

because they have passed the background investigations and screening

interviews that show they are emotionally and financially able to provide loving

and nurturing environments for the children. To keep children needing homes

and loving parents apart because they are of different races or ethnic

backgrounds is not fair to the children or the adoptive parents. Preventing or

delaying such adoptions is detrimental to each child's development. Children

require a consistent home environment to flourish, to grow to be productive

members of society. Legislation needs to support speedier adoptive placements

for minority children to give them the same quality of life afforded other

adoptees. Society needs to protect the right of adoptive parents by not denying

transracial adoptions as an option for couples seeking to adopt.

Student restates her position in a concluding paragraph.

Transracial Adoptions 9

References

Title the page
References.

Double-space
throughout. In
each citation
indent all lines,
after the first, five
spaces. Note APA
style placement of
date and format
for titles.

All in the family [Editorial]. (1994, Jan. 24). *New Republic,* pp. 6–7.

Bausch, R. S., & Serpe, R. T. (1997). Negative outcomes of interethnic adoption
of Mexican American children. *Social Work, 42.2,* 136–43.

Blackman, A., et al. (1994, Aug. 22). Babies for export. *Time, Time On-disc*
[CD-ROM], pp. 64–65.

Bolles, E. B. (1984). *The Penguin adoption handbook: A guide to creating your new
family.* New York: Viking.

Cole, W., Drummond, T., & Epperson, S. E. (1995, Aug. 14). Adoption in black
and white. *Time,* pp. 50–51.

Davis, R. (1995, Apr. 13). Suits back interracial adoptions. *USA Today,* p. A3.

Harnack, A. (Ed.) (1995). *Adoption: Opposing viewpoints* (p. 188). San Diego:
Greenhaven.

Haun, S. (1997, Sept. 30). Personal interview.

Jackson, R. L. (1995, Apr. 25). U.S. stresses no race bias in adoptions.
Los Angeles Times, p. A26.

Kennedy, R., & Moseley-Braun, C. (1995). At issue: interracial adoption—is the
multiethnic placement act flawed? *ABA Journal 81, ABA Journal On-Disc*
[CD-ROM], pp. 44–45.

Kuebelbeck, A. (1996, Dec. 31). Interracial adoption debated. *AP US and World.*
Retrieved October 10, 1999, from http://www.donet.com/~brandyjc/
p6at111.htm.

Losing Isaiah (1995) [film].

Russell, A. T. (1995). Transracial adoptions should be forbidden. In A. Harnack,
Ed., *Adoption: Opposing viewpoints* (pp. 189–96). San Diego: Greenhaven.

Simon, R. J., Alstein, H., & Melli, M. S. (1995). Transracial adoptions should be
encouraged. In A. Harnack (Ed.), *Adoption: Opposing viewpoints*
(pp. 198–204). San Diego: Greenhaven.

FOOTNOTE OR ENDNOTE STYLE

Instructors in history, philosophy, and art history frequently prefer the footnote or endnote form of documentation to any pattern using parenthetical documentation. The two chief guides for this pattern are the *MLA Handbook* (6th ed., 2003) and the *Chicago Manual of Style* (15th ed., 2003). The required information and the order of that information in a footnote (or endnote) are the same in the two manuals, but they do differ in minor ways in format. Both manuals state a preference for endnotes (citations placed at the end of the paper) rather than footnotes (citations placed at the bottom of appropriate pages), but some instructors may want to see footnotes, so always be sure to determine the precise guidelines for your assignment. Further learn your instructor's expectations with regard to a bibliography in addition to footnotes or endnotes. If the first footnote (or endnote) reference to a source contains complete bibliographic information, a list of works cited may not be necessary. Still, some instructors want both complete documentation notes and the alphabetized Works Cited page(s) following the text (with footnotes) or after the endnotes.

The following guidelines adhere to the *Chicago Manual of Style.* The few differences in format found in the *MLA Handbook* are explained where appropriate.

In-Text Citations

Use a raised (superscript, such as this [2]) arabic numeral immediately following all material from a source, whether the borrowed material is quoted or paraphrased. The number follows all punctuation except the dash, and it always follows material needing documentation at the end of a sentence or clause. Number footnotes or endnotes consecutively throughout the paper, beginning with "1." Use care to present material from sources with introductory tags and with a placing of superscript numbers so that readers can tell where borrowed material begins and where it ends. Regularly placing citation numbers only at the ends of paragraphs will not result in accurate documentation.

Location and Presentation of Footnotes

1. Place footnotes on the same page as the borrowed material. You need to calculate the number of lines needed at the bottom of the page to complete all the footnotes for that page. If you miscalculate, retype the page. (A word processor will make these calculations for you.)
2. Begin the first footnote four lines (two double spaces) below the last line of text.
3. Indent the first line of each footnote five spaces. Type the online, full-size numeral that corresponds to the superscript numeral in the text, followed by a period. (MLA style calls for indenting the first line five spaces and using a superscript numeral without a period.)

4. If a footnote runs to more than one line of text, single-space between lines and begin the second line flush with the left margin.

5. If more than one footnote appears on a page, double-space between notes.

Location and Presentation of Endnotes

1. List endnotes in consecutive order corresponding to the superscript numbers in the text.

2. Indent the first line of each endnote five spaces. Type the online number followed by a period, leave one space, and then type the reference. (MLA style calls for using a superscript numeral in the text as well as in the notes themselves.)

3. If an endnote runs to more than one line, double-space between lines and begin the second line flush with the left margin.

4. Double-space between endnotes.

5. Start endnotes on a new page titled "Notes." Endnotes follow the text and precede a list of works cited, if such a list is included.

Footnote/Endnote Form: First (Primary) Reference

Each first reference to a source contains all the necessary author, title, and publication information that would be found in a list of works cited or list of references. Subsequent references to the same source use a shortened form. Prepare all first-reference notes according to the following guidelines.

Form for Books

1. Cite the author's full name in signature order, followed by a comma.

2. Cite the title of the book in italics. (MLA style: underline the title.) Include the complete subtitle, if there is one, unless a list of works cited is also provided. No punctuation follows the title.

3. Give the facts of publication in parentheses: city of publication followed by a colon, publisher followed by a comma, and year of publication.

4. Give the precise page reference. Do not use "p." or "pp." *Chicago Manual* style: Place a comma after the closing parenthesis, before the page number. *MLA Handbook* style: Use no punctuation between the closing parenthesis and the page reference. All notes end with a period.

CHICAGO: 1. Daniel J. Boorstin, *The Americans: The Colonial Experience*

(New York: Vintage-Random, 1958), 46.

MLA: ¹ Daniel J. Boorstin, The Americans: The Colonial Experience

(New York: Vintage-Random, 1958) 46.

Form for Articles

1. Cite the author's full name in signature order, followed by a comma.
2. Cite the title of the article in quotation marks, and place a comma *inside* the closing quotation mark.
3. Give the facts of publication: the title of the journal, underlined; the volume in arabic numerals; and the date followed by a colon. Citations of scholarly journals require the volume number followed by the date in parentheses; citations of popular magazines and newspapers eliminate the volume number, giving the date only, not in parentheses.
4. Provide a precise page reference following the colon, without using "p." or "pp." All notes end with a period.

> 2. Everard H. Smith, "Chambersburg: Anatomy of a Confederate Reprisal,"
>
> *American Historical Review* 96 (April 1991): 434.

Sample Footnotes/Endnotes

Additional information must be added as necessary. Some of the common variations are illustrated here. Note that the examples are presented as endnotes; that is, the lines of each note are double-spaced. Remember that footnotes are single-spaced *within* each note but double-spaced *between* notes. The Chicago style of italicizing title, using an online numeral, and placing a comma after the facts of publication in a book citation has been followed in these examples.

A Work by Two or Three Authors

> 3. Charles A. Beard and Mary R. Beard, *The American Spirit* (New York:
>
> Macmillan, 1942), 63.

A Work by More Than Three Authors

> 4. Lester R. Brown et al., *State of the World 1990: A World-watch Institute*
>
> *Report on Progress Toward a Sustainable Society* (New York: Norton, 1990), 17.

An Edited Work

> 5. *The Autobiography of Benjamin Franklin,* ed. Max Farrand (Berkeley:
>
> University of California Press, 1949), 6–8.

(Begin with the title—or the editor's name—if the author's name appears in the title.)

6. Bentley Glass, Orvsei Temkin, and William L. Straus, Jr., eds., *Forerunners of Darwin: 1745–1859* (Baltimore: Johns Hopkins Press paperback edition, 1968), 326.

A Translation

7. Allan Gilbert, trans. and ed., *The Letters of Machiavelli* (New York: Capricorn Books, 1961), 120.

A Preface, Introduction, or Afterword

8. Ernest Barker, introduction to *The Politics of Aristotle,* trans. and ed. Ernest Barker (New York: Oxford University Press, 1962), xiii.

A Book in Two or More Volumes

9. Paul Tillich, *Systematic Theology,* 3 vols. (Chicago: University of Chicago Press, 1951–63), 1:52.

(Make the page reference first to the volume number, followed by a colon, and then the page number.)

A Book in Its Second or Subsequent Edition

10. Frank J. Sorauf and Paul Allen Beck, *Party Politics in America,* 6th ed. (Glenview, IL: Scott, Foresman/Little, Brown, 1988), 326.

A Book in a Series

11. Charles L. Sanford, ed., *Benjamin Franklin and the American Character,* Problems in American Civilization (Lexington, MA: D.C. Heath, 1955), 4.

A Work in a Collection

12. George Washington, "Farewell Address, 1796," in *A Documentary History of the United States,* ed. Richard D. Heffner (New York: New American Library, 1965), 64–65.

An Encyclopedia Article

13. *The Concise Dictionary of American Biography*, 1964 ed., s.v. "Anthony, Susan Brownell."

(Do not cite a page number for reference works arranged alphabetically; rather, cite the entry in quotation marks after "s.v." [*sub verbo*—"under the word"]. The edition number or year is needed, but no other facts of publication are required for well-known reference works.)

An Article in a Scholarly Journal

14. Ellen Fitzpatrick, "Rethinking the Intellectual Origins of American Labor History," *American Historical Review* 96 (April 1991): 426.

An Article in a Popular Magazine

15. Richard Leakey, "Extinctions Past and Present," *Time,* April–May 2000: 35.

An Editorial

16. "Means of Atonement," editorial, *Wall Street Journal*, 22 May 2000: A38.

A Review

17. Gabriel P. Weisberg, "French Art Nouveau," review of *Art Nouveau in Fin-de-Siècle France: Politics, Psychology, and Style* by Deborah Silverman, *Art Journal* 49 (Winter 1990): 427.

An Online News Service

18. Leslie Gevirtz, "US Leads 100-Year Game of Economic Development," *Reuters*, Nov/Dec. 1999, http://www.reuters.com/magazine/ (accessed January 4, 2000).

An Article from a Reference Database

19. *Encyclopaedia Britannica Online*, s.v. "Prohibition," http://search.eb.com/ (accessed January 24, 1998).

Footnote/Endnote Form: Short Forms

After the first full documentary footnote or endnote, subsequent references to the same source should be shortened forms. The simplest short form for any source with an author or editor is the author's or editor's last name followed by a comma and a precise page reference; thus: 20. Fitzgerald, 425. If there is no author cited, use a short title and page number. If two sources are written by authors with the same last name, then add first names or initials to distinguish between them.

> 21. Henry Adams, 16.
>
> 22. James T. Adams, 252.

If you use two or more sources by the same author, then add a short title to the note; thus:

> 23. Boorstin, *American Politics*, 167.
>
> 24. Boorstin, *The Americans*, 65–66.

The Latin abbreviations *loc. cit.* and *op. cit.* are no longer recommended, and ibid. is almost as obsolete, usually replaced now by the simple short form of author's last name and page number. Remember that ibid. can be used only to refer to the source cited in the immediately preceding note. The following footnotes, appearing at the bottom of a page from a history paper, illustrate the various short forms.

Sample Footnotes from a History Paper

While mid-twentieth-century historians may be more accurate, they may have lost the flavor of earlier American historians who had a clear ideology that shaped their writing.[20]

11. William Bradford, *Of Plymouth Plantation*, in *The American Puritans: Their Prose and Poetry*, ed. Perry Miller (New York: Anchor-Doubleday, 1956), 5.

12. Daniel J. Boorstin, *The Americans: The Colonial Experience* (New York: Vintage-Random, 1958), 16.

13. Ibid., 155.

14. James T. Adams, 136.

15. Henry Adams, *The Education of Henry Adams*, ed. D. W. Brogan (Boston: Houghton Mifflin, 1961), 342.

16. Boorstin, *American Politics*, 167.

17. Henry Adams, "The Tendency of History," 16.

18. Ibid., 71.

19. Henry Adams, *Education*, 408.

20. John Higham, "The Cult of the 'American Consensus': Homogenizing Our History," *Commentary* 27 (Feb. 1959): 94–96.

A
Collection
of
Readings

This section is divided into 11 chapters: each of the first 10 chapters on a current topic or set of interrelated issues open to debate and the last chapter a collection of some well-known arguments from the past. Although the number of articles varies in each chapter, all contain at least 5 articles in order to remind readers that complex issues cannot be divided into simple "for" or "against" positions. This point remains true even for the chapters on a rather specific topic, bioethics, for example. It is not sound critical thinking to be, simply, for or against any complicated public-policy issue.

There are questions following each article to aid your reading, analysis, and critical responses, and each chapter begins with a brief introduction and set of questions to focus your thinking as you read. Each introduction concludes with a list of a few websites that are relevant to the chapter's topic and may be of interest to you. However, please keep these two thoughts in mind as you read: (1) there is no way to include all possibly relevant Web addresses, and (2) the Internet is ever-changing. Although every effort has been made to include sites that are expected to last, websites in existence when this text was prepared may no longer be available.

Here are some general questions to guide your critical thinking as you read and reflect on the various issues:

1. What are my views on this issue? Do I already have a coherent position? If so, what can I gain by studying the writers who present a different point of view?

2. Which writers rely primarily on facts to support their claims? Which combine facts and logic? Which also use persuasive strategies? Which ones seem to be primarily interested in "pushing emotional buttons" in readers who are assumed to be in agreement with the author? Do I recognize any logical fallacies?

3. Which type of argument usually works best for me? Does my answer to this question depend in part on the particular issue?

CHAPTER 13

The Media:
Image and Reality

Although we may not agree with Marshall McLuhan that the medium is itself the message, we must still recognize the ways that the various media influence us, touching our emotions, shaping our vision of the world, altering our lives. The essays in this chapter explore and debate the effects of television, advertising, and the press on the ways we imagine and then construct our lives. Surely we are influenced by media images, by the "reality" they bombard us with. The questions become, first, how extensive is the influence, given the other influences in our lives? and second, what, if anything, can or should we do about it? The writers do not answer these questions in the same way.

PREREADING QUESTIONS

1. How well do we really know the sports figures, film stars, and other celebrities who are covered by the media? How much of what we see is "real," how much public relations?

2. How accurate is our press coverage? Do media outlets around the world "see" and show the same world to their viewers?

3. How does advertising shape our images of the world? How realistic are those images? What makes advertising so appealing?

4. What standards of reliability, objectivity, and fairness should be set for the media? What, if any, distortions are acceptable because they make the journalist's story more compelling?

Websites Related to This Chapter's Topic

Media Research Center

www.mediaresearch.org

Studies and reports on "liberal" media bias.

Electronic Databases

Databases such as Proquest and Expanded Academic ASAP plus many others containing articles in the social sciences are available through your library. They will lead you to many articles on the topic.

VERY FAMILIAR, LARGELY UNKNOWN | THOMAS BOSWELL

A graduate of Amherst College and a sports columnist with the *Washington Post,* Thomas Boswell (b. 1947) has won recognition for his sportswriting, especially for his essays on baseball. Boswell's two books are *How Life Imitates the World Series* (1982) and *Why Time Begins on Opening Day* (1984). The following column was published July 24, 2003.

PREREADING QUESTIONS   How well do we know other people—family and friends, for example? What strategies can we use to be more adept at telling the difference between reality and media distortion?

In psychology, much less criminology, it is commonplace to observe that no 1
one can understand another person completely. There's an element of mystery at the center of personality. Even our self-knowledge is limited.

In daily life, we only need to look in our own family and friends for exam- 2
ples of behavior so out of character that we must change what we believe about someone close to us.

However, in big-time sports, where we are constantly encouraged to be- 3
lieve we have gotten Up Close and Personal with famous athletes and coaches, it is easy to forget such an everyday lesson—right up to the moment when the handcuffs snap shut or the felony charges are filed.

Four centuries ago, Montaigne wrote: "Others do not see you, they guess 4
at you by uncertain conjectures; they see not so much your nature as your art. . . . It is a rare life that remains well ordered in private . . . to be disciplined within, where all is permissible, where all is concealed—that's the point."

5   These days, whether Kobe Bryant is being charged with sexual assault or a basketball player is ordered held without bond, accused of slaying a former teammate, we are getting that point poked into our chests over and over.

6   Does a week pass without some fresh news that proves we aren't close to understanding the sports figures we follow? This week, Alabama's ex-football coach explained on national TV that "it all started" when he had too much to drink in a topless bar. Too often, the tale is tragic, not comic. Right now, authorities are searching near Waco, Tex., for the body of Patrick Dennehy, the Baylor player whom Carlton Dotson Jr. is accused of killing.

7   We're aware of the image polishing and spin doctoring that surrounds politics and entertainment. But sports keeps fooling us—because it seems different. In moments of athletic drama, we think we see people with their hair down, see them as they really are. And, to a degree, that is true. When Michael Jordan collapsed hugging the NBA championship trophy, that was no act. Cal Ripken's trip around Camden Yards after he broke Lou Gehrig's record was not scripted. He was shaking hands with plenty of fans he already knew.

8   Yet even at such times, we are seeing only slices of the whole person. The final explosive meeting in May between Jordan and Wizards owner Abe Pollin would have been thought radically out of character for both. Yet it happened. So, now we must rework our understanding of both.

9   In most cases, the promotional machine of sports shapes, and exaggerates, the degree to which we think we know great athletes. At the moment, Tiger Woods is probably the world's top jock. Everybody imagines they know him. In fact, he is the least accessible, most shielded, most image-managed athlete in our history. Nobody else is close. Jack Nicklaus was so old shoe and open to inspection he sometimes got boring. Tiger is the next wave. He gives few unguarded hints of who he really is with spikes off.

10   Those who profit from packed stadiums and high TV ratings wish nothing better than that fans feel a kinship, an empathy, almost a personal friendship with the stars they pay top dollar to watch and cheer for. If any basketball fan anywhere doesn't feel that they know Kobe Bryant, there's an NBA marketer whose job is in jeopardy.

11   Teams, agents and athletes parcel out pieces of this sports personality product until, over the course of years, we feel we know our Cals, Mikes, Tigers or Kobes almost as well—sometimes better—than people in our own lives. Those who don't cooperate, who say, "Get out of my face," who don't want to play the "here's a little piece of my soul so you'll like me better" game—like Barry Bonds—are actually sometimes pilloried.

12   The media have a vested interest, as well as an unconscious bias. We're tempted to believe that those who reveal themselves are the people who have little to hide while those who wall us out must, at the least, be crabs. In sports, if you don't present a public face, and a palatable one, you may get booed. So, ironically, the incentive to create a fake face is even greater.

13   As soon as we buy into the word "hero," we've taken the bait. Athletes, as people, resemble us in a hundred more ways than they differ from us. And they're even more fascinating when we keep that in mind. "It is very hard to

find an ideal in history," wrote Ralph Waldo Emerson. "By courtesy we call saints and heroes such, but they are very defective characters."

When a star hits the skids, his natural supporters start reinforcing the best 14 of what the public already thinks it knows. Ever since the Bryant scandal broke, testimonials have arrived, including one this week from Coach Phil Jackson, praising his character. Jackson can speak to Bryant's exemplary behavior as a player, a teammate, a student of the game and even, perhaps, as the public relations torch bearer of his sport.

But when it comes to the character of two people in a hotel room, one of 15 whom is, at the least, committing adultery, here's what we know for sure: nothing. We don't know anything—that is pertinent to the charges—about either the alleged victim or assailant. Hence, evidence, juries and presumption of innocence.

Yet even with our elaborate legal system, it's a bedrock statistic that juries 16 seldom convict celebrities. The jury feels it knows the defendant. And we're hard pressed to believe the worst of those we know. We've already made an evaluation, probably a positive one. Our instincts fight the idea of guilt.

If the Bryant case comes to trial, one of his core advantages, whether he 17 deserves it or not, will be that the jury thinks of him as "Kobe," not "Mr. Bryant," Even though, ideally, it shouldn't be that way. The alleged victim will start from zero. She'll only be known in the context of the trial and against a backdrop of counterattack from Bryant's lawyers.

So don't feel too sorry for Bryant. In a sense, his defense began preparing 18 its case the first day he lit up the NBA. For the last eight years, almost anyone who doesn't live in a cave has come to believe they know "Kobe." Even though they don't. That's a huge home "court" advantage.

QUESTIONS FOR READING

1. What was the specific occasion for Boswell's column? That is, what sports star's actions led to this discussion of reality and media distortion?
2. Why are we more willing to believe that we really know sports figures than any other celebrities?
3. At best, how much do we see of a person?
4. Who serve as Boswell's examples of sports figures we really don't know well?
5. Who benefits from the public's belief that it really knows star athletes?
6. Why are we often suspicious of those athletes who don't want to reveal much of themselves through the media?
7. Why does Kobe Bryant have a "home court advantage" in his trial for sexual assault?

QUESTIONS FOR REASONING AND ANALYSIS

1. What is Boswell's claim?
2. What two different kinds of evidence does Boswell offer to support his claim—that is, what kinds of reasons and what type of data?

3. Does the author expect us to see his specific examples as inclusive or just the most recent proof of the problem? How do you know?

4. What does the author seek to accomplish in his first three paragraphs?

5. Evaluate Boswell's argument. Is his logic sound? His evidence sufficient?

QUESTIONS FOR REFLECTING AND WRITING

1. Do you agree with Boswell that we can never fully understand someone else, that we just guess at who they are? Why or why not?

2. How about understanding ourselves? Are we a partial mystery to ourselves? If so, why might that be the case? If not, why not?

3. Do you think that we are getting a realistic look at leading sports figures? We see them sweat and struggle in competition; does that mean we actually know them fairly well? If yes, defend your position as a rebuttal to Boswell. If no, think about ways that the media may distort their presentation of sports competition and their interviews of sports figures as a way to support this position.

PARALLEL UNIVERSES | ANNE APPLEBAUM

Currently a columnist and editorial board member of the *Washington Post*, Anne Applebaum (b. 1964) was a journalist and writer in Poland and London for 20 years before returning to the United States. Her articles are published in many magazines, she appears on TV talk shows, and she is the author of *Gulag: A History* (2003). The following was published in the *Washington Post* July 22, 2003.

PREREADING QUESTIONS What news sources do you use—what newspapers, news magazines, and TV news programs do you turn to? Do you read/listen to enough different sources to be able to get more than one outlook? Do you think that doing so is a good idea?

1   Late last week Tony Blair made a speech in Washington. Afterward various British journals of record summed up their prime minister's performance. The *Daily Mirror* found "something quite nauseating" about the speech, in which Blair once again "backed America in what many now view as a war based on lies." The *Daily Mail* sneered at "Blair the brilliant contortionist, trying to have it both ways." The *Guardian* meanwhile, declared that the speech represented a "significant softening" of the prime minister's position on Iraqi weapons, and described the event this way: Blair "stood before hundreds of members of Congress to admit that he may eventually be proved wrong."

2   Is that what he was doing? Funny, but if you'd been reading the American press, you'd have had quite a different impression. "Bush, Blair Defend Motives Behind War," read the headline in *The Post*, which failed to detect any "significant softening" in the prime minister's words. The *New York Post*—the closest thing Americans have to the *Daily Mail*—failed to see anything remotely "contortionist" in the speech either, writing that "Blair's address clearly reflected a

nuanced appreciation of America's role in the world." Far from sounding "nauseating," Blair "heralded the role the United States has played in fighting the broader war on terrorism," wrote the *Los Angeles Times.* Not since Mikhail Gorbachev simultaneously became an international superstar and the most hated politician in Russia has a political leader enjoyed such disparate reputations at home and abroad.

In part these remarkably different descriptions of the same speech reflect 3 the vagaries of domestic politics. The issues that actually make Blair unpopular in Britain, such as the travails of the National Health Service, are not issues here at all, and some of what we see as his better attributes are considered failings in Britain. Here he's thought eloquent; there he's thought slippery. Here he's thought statesmanlike; there he's thought to be too interested in foreign countries, and not enough interested in his own.

But they also reflect a larger phenomenon that is not much better under- 4 stood. America and Britain—along with America and France, America and Russia, America and Botswana, America and anywhere, really—live in parallel informational universes. By that I mean that the media produced in different cultures don't merely reflect different opinions about the news, they actually recount alternative versions of reality.

Different countries have always had different perspective on the news, of 5 course. But in the world of globalized information, where just about any newspaper or television program in any language is available at the click of a mouse, this isn't supposed to happen anymore. Nowadays we're all supposed to know what everybody else is thinking, to have access to the same images and information, and some of us do. Peasants in rural India gather around village television sets to watch reruns of *Dallas.* In different time zones, Japanese and German bankers watch the same images on their Reuters screens. It is often said now that events are monitored around the world in "real time," or that we all live in a "global informational village," as if such a thing had already come to pass.

During the Iraq war, a few Americans and Europeans, at least, began to 6 notice how tiny that village actually is. It wasn't hard to see that the war as broadcast by the BBC or Deutsche Welle was quite different from the war as broadcast by NBC or CNN. Fewer understood that this is not only a Euro-American problem: A German friend visited Poland during the war and was surprised by how much less blood seemed to appear on the Polish evening news. And the differences run much deeper than a disagreement over Iraq, or portrayals of a single event. It isn't just that Europeans have different opinions from Americans about the Israeli-Palestinian conflict, for example, they actually learn different facts and read about different events, and therefore they reach different conclusions. When George Tenet fell on his sword earlier this month over that now infamous piece of British intelligence that made it into the president's State of the Union speech, the story played here as "White House Dumps on CIA." In Britain, it played as "White House Dumps on Britain."

7   Strangest of all, the availability of alternative points of view doesn't appear to have mellowed anyone's prejudices—quite the contrary. Nowadays, we all live under the illusion that we are receiving many different types of information, but that we select only the most plausible. In fact, as information multiplies, it grows ever easier to choose to read (or watch) whatever best matches your particular bias, whether national or ideological. If you hate network television's right-wing bias, you can click onto say, www.globalexchange.org or www.moveon.org. If you hate network television's left-wing bias, you can always watch Fox. Having done so, you'll labor under the illusion that you've picked the most truthful version of events—but how would you know? Have you actually compared and contrasted the arguments of both sides and come to a judicious conclusion?

8   What is true here is even more true internationally. If British newspaper readers learned anything of Blair's rapturous reception here last week, they learned it from British articles denouncing the slavish U.S. media. If French television viewers learned anything about American perceptions of the war in Iraq, they learned it from French news items on the jingoistic U.S. media. The prophets of globalization once spoke of a seamless, borderless world, in which national differences would magically disappear. They were wrong.

QUESTIONS FOR READING

1. The author begins by discussing a speech by British Prime Minister Tony Blair. What, actually, is her subject in this essay?

2. What do we assume about the news coverage in different countries today? Why do we make these assumptions?

3. What specific differences are there in news coverage in different countries?

4. What is another consequence of having so many different news sources? Why has this abundance not made us more knowledgeable and wiser?

QUESTIONS FOR REASONING AND ANALYSIS

1. Applebaum begins with two paragraphs on Blair's speech in Washington. What does she include in these paragraphs? What does she gain by beginning with these details?

2. What is her claim? Where does she state it?

3. How does she qualify her claim? (Look again at paragraphs 3 and 5.)

4. Applebaum gives alternative news sources, in paragraph 7, for those who hate TV's right-wing bias *and* its left-wing bias. What is her primary point in this paragraph? What other point is she implying when she comments on the apparently contradictory biases of TV news? What is she implying about the Fox News Channel?

5. Applebaum provides additional evidence in paragraph 6. Evaluate her argument—remembering that she is writing a brief op-ed column, not a long scholarly essay for an academic journal, and that she expects her readers to be familiar with the events referred to and their coverage in the news.

QUESTIONS FOR REFLECTING AND WRITING

1. In paragraph 7, the author asserts that if you take your news from only one source, you are probably reinforcing your own prejudices and not getting "the most truthful version of events." Do you get news from more than one source? If not, do you now think that you should? If you disagree with Applebaum, how would you rebut her assertion?

2. Other analysts of television and American culture have observed that with the vast increase in numbers of TV channels, fewer and fewer Americans are watching the same shows and that this gives us less in common with colleagues and neighbors and family, pushing us into smaller and smaller "worlds." Are these observations consistent with your experience? How would you go about collecting data to support this analysis?

3. Applebaum asserts that differences in news coverage go beyond differences of opinion and actually provide "alternative versions of reality." Does this idea make sense to you? How would you go about collecting data to support the idea? If you disagree with the assertion, how would you rebut Applebaum?

WHITE LIES | KATHA POLLITT

Associate editor at *The Nation*, Katha Pollitt (b. 1949) contributes to periodicals, has collected her essays in *Reasonable Creatures: Essays on Women and Feminism* (1994), and has a book of poetry, *Antarctic Traveller* (1982). "White Lies" appeared in *The Nation* on June 16, 2003.

PREREADING QUESTIONS What are "white lies"? If you don't know this expression, look it up—it's important to understanding Pollitt's claim.

The radio went on in the middle of the night and there in my ear was the 1 voice of a young man. It was a soothing voice, deferential, quizzical, NPR-ish, the voice boy journalists in the high-end media use when they are trying to get Nazis to talk about their childhoods. And yet there was a kind of suppressed glee in it, too—as if he had just gotten the perfect quote from Adolf Jr. for his lead. Yes, the young man said ruefully, he knew people hated him; yes, he's become more religious. Well, naturally! This was Stephen Glass, the *New Republic* tale-spinner, pushing his autobiographical novel *The Fabulist,* and public contrition just goes with the territory. F. Scott Fitzgerald, who famously said there are no second acts in American lives, should only be alive to see how wrong he was.

There's one person besides his agent who should be overjoyed at Glass's 2 splashy re-emergence from obscurity, and that is Jayson Blair. Forced out at the *New York Times* on May 1 for a wide variety of journalistic sins—plagiarizing, making things up, getting things wrong, pretending to be eyewitness reporting from Maryland and Texas while never actually leaving the city— Blair, too, has acknowledged that he was "troubled," and has an agent trying to secure a six-figure advance for a tell-all book. While no one judged Glass as a case of whiteboyism run amok, Blair, who is black, is now exhibit A for affirmative-action bashers: You see what happens when guilty liberals coddle the unqualified? Janet Cooke, the black journalist fired from the *Washington Post* after winning a Pulitzer for a fabrication, tends to come in for a mention at this point—never mind that she was canned twenty-two long years ago. Glass's reappearance is a timely reminder that liars and manipulators come in all colors of the rainbow.

3   Everyone is asking how these two were able to deceive so many for so long. But is it so mysterious? As many a woman has learned to her chagrin, pathological liars are brilliant at deception. They know how to make a story sparkle, they breezily proffer instant explanations for any little inconsistency, they're scheming all the time while you, their mark, are preoccupied with a hundred other things. Besides, you want to believe them—they're so charming, attentive and flattering. According to numerous accounts, Blair was a champion sycophant to *Time* top editor Howell Raines and Gerald Boyd, his second-in-command; Glass was the quintessential young man in a hurry, smart and needy, someone in whom his editors could see their younger selves. As *George* editor Richard Blow, one of Glass's victims, confessed in *Salon*, these professional liars know how to play to your secret wishes and preconceptions. Glass's hilarious tales—young conservatives engaging in drug-fueled orgies, women stricken en masse with crushes on UPS men—played on the desire of his wonkish Beltway editors to feel superior and in-the-know.

4   As Blow acknowledges, to his credit, Glass pandered to his editors' tacit racism, too. He wrote a piece for *Harper's* alleging that blacks spend tons of cash on phone psychics and one for the *New Republic* that told of his cabdriver being robbed by a black man. One of the fabrications that finally brought him down was an article for *George* alleging that Clinton adviser Vernon Jordan had Monicas of his own. It's interesting how often race and class prejudice show up in these discredited stories. Janet Cooke's Pulitzer was for a feature about an 8-year-old black heroin addict. Ruth Shalit, the *New Republic's* star plagiarizer, attacked the *Washington Post* in an error-strewn piece for pandering to racial sensitivities. (Her editor, Andrew Sullivan, is now enjoying himself at the *Times's* expense—but while the *Times* prostrated itself with a 14,000-word article detailing Blair's derelictions, the *New Republic* issued only pro forma regret.) Jay Forman's mostly invented *Slate* article on the obscure Florida sport of monkey-fishing in the mangroves played to stereotypes about backwoods Southerners—they eat squirrels and sleep with their sisters, so why wouldn't they fish for monkeys, too?

5   Blair now joins a lengthening list of disgraced journalists—don't forget Mike Barnicle (plagiarized), Patricia Smith (made up quotes and people) and my favorite ethical line-crosser, Bob Greene (slept with a high schooler who interviewed him for her school paper). The *Times* has suspended Rick Bragg, a Raines protege whose lavishly overwritten tales of Southern life provoked many an eyeroll from acerbic New Yorkers, for excessive reliance on an uncredited volunteer stringer who did his actual reporting. Several other *Times* reporters are allegedly under investigation by management as well.

It sounds like management needs to take a look at itself, and not just about   6
such common journalistic failings as borrowed phrases and embellished
quotes. It's embarrassing to see *Times* brass flagellating themselves with tiny
Blair corrections ("The sister of Corporal Gardner is named Cara, not Kara")
while weighty issues of news content go unaddressed. For all their slapdash
dishonesty, none of Blair's stories affected the course of any event. That cannot be said of the paper's relentless pushing of Whitewater, which helped stall
a presidency but ended without a Clinton indictment, or its unfounded, life-
destroying pursuit of Wen Ho Lee.

At the present moment, the question of whether Rick Bragg personally wit-   7
nessed the "jumping mullet that belly-flop with a sharp clap into steel-gray water" is trivial compared with Judith Miller's credulous reports on Iraq. Here we
have a Pulitzer-winning reporter who alleges that an unnamed Iraqi scientist
has proof both of WMDs and of Saddam's connections with Al Qaeda and
Syria. Miller got this fascinating scoop from her Army handlers—she never
questioned him herself; indeed, she never even met him! She allowed the Army
to vet her copy and determine the timing of its publication. Result: a front-page
story that was trumpeted everywhere as the retroactive justification for war.

Where were the editors who should have reined in this Administration-   8
friendly flight of fancy? The person who put Miller's story on page one has more
to answer for than the harried administrator who didn't notice that Blair's travel
receipts were from a Starbucks in Brooklyn.

QUESTIONS FOR READING

1. Who is Stephen Glass? What did he do to become "famous"?
2. Who is Jayson Blair? What did he do to become "famous"?
3. How did they deceive their editors? What reasons does Pollitt give?
4. How many reporters, in all, does Pollitt name in the first five paragraphs? What do they all have in common?
5. How, in the author's view, do the errors of these reporters differ from the *New York Times's* coverage of Whitewater and Judith Miller's coverage of Iraq?

QUESTIONS FOR REASONING AND ANALYSIS

1. What is Pollitt's claim? Where does she state it?
2. Pollitt begins with several paragraphs of details about various reporters in dis-grace for plagiarizing. What does she gain by beginning with details rather than a general introduction leading to a statement of her claim? What are readers in-vited to expect her point to be? Except, how does her title warn us to be patient and read on?
3. What is the author's primary point of difference between the plagiarizing re-porters and Judith Miller?
4. What is Pollitt's opinion of journalists who plagiarize? Is she defending them in this article? Or using them to make a larger point?

QUESTIONS FOR REFLECTING AND WRITING

1. How many of the cases mentioned by Pollitt are you familiar with? Whether these reporters are known to you or not, what lesson can you draw about the consequences of plagiarizing in the world of journalism? (Note: Janet Cooke had to return her Pulitzer Prize, and she has not worked in journalism since her firing by the *Washington Post*.)

2. Is biased reporting a more serious "lie" than making up parts of your article or not acknowledging others whose facts you used? Why or why not? Be prepared to defend your position.

JOURNALISM AND THE LARGER TRUTH | ROGER ROSENBLATT

Fulbright scholar, college professor, editor, and writer, Roger Rosenblatt (b. 1940) first came to Washington as education director of the National Endowment for the Humanities. His career demonstrates the close connections between the worlds of academia, politics, and journalism. Rosenblatt is the author of several books, the latest on abortion in the United states, as well as many essays. The following essay, though published in *Time* July 2, 1984, remains relevant in the light of the recent firings of several journalists for plagiarism and/or making up "facts."

PREREADING QUESTIONS What, if any, connection do you see between "journalism" and "the larger truth"? What is the role of the journalist?

1   When journalists hear journalists claim a "larger truth," they really ought to go for their pistols. The *New Yorker*'s Alastair Reid[1] said the holy words last week: "A reporter might take liberties with the factual circumstances to make the larger truth clear." O large, large truth. Apparently Mr. Reid believes that imposing a truth is the same as arriving at one. Illogically, he also seems to think that truths may be disclosed through lies. But his error is more fundamental still in assuming that large truth is the province of journalism in the first place. The business of journalism is to present facts accurately—Mr. Reid notwithstanding. Those seeking something larger are advised to look elsewhere.

2   For one thing, journalism rarely sees the larger truth of a story because reporters are usually chasing quite small elements of information. A story, like a fern, only reveals its final shocking shape in stages. Journalism also reduces most of the stories it deals with to political considerations. Matters are defined in terms of where power lies, who opposes whom or what, where the special interests are. As a result, the larger truth of a story is often missed or ignored. By its nature, political thought limits speculative thought. Political realities themselves cannot be grasped by an exclusively political way of looking at things.

3   Then, too, journalism necessarily deals with discontinuities. One has never heard of the Falkland Islands.[2] Suddenly the Falklands are the center of the

---

[1] *New Yorker* staff writer who defended his revelation at a seminar that his nonfiction articles about Spain contain fictional embellishments. —Ed.

[2] Islands near Argentina fought over by Britain and Argentina in 1982. They remain a part of the United Kingdom. —Ed.

universe; one knows all there is to know about "kelpers" and Port Stanley; sheep jokes abound. In the end, as at the beginning, no one really knows anything about the Falkland Islands other than the war that gave it momentary celebrity—nothing about the people in the aftermath of the war, their concerns, isolation, or their true relationship to Argentina and Britain. Discontinuities are valuable because they point up the world's variety as well as the special force of its isolated parts. But to rely on them for truth is to lose one's grip on what is continuous and whole.

Journalism looks to where the ball is, and not where it is not. A college basketball coach, trying to improve the performance of one of his backcourt men, asked the player what he did when he practiced on his own. "Dribble and shoot," came the reply. The coach then asked the player to add up the total time he dribbled and shot during a scrimmage game, how many minutes he had hold of the ball. "Three minutes in all," came the reply. "That means," said the coach, "that you practice what you do in three minutes out of 40 in a game." Which means in turn that for every player, roughly 37 out of a possible 40 minutes are played away from the ball.

Journalism tends to focus on the poor when the poor make news, usually dramatic news like a tenement fire or a march on Washington. But the poor are poor all the time. It is not journalism's ordinary business to deal with the unstartling normalities of life. Reporters need a *story*, something shapely and elegant. Poverty is disorderly, anticlimactic and endless. If one wants truth about the poor, one must look where the ball is not.

Similarly, journalism inevitably imposes forms of order on both the facts in a story and on the arrangement of stories itself. The structures of magazines and newspapers impose one kind of order; radio and television another, usually sequential. But every form journalism takes is designed to draw the public's attention to what the editors deem most important in a day's or week's events. This naturally violates the larger truth of a chaotic universe. Oddly, the public often contributes its own hierarchical arrangements by dismissing editors' discriminations and dwelling on the story about the puppy on page 45 instead of the bank collapse on Page One. The "truth" of a day's events is tugged at from all sides.

Finally, journalism often misses the truth by unconsciously eroding one's sympathy with life. A seasoned correspondent in Evelyn Waugh's maliciously funny novel *Scoop* lectures a green reporter. "You know," he says, "you've got a lot to learn about journalism. Look at it this way. News is what a chap who doesn't care much about anything wants to read." The matter is not a laughing one. A superabundance of news has the benumbing effect of mob rule on the senses. Every problem in the world begins to look unreachable, unimprovable. What could one lone person possibly accomplish against a constant and violent storm of events that on any day include a rebellion of Sikhs, a tornado in Wisconsin, parents pleading for a healthy heart for their child? Sensibilities, overwhelmed, eventually grow cold; and therein monsters lie. Nobody wants to be part of a civilization that reads the news and does not care about it. Certainly no journalist wants that.

8   If one asks, then, where the larger truth is to be sought, the answer is where it has always been: in history, poetry, art, nature, education, conversation; in the tunnels of one's own mind. People may have come to expect too much of journalism. Not of journalism at its worst; when one is confronted with lies, cruelty and tastelessness, it is hardly too much to expect better. But that is not a serious problem because lies, cruelty and tastelessness are the freaks of the trade, not the pillars. The trouble is that people have also come to expect too much of journalism at its best, because they have invested too much power in it, and in so doing have neglected or forfeited other sources of power in their lives. Journalists appear to give answer, but essentially they ask a question: What shall we make of this? A culture that would rely on the news for truth could not answer that question because it already would have lost the qualities of mind that make the news worth knowing.

9   If people cannot rely on the news for facts, however, then journalism has no reason for being. Alastair Reid may have forgotten that the principal reason journalists exist in society is that people have a need to be informed of and comprehend the details of experience. "The right to know and the right to be are one," wrote Wallace Stevens[3] in a poem about Ulysses. The need is basic, biological. In that sense, everyone is a journalist, seeking the knowledge of the times in order to grasp the character of the world, to survive in the world, perhaps to move it. Archimedes[4] said he could move the world as long as he had a long enough lever. He pointed out, too, that he needed a ground to stand on.

---

[3]An American poet (1879–1955). —Ed.

[4]A Greek mathematician (287?–212 B.C.) known for his mechanical inventions. —Ed.

QUESTIONS FOR READING

1. What three objections does Rosenblatt have to journalists taking liberties with the facts?

2. Which one of these objections becomes Rosenblatt's main idea, the claim of his argument?

3. How many reasons does the author give in support of his claim? Find each one and restate it in your own words.

4. If journalism cannot give us the truth, where should we look for the truth?

QUESTIONS FOR REASONING AND ANALYSIS

1. Rosenblatt devotes two paragraphs to his fourth reason, developing it in part by using a comparison or analogy to basketball. Explain the point of the analogy.

2. Judging from the distinction he draws between the facts of journalism and the truth of literature, for example, what does Rosenblatt appear to mean by "truth"?

3. If journalists impose (or find) an order in their "stories," doesn't that structuring give a larger meaning to events? Why, according to the author, is the journalist's order not going to give us the truth?

QUESTIONS FOR REFLECTING AND WRITING

1. Why are some journalists tempted to embellish the events they cover, to create "stories" out of today's news? Can you account for their motivation?

2. In what ways does journalism have power? Does it have too much power? Is Rosenblatt accurate when he asserts that we now expect too much of journalism? Be prepared to support your views on these interrelated questions.

3. Do you agree with the author that we should not look for higher truths in journalism but rather in literature, art, history, conversation, our own thinking? Why or why not?

IN YOUR FACE . . . ALL OVER THE PLACE! | JEAN KILBOURNE

Writer and speaker Jean Kilbourne has been a visiting scholar at Wellesley College and an adviser on alcohol and tobacco advertising to two surgeons general. She is the author of *Can't Buy My Love* (2000) and editor of *Media Sharp* (2000). The following excerpt is from her book, *Deadly Persuasion*, published in 1999.

PREREADING QUESTIONS We know that TV shows are filled with stereotypes; what about advertising? Think about print or TV ads; what kinds of stereotypes come to mind?

In spite of the fact that we are surrounded by more advertising than ever 1 before, most of us still ridicule the idea that we might be personally influenced by it. The ridicule is often extremely simplistic. The argument essentially is, "I'm no robot marching down to the store to do advertising's bidding and therefore advertising doesn't affect me at all." This argument was made by Jacob Sullum, a senior editor at *Reason* magazine, in an editorial in the *New York Times*. Writing about "heroin chic," the advertising fad in the mid-1990s of using models who looked like heroin addicts, Sullum says, "Like you, I've seen . . . ads featuring sallow, sullen, scrawny youths. Not once have I had an overwhelming urge to rush out and buy some heroin." He concludes from this in-depth research that all critics of advertising are portraying "people not as independent moral agents but as mindless automatons," as if there were no middle ground between rushing out to buy heroin and being completely uninfluenced by the media images that surround us—or no possibility that disaffected teens are more vulnerable than middle-aged executives. After all, Sullum is *not* the target audience for heroin chic ads.

Of course, most of us feel far superior to the kind of person who would be 2 affected by advertising. *We* are not influenced, after all. We are skeptical, even cynical . . . but ignorant (certainly not stupid, just uninformed). Advertising is familiar, but not known. The fact that we are surrounded by it, that we can sing the jingles and identify the models and recognize the logos, doesn't mean that we are educated about it, that we understand it. As Sut Jhally says, "To not be influenced by advertising would be to live outside of culture. No human being lives outside of culture."

3   Advertisers want us to believe that we are not influenced by ads. As Joseph Goebbels said, "This is the secret of propaganda: Those who are to be persuaded by it should be completely immersed in the ideas of the propaganda, without ever noticing that they are being immersed in it." So the advertisers sometimes play upon our cynicism. In fact, they co-opt our cynicism and our irony just as they have co-opted our rock music, our revolutions and movements for liberation, and our concern for the environment. In a current trend that I call "anti-advertising," the advertisers flatter us by insinuating that we are far too smart to be taken in by advertising. Many of these ads spoof the whole notion of image advertising. A scotch ad tells the reader "This is a glass of Cutty Sark. If you need to see a picture of a guy in an Armani suit sitting between two fashion models drinking it before you know it's right for you, it probably isn't."

4   And an ad for shoes says, "If you feel the need to be smarter and more articulate, read the complete works of Shakespeare. If you like who you are, here are your shoes." Another shoe ad, this one for sneakers, says, "Shoe buying rule number one: The image wears off after the first six miles." What a concept. By buying heavily advertised products, we can demonstrate that we are not influenced by advertising. Of course, this is not entirely new. Volkswagens were introduced in the 1960s with an anti-advertising campaign, such as the ad that pictured the car and the headline "Lemon." But such ads go a lot further these days, especially the foreign ones. A British ad for Easy jeans says, "We don't use sex to sell our jeans. We don't even screw you when you buy them." And French Connection UK gets away with a double-page spread that says "fcuk advertising."

5   Cynicism is one of the worst effects of advertising. Cynicism learned from years of being exposed to marketing hype and products that never deliver the promised goods often carries over to other aspects of life. This starts early: A study of children done by researchers at Columbia University in 1975 found that heavy viewing of advertising led to cynicism, not only about advertising, but about life in general. The researchers found that "in most cultures, adolescents have had to deal with social hypocrisy and even with institutionalized lying. But today, TV advertising is stimulating *preadolescent* children to think about socially accepted hypocrisy. They may be too young to cope with such thoughts without permanently distorting their views of morality, society, and business." They concluded that "7- to 10-year-olds are strained by the very existence of advertising directed to them." These jaded children become the young people whose mantra is "whatever," who admire people like David Letterman (who has made a career out of taking nothing seriously), whose response to almost every experience is "been there, done that," "duh," and "do ya think?" Cynicism is not criticism. It is a lot easier than criticism. In fact, easy cynicism is a kind of naivete. We need to be more critical as a culture and less cynical.

6   Cynicism deeply affects how we define our problems and envision their solutions. Many people exposed to massive doses of advertising both distrust every possible solution *and* expect a quick fix. There are no quick fixes to the problems our society faces today, but there are solutions to many of them. The

first step, as always, is breaking through denial and facing the problems squarely. I believe it was James Baldwin who said, "Not everything that is faced can be changed, but nothing can be changed until it is faced." One of the things we need to face is that we and our children are indeed influenced by advertising.

Although some people, especially advertisers, continue to argue that ad- 7 vertising simply reflects the society, advertising does a great deal more than simply reflect cultural attitudes and values. Even some advertisers admit to this: Rance Crain of *Advertising Age* said great advertising "plays the tune rather than just dancing to the tune." Far from being a passive mirror of society, advertising is an effective and pervasive medium of influence and persuasion, and its influence is cumulative, often subtle, and primarily unconscious. Advertising performs much the same function in industrial society as myth performed in ancient and primitive societies. It is both a creator and perpetuator of the dominant attitudes, values and ideology of the culture, the social norms and myths by which most people govern their behavior. At the very least, advertising helps to create a climate in which certain attitudes and values flourish and others are not reflected at all.

Advertising is not only our physical environment, it is increasingly our spir- 8 itual environment as well. By definition, however, it is only interested in materialistic values. When spiritual values or religious images show up in ads, it is only to appropriate them in order to sell us something. Sometimes this is very obvious. Eternity is a perfume by Calvin Klein. Infiniti is an automobile and Hydra Zen a moisturizer. Jesus is a brand of jeans. "See the light," says an ad for wool, while a face powder ad promises "an enlightening experience" and absolute heaven." One car is "born again" and another promises to "energize your soul." In a full-page ad in *Advertising Age*, the online service Yahoo! proclaims, "We've got 60 million followers. That's more than some religions," but goes on to assure readers, "Don't worry. We're *not* a religion." When Pope John Paul II visited Mexico City in the winter of 1999, he could have seen a smiling image of himself on bags of Sabritas, a popular brand of potato chips, or a giant street sign showing him bowing piously next to a Pepsi logo with a phrase in Spanish that reads, "Mexico Always Faithful." In the United States, he could have treated himself to pope-on-a-rope soap.

But advertising's co-optation of spirituality goes much deeper than this. It 9 is commonplace these days to observe that consumerism has become the religion of our time (with advertising its holy text), but the criticism usually stops short of what is most important, what is at the heart of the comparison. Advertising and religion share a belief in transformation and transcendence, but most religions believe that this requires work and sacrifice. In the world of advertising, enlightenment is achieved instantly by purchasing material goods. As James Twitchell, author of *Adcult USA*, says, "The Jolly Green Giant, the Michelin Man, the Man from Glad, Mother Nature, Aunt Jemima, Speedy Alka-Seltzer, the White Knight, and all their otherworldly kin are descendants of the earlier gods. What separates them is that they now reside in manufactured products and that, although earlier gods were invoked by fasting, prayer, rituals, and penance, the promise of purchase calls forth their modern ilk."

10   Advertising constantly promotes the core belief of American culture: that we *can* re-create ourselves, transform ourselves, transcend our circumstances— but with a twist. For generations Americans believed this could be achieved if we worked hard enough, like Horatio Alger. Today the promise is that we can change our lives instantly, effortlessly—by winning the lottery, selecting the right mutual fund, having a fashion makeover, losing weight, having tighter abs, buying the right car or soft drink. It is this belief that such transformation is possible that drives us to keep dieting, to buy more stuff, to read fashion magazines that give us the same information over and over again. Cindy Craw- ford's makeup is carefully described as if it could transform us into her. On one level, we know it won't—after all, most of us have tried this approach many times before. But on another level, we continue to try, continue to believe that this time it will be different. This American belief that we can transform our- selves makes advertising images much more powerful than they otherwise would be.

11   The focus of the transformation has shifted from the soul to the body. Of course, this trivializes and cheapens authentic spirituality and transcendence. But, more important, this junk food for the soul leaves us hungry, empty, mal- nourished. The emphasis on instant salvation is parodied in an ad from *Ad- busters* for a product called Mammon, in which a man says, "I need a belief system that serves my needs right away." The copy continues, "Dean Sachs has a mortgage, a family and an extremely demanding job. What he doesn't need is a religion that complicates his life with unreasonable ethical de- mands." The ad ends with the words, "Mammon: Because you deserve to en- joy life—guilt free."

12   As advertising becomes more and more absurd, however, it becomes in- creasingly difficult to parody ads. There's not much of a difference between the ad for Mammon and the real ad for cruises that says "It can take several life- times to reach a state of inner peace and tranquillity. Or, it can take a couple of weeks." Of course, we know that a couple of weeks on a cruise won't solve our problems, won't bring us to a state of peace and enlightenment, but it is so tempting to believe that there is some easy way to get there, some ticket we can buy.

13   To be one of the "elect" in today's society is to have enough money to buy luxury goods. Of course, when salvation comes via the sale, it becomes im- portant to display these goods. Owning a Rolex would not impress anyone who didn't know how expensive it is. A Rolex ad itself says the watch was voted "most likely to be coveted." Indeed, one of advertising's purposes is to create an aura for a product, so that other people will be impressed. As one marketer said recently in *Advertising Age,* "It's no fun to spend $100 on athletic shoes to wear to high school if your friends don't know how cool your shoes are."

14   Thus the influence of advertising goes way beyond the target audience and includes those who could never afford the product, who will simply be en- vious and impressed—perhaps to the point of killing someone for his sneakers or jacket, as has sometimes happened in our poverty-stricken neighborhoods. In the early 1990s the city health commissioner in Philadelphia issued a public

health warning cautioning youths against wearing expensive leather jackets and jewelry, while in Milwaukee billboards depicted a chalk outline of a body and the warning, "Dress Smart and Stay Alive." Poor children in many countries knot the laces of their Nikes around their ankles to avoid having them stolen while they sleep.

Many teens fantasize that objects will somehow transform their lives, give them social standing and respect. When they wear a certain brand of sneaker or jacket, they feel, "This is important, therefore I am important." The brand gives instant status. No wonder they are willing, even eager, to spend money for clothes that advertise the brands. A *USA Today*–CNN–Gallup Poll found that 61 percent of boys and 44 percent of girls considered brand names on clothes "very important" or "somewhat important". As ten-year-old Darion Sawyer from Baltimore said, "People will tease you and talk about you, say you got on no-name shoes or say you shop at Kmart." Leydiana Reyes, an eighth-grader in Brooklyn, said, "My father always tells me I could buy two pairs of jeans for what you pay for Calvin Klein. I know that. But I still want Calvin Klein." And Danny Shirley, a fourteen-year-old in Santa Fe decked out in Tommy Hilfiger regalia, said, "Kids who wear Levi's don't really care about what they wear, I guess."   15

In the beginning, these labels were somewhat discreet. Today we see sweatshirts with fifteen-inch "Polo" logos stamped across the chest, jeans with four-inch "Calvin Klein" labels stitched on them, and a jacket with "Tommy Hilfiger" in five-inch letters across the back. Some of these outfits are so close to sandwich boards that I'm surprised people aren't paid to wear them. Before too long, the logo-free product probably will be the expensive rarity.   16

What people who wear these clothes are really buying isn't a garment, of course, but an *image*. And increasingly, an image is all that advertising has to sell. Advertising began centuries ago with signs in medieval villages. In the nineteenth century, it became more common but was still essentially designed to give people information about manufactured goods and services. Since the 1920s, advertising has provided less information about the product and focused more on the lives, especially the emotional lives, of the prospective consumers. This shift coincided, of course, with the increasing knowledge and acceptability of psychology, as well as the success of propaganda used to convince the population to support World War I.   17

Industrialization gave rise to the burgeoning ability of businesses to mass-produce goods. Since it was no longer certain there would be a market for the goods, it became necessary not just to mass-produce the goods but to mass-produce markets hungry for the goods. The problem became not too little candy produced but not enough candy consumed, so it became the job of the advertisers to *produce consumers*. This led to an increased use of psychological research and emotional ploys to sell products. Consumer behavior became recognized as a science in the late 1940s.   18

As luxury goods, prepared foods, and nonessential items have proliferated, it has become crucial to create artificial needs in order to sell unnecessary products. Was there such a thing as static cling before there were fabric   19 softeners and sprays? An ad for a "lip renewal cream" says, "I never thought of my lips as a problem area until Andrea came up with the solution."

20   Most brands in a given category are essentially the same. Most shampoos are made by two or three manufacturers. Blindfolded smokers or beer-drinkers can rarely identify what brand they are smoking or drinking, including their own. Whether we know it or not, we select products primarily because of the image reflected in their advertising. Very few ads give us any real information at all. Sometimes it is impossible to tell what is being advertised. "This is an ad for the hair dryer," says one ad, featuring a woman lounging on a sofa. If we weren't told, we would never know. A joke made the rounds a while ago about a little boy who wanted a box of tampons so that he could effortlessly ride bicycles and horses, ski, and swim.

21   Almost all tobacco and alcohol ads are entirely image-based. Of course, when you're selling a product that kills people, it's difficult to give honest information about it. Think of all the cigarette ads that never show cigarettes or even a wisp of smoke. One of the most striking examples of image advertising is the very successful and long-running campaign for Absolut vodka. This campaign focuses on the shape of the bottle and the word "Absolut," as in "Absolut Perfection," which features the bottle with a halo. This campaign has been so successful that a coffee-table book collection of the ads published just in time for Christmas, the perfect gift for the alcoholic in your family, sold over 150,000 copies. Collecting Absolut ads is now a common pastime for elementary-school children, who swap them like baseball cards.

22   How does all this affect us? It is very difficult to do objective research about advertising's influence because there are no comparison groups, almost no people who have not been exposed to massive doses of advertising. In addition, research that measures only one point in time does not adequately capture advertising's real effects. We need longitudinal studies, such as George Gerbner's twenty-five-year study of violence on television.

23   The advertising industry itself can't prove that advertising works. While claiming to its clients that it does, it simultaneously denies it to the Federal Trade Commission whenever the subject of alcohol and tobacco advertising comes up. As an editorial in *Advertising Age* once said, "A strange world it is, in which people spending millions on advertising must do their best to prove that advertising doesn't do very much!" According to Bob Wehling, senior vice-president of marketing at Procter & Gamble, "We don't have a lot of scientific studies to support our belief that advertising works. But we have seen that the power of advertising makes a significant difference."

24   What research can most easily prove is usually what is least important, such as advertising's influence on our choice of brands. This is the most obvious, but least significant, way that advertising affects us. There are countless examples of successful advertising campaigns, such as the Absolut campaign, that have sent sales soaring. A commercial for I Can't Believe It's Not Butter featuring a sculptress whose work comes alive in the form of romance-novel hunk Fabio boosted sales about 17 percent. Tamagotchis—virtual pets in an egg—were introduced in the United States with a massive advertising campaign and earned

$150 million in seven months. And Gardenburger, a veggie patty, ran a thirty-second spot during the final episode of *Seinfeld* and, within a week, sold over $2 million worth, a market share jump of 50 percent and more than the entire category sold in the same week the previous year. But advertising is more of an art than a science, and campaigns often fail. In 1998 a Miller beer campaign bombed, costing the company millions of dollars and offending a large segment of their customers. The 1989 Nissan Infiniti campaign, known as the "Rocks and Trees" campaign, was the first ever to introduce a car without showing it and immediately became a target for Jay Leno's monologues. And, of course, the Edsel, a car introduced by Ford with great fanfare in 1957, remains a universal symbol of failure.

The unintended effects of advertising are far more important and far more difficult to measure than those effects that are intended. The important question is not "Does this ad sell the product?" but rather "What else does this ad sell?" An ad for Gap khakis featuring a group of acrobatic swing dancers probably sold a lot of pants, which, of course, was the intention of the advertisers. But it also contributed to a rage for swing dancing. This is an innocuous example of advertising's powerful unintended effects. Swing dancing is not binge drinking, after all. 25

Advertising often sells a great deal more than products. It sells values, images, and concepts of love and sexuality, romance, success, and, perhaps most important, normalcy. To a great extent, it tells us who we are and who we should be. We are increasingly using brand names to create our identities. James Twitchell argues that the label of our shirt, the make of our car, and our favorite laundry detergent are filling the vacuum once occupied by religion, education, and our family name. 26

Even more important, advertising corrupts our language and thus influences our ability to think clearly. Critic and novelist George Steiner once talked with an interviewer about what he called "anti-language, that which is transcendentally annihilating of truth and meaning." Novelist Jonathan Dee, applying this concept to advertising, writes that "the harm lies not in the ad itself; the harm is in the exchange, in the collision of ad language, ad imagery, with other sorts of language that contend with it in the public realm. When Apple reprints an old photo of Gandhi, or Heineken ends its ads with the words 'Seek the Truth,' or Winston suggests that we buy cigarettes by proposing (just under the surgeon general's warning) that 'You have to appreciate authenticity in all its forms,' or Kellogg's identifies itself with the message 'Simple is Good,' these occasions color our contact with those words and images in their other, possibly less promotional applications." The real violence of advertising, Dee concludes, is that "words can be made to mean anything, which is hard to distinguish from the idea that words mean nothing." We see the consequences of this in much of our culture, from "art" to politics, that has no content, no connection between language and conviction. Just as it is often difficult to tell what product an ad is selling, so is it difficult to determine what a politician's beliefs are (the "vision thing," as George Bush so aptly called it, albeit unintentionally) or what the subject is of a film or song or work of art. As Dee says, "The men and women 27 who make ads are not hucksters; they are artists with nothing to say, and they have found their form." Unfortunately, their form deeply influences all the other forms of the culture. We end up expecting nothing more.

28   This has terrible consequences for our culture. As Richard Pollay says, "Without a reliance on words and a faith in truth, we lack the mortar for social cohesion. Without trustworthy communication, there is no communion, no community, only an aggregation of increasingly isolated individuals, alone in the mass."

29   Advertising creates a worldview that is based upon cynicism, dissatisfaction, and craving. The advertisers aren't evil. They are just doing their job, which is to sell a product, but the consequences, usually unintended, are often destructive to individuals, to cultures, and to the planet. In the history of the world, there has never been a propaganda effort to match that of advertising in the twentieth century. More thought, more effort, and more money go into advertising than has gone into any other campaign to change social consciousness. The story that advertising tells is that the way to be happy, to find satisfaction—and the path to political freedom, as well—is through the consumption of material objects. And the major motivating force for social change throughout the world today is this belief that happiness comes from the market.

30   So, advertising has a greater impact on all of us than we generally realize. The primary purpose of the mass media is to deliver us to advertisers. Much of the information that we need from the media in order to make informed choices in our lives is distorted or deleted on behalf of corporate sponsors. Advertising is an increasingly ubiquitous presence in our lives, and it sells much more than products. We delude ourselves when we say we are not influenced by advertising. And we trivialize and ignore its growing significance at our peril.

NOTES

1. "This argument was made by Jacob Sullum": Sullum, 1997, A31.
2. "As Sut Jhally says": Jhally, 1998.
3. "As Joseph Goebbels": Goebbels, 1933, March 28. Quoted in Jacobson and Mazur, 1995, 15.
4. "A study of children done by researchers at Columbia University": Bever, Smith, Bengen, and Johnson, 1975, 119.
5. "'7- to 10-year-olds are strained'": Bever, Smith, Bengen, and Johnson, 1975, 120.
6. "Rance Crain of *Advertising Age*": Crain, 1999, 23.
7. "When Pope John Paul II": Chacon and Ribadeneria, 1999. A8.
8. " 'The Jolly Green Giant' ": Twitchell, 1996, 30.
9. "'It's no fun to spend $100 on athletic shoes'": Peppers and Rogers, 1997, 32.
10. "the city health commissioner in Philadelphia": Worthington, 1992, 15.
11. "A USA Today–CNN–Gallup Poll": Jacobson and Mazur, 1995, 26.
12. "Leydiana Reyes": Leonhardt, 1997, 65.
13. "Danny Shirley": Espen, 1999, 59.
14. "sweatshirts with fifteen-inch 'Polo' logos": Ryan, 1996, D1.

15. "Consumer behavior": Woods, 1995.
16. "Most shampoos": Twitchell, 1996, 252.
17. "Blindfolded smokers": Twitchell, 1996, 125.
18. " 'A strange world it is' ": Bernstein, 1978, August 7.
19. "According to Bob Wehling": Crain, 1998, 24.
20. "A commercial for I Can't Believe It's Not Butter": Haran, 1996, 12.
21. "Tamagotchis": Goldner, 1998, S43.
22. "And Gardenburger": Gardenburger hits the spot, 1998, 17.
23. "In 1998 a Miller beer campaign": Crain, 1998, 24.
24. "The 1989 Nissan Infiniti": Horton, 1996, S28.
25. "the Edsel": Horton, 1996, S30.
26. "An ad for Gap khakis": Cortissoz, 1998, A10.
27. "James Twitchell argues": University of Florida news release, quoted by Orlando, 1999, *http://www.sciencedaily.com/releases/1999/05/ 990518114815. htm.*
28. "Critic and novelist George Steiner": Dee, 1999, 65–66.
29. "As Richard Pollay": Pollay, 1986.
30. "there has never been a propaganda effort": Jhally, 1998.

QUESTIONS FOR READING

1. What is Kilbourne's subject? (Be more precise than just "advertising.")

2. How is advertising like propaganda?

3. What is the nature of the "anti-advertising" ad? What is one of the consequences of anti-advertising?

4. What role does advertising play in our society? How does it promote "the core belief of American culture"? How is its message different from what that core belief used to emphasize?

5. How does advertising go beyond the target audience? How do we want others to react to what we have purchased? What are we purchasing with designer-labeled clothing?

6. In the second half of the twentieth century, what became advertising's purpose or task? How did this purpose change ads?

7. How does advertising affect language?

QUESTIONS FOR REASONING AND ANALYSIS

1. What is Kilbourne's claim? What *type* of argument is this—that is, what does it seek to accomplish?

2. Kilbourne provides a brief history of advertising. What does she accomplish by including this in her discussion?

3. List the effects of advertising discussed by Kilbourne. How does her discussion of effects support her claim? What evidence does the author provide throughout her analysis?

4. The author points out that it is difficult to study the effects of ads. Why is it difficult? Why does she include these comments in her argument?

QUESTIONS FOR REFLECTING AND WRITING

1. Evaluate Kilbourne's argument. Does she convince you? If not, what would you need to be convinced?

2. Do you find considerable cynicism today? If so, have you ever connected it to the endless distortions created by ads? If not, does this seem like a reasonable causal connection to you now?

3. Should advertising be banned from children's TV programs? Why or why not?

MADE IN HEAVEN | LEIGH MONTVILLE

A graduate of the University of Connecticut, Leigh Montville (b. 1943) has said that he always wanted to be a sports journalist. He has been writing a sports column for the *Boston Globe* most of his working life—as well as a general column of social commentary in the magazine section of the Sunday *Globe*. The following is one of his Sunday columns, first printed May 15, 1983.

PREREADING QUESTIONS Do you buy designer-labeled clothing and shoes? If so, why? Have you ever been jealous of someone else's expensive possessions? What, if any, role does advertising play in such jealousies?

1   And in the spring of one year in the sixth millennium of Creation, the Lord became bored. He watched the long line of human beings heading toward the world and knew He had to make some changes. Just to stay awake.

2   He had an idea.

3   "Put a tiny alligator on the left breast of every human who leaves the shop for the next week," He bellowed to his angels. "And make it snappy."

4   "An alligator?" the angels asked.

5   "An alligator," the Lord said. "Now."

6   The angels hurried to work. A change like this hadn't happened in a long time, not since the Lord requested redheads and peroxide blondes. An alligator . . . an alligator. One of the angels drew a stencil and the others began the work.

7   "Do you think He wants the alligator above or below the nipple?" one angel asked.

8   "We'll try a few spots," a second angel replied. "We'll see what works best."

9   The final choice was slightly above the left nipple. Thousands, then millions of people were sent to the world with the little alligators upon their breasts. The angels watched with horror. The Lord watched with renewed interest. He found that He was pleased.

10   "Look at that, will you?" He said. "Man seems to like having a little alligator above his left breast. Look how proud he is. He parades around with confidence he never had before."

Sure enough, race and creed and ethnic origin made no difference. The 11
people who wore the alligator were the most confident on the planet. They
admired each other's alligators. They pitied the poor folk who did not have
alligators.

"Let us try this," the Lord said. "Let us keep making alligators, but on Tues- 12
days and Thursdays, perhaps, let's produce people with a little polo player on
the left breast."

"A polo player, Lord?" the angels asked.   13

"Just do what I ask," the Lord said.   14

The appearance of people with polo players above their left breasts 15
seemed to be as exciting as the appearance of the people with alligators. The
Lord laughed as He watched everyone admiring everyone else. He wanted to
see more.

"Let us make people with little penguins above their left breasts," He told 16
the angels. "Let us make some people with a fox in that spot. A tiger. A hand
making a signal with the index finger and thumb. Every now and then, too,
make some people with the word 'Rugger' across the right biceps."

The new diversity soon dominated the world. Virtually everyone under age 17
58 bore an insignia or name above the left breast. Humankind viewed these
changes as blessings supplied by a Benevolent Being.

"You are a genius, Lord," the angels said.   18

"I have only begun," the Lord replied.   19

He turned his attention now to the right buttock. He thought and thought, 20
searching for the right expression. He decided upon names.

"Names, Lord?" the angels asked.   21

"Take these down," the Lord said in a flash of inspiration. "Calvin Klein. 22
Gloria Vanderbilt. Sasson. Sergio Valenti. Lee. and . . . let me think . . . yes,
Jordache."

The names on the right buttock were at least as successful as the animals 23
above the left breast. Some names were printed. Some were written in
script. People looked each other over, fore and aft, and cooed at the different markings.

"Love your alligator," one of them would say to a complete stranger. "And 24
love your Sergio Valenti, too."

"Wonderful, Lord," the angels said. "Man has not been so interested in his 25
surroundings for a long time."

"Take out your pads," the Lord said. "There is more work to do." 26

He now turned his attention to feet. He ordered some feet to be made with 27
three stripes down the sides. He ordered other feet made with two stripes.
With stars. He ordered feet made with little green tabs with the word "Bass"
or "Dexter" written on the tabs. He ordered feet made with metal plates on
the side that read "Candie's."

"Feet may be the ultimate," the Lord said. "I have a hunch we haven't seen 28
anything, compared to what will happen with feet."

He was right again, of course. The designs on the feet were the best of all. 29
People boasted about their feet. People admired each other's feet. To walk

down the street with an animal on the left breast, a name on the right buttock, and swirls on the feet was to be as close to heaven as possible.

30   "I am pleased," the Lord said as he sat upon a cloud and watched the activity." I am very, very pleased."

31   The angels were pleased because He was pleased. They stood in a line and awaited orders. There was nary a waver when the Lord decreed that some people should now be made with little plugs in their ears that played Top 40 music all day long.

32   Everyone simply went to work.

QUESTIONS FOR READING

1. At what point in your reading did you realize that this is a humorous piece?
2. What, exactly, is Montville poking fun at?
3. Montville mentions the brand names of one kind of shirt, six kinds of jeans, and three kinds of shoes. How many of the other brands can you name from their logos or designs?

QUESTIONS FOR REASONING AND ANALYSIS

1. From reading this piece, what can you conclude to be the chief characteristics of the parable format?
2. What details of the story contribute to its humor? What more serious point is Montville also making?
3. Why do parables often teach more effectively than lectures?

QUESTIONS FOR REFLECTING AND WRITING

1. What seem to be the reasons that people get pleasure from wearing designer-labeled clothes? What needs do these clothes help satisfy?
2. In the previous essay, Jean Kilbourne argues that buying in response to advertising does not really satisfy us. Are people entirely fooling themselves, suckered by advertising, or do they get some satisfaction from their spending? Explain your views on these interrelated questions.
3. How would you explain what image advertising is to a class of fifth-graders? What ads would you use as examples?

CHAPTER 14

Violence and American Society

Are we a violent society? Is the United States any different from other countries? These are two good questions with which to begin this chapter's exploration. Richard Harwood has written ("America's Unchecked Epidemic," 12/1/97) that statistics show that U.S. cities have no more crime than other similar cities in Western Europe but that we do have more violence, that is, a higher murder rate. Some social analysts argue that violence in the media is the cause, whereas others defend the media as only one of many influences on our lives and point out that although many watch violent television shows or listen to rap music, only a few act violently. Some argue that it is the American's love affair with guns that generates the violence—whereas gun owners insist that most handle their guns safely. One problem is agreeing on the causes; the other, even more difficult, problem is agreeing on solutions, because solutions are likely to mean restrictions of some sort. Emotions run high on the topics explored in this chapter; try to keep yours in check and read critically.

Prereading Questions

1. Are those concerned about the influence of media violence taking their concerns too seriously, or should we be concerned?

2. What groups seem especially vulnerable to the influences of media violence?

3. Do you have a position on "gun control"? Do you think that what you mean by this term is about the same as what most people mean?

4. What are the main sources of influence on your thinking about guns—family, friends, religion, reading on the topic? How strong are these influences—that is, how willing are you to listen to someone whose views may differ from yours?

Websites Related to This Chapter's Topic

Baby Bag

www.babybag.com/articles/amaviol.htm

Facts about media violence directed to parents but useful for others as well.

Interact/Jesuit Communication Project Site at the University of Oregon

http://interact.uoregon.edu/MediaLit/JCP/violence.html

Contains bibliographies and a list of video resources on media violence.

Handgun Control and the Center to Prevent Handgun Violence

www.handguncontrol.org

An organization founded in 1974 by Sarah Brady, the home page provides links to recent articles, news headlines, and facts about guns.

Center for Responsive Government

www.opensecrets.org/news/guns/index/htm

The center's web page, called Gun Control vs. Gun Rights, provides information on congressional votes and contributions by lobbies to representatives.

National Rifle Association

www.nra.org

This large gun lobby provides commentary and news updates on gun-control issues.

TELEVISION AND VIOLENT CRIME | BRANDON S. CENTERWALL

Brandon Centerwall (b. 1954) holds a medical degree from the University of California, San Diego, and a master's in public health, with a specialty in epidemiology, from Tulane University. He did his residency in psychiatry at the

University of Washington and is currently a professor there in the department of epidemiology. Centerwall has testified before Congressional committees on television violence and has published articles on various psychological issues, including the impact of television violence on behavior. The following article appeared in the Spring 1993 issue of *Public Interest.*

PREREADING QUESTIONS What knowledge do you have of studies of TV violence? Think about what you already know about the subject. What key challenge faces researchers of the impact of TV violence on viewers?

Children are born ready to imitate adult behavior. That they can, and do, 1 imitate an array of adult facial expressions has been demonstrated in newborns as young as a few hours old, before they are even old enough to know that they have facial features. It is a most useful instinct, for the developing child must learn and master a vast repertoire of behavior in short order.

But while children have an instinctive desire to imitate, they do not possess 2 an instinct for determining whether a behavior ought to be imitated. They will imitate anything, including behavior that most adults regard as destructive and antisocial. It may give pause for thought, then, to learn that infants as young as fourteen months demonstrably observe and incorporate behavior seen on television.

The average American preschooler watches more than twenty-seven hours 3 of television per week. This might not be bad if these young children understood what they were watching. But they don't. Up through ages three and four, most children are unable to distinguish fact from fantasy on TV, and remain unable to do so despite adult coaching. In the minds of young children, television is a source of entirely factual information regarding how the world works. There are no limits to their credulity. To cite one example, an Indiana school board had to issue an advisory to young children that, no, there is no such thing as Teenage Mutant Ninja Turtles. Children had been crawling down storm drains looking for them.

Naturally, as children get older, they come to know better, but their earli- 4 est and deepest impressions are laid down at an age when they still see television as a factual source of information about the outside world. In that world, it seems, violence is common and the commission of violence is generally powerful, exciting, charismatic, and effective. In later life, serious violence is most likely to erupt at moments of severe stress—and it is precisely at such moments that adolescents and adults are most likely to revert to their earliest, most visceral sense of the role of violence in society and in personal behavior. Much of this sense will have come from television.

THE SEEDS OF AGGRESSION

In 1973, a remote rural community in Canada acquired television for the 5 first time. The acquisition of television at such a late date was due to problems with signal reception rather than any hostility toward TV. As reported in *The Impact of Television* (1986), Tannis Williams and her associates at the University of British Columbia investigated the effect of television on the children of this community (which they called "Notel"), taking for comparison two similar towns that already had television.

6   The researchers observed forty-five first- and second-graders in the three towns for rates of inappropriate physical aggression before television was introduced into Notel. Two years later, the same forty-five children were observed again. To prevent bias in the data, the research assistants who collected the data were kept uninformed as to why the children's rates of aggression were of interest. Furthermore, a new group of research assistants was employed the second time around, so that the data gatherers would not be biased by recollections of the children's behavior two years earlier.

7   Rates of aggression did not change in the two control communities. By contrast, the rate of aggression among Notel children increased 160 percent. The increase was observed in both boys and girls, in those who were aggressive to begin with and in those who were not. Television's enhancement of noxious aggression was entirely general and not limited to a few "bad apples."

8   In another Canadian study, Gary Granzberg and his associates at the University of Winnipeg investigated the impact of television upon Indian communities in northern Manitoba. As described in *Television and the Canadian Indian* (1980), forty-nine third-, fourth-, and fifth-grade boys living in two communities were observed from 1973, when one town acquired television, until 1977, when the second town did as well. The aggressiveness of boys in the first community increased after the introduction of television. The aggressiveness of boys in the second community, which did not receive television then, remained the same. When television was later introduced in the second community, observed levels of aggressiveness increased there as well.

9   In another study conducted from 1960 to 1981, Leonard Eron and L. Rowell Huesmann (then of the University of Illinois at Chicago) followed 875 children living in a semirural U.S. county. Eron and Huesmann found that for both boys and girls, the amount of television watched at age eight predicted the seriousness of criminal acts for which they were convicted by age thirty (Figure 1). This remained true even after controlling for the children's baseline aggressiveness, intelligence, and socioeconomic status. Eron and Huesmann also observed second-generation effects. Children who watched much television at age eight later, as parents, punished their own children more severely than did parents who had watched less television as children. Second- and now third-generation effects are accumulating at a time of unprecedented youth violence.

10   All seven of the U.S. and Canadian studies of prolonged childhood exposure to television demonstrate a positive relationship between exposure and physical aggression. The critical period is preadolescent childhood. Later exposure does not appear to produce any additional effect. However, the aggression-enhancing effect of exposure in preadolescence extends into adolescence and adulthood. This suggests that any interventions should be designed for children and their caregivers rather than for the general adult population.

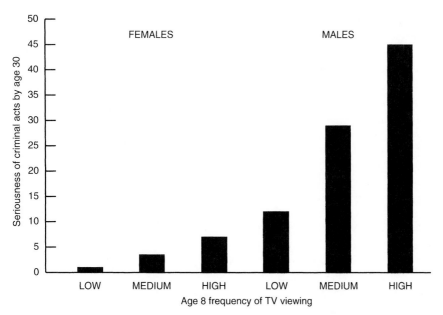

FIGURE 1 Relationship of television viewing frequency at age eight to seriousness of crimes committed by age thirty. Columbia County Cohort Study, 1960–1981. (Reprinted by permission from Leonard D. Eron and L. Rowell Huesmann, "The control of aggressive behavior by changes in attitudes, values, and the conditions of learning." Advances in the Study of Aggression. Orlando, Florida: Academic Press, 1984.)

These studies confirmed the beliefs of most Americans. According to a Harris poll at the time of the studies, 43 percent of American adults believe that television violence "plays a part in making America a violent society." An additional 37 percent think it might. But how important is television violence? What is the effect of exposure upon entire populations? To address this question, I took advantage of an historical accident—the absence of television in South Africa prior to 1975. **11**

THE SOUTH AFRICAN EXPERIENCE

White South Africans have lived in a prosperous, industrialized society for decades, but they did not get television until 1975 because of tension between the Afrikaner- and English-speaking communities. The country's Afrikaner leaders know that a South African television industry would have to rely on British and American shows to fill out its programming schedule, and they felt that this would provide an unacceptable cultural advantage to English-speaking South Africans. So, rather than negotiate a complicated compromise, the government simply forbade television broadcasting. The entire population of two million whites—rich and poor, urban and rural, educated and uneducated—was thus excluded from exposure to television for a quarter century after the medium was introduced in the United States. **12**

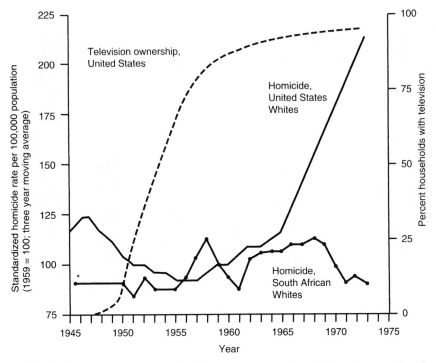

FIGURE 2 Television ownership and white homicide rates, United States and South Africa, 1945 through 1973. Asterisk denotes six-year average. Note that television broadcasting was not permitted in South Africa prior to 1975. (Reprinted by permission from Brandon S. Centerwall, "Exposure to television as a cause of violence," Public Communication and Behavior, Vol. 2, Orlando, Florida: Academic Press, 1989.)

13   In order to determine whether exposure to television is a cause of violence, I compared homicide rates in South Africa, Canada, and the United States. Since blacks in South Africa live under quite different conditions than blacks in the United States, I limited the comparison to white homicide rates in South Africa and the United States, and the total homicide rate in Canada (which was 97 percent white in 1951).* I chose the homicide rate as a measure of violence because homicide statistics are exceptionally accurate.

14   From 1945 to 1974, the white homicide rate in the United States increased 93 percent. In Canada, the homicide rate increased 92 percent. In South Africa, where television was banned, the white homicide rate declined by 7 percent (Figure 2).

---

* The "white homicide rate" refers to the rate at which whites are the victims of homicide. Since most homicide is intra-racial, this closely parallels the rate at which whites commit homicide.

CONTROLLING FOR OTHER FACTORS

Could there be some explanation other than television for the fact that vi-   15
olence increased dramatically in the U.S. and Canada while dropping in South
Africa? I examined an array of alternative explanations. None is satisfactory:

- *Economic growth.* Between 1946 and 1974, all three countries experienced substantial economic growth. Per capita income increased by 75
  percent in the United States, 124 percent in Canada, and 86 percent in
  South Africa. Thus differences in economic growth cannot account for
  the different homicide trends in the three countries.
- *Civil unrest.* One might suspect that anti-war or civil-rights activity was
  responsible for the doubling of the homicide rate in the United States
  during this period. But the experience of Canada shows that this was not
  the case, since Canadians suffered a doubling of the homicide rate without similar civil unrest.

Other possible explanations include changes in age distribution, urbaniza-   16
tion, alcohol consumption, capital punishment, and the availability of firearms.
As discussed in *Public Communication and Behavior* (1989), none provides a viable explanation for the observed homicide trends.

In the United States and Canada, there was a lag of ten to fifteen years   17
between the introduction of television and a doubling of the homicide rate. In
South Africa, there was a similar lag. Since television exerts its behavior-
modifying effects primarily on children, while homicide is primarily an adult activity, this lag represents the time needed for the "television generation" to
come of age.

The relationship between television and the homicide rate holds *within* the   18
United States as well. Different regions of the U.S., for example, acquired television at different times. As we would expect, while all regions saw increases in
their homicide rates, the regions that acquired television first were also the first
to see higher homicide rates.

Similarly, urban areas acquired television before rural areas. As we would   19
expect, urban areas saw increased homicide rates several years before the occurrence of a parallel increase in rural areas.

The introduction of television also helps explain the different rates of homi-   20
cide growth for whites and minorities. White households in the U.S. began acquiring television sets in large numbers approximately five years before
minority households. Significantly, the white homicide rate began increasing in
1958, four years before a parallel increase in the minority homicide rate.

Of course, there are many factors other than television that influence the   21
amount of violent crime. Every violent act is the result of a variety of forces
coming together—poverty, crime, alcohol and drug abuse, stress—of which
childhood TV exposure is just one. Nevertheless, the evidence indicates that
if, hypothetically, television technology had never been developed, there
would today be 10,000 fewer homicides each year in the United States,
70,000 fewer rapes, and 700,000 fewer injurious assaults. Violent crime would
be half what it is.

THE TELEVISION INDUSTRY TAKES A LOOK

22   The first congressional hearings on television and violence were held in 1952, when not even a quarter of U.S. households owned television sets. In the years since, there have been scores of research reports on the issue, as well as several major government investigations. The findings of the National Commission on the Causes and Prevention of Violence, published in 1969, were particularly significant. This report established what is now the broad scientific consensus: Exposure to television increases rates of physical aggression.

23   Television industry executives were genuinely surprised by the National Commission's report. What the industry produced was at times unedifying, but physically harmful? In response, the network executives began research programs that collectively would cost nearly a million dollars.

24   CBS commissioned William Belson to undertake what would be the largest and most sophisticated study yet, an investigation involving 1,565 teenage boys. In *Television Violence and the Adolescent Boy* (1978), Belson controlled for one hundred variables, and found that teenage boys who had watched above-average quantities of television violence before adolescence were committing acts of serious violence (e.g., assault, rape, major vandalism, and abuse of animals) at a rate 49 percent higher than teenage boys who had watched below-average quantities of television violence. Despite the large sum of money they had invested, CBS executives were notably unenthusiastic about the report.

25   ABC commissioned Melvin Heller and Samuel Polsky of Temple University to study young male felons imprisoned for violent crimes (e.g., homicide, rape, and assault). In two surveys, 22 and 34 percent of the young felons reported having consciously imitated crime techniques learned from television programs, usually successfully. The more violent of these felons were the most likely to report having learned techniques from television. Overall, the felons reported that as children they had watched an average of six hours of television per day—approximately twice as much as children in the general population at that time.

26   Unlike CBS, ABC maintained control over publication. The final report, *Studies in Violence and Television* (1976), was published in a private, limited edition that was not released to the general public or the scientific community.

27   NBC relied on a team of four researchers, three of whom were employees of NBC. Indeed, the principal investigator, J. Ronald Milavsky, was an NBC vice president. The team observed some 2,400 schoolchildren for up to three years to see if watching television violence increased their levels of physical aggressiveness. In *Television and Aggression* (1982), Milavsky and his associates reported that television violence had no effect upon the children's behavior. However, every independent investigator who has examined their data has concluded that, to the contrary, their data show that television violence did cause a modest increase of about 5 percent in average levels of physical aggressiveness. When pressed on the point, Milavsky and his associates conceded that their findings were consistent with the conclusion that television violence increased physical aggressiveness "to a small extent." They did not

concede that television violence actually caused an increase, but only that their findings were consistent with such a conclusion.

The NBC study results raise an important objection to my conclusions. 28 While studies have repeatedly demonstrated that childhood exposure to television increases physical aggressiveness, the increase is almost always quite minor. A number of investigators have argued that such a small effect is too weak to account for major increases in rates of violence. These investigators, however, overlook a key factor.

Homicide is an extreme form of aggression—so extreme that only one person in 20,000 committed murder each year in the United States in the mid- 29 1950s. If we were to rank everyone's degree of physical aggressiveness from the least aggressive (Mother Theresa) to the most aggressive (Jack the Ripper), the large majority of us would be somewhere in the middle and murderers would be virtually off the chart (Figure 3). It is an intrinsic property of such "bell curve" distributions that small changes in the average imply major changes at the extremes. Thus, if exposure to television causes 8 percent of the population to shift from below-average aggression to above-average aggression, it follows that the homicide rate will double. The findings of the NBC study and the doubling of the homicide rate are two sides of the same coin.

After the results of these studies became clear, television industry executives lost their enthusiasm for scientific research. No further investigations were 30 funded. Instead, the industry turned to political management of the issue.

THE TELEVISION INDUSTRY AND SOCIAL RESPONSIBILITY

The television industry routinely portrays individuals who seek to influence 31 programming as un-American haters of free speech. In a 1991 letter sent to

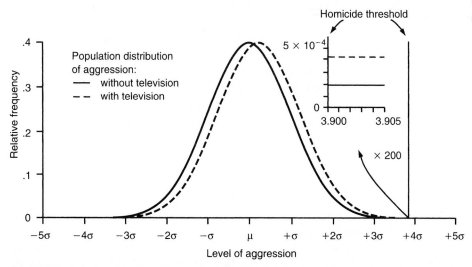

FIGURE 3 Relationships between television, aggression, and homicide in the general population: a model. (Reprinted by permission of Academic Press.)

7,000 executives of consumer product companies and advertising agencies, the president of the Network Television Association explained:

> Freedom of expression is an alienable right of all Americans vigorously supported by ABC, CBS, and NBC. However, boycotts and so-called advertiser "hit lists" are attempts to manipulate our free society and democratic process.

32   The letter went on to strongly advise the companies to ignore all efforts by anyone to influence what programs they choose to sponsor. By implication, the networks themselves should ignore all efforts by anyone to influence what programs they choose to produce.

33   But this is absurd. All forms of public discourse are attempts to "manipulate" our free society and democratic process. What else could they be? Consumer boycotts are no more un-American than are strikes by labor unions. The Network Television Association is attempting to systematically shut down all discourse between viewers and advertisers, and between viewers and the television industry. Wrapping itself in patriotism, the television industry's response to uppity viewers is to put them in their place. If the industry and advertisers were to actually succeed in closing the circle between them, the only course they would leave for concerned viewers would be to seek legislative action.

34   In the war against tobacco, we do not expect help from the tobacco industry. If someone were to call upon the tobacco industry to cut back production as a matter of social conscience and concern for public health, we would regard that person as simple-minded, if not frankly deranged. Oddly enough, however, people have persistently assumed that the television industry is somehow different—that it is useful to appeal to its social conscience. This was true in 1969 when the National Commission on the Causes and Prevention of Violence published its recommendations for the television industry. It was equally true in 1989 when the U.S. Congress passed an anti-violence bill that granted television industry executives the authority to hold discussions on the issue of television violence without violating antitrust laws. Even before the law was passed, the four networks stated that there would be no substantive changes in their programming. They have been as good as their word.

35   For the television industry, issues of "quality" and "social responsibility" are peripheral to the issue of maximizing audience size—and there is no formula more tried and true than violence for generating large audiences. To television executives, this is crucial. For if advertising revenue were to decrease by just 1 percent, the television industry would stand to lose $250 million in revenue annually. Thus, changes in audience size that appear trivial to most of us are regarded as catastrophic by the industry. For this reason, industry spokespersons have made innumerable protestations of good intent, but nothing has happened. In the more than twenty years that levels of television violence have been monitored, there has been no downward movement. There are no recommendations to make to the television industry. To make any would not only be futile but could create the false impression that the industry might actually do something constructive.

On December 11, 1992, the networks finally announced a list of voluntary   36
guidelines on television violence. Curiously, reporters were unable to locate
any network producers who felt the new guidelines would require changes in
their programs. That raises a question: Who is going to bell the cat? Who is going to place his or her career in jeopardy in order to decrease the amount of violence on television? It is hard to say, but it may be revealing that when Senator
Paul Simon held the press conference announcing the new inter-network
agreement, no industry executives were present to answer questions.

MEETING THE CHALLENGE

Television violence is everybody's problem. You may feel assured that your   37
child will never become violent despite a steady diet of television mayhem, but
you cannot be assured that your child won't be murdered or maimed by someone else's child raised on a similar diet.

The American Academy of Pediatrics recommends that parents limit their   38
children's television viewing to one or two hours per day. But why wait for a pediatrician to say it? Limiting children's exposure to television violence should
become part of the public health agenda, along with safety seats, bicycle helmets, immunizations, and good nutrition. Part of the public health approach
should be to promote child-care alternatives to the electronic babysitter, especially among the poor.

Parents should also guide what their children watch and how much. This is   39
an old recommendation that can be given new teeth with the help of modern
technology. It is now feasible to fit a television set with an electronic lock that
permits parents to preset the channels and times for which the set will be available; if a particular program or time of day is locked, the set will not operate
then. Time-channel locks are not merely feasible; they have already been designed and are coming off the assembly line.

The model for making them widely available comes from closed-captioning   40
circuitry, which permits deaf and hard-of-hearing persons access to television.
Market forces alone would not have made closed-captioned available to more
than a fraction of the deaf and hard-of-hearing. To remedy this problem, Congress passed the Television Decoder Circuitry Act in 1990, which requires that
virtually all new television sets be manufactured with built-in closed-captioning
circuitry. A similar law should require that all new television sets be manufactured with built-in time-channel lock circuitry—and for a similar reason. Market
forces alone will not make this technology available to more than a fraction of
households with children and will exclude most poor families, the ones who
suffer the most from violence. If we can make television technology available
to benefit twenty-four million deaf and hard-of-hearing Americans, surely we
can do no less for the benefit of fifty million American children.

A final recommendation: Television programs should be accompanied by   41
a violence rating so that parents can judge how violent a program is without
having to watch it. Such a rating system should be quantitative, leaving aesthetic and social judgments to the viewers. This approach would enjoy broad
popular support. In a *Los Angeles Times* poll, 71 percent of adult Americans

favored the establishment of a TV violence rating system. Such a system would not impinge on artistic freedom since producers would remain free to produce programs with high violence ratings. They could even use high violence ratings in the advertisements for their shows.

42 None of these recommendations would limit freedom of speech. That is as it should be. We do not address the problem of motor vehicle fatalities by calling for a ban on cars. Instead, we emphasize safety seats, good traffic signs, and driver education. Similarly, to address the problem of television-inspired violence, we need to promote time-channel locks, program rating systems, and viewer education about the hazards of violent programming. In this way we can protect our children and our society.

REFERENCES

Following is a partial list of studies and articles on this topic.

William A. Belson, *Television Violence and the Adolescent Boy.* Westmead, England: Saxon House (1978).

Brandon S. Centerwall, "Exposure to Television as a Cause of Violence," *Public Communication and Behavior,* Vol. 2. Orlando, Florida: Academic Press (1989), pp. 1–58.

Leonard D. Eron and L. Rowell Huesmann, "The Control of Aggressive Behavior by Changes in Attitudes, Values, and the Conditions of Learning," *Advances in the Study of Aggression.* Orlando, Florida: Academic Press (1984), pp. 139–171.

Gary Granzberg and Jack Steinbring (eds.), *Television and the Canadian Indian.* Winnipeg, Manitoba: University of Winnipeg (1980).

L. Rowell Huesmann and Leonard D. Eron, *Television and the Aggressive Child.* Hillsdale, New Jersey: Lawrence Erlbaum Associates (1986), pp. 45–80.

Candace Kruttschnitt, et al., "Family Violence, Television Viewing Habits, and Other Adolescent Experiences Related to Violent Criminal Behavior," *Criminology,* Vol. 24 (1986), pp. 235–267.

Andrew N. Meltzoff, "Memory in Infancy," *Encyclopedia of Learning and Memory.* New York: Macmillan (1992), pp. 271–275.

J. Ronald Milavsky, et al., *Television and Aggression.* Orlando, Florida: Academic Press (1982).

Jerome L. Singer, et al., "Family Patterns and Television Viewing as Predictors of Children's Beliefs and Aggression," *Journal of Communication,* Vol. 34, No. 2 (1984), pp. 73–89.

Tannis M. Williams. (ed.), *The Impact of Television.* Orlando, Florida: Academic Press (1986).

QUESTIONS FOR READING

1. Centerwall begins with some facts. How much television do preschoolers watch? How well do they understand what they are watching? What impressions of the world will they retain from TV?

2. What evidence of increased aggression from viewing TV violence does the author present? Summarize each study.

3. What does Centerwall seek to accomplish in the section "Controlling for Other Factors"?

4. What did the television-sponsored studies reveal? How does the TV industry now feel about research?

5. What is the industry's strategy now for avoiding control over its programming? What is the author's attitude toward the industry's argument?

6. List Centerwall's proposed solutions.

QUESTIONS FOR REASONING AND ANALYSIS

1. In his four-paragraph opening, Centerwall does not state a thesis, or even announce a purpose in writing. What subject is established? What thesis is implied?

2. What type of argument is this?

3. To make his argument successful, what causal relationship must Centerwall establish?

4. What strategy does Centerwall use in paragraph 34 to express the idea that we should not expect help from the TV industry? What motivates television executives?

5. Analyze the author's argument. Is his tone appropriate? Is his evidence clearly presented? Relevant and effective? Are potential counterarguments considered and rebutted? Are conciliatory strategies used?

QUESTIONS FOR REFLECTING AND WRITING

1. Which of Centerwall's reasons do you find most compelling? Why?

2. Which recommendations have been adopted or made available? Are they making a difference?

3. Do you agree with all of the author's recommendations? Will they make a difference? Why or why not?

4. Are there other suggestions you would offer?

GUNS, LIES, AND VIDEO | KAREN WRIGHT

Karen Wright is a freelance writer whose articles have appeared in *Discover*, the *New York Times Magazine*, *Scientific American*, and *Science*. The following article was published in the April 2003 issue of *Discover* magazine.

PREREADING QUESTIONS Have you played violent video games? Which do you think may have the greater influence on children: violence on television or violent video games? Why?

In a survey published earlier this year, seven of 10 parents said they would never let their children play with toy guns. Yet the average seventh grader spends at least four hours a week playing video games, and about half of those games have violent themes, like Nuclear Strike. Clearly, parents make a distinction between violence on a screen and that acted out with plastic M-16s. Should they?

2   Psychologists point to decades of research and more than a thousand studies that demonstrate a link between media violence and real aggression. Six formidable public-health organizations, including the American Academy of Pediatrics and the American Medical Association (AMA), issued a joint statement of concern in 2000. According to one expert's estimate, aggressive acts provoked by entertainment media such as TV, movies, and music could account for 10 percent of the juvenile violence in society. And scientists say they have reason to believe that video games are the most provocative medium yet.

3   "With video games, you're not only passively receiving attitudes and behaviors, you're rehearsing them," says pediatrician Michael Rich, a former filmmaker and the current head of the Center on Media and Child Health at Harvard University.

4   But the case isn't quite closed. Last year, psychologist Jonathan Freedman of the University of Toronto published an outspoken indictment of some of the field's most influential studies. The "bulk of the research does not show that television or movie violence has any negative effects," he argues in *Media Violence and Its Effect on Aggression.* In a 1999 editorial titled "Guns, Lies, and Videotape," the redoubtable British medical journal *The Lancet* admitted that "experts are divided on the subject," and that "both groups can support their views with a sizable amount of published work."

5   Those who grew up with the Three Stooges or Super Mario Brothers may have trouble seeing their youthful pastimes in a sinister light. But televised violence has been a topic of national consternation almost from the first broadcast. Congressional hearings on the subject date back to 1952; the first surgeon general's report addressing it was published in 1972. "We've been studying it at least since then, but the studies haven't given us definite answers," says Kimberly Thompson, director of the Kids Risk Project at the School of Public Health at Harvard. Thompson and others believe that the rise of TV viewing in American households may be at least partly responsible for the eightfold increase in violent crime in this country between 1960 and 1990. Today a typical kid spends two hours a day watching television, and children's programs average between 20 and 25 violent acts per hour—four times as many as adult programs. "The message that's going out to children is that violence is OK or it's funny or it's somehow heroic," says Jeffrey G. Johnson, a psychiatric epidemiologist at the College of Physicians and Surgeons at Columbia University in New York.

6   Common sense argues that such exposure must have *some* effect. Designing studies to measure it is another story. So far, for example, there aren't any universal standards defining or quantifying violent content. Many early investigations simply proved that aggressive kids like to watch aggressive TV, without illuminating which tendency leads to which. And it's obvious that poverty, abuse, and ready access to weapons can put a child on the wrong path too.

One way to distinguish among the potential causes of juvenile violence is 7
by studying large numbers of people over long periods of time. Last year, Johnson and his colleagues published results of a 17-year study following more than
700 kids from an average age of 6 to adulthood. They tallied the hours each
subject spent in front of the tube and compared those numbers with subsequent acts of aggression, ranging from threats to criminal assault. The trends
are clear, says Johnson: Kids who spent more than three hours a day watching
television at age 14 were more than four times as likely to have acted aggressively by age 22 than kids who watched TV for less than an hour. The connection held up even after researchers accounted for other possible culprits,
including poverty, neglect, and bad neighborhoods—and even among tube-
addled females, who, like the rest of the subjects, were predominantly white
and Catholic.

"It's not that TV just triggers aggression in aggressive people," Johnson 8
says. "We saw this in 'nice' girls too."

Some laboratory studies hint that violent programming may lead to a 9
malevolent state of mind. In one classic example, 5- to 9-year-olds were told
they could press buttons that would either further or foil their playmates' attempts to win a game. Children who watched segments of the 1970s crime
drama *The Untouchables* beforehand showed more willingness to hinder their
peers' efforts than did those who watched a track race.

A recent analysis asserts that the correlation between virtual and actual ag- 10
gression is stronger than those linking passive smoke and lung cancer, calcium
intake and bone density, and exposure to lead and IQ. "The correlation between media violence and aggression is stronger than many of these things
that we accept as fact—such as that if you eat lead paint chips, you'll become
mentally retarded," says Rich.

Rich and others think video games could have an even greater effect than 11
TV because they're interactive. The genre term "first-person shooter" says it
all. "Often the interface that the child has with the game is a gun," says Rich.
"A very realistic gun."

Yet only a handful of video-game studies have been published so far. At 12
Iowa State University in Ames, social psychologist Craig Anderson tested college students' willingness to provide help to others after playing 20 minutes
of benign games like Glider Pro or malignant ones like the pedestrian-plowing
Carmageddon. Anderson timed how long his subjects waited before responding to a person left whimpering in the hallway after a staged attack.
"The people who played a violent video game took about four times as long
to come to the aid of the victim than people who played a nonviolent game,"
says Anderson.

Skeptics like Freedman say such correlations don't amount to causation 13
and that other, well-established risk factors such as poverty and neglect are important to consider. All true, Rich concedes. "But it's only correlations that suggest we should all wear seat belts," he says. "And [exposure to media violence]
is one of the few risk factors that is easily controllable."

14   Laboratory studies have also been criticized for attributing to violent content behavior that could be a result of general physiological arousal. Any exciting program will cause an increase in heart rate, for example, and it's known that a racing heart can make an individual more bellicose. So Anderson took care to compare only video games that elevated his subject's heart rates to the same degree. And child psychologist John Murray of Kansas State University in Manhattan has used realtime MRI scans to observe whether violent content triggers unique patterns of brain activity. One group of Murray's kids watched fight scenes from *Rocky IV;* the other, an action-packed mystery called *Ghostwriter.* Only the boxing bouts activated an area in the right hemisphere called the right posterior cingulate, which may store long-term memories of trauma.

15   "We were surprised to find this, and worried," says Murray. He fears that violent programs may pack the same emotional punch as actual violence. "It's not 'just' entertainment," he says. "It becomes a story about how life is."

16   The advertising industry is built on the faith that media content and consumption can change human behavior, Rich points out. So why does society question the influence of dramatized violence? The obvious answer is that, despite the reams of paper devoted to its pernicious influence, violent entertainment remains entertaining. Americans appear to regard its consequences, whatever they may be, as an acceptable risk. Even hard-liners like Anderson, Rich, and the AMA don't recommend banning violent content. Instead, they lobby for greater parental awareness and control.

17   But maybe parents themselves should beware. The effect of violent media on adults is still unexplored territory. And television news, a staple of grown-up media consumption, carries some of the nastiest carnage on the airwaves.

18   "There is some evidence that violent media has a bigger effect on children." Anderson says. "But there's no age group that's immune."

QUESTIONS FOR READING

1. Which may be the most "provocative medium," TV or video games? Why?
2. What is the "state of affairs" with regard to studies of TV violence?
3. How does violence in children's programs compare with violence in adult programs?
4. Why is it difficult to get a good study of the effect of TV violence?
5. What are some other possible causes of juvenile aggression?
6. What were the results of Johnson's long-term study of TV watching and adult aggression?
7. What did John Murray's studies reveal about increased brain activity?
8. Why do we seem unwilling to respond to what the studies seem to suggest?

QUESTIONS FOR REASONING AND ANALYSIS

1. What is Wright's subject? What is her claim?

2. Does Wright take a strong stand on the topic? Does she have a clear "leaning" on the issue? How do you know? What seems to be her primary purpose in writing?

3. What *kind* of evidence is offered to support the claim?

4. How does Wright qualify her position on the effects of media violence? Why is the qualification important?

5. One can see this as a problem/solution argument. What solutions does the author offer? What solutions are not being pushed by those concerned about the effects of media violence?

QUESTIONS FOR REFLECTING AND WRITING

1. Are you convinced by all the studies that there is at least a strong correlation between experiencing a lot of media violence and increased aggression? Why or why not? If you disagree, how would you rebut the evidence that Wright presents?

2. If the correlation is stronger than that between wearing seat belts and surviving an accident, why aren't we doing something to reduce the amount of violence to which children are exposed? If you were media czar, what would you do?

3. Who is put in charge of controlling children's access to media violence? Is this approach working? If not, why not?

HOLLOW CLAIMS ABOUT FANTASY VIOLENCE | RICHARD RHODES

A graduate of Yale University, fiction writer and journalist Richard Rhodes (b. 1937) is the author of 18 books, has won many fellowships and awards, and has been a consultant to public television on nuclear issues. His study *The Making of the Atomic Bomb* (1986) won a Pulitzer Prize for nonfiction. One of his most recent books is *Why They Kill: The Discoveries of a Maverick Criminologist* (1997). The following column was published September 17, 2000, in the *New York Times*.

PREREADING QUESTIONS Given his title, what do you anticipate Rhodes's position on media violence and aggression to be? If media violence has little or no effect on violent behavior, what may be the causes of such behavior?

The moral entrepreneurs are at it again, pounding the entertainment in- 1
dustry for advertising its Grand Guignolesque confections to children. If exposure to this mock violence contributes to the development of violent behavior,
then our political leadership is justified in its indignation at what the Federal
Trade Commission has reported about the marketing of violent fare to children.
Senators John McCain and Joseph Lieberman have been especially quick to
fasten on the FTC report as they make an issue of violent offerings to children.

But is there really a link between entertainment and violent behavior?   2

The American Medical Association, the American Psychological Associa-   3
tion, the American Academy of Pediatrics and the National Institute of Mental

Health all say yes. They base their claims on social science research that has been sharply criticized and disputed within the social science profession, especially outside the United States. In fact, no direct, causal link between exposure to mock violence in the media and subsequent violent behavior has ever been demonstrated, and the few claims of modest correlation have been contradicted by other findings, sometimes in the same studies.

4   History alone should call such a link into question. Private violence has been declining in the West since the media-barren late Middle Ages, when homicide rates are estimated to have been 10 times what they are in Western nations today. Historians attribute the decline to improving social controls over violence—police forces and common access to courts of law—and to a shift away from brutal physical punishment in child-rearing (a practice that still appears as a common factor in the background of violent criminals today).

5   The American Medical Association has based its endorsement of the media violence theory in major part on the studies of Brandon Centerwall, a psychiatrist in Seattle. Dr. Centerwall compared the murder rates for whites in three countries from 1945 to 1974 with numbers for television set ownership. Until 1975, television broadcasting was banned in South Africa, and "white homicide rates remained stable" there, Dr. Centerwall found, while corresponding rates in Canada and the United States doubled after television was introduced.

6   A spectacular finding, but it is meaningless. As Franklin E. Zimring and Gordon Hawkins of the University of California at Berkeley subsequently pointed out, homicide rates in France, Germany, Italy and Japan either failed to change with increasing television ownership in the same period or actually declined, and American homicide rates have more recently been sharply declining despite a proliferation of popular media outlets—not only movies and television, but also video games and the Internet.

7   Other social science that supposedly undergirds the theory, too, is marginal and problematic. Laboratory studies that expose children to selected incidents of televised mock violence and then assess changes in the children's behavior have sometimes found more "aggressive" behavior after the exposure—usually verbal, occasionally physical.

8   But sometimes the control group, shown incidents judged not to be violent, behaves more aggressively afterward than the test group; sometimes comedy produces the more aggressive behavior; and sometimes there's no change. The only obvious conclusion is that sitting and watching television stimulates subsequent physical activity. Any kid could tell you that.

9   As for those who claim that entertainment promotes violent behavior by desensitizing people to violence, the British scholar Martin Barker offers this critique: "Their claim is that the materials they judge to be harmful can only influence us by trying to make us be the same as them. So horrible things will make us horrible—not horrified. Terrifying things will make us terrifying—not terrified. To see something aggressive makes us feel aggressive—not aggressed against. This idea is so odd, it is hard to know where to begin in challenging it."

Even more influential on national policy has been a 22-year study by two   10
University of Michigan psychologists, Leonard D. Eron and L. Rowell Huesmann, of boys exposed to so-called violent media. The Telecommunications
Act of 1996, which mandated the television V-chip, allowing parents to screen
out unwanted programming, invoked these findings, asserting, "Studies have
shown that children exposed to violent video programming at a young age
have a higher tendency for violent and aggressive behavior later in life than
children not so exposed."

Well, not exactly. Following 875 children in upstate New York from third   11
grade through high school, the psychologists found a correlation between a
preference for violent television at age 8 and aggressiveness at age 18. The
correlation—0.31—would mean television accounted for about 10 percent of
the influences that led to this behavior. But the correlation only turned up in
one of three measures of aggression: the assessment of students by their
peers. It didn't show up in students' reports about themselves or in psychological testing. And for girls, there was no correlation at all.

Despite the lack of evidence, politicians can't resist blaming the media for   12
violence. They can stake out the moral high ground confident that the First
Amendment will protect them from having to actually write legislation that
would be likely to alienate the entertainment industry. Some use the issue as a
smokescreen to avoid having to confront gun control.

But violence isn't learned from mock violence. There is good evidence—   13
causal evidence, not correlational—that it's learned in personal violent encounters, beginning with the brutalization of children by their parents or their
peers.

The money spent on the all the social science research I've described was   14
diverted from the National Institute of Mental Health budget by reducing support for the construction of community mental health centers. To this day there
is no standardized reporting system for emergency-room findings of physical
child abuse. Violence is on the decline in America, but if we want to reduce it
even further, protecting children from real violence in their real lives—not the
pale shadow of mock violence—is the place to begin.

QUESTIONS FOR READING

1. What is Rhodes's subject?
2. Who claims that "mock violence" causes violent behavior? On what basis?
3. What has been in decline since the Middle Ages? What causes do historians find
    for the decline?
4. How does Rhodes challenge Centerwall's studies?
5. What is the author's objection to lab studies of children's behavior after watch-
    ing violence on TV?
6. How does Rhodes account for the politicians' desire to blame the media for
    violence?

QUESTIONS FOR REASONING AND ANALYSING

1. What is Rhodes's claim? Where does he state it?

2. How is his argument organized? What is he doing in paragraphs 3–11? In paragraphs 12–14?

3. What does the author think is the primary cause of violence? What, then, should we do to reduce violence?

4. Analyze the author's word choice in paragraph 1. How does his language create tone and express his attitude?

QUESTIONS FOR REFLECTING AND WRITING

1. Karen Wright (p. 401) argues that common sense tells us that we must be influenced by media violence. Rhodes, in paragraph 9, presents the argument that the opposite should be true—we should react negatively to media violence. Who makes more sense to you? Why? How would you defend your view?

2. Rhodes argues that child abuse, especially by their parents, is the single most powerful cause of aggression; we learn violence from experiencing real violence. Do you agree? Why? Disagree? Why? You may want to do an Internet and/or electronic database search to find information on this topic.

BAD RAPS: MUSIC REBELS REVEL IN THEIR THUG LIFE | SUZANNE FIELDS

Suzanne Fields (b. 1936) is a syndicated op-ed columnist with a twice-weekly column in the *Washington Times.* She holds a Ph.D. in literature from Catholic University and is trained in social psychology. A collection of her columns was published by the *Washington Times* in 1996. Her article on rap music appeared on May 21, 2001, in *Insight on the News.*

PREREADING QUESTIONS From the title, what do you expect the article to be about? What do you expect Fields's attitude to be toward her subject?

1   Nothing in the culture wars makes a stronger argument for the defense of conservative values than rap music. Rap expresses the worst kind of images emanating from a postmodern society that has consigned a generation of young men and women to the darkest dramas of the desperately lost.

2   The megastars of this genre are not about to sing of "you and me and baby makes three." Their lyrics come from a world of broken families, absent fathers, illegitimate children and matriarchal dominance, often subsidized by welfare.

3   For the men who denigrate women as "bitches" and "ho's," this is not merely misogyny (though it is that), but alienation from common humanity and community. The lyrics employ vulgar street idioms because both the language and experience of poetry or romance are absent from the lives of the rappers and their audience as well.

4   Frank Sinatra grew up on the mean streets of New Jersey and he knew the Mafia well, but when he sang "You're the top, You're the Tower of Pisa. . . ."

You're the Mona Lisa" he aspired to sophistication and wanted others to see him as debonair. (Is there a rapper alive who knows the difference between the Tower of Pisa and a towering pizza?) When Frankie was bad, literally, he didn't want his fans to hear about it. He wasn't as innocent as his lyrics, but he cultivated that impression.

5   Rappers Sean "Puffy" Combs and Eminem, by contrast, must live like they sing. They're rich, but their attraction resides in perverse behavior on and off stage. When as adults they tap into adolescent rebellion, they dumb down both their emotions and their economic success.

6   Shelby Steele, a black scholar, has their number when he writes that to keep their audience they can't just sing about alienation—they had better experience it as well, either with the audience or for the audience.

7   "The rappers and promoters themselves are pressured toward a thug life, simply to stay credible," Steele writes in *The Wall Street Journal."* A rap promoter without an arrest record can start to look a lot like Dick Clark."

8   A rapper such as Eminem, who revels in affecting a white-trash identity, has defenders, too. They find irony, satire and poetic metaphor in his lyrics, but it's difficult to see how most of his fans take those lyrics as anything but straight. Lurking in them is a cruel depravity that seeks ways to go over the line by singing of macho brutality—of raping women, holding gay men with a knife at their throats and helping a group of friends to take a little sister's virginity.

9   These lyrics are powerful, but the power resides in psychological defensiveness that provides a perverse rationalization for brutality: If you don't love you can't be rejected, so you might as well hate and rape.

10   Every generation since Elvis has driven through adolescence on popular music—looking for the new sound and sensibility that rejects what their parents liked. Elvis was the cutting edge of the sexual revolution innovative then, but tame and hardly even titillating today. It's hard to believe that for his first appearance on the *Ed Sullivan Show,* the maestro wouldn't allow the cameras to focus below the singer's waist.

11   Elvis brilliantly combined the black, blues and sex rhythms of the honkytonks of the backroads South of his time, liberating teen-age rebels in dance and song. But nearly every music hero and heroine after him has had to push the envelope or raise the ante to be a big winner. For some teenagers the explicit meanness may provide an imaginary escape, the permission to act in a dark, forbidden drama of their imaginations. For these young men and women, the incentives to "act out" may be no more aggressive than dyeing hair purple or wearing ugly clothes. For others, "acting out" as in "men behaving badly," may be the preferred response in human relationships.

12   Rappers, rollers and rockers who tap into the big time with bite and bitterness draw millions to their records and concerts for different reasons. The teen-age and young-adult Zeitgeist is made up of rebels with and without causes. It didn't hurt Eminem that his mother sued him for $10 million for using lyrics such as "my mom smokes more dope than I do." (It might have been Eminem's press agent's idea.) That's on the same track in which he ponders which Spice Girl he would prefer to "impregnate."

13   There are lots of other popular singers who get less notice by being less bizarre. They make up a popular lifestyle that eventually will morph into a healthy nostalgia. The pity is that the nasty stuff of violent rap may never reach the nostalgic mode but congeal into a brutal life perspective.

14   In one of Eminem's hits he sings of a deranged fan. Eminem suggests the fan get counseling, but the fan doesn't. Instead he kills himself and his pregnant girlfriend. Fantasy or reality?

QUESTIONS FOR READING AND ANALYSIS

1. What are the subjects of rappers' lyrics?
2. What does Frank Sinatra have in common with modern rappers? How does he differ from them?
3. What is the relationship between Combs's and Eminem's music and their lifestyles? How are their lifestyles a series of contradictions?
4. What were the sources of Elvis's music? How was he innovative for his time?
5. What process does Fields expect to take place with teens growing up on rap music?

QUESTIONS FOR REASONING AND ANALYSIS

1. What is Fields's claim? Where does she state it?
2. The author quotes Shelby Steele, who says that rap promoters need an arrest record so as not to be like Dick Clark. Who is Dick Clark? What makes this reference effective?
3. What is effective about Fields's choice of Sinatra and Elvis to contrast with today's rappers?

QUESTIONS FOR REFLECTING AND WRITING

1. Do you listen to rap music? If so, how would you defend your choice? If not, why not?
2. Do you agree that teens influenced by rap music will be affected into adulthood by a music that alienates them from "common humanity"? If so, how do you suggest that we keep teens from this influence? If you disagree with Fields, what rebuttal would you offer?

SUPREMACY CRIMES | GLORIA STEINEM

Editor, writer, and lecturer, Gloria Steinem (b. 1934) has been cited in *World Almanac* as one of the 25 most influential women in America. She is the cofounder of *Ms. Magazine* and of the National Women's Political Caucus and is the author of a number of books and many articles. The following article appeared in *Ms.* in the August/September 1999 issue.

PREREADING QUESTIONS Who are the teens who commit most of the mass shootings at schools? Who are the adults who commit most of the hate crimes and sadistic killings? What generalizations can you make about these groups based on your knowledge from media coverage?

You've seen the ocean of television coverage, you've read the headlines: 1 "How to Spot a Troubled Kid," "Twisted Teens," "When Teens Fall Apart."

After the slaughter in Colorado that inspired those phrases, dozens of 2 copycat threats were reported in the same generalized way: "Junior high students charged with conspiracy to kill students and teaches" (in Texas); "Five honor students overheard planning a June graduation bombing" (in New York); "More than 100 minor threats reported statewide" (in Pennsylvania). In response, the White House held an emergency strategy session titled "Children, Violence, and Responsibility." Nonetheless, another attack was soon reported: "Youth With 2 Guns Shoots 6 at Georgia School."

I don't know about you, but I've been talking back to the television set, 3 waiting for someone to tell us the obvious: it's not "youth," "our children," or "our teens." It's our sons—and "our" can usually be read as "white," "middle class," and "heterosexual."

We know that hate crimes, violent and otherwise, are overwhelmingly com- 4 mitted by white men who are apparently straight. The same is true for an even higher percentage of impersonal, resentment-driven, mass killings like those in Colorado; the sort committed for no economic or rational gain except the need to say, "I'm superior because I can kill." Think of Charles Starkweather, who reported feeling powerful and serene after murdering ten women and men in the 1950s; or the shooter who climbed the University of Texas Tower in 1966, raining down death to gain celebrity. Think of the engineering student at the University of Montreal who resented females' ability to study that subject, and so shot to death 14 women students in 1989, while saying, "I'm against feminism." Think of nearly all those who have killed impersonally in the workplace, the post office, McDonald's.

White males—usually intelligent, middle class, and heterosexual, or trying 5 desperately to appear so—also account for virtually all the serial, sexually motivated, sadistic killings, those characterized by stalking, imprisoning, torturing, and "owning" victims in death. Think of Edmund Kemper, who began by killing animals, then murdered his grandparents, yet was released to sexually torture and dismember college students and other young women until he himself decided he "didn't want to kill all the coeds in the world." Or David Berkowitz, the Son of Sam, who murdered some women in order to feel in control of all women. Or consider Ted Bundy, the charming, snobbish young would-be lawyer who tortured and murdered as many as 40 women, usually beautiful students who were symbols of the economic class he longed to join. As for John Wayne Gacy, he was obsessed with maintaining the public mask of masculinity, and so hid his homosexuality by killing and burying men and boys with whom he had had sex.

6   These "senseless" killings begin to seem less mysterious when you consider that they were committed disproportionately by white, non-poor males, the group most likely to become hooked on the drug of superiority. It's a drug pushed by a male-dominant culture that presents dominance as a natural right; a racist hierarchy that falsely elevates whiteness; a materialist society that equates superiority with possessions; and a homophobic one that empowers only one form of sexuality.

7   As Elliott Leyton reports in *Hunting Humans: The Rise of the Modern Multiple Murderer,* these killers see their behavior as "an appropriate—even 'manly'—response to the frustrations and disappointments that are a normal part of life." In other words, it's not their life experiences that are the problem, it's the impossible expectation of dominance to which they've become addicted.

8   This is not about blame. This is about causation. If anything, ending the massive cultural cover-up of supremacy crimes should make heroes out of boys and men who reject violence, especially those who reject the notion of superiority altogether. Even if one believes in a biogenetic component of male aggression, the very existence of gentle men proves that socialization can override it.

9   Nor is this about attributing such crimes to a single cause. Addiction to the drug of supremacy is not their only root, just the deepest and most ignored one. Additional reasons why this country has such a high rate of violence include the plentiful guns that make killing seem as unreal as a video game; male violence in the media that desensitized viewers in much the same way that combat killers are desensitized in training; affluence that allows maximum access to violence-as-entertainment; a national history of genocide and slavery; the romanticizing of frontier violence and organized crime; not to mention extremes of wealth and poverty and the illusion that both are deserved.

10   But it is truly remarkable, given the relative reasons for anger at injustice in this country, that white, non-poor men have a near-monopoly on multiple killings of strangers, whether serial and sadistic or mass and random. How can we ignore this obvious fact? Others may kill to improve their own condition, in self-defense, or for money or drugs; to eliminate enemies; to declare turf in drive-by shootings; even for a jacket or a pair of sneakers—but white males addicted to supremacy kill even when it worsens their condition or ends in suicide.

11   Men of color and females are capable of serial and mass killing, and commit just enough to prove it. Think of Colin Ferguson, the crazed black man on the Long Island Railroad, or Wayne Williams, the young black man in Atlanta who kidnapped and killed black boys, apparently to conceal his homosexuality. Think of the Aileen Carol Wuornos, the white prostitute in Florida who killed abusive johns "in self-defense," or Waneta Hoyt, the upstate New York woman who strangled her five infant children between 1965 and 1971, disguising their cause of death as sudden infant death syndrome. Such crimes are rare enough to leave a haunting refrain of disbelief as evoked in Pat Parker's poem "jonestown": "Black folks do not/Black folks do not/Black folks do not commit suicide." And yet they did.

Nonetheless, the proportion of serial killings that are not committed by 12
white males is about the same as the proportion of anorexics who are not female. Yet we discuss the gender, race, and class components of anorexia, but
not the role of the same factors in producing epidemics among the powerful.

The reasons are buried deep in the culture, so invisible that only by re- 13
versing our assumptions can we reveal them.

Suppose, for instance, that young black males—or any other men of 14
color—had carried out the slaughter in Colorado. Would the media reports be
so willing to describe the murderers as "our children"? Would there be so little discussion about the boys' race? Would experts be calling the motive a mystery, or condemning the high school cliques for making those young men feel
like "outsiders"? Would there be the same empathy for parents who gave the
murderers luxurious homes, expensive cars, even rescued them from brushes
with the law? Would there be as much attention to generalized causes, such as
the dangers of violent video games and recipes for bombs on the Internet?

As for the victims, if racial identities had been reversed, would racism re- 15
main so little discussed? In fact, the killers themselves said they were targeting
blacks and athletes. They used a racial epithet, shot a black male student in the
head, and then laughed over the fact that they could see his brain. What if that
had been reversed?

What if these two young murderers, who were called "fags" by some of 16
the jocks at Columbine High School, actually had been gay? Would they have
got the same sympathy for being gay-baited? What if they had been lovers?
Would we hear as little about their sexuality as we now do, even though only
their own homophobia could have given the word "fag" such power to humiliate them?

Take one more leap of the imagination: suppose these killings had been 17
planned and executed by young women—of any race, sexuality, or class. Would
the media still be so disinterested in the role played by gender-conditioning?
Would journalists assume that female murderers had suffered from being shut
out of access to power in high school, so much so that they were pushed beyond their limits? What if dozens, even hundreds of young women around the
country had made imitative threats—as young men have done—expressing ad-
miration for a well-planned massacre and promising to do the same? Would we
be discussing their youth more than their gender, as is the case so far with these
male killers?

I think we begin to see that our national self-examination is ignoring some- 18
thing fundamental, precisely because it's like the air we breathe: the white male
factor, the middle-class and heterosexual one, and the promise of superiority
it carries. Yet this denial is self-defeating—to say the least. We will never reduce
the number of violent Americans, from bullies to killers, without challenging
the assumptions on which masculinity is based: that males are superior to females, that they must find a place in a male hierarchy, and that the ability to
dominate someone is so important that even a mere insult can justify lethal revenge. There are plenty of studies to support this view. As Dr. James Gilligan
concluded in *Violence: Reflections on a National Epidemic*, "If humanity is to

evolve beyond the propensity toward violence . . . then it can only do so by recognizing the extent to which the patriarchal code of honor and shame generates and obligates male violence."

19   I think the way out can only be found through a deeper reversal: just as we as a society have begun to raise our daughters more like our sons—more like whole people—we must begin to raise our sons more like our daughters—that is, to value empathy as well as hierarchy; to measure success by other people's welfare as well as their own.

20   But first, we have to admit and name the truth about supremacy crimes.

QUESTIONS FOR READING

1. What kinds of crimes is Steinem examining? What kinds of crimes is she excluding from her discussion?

2. What messages, according to Steinem, is our culture sending to white, non-poor males?

3. How does Elliott Leyton explain these killers' behavior?

4. What is the primary reason we have not examined serial and random killings correctly, in the author's view? What is keeping us from seeing what we need to see?

5. What do we need to do to reduce "the number of violent Americans, from bullies to killers"?

QUESTIONS FOR REASONING AND ANALYSIS

1. What is Steinem's claim? Where does she state it?

2. What kind of argument is this; that is, what *type* of claim is the author presenting?

3. What is her primary type of evidence?

4. How does Steinem qualify her claim and thereby anticipate and answer counterarguments? In what paragraphs does she present qualifiers and counterarguments to possible rebuttals?

5. How does the author seek to get her readers to understand that we are not thinking soundly about the mass killings at Columbine High School? Is her strategy an effective one? Why or why not?

QUESTIONS FOR REFLECTING AND WRITING

1. Steinem concludes by writing that we must first "name the truth" about supremacy violence before we can begin to address the problem. Does this make sense to you? How can this be good advice for coping with most problems? Think of other kinds of problems that this approach might help solve.

2. Do you agree with Steinem's analysis of the causes of serial and random killings? If yes, how would you add to her argument? If no, how would you refute her argument?

GUN REGISTRATION: IT'S COMMON SENSE | SARAH BRADY

An advocate for gun-control legislation since her husband was shot and severely disabled when President Ronald Reagan was shot, Sarah Brady (b. 1942), a graduate of the College of William and Mary and a former teacher, is chair of Handgun Control and the Center to Prevent Handgun Violence. This article was published June 11, 1999, shortly after the student shootings in Littleton, Colorado.

PREREADING QUESTIONS Should 18-year-olds be allowed to buy handguns? How would you account for America's high murder rate relative to other Western democracies?

In an interview on *Good Morning, America* last week, the president said 1 that we should consider registering guns just as we register cars. He's right, of course. In the same way that we require the registration of cars, we should require that the sale or transfer of firearms—at least handguns—be reported to law enforcement authorities.

Registration is a vital law enforcement tool. It's a crime-solver. By permit- 2 ting guns to be readily traced back to their last lawful owner, police can more readily identify who pulled the trigger and, if the shooter is a prohibited purchaser, who illegally sold or transferred the gun to the shooter. When police are unable to trace a gun, a criminal and his accomplice can, quite literally, get away with murder. And that's what happens all too often.

It took law enforcement officials two weeks to determine who sold the 3 TEC-9 assault pistol to the two shooters in Littleton, Colo. And if the seller hadn't identified himself, the police might never have made the link. The police in Littleton were not searching for the killers; the two killed themselves. But in many criminal investigations, the shooters and their accomplices are not identified and, thanks in part to weak gun laws, they may never be caught.

The gun lobby will insist that the president has made a critical miscalcula- 4 tion. No sitting president since Lyndon B. Johnson has dared suggest that firearms should be registered. The NRA would like everyone to believe that gun registration, in whatever form, is the third rail of American politics.

Some third rail. A public opinion survey conducted last year by the National 5 Opinion Research Center found that 85 percent of Americans, including 75 percent of gun owners, support mandatory registration of handguns.

It all comes down to common sense. Almost everywhere else in the world, 6 sales or transfers of firearms must be recorded. Some countries, such as Japan and Great Britain, have banned handguns altogether.

Meanwhile, in this country, it took a massacre the size of Littleton for con- 7 gressional leaders to acknowledge that background checks should be conducted at gun shows. And it was regarded as a giant step forward when the Senate a few weeks ago voted to prohibit the sale of AK-47s and Uzis to children. Requiring gun manufacturers to provide a simple safety lock with every handgun they sell was, by American standards, a major accomplishment.

So as the House of Representatives prepares to consider the Senate- 8 passed gun legislation, congressional leaders are urging caution. Some on both sides are suggesting that going beyond the Senate-passed bill may be going too far. Establishing a minimum 72-hour waiting period on handgun purchases so that law enforcement can do a more thorough background check? Not likely. Limiting handgun purchases to one handgun per month so that professional gun traffickers cannot go around buying 50 or 100 guns a month? Forget it, too controversial.

9   And while the House might consider prohibiting the sale of handguns at gun shows to those between the ages of 18 and 21, it might stop short of prohibiting 18-year-olds from actually possessing handguns. It doesn't seem to matter that 18- and 19-year-olds lead the nation in homicides. These youth shouldn't be limited, so the argument goes, to possessing rifles and shotguns. They need handguns.

10   Is it any wonder that the president seemed upset the other day when he was questioned about his commitment to tougher gun laws? This president has done far more than any other to advance our thinking about guns, and yet Congress is still playing political games. When the Senate took up the issue of guns a few weeks ago, the first amendment that passed was one that would have gutted our gun laws, stopping Brady background checks on criminals reclaiming guns at pawn shops and permitting federally licensed gun dealers to sell at gun shows in all 50 states. Now some in the House want to limit the time that can be taken for background checks at gun shows—even if the records are showing a problem, such as a felony arrest, that needs more investigation. Allowing felons to get guns in the interest of promoting quick gun sales makes no sense.

11   When is this insanity going to end? Anyone who bemoans the "inconvenience" that these new gun-show restrictions might impose on gun-show promoters should be required to talk to as many victims of gun violence as I have. Let them start with some of the 13 mothers who every day lose a child to gun violence. And then let them talk to some of the many children who have lost classmates.

12   The simple truth is that we don't need to ban guns in this country to reduce gun violence. All we need are common-sense gun laws. Since the Brady Law was passed in 1993, gun crimes have dropped sharply. But we still have so far to go. Common sense, when it comes to guns, remains in short supply. At least in Congress.

QUESTIONS FOR READING

1. How, according to Brady, can gun registration help police solve crimes?

2. What percentage of Americans support handgun registration? What percentage of gun owners support such registration?

3. What countries ban all handguns? How common are records of gun sales and transfers?

4. How many mothers lose a child to gun violence each day?

QUESTIONS FOR REASONING AND ANALYSIS

1. What is Brady's claim? Where does she state it?

2. Brady is, of course, associated with lobbying for gun control. What does she gain by asserting that "we don't need to ban guns in this country to reduce gun violence"?

3. When she writes, in paragraph 8, "Not likely" and "Forget it, too controversial," what is Brady really saying? Does she agree with members of Congress who have doubts about passing gun legislation?

QUESTIONS FOR REFLECTING AND WRITING

1. Are you among the majority who support gun registration? Why or why not?

2. Should sales of semiautomatics to children be banned? Should ownership be banned except for military personnel? Explain your position.

3. Should those attending gun shows be limited to the purchase of one gun? Why or why not?

FALSE CHOICES ON GUN SAFETY | JONATHAN COWAN

Jonathan Cowan is the president of Americans for Gun Safety, a nonprofit organization that supports the rights of Americans to own guns but seeks to improve gun safety. His article was published in the *Washington Post* on October 10, 2002.

PREREADING QUESTIONS What was happening in the greater Washington, DC, area in the fall of 2002 that might have led to a debate on gun safety or stricter enforcement of gun laws?

A sniper has taken aim, spreading death and fear in Maryland, Virginia and 1 the District of Columbia. Yet despite this terror campaign, there is no movement from Congress or the administration for tougher gun safety laws. This is in sharp contrast to the congressional response to the 1999 Columbine shootings, which led to an immediate Senate vote to require background checks for purchasers at gun shows. Why the difference, and what does it say about the future of gun safety in America?

Unfortunately, after the 2000 elections, most Democrats concluded that 2 calling for new gun laws could cost them critical white male votes. Meanwhile, the Bush White House sought to extend its balancing act on guns, taking specific steps to please the gun lobby but publicly maintaining support for limited new gun safety measures to preserve its "compassionate conservative" identity. Thus the bipartisan consensus on guns: Back a narrow agenda that emphasizes the protection of gun rights and tougher enforcement of existing laws, rather than the need for new gun laws.

While such an approach may seem to make political sense, it represents an 3 abdication of a critical responsibility of the national government: public safety. Moreover, it offers voters a false choice on two counts—gun rights or gun safety, and new gun laws or tougher enforcement. America can protect gun rights and promote gun responsibility only with new laws and vigorous enforcement of existing laws.

4   With more than 500,000 gun-related crimes each year, America cannot focus exclusively on punishing people once they commit gun-related crimes. It must also attempt to stop guns from falling into the wrong hands in the first place—which means breaking up the black market in illegal guns. According to data from the Bureau of Alcohol, Tobacco and Firearms (ATF), this market—a chain of crooked dealers and petty street traffickers—supplies most of the guns used in crime. Congress and the Bush administration must design a real national strategy aimed at waging a war against this mostly American illegal gun cartel.

5   A comprehensive national gun-trafficking strategy would have three components;

6   (1) A federal enforcement effort focused not just on punishing criminals after the fact—the thrust of the administration's worthy but one-sided Project Safe Neighborhoods—but also on busting up the chain of illegal guns, from manufacturers to dealers to street merchants. The president ought to create a fully staffed and funded national gun-trafficking task force, similar to the corporate fraud effort launched months ago.

7   (2) New federal enforcement tools that would beef up the ability of ATF to crack down on gun trafficking, including more tracing of crime guns and ballistics fingerprinting to link slugs and casings to the owners of the guns that fired them. Despite the bipartisan calls for tough enforcement, ATF is hamstrung by laws—such as the one limiting unannounced inspections of gun dealers to one a year—that appear to be intended to make it difficult to punish those at the top of the gun-trafficking chain.

8   (3) Legislation to close the most glaring loopholes in federal law. This would include requiring background checks at all gun shows for all gun sales and fixing the deeply flawed background check system—a system that has allowed thousands of criminals to obtain guns because they were among the 35 million prohibited buyers whose names were not yet in an instant-check database. During the 2000 campaign, candidate George W. Bush supported some version of these measures, and gun rights and gun safety supporters such as Sens. John McCain, Chuck Schumer, Joe Lieberman and Larry Craig and Reps. Carolyn McCarthy and John Dingell have bipartisan bills to do exactly this. Compromise in closing these dangerous loopholes ought to be achievable.

9   Opponents will say that new gun laws—or vigorous enforcement of existing laws—violate gun rights. But America has passed six major federal gun laws since the 1930s, and the number of guns in private hands has quintupled. They will say that gun laws don't work, but the Brady law has already stopped 700,000 prohibited buyers from purchasing guns. They will say that guns don't kill, people do—and they are right—but that doesn't mean we shouldn't try to keep guns out of the hands of people who are most likely to commit a crime or kill with a gun.

10   The country deserves a war on illegal guns, not empty rhetoric about tough enforcement and silence in the face of senseless shootings. Such a war may not

have saved the lives lost in the Washington area during the past week, but it will save others—without taking away the guns or diminishing the gun rights of a single law-abiding American.

QUESTIONS FOR READING

1. What is Cowan's subject?
2. What has been the post-2000-election bipartisan consensus on guns?
3. How has the political response to the sniper been different from the response to the Columbine shootings?
4. How many gun-related crimes occur each year in the United States?
5. How do most criminals obtain their guns?
6. What is Cowan's recommendation? Summarize his three-step plan in your own words.

QUESTIONS FOR REASONING AND ANALYSIS

1. What is Cowan's claim? Where does he state it? How does it challenge the current bipartisan consensus on guns?
2. What two points does the author present in paragraphs 3 and 4 as the primary defense of his proposed plan? Do these points make sense to you? Why or why not?
3. What rebuttals of his proposal does he anticipate? How does he answer them?

QUESTIONS FOR REFLECTING AND WRITING

1. Evaluate Cowan's proposal. Does his three-step plan seem sensible? Feasible? If you agree with Cowan, how would you try to sell the plan to your representative and senators? If you disagree with the proposal, what argument would you present to your elected officials to dissuade them from supporting the plan?
2. The powerful gun lobby seems to be a major stumbling block to new gun safety laws and to better enforcement of existing laws. What do you think of this situation? Should powerful lobbies control the ways that elected officials vote or the bills that are presented for consideration? Are lobbies and political action committees, with their money and single-issue approach, significantly altering a party system of compromise and consensus? If so, is this good or bad for our political system? These are some key questions on which to reflect and write.

CHAPTER 15

Sports Talk— Sports Battles

Title IX changed the appearance of the playing field. Not only has professional soccer achieved new status and appeal in this country, but women's soccer teams also have been front-page news. But has Title IX leveled the playing field? Two writers in this chapter debate the effect, for good or ill, of Title IX on college sports. In addition, Rick Reilly and award-winning cartoonist Pat Oliphant look at the place of women in professional tennis and golf—where it seems that the "paying field" is either not level or not even available to women.

Part of the issue with Title IX is that it funnels money for athletics away from men's college sports, and yet men's college sports is big business, bringing, for Division I schools at any rate, both fame and big bucks through television coverage of their men's football and basketball teams. To garner the fame and dollars, though, one must have great teams, not teams that have fun, build strong bodies, and enhance school spirit, but teams that win championships. Some would argue that men's college football and basketball teams have become farm leagues for the pros with the loss of the original idea of the college athlete and such romantic goals as building body, mind, and spirit. If this is true, is it a problem? If it is a problem, is there any way to return to an earlier time when college athletes were also expected to take serious courses and get a degree?

PREREADING QUESTIONS

1. What are the requirements of Title IX for college athletic departments? Has Title IX been successful in giving women greater opportunities to participate in sports, not just in college but in high schools and recreation youth leagues as well?

2. Should professional athletes be given equal pay in a sport or be paid according to their popularity or draw, regardless of gender?

3. Should the PGA play at clubs that restrict women from membership? Should private clubs—which get a tax break—be allowed to discriminate in membership selection on the basis of gender, race, or religion?

4. Should the NCAA demand higher academic credentials for would-be college athletes and expect college players to carry typical course loads leading to graduation?

Websites Related to This Chapter's Topic

NCAA Online

http://www.ncaa.org

All about the organization and about college sports—stats galore.

Gender Equity in Sports

http://balliwick.lib.uiowa.edu/ge/index.html#200

Site sponsored by the University of Iowa contains information on legal issues connected to Title IX plus resources and links.

There are also websites for the PGA (Professional Golf Association) and USTA (United States Tennis Association), in addition to ESPN.com and all of your favorite sports sites.

PAT OLIPHANT

Born in Australia (in 1936) and now a U.S. citizen, Pat Oliphant started drawing cartoons at age twenty. His cartoons are now syndicated in over 500 newspapers in this country and in many cities around the world as well. He has won numerous awards, including the Pulitzer Prize. The following cartoon appeared November 23, 2002.

'HELL, I DIDN'T EVEN KNOW THEY PLAYED GOLF, DID YOU, HOOTIE?'

QUESTIONS FOR READING

1. What is "happening" in the cartoon? Who is doing what to whom? Where is it happening?
2. Which figure speaks the caption? Who is Hootie?
3. What sports controversy is Oliphant depicting?

QUESTIONS FOR REASONING AND ANALYSIS

1. What actions in the cartoon make it funny? What elements of Oliphant's style of drawing make the cartoon funny?
2. What is Oliphant's reaction to the issue? That is, what is the cartoon saying?

QUESTIONS FOR REFLECTING AND WRITING

1. Why do women want to join men's clubs? What do they lose out on when they are excluded? Is the issue primarily symbolic, or are there other consequences to the exclusion?

2. Are respected organizations such as the PGA damaged when they use a facility that discriminates against gender, race, or religion? Image isn't everything, but is it important sometimes? Why or why not?

DISADVANTAGE, WOMEN | RICK REILLY

A graduate of the University of Colorado, Rick Reilly (b. 1958) is an award-winning sports writer and columnist. He is a senior writer for *Sports Illustrated* and has co-authored several autobiographies of sports figures. He has also written two novels, including *Missing Links* (1996). His latest nonfiction book is *Who's Your Caddy?* (2003). The following column was posted on SI.com July 10, 2001.

PREREADING QUESTIONS At the four major tennis tournaments, where the men and women are playing at the same time and the purses are the largest, are the players paid equally or not? Does this issue matter to you? Should it?

Did you hear what happened to Venus Williams after she won Wimbledon 1 on Sunday? She was robbed! She had $52,923 ripped right out of her purse! In broad daylight!

Instead of getting $705,109, which men's winner Goran Ivanisevic received 2 on Monday, she earned about a new Lexus less. You talk about a grass ceiling. Not only that, but it also happened to Jennifer Capriati this year at the French Open. The dinosaurs who run that tournament gave her $29,306 less than the men's winner, Gustavo Kuerten.

Leave it to tennis to jack the only group of players anybody wants to see. 3 You don't believe me? Let's compare, shall we?

In the women's Top 10, you have the riveting Slam Sisters—Venus and Ser- 4 ena Williams—the tempestuous Martina Hingis, the sports story of the year in Capriati, the tragic Monica Seles and the big Teddette bear, Lindsay Davenport, not to mention, at No. 11, the world's leading cause of whiplash, Anna Kournikova. In the men's Top 10 you have nine guys you couldn't pick out of a Pinto full of Domino's delivery men, plus Andre Agassi. Combined, most of the Top 10 men have the Q rating of a lamp. Seriously, is Yevgeny Kafelnikov a tennis player or something you cure with penicillin?

The women play amazing, long, topsy-turvy, edge-of-your-seat points. The 5 men hit 140-mph aces nobody can see, and then ask for a towel. Everything is serve and towel, serve and towel. It's like being at a cocktail party with Boris Yeltsin. In a third-round Wimbledon match Ivanisevic had 41 aces against Andy Roddick, who had 20. It is unclear how the rest of the points were won because the official statistician fell asleep. If men's tennis is to be saved, somebody had better start decompressing these guys' balls. Then something has to be done about the equipment.

The women we know by first names: *Can you believe what Martina said* 6 *about Serena?* They hate one another, insult one another's fathers, insult their own fathers, bump each other on changeovers, wear body-hugging Technicolor dresses designed by Edward Scissorhands and generally provide more story lines than six months' worth of *All My Children,* all of which will come splatter-ing out later this month in a new book about the women's tour, *Venus Envy.*

7   The men, on the other hand, stand around killing the grass. Except for Agassi, they all look like the slackers you have to shoo away from the door of your Starbucks. They are so dull, they make tennis writers bang their heads against their laptops. From what we know, there are no books coming out about the men. They are lucky to make the white pages.

8   Did you know that the French Open women's final on NBC last month drew almost twice as many viewers as the men's? Did you know that Capriati's quar-terfinal Wimbledon match last week pulled in 25% more viewers than Pete Sampras's fourth-rounder the day before? Did you know that of the 10 most-searched-for athletes on Lycos during one week leading up to Wimbledon, four were women's tennis stars: Kournikova (No. 1), Hingis (5), Jelena Dokic (7) and Serena Williams (8)? None were male tennis players. Did you know that John McEnroe has said, "*Men* may eventually have to sue for equal pay"?

9   Did you know that last year, for the first time in history, more women's matches were played on the Stadium court at the U.S. Open than men's matches? Did you know that this year the U.S. Open, for the first time, has scheduled a final for prime time, and it's the women's, not the men's? Did you know that in an MSNBC survey last year, almost 70% of respondents preferred women's tennis to men's?

10   So what if the men play five sets to the women's three? *Ishtar* is longer than *Casablanca.* Which would you rather see? The pooh-bahs at the Australian Open and U.S. Open figured all this out long ago and raised their women's prize money to match the men's.

11   To recap, the women are more popular, make more headlines and play more entertaining tennis than the men, yet the women made $790,919 less over the Wimbledon fortnight than the men and $428,637 less at the French.

12   Wait, I take it all back. The women should not make as much as the men—they should make *more.*

QUESTIONS FOR READING

1.   What is Reilly's subject? What is the issue?
2.   What is Reilly's view of the women tennis stars? What is his view of the male players? How do their games differ?
3.   Which majors pay the players equally? Which do not?

QUESTIONS FOR REASONING AND ANALYSIS

1.   Analyze Reilly's argument. What is his claim? What type of evidence does he provide? What are his reasons for defending his claim?
2.   What counterargument does Reilly anticipate? How does he rebut it?
3.   Examine his style and tone. What is clever about his opening? What rhetorical strategies does he use?

QUESTIONS FOR REFLECTING AND WRITING

1. Has Reilly presented a convincing argument? If yes, what makes it convincing to you? If no, how would you rebut his argument? (Think: What type of audience might accept your counterargument? What readers might reject your reasoning?)

2. If tennis players should get equal pay at the major tournaments, does it follow that all professional players should get equal pay in their sports, regardless of gender? Consider other sports—soccer or golf or basketball, for example. Plan your argument, using one or more of these other sports. (You may want to go online to seek some current stats similar to Reilly's.)

TITLE IX QUOTA CREEP | JESSICA GAVORA

A Washington writer, Jessica Gavora is a member of the Independent Women's Forum and an analyst and speechwriter in the Department of Justice. She is also the author of *Tilting the Playing Field: Schools, Sports, Sex and Title IX* (2001). Her article on Title IX appeared June 11, 2002, on National Review Online.

PREREADING QUESTIONS Do you have any evidence from your experience that high school girls may be counseled into taking voc-ed courses such as cosmetology and other "female" courses rather than encouraged to take "male" courses? Should girls be encouraged to take plumbing and engineering voc-ed courses?

The 30th anniversary of Title IX, to be officially marked next week, has 1 been dominated by news of quotas instituted under the federal anti-sex-discrimination law decimating men's Olympic sports. Less noted but perhaps even more alarming, however, is the spread of Title IX sex quotas out of sports into other areas of education.

The latest offering from the National Women's Law Center (NWLC) is a per- 2 fect example of quota creep under Title IX. Last week a NWLC "*study*" charged high-school vocational and technical programs with "enduring sex discrimination." The evidence offered by the ladies of the NWLC? The shocking fact that girls dominate voc-ed classes like cosmetology and child care while boys form majorities of would-be plumbers, pipe-fitters, and engineers.

The Law Center's logic in charging pervasive sex discrimination in voca- 3 tional education is the same as that which is resulting in widespread destruction of men's athletic programs. Evidence that women are discriminated against cannot be found in the real world of education, where they are ever more successful. So it is found in numbers. A world free of sex discrimination, in the view of the National Women's Law Center, is a world in which participants in any given educational program perfectly match the number of males and females in the school itself. In this androgynous view of human nature, all girls and women and all boys and men are equally interested in and capable of playing lacrosse, excelling in physics, becoming electrical engineers or scoring 1600 on the SAT. Any failure of this perfect equality of interests and abilities to manifest itself in equality of athletic and academic achievement, then, is prima facie proof of illegal discrimination under Title IX.

4   On the basis of "data" culled from 12 states, the NWLC found that females are 96 percent of the students in cosmetology classes, 87 percent of students in child care, and 86 percent of students in classes that lead to jobs as health assistants. Boys, on the other hand, are 94 percent of plumbing and electrician students, 93 percent of future welders and carpenters, and—gasp!—92 percent of those studying automotive technologies.

5   All of this is actionable, so say the girls of the National Women's Law Center, because these insidious patterns aren't the result of choice but of enduring bias against women.

6   "Biased counseling, the provision of incomplete information to students on the consequences of their career training choices, sexual harassment of girls who enroll in non-traditional classes and other forms of discrimination conspire today to create a vocational system characterized by pervasive sex segregation," reads the NWLC report.

7   The same misogynistic counselors who are steering girls into "traditionally female" vocational tracks, however, are failing utterly in their conspiracy to keep women down in other areas of the academy. Somehow, despite the insidious forces feminists believe are arrayed against them, girls and women have managed to penetrate areas of "traditionally male" education and become the dominant sex in American education.

8   In grade school and high school, girls of all kinds and all ages in all subjects excel relative to boys. Girls get better grades than boys do. More girls than boys take courses in chemistry, algebra, geometry, precalculus, and biology. Girls and boys are equally likely to take trigonometry and calculus. Boys and girls took high-school advanced-placement tests at the same rate in 1984 but today 74 out of every 1,000 high-school girls take an AP exam compared to 58 out of every 1,000 high school boys.

9   Similarly, when they get to college, women increasingly participate in—and excel in—subject areas traditionally dominated by men. Women earn 46 percent of bachelor's degrees in science and engineering and 49 percent of business degrees. Women were one percent of engineering grads in 1972 and 17 percent in 1997. In the physical and computer sciences women have climbed from 15 percent of graduates 30 years ago to almost 40 percent of graduates today.

10   In fact, if anyone has a plausible claim of sex discrimination, it's the boys. While an equal number of girls and boys graduate from high school every year,overwhelmingly more women go on to college than men. Women are 56 percent of undergraduates today, a number the Department of Education estimates will rise to 58 percent by 2009. But hey, who's counting?

11   The gender-equity litigation industry has a penchant for uncovering patterns of Title IX-actionable discrimination that come in neat, politically relevant numbers. Thus, on the 25th anniversary of Title IX, the NWLC filed sex-discrimination complaints against 25 colleges and universities alleged to be shortchanging girls in the provision of athletic scholarships.

This anniversary, apparently unable to find 30 instances of even their ex- 12
pansive notion of discrimination, the gals of the NWLC have settled for the
number 12—twelve investigations in each of the Department of Education's
twelve regional offices of its Office for Civil Rights (OCR). Having lost their allies in the Washington offices of the OCR, feminists must now rely on the career education bureaucrats who remain in control of the OCR's regional offices.

And it's not hard to predict what remedy will be advocated, once these "in- 13
vestigations" are complete, to correct the sex imbalance in the nation's voca-
tional-education system. When they fail to convince high-school girls, who are
a declining share of voc-ed students, to take more classes in welding and auto
mechanics, activists will begin to agitate for boys' representation in these
classes to be curtailed in order to reach gender parity. What is happening today in collegiate athletic programs will soon be coming to high schools across
the country. Boys will lose. No girls will gain. But the law will be complied with.

Is this scenario the stuff of fantasy? Asked recently if anyone thought men's 14
sports teams would one day be eliminated because of Title IX, former senator
Birch Bayh, the law's original sponsor, said no: "That was not the purpose of Title IX. And that has been a very unfortunate aspect of this. The idea of Title IX
was not to give fewer opportunities to men; it was to make more opportunities
for women."

A look back at the history of Title IX makes the law's 30th anniversary 15
appear ominous.

QUESTIONS FOR READING

1. What is the occasion for Gavora's writing? What is her subject?
2. What data has the National Women's Law Center found about high school vocational education courses? What is this group's response to the data? How do
   they account for the choices that girls and boys are making in the courses they
   choose?
3. What statistics does Gavora present to show how girls are performing in academic courses in high school and college?
4. What percentage of college undergraduates are women?
5. What is Gavora's prediction of a remedy for the imbalance in voc-ed courses?

QUESTIONS FOR REASONING AND ANALYSIS

1. What is Gavora's claim? Where does she state it?
2. Does the author provide evidence that Title IX is "decimating men's Olympic
   sports"?
3. Gavora's data demonstrating that girls are "winning" the academic race are
   sound. However, how might one challenge the assertion that boys are now the
   ones discriminated against? (Look at her data for college degrees; look at David
   Sadker's essay on this subject, pp. 148–49)

4. How would you characterize the author's style and tone? Examine her word choice, especially as she refers to the NWLC.

5. Examine paragraph 12. Does Gavora present evidence to demonstrate that the NWLC has "lost their allies in the Washington offices of the OCR"?

QUESTIONS FOR REFLECTING AND WRITING

1. Evaluate Gavora's argument. Has she convinced you of quota creep in high school voc-ed courses? If yes, why? If no, how would you rebut her argument?

2. What may be some of the reasons why girls and boys select the voc-ed courses that they choose—or select an academic track instead? Girls' numbers in voc-ed courses are dropping, but this is not true for boys. Which voc-ed courses can lead to good paying jobs—the traditionally female or traditionally male courses? List as many possible causes as you can and then reflect on which may be most significant.

3. What is your reaction to the author's word choice regarding her opponents on this issue? What audience is likely to be amused or delighted by her style and tone? What readers may be turned off to her rhetorical strategies? Why?

U.S. women's 4 × 400 meters relay team is a winner at the 2000 Olympics. Many successful women athletes have won college scholarships as a result of Title IX.
(Fauqere/DPPI/SIPA Press)

SOLVING THE TITLE IX PROBLEM | FRANK DEFORD

A native of Baltimore, Maryland, Frank Deford (b. 1938) is a sportswriter, biographer, and novelist. He has written biographies of athletes such as Billie Jean King, Bill Tilden, and Arthur Ashe. His eighth novel is *An American Summer.* A member of the Hall of Fame of the National Sportscasters and Sportswriters Association, Deford is a senior contributing columnist for *Sports Illustrated,* a commentator for NPR's *Morning Edition,* and a correspondent on HBO's *RealSports with Bryant Gumbel.* His column on Title IX appeared on *SI Online* June 19, 2002.

PREREADING QUESTIONS What is good about the enforcing of Title IX? What problems have come with its enforcement? Are these problems that can be solved?

No question about equality is more nettlesome than Title IX's application 1 to athletics. The law says, indisputably, that equally proportionate amounts of athletic department money must be spent on both sexes. Because of that, in the years since the law started to be rigorously enforced, the number of girls playing sports in high school is up almost tenfold and the number of young women playing sports in college is up five times.

But this great advance in female participation has come at a price for *male* 2 athletes. College wrestling has been emasculated: 170 teams cut. Collegiate male gymnastics is headed for extinction, and the elimination of men's tennis, track and swimming—even baseball—continues apace. Critics of Title IX— which is 30 years old this week—call it reverse discrimination and "affirmative androgyny."

Look, goes the men's argument, more boys than girls care about sports. To 3 demand matching amounts of athletic funding for females is a tortured distortion of fairness. Would it make any sense to require equal funding for males in, say, dress making?

But then the counter argument: The reason fewer girls want to play sports 4 is that they never had the opportunity before. Give them the same chances as boys, and just as many of them will want to play.

For me, that's a more persuasive case. In this professed land of opportu- 5 nity, where discrimination against women in sports was overwhelming for so long, it's simply dog-in-the-manger to deny females the option of organized athletics because they haven't had the chance to find out if they'd like it.

Anyway, all this obscures the elephant in the room: football. It is that rare 6 male sport that has no female analogue. It also uses far more bodies and gobbles up far more money than any other sport. No schools would have to eliminate wrestling and gymnastics if they'd just trim some of the fat off football.

But football is a favored sport and politically powerful. Alumni love it and 7 old-boy athletic directors protect it. Football is a banner that schools wave at the beginning of the educational year to rally the troops, students and alumni alike. It identifies and unifies and helps fund-raise . . . if for all the wrong reasons. So, even if school football is indefensibly expensive as a *sport,* it is a distinct part of our American culture that serves various non-athletic purposes.

Not even basketball fulfills those, and, anyway, basketball requires fewer players and there are women's teams as well as men's.

8   No, football is the cheese that stands alone, and it would make sense for it to be separated from all other sports. Football is primarily a spectator sport. It's show biz. It has nothing to do with wrestling, men's or women's track, tennis, gymnastics or all other sports, which are intended primarily to be *played* by students, not *watched* by ticket buyers. Call football what it is: either an arm of annual giving or a form of institutional advertising. But get it out of the athletic department. Then, for both men and women, Title IX would have what it doesn't have now: a level playing field.

QUESTIONS FOR READING

1.   What is Deford's subject?
2.   What has been the result of Title IX for females? For males?
3.   Which college sport creates the biggest problem for college athletic departments needing to achieve gender equity?
4.   What are the apparent purposes of football? How does it differ from other college sports?

QUESTIONS FOR REASONING AND ANALYSIS

1.   What is Deford's claim? Where does he state it? What does he gain by the placing of his claim?
2.   What is the argument against Title IX? What is the argument for Title IX? Which is the more persuasive for Deford? Why?
3.   Evaluate Deford's solution to the problems caused by Title IX given the cost of college football. How does he defend his solution?

QUESTIONS FOR REFLECTING AND WRITING

1.   Has the author offered, in your view, a sensible, feasible solution to the conflicts created by Title IX demands? If yes, why? If not, how would you refute his argument?
2.   Before Deford's solution could be implemented, it would have to stand a court test—that it does not violate the equity standard established by Title IX. How would you defend the solution in court?
3.   To implement Deford's solution, college administrators and athletic directors would also have to accept the idea of separating football from the other college sports. Why might they have trouble accepting this solution? How would you try to convince them to embrace the solution?

MY PLAN TO PUT THE COLLEGE BACK IN COLLEGE SPORTS | GORDON GEE

With degrees in both law and education from Columbia University, Gordon Gee is in his third year as president of Vanderbilt University. Active on many commissions and boards, Gee is also the former president of Brown University, Ohio State University, the University of Colorado, and West Virginia University. His views on college football were published in the *Washington Post* on September 21, 2003.

PREREADING QUESTIONS How important is college football to you? Why is it important to many students and alums? Is it *too* important—especially at Division I colleges?

I like to win. I also like to sleep at night. But after 23 years leading universities, I find it increasingly hard to do both. 1

This has been the most ignominious year in recent memory for college sports. We've seen coaches behaving badly, academic fraud, graft, possibly even murder. Clearly, the system is broken, and fixing it will require more than sideline cheering. 2

That's why, last week, we at Vanderbilt announced that we would replace our traditional athletic department with a new body that is more connected to the mission of the university and more accountable to the institution's academic leadership. We'll no longer need an athletic director. We're not eliminating varsity sports, mind you, or relinquishing our membership in the highly competitive Southeastern Conference. Rather, we're making a clear statement that the "student-athlete"—a term invented decades ago when college sports was faced with another seemingly endless parade of scandals—belongs back in the university. 3

Many athletic departments exist as separate, almost semi-autonomous fiefdoms within universities and there is the feeling that the name on the football jersey is little more than a "franchise" for sports fans. As Bill Bowen and Sarah Levin point out in their new book, *Reclaiming the Game: College Sports and Educational Values,* student-athletes are increasingly isolated, even at the best schools in the country. They do not participate in the extracurricular activities that are so important for personal growth. They miss out on opportunities to study abroad or have internships. They spend too much time in special athletic facilities that are off-limits to the rest of the student body. And their world can too often be defined by coaches' insatiable demands for practice and workout sessions. 4

True, this is the cost of staying competitive in college sports, where tens of millions of dollars are at stake. But should it be? Over the years I have gotten to know thousands of student-athletes. They are as different as any group of individuals could be. What they have in common, though, is a sense that they missed out on an important part of the college experience by focusing only on sports. They also lose out by being stripped of their responsibilities as citizens of the university when we say that "all will be forgiven" as long as their performance on the field is up to snuff. 5

6   This must change. At Vanderbilt, that means ensuring that every student, every athlete, is part of a vibrant academic and social community.

7   Shifting Vanderbilt's athletics program to our division of student life and university affairs is merely a step—perhaps bold, perhaps quixotic—in the much-needed reform of intercollegiate athletics. We took this step mindful that Vanderbilt is in an unusual position. It is a highly selective private university with an athletics program untarnished by scandal; our student-athletes graduate at rates that are among the best in the country; and we have loyal, generous supporters who have blessed us with excellent facilities. We can do things here that other universities can't or won't.

8   I will say this: After our announcement, I received many phone calls from college presidents who said, "You go, Gordon. Walk off the cliff, and if you succeed, we will be right behind."

9   In recent years, there have been a number of well-meaning and forceful efforts to reform college athletics, but they have not gone far enough. It is time for all those who are concerned about the future of our enterprise to get serious about addressing the crisis of credibility we now face. College presidents, working together, should commit themselves to the following reforms:

10   First, all students who participate in intercollegiate sports should be required to meet the requirements of a core curriculum. The "permanent jock-ocracy" has for too long made a mockery of academic standards when it comes to athletes. We need to end sham courses, manufactured majors, degree programs that would embarrass a mail-order diploma mill, and the relentless pressure on faculty members to ease student-athletes through their classes.

11   Second, colleges should make a binding four-year commitment to students on athletic scholarships. One of the dirty secrets of intercollegiate athletics is that such scholarships are renewed year-to-year. A bad season? Injury? Poor relationship with a coach? Your scholarship can be yanked with very little notice. Rather than cynically offering the promise of academic enrichment, colleges should back up the promise so long as a student remains in good academic standing.

12   Third, the number of athletic scholarships a school can award should be tied to the graduation rates of its athletes in legitimate academic programs. If a school falls below a threshold graduation rate, it should be penalized by having to relinquish a certain number of scholarships for the next year's entering class. A version of this proposal is part of a reform package now snaking its way through the NCAA.

13   Fourth, graduation rates should be tied to television and conference revenues. If money is the mother's milk of college athletics, then access to it should be contingent on fulfilling the most basic mission of a university—educating students.

14   Finally, college presidents and others need to take a good look at the system we have created for ourselves, in which the professional sports leagues have enjoyed a free feeder system that exploits young people and corrupts otherwise noble institutions. We have maintained the fantasy for far too long that a big-time athletics program is for the students, the alumni, and, at public

universities, even for the legislators. It is time for us to call it what it has sadly become: a prep league for the pros, who have taken far more than they have given back. We should demand nothing less than a system in which student-athletes are an integral part of the academic institutions whose names and colors they so proudly wear on game day.

QUESTIONS FOR READING

1. What is Gee's subject? (State it as a problem.)
2. Why, according to Gee, are there problems in college athletics? What, specifically, are the problems for the athletes themselves?
3. What is Gee changing at Vanderbilt?
4. What are the five reforms he recommends for all colleges?

QUESTIONS FOR REASONING AND ANALYSIS

1. What is Gee's claim? (State it as a problem/solution assertion.)
2. In paragraph 7, Gee explains the first move toward reform that he has made at Vanderbilt. He then describes his university. Why? How are his remarks conciliatory? What does he seek to accomplish?
3. Examine Gee's grounds. He does not provide statistics and refers to current problems in only a general way. Why? What does he expect his readers to know?
4. What is Gee's reasoning in support of his claim? What values have been lost in the development of college athletics? Why must they be reinstated?

QUESTIONS FOR REFLECTING AND WRITING

1. Do you agree with the author that many college athletes are shortchanged in their college experience and education? Do you agree that this is a problem? Why or why not?
2. If you agree with President Gee that there are problems, do you agree with his reform proposals? Study them both individually and as a package. Do you accept them all? If so, why? If not, how would you challenge his proposed solution? Do you think that some of the package is useful and workable, but not the whole package? If so, why? What would you support? What reject? Think of yourself as in a debate with Gee, discussing each item of his reform package, one at a time.
3. What is the role or purpose of the university? What is the role or purpose of sports as a part of the university?

EDUCATION, ATHLETICS: THE ODD COUPLE | SALLY JENKINS

A sportswriter for the *Washington Post* for a number of years, Sally Jenkins left in 1990 to work at *Sports Illustrated* and write a number of books, mostly about sports figures. She has a book written with Dean Smith about his years in college basketball.

In 2000 she published, with Lance Armstrong, *It's Not about the Bike: My Journey Back to Life*. She has also written *Men Will Be Boys: The Modern Woman Explains Football and Other Amusing Male Rituals* (1996). In 2000 Jenkins returned to the *Post*. The following column appeared there on September 13, 2002.

PREREADING QUESTIONS   Explain Jenkins's title; what does it suggest her attitude will be toward college and athletics? How big are the problems with college athletics?

1   It's knee-jerk time in college athletics again. Ohio State and Maurice Clarett are examples of everything wrong, while Vanderbilt has preserved the sanctity of the academic temple. For days now, we've enjoyed black and white thinking, moral certainty, and stern reform-mindedness. But the last thing we can apply to college sports any more is absolutism. Nothing is as good or bad as it seems—nor is the Ivy League, as it turns out.

2   Whatever you're sure of on the subject of college sports, you will certainly question it after the publication of a book called *Reclaiming the Game*, by William G. Bowen and Sarah A. Levin. The book, which will appear next week from Princeton University Press, takes a hard-eyed look at the Ivies and other so-called "elite" colleges and reaches some startling conclusions: Recruited athletes are four times more likely to be admitted to the Ivies than other students, they have lower SAT scores than their peers by 119–165 points, and they chronically under-perform academically. Seem familiar? It sounds like Division I-A.

3   In other words, even the Ivies are getting it wrong?

4   It depends on your view. Every scandal, controversy and ill in the NCAA always boils down to the same question: What are college athletics really for? What are they supposed to be, and what values should they represent? This is where the real trouble begins, because college athletics have increasingly become a matter of competing moralities. And they have always been extremely human, corrupt, and mistaken-prone endeavors, too.

5   People who want to apply pat reforms or even a consistent philosophy to college athletics are simply barking up the wrong tree—and perhaps the worst tree we can bark up these days is to assume that some schools have found the higher moral ground.

6   One of the more interesting conclusions reached by Bowen, a former president of Princeton who is now head of the Andrew W. Mellon Foundation, and co-author Levin, is that academic hypocrisy is rampant.

7   "Truth-telling is important, especially for institutions that pride themselves, as colleges and universities should, on inculcating respect for evidence and for their own unequivocal commitments to honest rendering of facts and to faithful reporting," they write. "But there is something unsettling about reading stories describing the 'purity' of athletics at the non-scholarship schools when so many of their leaders are well aware of the compromises that are being made in fielding teams. There is enough cynicism today about the capacity of institutions (whether they be corporations, churches, colleges and universities, governmental entities, or foundations) to be what they claim to be . . ."

8   It's difficult to read that passage and not think about Vanderbilt, which has presented itself as a paragon of academic virtue this week, while Ohio State, a

very good school, is having a difficult time fighting off the taint of academic scandal. Ohio State Athletic Director Andy Geiger suspended Clarett for accepting money against NCAA rules. Meantime, Vanderbilt Chancellor Gordon Gee announced he was doing away with his athletic department.

But it turns out Gee's great reform basically amounts to a symbolic name 9 change—he's not cutting any sports, or scholarships. He accompanied it with a speech that smacked of grandstanding. "For too long, college athletics has been segregated from the core mission of the university," Gee intoned.

Gee sounds like a personable, well-intentioned guy. But he doesn't sound 10 anymore personable or well-intentioned than Geiger, who insists Ohio State is basically clean and the Clarett affair was isolated.

"I hope we get investigated up the yin-yang," Geiger said. "I'd submit we 11 don't have a systemic issue, we have a maverick deal, and it's been more than difficult. But it's not because we're corrupt."

The funny thing is, Gee wasn't always so reform-minded and he's no 12 stranger to big athletic programs. He once was president of Ohio State, where he actually hired Geiger, and he also presided over West Virginia, and Colorado, when the Buffaloes enjoyed both national championship and scandal under Bill McCartney. You have to wonder if, now that he's at Vandy, he's simply playing to a new crowd.

Geiger has a varied resume too; he's been all over Division I-A, and his 13 record for integrity is pretty good. He was the former athletic director at Stanford University, until he got tired of what he calls "Stanford-speak" and decided he wanted to work for public universities. He went to Maryland, and then Ohio State.

Here is the central problem with any reform of college athletes: The proper 14 role of college sports on a campus depends entirely on what group is evaluating the question. Is the athletic scholarship a scam, or a tool of affirmative action? Some say Ohio State was wrong to give a scholarship to Clarett, a guy who didn't even want to be there. Others such as Geiger argue that to do away with scholarships and academic exceptions would be to kill opportunity. He also maintains that "athletics have some intellectual content unto themselves."

There are differences even within the same programs. Ohio State, for in- 15 stance, will have 105,000 people at the football stadium on Saturday, and about 200 at a women's soccer game. Yet both sports are supposed to be part of the same school, program, values, effort, and management.

Any truly intelligent discussion of college athletics may require what Ger- 16 maine Greer once called, in a discussion completely unrelated to football, "myriad-mindedness." Increasingly, if we're going to solve the "problem" of athletics we have to accept differing value systems and accept the tension between competing moralities. The NCAA is comprised of public schools, and private, of large corporatized universities and small precious intellectual havens, of Northeastern industrials and Midwestern agriculturals—and it's the clash between them that makes their games so interesting.

What are college sports for? Maybe we should first ask what a college is 17 for. The chief event that occurs in college is the emancipation of your head. The main undertaking of a student is understanding, and this is why no one expects him or her to come up with anything resembling consistency; they're too busy questioning and rejecting. College is also where scruple and low-level crime duel. Youth carouses un-enforced by parents or much else in the way of authority. Hopefully, the outcome of this formative emancipation is the development of one's own interior hall monitor. But sometimes it produces a communist, or a car wreck.

18   This is the risk we take by having colleges at all. The same principle could be applied to games that undergraduates play.

QUESTIONS FOR READING

1. What is Jenkins's subject? (Be more precise than college sports.)
2. What does the book *Reclaiming the Game* reveal? From the title, what do you think is the authors' view regarding college sports?
3. What, according to Jenkins, is at the core of all debates over college athletics?
4. Who are Andy Geiger and Maurice Clarett? What happened at Ohio State?
5. What is the connection between Geiger at Ohio State and Chancellor Gee at Vanderbilt? What seems to be the author's attitude toward Gee?
6. Why is discussion of reforming college athletics difficult, in Jenkins's view?
7. What, in her view, are colleges for?

QUESTIONS FOR REASONING AND ANALYSIS

1. What is Jenkins's thesis? What are the main points in her argument?
2. Why does Jenkins present information about Gee's past positions and appointments? How does this serve as evidence in support of her thesis?
3. Explain the concept of "myriad-mindedness" as it applies to solving problems of college sports.
4. Examine Jenkins's images in paragraph 17. What makes them effective in support of her concept of college?

QUESTIONS FOR REFLECTING AND WRITING

1. Evaluate Jenkins's argument. Do you agree with her approach to problems in college athletics? If yes, why? If no, how would you rebut her argument?
2. The sports pages offer an almost continual flow of rule breaking and scandals (including, in 2003, murder and attempted cover-up at Baylor University) in college athletics, yet Jenkins argues that it is not as bad as it seems. How might you defend her assessment? If you disagree, how would you respond to her?
3. What is the role or purpose of the university? What is the role or purpose of sports as part of the university? Do we have to " accept the tension between competing moralities," or can (should?) we agree on the basic values and goals of college and college sports?

CHAPTER 16

Open Society vs. Homeland Security: The American Balancing Act

The seven articles in this chapter explore issues relating to immigration into the United States, to noncitizens within the country, and to the effects of the melting pot. The authors differ in their views on immigrants—legal, illegal, and "short-term legal"—and on their approach to a number of interrelated issues that we often collect, perhaps foolishly, under the broad heading "immigration."

PREREADING QUESTIONS

1. What do you know about immigration laws and the status and problems of current immigrants in the United States?

2. How much of what you know is based on study? On experience? On ideas expressed by family and friends? On what you have seen and heard on TV? Of these various sources, which may be the most credible?

3. What do we gain by welcoming new immigrants to the United States?

4. Who gains and who loses from the presence of illegal aliens?

5. In what ways has immigration in the past thirty years changed the faces of America? What will be the impact on situations that have involved racial/ethnic preferences?

6. If you are a recent immigrant, how might your views on these topics differ from those whose families have been U.S. citizens for at least two generations—or vice versa?

Websites Relevant to This Chapter's Topic

Federation for American Immigrations Reform (FAIR)

http://www.fairus.org

This is a source of facts, legislation, and issues. FAIR is an advocate for more restricted and controlled immigration.

ACLU and Immigrants' Rights

www.aclu.org/issues/immigrant.hmir.html

Among its many activities, the American Civil Liberties Union advocates immigrants' rights. Their site provides news updates, reference sources, and briefing papers.

THE BORDER PATROL STATE | LESLIE MARMON SILKO

An English professor (University of Arizona) and writer, Leslie Marmon Silko (b. 1948) is the recipient of several grants and awards for her poetry. Her first novel, *Ceremony* (1977), was praised for its portrayal of life on an Indian reservation. Other works include *Storyteller* (1981), a collection of her poems and short stories, and the novel *Almanac of the Dead* (1991). "The Border Patrol State," based in part on her own experience driving in the Southwest, was published on October 17, 1994, in *Nation* magazine.

PREREADING QUESTIONS Have you ever been bullied by a person or group at school or in your neighborhood? If so, how did the situation make you feel? If not, can you try to imagine how someone might feel in that situation?

1   I used to travel the highways of New Mexico and Arizona with a wonderful sensation of absolute freedom as I cruised down the open road and across the

vast desert plateaus. On the Laguna Pueblo reservation, where I was raised, the people were patriotic despite the way the U.S. government had treated Native Americans. As proud citizens, we grew up believing the freedom to travel was our inalienable right, a right that some Native Americans had been denied in the early twentieth century. Our cousin, old Bill Pratt, used to ride his horse 300 miles overland from Laguna, New Mexico, to Prescott, Arizona, every summer to work as a fire lookout.

In school in the 1950s, we were taught that our right to travel from state to state without special papers or threat of detainment was a right that citizens under communist and totalitarian governments did not possess. That wide open highway told us we were U.S. citizens; we were free. . . .

Not so long ago, my companion Gus and I were driving south from Albuquerque, returning to Tucson after a book promotion for the paperback edition of my novel *Almanac of the Dead.* I had settled back and gone to sleep while Gus drove, but I was awakened when I felt the car slowing to a stop. It was nearly midnight on New Mexico State Road 26, a dark, lonely stretch of two-lane highway between Hatch and Deming. When I sat up, I saw the headlights and emergency flashers of six vehicles—Border Patrol cars and a van were blocking both lanes of the highway. Gus stopped the car and rolled down the window to ask what was wrong. But the closest Border Patrolman and his companion did not reply; instead, the first agent ordered us to "step out of the car." Gus asked why, but his question seemed to set them off. Two more Border Patrol agents immediately approached our car, and one of them snapped, "Are you looking for trouble?" as if he would relish it.

I will never forget that night beside the highway. There was an awful feeling of menace and violence straining to break loose. It was clear that the uniformed men would be only too happy to drag us out of the car if we did not speedily comply with their request (asking a question is tantamount to resistance, it seems). So we stepped out of the car and they motioned for us to stand on the shoulder of the road. The night was very dark, and no other traffic had come down the road since we had been stopped. All I could think about was a book I had read—*Nunca Más*—the official report of a human rights commission that investigated and certified more than 12,000 "disappearances" during Argentina's "dirty war" in the late 1970s.

The weird anger of these Border Patrolmen made me think about descriptions in the report of Argentine police and military officers who became addicted to interrogation, torture and the murder that followed. When the military and police ran out of political suspects to torture and kill, they resorted to the random abduction of citizens off the streets. I thought how easy it would be for the Border Patrol to shoot us and leave our bodies and car beside the highway, like so many bodies found in these parts and ascribed to "drug runners."

Two other Border Patrolmen stood by the white van. The one who had asked if we were looking for trouble ordered his partner to "get the dog," and from the back of the van another patrolman brought a small female German shepherd on a leash. The dog apparently did not heel well enough to suit him, and the handler jerked the leash. They opened the doors of our car and pulled the dog's head into it, but I saw immediately from the expression in her eyes that the dog hated them, and that she would not serve them. When she showed no interest in the inside of our car, they brought her around back to the trunk, near where we were standing. They half-dragged her up into the trunk, but still she did not indicate any stowed-away human beings or illegal drugs.

7   Their mood got uglier; the officers seemed outraged that the dog could not find any contraband, and they dragged her over to us and commanded her to sniff our legs and feet. To my relief, the strange violence the Border Patrol agents had focused on us now seemed shifted to the dog. I no longer felt so strongly that we would be murdered. We exchanged looks—the dog and I. She was afraid of what they might do, just as I was. The dog's handler jerked the leash sharply as she sniffed us, as if to make her perform better, but the dog refused to accuse us: She had an innate dignity that did not permit her to serve the murderous impulses of those men. I can't forget the expression in the dog's eyes; it was as if she were embarrassed to be associated with them. I had a small amount of medicinal marijuana in my purse that night, but she refused to expose me. I am not partial to dogs, but I will always remember the small German shepherd that night.

8   Unfortunately, what happened to me is an everyday occurrence here now. Since the 1980s, on top of greatly expanding border checkpoints, the Immigration and Naturalization Service and the Border Patrol have implemented policies that interfere with the rights of U.S. citizens to travel freely within our borders. I.N.S. agents now patrol all interstate highways and roads that lead to or from the U.S.-Mexico Border in Texas, New Mexico, Arizona and California. Now, when you drive east from Tucson on Interstate 10 toward El Paso, you encounter an I.N.S. check station outside Las Cruces, New Mexico. When you drive north from Las Cruces up Interstate 25, two miles north of the town of Truth or Consequences, the highway is blocked with orange emergency barriers, and all traffic is diverted into a two-lane Border Patrol checkpoint—ninety-five miles north of the U.S.-Mexico border.

9   I was detained once at Truth or Consequences, despite my and my companion's Arizona driver's licenses. Two men, both Chicanos, were detained at the same time, despite the fact that they too presented ID and spoke English without the thick Texas accents of the Border Patrol agents. While we were stopped, we watched as other vehicles—whose occupants were white—were waved through the checkpoint. White people traveling with brown people, however, can expect to be stopped on suspicion they work with the sanctuary movement, which shelters refugees. White people who appear to be clergy, those who wear ethnic clothing or jewelry and women with very long hair or very short hair (they could be nuns) are also frequently detained; white men with beards or men with long hair are likely to be detained, too, because Border Patrol agents have "profiles" of "those sorts" of white people who may help political refugees. (Most of the political refugees from Guatemala and El Salvador are Native American or mestizo [of mixed Indian and European heritage] because the indigenous people of the Americas have continued to

resist efforts by invaders to displace them from their ancestral lands.) Alleged increase in illegal immigration by people of Asian ancestry means that the Border Patrol now routinely detains anyone who appears to be Asian or part Asian, as well.

Once your car is diverted from the Interstate Highway into the checkpoint 10 area, you are under the control of the Border Patrol, which in practical terms exercises a power that no highway patrol or city patrolman possesses: They are willing to detain anyone, for no apparent reason. Other law-enforcement officers need a shred of probable cause in order to detain anyone. On the books, so does the Border Patrol; but on the road, it's another matter. They'll order you to stop your car and step out; then they'll ask you to open the trunk. If you ask why or request a search warrant, you'll be told that they'll have to have a dog sniff the car before they can request a search warrant, and the dog might not get there for two or three hours. The search warrant might require an hour or two past that. They make it clear that if you force them to obtain a search warrant for the car, they will make you submit to a strip search as well.

Traveling in the open, though, the sense of violation can be even worse. 11 Never mind high-profile cases like that of former Border Patrol agent Michael Elmer, acquitted of murder by claiming self-defense, despite admitting that as an officer he shot an "illegal" immigrant in the back and then hid the body, which remained undiscovered until another Border Patrolman reported the event. (Last month, Elmer was convicted of reckless endangerment in a separate incident, for shooting at least ten rounds from his M-16 too close to a group of immigrants as they were crossing illegally into Nogales in March 1992.) Or that in El Paso, a high school football coach driving a vanload of his players in full uniform was pulled over on the freeway and a Border Patrol agent put a cocked revolver to his head. (The football coach was Mexican-American, as were most of the players in his van; the incident eventually caused a federal judge to issue a restraining order against the Border Patrol.) We've a mountain of personal experiences like that which never make the newspapers. A history professor at U.C.L.A. told me she had been traveling by train from Los Angeles to Albuquerque twice a month doing research. On each of her trips, she had noticed that the Border Patrol agents were at the station in Albuquerque scrutinizing the passengers. Since she is six feet tall and of Irish and German ancestry, she was not particularly concerned. Then one day when she stepped off the train in Albuquerque, two Border Patrolmen accosted her, wanting to know what she was doing, and why she was traveling between Los Angeles and Albuquerque twice a month. She presented identification and an explanation deemed "suitable" by the agents, and was allowed to go about her business.

Just the other day, I mentioned to a friend that I was writing this article and 12 he told me about his 73-year-old father, who is half Chinese and had set out alone by car from Tucson to Albuquerque the week before. His father had become confused by road construction and missed a turnoff from Interstate 10 to Interstate 25; when he turned around and circled back, he missed the turnoff a second time. But when he looped back for yet another try, Border Patrol agents stopped him and forced him to open his trunk. After they satisfied themselves that he was not smuggling Chinese immigrants, they sent him on his way. He was so rattled by the event that he had to be driven home by his daughter.

13   This is the police state that has developed in the southwestern United States since the 1980s. No person, no citizen, is free to travel without the scrutiny of the Border Patrol. In the city of South Tucson, where 80 percent of the respondents were Chicano or Mexicano, a joint research project by the University of Wisconsin and the University of Arizona recently concluded that one out of every five people there had been detained, mistreated verbally or nonverbally, or questioned by I.N.S. agents in the past two years.

14   Manifest Destiny may lack its old grandeur of theft and blood—"lock the door" is what it means now, with racism a trump card to be played again and again, shamelessly, by both major political parties. "Immigration," like "street crime" and "welfare fraud," is a political euphemism that refers to people of color. Politicians and media people talk about "illegal aliens" to dehumanize and demonize undocumented immigrants, who are for the most part people of color. Even in the days of Spanish and Mexican rule, no attempts were made to interfere with the flow of people and goods from south to north and north to south. It is the U.S. government that has continually attempted to sever contact between the tribal people north of the border and those to the south.*

15   Now that the "Iron Curtain" is gone, it is ironic that the U.S. government and its Border Patrol are constructing a steel wall ten feet high to span sections of the border with Mexico. While politicians and multinational corporations extol the virtues of NAFTA [the North American Free Trade Agreement] and "free trade" (in goods, not flesh), the ominous curtain is already up in a six-mile section of the border crossing at Mexicali; two miles are being erected but are not yet finished at Naco; and at Nogales, sixty miles south of Tucson, the steel wall has been all rubber-stamped and awaits construction. Like the pathetic multi-million-dollar "antidrug" border surveillance balloons that were continually deflated by high winds and made only a couple of meager interceptions before they blew away, the fence along the border is a theatrical prop, a bit of pork for contractors. Border entrepreneurs have already used blowtorches to cut passageways through the fence to collect "tolls" and are doing a brisk business. Back in Washington, the I.N.S. announces a $300 million computer contract to modernize its record-keeping and Congress passes a crime bill that shunts $255 million to the I.N.S. for 1995, $181 million earmarked for border control, which is to include 700 new partners for the men who stopped Gus and me in our travels, and the history professor, and my friends' father, and as many as they could from South Tucson.

16   It is no use; borders haven't worked, and they won't work, not now, as the indigenous people of the Americas reassert their kinship and solidarity with

---

* The Treaty of Guadalupe Hidalgo, signed in 1848, recognizes the right of the Tobano O'Odom (Papago) people to move freely across the U.S.-Mexico border without documents. A treaty with Canada guarantees similar rights to those of the Iroquois nation in traversing the U.S.-Canada border.

one another. A mass migration is already under way; its roots are not simply economic. The Uto-Aztecan languages are spoken as far north as Taos Pueblo near the Colorado border, all the way south to Mexico City. Before the arrival of the Europeans, the indigenous communities throughout this region not only conducted commerce, the people shared cosmologies, and oral narratives about the Maize Mother, the Twin Brothers and their Grandmother, Spider Woman, as well as Quetzalcoatl the benevolent snake. The great human migration within the Americas cannot be stopped; human beings are natural forces of the Earth, just as rivers and winds are natural forces.

Deep down the issue is simple: The so-called "Indian Wars" from the days 17 of Sitting Bull and Red Cloud have never really ended in the Americas. The Indian people of southern Mexico, of Guatemala and those left in El Salvador, too, are still fighting for their lives and for their land against the "cavalry" patrols sent out by the government of those lands. The Americas are Indian country, and the "Indian problem" is not about to go away.

One evening at sundown, we were stopped in traffic at a railroad crossing 18 in downtown Tucson while a freight train passed us, slowly gaining speed as it headed north to Phoenix. In the twilight I saw the most amazing sight: Dozens of human beings, mostly young men, were riding the train; everywhere, on flat cars, inside open boxcars, perched on top of boxcars, hanging off ladders on tank cars and between boxcars. I couldn't count fast enough, but I saw fifty or sixty people headed north. They were dark young men, Indian and mestizo; they were smiling and a few of them waved at us in our cars. I was reminded of the ancient story of Aztlán, told by the Aztecs but known in other Uto-Aztecan communities as well. Aztlán is the beautiful land to the north, the origin place of the Aztec people. I don't remember how or why the people left Aztlán to journey farther south, but the old story says that one day, they will return.

QUESTIONS FOR READING

1. What feelings did Silko sense among the Border Patrolmen? How is the mood of her experience developed by the details regarding the dog?
2. Where are drivers being stopped? What kinds of people are detained? What do they have in common?
3. What, in Silko's view, is the political purpose in reference to immigration and illegal aliens?
4. Why, according to the author, will borders fail to work in the Southwest?

QUESTIONS FOR REASONING AND ANALYSIS

1. What is Silko's claim?
2. What does the author accomplish in her first two paragraphs? Can you predict what kind of discussion or argument will follow her opening?
3. In the closing paragraph, Silko describes Mexicans riding on a train from Tucson to Phoenix. For her, the picture is a positive one. Why? Is it likely to be a positive picture for all readers? Why or why not?

4. In your view, what images are especially powerful in this essay? Why?

5. What type of evidence does the author present to support her claim? Is her approach effective? Why or why not?

QUESTIONS FOR REFLECTING AND WRITING

1. Should Americans of color be harassed by police officers in situations in which they might be breaking the law? Why or why not?

2. Should the Mexican-American border be open? In what sense do you mean "open"? Explain your position.

DON'T WOBBLE ON IMMIGRATION | BEN WATTENBERG

A senior fellow at the American Enterprise Institute, Ben Wattenberg (b. 1933) is moderator of the weekly PBS television program *Think Tank*. He also writes a weekly syndicated newspaper column and is the author of *The Birth Dearth*. The following article on immigration was published in the *Washington Post,* March 30, 2002.

PREREADING QUESTIONS Is it logical for a country of immigrants to fear immigration? Why or why not?

1   President Bush and others have said we are at war to save our civilization— that is, Western civilization. The events of Sept. 11 were perpetrated by Muslim radicals. All were foreigners; some were here illegally.

2   Understandably, many immigrants have been detained. Deportations of illegal immigrants have accelerated here and in Europe. There is speculation about an anti-immigrant backlash. The quadrennial candidate Pat Buchanan's book was high on bestseller lists. Its title says it all: *The Death of the West: How Dying Populations and Immigrant Invasions Imperil Our Country and Civilization.*

3   If we're talking about the survival and, one hopes, the extension, of Western civilization, we should be talking about immigration and demographics. Let's get some numbers straight. Birth and fertility rates in Europe and Japan are unprecedented and incredible.

4   Over time, it takes 2.1 children per woman just to keep a society at zero growth, the "replacement level," absent immigration. The total fertility rate of Europe and Japan is 1.3 children per woman—on a 50-year slide. Europe has begun "de-populating"; Japan will follow soon, according to U.N. projections, which show Europe losing 124 million people by 2050, while its median age climbs to about 50.

5   Economic markets are responsive to change, but this decline could pose a challenge. How would you like to be a home builder in a society that is losing significant population every year? Where do the public funds for the military come from when there aren't even enough worker bees to provide pensions for the senior bees? These are not the best of all possible allies. America may have to move further toward a go-it-alone position.

6   Fortunately, the other part of the West, the English-speaking settler nations—Canada, Australia and the United States—have different demographic

portraits. Why? Because, in moderate numbers, they take in immigrants. And the numbers are only moderate. In our peak immigration decade of 1900–1910, America accepted immigrants amounting to 1 percent of its population, each year. The rate today is one-third that.

America's fertility rate has averaged about two children per woman in re- 7 cent years—below replacement. Over time, if it weren't for immigration, America would stop growing and perhaps begin slowly depopulating. Such a no-growth, aging America could find it hard to lead in what may be a long struggle among civilizations, some of which, unlike the West, are projected to grow for several decades before leveling off.

The flash point of American immigration today concerns Mexicans. To 8 those, such as Buchanan, who fear immigration, they appear as an inexorable Third World tan tide, intent on recapturing the American Southwest, ready to swamp Western values, the splitting wedge in a majority nonwhite America of the future.

Bunk. America takes in about a million immigrants each year, of whom 9 about 45 percent are from Latin America, of whom Mexicans account for somewhat less than half, perhaps 25 percent to 30 percent of the total when illegals are counted. The other 70 percent to 75 percent of immigrants to this country come from everywhere, including 30 percent from Asia.

Nonwhite? Half of Mexicans are classified white. Third World? Mexico's per 10 capita income is above $5,000; it now has "investment grade" bond status. Mexico is a member of the Organization for Economic Cooperation and Development, the "First World" economic club. It is a real democracy. Its fertility rate has fallen from 6.5 to 2.5 children per woman in 30 years, and it is expected to go below replacement soon.

Invasion? How many invaders compete to mow the lawns and clean the 11 dishes of those they have invaded? Mexican Americans serve disproportionately in this country's armed services and have won a disproportionate share of medals for gallantry in combat.

Assimilation? By the third generation just about all Mexican Americans 12 speak English, and Mexican grandparents often complain that their grandchildren speak no Spanish.

Not Western? Scholars say the *padrones* of Latin America, the hegemonic 13 roots of the culture, are language and religion. The languages are Spanish or Portuguese, European tongues. The religion is Catholic, with growing evangelical Protestant sects.

Now is not the time to go wobbly on immigration. It is the key to Ameri- 14 can growth and prosperity. If we are indeed in for a war to preserve Western civilization, we'll need every straight-shooting, red-blooded, patriotic soul we can get. (Remember immigrants *choose* the American way of life.)

Immigrants are also our best salesmen; no one tells the American story bet- 15 ter. And we're going to need all the salesmen we can get as we go about the business of recruiting economic, cultural and military allies—allies who believe in liberty, as we do.

QUESTIONS FOR READING

1. What is America's fertility rate? Without immigration, what will happen to the United States?
2. What is the rate of immigration, per year, in the United States today?
3. What, according to the author, seems to be the problem that some see with immigration? What do these people fear?
4. What percentage of yearly immigrants are Mexican? What percent are Asian?
5. What is happening in Mexico today?
6. What are Wattenberg's answers to fears of "invasion," "assimilation," and "not Western"?

QUESTIONS FOR REASONING AND ANALYSIS

1. Where does Wattenberg state his claim?
2. One could say that Wattenberg's only defense of his claim is in his last two paragraphs. What does he do in the first 13 paragraphs to support his argument?
3. The author begins paragraph 9 with the word *bunk*. What does he mean here?
4. Wattenberg begins four paragraphs (10–13) with a one- or two-word question. What is effective about this strategy?

QUESTIONS FOR REFLECTING AND WRITING

1. Evaluate Wattenberg's argument. Does he effectively respond to the anxieties of many who oppose immigration? Why or why not?
2. Have you thought about immigration in the context of replacing the Western depopulation trend? Is this a helpful way to examine the issue?
3. What do you want the administration to do about illegal Mexican immigrants? How can you make your views known to the federal government? Reflect on specific actions you can take to voice your opinions on this topic.

CONFRONTING THE PROBLEM OF ILLEGAL MEXICAN MIGRATION TO THE U.S. | DANIEL T. GRISWOLD

A former editorial page editor, Daniel Griswold holds an undergraduate degree in journalism from the University of Wisconsin and a master's from the London School of Economics. He is currently associate director of the Center for Trade Policy Studies at the Cato Institute in Washington, DC. He frequently appears on radio and TV talk shows, including the Fox News Channel and Voice of America. He has coedited *Economic Casualties: How U.S. Foreign Policy Undermines Trade, Growth, and Liberty* (1999). The following article was published March 2003 in *USA Today Magazine*.

PREREADING QUESTIONS What, in your view, are some of the problems of illegal aliens from Mexico? Do you have any solutions to these problems?

America's immigration laws are colliding with reality, and reality is winning. 1
Today, approximately 8,000,000 people live in the U.S. without legal documents, and each year the number grows by an estimated 250,000 as more enter illegally or overstay their visas. Over half of the illegal immigrants entering and already here come from Mexico.

In February 2001, Pres. George W. Bush and his Mexican counterpart, 2
Vicente Fox, agreed at a conference in Guanajuato, Mexico, to work together to fix the problem. Then, on Sept. 7, 2001, after meeting for three days in Washington, Bush and Fox "renewed their commitment to forging new and realistic approaches to migration to ensure it is safe, orderly, legal, and dignified." They endorsed an immigration policy that includes "matching willing workers with willing employers; serving the social and economic needs of both countries; respecting the human dignity of all migrants, regardless of their status; recognizing the contribution migrants make to enriching both societies; [and] shared responsibility for ensuring migration takes place through safe and legal channels." However, the terrorist attacks on the World Trade Center and Pentagon four days later knocked those plans off the burner entirely. Now, more than a year after those events, the underlying reality of migration that brought the two presidents together remains fundamentally unchanged and must be addressed.

Immigration is the most conspicuous piece of unfinished business between 3
the U.S. and Mexico. On almost every other front, U.S.-Mexican relations have made dramatic progress in recent years, but a glaring exception to the trend is immigration policy. While the U.S. government has encouraged closer trade, investment, and political ties with Mexico, it has labored in vain to keep a lid on the flow of labor across the border. Since the mid 1980s, in its effort to stop illegal immigration, Washington has imposed new and burdensome regulations on American employers and dramatically increased spending on border control. Despite those aggressive efforts, America's border policy has failed to achieve its principal objective—to stem the flow of undocumented workers into the U.S. labor market.

The U.S. and Mexico share a 2,000-mile land border, by far the longest in 4
the world between an industrialized and less developed country. By the early 1980s, the perception became widespread that America was being flooded with illegal immigrants from Mexico. In 1986, Congress passed the landmark Immigration Reform and Control Act (IRCA), which contained three major provisions aimed at regaining "control of our borders." To dampen demand for undocumented labor, it required U.S. companies to check documentation of all prospective employees and, for the first time in American history, authorized fines against firms that knowingly hire illegal immigrants. To cut off the supply of unauthorized workers, it increased spending on the Border Patrol. Moreover, to address the issue of the millions of illegal aliens already in the U.S., it granted permanent legal status, or "amnesty," to 2,800,000 unauthorized immigrants who had been in the country continuously since Jan. 1, 1982.

After initial declines, the number of Mexicans entering the U.S. began to 5
rise again by the early 1990s. Soon after taking office in 1993, the Clinton

Administration tried to stem the rising tide through enhanced border enforcement in a policy it dubbed "prevention through deterrence." The policy focused on the major entry points along the U.S.-Mexican border: San
Diego, Calif.; El Paso and Laredo, Tex., and Nogales, Ariz. The 1996 Illegal
Immigration Reform and Immigrant Responsibility Act further ramped up resources for border control, including funds for additional layers of fencing in
San Diego, and imposed tougher penalties on smugglers, undocumented
workers, and those who overstay their visas. From 1986 to 1998, the amount
of tax dollars that Congress appropriated for the Immigration and Naturalization Service increased eightfold and for the Border Patrol sixfold. The
number of Border Patrol agents assigned to the southwestern border doubled to 8,500.

6   By any real measure of results, the effort since 1986 to constrict illegal immigration has failed. The number of undocumented immigrants in the U.S. has
doubled since then, from an estimated 4,000,000 to 8,000,000. The length of
the U.S.-Mexican border and the volume of legal border crossings virtually
guarantee that current American border control policy will fail. Moreover,
Washington's expensive and coercive efforts to curb Mexican migration have
caused a number of perverse and unintended consequences.

WHY MEXICANS MIGRATE NORTH

7   To understand why U.S. border policy has failed, we must first understand
why Mexican workers migrate despite the American government's expensive
campaign to keep them out. Most Mexicans who migrate to the U.S. do not
come intending to settle permanently. They come to solve temporary problems of family finance—by saving dollars and sending them back home in the
form of remittances. Their goal is to rejoin their families and communities after
a few months or years as sojourners in the American labor market. From the
end of the Bracero program in 1964 until the passage of the IRCA in 1986—a
period during which Mexicans were practically, if not legally, free to cross the
border and work—the flow of labor was largely circular. During that period,
Douglas Massey of the University of Pennsylvania estimates that 28,000,000
Mexicans entered the U.S. and 23,400,000 eventually returned to Mexico, for
a net immigration total of 4,600,000. In other words, when free to enter and
work in the U.S., more than 80% of Mexican migrants still chose eventually to
return to their homeland. "Given the relatively porous border" during that
period, Massey concludes, "migrants knew that they could return to the United
States for additional labor whenever the need arose, thus encouraging a pattern of circular rather than settled migration."

8   Immigration is ultimately driven by demand for labor in the U.S. market.
Mexicans migrate to the U.S. not simply because wages are higher, but because Americans want to hire them. Drawing on their social capital, migrants
commonly enter the U.S. labor market after learning that specific jobs are available in specific locations. For a Mexican worker, being unemployed or under-
employed is far more expensive in the U.S. than back in Mexico. If jobs are not
available for migrants in the U.S., a journey north of the border will be far less

attractive no matter what the wage differential. If jobs are available, current American border policy will not keep them out.

While it has failed to stop the flow of workers, Washington's campaign 9 against economic migration from Mexico has spawned an underworld of smuggling, document fraud, and other criminal activity. To make the difficult crossing through unfamiliar territory, migrants have been forced to hire the services of smuggling networks or individual guides known as "coyotes." As a direct consequence of the government's "prevention through deterrence" campaign, the share of illegal immigrants who use smugglers to enter from Mexico increased from 70% in the early 1990s to nearly 90% by the end of the decade. Fees that coyotes charge also increased during that period, from an estimated average of $500 to $1,000 or more. To circumvent employer sanctions in the U.S., undocumented migrants are supplied with false documents by a well-developed underground cottage industry.

Once in the U.S., illegal Mexican workers must remain longer to pay the 10 higher price of crossing the border, and they are reluctant to repeat the increasingly expensive and dangerous trip more often than necessary. Yet, the cost of crossing the border continues to be low enough that hundreds of thousands of Mexicans succeed in entering the U.S. illegally each year. Those who do are staying longer and adding to the stock of Mexican migrants already in the country. Before passage of the IRCA in 1986, the median stay in the U.S. of undocumented migrants from Mexico was 2.6 years; by 1998, after the border crackdown of the Clinton years, the median stay had risen to 6.6 years. The border policy aimed at reducing illegal immigration to the U.S. has perversely encouraged illegal immigrants to stay.

Another consequence of the suppression policy has been to divert migra- 11 tion flows from a few traditional urban crossing points to more scattered rural areas—to the frustration of rural residents and the peril of migrants. Up until the mid 1980s, the large majority of Mexican migrants entered the U.S. via three narrow, urban gates—San Diego, Nogales, and El Paso and Laredo, Tex. In response to enhanced border enforcement in those cities, migration patterns shifted to remote rural areas such as the Arizona-Mexico border, where patrols are more scattered, but conditions are also more dangerous. The diverted flow has caused headaches for Americans living in those areas as migrants have trespassed on private property, disturbed livestock, and destroyed property. The remote topography and hostile desert climate have resulted in the deaths of thousands of migrants since the crackdown began. In 2001, 336 migrants were found dead along the border from dehydration and other causes, down slightly from 377 deaths in 2000, but up sharply from the death toll in earlier years.

Employer sanctions have artificially depressed wages of undocumented 12 workers by reducing their bargaining power and complicating the task of hiring them. Sanctions have increased the paperwork for businesses and encouraged hiring through subcontractors and off-the-books cash payments. A Labor Department study on the effect of employer sanctions contained in the 1986 IRCA bill concluded that "employer sanctions are viewed as a tax on the employment of unauthorized workers and are incorporated directly into the labor demand schedule of the firms. As a result, the direct effect of employer sanctions is to lower wages."

13   The migration of Mexican workers to the U.S. is a rational and mutually beneficial response to underlying economic needs on both sides of the border. Immigration—like the international flow of goods, services, and capital—typically benefits most people in both the sending and receiving countries.

14   Immigration aids the U.S. economy by providing workers to fill gaps in the labor market. Immigrants tend to fill occupations where the gap between the supply of workers and the demand for them is greatest, typically in the highest- and lowest-skilled jobs. That hourglass shape of the immigration labor pool complements the native workforce, where a much larger share of workers falls in the middle range in terms of skills and education. As a result, immigrants do not typically compete for the kinds of jobs held by the vast majority of American workers. Instead, they migrate to those segments of the job market where most Americans are over- or underqualified.

15   America's recent history confirms that its economy can prosper during times of robust immigration. During the long boom of the 1990s, and especially in the second half of the decade, the national unemployment rate fell below four percent and real wages rose both up and down the income scale during a time of high immigration levels. According to a study by the Council of Economic Advisers, household incomes rose strongly from 1993 through 1999 across all income groups, including the poorest one-fifth of American households. The poverty rate fell by three percent during the 1990s, and almost 10% among African-Americans. Those remarkable gains occurred during a decade of large immigration inflows, including low-skilled workers from Mexico.

BENEFITS FOR THE U.S.

16   Low-skilled immigrants, a category that describes most migrants from Mexico, benefit the U.S. economy by filling jobs for which the large majority of American workers are overqualified and that they are unwilling to take. Important sectors of the U.S. economy have turned to low-skilled immigrant workers, documented and undocumented, to cover persistent job vacancies. Hotels and motels, restaurants, construction, manufacturing, health care, retailing, and other services are major employers of low-skilled immigrant labor. Of the roughly 5,000,000 undocumented workers in the American labor force, the Pew Hispanic Center estimates that 1,000,000 are employed in manufacturing; 600,000 in construction; 700,000 in restaurants; and 1,000,000 to 1,400,000 in agriculture. More than half (58%) of those workers are from Mexico.

17   The demand for less-skilled labor will continue to rise in the years ahead. According to the Department of Labor, while the fastest-growing occupations in the next decade in percentage terms will require high degrees of skill and education, the largest growth in absolute numbers will be in those categories that require only "short-term-on-the-job training" of one month or less. In fact, of the top-30 categories with the largest expected job growth between 2000 and 2010, more than half fall into that least-skilled category. Those include

combined food preparation and servicing workers; waiters and waitresses; retail salespersons; cashiers; security guards; nursing aides, orderlies, and attendants; janitors and cleaners; home health aides; manual laborers and freight, stock, and materials movers; landscaping and groundskeeping workers; and manual packers and packagers—all occupations where low-skilled immigrants from Mexico can be expected to help meet the rising demand. Across the American economy, the Labor Department estimates that the total number of jobs requiring only short-term training will increase from 53,200,000 in 2000 to 60,900,000 by 2010, a net increase of 7,700,000 jobs.

Meanwhile, the supply of American workers suitable for such work is falling   18 because of an aging workforce and rising education levels. The median age of American workers continues to increase as the large cohort of baby boomers approaches retirement age. From 1990 to 2010, the median age of U.S. workers is expected to increase from 36.6 to 40.6. Younger and older workers alike are now more educated as the share of adult native-born men without a high school diploma has plunged—from 53.6% in 1960 to nine percent in 1998, for example. During that same period, the share with college degrees went up from 11.4% to 29.8%. With the number of low-skilled jobs expected to grow by more than 700,000 a year, and a shrinking pool of Americans willing to fill those jobs, Mexican migrants provide a ready and willing source of labor to fill the growing gap between demand and supply on the lower rungs of the labor ladder.

Legalization of undocumented workers would restore the normal incentive   19 for them to upgrade their skills and increase their bargaining power with employers. As evidence, a 1995 Labor Department study found that undocumented workers who were legalized in the 1980s as part of the IRCA "amnesty" provisions responded by investing in their skills and education. "For many, legalization appears to have been a turning point. Suddenly, there was a surge of investment in language skills, education, and training," the study found. Specifically, 43% of Mexican men undertook some skill-enhancement training following legalization," more than a doubling of the previous rate of human-capital accumulation for most origin groups."

Another beneficial consequence was an increase in wages paid to newly le-   20 galized workers. The same study found that real wages paid to undocumented workers were flat for most of the decade until 1987–88, but then rose 15% in the five years following legalization. Legalization put previously undocumented workers on an equal footing with documented ones, allowing them to withhold their labor more credibly or consider other job offers instead of forcing them to accept what a limited group of employers were offering. Legalization eliminated the need for off-the-books payments, middlemen, and other subterfuges that had acted as a tax on their labor.

A final benefit of legalized immigration would be the almost certain re-   21 duction of illegal immigration. If a wide enough channel were opened so that the supply of workers from Mexico could be legally matched with the demand for their labor in the U.S., the rationale for the current illegal flow of Mexican migrants would vanish. Why would Mexican workers bear the cost and risk of sneaking across the border, and then pay a tax on their wages and working conditions for their undocumented status, when they could instead enter the country and work legally?

22   The experience of the Bracero program demonstrates that workers prefer the legal channel. Faced with large-scale illegal immigration in the early 1950s, the Immigration and Naturalization Service more than doubled the number of Bracero visas, enough to meet growing demand, especially in the agricultural sector. As a result, illegal immigration from Mexico plummeted to almost nothing during the second half of the decade. Illegal migration was supplanted by legal migration.

23   Long-time opponents of immigration have seized on 9/11 to argue against legalization of Mexican migration in favor of drastic cuts in existing levels of legal immigration. The connection between the Sept. 11 attacks and illegal immigration from Mexico is nonexistent, though.

24   None of the 19 hijackers entered the country illegally or as immigrants. They all arrived in the U.S. with valid temporary nonimmigrant tourist or student visas. None of them arrived via Mexico, and none were Mexican. Sealing the Mexican border with a three-tiered, 2,000-mile replica of the Berlin Wall patrolled by thousands of American troops would not have kept a single Sept. 11 terrorist out of the U.S.

25   Washington can take necessary steps to secure our borders without sacrificing the benefits of immigration. On May 14, 2002, Bush signed the Enhanced Border Security and Visa Entry Reform Act of 2002. Passed unanimously by Congress, the legislation focuses on identifying potential terrorists abroad and keeping them out of the U.S. Notably absent from the bill were any provisions rolling back levels of legal immigration or bolstering efforts to curb undocumented migration from Mexico.

26   Members of Congress rightly understood, when crafting the legislation, that Mexican migration is not a threat to national security. Indeed, legalizing and regularizing the movement of workers across the U.S.-Mexican border would enhance our national security by bringing much of the underground labor market into the open, encouraging newly documented workers to cooperate fully with law enforcement officials, and freeing resources for border security and the war on terrorism. It would begin to drain the swamp of smuggling and document fraud that facilitates illegal immigration, and would encourage millions of currently undocumented workers to make themselves known to authorities by registering with the government, reducing cover for terrorists who manage to enter the country and overstay their visas.

27   Legalization would allow the government to devote more of its resources to keeping terrorism out of the country. Before Sept. 11, the U.S. government had stationed more than four times as many border enforcement agents on the Mexican border as along the Canadian one, even though the latter is more than twice as long and has been the preferred border of entry for Middle Easterners trying to enter the U.S. illegally. A system that allows Mexican workers to enter the U.S. legally would free up thousands to government personnel and save an estimated $3,000,000,000 a year—resources that would then be available to fight terrorism.

MAKING WORK LEGAL

The realities of the North American labor market demand a system of le- 28 gal, regulated migration to and from Mexico that conforms to how millions of people on both sides of the border arrange their lives. A reformed immigration system must create a legal channel through which Mexican nationals can enter and remain in the U.S. for a definite time to work.

A temporary work visa (TWV) should be created that would allow Mexican 29 nationals to remain in the U.S. to work for a limited period. The visa could authorize work for a definite period—perhaps three years—and would be renewable for an additional limited period; permit unlimited multiple entries for as long as the visa was valid; allow complete mobility between employers and sectors of the American economy; and entitle the holder to "national treatment."

Mobility is essential so that workers can exercise full freedom to change 30 jobs to realize maximum pay and working conditions, under the theory that their best projection against below-market pay and working conditions is the ability to leave for a better offer. On an economy-wide scale, full mobility would allow the supply of labor to shift between sectors to meet changing demand. The visa must also confer on the immigrant worker national treatment—that is, the same legal protections extended by law to native workers. That would ensure that temporary workers do not enjoy any unfair legal advantage or suffer any legal disadvantage compared to other workers. Mobility and national treatment will protect immigrant workers from the real and perceived abuses of past "guest worker" programs that tied them to specified employers, making visa holders overly dependent on the good will of their employers.

To encourage work and protect taxpayers, holders of a TWV should be in- 31 eligible for Federal means-tested welfare programs. The immigrant provisions of the 1996 welfare reform act should be affirmed, both in the law establishing the temporary worker visa and in any reauthorization of Federal welfare law. Decoupling the visa from welfare would benefit immigrant workers in two ways: It would help low-income families avoid the welfare trap, and it would insulate the temporary visa program from charges that it is a burden to taxpayers. Pro-immigration groups that lobby for restoration of welfare benefits for new and future immigrants are ultimately hurting the interests of the very people they claim to respect.

The number of visas issued should be sufficient to meet demand in the U.S. 32 labor market. Using the current estimated net inflow of undocumented workers, 300,000 visas per year would be a reasonable starting point. Distribution of visas could be rationed through a one-time application fee. The fee should be set high enough to offset costs and regulate demand, but low enough to undercut smugglers, perhaps in the range of $1,000. In addition, a program should be created to allow undocumented workers already in the U.S. to earn legal status based on years of work and other productive behavior. They should be issued TWVs immediately, provided they register with the government and do not pose a threat to America's internal or national security. Those who have lived and worked in the U.S. for more than a certain period should be eligible to apply for permanent residence status and, ultimately, citizenship. Like new entrants, undocumented workers already in the country would be required to pay the same application fee.

33   Legalizing undocumented workers already in the U.S. would not be a mere repeat of the 1980s IRCA "amnesty." Undocumented workers would not be granted automatic permanent residence status. All eligible immigrants could be issued temporary worker visas, valid for a limited period only. To gain permanent residence status, they would then need to apply for permanent residency through existing channels. They would not receive preferential treatment, but would be processed along with other legally qualified applicants for permanent residency.

34   The Federal government's 15-year campaign against Mexican migration has failed by any objective measure. The President and Congress should return to the task of reforming the nation's dysfunctional immigration system into one that is economic, humane, and compatible with how Americans actually arrange their lives.

QUESTIONS FOR READING

1. What have our immigration laws and recent policies failed to accomplish?

2. What specific actions were taken in the 1980s and 1990s? How do we know that these have not worked? What negative consequences have resulted from government efforts to stop Mexican migration?

3. Why do Mexicans come illegally to the United States?

4. What does the United States gain from Mexican illegals? Why are Mexican migrants not an economic threat to most Americans?

5. What are the advantages of legalizing Mexican migrants?

6. How would Griswold handle the process of "legal" Mexican migrants? List the specific points of his proposal.

QUESTIONS FOR REASONING AND ANALYSIS

1. What is Griswold's claim? Where does he state it most directly and fully?

2. What counterargument does the author anticipate? How does he rebut it?

3. Evaluate Griswold's argument. Is his reasoning sound? Are his data credible? Has he changed your thinking on this issue?

QUESTIONS FOR REFLECTING AND WRITING

1. What statistics in this essay are most surprising to you? Why?

2. Are there any specific points in his proposed solution with which you disagree? If so, on what basis? If not, are you then prepared to accept his proposals? Explain your position.

3. Griswold ends by asserting that his claim makes economic sense, is more humane than the current situation, and is a practical solution to the way Americans want to live. In your view, are these the important points to defend in this debate? Is

one more important than another? Explain your views. Does Griswold support all three points effectively in his argument? If yes, support your judgment. If not, which one is least successfully defended? Defend your analysis.

WHEN IMMIGRATION REFORM HELPS HOMELAND SECURITY | MARCELA SANCHEZ

Washington Post journalist Marcela Sanchez reports on issues shaping events in Latin America in her weekly online column "Desde Washington." Sanchez is also Washington correspondent for several newspapers and TV newscasts in Colombia. She is a frequent commentator on *Foro Interamericano* of Worldnet TV. Her article on immigration appeared at washingtonpost.com on July 3, 2003.

PREREADING QUESTIONS What kinds of immigration reform might aid homeland security—other than deportation, student raids, and profiling/harassing? Try to anticipate Sanchez's argument.

1   Tucked away in Tom Ridge's bulging portfolio as the Cabinet secretary charged with securing U.S. territory from future terrorist attacks is the ambitious yet unstated goal of legitimizing illegal immigrants currently in this country.

2   Neither Ridge nor anyone in the White House will say this publicly, yet logic makes it apparent. Terrorists, after all, are people, and it is among people, particularly those 8 million to 9 million living here with no legal status, that those terrorists can easily hide.

3   There are those who say legitimacy is not an option for those who have shown no respect for U.S. immigration laws. Deport them, one and all, or lock them up and throw away the key. That would send the necessary warning to the world.

4   Politically and logistically, however, such solutions are practically impossible. Immigration agents currently deport an average of 407 criminals or other illegal aliens every day. At that rate, it would take more than 50 years to oust all the scofflaws, a majority of them Mexican. So like it or not, millions will have to somehow be brought into the fold.

5   In fact, this is already happening outside the federal realm. Mexican consular officials in this country have been issuing identification cards—known as *matriculas consulares*—to thousands of Mexicans here illegally. The cards effectively document the undocumented. They provide no official change in status for the immigrant but offer a foothold in society and open doors to a few basic services such as bank accounts.

6   Already, 14 states and more than 900 police and sheriff's departments around the country accept the cards as legitimate identification. Absent alternatives, the *matriculas* have become a welcome tool for those authorities to get a better handle on who's on the streets of their communities.

7   This local and state process has not escaped the notice of the federal government, the FBI and Ridge himself. Just last week the FBI warned that the documents are vulnerable to fraud and misuse by criminals and terrorists. No

surprise there. The 9/11 hijackers proved that even U.S.-issued documents were vulnerable.

8 Ridge, for his part, says his main concern is preserving the integrity of the *matriculas.* Publicly, he has been sympathetic to the idea of regularizing the status of illegal immigrants, and this week told a group of Hispanic reporters that as a member of Congress in 1986 he voted in favor of amnesty for more than a million illegal immigrants then living in the country.

9 So the question now is, who at the federal level is going to shape this process already under way and what form it will ultimately take. Washington could deport and arrest more immigrants but that would do a disservice to national security by pushing millions of illegals deeper into the shadows and making it even harder to find the few ill-intentioned among them. Or Washington could act according to today's national security nuances by distinguishing, as Ridge seems to do, between those who want to destroy a way of life and those who want to take part in it.

10 Republican Richard Lugar, chairman of the Senate Foreign Relations Committee, called this week for an end to American reluctance to adopt positive immigration reforms. Some of his colleagues, Republican and Democrat, already are pushing new bills to create, for instance, a guest worker program that would match many of those here illegally with employers who want to hire them.

11 Others, such as Demetrios Papademetriou of the Migration Policy Institute, a Washington think tank, suggest a U.S.-vetted registration process similar to the one now used for those from Arab countries. Those who cooperate could be offered "eventual regularization of their status," he said.

12 So far there is no clear indication if, when and how President Bush will take the lead on this issue. As all politicians and their pollsters know, there would be much to gain for Bush and the Republican Party if he were to take radical and concrete steps to regularize the status of illegal Hispanic immigrants. Such an act might do for today's GOP what Lincoln did 140 years ago when he turned it into the party of the emancipated.

13 But at this moment and in this White House, where punitive voices on this issue shout down conciliatory ones all too often, legitimization may be further swept under the rug. Reluctance to take such a political risk would bring about mostly half-baked measures. And so, ironically, the lack of political resolve over immigration would trump homeland security—and play into the hands of terrorists.

QUESTIONS FOR READING

1. Why is deportation, in the author's view, not practical?
2. As deportation is not a practical solution, what "type" of solution will be necessary?
3. What specific solution strategy does Sanchez suggest? What are some variations of this basic plan?

4. What advantages do these solutions hold for the Republican Party, in the author's view? How hopeful is Sanchez that the Bush administration will actually employ the solutions she discusses?

QUESTIONS FOR REASONING AND ANALYSIS

1. Study all of Sanchez's reasons for rejecting deportation. Has she made a good case for rejecting this solution? Why or why not?

2. List all of the specific solutions that would help authorities to keep track of immigrants, especially illegal aliens, covered by Sanchez. Has she made a good case for using one or some combination of these solutions? Why or why not?

3. What is Sanchez's attitude toward the Bush administration? How do you know?

QUESTIONS FOR REFLECTING AND WRITING

1. Should the identification cards used for illegal Mexicans be continued? Developed and expanded in some way? Stopped? Take a stand.

2. How serious a threat to homeland security are illegal Mexicans? Can they be, for all practical purposes, eliminated from discussions of security? Why or why not?

SHOW ME THE MONEY: PATRIOT ACT HELPS THE FEDS IN CASES WITH NO TIE TO TERROR | MICHAEL ISIKOFF

Possessing a master's degree in journalism from Northwestern University, Michael Isikoff has been an investigative correspondent for *Newsweek* magazine since 1994. He is the author of *Uncovering Clinton: A Reporter's Story* (1999), the winner of many awards for his reporting, and a frequent guest on TV news programs such as *Meet the Press*. The following article appeared in *Newsweek* on December 1, 2003.

PREREADING QUESTIONS   What is the Patriot Act? When and why was it passed? What was its stated purpose?

For FBI agents in Las Vegas, cases don't get any juicier. Earlier this year the   1 Feds were closing in on Michael Galardi, the city's biggest strip-club baron, who was suspected of bribing local officials. Facing prosecution, Galardi cut a deal and confessed to funneling hundreds of thousands of dollars to Clark County commissioners. Galardi told agents that he gave one official $20,000 to help buy a new SUV; another received $400 worth of lap dances at one of his clubs. In exchange, the commissioners had allegedly done Galardi favors, such as spiking a proposed lap-dance ordinance that would have put stricter limits on how much the customers could touch. To make their case, the agents working "Operation G-String" needed to see the financial records of local officials. To do that, the FBI turned to a new weapon in its arsenal: The USA Patriot Act.

2   Whisked through Congress in the weeks after 9/11, the Patriot Act—which gives federal law enforcement wide-ranging powers to track and eavesdrop on suspected terrorists—was promoted as an urgently needed law to thwart future attacks. When civil libertarians complained the law could lead to abuses, Attorney General John Ashcroft derided them as "hysterics." He insisted that any weakening of the act would "risk American lives." Some early fears that the Patriot Act would be abused have been overblown. One much-criticized provision that allows the FBI to monitor the books people check out of libraries hasn't actually been used at all. Yet Operation G-String shows how the Feds are using their new powers in cases that have nothing to do with terrorism—something most members of Congress never anticipated.

3   In Las Vegas, the Feds used a little-known provision in the Patriot Act that allows them to quickly obtain financial records of suspected terrorists or money launderers. Law-enforcement agencies can submit the name of any suspect to the Treasury Department, which then orders financial institutions across the country to search their records for any matches. If they get a "hit"—evidence that the person has an account—the financial institution is slapped with a subpoena for the person's records.

4   The Feds might have gotten the same records even without the new law—but only if they had hard evidence that a suspect was doing business at a particular bank. In effect, the Patriot Act allows the Feds to search every financial institution in the country for the records of anybody they have suspicions about—the very definition, critics say, of a fishing expedition. "It's the functional equivalent of a national subpoena," says Peter Dijinis, a banking lawyer. Even the law's architects acknowledge just how far-reaching the provision is. "It's an extraordinary power," says David Aufhauser, a former general counsel at Treasury, who insists it's being used responsibly.

5   It's the Patriot Act's money-laundering language that has allowed the Feds to stretch the way the law can be used. Essentially, money laundering is an effort to disguise illicit profits. But it's such a broad statute that prosecutors can use it in the pursuit of more than 200 different federal crimes. Treasury Department figures reviewed by *Newsweek* show that this year the Feds have used the Patriot Act to conduct searches on 962 suspects, yielding "hits" on 6,397 financial records. Of those, two thirds (4,261) were in money-laundering cases with no apparent terror connection. Among the agencies making requests, *Newsweek* has learned, were the IRS (which investigates tax fraud), the Postal Service (postal fraud) and the Secret Service (counterfeiting). One request came from the Agriculture Department—a case that apparently involved food-stamp fraud.

6   Operation G-String went a step further. It was the first time the FBI used the Patriot Act's powers against local pols. To the Feds, it was a great success. Three local commissioners and a lobbyist were indicted this month. (The FBI also pulled records on one Vegas council member—and several officials' ex-spouses—who were never charged.) An FBI official defended the searches as "entirely lawful." Even so, Rep. Shelley Berkley, a Nevada Democrat, complained to the local FBI

chief. She says she was told the agents were only "using the tools that Congress gave them." The conversation left Berkley unsettled. In the urgent push to pass the Patriot Act, she says, "never . . . did the FBI say we needed additional tools to keep this nation safe from strip-club operators."

QUESTIONS FOR READING

1. In what case did the FBI use their new powers from the Patriot Act? What power did they use?
2. Who has complained about possible abuses of the Patriot Act? Why? What has been the response of Attorney General Ashcroft?
3. What is the process by which the FBI can obtain an individual's financial records? How does the new law make the task of obtaining financial records easier for the FBI?
4. What does the term *money laundering* mean?
5. What was new in the FBI's use of the Patriot Act in the Las Vegas case?

QUESTIONS FOR REASONING AND ANALYSIS

1. Examine Isikoff's organization. How does he begin? How does he end? What does he cover in the middle of the essay? What is the effect of his choice of structure?
2. Look again at the opening paragraph. What is the paragraph's tone? How do word choice and sentence structures work to create its tone?
3. What is Isikoff's attitude toward the use of the Patriot Act to solve the Operation G-Strong case? How do you know? What, then, is the author's implied claim?

QUESTIONS FOR REFLECTING AND WRITING

1. Have you been bothered by powers given to the government in the Patriot Act? If not, why not? (The powers will be used responsibly? The powers are essential to fighting terror? Something else?) If yes, why? (You define yourself as a civil libertarian? Something else?) Explain.
2. Is the FBI using the provisions of the Patriot Act responsibly when it searches records to solve a case of bribing city officials? Be prepared to explain and defend your position.
3. How should we balance individual rights and freedoms with the need to protect society against possible terrorism? What can you contribute to this debate?

THE NEW CAMPUS RAIDS | JUNGWON KIM

Jungwon Kim is a radio reporter and an editor for *Amnesty Now*, the magazine of the activist organization Amnesty International. *The Nation* published this article June 2, 2003.

PREREADING QUESTIONS What kinds of campus raids are likely to be Kim's concern? Given Kim's position with *Amnesty Now,* what do you anticipate his position on the raids to be?

1   On February 26, the small town of Moscow, Idaho, saw more commotion than it had since a truck camper exploded in a vacant lot last September. While the town was still sleeping, two military planes landed at a nearby airport, and at 4:30 am, at least 100 armed federal agents raided a University of Idaho student apartment—all to arrest a single Saudi graduate student, Sami al-Hussayyen. As dawn broke, they interrogated at least twenty other Middle Eastern students and their spouses in their homes, sometimes in front of their children. Within hours, the Feds indicted al-Hussayyen on felony charges of visa fraud, accusing him of supporting a Detroit-based Muslim charity that, they alleged, had links to overseas terrorists. (The group has not been formally charged.)

2   Word of the raid spread quickly among foreign students across the country, as did news in December that six Middle Easterners studying in Colorado were jailed when they complied with the INS's "special registration" program, required of men from twenty-five predominantly Muslim countries. Their offense: dropping below the twelve-hour course minimum required for a student visa, even though they had permission from their schools. Another round of "enforcement action," to use agency parlance, had apparently begun.

3   Thanks to Hani Hanjour, the 9/11 hijacker who entered the United States on a student visa, South Asian and Middle Eastern students joined the government's suspect list soon after the attacks. Since then, says the ACLU's Lucas Guttentag, attorneys have observed "a persistent pattern of discriminatory investigations and enforcement against Muslims and South Asians, especially foreign students from Middle Eastern countries." An untold number disappeared in the mass INS sweeps immediately after 9/11. Then came the "special registration" arrests, which included many students. And round three has just begun: The Homeland Security Department's new immigration enforcement agency, the Bureau of Immigration and Customs Enforcement (ICE), introduced a massive database in January that will soon track the country's 1.2 million foreign students and visiting scholars in real time.

4   Some of the tactics used with students are constitutionally questionable. In the Idaho raids, for example, combined teams of FBI and INS agents interrogated students, blurring the line between criminal and civil questioning. Under immigration law, foreign students must answer any question relating to their visa status, yet anyone questioned by the FBI—even a noncitizen—has the right to remain silent. UI law professor Elizabeth Brandt, who coordinated the students' legal representation, said the FBI was "bootstrapping" INS authority to pressure students to answer questions related to criminal activity.

5   Indeed, a Moscow attorney present at one interrogation described "threats of criminal prosecution, threats of being placed in deportation proceedings, threats of immediate arrest." The lawyer, who asked not to be

named, said many of those interrogated were not given Miranda warnings, and at least one was refused when she asked to call a lawyer. The attorney said veteran defense lawyers present at the interrogations were "really shaken."

Justice Department spokesman Jorge Martinez would not comment on 6 the Idaho raid except to say, "The FBI has clear guidance on how to handle those issues, Miranda rights." On April 25 al-Hussayyen was ordered deported for visa fraud, and ICE is holding him in solitary confinement as he awaits a criminal trial.

Since the Idaho and Colorado incidents, there has been a lull in the flashy 7 raids. But foreign students are still on edge, as listservs carry whispers from campus to campus of interrogations, deportations and disappeared students.

Muslim foreign students say the pressure of continual scrutiny has led 8 them to curtail travel plans and political activities. For some, this has meant agonizing professional sacrifices. Berkeley sophomore Imad Ahmed may turn down an internship with his "idol," an internationally esteemed human rights lawyer in Lahore. Although Ahmed is a British citizen and left Pakistan as an infant, he had to register with the INS and worries that he might have trouble re-entering the United States if he leaves.

Others are simply looking for a way out, believing the climate will only get 9 worse. "I've had many friends leave," says Sharmeen Obaid, a Pakistani graduate student at Stanford University. "One quit a bank job in New York. The rest were in the process of applying for jobs but decided to go back."

Those who remain will likely see another wave of roundups after August 1, 10 the compliance deadline for colleges to put information on all foreign students into the new ICE database. Once it's up and running, students will have to be vigilant about filing paperwork and keep schools notified of their every move, as the system's real-time reporting eliminates any slack that once allowed students and administrators to correct mistakes.

Immigration authorities have already picked up at least two students in 11 good standing because of errors in the glitch-prone system. To this, ICE spokesman Chris Bentley responds, "Are these procedures foolproof? Obviously the answer is no. Could someone be arrested if the database says he is out of status? Yes."

In New York City, a Bangladeshi community-college student lives a life in 12 limbo as he awaits deportation for a minor visa violation. Coming to America "was the best opportunity of my life," he said. "But after the buildings fell, I knew this would come. The worst has happened."

QUESTIONS FOR READING

1. What is Kim's subject?
2. What did the INS do right after 9/11?
3. What database has been created by the Homeland Security Department? What will it accomplish?

4. Explain the difference between questioning by the INS of those on student visas and questioning by the FBI. How was this difference apparently blurred in the Idaho raids?

5. What students feel most threatened by post-9/11 events on campuses?

QUESTIONS FOR REASONING AND ANALYSIS

1. How would you state Kim's claim?

2. Analyze Kim's evidence. Is it credible? Is it convincing?

3. Look at Kim's word choice. How does he present details of the raid for maximum effect? In paragraph 2, why does he put the words "enforcement action" in quotation marks? Find other examples of this use of quotation marks.

4. What is effective about Kim's opening paragraph? What does he accomplish with it?

QUESTIONS FOR REFLECTING AND WRITING

1. Do the actions taken against those on student visas distress you at all? Why or why not?

2. What civil liberties are you willing to give up in the attempt to increase homeland security and prevent terrorist attacks? Think specifically about what curtailing of freedoms will likely decrease terrorism. If you don't think that any tradeoff is acceptable—or useful—explain why not.

NO COMPROMISES: WHY WE'RE GOING TO LOSE THE WAR ON TERROR—AND HOW WE COULD WIN | KARINA ROLLINS

A University of Maryland graduate, Karina Rollins spent much of her youth with her parents in Germany. Included in her journalism career was a spell at *The National Review,* and she has been published in many magazines. Currently she is a senior editor at *The American Enterprise* magazine, a regular on C-SPAN's *Washington Journal,* and a panelist on national German TV. Her article appeared in the January/February 2003 issue of *The American Enterprise.*

PREREADING QUESTIONS Do you have concerns about our security in this country? If so, what are they? If not, why not? What role does—or should—technology play, for good or for bad, in the problem of terrorism?

1   After 19 terrorists hijacked commercial airplanes, crashed them into the World Trade Center and the Pentagon, and killed over 3,000 Americans, the U.S. government sprang into action: The director of the Federal Bureau of Investigation held a friendly meeting with an American Muslim group with known ties to terrorists. The State Department printed up thousands of copies of a poster series, "Mosques of America," and sponsored an imam-exchange program. None of which attracted any criticism from the attorney general or the President; all of which would be amusing if it were a sketch on *Saturday Night Live.*

The nation's new and improved airport security is a joke; all the stories 2 about little blue-haired ladies' shoes searched for explosives are true. Americans know the hassle and make-work and plastic forks don't add to their safety. One of the biggest laugh lines of a Washington, D.C., political comedy troupe, The Capitol Steps, comes at the beginning of a skit about airport security. A man in a giant turban walks on stage and hangs a big sign that reads simply, "O'Hare Security." It brings down the house.

Former senators Warren Rudman and Gary Hart, cochairmen of the Commission on National Security in the 21st Century, concluded that "A year after 9/11, America remains dangerously unprepared to prevent and respond to a catastrophic terrorist attack on US soil." Rudman and Hart lament that enormous amounts of money are spent on airports, while port and cargo security take a back seat; that police, firemen, and emergency medical workers still can't communicate well with each other or their counterparts in nearby cities; that public health facilities are unprepared for a biological or chemical attack; that local police work in an intelligence vacuum and don't have access to terrorist watch lists; and that there has been no national debate about how to protect factories and power plants. Cyberspace is still glaringly unprotected as well.

The Homeland Security bill has now, after many distractions, finally been 4 passed. It will be the job of the new department to close the gaping security holes, and it will surely be successful in implementing some effective safety mechanisms. But it could take years for the department to become operational. Besides, addressing such practical matters is only half the solution; there is an entire worldview in Washington that must change drastically.

The administration publicly characterizes al-Qaeda and its sympathizers as 5 a group of criminals, ignoring the religious nature of their plans to destroy the West. If the government—and the American people—are to win the war on terror, both must understand that our enemies have succeeded in launching a holy war—a war that will most certainly last beyond the lifetime of anyone reading these pages.

More than a year after 9/11, too many clear and present dangers continue 6 to loom over Americans. Following are prescriptions to address some of the biggest problems:

RETURN TO COMMON SENSE AND PURGE POLITICAL CORRECTNESS

Transportation Secretary Norman Mineta frets that being more suspicious 7 of Arab males than 12-year-old girls will lead to World War II-style internment camps for Muslims. When asked several months ago on *60 Minutes* if elderly white women and young Muslim men should be treated the same at the airport security gate, he answered "Basically, I would hope so." The President praises Mr. Mineta for outstanding performance.

As William Lind of the Free Congress Foundation realizes, "The same gov- 8 ernment that wants to invade Iraq is too intimidated by political correctness to provide homeland security by profiling terrorists. The government's feeble efforts to protect our own perimeter spread fear and erode loyalties by telling patriotic citizens that their own government does not or cannot differentiate between patriots and terrorists." In a small bit of encouraging news, the government has announced plans to fingerprint and photograph men who are citizens of countries on an adjustable terror watch list. No, racial profiling isn't the answer. But terrorist profiling is. And that means being wary of young Arab-looking men. It's reality.

ELIMINATE TERRORIST TRAINING CAMPS—FOR REAL

9   The United States "should immediately tell all nations that have terrorist training camps on their territory that they should get rid of them," declares Cliff May, president of the Foundation for the Defense of Democracies. "We should tell these countries we would like them to take care of the camps on their own. If they don't, we should tell them: 'We are going to violate your sovereignty to eliminate them if you do not.' We should give them a limited amount of time. If they don't comply, we should have contingency plans to eliminate the camps through bombing or commando raids.

10   "There is a lot of talk about the recruitment of terrorists, but you can't become a terrorist unless you're trained to be one. You need training to become a sniper or a suicide bomber. You have to go someplace where they teach you. It is vital that there be no such places in the world within the next six months."

GIVE SECURITY CLEARANCES TO LOCAL POLICE
AND PLAN STATEWIDE RESPONSES

11   "What's important is trust and inclusion," says Edward Davis, police superintendent of Lowell, Massachusetts.

12   "That only happens through face-to-face contact. It's important that local police have security clearances. I have one and it makes me feel like I'm in the game. The joint task forces are working pretty well here in Massachusetts.

13   "And there has to be more discussion of regional responses to incidents. Jurisdictional issues have to be ironed out. There should be response scenarios that are clear, that can be trained, and that take care of the communications and coordination problems that can happen. If I had 1,000 police officers here tomorrow, I wouldn't really know how to coordinate them. You need a plan in advance. Not a complicated one, but a plan nonetheless. We need to do a better job planning for responses on a statewide level."

ISSUE NATIONAL I.D. CARDS

14   National I.D. cards are a scary thought for many Americans, conjuring up images of Big Brother and George Orwell's dystopia. Enough with the hysteria already. "Like it or not," points out my colleague Eli Lehrer, who founded the Heritage Foundation's Excellence in Policing Project and has written extensively about national identity cards, "Americans already have national I.D. cards. When they travel overseas, open a bank account, start a new job, or buy a gun, U.S. citizens need to provide state-issued identification. A citizen who gets stopped by the police and can't produce a driver's license, passport, or Social Security card will often have to spend the night in jail." It's hard to argue that this constitutes government power run amok.

A national I.D. card, far from robbing Americans of freedom or privacy, 15 would simply make it much easier for police to tell the majority of law-abiding people from the small proportion of criminals and terrorists in our midst who are capable of doing real harm. It would make us safer—and that makes us freer.

STOP PRETENDING THAT SAUDI ARABIA IS OUR FRIEND

As former assistant secretary of defense Frank Gaffney, Jr., now president 16 of the Center for Security Policy, explains: "Saudi Arabia's alignment with America's enemies extends far beyond the anti-U.S. and anti-Western propaganda that is also ceaselessly disseminated by the kingdom's government-run media. For some fifty years, Saudi officials, royal family, and what passes for private sector institutions have been expending untold sums to promote the state religion—a virulently intolerant strain of Islam known as Wahabism. Washington has long ignored the individual and cumulative effects of such spending on Wahabi proselytizing, recruiting, indoctrination, training, and equipping of adherents who embrace the sect's injunction to convert or kill infidels.

"In the wake of terrorism made possible—or at least abetted—at home 17 and abroad by such Saudi-connected activities, the United States can no longer afford to turn a blind eye to this profoundly unfriendly behavior. That is particularly true insofar as there is reason to believe that Wahabi enterprises are giving rise to perhaps the most insidious enemy of all: an Islamist Fifth Column operating within this country."

As of the printing of this issue, the White House continues to call the Saudis 18 "good partners" in the war on terror.

PRAY THAT THE STATE DEPARTMENT DOESN'T DESTROY US

The State Department is directly responsible for issuing visas to the 19 Sep- 19 tember 11 hijackers, almost all of which should have been flatly rejected. The consular officers who issued the visas each received bonuses of $10,000 to $15,000. The State Department's Visa Express program, which let Saudi citizens apply for visas at Saudi travel agencies and provided even fewer safeguards than the regular system, continued for almost a whole year after 9/11.

The Homeland Security Act includes stricter visa controls for Saudi 20 citizens—but only by accident. If the State Department had had its way, those controls would have been wiped clear off the bill: State objected to the singling out of Saudi Arabia—the country from which came 15 of the 19 September 11 hijackers. Joel Mowbray, who first broke the visa scandal story in *National Review*, reports that the department was assured, incredibly, that the Saudi provision would be struck from the legislation. Only due to "the last-minute confusion and the rush to get the mammoth bill passed during the lameduck session," he says, "did the provision stay put."

Unfazed by even the most egregious breaches of security, Secretary of 21 State Colin Powell continues to wax poetic: "From the mountains of Afghanistan to the valleys of Bosnia to the plains of Africa to the forests of Asia and around the world we are on the ground working with our Muslim partners to expand the circle of peace, the circle of prosperity, the circle of freedom."

22   Secretary Powell also wants more of these "partners" on the ground right here in the U.S., pledging to expand programs to bring more Islamic political and religious leaders as well as journalists and teachers to America.

GET SERIOUS ABOUT BORDER CONTROL AND IMMIGRATION

23   The Immigration and Naturalization Service is guilty of the same reckless sloppiness in approving documents as the State Department. Of course, the INS is also understaffed and underfunded—something which could start to be fixed immediately (and should have been started on September 12, 2001). The administration seems to lack any real sense of urgency about the country's porous borders, and the lack of cooperation from our Mexican and, especially, Canadian neighbors.

24   "When it comes to immigration, the President's approach is guided by compassion and fairness," says Sharon Castillo, a spokesman for the Republican National Committee. No word on how fair it is to Americans who died at the hands of terrorists who could have been kept out of the country.

RECOGNIZE THE THREAT POSED BY MUSLIM ORGANIZATIONS, ISLAMIC CENTERS, AND MOSQUES IN OUR MIDST

25   Terror expert Steven Emerson founded The Investigative Project to collect data on militant Muslim groups in the U.S. In his book *American Jihad: The Terrorists Living Among Us,* he points to nine "terrorist support networks" based in America: Muslim Arab Youth Association, the American Islamic Group, Islamic Cultural Workshop, the Council on American-Islamic Relations, the American Muslim Council, Islamic Circle of North America, the Muslim Public Affairs Council, the American Muslim Alliance, and the Islamic Society of North America.

26   These groups, Emerson says, use "the laws, freedoms, and loopholes of the most liberal nation on earth to help finance and direct one of the most violent international terrorism groups in the world. Operating in the freewheeling and tolerant environment of the United States, bin Laden was able to set up a whole array of 'cells' in a loosely organized network that included Tucson, Arizona; Brooklyn, New York; Orlando, Florida; Dallas, Texas; Santa Clara, California; Columbia, Missouri; and Herndon, Virginia."

START POINTING FINGERS

27   No reform or security measure is going to mean very much if the people who egregiously violate the most basic rules, and those in charge of them, aren't held accountable, which in most cases means being fired. After 9/11, the administration and members of Congress bent over backwards to insist that no one was "finger pointing" or "seeking to lay blame." But accountability is precisely what's needed.

28   Minneapolis FBI special agent Coleen Rowley and her team did everything in their power to get authorization from FBI headquarters merely to search the computer of Zacarias Moussaoui, the so-called twentieth hijacker. They were stalled and denied at every turn, despite providing clear evidence for the ne-

cessity of the search. One supervisory special agent in particular was responsible for the travesty. FBI Director Robert Mueller's response when Rowley's memo made the front pages: announcing plans to hire more agents and buy new computers. Oh, and he promoted that supervisory agent.

Calling for Mueller's resignation back in May, the *Wall Street Journal* 29 pointed out the obvious: "If Mueller had wanted to send a message to change the FBI mindset he would have fired the supervisory special agent who ignored the Minneapolis warnings on Moussaoui." To make matters worse, Mueller and Attorney General John Ashcroft did not inform the President of the debacle for seven months. As long as Robert Mueller is allowed to keep his job, the FBI's credibility is non-existent. The White House's response; praise all around.

So, how safe are we? 30

QUESTIONS FOR READING

1. What is Rollins's subject? (State it as a problem.)
2. What specific issues does she see within the larger problem?
3. What two problems concern her with the Department of Homeland Security and the current administration?
4. State in your own words each of Rollins's proposed solutions.

QUESTIONS FOR REASONING AND ANALYSIS

1. What is Rollins's claim? Where does she state it?
2. Analyze the author's opening two paragraphs. What rhetorical strategy is she using? Does it get your attention? Will it be effective for her anticipated audience?
3. How would you describe the author's style and tone in general throughout her essay? What, presumably, does she want to suggest with her style and tone?
4. Evaluate Rollins's eight proposed solutions. She develops each one largely by quoting various people. Are her sources credible and relevant? Convincing? Are you prepared to accept all eight proposals? Why or why not?

QUESTIONS FOR REFLECTING AND WRITING

1. Would you agree that the author has "done her homework"? If no, why not? If yes, does this make her argument more compelling, or is it what we should expect of anyone presenting a serious argument? Explain your views.
2. If you are not in agreement with one or more of Rollins's proposals, how would you rebut each one? Prepare your counterarguments.
3. Are there actions we should take that Rollins has left out of her agenda? If so, what are they? Note, for example that she mentions in paragraph 3 that "Cyberspace is still glaringly unprotected." However, she does not offer proposals for protecting cyberspace. How does an "unprotected" cyberspace aid terrorism? Do you think that cyberspace needs protecting? If not, why not? If so, what are your recommendations?

CHAPTER 17

Criminal Justice Issues

The following six articles explore and debate three current criminal justice issues: trying juveniles as adults, filming jury deliberations, and capital punishment as a sentencing option in some crimes. One response to the recent numbers of teenagers committing murder, sometimes multiple murders, has been to try them as adults so that adult sentencing, rather than juvenile detention, can be applied. We need to think, as individuals and as a society, about our approach to juvenile offenders. Once filming was allowed in some court cases, it was only a matter of time before the argument was extended to include cameras in the jury room as well. This issue poses challenging questions because we are forced to infer the consequences of jury-room cameras. How, if at all, will jurors change their deliberations knowing they are being filmed—recorded, presumably, for use by the media? Finally, two highly regarded writers debate the social, moral, and philosophical questions relevant to capital punishment.

PREREADING QUESTIONS

1. Why have we separated juveniles from the adult system? Why have some people changed their views on trying juveniles as adults?
2. What are some of the effects of appearing in front of cameras, for many people? What are the possible dangers of recording jury deliberations?
3. What are the current laws on the use of the death penalty?
4. In capital cases, what kinds of evidence do we need in order to decide on guilt beyond a reasonable doubt?
5. If you wanted to change any of the current laws to make them reflect your position, how would you go about trying to get the laws changed?

Websites Related to This Chapter's Topic

Justice Center Website: Focus on the Death Penalty

www.uaa.alaska.edu/just/death/index.html

From the University of Alaska, Anchorage, a site that gives information—
  statistics and court decisions—as well as many good links.

University of San Diego, Ethics Across the Curriculum

http://ethics.acusd.edu/death_penalty.html

Site with legislative information, statistics, and links.

Cornell Law School—Cornell Death Penalty Project

www.lawschool.cornell.edu/library/death

Contains information on court decisions and results of relevant studies.

Website of child defense attorney Andrew Vachss

http://www.vachss.com

Links to agencies and websites that deal with trying juveniles as adults.

ADULT CRIME, ADULT TIME | LINDA J. COLLIER

An attorney, Linda J. Collier is currently dean of public services and social sciences at Delaware County Community College in Pennsylvania. She has been the director of student legal services at Pennsylvania State University and special assistant for legal affairs to two college presidents, in addition to teaching courses in sociology and criminal justice. The following essay, published in the *Washington Post* in 1998, is written in response to the case of a 12-year-old and a 14-year-old shooting four students and a teacher at their school in Jonesboro, Arkansas, that same year.

PREREADING QUESTIONS Why do some think that the juvenile justice system is inadequate? What kinds of cases was it originally designed to handle?

When prosecutor Brent Davis said he wasn't sure if he could charge   1
11-year-old Andrew Golden and 13-year-old Mitchell Johnson as adults after

Tuesday afternoon's slaughter in Jonesboro, Ark., I cringed. But not for the reasons you might think.

2   I knew he was formulating a judgment based on laws that have not had a major overhaul for more than 100 years. I knew his hands were tied by the long-standing creed that juvenile offenders, generally defined as those under the age of 18, are to be treated rather than punished. I knew he would have to do legal cartwheels to get the case out of the juvenile system. But most of all, I cringed because today's juvenile suspects—even those who are accused of committing the most violent crimes—are still regarded by the law as children first and criminals second.

3   As astonishing as the Jonesboro events were, this is hardly the first time that children with access to guns and other weapons have brought tragedy to a school. Only weeks before the Jonesboro shootings, three girls in Paducah, Ky., were killed in their school lobby when a 14-year-old classmate allegedly opened fire on them. Authorities said he had several guns with him, and the alleged murder weapon was one of seven stolen from a neighbor's garage. And the day after the Jonesboro shootings, a 14-year-old in Daly City, Calif., was charged as a juvenile after he allegedly fired at his middle-school principal with a semiautomatic handgun.

4   It's not a new or unusual phenomenon for children to commit violent crimes at younger and younger ages, but it often takes a shocking incident to draw our attention to a trend already in progress. According to the U.S. Department of Justice, crimes committed by juveniles have increased by 60 percent since 1984. Where juvenile delinquency was once limited to truancy or vandalism, juveniles now are more likely to be the perpetrators of serious and deadly crimes such as arson, aggravated assault, rape and murder. And these violent offenders increasingly include those as young as the Jonesboro suspects. Since 1965, the number of 12-year-olds arrested for violent crimes has doubled and the number of 13- and 14-year-olds has tripled, according to government statistics.

5   Those statistics are a major reason why we need to revamp our antiquated juvenile justice system. Nearly every state, including Arkansas, has laws that send most youthful violent offenders to the juvenile courts, where they can only be found "delinquent" and confined in a juvenile facility (typically not past age 21). In recent years, many states have enacted changes in their juvenile crime laws, and some have lowered the age at which a juvenile can be tried as an adult for certain violent crimes. Virginia, for example, has reduced its minimum age to 14, and suspects accused of murder and aggravated malicious wounding are automatically waived to adult court. Illinois is now sending some 13-year-olds to adult court after a hearing in juvenile court. In Kansas, a 1996 law allows juveniles as young as 10 to be prosecuted as adults in some cases. These are steps in the right direction, but too many states still treat violent offenders under 16 as juveniles who belong in the juvenile system.

6   My views are not those of a frustrated prosecutor. I have represented children as a court-appointed guardian *ad litem*, or temporary guardian, in the Philadelphia juvenile justice system. Loosely defined, a guardian *ad litem* is re-

sponsible for looking after the best interest of a neglected or rebellious child who has come into the juvenile courts. It is often a humbling experience as I try to help children whose lives have gone awry, sometimes because of circumstances beyond their control.

My experience has made me believe that the system is doing a poor job at 7 treatment as well as punishment. One of my "girls," a chronic truant, was a foster child who longed to be adopted. She often talked of how she wanted a pink room, a frilly bunk bed and sisters with whom she could share her dreams. She languished in foster care from ages 2 to 13 because her drug-ravaged mother would not relinquish her parental rights. Initially, the girl refused to tolerate the half-life that the state had maintained was in her best interest. But as it became clear that we would never convince her mother to give up her rights, the girl became a frequent runaway. Eventually she ended up pregnant, wandering from place to place and committing adult crimes to survive. No longer a child, not quite a woman, she is the kind of teenage offender for whom the juvenile system has little or nothing to offer.

A brief history: Proceedings in juvenile justice began in 1890 in Chicago, 8 where the original mandate was to save wayward children and protect them from the ravages of society. The system called for children to be processed through an appendage of the family court. By design, juveniles were to be kept away from the court's criminal side, the district attorney and adult correctional institutions.

Typically, initial procedures are informal, non-threatening and not open to 9 public scrutiny. A juvenile suspect is interviewed by an "intake" officer who determines the child's fate. The intake officer may issue a warning, lecture and release; he may detain the suspect; or, he may decide to file a petition, subjecting the child to juvenile "adjudication" proceedings. If the law allows, the intake officer may make a recommendation that the juvenile be transferred to adult criminal court.

An adjudication is similar to a hearing, rather than a trial, although the ju- 10 venile may be represented by counsel and a juvenile prosecutor will represent the interests of the community. It is important to note that throughout the proceedings, no matter which side of the fence the parties are on, the operating principle is that everyone is working in the best interests of the child. Juvenile court judges do not issue findings of guilt, but decide whether a child is delinquent. If delinquency is found, the judge must decide the child's fate. Should the child be sent back to the family—assuming there is one? Declare him or her "in need of supervision," which brings in the intense help of social services? Remove the child from the family and place him or her in foster care? Confine the child to a state institution for juvenile offenders?

This system was developed with truants, vandals and petty thieves in mind. 11 But this model is not appropriate for the violent juvenile offender of today. Detaining a rapist or murderer in a juvenile facility until the age of 18 or 21 isn't even a slap on the hand. If a juvenile is accused of murdering, raping or assaulting someone with a deadly weapon, the suspect should automatically be sent to adult criminal court. What's to ponder?

12   With violent crime becoming more prevalent among the junior set, it's a mystery why there hasn't been a major overhaul of juvenile justice laws long before now. Will the Jonesboro shootings be the incident that makes us take a hard look at the current system? When it became evident that the early release of Jesse Timmendequas—whose murder of 7-year-old Megan Kanka in New Jersey sparked national outrage—had caused unwarranted tragedy, legislative action was swift. Now New Jersey has Megan's law, which requires the advance notification of a sexual predator's release into a neighborhood. Other states have followed suit.

13   It is unequivocally clear that the same type of mandate is needed to establish a uniform minimum age for trying juveniles as adults. As it stands now, there is no consistency in state laws governing waivers to adult court. One reason for this lack of uniformity is the absence of direction from the federal government or Congress. The Bureau of Justice Statistics reports that adjacent states such as New York and Pennsylvania respond differently to 16-year-old criminals, with New York tending to treat offenders of that age as adults and Pennsylvania handling them in the juvenile justice system.

14   Federal prosecution of juveniles is not totally unheard of, but it is uncommon. The Bureau of Justice Statistics estimates that during 1994, at least 65 juveniles were referred to the attorney general for transfer to adult status. In such cases, the U.S. attorney's office must certify a substantial federal interest in the case and show that one of the following is true: The state does not have jurisdiction; the state refuses to assume jurisdiction or the state does not have adequate services for juvenile offenders; the offense is a violent felony, drug trafficking or firearm offense as defined by the U.S. Code.

15   Exacting hurdles, but not insurmountable. In the Jonesboro case, prosecutor Davis has been exploring ways to enlist the federal court's jurisdiction. Whatever happens, federal prosecutions of young offenders are clearly not the long-term answer. The states must act. So as far as I can see, the next step is clear: Children who knowingly engage in adult conduct and adult crimes should automatically be subject to adult rules and adult prison time.

QUESTIONS FOR READING

1. What are some of the problems with current state laws governing juvenile crimes?
2. Briefly summarize the author's history of the juvenile justice system.
3. In addition to failing to punish properly, in the author's view, what else do juvenile court systems fail to do?
4. Where does Collier look for help in correcting the juvenile justice system?

QUESTIONS FOR REASONING AND ANALYSIS

1. What is Collier's claim? Where does she state it?
2. In paragraph 11, when she writes "What's to ponder?" what response does she want from readers?

3. Although Collier is writing in response to the Jonesboro murders, she refers to other juvenile murders in paragraph 3. What does she seek to gain by this?

4. The author asserts that she is not writing as a "frustrated prosecutor" and describes her experience as a court-appointed guardian. What does she gain by this discussion in paragraphs 6 and 7?

QUESTIONS FOR REFLECTING AND WRITING

1. Could the example of one of Collier's court-appointed "girls" be used to argue for, rather than against, the juvenile justice system? Explain your answer.

2. Do you think that juveniles should be tried as adults? If so, in what situations? If not, why not?

KIDS WHO KILL ARE STILL KIDS | RICHARD COHEN

Richard Cohen is a journalist with a syndicated column. The following column appeared in newspapers on August 3, 2001.

PREREADING QUESTIONS   Should we, as a country, have a cutoff age for capital sentencing? If so, what should the cutoff age be?

When I was about 12, I heaved a cinder block over my neighbor's fence and   1
nearly killed her. I didn't know she was there. When I was about the same age, I started a small fire in a nearby field that spread until it threatened some nearby houses. I didn't mean to do it. When I was even younger, I climbed on top of a toolshed, threw a brick in the general direction of my sister and sent her, bleeding profusely and crying so that I can still hear her, to the hospital. I didn't mean to do that, either.

I tell these stories to remind us all that kids are kids and to suggest that   2
even the worst of them—even the ones who commit murder—are still kids. I would be lying if I said that I knew what to do with them—how long they should be jailed and where—but I do know that something awful has come over this country. It seems the more incomprehensible the crime, the more likely it is that a child will be treated as an adult.

This is what happened to Nathanial Brazill, 14, who was recently sentenced   3
to 28 years in prison for the murder of a teacher, Barry Grunow. Brazill was only 13 when he shot the teacher on the final day of school. Grunow, a much-beloved teacher, had stopped Brazill from talking to two girls and disrupting the class. Earlier in the day, the boy had been suspended for throwing water balloons. He had gone home, gotten a gun and returned to school. Grunow was Brazill's favorite teacher.

I always feel in columns of this sort the necessity to say something about   4
the victim and how his life was taken from him. I feel a particular need to do so in this case because Grunow seemed to be an exceptional teacher, a good person. Anyway—and this is only me talking—I feel a certain awe, a humility,

toward people who dedicate their lives to teaching kids instead of, say, peddling tech stocks or mouthing off on television about Gary Condit.[1]

5   But Grunow is gone and nothing can be done to bring him back. That is not merely a cliché but also an important point. Because always in these cases when it comes time to justify why a minor was treated as an adult, someone says something about sending a message to other kids. This is absurd.

6   Consider what Brazill did. He shot his teacher before oodles of witnesses. He shot a man he liked. He shot someone without any chance of his getting away. He shot someone for almost no reason at all. He shot someone not in the course of a robbery or a sex crime or because he put a move on his girlfriend but because he is a screwed-up kid, damaged, full of anger and with not much self-control. He shot someone without fully comprehending the consequences. He shot someone, because, among other things, he was just 13 years old.

7   And yet, he was prosecuted—and sentenced to three years more than the mandatory minimum—as an adult. If there is one thing he is not, it is an adult. But Brazill and, earlier, 13-year-old Lionel Tate were sentenced as if they were button men for some crime family. Tate was given life without parole for the killing of a 6-year-old girl he maintained died in a wrestling accident. These boys were tried as adults but, I'd guess, their ability to participate in their own defense would be labeled juvenile.

8   Amnesty International says about 200,000 children have been tried as adults by American courts. Florida alone reports that 3,300 kids were prosecuted as adults in fiscal 1999–2000. This sends a message—but it's to the adult community: We're getting tough. Kids, however, are unlikely to get the message. I mean, you know how kids are.

9   Where is the deterrence in this policy? Will other 13-year-olds now hesitate before killing their teacher? Hardly. Who is being punished? The child at first, but later the adult he becomes.

10   Brazill will be over 40 when he gets out of jail. When he's, say, 35, will he have anything in common with the child who pulled the trigger? No more, I'd say, than I do with the jerk who nearly killed Richie Miller's mother with a cinder block. I didn't set out to hurt anyone, it's true. But neither did Brazill, he says. He just pulled the trigger and the man, somehow, died. It is, when you think about it, a childish explanation.

---

[1]Former member of Congress from California. —Ed.

QUESTIONS FOR READING

1. How many years was Brazill sentenced to? What was his crime?
2. What is Cohen's explanation of Brazill's behavior?
3. What message is supposed to be sent by trying children as adults? What is Cohen's assessment of the success of this strategy?

QUESTIONS FOR REASONING AND ANALYSIS

1. Cohen tells readers that 200,000 children have been tried as adults. Why does he include this statistic?

2. The author begins by reporting some of his actions as a youngster. What does he seek to gain from this beginning?

3. What is Cohen's claim? Evaluate his argument: Is his evidence convincing? Why or why not?

QUESTIONS FOR REFLECTING AND WRITING

1. The U.S. and Iran are the only two countries that allow for the execution of juveniles. Forty percent of the U.S. states allow the execution of people as young as 16. What should be the cutoff age for capital punishment regardless of the crime? Be prepared to support your position?

2. When you were young, did you do anything that hurt another person, either accidentally—or not so accidentally? If so, what were the consequences? How do you feel now about the incident?

3. How should the two boys Cohen uses as examples have been tried and sentenced, in your view? Be prepared to support your position.

JUSTICE FILMED IS JUSTICE DISTORTED | MARTIN KIMEL

Sometimes a commentator on Public Radio International's *Marketplace* program, Martin Kimel (b. 1960) is a securities lawyer in Washington, DC. He has written both humorous and serious articles for various newspapers and magazines. His article on cameras in the courtroom was published by the *Washington Post* on December 22, 2002.

PREREADING QUESTIONS Have you ever sat on a jury? Would you like to be called for jury duty when you are finished with college? Would you be bothered by a camera filming jury deliberations?

A Texas appeals court will soon decide whether a trial judge made a mistake when he ruled that the PBS program *Frontline* may televise the jury deliberations in a death-penalty case. In the meantime, jury selection has been suspended in the Houston trial of Cedric Ryan Harrison, who allegedly shot a man to death during a carjacking.

As a lawyer who once served as a juror in a murder trial here in Washington, I find the trial judge's decision to allow a camera in the jury room one of the most astonishing rulings in decades.

It's safe to assume that the country's criminal courts will not be busy over the holidays wiring their jury rooms for the benefit of the television networks; the trial judge's decision is not necessarily the start of a trend. But it is disturbing nonetheless because it is the most serious challenge so far to the time-honored principle of jury confidentiality. Televising jury deliberations in cases involving violent felonies (including capital-murder trials) is a terrible idea. It could change the makeup of juries, both by dissuading some thoughtful people from serving and by attracting the kind of jurors who would say anything to get their 15 minutes of fame on *Jerry Springer*. Perhaps more important, it would affect how jurors will act once they begin deliberations.

4   Take the trial I sat on some years back. The defendant was charged with murder for shooting an 18-year-old woman three times at close range, and with assault with intent to kill for shooting her cousin twice. He survived to testify against the defendant, though the defense argued that the cousin had been too high on crack to identify anyone reliably. (The cousin denied using crack that night.)

5   Out of fear of reprisal, we jurors were grateful that the judge preserved our anonymity throughout the trial by referring to us by juror numbers alone. Even with jury confidentiality, a defendant who is convicted knows that every juror voted against him because of the nearly universal requirement that felony verdicts be unanimous. At least we didn't have to worry about our faces being broadcast widely. Without that kind of confidentiality, jurors may fear that a negative comment about a defendant or witness could come back to haunt them, especially as their faces would be known to the world.

6   Surprisingly, only 14 of the 110 potential jurors summoned for the Harrison trial told the judge during jury selection that the presence of a camera in the jury room might affect their decision-making. Even assuming that the others honestly believed that they wouldn't be affected, it's a good bet that none of the 12 jurors, plus alternates, who will be chosen have participated in a murder trial before. While these jurors may believe they wouldn't be influenced by a camera, my experience suggests that they probably have no idea what they are in for. Deciding whether to send a person to prison even for a short time is an awesome responsibility, still more so when the issue is life imprisonment or death.

7   In the course of finding our defendant guilty of both first-degree murder and assault with intent to kill, more than a few tears were shed in the jury room. It was a stressful experience, and I fear that we might well have ended with a hung jury had the unblinking eye of a camera been trained on us.

8   There are several ways that filming deliberations might affect how jurors reach a verdict. For instance, passing judgment on minority defendants can raise sensitive issues that could well be exacerbated in a public setting. My trial involved black victims and a black defendant. Six jury members were black; five were white; one was Asian. Overwhelming evidence convinced a middle-aged African American juror that the defendant was guilty, but she said she didn't want to send another young black man to jail. Had we been on national TV, I wonder whether the five other non-black jurors and I, for fear of appearing racially insensitive, might have thought twice before trying to persuade her that she shouldn't base her vote on sentiment.

9   A similar dynamic applies to discussions among jurors of different backgrounds. The jury box may be the only place in the country where citizens of diverse races, ethnicities and economic backgrounds come to work together as equals, notwithstanding potentially great disparities in education. My jury of

six men and six women included a cook, a paralegal, a government worker, a federal law enforcement officer and a physician. During more than a week and a half of testimony, my fellow jurors and I developed a rapport that allowed us to speak fairly openly with each other. I doubt that this could have happened if we had known we were all going to be on television. Moreover, the knowledge that a TV editor could take an inoffensive exchange or comment out of context would have affected my behavior. And when you need a unanimous verdict from 12 people, affecting even one juror's conduct can change the outcome of a trial.

Videotaping jury deliberations in cases involving violent felonies also   10 would provide creative defense lawyers with all sorts of extraneous grist for their appellate mills. The Texas defendant who agreed to let *Frontline* film his jury's deliberations agreed not to use the videotape on appeal (though he didn't expressly waive his right to challenge any jury misconduct), but good luck to the prosecutor trying to hold him to that if the jury finds him guilty. And if the defendant does appeal, he could retain a new attorney who would surely argue that his or her client had been the victim of ineffective assistance of counsel in letting him sign such a waiver.

From my own experience as a juror, I can imagine the defense counsel ar-   11 guing on appeal that the rest of the jury exercised undue influence when we persuaded the sentimental holdout juror to follow her head in deciding how to vote, or trying to make much of our forewoman's speculating at one point about why the defendant's wife never attended his trial. (We all agreed that this was a fact we couldn't consider.) Given the cleverness of attorneys, even a joke—such as the way one of my fellow jurors referred to the defendant's folksy lawyer as "Matlock"—could provide an excuse for frivolous appeals. Jurors are not blow-dried, scripted TV personalities. But if they are put on TV, could they eventually be held to the same standards as Ted Koppel?

Finally, while there are many specific reasons to maintain jury confidential-   12 ity, there is no compelling reason to film jury deliberations.

At its best, the jury system gathers citizens together so they can bring their   13 collective wisdom to bear on serious questions of guilt and innocence. Juries provide an important check on the power of government and lend moral authority to the verdicts rendered by our judicial system. We should think twice before doing anything that would weaken them, which abandoning the long-standing practice of jury confidentiality surely would do.

QUESTIONS FOR READING

1. What is the specific occasion for Kimel's article?
2. What two sources of personal knowledge and experience does the author use?
3. What are the specifics of Kimel's jury experience? (What was the case? The makeup of the jury?)

QUESTIONS FOR REASONING AND ANALYSIS

1. What is Kimel's claim? Where does he state it?

2. What are the author's specific arguments? List them, in your own words.

3. Evaluate Kimel's sources—his backing—for the grounds he provides.

4. Which point in Kimel's argument is, in your view, most compelling? Why?

QUESTIONS FOR REFLECTING AND WRITING

1. If you were called for jury duty and knew that your deliberations would be filmed, would you agree to serve, or would you tell the judge that filming would affect your decision making? Explain your position and reasoning.

2. If you were a judge, would you support cameras in the jury room? If so, how would you instruct jurors? If not, how would you defend your position?

THE CASE FOR LETTING CAMERAS INTO THE SACRED JURY ROOM | TERESA WYSZOMIERSKI

A New York-based attorney specializing in finance, Teresa Wyszomierski is vice president of Moody's Investors Service. Her defense of cameras in the jury room was published on January 31, 2003, by the *Chicago Tribune*.

PREREADING QUESTIONS If you were going to defend the use of cameras filming jury deliberations, how would you build that argument? What might be one or two good reasons for using cameras?

1   Last fall, a Texas judge tried to pry the lid off the "black box" of American jurisprudence—jury deliberations—by allowing PBS's *Frontline* to videotape jurors as they reach a verdict in the capital murder trial of Cedric Harrison. Jury selection in that Texas case has been halted pending an appeal by the prosecution, which objected to the filming.

2   As an attorney who recently served as a juror in a murder case, I think the *Frontline* documentary should get the go-ahead. In fact, I think jury deliberations should be filmed on a routine basis to make sure our legal system works as advertised, because right now it doesn't.

3   For example, all prospective jurors promise the judge they will accept his or her "charge" or instructions as to what the law is and how it should be applied. Unfortunately, most jurors can't keep this promise because they don't understand the judge's charge.

4   Jurors are often confused by the instructions because they are often conveyed in incomprehensible legalese. In addition, the charge is usually the first time jurors are introduced to abstract concepts like "proof of guilt beyond a reasonable doubt."

5   The murder case I was on involved two co-defendants charged with seven crimes each. Despite my legal training, I doubted that I would be able to accurately remember all the elements of these crimes after only one oral reading.

The judge wouldn't let me take notes, so I visited the New York Unified Court System Web site beforehand to review the state's penal code charges for the crimes in question.

6   It's a good thing I did. None of the other jurors could remember the judge's long and detailed charge and were grateful that I could. This kept our deliberations focused and ensured that we were applying the law as instructed by the judge.

7   But what if I hadn't done this preparation, as most jurors don't? A well-meaning, but confused, jury could easily have convicted an innocent defendant. Shouldn't a wronged defendant be allowed to discover such a life-altering error, especially when the death penalty is at issue?

8   And what about juries that aren't confused, but choose to deliberately ignore a judge's instructions? So-called "jury nullification" can also spell disaster for justice, as when Southern juries in years past refused to convict those who lynched blacks.

9   The prosecutor in the Harrison case has argued that having a camera in the jury room would discourage potential jurors from serving. But before jury selection in the Harrison case was halted pending appeal, only 14 of the 110 prospective jurors expressed reservations about the filming.

10   The prospect of unwanted notoriety after a televised broadcast probably contributed to this group's reluctance. But this would be less of a concern if jury deliberations were taped solely to facilitate appellate review, and not for entertainment purposes.

11   And if prospective jurors elect not to serve because they're afraid that their decision won't withstand objective scrutiny, then it's best that they be excluded. Our legal system will benefit if taping deliberations forces jurors to render a more carefully considered verdict.

12   The prosecution has also speculated that jurors willing to be filmed are more apt to posture and play to the camera. Alternatively, a *New York Times* editorial hypothesized that "jurors, especially less educated and articulate ones, may be wary of speaking out if they know they are being judged."

13   But such condescending speculation ignores practical experience. Jury deliberations have been taped and televised before by PBS, ABC, and CBS with no discernible impact on the deliberative process.

14   And by observing a few procedural safeguards, the potentially disruptive influence of a camera in the jury room can be eliminated. Prospective jurors should be informed that their deliberations will be filmed, and the camera should be hidden so as not to be a distraction. In addition, the jury's deliberations should not be broadcast live, but only after the verdict has been rendered.

15   It is likely that videotaping jury deliberations will lengthen the appeals process. But so be it. Legally defective deliberations have compromised the integrity of our system for too long. It's time for the jury room to come out of the closet.

QUESTIONS FOR READING

1. What is the occasion for this article?

2. What two sources of knowledge and personal experience does the author draw on?

3. What are the specifics of Wyszomierski's jury experience? What was the case? What particular point does the author make about her jury experience?

4. What does the author concede as a consequence of cameras? How does she defend tolerating this consequence?

QUESTIONS FOR REASONING AND ANALYSIS

1. What is Wyszomierski's claim? Where does she state it? How is her position qualified?

2. What are the particular reasons she offers in defense of her claim? List them in your own words. Which ones are rebuttals of counterarguments?

3. Evaluate her grounds. Do some of her reasons provide better support than others? Explain and defend your evaluation.

QUESTIONS FOR REFLECTING AND WRITING

1. Wyszomierski begins with the assumption that our legal system is flawed. Do you agree with that assumption? Why or why not? If you agree, do you think that filming jury deliberations will improve the system? Why or why not?

2. Who, in your view, has the more convincing argument: Kimel or Wyszomierski? Why? Prepare a comparative analysis of the two arguments.

THE ULTIMATE PUNISHMENT: A DEFENSE | ERNEST VAN DEN HAAG

A naturalized citizen born in 1914 in the Netherlands, Ernest van den Haag holds a doctorate from New York University and has been a psychoanalyst. In addition, he has written many articles in both American and European journals and several books on sociological issues, including violence and crime. "The Ultimate Punishment: A Defense" is reprinted (with some footnotes omitted) from the May 7, 1986, issue of the *Harvard Law Review*. Van den Haag effectively organizes his defense around the arguments put forward by his opponents.

PREREADING QUESTIONS Do you have a position on capital punishment? If so, what is it? If not, do you think you should take a stand on this issue? Why or why not?

1   In an average year about 20,000 homicides occur in the United States. Fewer than 300 convicted murderers are sentenced to death. But because no more than thirty murderers have been executed in any recent year, most convicts sentenced to death are likely to die of old age.[1] Nonetheless, the death penalty looms large in discussions: it raises important moral questions independent of the number of executions.

The death penalty is our harshest punishment. It is irrevocable: it ends the existence of those punished, instead of temporarily imprisoning them. Further, although not intended to cause physical pain, execution is the only corporal punishment still applied to adults. These singular characteristics contribute to the perennial, impassioned controversy about capital punishment.

I. DISTRIBUTION

Consideration of the justice, morality, or usefulness of capital punishment is often conflated with objections to its alleged discriminatory or capricious distribution among the guilty. Wrongly so. If capital punishment is immoral *in se*, no distribution among the guilty could make it moral. If capital punishment is moral, no distribution would make it immoral. Improper distribution cannot affect the quality of what is distributed, be it punishments or rewards. Discriminatory or capricious distribution thus could not justify abolition of the death penalty. Further, maldistribution inheres no more in capital punishment than in any other punishment.

Maldistribution between the guilty and the innocent is, by definition, unjust. But the injustice does not lie in the nature of the punishment. Because of the finality of the death penalty, the most grievous maldistribution occurs when it is imposed upon the innocent. However, the frequent allegations of discrimination and capriciousness refer to maldistribution among the guilty and not to the punishment of the innocent.

Maldistribution of any punishment among those who deserve it is irrelevant to its justice or morality. Even if poor or black convicts guilty of capital offenses suffer capital punishments, and other convicts equally guilty of the same crimes do not, a more equal distribution, however desirable, would merely be more equal. It would not be more just to the convicts under sentence of death.

Punishments are imposed on persons, not on racial or economic groups. Guilt is personal. The only relevant question is: does the person to be executed deserve the punishment? Whether or not others who deserved the same punishment, whatever their economic or racial group, have avoided execution is irrelevant. If they have, the guilt of the executed convicts would not be diminished, nor would their punishment be less deserved. To put the issue starkly, if the death penalty were imposed on guilty blacks, but not on guilty whites, or, if it were imposed by a lottery among the guilty, this irrationally discriminatory or capricious distribution would neither make the penalty unjust, nor cause anyone to be unjustly punished, despite the undue impunity bestowed on others.

Equality, in short, seems morally less important than justice. And justice is independent of distributional inequalities. The ideal of equal justice demands that justice be equally distributed, not that it be replaced by equality. Justice requires that as many of the guilty as possible be punished, regardless of whether others have avoided punishment. To let these others escape the deserved punishment does not do justice to them, or to society. But it is not unjust to those who could not escape.

8   These moral considerations are not meant to deny that irrational discrimination, or capriciousness, would be inconsistent with constitutional requirements. But I am satisfied that the Supreme Court has in fact provided for
adherence to the constitutional requirement of equality as much as possible.
Some inequality is indeed unavoidable as a practical matter in any system.[2] But,
ultra posse neo obligatur. (Nobody is bound beyond ability.)

9   Recent data reveal little direct racial discrimination in the sentencing of
those arrested and convicted of murder. The abrogation of the death penalty
for rape has eliminated a major source of racial discrimination. Concededly,
some discrimination based on the race of murder victims may exist; yet, this
discrimination affects criminal victimizers in an unexpected way. Murderers of
whites are thought more likely to be executed than murderers of blacks. Black
victims, then, are less fully vindicated than white ones. However, because most
black murderers kill blacks, black murderers are spared the death penalty more
often than are white murderers. They fare better than most white murderers.
The motivation behind unequal distribution of the death penalty may well have
been to discriminate against blacks, but the result has favored them. Maldistribution is thus a straw man for empirical as well as analytical reasons.

II. MISCARRIAGES OF JUSTICE

10   In a recent survey Professors Hugo Adam Bedau and Michael Radelet
found that 7000 persons were executed in the United States between 1900
and 1985 and that 25 were innocent of capital crimes. Among the innocents
they list Sacco and Vanzetti as well as Ethel and Julius Rosenberg. Although
their data may be questionable, I do not doubt that, over a long enough period, miscarriages of justice will occur even in capital cases.

11   Despite precautions, nearly all human activities, such as trucking, lighting,
or construction, cost the lives of some innocent bystanders. We do not give up
these activities, because the advantages, moral or material, outweigh the unintended losses. Analogously, for those who think the death penalty just, miscarriages of justice are offset by the moral benefits and the usefulness of doing
justice. For those who think the death penalty unjust even when it does not
miscarry, miscarriages can hardly be decisive.

III. DETERRENCE

12   Despite much recent work, there has been no conclusive statistical demon-
stration that the death penalty is a better deterrent than are alternative punishments. However, deterrence is less than decisive for either side. Most
abolitionists acknowledge that they would continue to favor abolition even if
the death penalty were shown to deter more murders than alternatives could
deter. Abolitionists appear to value the life of a convicted murderer or, at least,
his nonexecution, more highly than they value the lives of the innocent victims
who might be spared by deterring prospective murderers.

13   Deterrence is not altogether decisive for me either. I would favor retention
of the death penalty as retribution even if it were shown that the threat of execution could not deter prospective murderers not already deterred by the

threat of imprisonment.[3] Still, I believe the death penalty, because of its finality, is more feared than imprisonment, and deters some prospective murderers not deterred by the threat of imprisonment. Sparing the lives of even a few prospective victims by deterring their murderers is more important than preserving the lives of convicted murderers because of the possibility, or even the probability, that executing them would not deter others. Whereas the lives of the victims who might be saved are valuable, that of the murderer has only negative value, because of his crime. Surely the criminal law is meant to protect the lives of potential victims in preference to those of actual murderers.

Murder rates are determined by many factors; neither the severity nor the probability of the threatened sanction is always decisive. However, for the long run, I share the view of Sir James Fitzjames Stephen: "Some men probably abstain from murder because they fear that if they committed murder they would be hanged. Hundreds of thousands abstain from it because they regard it with horror. One great reason why they regard it with horror is that murderers are hanged." Penal sanctions are useful in the long run for the formation of the internal restraints so necessary to control crime. The severity and finality of the death penalty is appropriate to the seriousness and the finality of murder. **14**

IV. INCIDENTAL ISSUES: COST, RELATIVE SUFFERING, BRUTALIZATION

Many nondecisive issues are associated with capital punishment. Some believe that the monetary cost of appealing a capital sentence is excessive. Yet most comparisons of the cost of life imprisonment with the cost of execution, apart from their dubious relevance, are flawed at least by the implied assumption that life prisoners will generate no judicial costs during their imprisonment. At any rate, the actual monetary costs are trumped by the importance of doing justice. **15**

Others insist that a person sentenced to death suffers more than his victim suffered, and that this (excess) suffering is undue according to the *lex talionis* (rule of retaliation). We cannot know whether the murderer on death row suffers more than his victim suffered; however, unlike the murderer, the victim deserved none of the suffering inflicted. Further, the limitations of the *lex talionis* were meant to restrain private vengeance, not the social retribution that has taken its place. Punishment—regardless of the motivation—is not intended to revenge, offset, or compensate for the victim's suffering, or to be measured by it. Punishment is to vindicate the law and the social order undermined by the crime. This is why the kidnapper's penal confinement is not limited to the period for which he imprisoned his victim; nor is a burglar's confinement meant merely to offset the suffering or the harm he caused his victim; nor is it meant only to offset the advantage he gained.[4] **16**

Another argument heard at least since Beccaria is that, by killing a murderer, we encourage, endorse, or legitimize unlawful killing. Yet, although all punishments are meant to be unpleasant, it is seldom argued that they legitimize the unlawful imposition of identical unpleasantness. Imprisonment is not thought to legitimize kidnapping; neither are fines thought to legitimize robbery. The difference between murder and execution, or between kidnapping **17** and imprisonment, is that the first is unlawful and undeserved, the second a lawful and deserved punishment for an unlawful act. The physical similarities of the punishment to the crime are irrelevant. The relevant difference is not physical, but social.[5]

V. JUSTICE, EXCESS, DEGRADATION

18   We threaten punishments in order to deter crime. We impose them not only to make the threats credible but also as retribution (justice) for the crimes that were not deterred. Threats and punishments are necessary to deter and deterrence is a sufficient practical justification for them. Retribution is an independent moral justification. Although penalties can be unwise, repulsive, or inappropriate, and those punished can be pitiable, in a sense the infliction of legal punishment on a guilty person cannot be unjust. By committing the crime, the criminal volunteered to assume the risk of receiving a legal punishment that he could have avoided by not committing the crime. The punishment he suffers is the punishment he voluntarily risked suffering and, therefore, it is no more unjust to him than any other event for which one knowingly volunteers to assume the risk. Thus, the death penalty cannot be unjust to the guilty criminal.

19   There remain, however, two moral objections. The penalty may be regarded as always excessive as retribution and always morally degrading. To regard the death penalty as always excessive, one must believe that no crime—no matter how heinous—could possibly justify capital punishment. Such a belief can be neither corroborated nor refuted; it is an article of faith.

20   Alternatively, or concurrently, one may believe that everybody, the murderer no less than the victim, has an imprescriptible (natural?) right to life. The law therefore should not deprive anyone of life. I share Jeremy Bentham's view that any such "natural and imprescriptible rights" are "nonsense upon stilts."

21   Justice Brennan has insisted that the death penalty is "uncivilized," "inhuman," inconsistent with "human dignity" and with "the sanctity of life," that it "treats members of the human race as nonhumans, as objects to be toyed with and discarded," that it is "uniquely degrading to human dignity" and "by its very nature, [involves] a denial of the executed person's humanity." Justice Brennan does not say why he thinks execution "uncivilized." Hitherto most civilizations have had the death penalty, although it has been discarded in Western Europe, where it is currently unfashionable probably because of its abuse by totalitarian regimes.

22   By "degrading," Justice Brennan seems to mean that execution degrades the executed convicts. Yet philosophers, such as Immanuel Kant and G.F.W. Hegel, have insisted that, when deserved, execution, far from degrading the executed convict, affirms his humanity by affirming his rationality and his responsibility for his actions. They thought that execution, when deserved, is required for the sake of the convict's dignity. (Does not life imprisonment violate human dignity more than execution, by keeping alive a prisoner deprived of all autonomy?)

23   Common sense indicates that it cannot be death—our common fate—that is inhuman. Therefore, Justice Brennan must mean that death degrades when

it comes not as a natural or accidental event, but as a deliberate social imposition. The murderer learns through his punishment that his fellow men have found him unworthy of living; that because he has murdered, he is being expelled from the community of the living. This degradation is self-inflicted. By murdering, the murderer has so dehumanized himself that he cannot remain among the living. The social recognition of his self-degradation is the punitive essence of execution. To believe, as Justice Brennan appears to, that the degradation is inflicted by the execution reverses the direction of causality.

Execution of those who have committed heinous murders may deter only 24 one murder per year. If it does, it seems quite warranted. It is also the only fitting retribution for murder I can think of.

NOTES

1. Death row as a semipermanent residence is cruel, because convicts are denied the normal amenities of prison life. Thus, unless death row residents are integrated into the prison population, the continuing accumulation of convicts on death row should lead us to accelerate either the rate of executions or the rate of commutations. I find little objection to integration.

2. The ideal of equality, unlike the ideal of retributive justice (which can be approximated separately in each instance), is clearly unattainable unless all guilty persons are apprehended, and thereafter tried, convicted and sentenced by the same court, at the same time. Unequal justice is the best we can do; it is still better than the injustice, equal or unequal, which occurs if, for the sake of equality, we deliberately allow some who could be punished to escape.

3. If executions were shown to increase the murder rate in the long run, I would favor abolition. Sparing the innocent victims who would be spared, *ex hypothesi,* by the nonexecution of murderers would be more important to me than the execution, however just, of murderers. But although there is a lively discussion of the subject, no serious evidence exists to support the hypothesis that executions produce a higher murder rate. *Cf.* Phillips, *The Deterrent Effect of Capital Punishment: New Evidence on an Old Controversy,* 86 AM. J. Soc. 139 (1980) (arguing that murder rates drop immediately after executions of criminals).

4. Thus restitution (a civil liability) cannot satisfy the punitive purpose of penal sanctions, whether the purpose be retributive or deterrent.

5. Some abolitionists challenge: If the death penalty is just and serves as a deterrent, why not televise executions? The answer is simple. The death even of a murderer, however well-deserved, should not serve as public entertainment. It so served in earlier centuries. But in this respect our sensibility has changed for the better, I believe. Further, television unavoidably would trivialize executions, wedged in, as they would be, between game shows, situation comedies and the like. Finally, because televised executions would focus on the physical aspects of the punishment, rather than

the nature of the crime and the suffering of the victim, a televised execution would present the murderer as the victim of the state. Far from communicating the moral significance of the execution, television would shift the focus to the pitiable fear of the murderer. We no longer place in cages those sentenced to imprisonment to expose them to public view. Why should we so expose those sentenced to execution?

QUESTIONS FOR READING

1. What does van den Haag mean by "distribution"? That is, what issue in the death-penalty debate does the author examine in section one?

2. On what grounds does van den Haag dismiss the issue of possible maldistribution of death sentencing among the guilty? State his argument in your own words.

3. Does van den Haag believe that a significant racial bias can be found in the distribution of capital punishment? Does he offer evidence to support his views?

4. According to van den Haag, what kind of logical fallacy is illustrated by the argument of maldistribution?

5. On what two grounds does the author dismiss challenges to the death penalty based on miscarriages of justice?

6. What do studies show about the death penalty's potential as a deterrent to murder?

7. What is the position on deterrence of those who oppose the death penalty? What does van den Haag conclude about the values of abolitionists?

8. Why does van den Haag dismiss deterrence as an issue in the debate?

9. Why should costs be considered an irrelevant issue?

10. What is the purpose of punishing a criminal, according to van den Haag? Why is this purpose important to our understanding of death sentencing?

11. How does the author refute the idea that death sentencing legitimizes murder? Those who make this claim are using what type of argument? What strategy does van den Haag use to reveal a weakness in this type of argument?

12. What, finally, is the author's justification of legal punishment, including the death penalty?

QUESTIONS FOR REASONING AND ANALYSIS

1. To argue that the death penalty is always excessive, what must one believe? Why does van den Haag believe that the death penalty does not degrade? Explain his argument in your own words.

2. Where does the author place his claim, the thesis of his essay? What does he accomplish by this choice?

3. Consider the author's word choice in the second section. What words does he avoid using that a writer opposed to the death penalty might use instead of "miscarriage of justice" or to refer to the persons executed because of the miscarriage?

QUESTIONS FOR REFLECTING AND WRITING

1. Van den Haag is prepared to accept some miscarriages of justice (some innocent people will be punished) to achieve the advantages of capital punishment. Are you? If you agree with the author, explain why. If you disagree, how would you challenge van den Haag?

2. Van den Haag argues that capital punishment is a form of retribution for murder; it is not revenge but justice. Do you agree with his distinction between retribution and revenge? Explain your views.

3. Evaluate van den Haag's argument. Is it reasoned, thorough, and appropriately serious? Is it logical? Do you think he is right? Why or why not?

DEATH IS DIFFERENT | HUGO ADAM BEDAU

A native of Oregon with a doctorate from Harvard University, Hugo Adam Bedau (b. 1926) has taught for many years in the philosophy department at Tufts University. He is the author of articles and books on justice and capital punishment, including *The Courts, the Constitution and Capital Punishment* (1977) and *Death Is Different* (1987). In the following essay, the concluding chapter of *Death Is Different*, Bedau provides a thorough review of the debating points in the argument over capital punishment.

PREREADING QUESTIONS On what should a stand on the death penalty be based? On social/political concerns? On moral or religious beliefs? On practical considerations that include human error? Why?

Insofar as fundamental moral questions are raised by the death penalty, 1 their resolution does not turn on what a majority of the Supreme Court says the Constitution permits or forbids. Nor does it rest on what the tea leaves of public-opinion polls can be construed to mean. Morally speaking, what are at stake are the *reasons* that can be brought forward to support or to criticize this punishment. These reasons—familiar from public debates, letters to the editor, and radio and television talk shows—have not significantly altered over the past generation, and perhaps not even during the past century.

In order of increasing importance, the main reasons for support seem to 2 me to be these six: (1) the death penalty is a far less expensive method of punishment than the alternative of life imprisonment; the death penalty is more effective in preventing crime than the alternative because (2) it is a more effective deterrent, and because (3) it more effectively incapacitates; (4) the death penalty is required by justice; (5) in many cases there is no feasible alternative punishment; and (6) the death penalty vindicates the moral order and thus is an indispensable symbol of public authority. I want to evaluate each of these reasons and elaborate especially on those of salient current importance.

THE TAXPAYER'S ARGUMENT

Is the death penalty really so much less expensive than long-term impris- 3 onment? The answer depends on how one allocates the costs imposed under the two alternatives. The few attempts that have been made to do this in a manner comparable to the way economists try to answer other questions about the costs of alternative social policies are in agreement. In the words of the most recent study, "A criminal justice system that includes the death penalty costs more than a system that chooses life imprisonment."[1] Why this is true is easily understood. It is mainly a consequence of the commendable desire to afford every protection to a defendant whose life is at stake, and virtually every such defendant avails himself of all these protections. If the defendant is indigent, as are most of those accused of crimes that put them in jeopardy of the death penalty, then society has to foot the bill for the defendant's attorney as well as for the costs involved in the prosecution, jury selection, trial, and appeals. Although in theory these costs would need to be paid even if the defendant were not on trial for his life, in practice the evidence shows that non-death-penalty trials and appeals are generally less protracted and therefore less expensive. So the taxpayer's argument, as I have called it, is simply wrong on the facts.

4   But, of course, even if it were sound, no decent citizen or responsible legislator would support the death penalty by relying on this argument alone. Those who seriously advance it do so only because they also believe that the criminals in question ought to be executed whatever the cost to society and however galling the expenditure may be. As a consequence, the taxpayer's argument is really no more than a side issue, since defenders and critics of the death penalty agree that economic costs should take a back seat to justice and social defense where human life is concerned.

UNIQUELY EFFECTIVE DETERRENT

5   No one has ever offered any scientific evidence that the death penalty is an effective deterrent, or more effective than the alternative of long-term imprisonment, to any such crime as rape, arson, burglary, kidnapping, aircraft hijacking, treason, espionage, or terrorism (which itself typically involves one or more of these other crimes). All arguments for the death penalty that rest on belief in its superior deterrent capacity to prevent or reduce the incidence of these crimes depend entirely on guesswork, common sense, or analogy to its allegedly superior deterrent effects on the crime of murder.

6   What, then, is the evidence that the death penalty is an effective deterrent to murder? There is little or none. Murder comes in many different forms (gangland killings, murder among family members, murder during armed robbery or burglary, murder in jail or prison, murder for hire, murder to escape custody or avoid arrest), but very little of the research on deterrence has concentrated exclusively on one of these types to the exclusion of all the rest. The threat of executions is conceivably a much better deterrent to some types of murder than to others; but no research currently exists to confirm such a hypothesis.

7   It doesn't really matter. Deterrence is increasingly a make-weight in the argument for the death penalty. Public opinion surveys indicate that most of those who profess support for the death penalty would support it even if they were convinced—contrary to what they believe—that it is not a better deter-

rent than life imprisonment.[2] I find this plausible. Although from time to time there is sporadic evidence in favor of the deterrent power of executions (hardly anyone who thinks about it attaches much differential deterrent efficacy to the death penalty *statutes,* all by themselves), none of it survives careful scrutiny very long.[3] If anything, there is a steadily accumulating body of evidence to suggest that on balance the death penalty may cause (or encourage, or set the example for) more homicides than it prevents, because its "brutalizing" effect out-performs its deterrent effect.[4]

Furthermore, and quite apart from the status of the evidence on the issue 8 of deterrence vs. brutalization, one would expect that the rationale for deterrence in our society is of slowly declining importance. In previous centuries and up to a generation ago, when our society punished many *non*homicidal crimes with death, deterrence was the most plausible reason for hanging a counterfeiter or a horse thief or a claim jumper. Today, however, with the death penalty applied exclusively to murder, nondeterrent considerations naturally play an increasingly prominent role all the time. Indeed, social science research, public opinion, and Supreme Court rulings all neatly converge at this point. Despite more than a decade of effort to obtain convincing support for rational belief in the superior deterrent power of the death penalty, the evidence points the other way. During the same period, advocates of capital punishment—both those who are and those who are not aware of this lack of evidence—shifted the basis of their support for executions from deterrence to other reasons. Meanwhile, the Supreme Court has said in effect that the death penalty is unconstitutional except where it is not disproportionate to the crime and regardless of its deterrent effects.

From a public-policy perspective, one can say this: During the past fifteen 9 years, the legislative re-enactment of death penalty statutes has been no more than a series of stabs in the dark, insofar as these laws have been predicated on their supposed superior deterrence. A legislature ought to have better reasons than this for trying to protect the life of its citizens by imposing the threat of the death penalty. On moral grounds, general deterrence is certainly a legitimate function of the criminal law and therefore a justifiable basis on which to construct a system of punishments under law. Nevertheless, the choice of more rather than less severity in punishment for particular crimes on grounds of better deterrence alone encounters two different objections. One is that we violate moral principles if we are willing to use punitive methods, regardless of their savagery, in order to secure slight improvements in deterrence; the other is that there simply is no adequate evidence in favor of the superior deterrent efficacy of the death penalty.

INCAPACITATION AND PREVENTION

No one can dispute that capital punishment, when carried out, does ef- 10 fectively incapacitate each offender who is executed. (This has nothing to do with deterrence, however, because deterrence operates by threat and intimidation, not by destroying the capacity to break the law.) Does this incapacitation make a significant dent in the crime rate? The Department of Justice has reported that as of the end of 1984 "approximately 2 of every 3 offenders under sentence of death had a prior felony conviction; nearly 1 out of 10 had previously been convicted for homicide."[5] These data indicate that more than a hundred of those currently under sentence of death may be some of the worst offenders in the nation—and that several hundred more served a prison term for robbery, assault, or some other crime, and then, after their release, went on to commit the even graver crime of murder. (Of course, these data simultaneously show that the vast majority of condemned prisoners are *not* recidivist murderers.) But do these data also show that society needs the incapacitating power of death to prevent more crimes from being committed by convicted capital offenders?

11   If parole boards and release authorities knew in advance which inmates would murder after their release, the inmates in question would obviously be prevented from committing these offenses by being kept in some form of custody. Yet we have no reliable methods for predicting future dangerousness, and especially not for the propensity of a convicted murderer to murder again.[6] Consequently, the only effective general-policy alternatives to the present one are a system of mandatory death penalties and a system of mandatory prison terms for life. Even then, if the Bureau's own statistics are reliable, this would prevent only a tiny fraction of the twenty thousand or so murders committed in this nation each year. The truth is, as all release statistics agree, very few of the persons convicted of homicide and sent to prison are ever convicted of homicide again. Either to kill all those convicted of murder or to keep them all in prison forever, because of a few exceptions that cannot be identified in advance, would be an expensive and unjustified policy that very few of us, on reflection, would want to support.

12   Opponents of the death penalty encounter their stiffest objections when they try to explain why even the multiple or serial or recidivist murderer should not be executed. Few would disagree that "the thirst for revenge is keenest in the case of mass murder, . . . especially when it includes elements of sadism and brutality against innocent victims."[7] Revenge apart, incapacitation probably has its most convincing application in such cases. It is hardly surprising that many who generally oppose the death penalty would be willing to make an exception for such killers.

13   Let us note first that if the death penalty were confined to such cases, abolitionists would have scored a major victory. The immediate consequence of such a policy would be an unprecedented reduction in the annual number of death sentences—a drop from more than two hundred per year to fewer than twenty, if we can rely on the Bureau of Justice Statistics report quoted above. Any policy change that reduced death sentences by more than 90 percent should be welcomed by opponents of the death penalty as a giant step in the right direction.

14   More controversial is whether abolitionists could accommodate such an exception on moral grounds. The best way to do so, it seems to me, is to argue much as George Bernard Shaw did earlier in this century in his little book *The Crime of Imprisonment* that the execution of such murderers is society's

only alternative—we have no nonlethal methods of sedation or restraint that suffice to make certain that such offenders will not and cannot kill yet again. However, this is a factual question, and I (unlike Shaw) think that once the offender is in our custody, we are never in the position where our only recourse is to lethal methods. Others who have studied the problem more carefully agree;[8] there are reasonably humane methods at our disposal for coping with the most difficult and dangerous prisoners.

In the end, however, I think one must admit that the refusal to execute a 15 murderer who has repeated his crime—not to mention those who embody murderous evil on a gigantic scale, such as an Adolph Eichmann or a Lavrenti Beria—is evidence of a position on the death penalty that owes something to fanatic devotion as well as to cool reason. Dedicated pacifists and devoutly religious opponents of the death penalty may well be able to embrace such categorical opposition to executions without fear of rebuke from reason. Conscientious liberals, however, cannot so easily refuse to compromise. Do they not already compromise on other life-and-death issues—often tolerating suicide, euthanasia, abortion, the use of lethal force in social and self-defense—thereby showing that they refuse to accept any moral principle that categorically condemns all killing? If so, what is so peculiarly objectionable, from the moral point of view as they see it, in an occasional state-authorized killing of that rare criminal, the murderer who has murdered more than once? I cannot point to any clear and defensible moral principle of general acceptability that is violated by such a compromise, a principle that *absolutely forbids* such executions. If one nonetheless opposes all executions, as I do, then it must be on other grounds.

RETRIBUTIVE AND VINDICTIVE JUSTICE

Today there is substantial agreement that retribution is an essential aspect 16 of the criminal justice system, and that a general policy of punishment for convicted criminals is the best means to this end. Less argument exists on whether retribution alone justifies the practice of punishment; and there is no consensus on how to construct a penalty schedule on retributive grounds, matching the severity of punishments to the gravity of crimes. Regrettable confusion of the dangerous (though normal) emotion of anger and the desire for revenge it spawns—neither of which has any reliable connection to justice—with moral indignation at victimization—which does—often clouds the thinking of those who defend the "morality" of capital punishment.[9] There is also disagreement on whether other considerations of justice—such as equality, fairness of administration, and respect for the rights of the accused—should yield or prevail when they conflict with the demands of retribution.

These issues are inescapably philosophical, and I have my own views on 17 them, which I have explained elsewhere.[10] In a word, the most that principles of retribution can do for the death penalty is to *permit* it for murder; principles of retribution are strained beyond their capacity if they are invoked to justify the death penalty for any other crime. Thus if retribution is the moral principle on which defenders of the death penalty want to rest their case, then morality requires that nonhomicidal crimes must be punished in some less severe manner. However, the principles of retribution do not *require* us to punish murder by death; what they require is the severest punishment for the gravest crime consistent with our other moral convictions. Consequently, the appeal to retribution in the present climate of discussion—and it is a widespread appeal—fails to justify the death penalty.

18   In fact I think there is considerable self-deception among those who think they rest their defense of the death penalty on the moral principles of just retribution. Those principles cannot explain why society actually executes those few whom it does, and why it sentences to death no more than a small percentage of the murderers it convicts. Retribution is another fig leaf to cover our nakedness, I am afraid, even if it appears to be a respectable line of moral reasoning when taken in the abstract.

19   In recent years, neo-conservative writers of various sorts—such as columnist George F. Will, New York's Mayor Edward Koch, and academicians Walter Berns and Ernest van den Haag—have made much of the vindictive powers of the death penalty and of the civilizing and moralizing influence it thus wields. Van den Haag writes, "The [death] penalty is meant to vindicate the social order."[11] Berns elaborates the point: "The criminal law must be made awful, by which I mean, awe-inspiring. . . . It must remind us of the moral order by which alone we can live as *human* beings, and in our day the only punishment that can do this is capital punishment."[12] The language is resonant, but the claim is unconvincing.

20   One purpose of *any* system of punishment is to vindicate the moral order established by the criminal law—and properly so, because that order protects the rights of the law-abiding and because in a liberal society those rights are the basis for self-esteem and mutual respect. To go further, however, and insist that lethal punishment is the "only" appropriate response by society to the gravest crimes is wrong on two counts. The claim itself relies on naked moral intuitions about how to fit punishment to crimes, and such intuitions—with their deceptive clarity and superficial rationale—are treacherous. The least bit of historical sophistication would tell us that our forebears used the same kind of intuitive claims on behalf of maiming and other savageries that we would be ashamed to preach today. Furthermore, the claim makes sense only against the background of a conception of the state as a mystical entity of semi-divine authority, a conception that is hardly consistent with our pluralistic, liberal, non-theocratic traditions.

THE ALTERNATIVE

21   Imprisonment as it is currently practiced in this country is anything but an ideal alternative to the death penalty. Life imprisonment without the possibility of parole has been opposed by all experienced prison administrators as a virtually unmanageable option. The more one knows about most American prisons the more one judges long-term imprisonment to be a terrible curse for all concerned.[13] Defenders of the death penalty rightly point out that persons in prison can and sometimes do murder other inmates, guards, or visitors—

although such crimes occur much less frequently than some of those defenders imply. (Nor do they occur with greater frequency in the prisons of states that do not punish these crimes with death than in the prisons of states that do.[14]) So imprisonment for ten or twenty years, not to mention for life, is vulnerable to many objections. Indeed, a cynic might even go so far as to say that one of the best reasons for the death penalty is the alternative to it. Nevertheless, I think this alternative is still superior to execution—and will have to suffice until something better is proposed—for at least three important reasons.

First, society avoids the unsolvable problem of picking and choosing 22 among the bad to try to find the worst, in order to execute them. Experience ought long ago to have taught us that it is an illusion to expect prosecutors, juries, and courts to perform this task in a fashion that survives criticism. Deciding not to kill any among the murderers we convict enables us to punish them all more equitably, just as it relieves us of the illusion that we can choose the worst among the bad, the irredeemable from the others, those who "deserve to die" from those who really do not.

Second, we avoid the risk and costly error of executing the innocent, in fa- 23 vor of the equally risky but far less costly error of imprisoning the innocent. Arresting, trying, convicting, and punishing the innocent is an unavoidable problem, whose full extent in our history is only now beginning to be understood. Recent research on persons erroneously convicted of capital crimes in this century in the United States has identified some 350 such cases.[15] Scores of these convictions occurred in states where there was no death penalty; dozens of these errors were corrected and in some instances the wrongly convicted defendant was indemnified. Not so in all cases in the death penalty states. Where is the necessity—moral or empirical—to run the risk of executing the innocent?[16]

Third, there is a crucial symbolic significance in drawing the line at punish- 24 ments that deprive the offender of his liberty. Just as we no longer permit the authorities to use torture to secure confessions or to attack the body of the convicted offender with whips, branding irons, or other instruments that maim and stigmatize, nor to carry out the death penalty by the cruelest means our fevered imaginations can devise—even though some still cry out that social defense and just retribution require it—so we should repudiate the death penalty. It belongs alongside these other barbaric practices, which our society has rejected in principle.

For at least these reasons, the alternative of imprisonment is preferable to 25 death as punishment in all cases.[17]

THE SYMBOLISM: DEATH OR LIFE?

During earlier centuries, the death penalty played a plausible, perhaps 26 even justifiable, role in society's efforts to control crime and mete out just deserts to convicted offenders. After all, the alternative of imprisonment—the modern form of banishment—had yet to be systematically developed. Consequently, society in an earlier age could tolerate the death penalty with a clearer conscience than we can today. For us, however, the true dimension in which we assess this mode of punishment is neither its crime-fighting effectiveness nor its moral necessity, but its symbolism. Mistaken faith in deterrent efficacy, confusion over the requirements of justice, indifference to unfair administration, ignorance of nonlethal methods of social control—all these can explain only so much about the current support for the death penalty. The rest of the explanation lies elsewhere, in what executions symbolize, consciously or unconsciously, for those who favor them.

27   This symbolism deserves a closer look.[18] The death penalty, today as in the past, symbolizes the ultimate power of the state, and of the government of society, over the individual citizen. Understandably, the public wants visible evidence that the authority of its political leaders is intact, their powers competent to deal with every social problem, and their courage resolute in the face of any danger. Anxiety about war, fear of crime, indignation at being victimized provoke the authorities to use the power of life and death as a public gesture of strength, self-confidence, and reassurance. Not surprisingly, many are unwilling to abandon the one symbol a society under law in peacetime has at its disposal that, above all others, expresses this power with awe-inspiring finality: the death penalty.

28   This is precisely why, in the end, we should oppose the death penalty in principle and without exception. As long as capital punishment is available under law for any crime, it is a temptation to excess. Tyrannical governments, from Idi Amin's Uganda to the Ayatollah's Iran, teach this lesson. At best the use of the death penalty here and elsewhere has been and continues to be capricious and arbitrary. The long history of several of our own states, notably Michigan and Wisconsin, quite apart from the experience of other nations, proves that the government of a civilized society does not *need* the death penalty. The citizenry should not clamor for it. Their political leaders should know better—as, of course, the best of them do—than to cultivate public approval for capital statutes, death sentences, and executions. Instead a civilized government should explain why such practices are ill-advised, and why they are ineffective in reducing crime, removing its causes, and responding to victimization.

NOTES

1. Comment, "The Cost of Taking a Life: Dollars and Sense of the Death Penalty," *U. C. Davis Law Review* 18 (1985):1221–74, at 1270.
2. See *The Gallup Report,* January-February 1986, nos. 244–45, pp. 10–16; and Phoebe C. Ellsworth and Lee Ross, "Public Opinion and Capital Punishment: A Closer Examination of the Views of Abolitionists and Retentionists," *Crime & Delinquency* 29 (1983):116–69, at 147.
3. The findings reported by Isaac Ehrlich, "The Deterrent Effect of Capital Punishment: A Question of Life and Death," *American Economic Review* 65 (1975):397–417 ("[each] additional execution . . . may have resulted . . . in 7 or 8 fewer murderers") have been extensively criticized; see, e.g., Lawrence R. Klein, Brian Forst, and Victor Filatox, "The Deterrent Effect of Capital Punishment: An Assessment of the Esti-

mates," in Alfred Blumstein, Jacqueline Cohen, and Daniel Nagin, eds., *Deterrence and Incapacitation: Estimating the Effects of Criminal Sanctions on Crime Rates* (1978), pp. 336–60. The findings reported by James A. Yunker, "Is the Death Penalty a Deterrent to Homicide? Some Time Series Evidence," *Journal of Behavioral Economics* 5 (1976): 45–81 ("one execution will deter 156 murders") have been evaluated and found wanting by James Alan Fox, "The Identification and Estimation of Deterrence: An Evaluation of Yunker's Model," *Journal of Behavioral Economics* 6 (1977):225–42. The findings reported by David P. Phillips, "The Deterrent Effect of Capital Punishment: New Evidence on an Old Controversy," *American Journal of Sociology* 86 (1980): 139–48 (". . . in the two weeks following a public execution the frequency of homicide drops by 35.7%") has been refuted by William J. Bowers, "Deterrence or Brutalization: What Is the Truth About Highly Publicized Executions?" (unpublished). The latest claims in this vein are by Stephen K. Layson, "Homicide and Deterrence: A Reexamination of the United States Time-Series Evidence," *Southern Economic Journal* 52 (1985):68–89 ("the tradeoff of executions for murders is approximately—18.5," i.e., each execution results in a net decrease of 18.5 murders); for criticism see James Alan Fox, "Persistent Flaws in Econometric Studies of the Death Penalty: A Discussion of Layson's Findings," testimony submitted to the Subcommittee on Criminal Justice, House of Representatives, U.S. Congress, 7 May 1986.

4. See Bowers, "Deterrence or Brutalization."
5. United States, Department of Justice, Bureau of Justice Statistics, *Capital Punishment* 1984 (1985), p. 1.
6. Mark H. Moore et al., *Dangerous Offenders: The Elusive Target of Justice* (1984), and Ted Honderich et al., "Symposium: Predicting Dangerousness," *Criminal Justice Ethics* 2 (Winter/Spring 1983):3–17.
7. Jack Levin and James Alan Fox, *Mass Murder: America's Growing Menace* (1985), p. 222. The authors do not support the death penalty for serial, mass, or recidivist murderers.
8. See especially Norval Morris, *The Future of Imprisonment* (1974), pp. 85–121.
9. This is especially true of Walter Berns, *For Capital Punishment: Crime and the Morality of the Death Penalty* (1979), pp. 153ff. The arousal of "anger" is not evidence that anything morally wrong is its cause. There is no reason to believe that the punitive policies adopted by a society "angry" at criminals will be fair or effective in reducing crime. The revenge that "anger" can motivate has no claim as such to the title of just retribution. Moral indignation is another matter. As a feeling, it may be indistinguishable from anger, but its claim for a different status rests on its essential connection to a moral principle; one's indignation is aroused only if an important moral principle has been violated. Even when this happens, the policies inspired by moral indignation are not thereby guaranteed to be just or effective; and the

capacity for self-deception about the legitimacy of one's indignation is legendary.

10. See Bedau, "Classification-Based Sentencing: Some Conceptual and Ethical Problems," *New England Journal of Criminal and Civil Confinement* 10 (1984):1–26; Bedau, "Prisoners' Rights," *Criminal Justice Ethics* 1 (Winter/Spring 1982):26–41; Bedau, "Retribution and the Theory of Punishment," *Journal of Philosophy* 75 (1978):601–20; Bedau, "Penal Theory and Prison Reality Today," *Juris Doctor* 2 (December 1972):40–83.

11. Ernest van den Haag, "The Death Penalty Vindicates the Law," *American Bar Association Journal* 71 (April 1985):38–42 at 42; cf. van den Haag, "Refuting Reiman and Nathanson," *Philosophy & Public Affairs* 14 (1985):165–76 ("punishment must vindicate the disrupted public order").

12. Berns, *For Capital Punishment,* p. 173.

13. See, e.g., Robert Johnson and Hans Toch, eds., *The Pains of Imprisonment* (1982).

14. See Wendy Phillips Wolfson, "The Deterrent Effect of the Death Penalty upon Prison Murder," in Bedau, ed., *The Death Penalty in America,* 3d ed. (1982), pp. 159–73.

15. Hugo Adam Bedau and Michael L. Radelet, "Miscarriages of Justice in Potentially Capital Cases," presented at the annual meeting of the American Society of Criminology, November 1985.

16. Ernest van den Haag argues, with evident complacency, that the death penalty does "lead to the unintended death of some innocents in the long run"; he goes on to add that this leaves the death penalty precisely where other things of the same sort are: "in the long run nearly all human activities are likely to lead to the unintended deaths of innocents." Van den Haag, "The Death Penalty Vindicates the Law," p. 42. This tends to obscure three important points. First, lawful activities that take "statistical lives" (e.g., coal mining) are not designed to kill anyone, whereas every death by capital punishment (whether of a guilty or an innocent person) is intentional. Second, society permits dangerous commercial and recreational activities on various grounds— it would be wrongly paternalistic to interfere with what people choose to do at their own risk (e.g., scaling dangerous cliffs), and society can better afford the cost of the risky activity than the cost of its complete prevention or stricter regulation (e.g., public highways crowded with long truck-trailer rigs rather than separate highways for cars and trucks). But these reasons have no bearing on the choice between the death penalty and imprisonment, unless the combined deterrent/incapacitative effects of executions are demonstrably superior to those of the alternative. Since no defender of the death penalty has sustained the burden of the proof on this point—see the papers cited in n. 3 supra—van den Haag's argument is undermined. Van den Haag's position would be less vulnerable to objection if the only executions he

favored were of persons convicted of several—serial, multiple, or recidivist—murders. But he does not confine his support for the death penalty to such cases.

17. Michael Davis has recently argued that the death penalty is no more "irrevocable," in any important sense of that term, than many other punishments, including life in prison. See Davis, "Is the Death Penalty Irrevocable?" *Social Theory and Practice* 10 (1984):143–56. Insofar as he addresses the arguments I put forward in Chapter 1, to explain why death is a "more severe" punishment than imprisonment, he does not seem to disagree. On his interpretation, however, the issue of revocability has nothing to do with severity (see p. 147). Basic to his argument that the punishments of death and of life in prison are equally (ir)revocable is the idea that (a) an irrevocable punishment is such that if it is erroneously imposed on someone, then there is no way to compensate the person for the injustice he suffers, and (b) anyone has interests that are not extinguished with the end of natural life (see p. 146). But as compensating a person is not always identical with conferring a benefit on something he is interested in—rather, it is sometimes a matter of benefiting *him,* directly and in his own person—the truth of (a) and (b) do not entail that there is no difference, relative to irrevocability, that distinguishes the punishment of death from a life behind bars.

18. See Barbara Ann Stolz, "Congress and Capital Punishment: An Exercise in Symbolic Politics," *Law & Policy Quarterly* 5 (1983):157–80; and Tom R. Tyler and Renee Weber, "Support for the Death Penalty: Instrumental Response to Crime or Symbolic Attitude?" *Law & Society Review* 17 (1982):21–45. Tyler and Weber bifurcate all defenses of the death penalty into the "instrumental" and the "symbolic." Thus a retributive defense of the death penalty is, for them, merely "symbolic." Nor do they make it clear whether the "symbolic" role of this punishment is a conscious and intentional one. Stolz is concerned with the conscious symbolism of enacting national (more precisely, federal) criminal penalties; how much of what she reports could be transferred without loss to the reasons for enactment of state death penalty laws or to the reasons the public supports executions (state or federal) is not clear.

QUESTIONS FOR READING

1. According to Bedau, on what should the resolution of the death-penalty debate rest? Why?

2. How does Bedau organize his discussion?

3. What are the six arguments in support of capital punishment? Compare these to the arguments of van den Haag. Has Bedau covered the arguments presented by van den Haag?

4. What is Bedau's position on deterrence? Is there evidence that the death penalty deters murder? Is deterrence a justifiable use of criminal law? Is capital punishment justifiable as a possible deterrent?

5. What are the facts on recidivist murderers? What kind of murderer do many people want executed, even those who generally oppose the death penalty? What would be accomplished if only this kind of murderer were executed? Which group of people will still be unhappy? Why?

6. What are Bedau's arguments for rejecting capital punishment as the necessary response to grave crimes?

7. The author gives three reasons for preferring imprisonment to death. Explain each in your own words.

8. What does the death penalty symbolize, according to Bedau? Why is that the very reason to oppose the death penalty?

QUESTIONS FOR REASONING AND ANALYSIS

1. Bedau begins his discussion of the alternative to the death penalty by agreeing that it is not an ideal alternative. By so doing, what does he accomplish? How does this strengthen his argument?

2. Does retribution *allow* for the death penalty? Does it *require* it? What distinction does Bedau make between *retribution* and *revenge?* What does the author's distinctions among words illustrate about the nature of good argument?

3. What are two reasons for dismissing the "taxpayer's argument"? Compare Bedau and van den Haag on the role of cost in one's position on the death penalty. Do they agree? What might you conclude from your comparison?

QUESTIONS FOR REFLECTING AND WRITING

1. Compare Bedau's views on deterrence to van den Haag's. Who makes the better case? Why?

2. Which of the three reasons for supporting imprisonment over death sentencing do you think is the strongest? Why?

3. Could you accept the compromise position of death sentencing only for multiple murders? Is this a position we should work to make the practice in this country? Why or why not?

4. Do you think that the motive of revenge justifies the death penalty? If so, how would you refute Bedau on this issue?

5. Has Bedau led you to change your views on capital punishment in any way? Explain.

CHAPTER 18

Affirmative Action for Colleges?

Improving Public Schools?

Debates Over Fairness in Education

To say that the issues in education are both numerous and serious is certainly an understatement. Clinton wanted to be the "education president." Bush has his "No Child Left Behind" initiative. And yet criticism continues amid a few voices defending the U.S. schools. America's best schools and colleges attract students from around the world. But the variation in funding, facilities, quality teachers, and test scores from one school to the next should be unacceptable to politicians and parents alike. Elite colleges have demanding entrance requirements, but the majority of colleges have few requirements beyond a high school diploma. At many colleges, up to one-third of the freshman class is taking at least one remedial course, and fewer than half of those who start college actually graduate. Are we failing at the goal of universal education? Is this goal unrealistic? Can we make changes that will improve K–12 education? Is affirmative action still the way to make access to college more fair? These questions—and others raised by the six authors in this chapter—should be the concern of all citizens, for we all benefit, economically and socially, by an educated citizenry.

The first three authors examine the issue of affirmative action in college admissions, a policy that the Supreme Court has recently defended, at least in some forms. The last three authors explore problems related to K–12 education, including vouchers, teacher preparedness, and disparities of school funding.

PREREADING QUESTION

The topics of the six authors are connected to one another and to the questions about U.S. education raised here. Think about each author's particular argument, but also reflect on the ways that each one comments on the larger educational problems facing us in this new century.

Websites Relevant to This Chapter's Topic

U.S. Department of Education

www.ed.gov

This government site contains links to many resources on educational issues.

National Education Association

www.nea.org

This site contains definitions, resources on education, links to debates on bilingual education, charter schools, vouchers, and more.

American Federation of Teachers

www.aft.org

This union's site contains many resources and links. Go to their higher education page for resources on college issues, including distance learning.

Educational Policy Studies

http://w3.ed.uiuc.edu/EPS/Ed_Resources/category.lasso/

This site, maintained by the University of Illinois, contains a wealth of information on the many philosophies of education.

A VICTORY FOR WHITE GUILT | SHELBY STEELE

With a Ph.D. from the University of Utah, Shelby Steele (b. 1947) is a research fellow at Stanford University's Hoover Institution. He has written many essays on race, some of which have been collected in his book *The Content of Our Character* (1990). His latest book is *A Dream Deferred: The Second Betrayal of Black Freedom in America* (1998). The following article was published June 26, 2003, in the *Wall Street Journal*.

PREREADING QUESTIONS What is your position on race-based preferences in college admissions? Is diversity an important goal for colleges to seek?

At last the Supreme Court has ruled on the use of racial preferences in 1 university admissions. And now that it has happened, one wonders why the court took up the matter in the first place—unless its goal was to make a bad situation worse. If the two Michigan decisions disallowed the formulaic practice of affirmative action, they simultaneously opened the door to a new non-formulaic subjectivity in which admissions officers are even less accountable in their use of race as a factor in admissions than before. At least in the past they worried that race would be ruled unconstitutional, and this had begun to have a chilling effect on racial preferences. But the court has now removed that anxiety. Universities can, with confidence, take the matter of race and admissions into the proverbial smoke-filled room where, with Cheshire grins, they can titter at the phrase "narrow tailoring."

And apparently the words diversity and race are synonymous in the mind 2 of Justice O'Connor, who delivered the opinion of the court in *Grutter v. Bollinger.* "Compelling interest in a diverse student body is not prohibited by the constitution," she wrote. So diversity, this most spurious of notions, is now undergirded with constitutionality along with race. And when race and diversity stand together as legitimate—even constitutional—principles, we have indeed arrived at the threshold of legally sanctioned racialism. Because diversity works by group preferences, all the individuals in these beatific diverse environments must pursue a good part of their self-interest through their racial groups. The incentive is to make a tribe of one's race. You end up with a racialist diversity going more toward segregation than integration.

STIGMATIZATION OF BLACKS

A remarkable feature of this opinion is the way it ignores the vast array 3 of contradictions and unintended consequences that attach to affirmative action—a few of which are its racial divisiveness, its stigmatization of blacks as inferior, its facilitation of identity politics, its encouragement of a victim-focused identity in minorities, its reverse discrimination against whites and Asians, its preference for precisely the least needy minorities, its damage to the principle of excellence, its fostering of a parasitic diversity industry, its cynical refusal to allow the best and brightest minorities to compete openly with their white and Asian counterparts, its flaunting of the Constitution's equal protection clause, and of course its utter failure to close the academic gap between whites and blacks.

4   Affirmative action was conceived on—and apparently will continue to thrive on—the mere announcement of its good intentions. No amount of failure, blatant corruption, or even lack of support from most whites and (by one poll) 84% of blacks has been sufficient to bring it down. Now the highest court in the land has come under its spell. Why is this policy so free from accountability to performance, so able to sail on in thrall to its own good intentions?

5   I think we have to conclude that racial preferences serve their true purpose very well, and that they continue against all reason because American institutions need them. And it was institutions—universities, corporations, professional organizations, the military—that submitted over 100 amicus briefs saying quite frankly that they needed to be able to practice race-based preferential treatment for blacks and Hispanics. The fact is that American institutions feel a moral accountability to our racial history that individuals only feel when they speak out on race in the public square. Our institutions (including the Supreme Court) stand permanently in that public square.

6   In a society where full racial equality is not yet with us, and where institutions often exhibit the very racial stratifications that racism created, American institutions can easily be seen as racist until they prove otherwise. I have called this situation white guilt, not because it has much to do with guilt but because it makes institutions (and individuals in the public square) behave as though they were guilty. They scramble to show deference to minorities because only deference erects the firewall that protects them from stigmatization as racist. Without this protection they can easily lose their legitimacy in our democratic society.

7   So our institutions engineer the visibility of black and brown faces. This is why the *New York Times* was so mindlessly devoted to a black reporter whose incompetence was matched only by his compulsive lying. Today there are not enough well-trained black and brown faces to meet demand. Until he got caught, Jayson Blair was a precious commodity despite his incompetence. He even added an impression of journalistic excellence to the *Times* because institutions like this—and virtually all American universities—have made diversity an aspect of professional excellence.

8   Of course the people who run America's institutions do not want to feel that they are merely acting out a cynicism—using blacks and browns as a firewall. So, under layers of euphemistic, unexamined, and empty language (Justice O'Connor is a veritable fount of such—"learning outcomes," "diversity factors," "soft variables," "selection index," "nuanced judgments"), they conceal the cynicism of what they do by making diversity into a bureaucratic faith, a managerial religion. And this faith is built entirely around their good intentions. When blasphemers to this faith point to the array of ugly unintended consequences, these institutional leaders have only to shift their gaze to the post-card beauty of what they intend.

9   The Supreme Court has now joined their faith. And in so doing it has enshrined yet another ugly unintended consequence of the diversity faith: anti-

Americanism as a source of virtue and power. Precisely because racial preferences have to be implemented by so many jerry-built schemes that step over
the merit-based procedures of institutions, not to mention the 14th Amendment, they require an especially powerful source of moral authority. And this
has been found in the summary indictment of America that emerged in the '60s
from the convergence of so many social protest movements—civil rights, anti-
war, feminism, farm workers, environmentalism, etc. The compound effect of
all this protest was to cast America as a spiritually empty, greedy, racist and im-
perialistic nation—a malevolent force in the world.

Thus, anti-Americanism—a reflexive and smug faithlessness in the moral
character of America—became the first step to redemption. It became a virtuous attitude in itself, a way to establish one's credentials as a concerned and
socially responsible person. Anti-Americanism, as a credential of virtue, found
its political home on the left, and nowhere more securely than in the precincts
of academe. 10

Today the diversity faith is predicated on an updated and subtler anti-
Americanism, but an anti-Americanism nonetheless. Since there is no anti-
black discrimination in American universities, preferences have to be justified
by the idea that America is still a malevolent society where blacks are concerned. And still today—at least in the public square—one must be committed
to this view of America in order to credential one's virtue. 11

Anti-Americanism is also a formula for power because it truly delivers moral
authority and legitimacy to institutions. And in case you think this power is
meager, a shadow of its '60s vitality, consider that the Supreme Court of the
United States has just submitted to it. 12

AN HONEST ASSESSMENT

The most striking feature of Justice O'Connor's written opinion is that it
has no context. Cases of this magnitude, with issues that have not been examined for a generation, call for context—an honest assessment of the fairness of American society. Is the old malevolence of racism still with us to the
point that minority aspiration is stifled? In the past Justice O'Connor's jurisprudence always spoke of "narrowly tailoring" to need, usually to a specific
pattern of discrimination. How can giving a preference to people (very often
from the upper middle class) who have suffered no discrimination be a narrowly tailored remedy? And what can "compelling interest" mean when no
wrong has occurred? Does Justice O'Connor seek to help wronged people or
disadvantaged people? If the latter, why the racial preferences? Or why not a
preference for poor whites who have endured generations of disadvantage
and stigmatization? 13

Here is a justice known for "strict scrutiny" when actual discrimination is in
question. Yet when no discrimination is in question she forgoes strictness, and
gives both race and diversity constitutional stature. And in the process she be-
trays all her own careful jurisprudence around race. 14

15   Finally Justice O'Connor went with the doubting spirit of anti-Americanism, with a faithlessness in a society that has made more racial progress in the last 40 years than any society in human history. Through our struggles with race, we have grown into a self-examining and racially disciplined society. We deserve justices who can feel certain about the capacity of whites to be fair and the capacity of minorities to compete.

QUESTIONS FOR READING

1. What is the occasion for Steele's writing? What is he reacting to in the essay?
2. What is the new ruling? What does it allow?
3. What is Steele's reaction to the ruling? What unintended consequences does he list?
4. What are black attitudes toward affirmative action?
5. Why do institutions want race-based preferences to continue? What does Steele call this? How do institutions hide from any accusation of cynicism?
6. When signing on to diversity, institutions, in the author's view, are actually embracing what idea about America?
7. What are Steele's views on Justice O'Connor?

QUESTIONS FOR REASONING AND ANALYSIS

1. What is Steele's claim? You may need several sentences to tie his ideas together.
2. Steele argues that in order to embrace affirmative action to achieve diversity, institutions must believe that America is without moral character. The result of this anti-American belief is that the institutions obtain significant power and legitimacy. Does this reasoning make sense to you? Have you thought about the idea that institutions seek, whether consciously or not, moral authority—that they care about their image as, in this case, above any appearance of racism?
3. Steele supports his claim mostly through what kind of evidence? What impact does this have on readers? Does it follow that such arguments are less viable than other kinds of arguments? What *should* be the attitude of readers toward arguments that demand careful reading and concentration?

QUESTIONS FOR REFLECTING AND WRITING

1. Do you agree with Steele? If so, explain why. If not, how would you rebut his argument?
2. If diversity is a legitimate goal for colleges, is affirmative action the best way to achieve that goal? Steele does not believe that it has done anything to "close the academic gap between whites and blacks." Do you agree with that assessment? Why or why not?

AFFIRMING EXPLOITATION | RUBEN NAVARRETTE, JR.

A frequent speaker on college campuses, Ruben Navarrette (b. 1967) is a syndicated columnist and editorial board member of the *Dallas Morning News*. He holds a master's in public administration from the Kennedy School of Government and is the author of *A Darker Shade of Crimson: Odyssey of a Harvard Chicano* (1993). The following column was published April 22, 2003, in the *Washington Post*.

PREREADING QUESTIONS Does affirmative action exploit minorities? It is presumably designed to aid minorities; in what ways might it end up hurting them, or exploiting them?

In deciding whether race and ethnicity may be considered in college and 1 university admissions—the question at the heart of two cases involving the University of Michigan—the Supreme Court should do a cost-benefit analysis.

Supporters of affirmative action love to talk about the benefit of colleges 2 and universities having diverse student bodies. They insist that diversity offers a real-world experience to students who step onto the campus having had limited exposure to other races, ethnicities and cultures. And they may be right.

Yet they never acknowledge the costs. While boasting about how racial 3 preferences enhance the education of white students, they never stop to consider that this enhancement comes at the expense of the education of blacks and Latinos. How could they? That would mean accepting the possibility that a program created nearly 40 years ago to help minorities may now be harming them. It would also mean that by keeping it going, these supporters are accomplices in a brand of exploitation not altogether different from what was going on in our society before programs like affirmative action were created. Not long ago, exclusionary admissions policies that kept blacks and Latinos out of college put minority students at a disadvantage for the benefit of whites.

Now racial preferences that intend to let more blacks and Latinos into college—even if it means lowering standards—do much the same thing. And yet, 4 where's the outrage? For all their talk about compassion, liberals—affirmative action's most vocal defenders—aren't bothered that students admitted under these lower standards often struggle and drop out. For all their lip service about helping people become self-sufficient, liberals don't seem worried that the message sent by those who protest to preserve affirmative action is that they don't believe Latinos and African Americans can succeed without it.

Liberals don't even seem concerned about what's behind their own warning that, without racial preferences, the number of minority students on the nation's elite college campuses would plummet. Frankly, I don't believe that, but 5 even if I did, I would want to know why that is. The thinking goes that without the additional boost provided by racial preferences, there would not be enough qualified blacks and Latinos in the applicant pipeline who could get into the top-tier schools on the natural.

Yet whose fault is that? A prime suspect is the public school system. That 6 would be the same public school system in which only about half of black and

Latino ninth-graders ever graduate from high school. And the same system that liberals support and defend by fighting against merit pay for teachers, vouchers for students and just about any other attempt to impose accountability.

7   Starting to get the picture?

8   Those most intent on preserving the educational status quo have a personal interest in also preserving racial preferences. To the degree that there are failures and shortcomings in K–12 public education, racial preferences at the college level help to conceal them.

9   Were minority students suddenly to vanish from college and university campuses, and the campuses return to being all white—as liberals warn would happen without preferences—Americans might start asking tough questions about the quality of elementary and secondary schooling in this country, especially for minorities. They might even ask whether teachers and administrators—the vast majority of whom are white—have the same level of expectations for black and Latino students as they do for white students, or whether guidance counselors are "tracking" minority students away from college-prep and Advanced Placement courses and toward vocational studies and other less-challenging curriculums.

10   Take it from someone who spent four years in the classrooms of central California trying to inspire Latino students in a climate of abysmally low expectations—those are mighty good questions. So good that blacks and Latinos who are genuinely concerned with educational achievement, as opposed to political gains and the symbolism of holding on to a concession from the civil rights movement, should be asking them now.

11   The answers just may prompt those black and Latino activists to switch sides and oppose what they now support and to question whether their allies are really their adversaries. The answers may also teach them the most important lesson in all of this—that whatever happens at the Supreme Court, it will be of far less consequence than what happens every day in the nation's kindergarten classrooms.

QUESTIONS FOR READING

1.   What is Navarrette's subject? What is the date of his article—before or after the Supreme Court ruling?

2.   What are the benefits of diversity on college campuses?

3.   What are the costs of affirmative action to blacks and Latinos? How are they being exploited, in the author's view?

4.   What message does race-based preferences send? What assumption must supporters of the policy be making?

5.   What flaws in K–12 education may affirmative action actually be hiding?

6.   What does Navarrette want both black and white supporters of affirmative action to do? Where would he like to see some changes?

QUESTIONS FOR REASONING AND ANALYSIS

1. What is the author's claim?

2. What are the two major supports for his claim? That is, what are the two ways that affirmative action exploits blacks and Latinos?

3. Analyze the argument as a problem/solution argument. What is the problem? What is the cause(s) of the problem? What, then, is the general solution? What specific solutions does Navarrette either state or imply? To start the process of solving the problem, what do supporters of affirmative action need to do?

QUESTIONS FOR REFLECTING AND WRITING

1. Does Navarrette provide a new way of looking at affirmative action for you? Does his argument make sense? Is affirmative action one of those ideas that seems good in theory but actually has unintended negative consequences? Be prepared to explain your response to his approach to this issue.

2. Do you agree with the author's position on affirmative action? If so, why? If not, how would you rebut his argument?

3. Do you agree that the bigger problem is in K–12 education for blacks and Latinos? If so, why? If not, why not?

AFFIRMATIVE ACTION: THERE'S A THIRD WAY | RICHARD D. KAHLENBERG

A senior fellow at the Century Foundation, Richard Kahlenberg graduated from Harvard College in 1985 and Harvard Law in 1989. He is a frequent guest on TV and radio programs and is the author of *All Together Now: Creating Middle Class Schools Through Public School Choice* (2001) and *The Remedy: Class, Race, and Affirmative Action* (1996). The following article appeared in the *Washington Post* on March 31, 2003.

PREREADING QUESTIONS Race-based preferences for college admission actually benefit which groups? Who is excluded? Why?

With the issue of affirmative action going before the Supreme Court to- 1
morrow for oral argument, the debate has come to focus almost entirely on two different approaches: racial preference plans of the kind used by the University of Michigan (and favored by Democrats and most of the business and education establishment) and the "top 10 percent" plan used by the University of Texas (which is supported by the Bush administration and a few other groups). Unfortunately, little attention has been paid to a third alternative that has few political patrons but is supported by two-thirds of Americans: affirmative action for low-income students of all races.

Americans have always been uncomfortable with racial preference schemes 2
such as that used at Michigan, which automatically adds 20 bonus points out of a possible 150 to every minority candidate's application. Why should Vernon Jordan's kids get a break? In practice, affirmative action programs often benefit the

most advantaged students of color. William Bowen and Derek Bok found that 86 percent of black students at the 28 elite universities they studied were from middle- or upper-status families.

3   But the Texas plan and similar plans in California and Florida, which automatically admit students in the tops of their high school classes irrespective of SAT scores, have their own problems. The concept has little independent justification beyond its ability to serve as a proxy for race, which makes the scheme legally vulnerable. The program's success is perversely contingent on the continued segregation of high schools and would produce far less racial diversity in states less segregated than Texas, California and Florida. By completely ignoring SAT and ACT scores, research shows, the program will result in large dropout rates at more selective colleges. And the programs won't work at graduate schools, where the affirmative action debate is especially intense.

4   But there is a third way. A recent *Newsweek* poll found that 65 percent of Americans support providing a preference to low-income students of all races. Economic affirmative action is actively used in Texas, California and Florida, alongside the percentage plans, and has been at least as important in promoting racial diversity.

5   How would it work on a national scale? According to a study by Anthony Carnevale of the Educational Testing Service and Stephen Rose of ORC Macro, economic affirmative action at the nation's most selective 146 colleges would result in a 2-percentage-point decline in racial diversity and a 28-point increase in economic diversity. In a paper being published this week by the Century Foundation, Carnevale and Rose find that a race-blind economic affirmative action program would boost African American and Latino admissions from 4 percent (under a system of grades and test scores) to 10 percent, which is somewhat below the current 12 percent representation. The study's authors advocate combining race and class preferences in order to avoid the 2-point drop, but experience suggests most colleges will adopt economic affirmative action only when barred from using race.

6   While economic affirmative action, properly defined, would produce almost as much racial diversity as using race, it would produce far more economic diversity than racial affirmative action has. Today, even with extensive race-sensitive admissions policies, our selective colleges are economically segregated, a fact that supporters of affirmative action rarely acknowledge. Carnevale and Rose find that at the top 146 colleges, the lowest 25 percent of the population by economic status has just a 3 percent representation and the bottom economic half just a 10 percent representation. Meanwhile, the top economic quarter has a 74 percent representation. In other words, you are 25 times as likely to run into a wealthy student as a low-income student in our nation's elite colleges.

7   While universities routinely claim to give an admissions preference to disadvantaged students, in fact the representation of poor and working-class students would rise, not fall, if grades and test scores were the sole basis for admissions, the researchers find. Economic affirmative action would give the bottom half a representation of 38 percent. If diversity is defined broadly, to

value differences in both economic and racial backgrounds—kids from trailer homes and ghettoes and barrios as well as suburban minorities—economic affirmative action would provide a large net gain in the total student diversity at elite colleges.

But would economic affirmative action jeopardize high standards? [8] Carnevale and Rose find that under a system of economic preferences—which also would eliminate legacy and athletic preferences—graduation rates would climb slightly, from 86 percent today to almost 90 percent. One reason to be confident in their simulation is that economic affirmative action is not meant to be a challenge to merit but rather a better approximation of it. A 3.6 GPA and an SAT score of 1200 surely mean something more to a low-income, first-generation college applicant who attended terrible schools than to a student whose parents have graduate degrees and pay for the finest private schooling.

President Bush's legal briefs mention economic affirmative action, but only [9] in passing, perhaps because he thinks it smacks of "class warfare." But several members of the U.S. Supreme Court, including Justices Clarence Thomas, Antonin Scalia and Sandra Day O'Connor, have in the past endorsed economic affirmative action as an alternative to racial preferences. The irony is that it may be unelected conservative judges who finally pave the way for a popular plan benefiting America's low-income and working-class students.

QUESTIONS FOR READING

1. What are the two affirmative action strategies in use?
2. What is Kahlenberg's "third alternative"?
3. What has been one consequence of racial preference plans such as that used by the University of Michigan? What is the only reason that the "top 10 percent" plan works in some states? What is a risk of plans that ignore SAT scores altogether?
4. How many Americans support economic affirmative action? How would this plan affect black and Latino representation at many select colleges?
5. How well are low-income students represented at the country's top 146 schools? How would that change with economic affirmative action?

QUESTIONS FOR REASONING AND ANALYSIS

1. What is Kahlenberg's claim?
2. Analyze his argument using Toulmin's terms. What kinds of evidence does he provide? What are his sources (backing)? What key assumption does he make when he argues for his choice of affirmative action? How does he rebut potential counterarguments to his plan?
3. How hopeful is the author that colleges will switch from race-based affirmative action to economic affirmative action? How do you know?
4. How would you describe the author's tone? How does his tone differ from Shelby Steele's? How does Kahlenberg's tone help him to advance his argument?

QUESTIONS FOR REFLECTING AND WRITING

1. Are you one of the two-thirds of Americans who support economic affirmative action? Why or why not?

2. The bottom half of families, economically, are not well represented on elite college campuses. Is this a problem, in your view? Why or why not?

3. Both Navarrette and Kahlenberg mention dropout rates among students admitted on racial and ethnic preferences. How serious a problem is this, in your view? What are the advantages of giving people a chance? What are the disadvantages to those who drop out and to the college? (See if you can find some recent stats on dropout rates in general and completion rates as well. What, for example, is the completion rate of college athletes?)

DOING THE NUMBERS ON PUBLIC SCHOOLS ADDS UP TO ZERO | DANIEL HENNINGER

A graduate of Georgetown University's School of Foreign Service, Daniel Henninger is deputy editor of *The Wall Street Journal*'s editorial page. Henninger has received numerous awards for his commentary, including sharing in *The Wall Street Journal*'s Pulitzer Prize (2002) for coverage of the 9/11 attacks. The following column appeared May 2, 2003.

PREREADING QUESTIONS Based on his title, what do you expect Henninger's opinion of public schools to be? How do you know?

1   What with Americans being such an opinionated people, it isn't often that an issue of public policy ever arrives at the steady state of national agreement. Even as skulls were brought up from Saddam's torture chambers, e-mails still rolled in from the war's opponents to re-argue the wrongness of the effort. So imagine how surprising it was to discover this past week that there is one subject about which the people of this country are in about as much agreement as statistical science ever achieves: America's public schools. They are widely and deeply regarded as awful.

2   Public Agenda, a New York-based nonprofit that does opinion surveys on a range of issues, compiled an analysis of a decade of polling on public education, and news reports about the study were eye-catching. Mainly the message was that while accountability matters in the public mind, what really upsets people is the generalized disorderliness in public schools. Having opinions of my own on what caused many schools to shift from being temples of learning to temples for having-fun-with-my-friends, I thought the Public Agenda report, "Where We Are Now," deserved a closer look.

3   Please join me for a tour of the second circle of hell. George Bush has a plan of action called No Child Left Behind, but if Saddam's weapons of mass destruction were sufficient reason to invade Iraq, he should now send in the Marines to occupy and reconstruct the nation's dysfunctional public schools.

4   Teachers, principals, parents, employers, college professors and students all have a uniformly low opinion of what's going on in our schools. Unless

bracketed, the language here is taken largely from the study's own wording of questions and results:

Some 71% of respondents believe most public-school students do the bare 5 minimum to get by; 83% of teachers say parents who fail to set limits and create structure at home are a serious problem, and 81% think parents who refuse to hold their kids accountable for behavior or academic performance are a serious problem. Of teachers, 43% say they spend more time keeping order than teaching. Instead of more pay (12%), 86% of teachers said they'd rather have a school where student behavior and parental support were better.

Some 61% of African-American parents think inner-city kids should be 6 expected to achieve the same standards as wealthier kids. Priorities: 82% of African-American parents think the biggest priority is raising academic standards; 8% want more focus on diversity and integration. Nearly all parents, 92%, think you should have to pass a standardized test to be promoted—and, if you fail, you should have to go to summer school or repeat the grade.

Employers who think local public schools are doing a good or excellent 7 job: 42%. Some 59% of college professors rate public schools as fair or poor. Professors who say a high-school diploma means students have learned the basics: 31%. [In the 1970s, a friend who began teaching at the University of Texas told me most of his freshmen thought they were A students; "they're not."] Only 47% of professors and 41% of employers think public-school graduates have the skills to succeed in the work world. About 74% of employers and professors think public-school graduates' writing skills are fair or poor; same number for grammar and spelling. About 64% say graduates' basic math is fair or poor; 69% of employers feel personal organization is fair or poor.

Only 19% of teachers say parental involvement is strong in their school 8 [parental involvement is one of the established keys to a successful school]; 87% of teachers think parents ought to limit their kids' TV time or should check their homework [clearly the inference is most parents do neither].

Disrespect is pandemic.   9

Of all Americans surveyed, 9% say, "The kids I see in public are respectful 10 toward adults." Only 18% of teachers and 30% of students say, "Students treat each other with respect in my high school;" 19% of students say, "In my high school, most students treat teachers with respect." Americans who feel their schools have a serious discipline problem: 76%.

Any stairwell of public-school hell we've left off the tour? Oh yes, we've left 11 off the politics from hell.

Asked why talented teachers quit, school superintendents say: low pay and 12 prestige—5%; politics and bureaucracy—81%. Sixty-seven percent of principals wish they were able to reward good teachers and remove bad ones [that is, they can't do either now]. Over 80% of principals and superintendents say they have more new mandates and responsibilities than they can handle. Eighty-four percent of superintendents say they spend too much time on special ed., and 50% say they spend too much on legal issues and litigation.

A wag might ask: If we're so stupid, how come the U.S. earned an A in 13 technology and human performance in Iraq? Short answer: The armed services don't let stupid people enlist anymore. The army now provides it own education, which is largely what most employers do as well today. A job is now a re-education camp for many public-school grads.

14   How the schools got this way—how respect for teachers died, disorder rose, basic learning fell, bureaucracy rose, why the best teachers quit, parents stopped caring and why professors think freshmen are academically delusional—is a subject for another column and maybe another lifetime (it takes more than one paragraph to explain how Supreme Court Justices with high IQs render legal decisions reflecting no common sense).

15   But for now, amid the overwhelming agreement found in the Public Agenda surveys, I have one small, recurring question: Tell me again why we're supposed to think charter schools and school choice are bad ideas.

QUESTIONS FOR READING

1. What is America's attitude toward public schools?
2. What matters most to teachers? What, in the eyes of teachers, are serious problems?
3. What do African American parents want?
4. What are the views of employers and college professors with regard to high school graduates' preparation for college or the workforce?
5. What view do students and teachers both hold with regard to the showing of respect in their schools?
6. What bothers principals and superintendents?
7. Where are most grads now getting "educated"?

QUESTIONS FOR REASONING AND ANALYSIS

1. Much of Henninger's column is a report of a report—by Public Agenda—on public schools. What is his claim? Or, what claim seems to be implied? On what evidence do you draw your implications?
2. List the several distinct problems that emerge from the survey. What seem to be at least some of the causes for these problems, as stated or implied by the results of the surveys? What examination of causes requires another column—or lifetime? (For example, why have parents stopped caring?)
3. What solutions are stated or implied by the author?

QUESTIONS FOR REFLECTING AND WRITING

1. What statistic surprises you the most? Why?
2. Select one of the issues listed by the author in paragraph 14 and discuss what you think are the causes of and possible solutions for that particular problem.
3. Are charter schools and school choice good or bad ideas? Why? Be prepared to defend your position. If these are not solutions to problems in public education, what solutions do you recommend? Why?

PUT TEACHERS TO THE TEST | DIANE RAVITCH

Educated at Wellesley College and Columbia University, Diane Ravitch (b. 1938) has been an adjunct professor at Columbia's Teachers College and an assistant secretary in the Department of Education in the first Bush administration. Currently she teaches at New York University and is a visiting fellow at the Brookings Institution. Ravitch has written extensively, in articles and books, on the problems in American schools. The following article was published on February 25, 1998, in the *Washington Post.*

PREREADING QUESTIONS How important are teachers in the education process? How well do we train and certify our K–12 teachers?

Last summer, a suburban school district in New York advertised for 35 new 1 teachers and received nearly 800 applications. District officials decided to narrow the pool by requiring applicants to take the 11th-grade state examination in English. Only about one-quarter of the would-be teachers answered 40 of the 50 multiple-choice questions correctly.

As Congress considers reauthorization of the Higher Education Act, 2 teacher education has emerged as a major issue. Many states—and now President Clinton—are clamoring to reduce class size, but few are grappling with the most important questions: If we are raising standards for students, don't we also need to raise standards for teachers? Shouldn't state and local officials make sure that teachers know whatever they are supposed to teach students?

Almost every state claims that it is strengthening standards for students, 3 but the states have been strangely silent when it comes to ensuring that teachers know what they are supposed to teach. Most instead certify anyone with the right combination of education courses, regardless of their command of the subject they expect to teach, and many states require future teachers to pass only a basic skills test.

Today, in some states it may be harder to graduate from high school than 4 to become a certified teacher. Something is wrong with this picture.

Last summer the U.S. Department of Education reported that approxi- 5 mately one-third of the nation's public school teachers of academic subjects in middle school and high school were teaching "out of field," which means that they had earned neither an undergraduate major nor a minor in their main teaching field.

Fully 39.5 percent of science teachers had not studied science as a major 6 or minor; 34 percent of mathematics teachers and 25 percent of English teachers were similarly teaching "out of field." The problem of unqualified teachers was particularly acute in schools where 40 percent or more of the students were from low-income homes; in these schools, nearly half the teaching staff was teaching "out of field."

Many states now routinely certify people who do not know what they are 7 supposed to teach. No one should get a license to teach science, reading, mathematics or anything else unless he or she has demonstrated a knowledge of what students are expected to learn.

8   A majority of the nation's teachers majored in education rather than an academic subject. This is troubling, even though most of those who majored in education are elementary teachers. There is a widely accepted notion that people who teach little children don't need to know much other than pedagogical methods and child psychology; that is wrong. Teachers of little children need to be well-educated and should love learning as much as they love children. Yes, even elementary school teachers should have an academic major.

9   The field of history has the largest percentage of unqualified teachers. The Department of Education found that 55 percent of history teachers are "out of field," and that 43 percent of high school students are studying history with a teacher who did not earn either a major or minor in history. This may explain why nearly 60 percent of our 17-year-olds scored "below basic" (the lowest possible rating) on the most recent test of U.S. history administered by the federally funded National Assessment of Educational Progress. Only one out of every five teachers of social studies has either a major or minor in history. Is it any wonder that today's children have no idea when the Civil War occurred, what Reconstruction was, what happened during the progressive era, who FDR was, what the *Brown* decision decided, or what Stalin did? Many of their teachers don't know those things either.

10   There are many conditions over which school officials have no control, but they have complete control over who is allowed to teach. Why should anyone be certified to teach science or history who doesn't know what he or she is expected to teach the children?

11   Many state officials say that they have an abundance of people who want to teach and that this is actually an excellent time to raise standards. For career-changers with a wealth of experience in business or the military, however, obsolete certification requirements get in the way. Instead of requiring irrelevant education courses, states should examine prospective teachers for their knowledge of their academic field and then give them a chance to work in the schools as apprentice teachers.

12   As Congress ponders ways to improve the teaching profession, it should consider incentives for colleges of liberal arts to collaborate with schools of education in preparing future teachers. Representatives from both parts of the same campus should sit down together, study state academic standards and figure out how to prepare teachers who know both their subject and how to teach it well. Teachers need a strong academic preparation as well as practical classroom experience to qualify for one of the toughest jobs in America.

13   Every classroom should have a well-educated, knowledgeable teacher. We are far from that goal today. Congress can address this problem by focusing on the quality, not quantity, of the nation's teaching corps.

QUESTIONS FOR READING

1.   What kinds of evidence does Ravitch provide to support her claim? What key assumption is a part of her argument?

2. What solutions does the author present? What should school officials do? The states? Congress? How does she defend the feasibility of her solutions?

QUESTIONS FOR REASONING AND ANALYSIS

1. What strategy does Ravitch use in her opening paragraph? What makes her opening effective?

2. What is the claim of Ravitch's argument? What type of argument is this?

QUESTIONS FOR REFLECTING AND WRITING

1. Are you surprised by any of Ravitch's statistics? Why or why not?

2. Did you have any teachers teaching "out of field"? If so, how effective were they?

3. Do you agree that K–6 teachers should have a major in an academic subject? Why or why not? (What does Ravitch think they will gain from an academic major?)

4. Should all teachers have to pass a basic test in reading, writing, math, history, and science? If not, why not? If so, at what level? Think of some representative types of questions that you would put on such a test.

A GRAND COMPROMISE | JAMES P. PINKERTON

A senior fellow at the New America Foundation, James Pinkerton (b. 1958) is also a columnist for *Newsday*. Previously he worked in the White House as a domestic policy advisor to Presidents Reagan and George H. W. Bush. He is the author of *What Comes Next: The End of Big Government—and the New Paradigm Ahead* (1995). "A Grand Compromise" was published in the January/February 2003 issue of *Atlantic Monthly*.

PREREADING QUESTIONS To have a grand compromise on education requires reconciling the views of what two groups? How do their views on education differ, particularly with regard to some of the issues raised in the previous essays in this chapter?

In 1983 a federal education commission warned that "a rising tide of mediocrity" threatened the well-being of the republic. That tide has not ebbed. Nearly two decades later, in 2000, the Program for International Student Assessment found that American fifteen-year-olds ranked fourteenth in science literacy and eighteenth in mathematics literacy among the thirty-two countries administering the test, scoring below the average for developed countries in both categories. And although President George W. Bush and Congress recently united behind the grandiosely titled No Child Left Behind Act of 2001, few observers outside Washington, D.C., believe that the legislation will have anything more than a marginal effect on student performance. 1

All Presidents claim to be "education Presidents," but the schools drift along, up a bit, down a bit, always costing more money, but never making the sort of dramatic gains witnessed elsewhere in American life. Why should this be? 2

3   U.S. schools today are the product of three different educational eras: the agricultural (which produced the nine-month school year), the industrial (which emphasized rote learning and regimentation to fit the rhythms of mass production), and what might be called the experimental (which promoted a range of nostrums, from sex education to Whole Language, often at the expense of basic skills). Each of these has left its own layer of sediment to muck things up in the present. The worst legacy of the past, however, is localized school funding, which not only produces great regional inequalities in spending per pupil but also nurtures the persistent incompetence of many schools.

4   Today about 45 percent of school funding comes from local sources, such as property taxes. In Virginia, for example, average per-pupil spending in rural Hanover County is only half that in suburban Arlington County. In New Jersey, which has been struggling to equalize school funding for three decades, the schools in Elizabeth spend 70 percent more per pupil than do the schools in Toms River.

5   Beyond state lines the disparities grow even worse: among school districts with enrollments of 15,000 or more, spending ranges from $3,932 per pupil in DeSoto County, Mississippi, to $14,244 in Elizabeth, New Jersey. Rectifying such imbalances requires a national solution. "Most of the resource inequality cannot be resolved at the state level," David Grissmer and Ann Flanagan, analysts for the Rand Corporation, have written. "States spending the least are southern and western states that also have a disproportionate share of the nation's minority and disadvantaged students." Yet the federal government does little to address this systemic inequality, and continues to contribute only about seven percent of the total spent on elementary and secondary schools.

6   So what's an "education President" to do? Happily, the means of reforming elementary and secondary education does not lie in some obscure theory, or in some other country. It has been right in front of our eyes for decades: the model of the Pell Grant program.

7   Colleges and universities compete, in effect, in a single national market. The federal government pumps $10 billion a year into college education through Pell Grants. The GI Bill and other aid programs add billions more. Pell Grants have an inherently equalizing effect on per-student funding: every qualifying student in the country has access to the same amount—a maximum of $4,000 a year—and can spend it at the accredited college of his or her choice. Thus much of higher education is more equitably funded than K–12 education. Moreover, because Pell recipients decide where their grants are applied, the program is driven by students, not administrators.

8   Why not build on the Pell model, and apply it to elementary and secondary education? Total K–12 public school spending, for some 47 million students, is currently about $350 billion a year, slightly more than $7,000 per pupil per year. Expanding on the Pell model would mean giving every American elementary and secondary school student $7,000 to spend at the school of his or her choice. Unlike Pell Grants, this money would be given to all students, regardless of the level of need. This would create, in effect, a grand compromise

between left and right, guaranteeing more-equal funding (which the left wants) and more choice for students (which the right wants).

Making this happen, of course, would require a radical reshuffling of finan- 9 cial responsibilities among the various levels of government. But such a reshuffling is not unprecedented; after all, though states and localities once bore the cost of raising militias, national defense is now a federal responsibility. Since 9/11, of course, federal responsibility for homeland defense has increased, to the point where a new Cabinet department has been legislated.

Education is no less a national priority than defense. Education reformers 10 should not shrink from the full implications of their goals; it's time for the federal government to do more for education—and for state and local governments to do less. It is true that the $350 billion a year in spending that the federal government would have to take on from state and local governments is no small amount. But at three percent of GDP, it is less than the annual U.S. military budget, and less than what the federal government spends on health care each year. And because state and local governments would be able either to spend the money currently allotted to education on other priorities or to rebate money to taxpayers, any federal tax increases or spending cuts made to accommodate this new system would be at least partially offset.

Of course, many conservatives and some liberals might object to the loss 11 of local control over schools. But local control is in some ways detrimental to education and to equity. In the Jim Crow South, after all, local control was synonymous with "separate but equal"; today an insistence on local funding ought not to be a cover for maintaining separate and obviously unequal schools.

Moreover, conservatives ought to be pleased with the second element of 12 the grand compromise: expanded choice. The current method of funding K–12 education balkanizes school districts into pockets of excellence or indifference; a federal grant program would make all schools part of a national system, in which no child would be forced by accident of region or neighborhood to attend a bad school.

Because students in such a system could attend the schools of their choice, 13 they would create a self-correcting market. If a given school was inadequate, students could go elsewhere, taking their funding with them. The fragmentary evidence of the past few years suggests that schools faced with competition will struggle to retain "market share."

Of course, if schools in Mississippi are substandard at $4,000 per pupil, 14 there is no guarantee that they would be better at $7,000 per pupil. One of the bitter lessons of the twentieth-century welfare state is that a bureaucracy has an apparently infinite capacity to absorb extra money without producing additional output. But under this proposal schools would have a compelling interest in responding to an exodus of students; a school that failed to respond positively would lose its financial base.

Critics of this plan will say that it is a form of vouchers—and they will be 15 correct. But this plan can't be derided as an attempt to undermine the public schools by bleeding away their students. Rather, it's an attempt to lift all schools into the mainstream by equalizing funding across the country, improving the odds that every child receives an education appropriate for this century.

16   What schools would be eligible to receive this grant money? Public schools only? Religious schools? Home schools? Ideally, every kind of school, though as a practical matter certain schools would not be made eligible right away. The politics of reform must sometimes yield to the slower-moving politics of the possible. But once the principle of federally funded choice was established, its application would expand as the education market reacted to the new incentives.

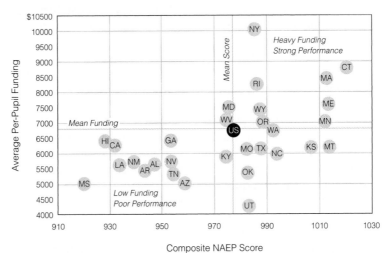

PUBLIC SCHOOL FUNDING VS. PERFORMANCE Funding disparities between states partly explain the gaps in student achievement (Source: Census Bureau; National Center for Educational National Assessment of Educational Progress).

17   This is just the outline of a grand compromise on education. If the right celebrates "liberty" untrammeled by bureaucracy and the left celebrates "rights" guaranteed, if necessary, by the government, the two can come together in behalf of a system of federally funded equal opportunity. Although neither side will like everything about this proposal, both might yet decide they like the status quo even less. And federally funded choice is a bold assault on the orthodoxies of the status quo.

QUESTIONS FOR READING

1. What are the legacies of the three educational eras? What is the fourth and worst legacy, according to the author?

2. What are the elements of the Pell Grant program for colleges?

3. What is Pinkerton's compromise? What does he propose?

4. What changes will be needed to make the compromise work?

5. What financial challenge does the author anticipate? How does he rebut it?

6. What other counterarguments does Pinkerton bring up and rebut?

QUESTIONS FOR REASONING AND ANALYSIS

1. What are the values and goals of the right? Of the left? Does Pinkerton's grand compromise give each side what it wants to see in education? Why or why not?

2. Explain the graph. What does it show? What can we learn from this visual?

3. Analyze Pinkerton's argument that education should be financed and controlled primarily at the federal, not the local, level. What are his reasons? Does he make a convincing case for change? Why or why not?

4. How does the author's "voucher" plan differ from current plans? Do you agree with Pinkerton that his is a better "voucher" plan? Why or why not?

QUESTIONS FOR REFLECTING AND WRITING

1. What statistic surprises you the most? Why?

2. Should students be allowed to use vouchers at private and parochial schools? Why or why not?

3. Is Pinkerton's plan feasible? Can we get people to give up local funding and control of schools? If so, how? If not, why not? *Should* we seek the changes Pinkerton argues for? Why or why not?

CHAPTER 19

Censorship
and
Free Speech

Six writers in this chapter explore contemporary situations that generate debates about censorship—and First Amendment rights. These situations include censoring books in school libraries, removing some controversial passages in assigned books, "policing" the Internet, and restricting student "speech." As you explore these specific issues, keep in mind that the Supreme Court continues to hand down rulings that shape our interpretation of First Amendment rights, so what is protected speech under the First Amendment is never absolute—it continues to evolve or be reinterpreted, depending on your point of view. Also keep in mind that many would argue that there is no such thing as absolute freedom in any society and that the First Amendment does not pretend to offer absolute freedoms. For example, you cannot go into a crowded theater and yell "Fire!" when there is no fire. You will be arrested for this behavior that puts others at risk.

PREREADING QUESTIONS

1. Have you considered positions between the extremes of absolutely no censorship of published materials (in any medium) and of laws prohibiting the publication of obscene, pornographic, or treasonable works or hate speech? What are some possible restrictions that may be agreed upon by most people?

2. What are some ways to control what is published (in any medium) without always resorting to legal restrictions? Are any of these possibilities feasible?

Websites Relevant to This Chapter's Topic

MIT Student Association for Freedom of Expression (SAFE)

http://web.mit.edu/safe/www/safe

Good information and links; site opposes censorship.

Index on Censorship

www.oneworld.org/index_oc

A bimonthly magazine supporting freedom of speech.

National Coalition Against Censorship (NCAC)

www.ncac.org

Organization promoting free speech. Site contains articles and news alerts.

The Censorship Pages, Sponsored by Books A to Z

www.booksatoz.com/censorship

Contains links to resources and lists of frequently banned books.

EXPELLING *HUCK FINN* | NAT HENTOFF

A staff writer for the *Village Voice* and a syndicated columnist for many years, Nat Hentoff (b. 1925) is also an author of articles and books on jazz and education. He is perhaps best known for his "Sweet Land of Liberty" columns on First Amendment issues. "Expelling *Huck Finn*" was published in the *Washington Post* on November 27, 1999.

PREREADING QUESTIONS What restrictions on free speech—and publication—are part of current law? Do you have a position on censorship? If so, what is it?

The Pennsylvania State Conference of the NAACP has instructed its   1
branches to file grievances with the state's human rights commission demanding that local school boards and district superintendents remove Mark Twain's *Adventures of Huckleberry Finn* from mandatory reading lists.

2   The charge, supported by the national NAACP, is that "tax dollars should not be used to perpetuate a stereotype that has psychologically damaging effects on the self-esteem of African American children."

3   Some years ago I was talking to African American eighth-graders in a Brooklyn public school who had been reading *Huckleberry Finn* in class—along with the history of racism in such towns as Hannibal, Mo., where Twain had grown up.

4   The students recently had been discussing the passage in which Huck, on the raft with Jim, was tormented by what he had been raised to believe—that he would go to hell if he did not report this runaway slave to the owner.

5   Huck wrote a note doing just that, but finally, destroying the note, he said to himself, "All right, then, I'll *go* to hell!"

6   "Do you think we're so dumb," one of the Brooklyn eighth-graders said to me, "that we don't know the difference between a racist book and an anti-racist book? Sure, the book is full of the word 'Nigger.' That's how those bigots talked back then."

7   As Twain said years later, Huck, after writing the note, was struggling between "a sound heart" and "a deformed conscience" that he had to make right.

8   "The people whom Huck and Jim encounter on the Mississippi"—Russell Baker wrote in the *New York Times* in 1982—"are drunkards, murderers, bullies, swindlers, lynchers, thieves, liars, frauds, child abusers, numskulls, hypocrites, windbags and traders in human flesh. All are white. The one man of honor in this phantasmagoria is 'Nigger Jim,' as Twain called him to emphasize the irony of a society in which the only true gentleman was held beneath contempt."

9   Michael Meyers—assistant national director of the NAACP under Roy Wilkins from 1975 to 1984—wrote to Julian Bond, the present NAACP chairman, about the organization's desire to censor *Huck Finn*.

10   Calling the book "a great anti-slavery classic," Meyers—now the executive director of the New York Civil Rights Coalition—asked Bond whether there is an actual NAACP policy "that encourages NAACP branches to either support or seek book banning or censorship." Bond, as Meyers noted in his letter, is on the ACLU's national advisory council, as is the NAACP's president, Kweisi Mfume. If such a policy exists, Meyers wrote, "what are you doing—or what are you prepared to do—to change such a policy?"

11   Bond answered that "the NAACP does not have a policy for every occasion. Might I ask you for a policy we might adopt that could allow the NAACP to express outrage at racist expression while protecting free speech?"

12   Meyers was puzzled by the response because, he says, *Huckleberry Finn*—as the youngsters in Brooklyn emphatically understood—is *anti*-racist.

13   In 1998 Judge Stephen Reinhardt, writing for a unanimous three-judge panel of the 9th Circuit Court of Appeals, rejected a lawsuit by an African American parent, who is also a teacher, asking that *Huckleberry Finn* be removed from mandatory reading lists in the Phoenix, Ariz., schools.

"Words can hurt, particularly racist epithets," Reinhardt wrote, "but a nec- 14 essary component of any education is learning to think critically about offensive ideas. Without that ability, one can do little to respond to them." Part of learning to think critically about offensive speech is to understand the context in which it is used.

Bond might consider sending Judge Reinhardt's decision (*Kathy Monteiro* 15 *v. the Tempe Union High School District*) to the Pennsylvania State Conference of the NAACP. He might also inform it of "The Jim Dilemma: Reading Race in *Huckleberry Finn*" by Jocelyn Chadwick-Joshua, an African American who has been instructing black and white teachers about the book for years.

She writes: "Without the memory of what a word once meant and what it 16 can continue to mean, we as a society are doomed to repeat earlier mistakes about ourselves, each other, and serious issues involving us all."

QUESTIONS FOR READING

1. What is Hentoff's subject?
2. What is the occasion for Hentoff's column? That is, what has happened to lead the author to write?
3. What is Meyers's view of the novel? Is the issue really a conflict between censorship and racist writing? What, in Hentoff's view, does the NAACP need to understand?

QUESTIONS FOR REASONING AND ANALYSIS

1. Hentoff devotes four paragraphs to his experience in a Brooklyn school. What are we to infer from his experience with Brooklyn students?
2. Many scholars of American literature and culture will argue that *Huck Finn* is essential reading. Should books that are so important be required reading?
3. What is Hentoff's claim?

QUESTIONS FOR REFLECTING AND WRITING

1. Have you read *Huck Finn*? If so, was your understanding similar to that of the Brooklyn students—or were you offended by the novel? Explain your reactions.
2. Some parents have worked to ban *Huck Finn* from school libraries. Should it be banned? Should any book be banned from a library? Explain your views.

IF YOU ASSIGN MY BOOK, DON'T CENSOR IT | MARK MATHABANE

A former White House Fellow at the Department of Education, Mark Mathabane is best known for his widely read—and at times controversial—novel *Kaffir Boy*. Mathabane lives and writes in North Carolina; his most recent novel is *Ubuntu*. The following article appeared in the *Washington Post* on November 28, 1999.

PREREADING QUESTIONS   Should cutting out parts of or changing parts of a book be seen as censorship? Should publishers—or teachers—change texts in these ways?

1   A few weeks ago, school officials at Kearsley High School in Flint, Mich., decided to censor *Kaffir Boy*, my story of growing up in a South African ghetto during apartheid. On the recommendation of a special committee of administrators, teachers and staff, the school has begun taping over several sentences and parts of sentences in its copies of the book after a half-dozen parents objected to my graphic description of one of the most harrowing experiences of my life: When I was 7 years old and trapped in the poverty-stricken ghetto of the Alexandra township, 10 miles north of Johannesburg, hunger drove me to tag along with a ring of boys who prostituted themselves for food. One parent called my description "pornography," according to the *Flint Journal,* adding that *Kaffir Boy* belonged in an adult bookstore rather than in a 10th-grade English class.

2   I wasn't altogether surprised by the parents' objections. The raw emotions and experiences in *Kaffir Boy,* which constitute the core of its power and appeal, have made the book controversial ever since its publication in the United States in 1986. When it became required reading for thousands of high school students nationwide several years ago, it was challenged by parents in school districts in a dozen states and, in some cases, withdrawn. No, what surprises—and disturbs—me is the decision at Kearsley to censor the text, altering a passage that marks a crucial turning point in the book—and in my life.

3   As a parent of three public school students, ages 6, 8 and 10, I pay attention to what they are assigned to read. I've read them portions of *Kaffir Boy* and my other books, which deal with issues of hunger, child abuse, poverty, violence, the oppression of women and racism. I'm always careful to provide context, to talk to them in a language they can understand.

4   Every year I also talk to thousands of students about my work and my life in South Africa. I tell them how fortunate they are to live in America, how important it is not to take this nation's freedoms for granted. I recall for them how my peers and I were forbidden by the government in Pretoria to read the U.S. Constitution and the Bill of Rights. I recall how empowered I felt after I clandestinely secured a copy of the Declaration of Independence. And I recall how, during the Soweto uprising of 1976, hundreds of students died fighting for recognition of their unalienable rights to "life, liberty and the pursuit of happiness."

5   When I came to America in 1978, I was stunned—and exhilarated—to find out that I could walk into any library and check out books that were uncensored and read them without fear of being harassed, thrown in jail or killed.

6   I have that experience in mind when I think about my own children's reading lists. In large part, I trust their teachers to have the judgment to assign books that are not only consistent with educational goals, but also with my children's maturity level. Should my children bring home a book I find objectionable, the responsible thing for me to do would be to request that my child be assigned a different one.

That's why I have no problem with parents who make such a request about $_7$ *Kaffir Boy.* The parents of a sophomore at West Mecklenburg High School in Charlotte, N.C., where the book has also been challenged, did just that. They were not only uncomfortable with the prostitution scene, but also with my use of racially graphic language such as the word "kaffir" (a pejorative term for "black").

But I strongly disagree with censoring portions of the book. They have no $_8$ right to decide the issue for other students. Should those students be deprived of what I believe is a key scene in order to make a few parents comfortable?

I don't think so. Books aren't written with the comfort of readers in mind. I $_9$ know I didn't write *Kaffir Boy* that way. I wrote it to reflect reality, to show the world the inhumanity of the apartheid system. It wasn't an easy book for me to write. The memories gave me nightmares. What's more, after the book was published in the United States, members of my family in South Africa were persecuted by the Pretoria regime, which subsequently banned the book there.

Kaffir Boy is disturbing, but it isn't pornographic. As Kari Molter, chair- $_{10}$ woman of the English department at Kearsley High, said, the prostitution scene, which makes up three pages, is "frightening," but it is "an important scene." I included it in the book not to titillate readers, but to reveal a disturbing truth about life under apartheid.

That disturbing truth included the terror and helplessness I felt as a child $_{11}$ during brutal midnight police raids; the grinding, stunting poverty in which I, my family and millions of other blacks were steeped; the emasculation of my father by a system that denied him the right to earn a living in a way that gave him dignity; the hopelessness and psychic pain that led me to contemplate suicide at age 10; the sacrifices and faith of my long-suffering mother as she battled to save me from the dead-end life of the street and its gangs.

Not the least disturbing of those truths is the passage about prostitution. $_{12}$ My father, the only breadwinner in a family of nine, had been arrested for the crime of being unemployed. There was no food in our shack, and my mother couldn't even get the usual cattle blood from the slaughterhouse to boil as soup. Desperate for food, one afternoon I linked up with a group of 5-, 6- and 7-year-old boys on the way to the nearby men's hostel. Their pimp, a 13-year-old boy named Mphandlani, promised that at the hostel we would get money and "all the food we could eat" in exchange for playing "a little game" with the migrant workers who lived there.

Once inside the hostel, I stood by in confusion and fear as the men and $_{13}$ boys began undressing. In the book, I give some physical descriptions of what happened. When Mphandlani told me to undress, too, I refused. One of the men came after me, and I bolted out of the hostel. I fled because I knew that what the men were doing to the boys was wrong, and recalled my parents telling me never to do wrong things. I was called a fool—and shunned—by those boys afterward.

Resisting peer pressure is one of the toughest things for young people to $_{14}$ do. That is the lesson of the prostitution scene. It's a lesson that seems to be lost on the people who want to censor my book. Teenagers understand what peer pressure is. They confront tough choices every day, particularly if they happen to live in environments where child abuse, poverty, violence and death are commonplace, where innocence dies young, and where children can't afford to be children.

15   Many students have connected powerfully with the story of *Kaffir Boy*. The book, they've told me in letters and e-mail, teaches them to never give up in the face of adversity, not to take freedom—or food—for granted, to regard education as a powerful weapon of hope, and always to strive to do the right thing.

16   Could *Kaffir Boy* have had this impact without the prostitution scene? I doubt it. It was an event that changed me forever. Could I have made that point using less graphic language? Perhaps. But language is a very sacred thing for a writer. When I write, I strive for clarity and directness, so the reader understands precisely what I mean. To fudge language in order to avoid offending the sensibilities of one group or another leads to doublespeak, which is the death of honesty.

17   That very honesty is what prompted a senior from Sentinel High School in Missoula, Mont., to send me a letter a few days ago. In it she wrote that *Kaffir Boy* made her realize "that no matter what, there is always hope." It is this hope that I'm seeking to keep alive with my books.

18   I owe my life to books. While I was in the ghetto, groaning under the yoke of apartheid, wallowing in self-pity, believing that I was doomed to die from the sheer agony of frustrated hopes and strangled dreams, books became my best friends and my salvation. Reading broadened my horizons, deepened my sensibilities and, most importantly, made me think. Books liberated me from mental slavery and opened doors of opportunity where none seemed to exist.

19   Censorship is not the solution to the legitimate concern some parents have about what is appropriate for their children to read. I wish child abuse and racism weren't facts of life, but they are. Only by knowing about them can we combat them effectively.

20   What's more, there are alternatives to censorship. One possible solution lies in schools developing reading-list guidelines, such as those being drawn up by the Charlotte-Mecklenburg school system in the wake of objections to *Kaffir Boy*. Under the guidelines, teachers will still choose their own books, but they will be required to give students and parents a summary of the contents and potential concerns, such as profanity or sexually explicit scenes. I don't mind if my book doesn't make the list, or if some parents choose another title for their offspring, but if students do read it, let them read it the way I wrote it.

QUESTIONS FOR READING

1.   What is the author's occasion for writing? What is the specific issue with regard to *Kaffir Boy*?

2.   What does Mathabane approve of parents doing? What does he object to?

3. Why is the prostitution scene disturbing? Why is it not, in the author's view, pornographic? What definition of pornography emerges from Mathabane's discussion?

4. How does the author defend his choice of language in *Kaffir Boy*?

5. What did books do for the author?

6. What can schools do, instead of censoring, to help parents guide their children's reading?

QUESTIONS FOR REASONING AND ANALYSIS

1. What does the author seek to accomplish in paragraphs 3–7 when he writes of his children and the U.S. freedoms that he admired from a distance in South Africa?

2. What is Mathabane's claim?

3. Mathabane would rather students not read his book than read it with parts removed. Can you understand his position? Why does he think it inappropriate to change someone's words?

4. Has the author presented an effective argument against altering books? Against censorship? Explain.

QUESTIONS FOR REFLECTING AND WRITING

1. Have you read *Kaffir Boy*? If so, did you find it disturbing? Did you find it moving and encouraging, as the author suggests?

2. Are there other assigned readings that bothered you—or that your parents did not want you to read? If so, how did you handle the situation?

3. Do you agree with Mathabane's definition of pornography? If not, why not?

PARENTAL NEGLECT LEADS TEENAGERS TO BE SEDUCED ON THE INTERNET | MICHELLE MALKIN

A Fox News commentator, Michelle Malkin (b. 1970) is a syndicated columnist and author of *Invasion: How America Still Welcomes Terrorists, Criminals, and Other Foreign Menaces to Our Shores* (2002). The daughter of Filipino immigrants, Malkin is a graduate of Oberlin College; she appears frequently on various television talk shows. The following article was published June 5, 2000, in *Insight on the News*.

PREREADING QUESTIONS How much time do you spend each day "surfing the Net"? Do you spend time in chat rooms? Do you have a cyber pal? Have you ever met—or would you meet—a stranger from the Internet?

When she was just 13 years old, Katie Tarbox was sexually molested by a 41-year-old man who had befriended her in one of the world's most popular gathering places for perverts and predators: an online chat room for teens. The man's screen name was "VALLEYGUY." He told Katie his name was "Mark." He bragged that he was a wealthy 23-year-old with "a four-seater Mercedes convertible—I love it—a BMW convertible, and a Jeep." When that didn't impress Katie, he boasted: "I have sexy green eyes. Girls love to look into them. What do you look like?"

2   Despite her apprehension about the "animals" and "weirdos" who populated America Online, or AOL, chat rooms, Katie developed a secret relationship with "Mark" during a six-month period. He listened sympathetically to the vulnerable girl's adolescent fears and frustrations. They talked about movies and music. She played the piano for him over the phone. In March 1996, she agreed to meet him face to face in Dallas—where her New Canaan, Conn., swim team was traveling for a national competition.

3   The sordid details of their encounter, and the subsequent federal prosecution of Katie's cyber-seducer (a Calabasas, Calif., financial analyst whose real name was Francis John Kufrovich), are laid out in the teen-ager's new book, *Katie.com*. Published recently by Dutton Books, this true-life horror story should be required reading for parents in the Internet age.

4   Feminists and women's magazine reviewers will focus on Katie's youthful critique of our beauty-obsessed culture. The author, now 17 and college-bound, writes candidly of her insecurities about clothes, weight, hair and skin: "At 13, I accepted the image of beauty I saw on the covers of fashion magazines. I thought the Calvin Klein models inside were beautiful. I though ultra-thinness was beautiful. Beauty was painful. And it was very expensive."

5   But low self-esteem and societal pressures weren't the main factors in driving Katie to seek companionship on the Net. In a painfully straightforward manner more incisive than any academic, pundit, or sociologist's work, Katie indicts parental absenteeism: "Home was a place where I always felt alone." On most days, Katie reveals, "I'd spend a couple of hours online. Usually, my parents weren't home to even know what I was doing."

6   Katie's mother and stepfather gave her obligatory warnings about not disclosing her real name and address on AOL. But aside "from these warnings, they didn't have much else to say."

7   The young girl's 200-page memoir is filled with sad longing for her parents' company. Katie describes "a dreadful thing called 'year-end' " that consumed her mother's attention. "Because she worked on the financial side of [her] company, she was responsible for composing a year-end report. Sometimes, she would come home as late as 1 in the morning, and she went to the office on weekends."

8   On a trip with her school singing group to Washington, Katie "hoped that her mother would be able to attend these performances, considering it would be one of the last times I would sing with the choir. But as always, business was a conflict, and she was not able to make it." Her stepfather, she writes, "could have defined what a father is for me. Instead, he always told me to go to my mother for answers or for help, and she was usually working, so I was left on my own."

9   When neither parent was around to celebrate her 14th birthday, Katie turned to the one adult she could depend on—Francis John Kufrovich, aka

"Mark," lurking in the AOL chat room. They corresponded in the middle of the night as Katie baked herself birthday cupcakes. "He was someone to talk to, Mom," Katie later explained. "You haven't been around a lot with all your business trips, and the fact that you live at work doesn't help."

Even after Kufrovich's arrest and conviction, Katie's mom still doesn't seem 10 to have her priorities straight. Instead of accompanying Katie to her molester's plea hearing, "she was in Florida on business."

Katie's book offers tips and Website addresses to help families defend 11 themselves on the Internet. But no software program, no filtering tool and no amount of law-enforcement resources can protect children from the cyberpredator's best friend: parental neglect.

QUESTIONS FOR READING

1. What is the occasion for Malkin's article? What is she responding to?
2. What happened to Katie Tarbox?
3. According to the author, how will feminists and women's magazine reviewers respond to Katie's story? What causes will they put forward to explain what happened?
4. What cause does Malkin find?
5. How does Katie describe her parents?

QUESTIONS FOR REASONING AND ANALYSIS

1. Malkin begins her essay by recounting Katie's sexual molestation. What makes this an effective opening?
2. Malkin dismisses low self-esteem and societal pressures as causes of Katie's involvement with "Mark" as the explanations of others. Does she provide any evidence that these are the causes that feminists will emphasize? Should these possible causes be dismissed altogether? Why or why not?
3. Katie wrote her book at age seventeen. Judging from your own experience, would you expect her to have enough maturity to analyze her family relationships with some accuracy? Or is she still hurting and wanting to hurt her mother and stepfather? Can we tell from the passages quoted by Malkin?
4. What is Malkin's claim? Has she supported her claim convincingly with Katie's story and her analysis of that story? Why or why not?

QUESTIONS FOR REFLECTING AND WRITING

1. Does Katie's story offer a powerful warning to you to stay away from chat-room "weirdos"? Why or why not?
2. How serious a problem is parental neglect? Are many parents too busy—or too afraid—to know what their teens are doing, both online and when they are out of the house?

3. Is adequate software in place to protect youngsters from Internet predators? Could parents control access if they chose to do so? Should the government block chat rooms and pornographic sites from those under eighteen? If so, how? If not, why not?

PROTECTING OUR CHILDREN FROM INTERNET SMUT: MORAL DUTY OR MORAL PANIC? | JULIA WILKINS

Julia Wilkins (b. 1968) holds a master's degree in social policy and is currently a special education teacher. She has published several articles on education and is the author of two books: *Math Activities for Young Children: A Resource Guide for Parents and Teachers* (1995) and *Non-Competitive Motor Activities: A Guide for Elementary Classroom Teachers* (1996). In the following article, which appeared in the September/October 1997 issue of *The Humanist,* Wilkins applies the sociological concept "moral panic" to Internet pornography.

PREREADING QUESTIONS Do you think that the media exaggerate or distort reality? If so, why would they do that? If not, how would you support your position?

1   The term *moral panic* is one of the more useful concepts to have emerged from sociology in recent years. A moral panic is characterized by a wave of public concern, anxiety, and fervor about something, usually perceived as a threat to society. The distinguishing factors are a level of interest totally out of proportion to the real importance of the subject, some individuals building personal careers from the pursuit and magnification of the issue, and the replacement of reasoned debate with witchhunts and hysteria.

2   Moral panics of recent memory include the Joseph McCarthy anti-Communist witchhunts of the 1950s and the satanic ritual abuse allegations of the 1980s. And, more recently, we have witnessed a full-blown moral panic about pornography on the Internet. Sparked by the July 3, 1995, *Time* cover article "On a Screen Near You: Cyberporn," this moral panic has been perpetuated and intensified by a raft of subsequent media reports. As a result, there is now a widely held belief that pornography is easily accessible to all children using the Internet. This was also the judgment of Congress, which, proclaiming to be "protecting the children" voted overwhelmingly in 1996 for legislation to make it a criminal offense to send "indecent" material over the Internet into people's computers.

3   The original *Time* article was based on its exclusive access to Marty Rimm's *Georgetown University Law Journal* paper, "Marketing Pornography on the Information Superhighway." Although published, the article had not received peer review and was based on an undergraduate research project concerning descriptions of images on adult bulletin board systems in the United States. Using the information in this paper, *Time* discussed the type of pornography available online, such as "pedophilia (nude pictures of children), hebephelia (youths) and . . . images of bondage, sadomasochism, urination, defecation, and sex acts with a barnyard full of animals." The article proposed that pornog-

raphy of this nature is readily available to anyone who is even remotely computer literate and raised the stakes by offering quotes from worried parents who feared for their children's safety. It also presented the possibility that pornographic material could be mailed to children without their parents' knowledge. *Time*'s example was of a ten-year-old boy who supposedly received pornographic images in his e-mail showing "10 thumbnail size pictures showing couples engaged in various acts of sodomy, heterosexual intercourse and lesbian sex." Naturally, the boy's mother was shocked and concerned, saying, "Children should not be subject to these images." *Time* also quoted another mother who said that she wanted her children to benefit from the vast amount of knowledge available on the Internet but was inclined not to allow access, fearing that her children could be "bombarded with X-rated pornography and [she] would know nothing about it."

From the outset, Rimm's report generated a lot of excitement—not only 4 because it was reportedly the first published study of online pornography but also because of the secrecy involved in the research and publication of the article. In fact, the *New York Times* reported on July 24, 1995, that Marty Rimm was being investigated by his university, Carnegie Mellon, for unethical research and, as a result, would not be giving testimony to a Senate hearing on Internet pornography. Two experts from *Time* reportedly discovered serious flaws in Rimm's study involving gross misrepresentation and erroneous methodology. His work was soon deemed flawed and inaccurate, and *Time* recanted in public. With Rimm's claims now apologetically retracted, his original suggestion that 83.5 percent of Internet graphics are pornographic was quietly withdrawn in favor of a figure less than 1 percent.

Time admitted that grievous errors had slipped past their editorial staff, as 5 their normally thorough research succumbed to a combination of deadline pressure and exclusivity agreements that barred them from showing the unpublished study to possible critics. But, by then, the damage had been done: the study had found its way to the Senate.

GOVERNMENT INTERVENTION

Senator Charles Grassley (Republican—Iowa) jumped on the pornography 6 bandwagon by proposing a bill that would make it a criminal offense to supply or permit the supply of "indecent" material to minors over the Internet. Grassley introduced the entire *Time* article into the congressional record, despite the fact that the conceptual, logical, and methodological flaws in the report had already been acknowledged by the magazine.

On the Senate floor, Grassley referred to Marty Rimm's undergraduate re- 7 search as "a remarkable study conducted by researchers at Carnegie Mellon University" and went on to say:

> The university surveyed 900,000 computer images. Of these 900,000 images, 83.5 percent of all computerized photographs available on the Internet are pornographic. . . . With so many graphic images available on computer networks, I believe Congress must act and do so in a constitutional manner to help parents who are under assault in this day and age.

8　　Under the Grassley bill, later known as the Protection of Children from Pornography Act of 1995, it would have been illegal for anyone to knowingly or recklessly transmit indecent material to minors. This bill marked the beginning of a stream of Internet censorship legislation at various levels of government in the United States and abroad.

9　　The most extreme and fiercely opposed of these was the Communications Decency Act, sponsored by former Senator James Exon (Democrat—Nebraska) and Senator Dan Coats (Republican—Indiana). The CDA labeled the transmission of "obscene, lewd, lascivious, filthy, indecent, or patently offensive" pornography over the Internet a crime. It was attached to the Telecommunications Reform Act of 1996, which was then passed by Congress on February 1, 1996. One week later, it was signed into law by President Clinton. On the same day, the American Civil Liberties Union filed suit in Philadelphia against the U.S. Department of Justice and Attorney General Janet Reno, arguing that the statute would ban free speech protected by the First Amendment and subject Internet users to far greater restrictions than exist in any other medium. Later that month, the Citizens Internet Empowerment Coalition initiated a second legal challenge to the CDA, which formally consolidated with *ACLU v. Reno*. Government lawyers agreed not to prosecute "indecent" or "patently offensive" material until the three-judge court in Philadelphia ruled on the case.

10　　Although the purpose of the CDA was to protect young children from accessing and viewing material of sexually explicit content on the Internet, the wording of the act was so broad and poorly defined that it could have deprived many adults of information they needed in the areas of health, art, news, and literature—information that is legal in print form. Specifically, certain medical information available on the Internet includes descriptions of sexual organs and activities which might have been considered "indecent" or "patently offensive" under the act—for example, information on breastfeeding, birth control, AIDS, and gynecological and urinological information. Also, many museums and art galleries now have websites. Under the act, displaying art like the Sistine Chapel nudes could be cause for criminal prosecution. Online newspapers would not be permitted to report the same information as is available in the print media. Reports on combatants in war, at the scenes of crime, in the political arena, and outside abortion clinics often provoke images or language that could be constituted "offensive" and therefore illegal on the net. Furthermore, the CDA provided a legal basis for banning books which had been ruled unconstitutional to ban from school libraries. These include many of the classics as well as modern literature containing words that may be considered indecent.

11　　The act also expanded potential liability for employers, service providers, and carriers that transmit or otherwise make available restricted communications. According to the CDA, "knowingly" allowing obscene material to pass through one's computer system was a criminal offense. Given the nature of the Internet, however, making service providers responsible for the content of the traffic they pass on to other Internet nodes is equivalent to holding a telephone carrier responsible for the content of the conversations going over that carrier's lines. So, under the terms of the act, if someone sent an indecent electronic comment from a workstation, the employer, the e-mail service provider, and the carrier all could be potentially held liable and subject to up to $100,000 in fines or two years in prison.

On June 12, 1996, after experiencing live tours of the Internet and hearing arguments about the technical and economical infeasibility of complying with the censorship law, the three federal judges in Philadelphia granted the request for a preliminary injunction against the CDA. The court determined that "there is no evidence that sexually oriented material is the primary type of content on this new medium" and proposed that "communications over the Internet do not 'invade' an individual's home or appear on one's computer screen unbidden. Users seldom encounter content 'by accident.' " In a unanimous decision, the judges ruled that the Communications Decency Act would unconstitutionally restrict free speech on the Internet. 12

The government appealed the judges' decision and, on March 19, 1997, the U.S. Supreme Court heard oral arguments in the legal challenge to the CDA, now known as *Reno v. ACLU.* Finally, on June 26, the decision came down. The Court voted unanimously that the act violated the First Amendment guarantee of freedom of speech and would have threatened "to torch a large segment of the Internet community." 13

Is the panic therefore over? Far from it. The July 7, 1997, *Newsweek,* picking up the frenzy where *Time* left off, reported the Supreme Court decision in a provocatively illustrated article featuring a color photo of a woman licking her lips and a warning message taken from the website of the House of Sin. Entitled "On the Net, Anything Goes," the opening words by Steven Levy read, "Born of a hysteria triggered by a genuine problem—the ease with which wired-up teenagers can get hold of nasty pictures on the Internet—the Communications Decency Act (CDA) was never really destined to be a companion piece to the Bill of Rights." At the announcement of the Court's decision, anti-porn protesters were on the street outside brandishing signs which read, "Child Molesters Are Looking for Victims on the Internet." 14

Meanwhile, government talk has shifted to the development of a universal Internet rating system and widespread hardware and software filtering. Referring to the latter, White House Senior Adviser Rahm Emanuel declared, "We're going to get the V-chip for the Internet. Same goal, different means." 15

But it is important to bear in mind that children are still a minority of Internet users. A contract with an Internet service provider typically needs to be paid for by credit card or direct debit, therefore requiring the intervention of an adult. Children are also unlikely to be able to view any kind of porn online without a credit card. 16

In addition to this, there have been a variety of measures developed to protect children on the Internet. The National Center for Missing and Exploited Children has outlined protective guidelines for parents and children in its pamphlet, *Child Safety on the Information Superhighway.* A number of companies now sell Internet newsfeeds and web proxy accesses that are vetted in 17 accordance with a list of forbidden topics. And, of course, there remain those blunt software instruments that block access to sexually oriented sites by looking for keywords such as *sex, erotic,* and *X-rated.* But one of the easiest solutions is to keep the family computer in a well-traveled space, like a living room, so that parents can monitor what their children download.

FACT OR MEDIA FICTION?

18   In her 1995 *CMC* magazine article, "Journey to the Centre of Cybersmut," Lisa Schmeiser discusses her research into online pornography. After an exhaustive search, she was unable to find any pornography, apart from the occasional commercial site (requiring a credit card for access), and concluded that one would have to undertake extensive searching to find quantities of explicit pornography. She suggested that, if children were accessing pornography online, they would not have been doing it by accident. Schmeiser writes: "There will be children who circumvent passwords, Surfwatch software, and seemingly innocuous links to find the 'adult' material. But these are the same kids who would visit every convenience store in a five-mile radius to find the one stocking *Playboy.*" Her argument is simply that, while there is a certain amount of pornography online, it is not freely and readily available. Contrary to what the media often report, pornography is not that easy to find.

19   There *is* pornography in cyberspace (including images, pictures, movies, sounds, and sex discussions) and several ways of receiving pornographic material on the Internet (such as through private bulletin board systems, the World Wide Web, newsgroups, and e-mail). However, many sites just contain reproduced images from hardcore magazines and videos available from other outlets, and registration fee restrictions make them inaccessible to children. And for the more contentious issue of pedophilia, a recent investigation by the *Guardian* newspaper in Britain revealed that the majority of pedophilic images distributed on the Internet are simply electronic reproductions of the small output of legitimate pedophile magazines, such as *Lolita,* published in the 1970s.

20   Clearly the issue of pornography on the Internet is a moral panic—an issue perpetuated by a sensationalistic style of reporting and misleading content in newspaper and magazine articles. And probably the text from which to base any examination of the possible link between media reporting and moral panics is Stanley Cohen's 1972 book, *Folk Devils and Moral Panic,* in which he proposes that the mass media are ultimately responsible for the creation of such panics. Cohen describes a moral panic as occurring when "a condition, episode, person or group of persons emerges to become a threat to societal values and interests; . . . the moral barricades are manned by editors . . . politicians and other 'right thinking' people." He feels that, while problematical elements of society can pose a threat to others, this threat is realistically far less than the perceived image generated by mass media reporting.

21   Cohen describes how the news we read is not necessarily the truth; editors have papers to sell, targets to meet, and competition from other publishers. It is in their interest to make the story "a good read"—the sensationalist ap-

proach sells newspapers. The average person is likely to be drawn in with the promise of scandal and intrigue. This can be seen in the reporting of the *National Enquirer* and *People,* with their splashy pictures and sensationalistic headlines, helping them become two of the largest circulation magazines in the United States.

Cohen discusses the "inventory" as the set of criteria inherent in any reporting that may be deemed as fueling a moral panic. This inventory consists of the following: 22

EXAGGERATION IN REPORTING

Facts are often overblown to give the story a greater edge. Figures that are not necessarily incorrect but have been quoted out of context, or have been used incorrectly to shock, are two forms of this exaggeration. 23

Looking back at the original *Time* cover article, "On a Screen Near You: Cyberporn," this type of exaggeration is apparent. Headlines such as "The Carnegie Mellon researchers found 917,410 sexually explicit pictures, short stories and film clips online" make the reader think that there really is a problem with the quantity of pornography in cyberspace. It takes the reader a great deal of further exploration to find out how this figure was calculated. Also, standing alone and out of context, the oft-quoted figure that 83.5 percent of images found on Usenet Newsgroups are pornographic could be seen as cause for concern. However, if one looks at the math associated with this figure, one would find that this is a sampled percentage with a researcher leaning toward known areas of pornography. 24

THE REPETITION OF FALLACIES

This occurs when a writer reports information that seems perfectly believable to the general public, even though those who know the subject are aware it is wildly incorrect. In the case of pornography, the common fallacy is that the Internet is awash with nothing but pornography and that all you need to obtain it is a computer and a modem. Such misinformation is integral to the fueling of moral panics. 25

Take, for example, the October 18, 1995, *Scotland on Sunday,* which reports that, to obtain pornographic material, "all you need is a personal computer, a phone line with a modem attached and a connection via a specialist provider to the Internet." What the article fails to mention is that the majority of pornography is found on specific Usenet sites not readily available from the major Internet providers, such as America Online and Compuserve. It also fails to mention that this pornography needs to be downloaded and converted into a viewable form, which requires certain skills and can take considerable time. 26

MISLEADING PICTURES AND SNAPPY TITLES

Media representation often exaggerates a story through provocative titles and flashy pictorials—all in the name of drawing in the reader. The titles set the tone for the rest of the article; the headline is the most noticeable and important part of any news item, attracting the reader's initial attention. The recent 27

Newsweek article is a perfect example. Even if the headline has little relevance to the article, it sways the reader's perception of the topic. The symbolization of images further increases the impact of the story. *Time's* own images in its original coverage—showing a shocked little boy on the cover and, inside, a naked man hunched over a computer monitor—added to the article's ability to shock and to draw the reader into the story.

28   Through sensationalized reporting, certain forms of behavior become classified as *deviant*. Specifically, those who put pornography online or those who download it are seen as being deviant in nature. This style of reporting benefits the publication or broadcast by giving it the aura of "moral guardian" to the rest of society. It also increases revenue.

29   In exposing deviant behavior, newspapers and magazines have the ability to push for reform. So, by classifying a subject and its relevant activities as deviant, they can stand as crusaders for moral decency, championing the cause of "normal" people. They can report the subject and call for something to be done about it, but this power is easily abused. The *Time* cyberporn article called for reform on the basis of Rimm's findings, proclaiming, "A new study shows us how pervasive and wild [pornography on the Internet] really is. Can we protect our kids—and free speech?" These cries to protect our children affected the likes of Senators James Exon and Robert Dole, who took the *Time* article with its "shocking" revelations (as well as a sample of pornographic images) to the Senate floor, appealing for changes to the law. From this response it is clear how powerful a magazine article can be, regardless of the integrity and accuracy of its reporting.

30   The *Time* article had all of Cohen's elements relating to the fueling of a moral panic: exaggeration, fallacies, and misleading pictures and titles. Because certain publications are highly regarded and enjoy an important role in society, anything printed in their pages is consumed and believed by a large audience. People accept what they read because, to the best of their knowledge, it is the truth. So, even though the *Time* article was based on a report by an undergraduate student passing as "a research team from Carnegie Mellon," the status of the magazine was great enough to launch a panic that continues unabated—from the halls of Congress to the pulpits of churches, from public schools to the offices of software developers, from local communities to the global village.

QUESTIONS FOR READING

1. What does the term *moral panic* mean?
2. What is Wilkins's subject?
3. What events have led to the current "moral panic" over Internet pornography? What, eventually, was *Time* magazine's position on the Rimm study?
4. What law was passed by Congress? What would the law have banned on the Internet? What has happened to this law?

5. Has the moral panic over Internet pornography faded away? How does the author answer this question?

6. In what ways are children best protected from Internet pornography? How serious is the problem of children accessing porn on the Internet, according to Lisa Schmeiser?

7. In his book *Folk Devils and Moral Panic,* where does Stanley Cohen place the blame for moral panic?

8. What strategies are used to fuel a moral panic?

QUESTIONS FOR REASONING AND ANALYSIS

1. What is Wilkins's claim? What is she *not* arguing?

2. How does Wilkins's argument differ from the first two in this chapter? How does her purpose differ?

QUESTIONS FOR REFLECTING AND WRITING

1. Does the author convince you that media coverage of Internet pornography represents an example of moral panic? Why or why not?

2. Have you found pornography on the Internet? If so, was it easy to access? Do you consider it damaging—relative to *Playboy* or X-rated films? Explain.

3. Will a "decency" law work for the Internet? Why or why not? What are the potential problems?

4. Should there be an Internet V-chip for parents? Other strategies to block access? Explain your position.

WHAT LIMITS SHOULD CAMPUS NETWORKS PLACE ON PORNOGRAPHY? | ROBERT O'NEIL

A former president of the University of Wisconsin system and the University of Virginia, Robert O'Neil holds a law degree from Harvard University and currently teaches constitutional and commercial law at the University of Virginia. He is also the founding director of the Thomas Jefferson Center for the Protection of Free Expression and an authority on First Amendment issues. His article was published in the *Chronicle of Higher Education* on March 21, 2003.

PREREADING QUESTIONS   Should pornography be restricted on the Internet? Should access to pornography be restricted at the office? Do you have a position on these issues?

What if you were about to present a PowerPoint lecture to a large under-   1
graduate class, but found instead on your computer a series of sexually explicit ads and material from pornographic Web sites? That's essentially what happened recently to Mary Pedersen, a nutrition-science professor at California Polytechnic State University at San Luis Obispo. That incident and the increasing

presence of such imagery at Cal Poly have led to a novel, although undoubtedly predictable, struggle over computer content—one that is quite likely to be replicated at countless campuses in the coming months.

2   A concerned faculty group at Cal Poly has announced its intention to bring before the Academic Senate, sometime this spring, a "Resolution to Enhance Civility and Promote a Diversity-Friendly Campus Climate." Specifically, the measure would prohibit using the university's computers or network to access or download digital material generally described as "pornography." The resolution would also forbid the "transmission" of hate literature and obscenity on the Cal Poly network.

3   The sponsoring faculty members have offered several reasons for proposing such drastic action. First and foremost, they contend that the ready availability of sexually explicit imagery can create occasional but deeply disturbing encounters like Pedersen's discovery of unwelcome and unexpected material on her classroom computer. The pervasive presence of such images, proponents of the resolution argue, is inherently demeaning to female faculty members, administrators, and students.

4   Indeed, they suggest that the university might even be legally liable for creating and maintaining a "hostile workplace environment" if it fails to take steps to check the spread of such offensive material. That concern has been heightened by a putative link to a growing number of sexual assaults in the environs of the university.

5   Those who call for tighter regulation cite several other factors to support anti-pornography measures. In their view, a college or university must maintain the highest of standards, not only in regard to the integrity of scholarship and relations between teachers and students, but also in the range of material to which it provides electronic access. The clear implication is that the ready availability of sexually explicit and deeply offensive imagery falls below "the ethical standards that the university claims to uphold."

6   Critics of easy access to such material also claim that it can divert time, talent, and resources from the university's primary mission. Kimberly Daniels, a local lawyer who is advising the resolution's sponsors, told the student newspaper that "it is offensive that Cal Poly is taking the position that it is acceptable for professors to view pornography during work hours in their work office." That risk is not entirely conjectural. In fact, one professor left the institution last year after being convicted on misdemeanor charges for misusing a state-owned computer, specifically for the purpose of downloading in his office thousands of sexually explicit images. Local newspapers have also reported that the FBI is investigating another former Cal Poly professor who allegedly used a campus computer to view child pornography.

7   Finally, the concerned faculty group insists that the free flow of pornographic materials may expose the Cal Poly computer network to a greater risk of virus infection. They cite a student's recent experience in opening a salacious virus-bearing attachment that the student mistakenly believed had been sent by one of his professors.

The proposed Academic Senate resolution has touched off an intense de- 8
bate. The university's existing computer-use policy presumes that access and
choice of material are broadly protected, although it adds that "in exceptional
cases, the university may decide that such material directed at individuals presents such a hostile environment under the law that certain restrictive actions
are warranted." The new proposal would focus more sharply on sexually explicit imagery, and would require those who wish to view such material
through the campus network to obtain the express permission of the university's president.

Defenders of the current approach, including the senior staff of the uni- 9
versity's office of information technology, insist that a public university may not
banish from its system material that is offensive, but legal, without violating
First Amendment rights. Those familiar with the operations of such systems
also cite practical difficulties in the enforcement of any such restrictions, given
the immense volume of digital communications that circulate around the clock
at such a complex institution.

The debate at Cal Poly echoes what occurred some six years ago in Vir- 10
ginia. The General Assembly enacted what remains as the nation's only ban on
public employees' use of state-owned or state-leased computers to access sexually explicit material—at least without express permission of a "superior" for
a "bona fide research purpose." Six state university professors immediately
challenged the law on First Amendment grounds. A district judge struck down
the statute, but the U.S. Court of Appeals for the Fourth Circuit reversed that
ruling. The law had been modified before that judgment, and many Virginia
professors have since received exemptions or dispensations, but the precedent created by the appeals-court decision remains troubling for advocates of
free and open electronic communications.

The Virginia ruling complicates the Cal Poly situation. The First Amend- 11
ment challenge of those who oppose the Academic Senate resolution is less
clear than it might at first appear. Two premises underlying that resolution—
the need to protect government-owned hardware and the imperative to combat sexual hostility in the public workplace—contributed both to the passage
of the Virginia ban, and to its eventual success in the federal courts. What's
more, the U.S. Equal Employment Opportunity Commission some months ago
gave its blessing to a hostile-workplace complaint filed by Minneapolis Public
Library staff members who were offended by persistent display of graphic sexual images on reading-room terminals.

Thus, there is more than a superficial basis for the claims of Cal Poly's porn- 12
banishers that (in the words of one faculty member) "the First Amendment
doesn't protect . . . subjecting others to inappropriate material in the workplace." Even the information-technology consultant who has championed the
current computer-use policy at the university has conceded that access to controversial material is fully protected only "as long as it isn't offending others."

Although the desire to reduce the potential for offense and affront to other 13
users of a campus computer network seems unobjectionable, its implications

deserve careful scrutiny. In the analogous situation of public terminals in a library reading room, it is one thing to ask a patron who wishes to access and display sexually explicit material—or racially hateful material, for that matter—to use a terminal facing away from other users and staff members. It is quite another matter to deny access to such material altogether on the plausible premise that, if it can be obtained at all, there is a palpable risk that its visible display will offend others. To invoke an analogy that is now before the U.S. Supreme Court in a challenge to the Children's Internet Protection Act: It is one thing for a library to provide—even be compelled to provide—filtered access for parents who wish it for their children, but quite another to deny all adult patrons any unfiltered access.

14   What Cal Poly should seek to do, without impairing free expression, is to protect people from being gratuitously assaulted by digital material that may be deeply offensive, without unduly restricting access of those who, for whatever reason, may wish to access and view such material without bothering others. The proposal in the resolution that permission may be obtained from the university's president, for bona-fide research purposes, is far too narrow. Among other flaws, such a precondition might well deter sensitive or conscientious scholars, whether faculty members or students, who are understandably reluctant to reveal publicly their reasons for wishing to access sexually explicit images or hate literature.

15   A responsible university, seeking to balance contending interests of a high order, might first revisit and make more explicit its policies that govern acceptable computer use and access, by which all campus users are presumably bound. Such policies could condemn the flaunting of thoughtless dissemination of sexually explicit material and digital hate literature, expressing institutional abhorrence of such postings, without seeking to ban either type of material. The computer network might also establish a better warning system through which to alert sensitive users to the occasional and inevitable presence of material that may offend. Finally, a broader disclaimer might be in order, recognizing the limited practical capacity of a university server to control (or even enable users to avoid) troubling material.

16   What is needed is a reasonable balance that avoids, as Justice William O. Douglas warned a half-century ago, "burning down the house to roast the pig." That aphorism has special felicity here; in the offensive flaunting of sexually explicit imagery, there is a "pig" that doubtless deserves to be roasted. But there is also a house of intellect that must remain free and open, even to those with aberrant tastes and interests.

QUESTIONS FOR READING

1. What is the occasion for O'Neil's article? What is he responding to?
2. What is the resolution some Cal Poly faculty want passed by their Academic Senate? How do they want to limit access?
3. List the arguments for their resolution in your own words.

4. What are the arguments of those supporting the current Cal Poly Internet guidelines?

5. What arguments were used to support the Virginia ban?

6. How do these First Amendment debates affect terminals in public libraries? What is the current ruling on public libraries?

QUESTIONS FOR REASONING AND ANALYSIS

1. What is O'Neil's claim? Where does he state it? What, specifically, does he think that a university's position or strategy should be regarding "offensive" materials obtained through the university's server?

2. What organization does O'Neil use in the development of his argument? (Note where he states his claim.) What does he gain by his approach?

3. Where, essentially, does the author stand on censorship versus First Amendment freedoms?

4. Examine O'Neil's conclusion. How does he use Justice Douglas's metaphor effectively to conclude his argument?

QUESTIONS FOR REFLECTING AND WRITING

1. Evaluate O'Neil's argument. Is he clear and thorough in his analysis of the conflicting positions in this debate? Does he, in your view, have the stronger argument? If so, why? If not, why not?

2. Analyze the author's use of a conciliatory approach. Where does he acknowledge the merits of the opponents' views? How does his claim seek common ground? What might you conclude about the effectiveness of the conciliatory approach when engaged in First Amendment issues?

A LITTLE CIVILITY, PLEASE | MARK DAVIS

Mark Davis, a Texas native and graduate of the University of Maryland, is a popular radio talk show host (the "Mark Davis Show") in the Dallas/Fort Worth area and a columnist for the Dallas *Star-Telegram*. The following column was posted on *Star-Telegram.com* on March 5, 2003.

PREREADING QUESTIONS The courts have established that schools have rights that would seem to violate students' First Amendment rights. Should they? If so, in what areas? If not, why not?

Try something for me. 1

Send your teen-ager to school wearing a T-shirt that says, "Martin Luther 2 King Jr. Was Evil" or "Jews Lie: There Was No Holocaust."

Then wait for supporters to suggest that your child was not engaged in the 3 spread of hate but rather in the sparking of vigorous debates.

First, your kid would have been yanked from school so fast that his eyeballs 4 would have popped out.

5   But just let him (or you) argue that all this does is get people talking about the civil rights era or anti-Semitism, and the shock will be replaced by laughter.

6   That is exactly the argument made by defenders of Bretton Barber, a Michigan high school junior. The intellectual opening salvo he offered in his school on Feb. 17 was a T-shirt bearing the face of President Bush, framed by the words "International Terrorist."

7   A regular William F. Buckley, this kid.

8   His intent was obviously not to start a constructive discussion. Conversely, the school did not seek to squelch debate by ordering young Barber to turn the shirt inside out or go home.

9   If his T-shirt was more generalized and less hateful, with a slogan such as "No War" or even the famous Steve Nash shirt, "Shoot for Peace," I'd say the school should relax.

10   In the 1960s, students wearing black armbands to protest the Vietnam War won U.S. Supreme Court approval. In the case of Tinker v. Des Moines, the court ruled that students "did not shed their constitutional rights to freedom of expression at the schoolhouse gate."

11   Well, not all of them, anyway. In the years since, we have properly learned that schools do indeed have the right to establish dress guidelines. Most people have shed the absurd notion that an 11th-grader in a public school has the exact same First Amendment rights as an adult in the outside world.

12   The student newspaper can be barred from calling for the principal's ouster. Student assemblies can be squelched if they feature racial or religious bigotry.

13   And T-shirts can be nixed if they are—here's the tough word—*disruptive.*

14   Well, how exactly does a T-shirt disrupt? Do the words on the fabric leap from the wearer's chest and block the students' view of the teacher and blackboard?

15   No, but an atmosphere that fails to preserve a sense of order and decorum sends the message that various other behavioral extremes might also be tolerated. That is bad.

16   An armband is one thing. Hate speech, even under the guise of political discourse, is quite another.

17   How bizarre is it that most who would stand up for Barber's hamhanded "protest" condemning the president would recoil in shock if a kid wore a logo for Marlboro cigarettes or a Confederate flag emblem?

18   Gosh, wouldn't these be lost opportunities to discuss tobacco and the Civil War?

19   Passionate debate on controversial issues is good for students and should be encouraged. But within that exercise must be rules of decorous speech and behavior.

20   This should have nothing to do with whether we agree or disagree with the sentiment expressed. A student wearing a "Clinton is a Pervert" shirt around 1999 or so would have received no argument from me with regard to content, but I would have supported any school banning it.

The *Star-Telegram* is not the only newspaper to stick up for Bretton Barber.   21
I would expect a certain First Amendment zeal from journalists, and I am not
immune to it myself.

But his scolding is not, as an editorial stated, a missed opportunity for dis-   22
cussion. It is an opportunity far too rarely claimed, namely to teach a kid what
is and is not permissible within the borders of civilized debate.

Young Barber should be welcome to suggest and participate in vigorous   23
discussions on important issues on his own time or in an appropriate class.

QUESTIONS FOR READING

1.   What is Davis's occasion for writing? That is, what student action has received
     media attention?
2.   What are some of the controls that the courts have given to K–12 schools since
     the 1960s? What, specifically, can lead to a prohibiting of T-shirts?
3.   What is Davis's newspaper's position on Bretton Barber? Why is Davis not
     surprised by his paper's position?

QUESTIONS FOR REASONING AND ANALYSIS

1.   What is Davis's claim? Where does he state it?
2.   What is Davis's evidence? How does he defend his position?
3.   How does he rebut the potential counterargument that students should be
     encouraged to debate controversial issues?
4.   Study the examples Davis gives of T-shirt slogans that would quickly be
     squelched. What do they have in common? What is Davis's point in using those
     examples?
5.   What strategy does Davis use in paragraphs 7 and 18?

QUESTIONS FOR REFLECTING AND WRITING

1.   Do you agree with Davis's position on T-shirt slogans? If so, why? If not, how
     would you rebut his argument?
2.   Why have the courts defended the right of K–12 schools to limit the First
     Amendment rights of students? Is this different from the issue of controlling
     access to certain websites through a college server? (See Robert O'Neil,
     pp. 537–40.) Should it be different? Why or why not?

CHAPTER 20

Access and Privacy in a Technological Age

New technologies bring changes, not all of them unquestionably good. Five writers in this chapter examine some of the characteristics—or problems, depending on your perspective—of Internet technology. With more of the world run by computers, is there any way to keep privacy? Given existing technology, is there any way to stop downloading exchanges of copyrighted material—and should we be trying to do this? Do we have the technology to create national identification cards that are not easily faked by a black market? Even with the technology, do we want to have national IDs that may provide others with even more information about us than is already collected, thanks to computer technology? Technology and homeland security and privacy issues all "bump into one another" in this new, wired century. Some writers in this chapter look at one specific issue raised by these questions; others take a broader view of privacy and security issues. All present arguments needing our attention and reflection as we seek to adjust our lives both to new technology and to new fears in a post–9/11 world.

PREREADING QUESTIONS

1. Is it possible for the code makers to stay ahead of the hackers, or will "secure" sites always be reachable by gifted "techies"?

2. Even though we are all now a part of the global economy, that seems an abstract concept to many people. How does the computer affect your life in more immediate ways? Try listing the many ways that computers affect our daily lives.

3. Do you shop online? Do you believe that your credit card is secure? Do you download music from a "free" site? Do you think this is moral? Why or why not? Should it be legal? If it is legal, would anyone want to write music?

4. How can computer technology be used to increase homeland security? How *should* it be used?

5. How do you envision computer applications affecting your life in the next twenty years? In the next fifty years? Will the effects be good or bad—or both? Why?

Websites Relevant to This Chapter's Issues

Electronic Privacy Information Center: Internet Censorship

> www.epic.org/free_speech/censorship/
>
> This site focuses on legislation and court cases related to Internet censorship.

The Privacy Pages

> www.2020tech.com/maildrop/privacy.html
>
> Sponsored by the Orlando Mail Drop, this site contains many links to organizations and periodicals; it gives current news updates and information on security software and other privacy issues.

Net Freedom

> http://www.netfreedom.org
>
> Site that supports a position against all forms of censorship and content regulation on the Internet.

Recording Industry Association of America

> www.riaa.org
>
> Contains current information on piracy and first-amendment issues.

Department of Homeland Security

> http://www.dhs.gov/
>
> Contains information on the new department and its work.

NATIONAL IDs WON'T WORK | LORRAINE WOELLERT

Lorraine Woellert covers politics from Washington. She is legal affairs correspondent for *Business Week* and international-business correspondent for the *Washington Times.* Her argument against national IDs was published in *Business Week,* November 5, 2001.

PREREADING QUESTIONS Do you have a position on a national ID? Do you think that this is an important issue for Americans to debate in these times? Why or why not?

1   With the public still shaken by the World Trade Center attack and spooked by a growing number of anthrax scares, the clamor for tighter security is growing. Suitcase searches, closed streets, and a cop on every corner just aren't enough to settle jittery psyches. So we keep looking for ways to reassure ourselves and to soothe complicated new fears.

2   One idea—a national identification card that presumably would separate law-abiding citizens from dangerous infiltrators—is being promoted as a tool to reduce the threat of terrorism. But it's no silver bullet. A national ID card would rip at the fabric of our constitutional freedoms. It would cost billions and be technologically imperfect. Most troubling, it would lull the populace into a false sense of security.

3   First off, what would you need to get an ID card? A birth certificate and driver's license? Anyone—including terrorists—can obtain or alter such documents. Several of the men suspected of the September 11 attacks had forged identities. What would have prevented them from obtaining ID cards? And what of domestic terrorists Theodore Kaczynski and Timothy McVeigh?

4   To guard against counterfeiting, the card would need to be encoded with biometric data such as a fingerprint, retinal scan, or blood sample—yet these come with high failure rates. "Biometrics are fallible," says Professor David J. Farber, a technology expert at the University of Pennsylvania. He says fingerprints are reasonably good if you have an expensive reader. But hand readers fail frequently, facial recognition is new and buggy, and retinal scans are costly. "If this is a first-line defense, you can afford a lot of errors, but only if they're errors that reject. If they're errors that accept, [the cards are] useless," he says. In any case, these systems count on a nonforgeable ID card, and the technology involved for that can be prohibitively expensive, adds Farber.

5   Even simple data-storage cards, at $10 to $35, don't come cheap. Multiply that by 280 million Americans. Add the cost of card readers. Pay staff and overhead. The bottom line: a multibillion-dollar system that will take years to deploy and a well-funded bureaucracy to operate.

6   Then there's the Big Brother problem. A national ID card would eventually become as ubiquitous as the Social Security number and could be required for everyday life in the new age of terror. Want to enter the Lincoln Tunnel to New York? Send a package? Register for school? Buy a computer? No can do without an ID card. "This will quickly become a mandatory system," says Barry Steinhardt, associate director of the American Civil Liberties Union.

CHECKS

Taken to the extreme, a smart card could record your ethnicity, religion, po- 7
litical leanings, or favorite cereal. And at every turn, government agencies, employers, banks, insurance and health-care companies, and grocery stores would pressure you to add data to your life-on-a-chip. A prospective employer using the card to check your citizenship might notice that you vote in Democratic primaries—since the ID is required when you go to the polls. Hmm, maybe you aren't a good fit for this company. What about that prescription you're taking to control schizophrenia—part of the medical record that your health-care provider insists must be on your card? Airport security might decide you're unfit to fly. "We need to very carefully think through what our objective is," says William P. Crowell, former director of the National Security Agency and head of Cylink Corp., a Santa Clara (Calif.) technology company. "Let's make sure . . . use of the card is limited to [that] purpose before moving ahead."

Therein lies the irony: The more robust the card is, the more faith the pub- 8
lic will put in it. That, in turn, increases its vulnerability. "The more people assume the card is good, the less they will check you out, and the easier it becomes to slip someone past the system," says Professor Jonathan S. Shapiro of Johns Hopkins University. In other words, that false sense of security might only leave us more vulnerable to further terrorist attacks.

QUESTIONS FOR READING

1. What is the issue or anxiety to which Woellert is responding? What problems do Americans want a solution to?

2. What is one solution that has been suggested?

3. What are Woellert's objections to this solution?

QUESTIONS FOR REASONING AND ANALYSIS

1. Analyze Woellert's argument. Examine the support for each of her reasons to reject a national ID. What evidence does she present? What backing does she provide?

2. What assumption do the author and her sources make regarding technology? Is this a reasonable assumption? Today? In five years?

3. What assumption does Woellert make regarding the uses of an ID card? Are these assumptions reasonable? Why or why not?

QUESTIONS FOR REFLECTING AND WRITING

1. The author finds a terrible irony in the desire for a good ID card: The more reliable it is, the more people will foolishly trust it. How would you respond to her reasoning and her sense of people?

2. The author quotes a source as saying that we need to be quite sure what we would want a national ID card to do for us. What do you think such a card should do? Consider the possibilities suggested by Woellert and your own thoughts. Decide what you think such a card should be used for, if we were to have one at all, and argue in support of those uses.

THE CASE FOR A NATIONAL ID CARD | MARGARET CARLSON

With a law degree from the George Washington University, Margaret Carlson joined *Time* magazine in 1988 and became a columnist in 1994. Her columns focus on cultural and political issues. She is also a panelist on CNN's *Inside Politics* and *The Capitol Hill Gang.* The following *Time* column appeared January 21, 2002.

PREREADING QUESTIONS Do you favor an ID card of some kind? If so, who should administer it and what should it provide? If not, why not?

1   After representative John Dingell was asked to drop his pants at Washington's National Airport last week, some people felt safer. Others, like me, decided that we'd lost our collective minds. A near strip search of a 75-year-old Congressman whose artificial hip has set off a metal detector—while suspected al-Qaeda operative Richard Reid slips onto a Paris-to-Miami flight with a bomb in his shoe—isn't making us safer. It's making us ridiculous for entrusting our security to an unskilled police force that must make split-second decisions on the basis of incomplete data.

2   Incidents like this—and airport waits longer than the flight itself—have pushed me into the camp of the national ID card. Yes, a tamperproof ID smacks of Big Brother and Nazis intoning "Your papers, please," but the Federal Government already holds a trove of data on each of us. And it's less likely to mess up or misuse it than the credit-card companies or the Internet fraudsters, who have just as much data if not more. (Two years ago, for a *Time* article, I ordered dinner for 30 entirely online, and I am still plagued by vendors who know I like my wine French and my ham honey-baked.)

3   The idea of a national ID card leaped into the headlines just after Sept. 11. Oracle chairman Larry Ellison offered to donate the pertinent software. Ellison went to see Attorney General John Ashcroft, who was noncommittal despite his obvious enthusiasm for expanding government powers into other areas that trouble civil libertarians.

4   Enter Richard Durbin. In concert with the American Association of Motor Vehicle Administrators (yes, the dreaded DMVS have their own trade group), the Illinois Senator is proposing legislation that would create a uniform standard for the country's 200 million state-administered driver's licenses. Durbin noticed that the driver's license has become "the most widely used personal ID in the country. If you can produce one, we assume you're legitimate," he says. At present, nearly anyone can get a license; 13 of the 19 hijackers did. Having those licenses "gave the terrorists cover to mingle in American society without being detected."

5   Since we're using the driver's license as a de facto national ID, Durbin argues, let's make it more reliable. As it stands, the chief requirement is that one knows how to drive. This is fine if the only intent is to ensure that someone behind the wheel has mastered turn signals, but it shouldn't be sufficient

to get someone into a federal building, the Olympics or an airplane. All a terrorist needs to do is shop around for a lax state (Florida still doesn't require proof of permanent residency) or resort to a forger with a glue gun and laminator.

A high-tech, hard-to-forge driver's license could become a national 6 E-ZPass, a way for a law-abiding citizen to move faster through the roadblocks of post-9/11 life. It's no digitalized Supercard, but the states would have uniform standards, using bar codes and biometrics (a unique characteristic, like a palm print) and could cross-check and get information from other law-enforcement agencies. Polls show 70% of Americans support an even more stringent ID. But Japanese-American members of Congress and Transportation Secretary Norman Mineta are keenly sensitive to anything that might single out one nationality. Yet an ID card offers prospects of less profiling. By accurately identifying those who are in the U.S. legally and not on a terrorist watch list, the card would reduce the temptation to go after random members of specific groups.

It is not ideal to leave a national problem to the states, but because of 7 the general squeamishness about federal "papers" in the Congress, Durbin's proposal—congressional oversight of state DMVs—may be the best way to go. And if the government doesn't act, corporations will. Delta and American Airlines already provide separate lines for premium passengers; Heathrow Airport in London has an iris scan for people who have registered their eyeballs. An airline-industry association is at work on a Trusted Traveler card. Do we really want frequent-flyer status to be the basis for security decisions, or more plastic cards joining the too many we already have?

This ID would require one virtual strip search instead of many real ones. 8 Durbin says the card would remove the anonymity of a Mohamed Atta but not the privacy of others. With a card, Dingell could have confirmed his identity (though he made a point of not pulling rank). With the presumption that he wasn't a terrorist a once-over with a wand—with his pants on—would have lent credence to his claim that he possessed an artificial hip, not a gun. The Durbin card would at least let us travel with our clothes on.

QUESTIONS FOR READING

1. What situation has led to Carlson's writing on the subject of a national ID card?

2. What does Senator Durbin want to use as a reliable national ID card? What is his reasoning?

3. What would be the primary purpose of Carlson's ID card?

4. What might make driver's licenses more acceptable to Americans than some other type of card?

5. What other groups are exploring some kind of ID card?

QUESTIONS FOR REASONING AND ANALYSIS

1. What, specifically, is Carlson's claim? That is, what kind of ID card does she want?

2. How does she support her view of an ID card? List the points in her reasoning. Do her arguments make sense to you?

3. What counterargument does she introduce and how does she rebut it? Do you accept her rebuttal? Why or why not?

4. Examine her opening and closing paragraphs. How does she cleverly use the Representative Dingell incident to support her argument and get her reader's attention?

QUESTIONS FOR REFLECTING AND WRITING

1. Contrast the arguments of Woellert and Carlson, lining up their arguments and counterarguments. Who, in your view, has the more convincing argument? Why?

2. Both Woellert and Carlson observe that the Federal Government (and credit-card companies and Internet vendors) already have a great deal of information about each one of us. But the authors respond to this point differently in their arguments. Whose response makes the most sense to you? Should we be concerned about Big Brother? Why or why not?

PRIVACY UNDER ATTACK | SIMSON GARFINKEL

Simson Garfinkel is the author of a number of articles and books on Internet privacy issues, including *PGP—Pretty Good Privacy* (1994), *Web Security, Commerce, and Privacy* (2002), *Architects of the Information Society* (a 1999 brief history of MIT's technological achievements), and *Database Nation: The Death of Privacy in the 21st Century* (2001). The following passage is from Chapter 1 of *Database Nation*.

PREREADING QUESTION Some are observing that we live in a "transparent society," a world in which we are constantly watched by cameras and monitored by electronic surveillance strategies when we phone or use the Internet or shop. Does this concern you, or do you see a transparent society as a safer society?

1   You wake to the sound of a ringing telephone—but how could that happen?

2   Several months ago, you reprogrammed your home telephone system so the phone would never ring before the civilized hour of 8:00 a.m. But it's barely 6:45 a.m. Who could be calling at this time? More importantly, who was able to bypass your phone's programming?

3   You pick up the telephone receiver, then slam it down a moment later. It's one of those marketing machines playing a prerecorded message. Computerized telemarketing calls have been illegal within the United States for more than a decade now, but ever since international long-distance prices dropped below 10 cents a minute, calls have been pouring in to North America from all over the world. And they're nearly all marketing calls—hence the popularity of programmable phones today. What's troubling you now is how this call got past the filters you set up. Later on, you'll discover how: the company that sold

you the phone created an undocumented "back door"; last week, the phone codes were sold in an online auction. Because you weren't paying attention, you lost the chance to buy back your privacy.

Oops. 4

Now that you're awake, you decide to go through yesterday's mail. There's 5 a letter from the neighborhood hospital you visited last month. "We're pleased that our emergency room could serve you in your time of need," the letter begins. "As you know, our fees (based on our agreement with your HMO) do not cover the cost of treatment. To make up the difference, a number of hospitals have started selling patient records to medical researchers and consumer marketing firms. Rather than mimic this distasteful behavior, we have decided to ask you to help us make up the difference. We are recommending a tax-deductible contribution of $275 to help defray the cost of your visit."

The veiled threat isn't empty, but you decide you don't really care who finds 6 out about your sprained wrist. You fold the letter in half and drop it into your shredder. Also into the shredder goes a trio of low-interest credit card offers.

Why a shredder? A few years ago you would have never thought of shred- 7 ding your junk mail—until a friend in your apartment complex had his identity "stolen" by the building's superintendent. As best as anybody can figure out, the super picked one of those preapproved credit-card applications out of the trash, called the toll-free number, and picked up the card when it was delivered. He's in Mexico now, with a lot of expensive clothing and electronics, all at your friend's expense.

On that cheery note, you grab your bag and head out the door, which au- 8 tomatically locks behind you.

When you enter the apartment's elevator, a hidden video camera scans 9 your face, approves your identity, and takes you to the garage in the basement. You hope nobody else gets in the elevator—you don't relish a repeat of what happened last week to that poor fellow in 4G. It turns out that a neighbor recently broke up with her violent boyfriend and got a restraining order against him. Naturally, the elevator was programmed to recognize the man and, if he was spotted, to notify the police and keep the doors locked until they arrived. Too bad somebody else was in the elevator when it happened. Nobody realized the boyfriend was an undiagnosed (and claustrophobic) psychotic. A hostage situation quickly developed. Too bad for Mr. 4G. Fortunately, everything was captured on videotape.

Your car computer suggests three recommended approaches to your of- 10 fice this morning. You choose wrong, and a freak accident leaves you tied up in traffic for more than half an hour. As you wait, the computer plays an advertisement for a nearby burger joint every five minutes. You can't turn it off, of course: your car computer was free, paid for by the advertising.

Arriving late at work, you receive a polite email message from the com- 11 pany's timecard system; it knows when you showed up, and it gives you several options for making up the missed time. You can forgo lunch today, work an extra 45 minutes this evening, or take the 45 minutes out of your ever-dwindling vacation time. The choice is yours.

12   You look up and force a smile. A little video camera on your computer screen records your smile and broadcasts it to your boss and your coworkers. They've told you that Workplace Video Wallpaper™ builds camaraderie—but the company that sells the software also claims that the pervasive monitoring cuts down on workplace violence, romances, and even drug use. Nowadays, everybody smiles at work—it's too dangerous to do otherwise.

13   The cameras are just one of the ways you're being continually monitored at work. It started with electronic tags in all the company's books and magazines, designed to stop the steady pilferage from the library. Then, in the aftermath of a bomb scare, employees were told they'd have to wear badges at all times, and that desks and drawers would be subject to random searches. (Rumor has it that the chief of security herself called in the bomb threat—a ploy to justify the new policies.)

14   Next month, the company is installing devices in the bathrooms to make sure people wash their hands. Although the devices were originally intended for the healthcare and food industries, a recent study found that routine washing can also cut down on disease transmission among white-collar workers. So the machines are coming, and with them you'll lose just a little bit more of your privacy and your dignity.

15   This is the future—not a far-off future, but one that's just around the corner. It's a future in which what little privacy we now have will be gone. Some people call this loss of privacy "Orwellian," harking back to *1984*, George Orwell's classic work on privacy and autonomy. In that book, Orwell imagined a future in which privacy was decimated by a totalitarian state that used spies, video surveillance, historical revisionism, and control over the media to maintain its power. But the age of monolithic state control is over. The future we're rushing towards isn't one where our every move is watched and recorded by some all-knowing "Big Brother." It is instead a future of a hundred kid brothers that constantly watch and interrupt our daily lives. George Orwell thought that the Communist system represented the ultimate threat to individual liberty. Over the next 50 years, we will see new kinds of threats to privacy that don't find their roots in totalitarianism, but in capitalism, the free market, advanced technology, and the unbridled exchange of electronic information.

WHAT DO WE MEAN BY PRIVACY?

16   The concept of privacy is central to this . . . [essay], yet I wish I had a better word to express the aspect of individual liberty that is under attack by advanced technology as we enter the new millennium.

17   For decades, people have warned that pervasive databanks and surveillance technology are leading inevitably to the death of privacy and democracy. But these days, many people who hear the word "privacy" think about those kooks living off in the woods with their shotguns: these folks get their mail at post office boxes registered under assumed names, grow their own food, use cash to buy what they can't grow for themselves, and constantly worry about being attacked by the federal government—or by space aliens. If you are not

one of these people, you may well ask, "Why should I worry about my privacy? I have nothing to hide."

The problem with this word "privacy" is that it falls short of conveying 18 the really big picture. Privacy isn't just about hiding things. It's about self-possession, autonomy, and integrity. As we move into the computerized world of the twenty-first century, privacy will be one of our most important civil rights. But this right of privacy isn't the right of people to close their doors and pull down their window shades—perhaps because they want to engage in some sort of illicit or illegal activity. It's the right of people to control what details about their lives stay inside their own houses and what leaks to the outside.

To understand privacy in the next century, we need to rethink what privacy 19 really means today:

- It's not about the man who wants to watch pornography in complete anonymity over the Internet. It's about the woman who's afraid to use the Internet to organize her community against a proposed toxic dump—afraid because the dump's investors are sure to dig through her past if she becomes too much of a nuisance.

- It's not about people speeding on the nation's highways who get automatically generated tickets mailed to them thanks to a computerized speed trap. It's about lovers who will take less joy in walking around city streets or visiting stores because they know they're being photographed by surveillance cameras everywhere they step.

- It's not about the special prosecutors who leave no stone unturned in their search for corruption or political misdeeds. It's about good, upstanding citizens who are now refusing to enter public service because they don't want a bloodthirsty press rummaging through their old school reports, computerized medical records, and email.

- It's not about the searches, metal detectors, and inquisitions that have become a routine part of our daily lives at airports, schools, and federal buildings. It's about a society that views law-abiding citizens as potential terrorists, yet does little to effectively protect its citizens from the real threats to their safety.

Today, more than ever before, we are witnessing the daily erosion of per- 20 sonal privacy and freedom. We're victims of a war on privacy that's being waged by government eavesdroppers, business marketers, and nosy neighbors.

Most of us recognize that our privacy is at risk. According to a 1996 na- 21 tionwide poll conducted by Louis Harris & Associates, one in four Americans (24%) has "personally experienced a privacy invasion"[1]—up from 19% in 1978. In 1995, the same survey found that 80% of Americans felt that "consumers have lost all control over how personal information about them is circulated and used by companies."[2] Ironically, both the 1995 and 1996 surveys were paid for by Equifax, a company that earns nearly two billion dollars each year from collecting and distributing personal information.

22   We know our privacy is under attack. The problem is that we don't know how to fight back.

THE ROLE OF TECHNOLOGY

23   Today's war on privacy is intimately related to the dramatic advances in technology we've seen in recent years. As we'll see time and again . . . , unrestrained technology ends privacy. Video cameras observe personal moments; computers store personal facts; and communications networks make personal information widely available throughout the world. Although some specialty technology may be used to protect personal information and autonomy, the overwhelming tendency of advanced technology is to do the reverse.

24   Privacy is fundamentally about the power of the individual. In many ways, the story of technology's attack on privacy is really the story of how institutions and the people who run them use technology to gain control over the human spirit, for good and ill. That's because technology by itself doesn't violate our privacy or anything else: it's the people using this technology and the policies they carry out that create violations.

25   Many people today say that in order to enjoy the benefits of modern society, we must necessarily relinquish some degree of privacy. If we want the convenience of paying for a meal by credit card, or paying for a toll with an electronic tag mounted on our rear view mirror, then we must accept the routine collection of our purchases and driving habits in a large database over which we have no control. It's a simple bargain, albeit a Faustian one.

26   I think this tradeoff is both unnecessary and wrong. It reminds me of another crisis our society faced back in the 1950s and 1960s—the environmental crisis. Then, advocates of big business said that poisoned rivers and lakes were the necessary costs of economic development, jobs, and an improved standard of living. Poison was progress: anybody who argued otherwise simply didn't understand the facts.

27   Today we know better. Today we know that sustainable economic development *depends* on preserving the environment. Indeed, preserving the environment is a prerequisite to the survivability of the human race. Without clean air to breathe and clean water to drink, we will all surely die. Similarly, in order to reap the benefits of technology, it is more important than ever for us to use technology to protect personal freedom.

28   Blaming technology for the death of privacy isn't new. In 1890, two Boston lawyers, Samuel Warren and Louis Brandeis, argued in the *Harvard Law Review* that privacy was under attack by "recent inventions and business methods." They contended that the pressures of modern society required the creation of a "right of privacy," which would help protect what they called "the right to be let alone."[3] Warren and Brandeis refused to believe that privacy had to die for technology to flourish. Today, the Warren/Brandeis article is regarded as one of the most influential law review articles ever published.[4] And the article's significance has increased with each passing year, as the technological invasions that worried Warren and Brandeis have become more commonplace.

Privacy-invasive technology does not exist in a vacuum, of course. That's 29 because technology itself exists as a junction between science, the market, and society. People create technology to fill specific needs, real or otherwise. And technology is regulated, or not, as people and society see fit.

Few engineers set out to build systems designed to crush privacy and au- 30 tonomy, and few businesses or consumers would willingly use or purchase these systems if they understood the consequences. What happens more often is that the privacy implications of a new technology go unnoticed. Or if the privacy implications are considered, they are misunderstood. Or if they are understood correctly, errors are made in implementation. In practice, just a few mistakes can turn a system designed to protect personal information into one that destroys our secrets.

How can we keep technology and the free market from killing our privacy? 31 One way is by being careful and informed consumers. But I believe that government has an equally important role to play.

THE ROLE OF GOVERNMENT

With everything we've heard about Big Brother, how can we think of gov- 32 ernment as anything but the enemy of privacy? While it's true that federal laws and actions have often damaged the cause of privacy, I believe that the federal government may be our best hope for privacy protection as we move into the new millennium.

The biggest privacy failure of American government has been its failure to 33 carry through with the impressive privacy groundwork that was laid in the Nixon, Ford, and Carter administrations. It's worth taking a look back at that groundwork and how it may serve us today.

The 1970s were a good decade for privacy protection and consumer rights. 34 In 1970, Congress passed the Fair Credit Reporting Act. Elliot Richardson, who at the time was President Nixon's secretary of health, education, and welfare (HEW), created a commission in 1972 to study the impact of computers on privacy. After [months] of testimony in Congress, the commission found all the more reason for alarm and issued a landmark report in 1973.

The most important contribution of the Richardson report was a bill of 35 rights for the computer age, which it called the Code of Fair Information Practices (see the shaded box). That Code remains the most significant American thinking on the topic of computers and privacy to this day.

CODE OF FAIR INFORMATION PRACTICES

The Code of Fair Information Practices is based on five principles:

- There must be no personal data record-keeping systems whose very existence is secret.

- There must be a way for a person to find out what information about the person is in a record and how it is used.

(continued)

- There must be a way for a person to prevent information about the person that was obtained for one purpose from being used or made available for other purposes without the person's consent.

- There must be a way for a person to correct or amend a record of identifiable information about the person.

- Any organization creating, maintaining, using, or disseminating records of identifiable personal data must assure the reliability of the data for their intended use and must take precautions to prevent misuses of the data.

Source: Department of Health, Education, and Welfare, 1973.

36   The biggest impact of the HEW report wasn't in the United States, but in Europe. In the years after the report was published, practically every European country passed laws based on these principles. Many created data protection commissions and commissioners to enforce the laws.[5] Some believe that one reason for this interest in electronic privacy was Europe's experience with Nazi Germany in the 1940s. Hitler's secret police used the records of governments and private organizations in the countries he invaded to round up people who posed the greatest threat to the German occupation; postwar Europe realized the danger of allowing potentially threatening private information to be collected, even by democratic governments that might be responsive to public opinion.

37   But here in the United States, the idea of institutionalized data protection faltered. President Jimmy Carter showed interest in improving medical privacy, but he was quickly overtaken by economic and political events. Carter lost the election of 1980 to Ronald Reagan, whose aides saw privacy protection as yet another failed Carter initiative. Although several privacy protection laws were signed during the Reagan/Bush era, the leadership for these bills came from Congress, not the White House. The lack of leadership stifled any chance of passing a nationwide data protection act.

38   In fact, while most people in the federal government were ignoring the cause of privacy, some were actually pursuing an antiprivacy agenda. In the early 1980s, the federal government initiated numerous "computer matching" programs designed to catch fraud and abuse. (Unfortunately, because of erroneous data, these programs often penalized innocent individuals.[6]) In 1994, Congress passed the Communications Assistance to Law Enforcement Act, which gave the government dramatic new powers for wiretapping digital communications. In 1996, Congress passed a law requiring states to display Social Security numbers on driver's licenses, and another law requiring that all medical patients in the U.S. be issued unique numerical identifiers, even if they paid their own bills. Fortunately, the implementation of those 1996 laws has been delayed, largely thanks to a citizen backlash.

Continuing the assault, both the Bush and Clinton administrations waged   39
an all-out war against the rights of computer users to engage in private and secure communications. Starting in 1991, both administrations floated proposals
for use of "Clipper" encryption systems that would have given the government
access to encrypted personal communications. President Clinton also backed
the Communications Decency Act (CDA), which made it a crime to transmit
sexually explicit information to minors—and, as a result, might have required
Internet providers to deploy far-reaching monitoring and censorship systems.
When a court in Philadelphia found the CDA unconstitutional, the Clinton administration appealed the decision all the way to the Supreme Court—and lost.

Finally, the U.S. government's restrictions on the export of encryption tech-   40
nology have effectively restrained the widespread use of this technology for
personal privacy protection within the United States.

As we move forward. . . , the United States needs to take personal privacy   41
seriously again. . . .

FIGHTING BACK

Privacy is certainly on the ropes in America today, but so was the environ-   42
ment in 1969. Thirty years ago, the Cuyahoga River in Ohio caught on fire and
Lake Erie was proclaimed dead. Times have certainly changed. Today it's safe
to eat fish that are caught in the Cuyahoga, Lake Erie is alive again, and the
overall environment in America is the cleanest it's been in decades.

There are signs around us indicating that privacy is getting ready to make   43
a comeback as well. The war against privacy is commanding more and more attention in print, on television, and on the Internet. People are increasingly
aware of how their privacy is compromised on a daily basis. Some people have
begun taking simple measures to protect their privacy, measures like making
purchases with cash and refusing to provide their Social Security numbers—or
providing fake ones. And a small but growing number of people are speaking
out for technology *with* privacy, and putting their convictions into practice by
developing systems or services that protect, rather than attack, our privacy.

Over the past few decades, we've learned that technology is flexible, and   44
that when it invades our privacy, the invasion is usually the result of a conscious
choice. We now know, for instance, that when a representative from our bank
says:

> I'm sorry that you don't like having your Social Security number printed on
> your bank statement, but there is no way to change it.

that representative is actually saying:

> Our programmers made a mistake by telling the computer to put your
> Social Security number on you bank statement, but we don't think it's a
> priority to change the program. Take your business elsewhere.

Today we are relearning this lesson and discovering how vulnerable busi-   45
ness and government can be to public pressure. . . .

Technology is not autonomous; it simply empowers choices made by gov-   46
ernment, business, and individuals. One of the big lessons of the environmental

movement is that it's possible to shape these choices through the political process. This, I believe, justifies the involvement of government on the privacy question.

NOTES
1. Harris-Equifax, *Consumer Privacy Survey.* Conducted for Equifax by Louis Harris and Associates in association with Dr. Alan Westin of Columbia University, Equifax, Atlanta, GA, 1996.
2. Harris-Equifax, *Consumer Privacy Survey.* Conducted for Equifax by Louis Harris and Associates in association with Dr. Alan Westin of Columbia University, Equifax, Atlanta, GA, 1995.
3. Samuel Warren and Louis Brandeis, "The Right of Privacy," *Harvard Law Review* 4 (1980), 193. Although the phrase "the right to be let alone" is commonly attributed to Warren and Brandeis, the article attributes the phrase to the nineteenth-century judge Thomas M. Cooley.
4. Turkington et al., *Privacy: Cases and Materials.*
5. David H. Flaherty, *Protecting Privacy in Surveillance Societies* (University of North Carolina Press, 1989).

   In 1989, David H. Flaherty, the privacy commissioner of British Columbia, published a revised set of 12 Data Protection Principles and Practices for Government Personal Information Systems. These 12 principles are (emphasis supplied by David Flaherty in May 1997):

   The principles of *publicity and transparency* (openness) concerning government personal information systems (no secret databanks).

   The principles of *necessity* and relevance governing the collection and storage of personal information.

   The principle of reducing the collection, use, and storage of personal information to the maximum extent possible.

   The principle of *finality* (the purpose and ultimate administrative uses for personal information need to be established in advance).

   The principle of establishing and requiring *responsible keepers* for personal information systems.

   The principle of controlling *linkages,* transfers, and interconnections involving personal information.

   The principle of requiring informed *consent* for the collection of personal information.

   The principal of requiring accuracy and completeness in personal information systems.

   The principle of *data trespass,* including civil and criminal penalties for unlawful abuses of personal information.

   The requirement of special rules for protecting sensitive personal information.

   The right of access to, and correction of, personal information systems.

The *right to be forgotten,* including the ultimate anonymization or destruction of almost all personal information.

6. One federal match program compared a database that had the names of people who had defaulted on their student college loans with another database that had the names of federal employees. The match then automatically garnished the wages of the federal employees to pay for the defaulted loans. The problem with this match, and others, was that there were many false matches that were the result of incorrect data or similar-sounding names. And because the wages were automatically garnished, victims of this match were required to prove their innocence—that is, to prove that the match was erroneous.

QUESTIONS FOR READING

1. What is Garfinkel's subject? What is the problem he explores?
2. How do some people define privacy? How does the author define it as it applies to our lives in the twenty-first century?
3. What is the primary cause of the invasion of privacy in our time? How does Garfinkel qualify and explain the exact nature of this cause? (What is, in and of itself, not the villain?)
4. What solution does Garfinkel present?
5. What are the key points in the Code of Fair Information Practices?
6. Why hasn't the federal government established laws and commissions to oversee personal privacy similar to those established in some European countries?

QUESTIONS FOR REASONING AND ANALYSIS

1. What is Garfinkel's claim? Where does he state it?
2. Examine Garfinkel's long introduction. What does he accomplish with his futuristic scenario?
3. In paragraphs 26 and 27, and again in paragraph 42, the author develops an analogy. What is the analogy and what is the point he wants to make through the comparison?
4. Solutions to the loss of privacy because of technology are possible only if one believes a basic assumption that Garfinkel repeats throughout his chapter. What is the key assumption about technology on which his argument rests?

QUESTIONS FOR REFLECTING AND WRITING

1. Do you agree with Garfinkel's basic assumption? Or would you argue that computer technology is not just faster and easier but so much so that it is different in kind from previous strategies for collecting data about individuals? That is, is the technology itself a significant part of the problem, or is it a matter of how it is used? Be prepared to debate this point.

2. Do you agree with the problem—has modern technology created the invasion of privacy and autonomy that Garfinkel asserts? David Brin, in his 1998 book *The Transparent Society*, has argued that we need less rather than more privacy, that privacy has usually benefited the rich and powerful or the government, not the average person. Who has the better sense of the situation? Why?

3. If you agree with the problem and the cause, do you agree with the author's solutions? Why or why not?

ISSUE IS PIRACY, NOT PRIVACY | CARY SHERMAN

A graduate of Harvard Law School, Cary Sherman is now the president of the Recording Industry Association of America. Sherman is a musician and songwriter as well as an expert on intellectual property law. His article appeared in *USA Today*, January 29, 2003.

PREREADING QUESTIONS Have you downloaded music, movies, or texts from the Internet? Do you think doing so is breaking the law? Do you think it is immoral?

1   Today's debate: Online music files.

2   Opposing view: First Amendment does not protect the theft of other people's property.

3   Ever since a federal court ordered Verizon to identify a subscriber who illegally distributed hundreds of hit songs on the Internet, the company has claimed the ruling somehow violates the individual's right to privacy.

4   Strangely, when it was arguing its case in court, Verizon never uttered a word about privacy. Indeed, Verizon acknowledged that it will identify certain infringers when it suits Verizon. That's because it knows the issue here isn't about privacy; it's about piracy.

5   The fact is, our right to privacy does not include a right to commit illegal acts anonymously. You or I may have a right to keep our banking transactions private, but when we stick a gun in a teller's face and ask for the contents of the cash drawer, the bank is more than entitled to take our picture with a security camera.

6   The same is true on the Internet. Offering to upload music files without permission so millions of strangers can copy them off the Internet is neither a private act nor a legal one. Should those who engage in this gratuitous giveaway of other people's property be able to conceal their identity behind computer numbers or made-up screen names?

7   The Recording Industry Association of America is a stalwart defender of the First Amendment. But music piracy is not the kind of expression the First Amendment seeks to protect. In the words of the opinion, we're not talking about a consumer who "is anonymously using the Internet to distribute speeches of Lenin, biblical passages . . . or criticisms of the government." Rather we're talking about someone who is distributing illegal copies of popular songs—the very antithesis of protected activity.

8   There is a good reason Congress enacted the Digital Millennium Copyright Act, the law that requires Internet service providers to promptly identify the infringer when copyright owners file a sworn declaration that a subscriber is

illegally distributing copyrighted materials: In a digital age, when anyone with a decent computer and a shortage of scruples can instantaneously flood the world with an infinite number of perfect copies of any song, movie or text he can get his hands on, copyrights would be worthless without this most basic level of protection.

QUESTIONS FOR READING

1.   What is Sherman's subject?
2.   What has the court ruled that Verizon must do? What is Verizon's position on the issue?
3.   What law relevant to this debate has the Congress passed?

QUESTIONS FOR REASONING AND ANALYSIS

1.   What is Sherman's claim?
2.   In paragraph 7, Sherman asserts that the RIAA supports the First Amendment. Why does he make this point?
3.   In paragraph 5, the author uses an analogy; what is the analogy and what point does he make with it?

QUESTIONS FOR REFLECTING AND WRITING

1.   What is the idea of copyrights? How do they work? Why do we have them? Should people be able to copyright their music, movies, and texts? Why or why not?
2.   If you agree with the idea of copyrights, then presumably you agree with Sherman's view that downloading music from the Internet is stealing, right? Or not right?
3.   What is your review on music "sharing"? Can you justify it? Why or why not? Can you justify it and be consistent with a support for copyrights? Why or why not? Be prepared to debate this issue on practical and ethical grounds, not on emotion.
4.   Think back to Simson Garfinkel's argument. Is the technology in control of this problem, or can (and should) we make choices about using the technology—or finding a technological way to block music sharing? Or will the new policing of this activity and the issuing of fines be the only deterrent strategy we need? Explain your position.

TINY CELL PHONE OR BIG BROTHER? | LAUREN WEINSTEIN

Lauren Weinstein has been involved with the Internet for more than thirty years, beginning with ARPANET, the UCLA ancestor of the Internet. He is cofounder of People for Internet Responsibility and moderator of Privacy Forum. He has been a commentator on NPR and is a frequent columnist for *Wired News*. The following article appeared on January 6, 2003, at WiredNews.com.

PREREADING QUESTIONS What are some of the capabilities of the newest wireless phones? List as many components of this technology as you can. Consider: What components may pose a challenge to personal privacy?

1   You've seen the slew of commercials for them. You may already have one in your pocket or hanging from your belt. New generations of cell phones appear before you've even figured out all the features of your current model.

2   There's much more to consider regarding cellular technology beyond incomprehensible user manuals and the highly visible phone radiation and "driving while yakking" controversies.

3   The latest of these tiny wireless phones (the term "cellular" is now out of favor, we're told) sport multimedia color displays, video camera options, precision location tracking and a host of other heavily promoted features set to hit the mainstream this year.

4   Yet little thought has been given to how these advanced capabilities could affect society.

5   Commercials for these devices tend to emphasize their most benign aspects. Commuters play games, separated lovers send text messages and a housewife lures her husband away from the poker game with photos of her culinary masterpieces.

6   These are credible enough applications, but they're unlikely to be the big moneymakers for the wireless companies and their cohorts.

7   The serious income streams from the new wireless systems are likely to result from attempts to satisfy appetites not for home-cooked meals, but for other types of activities. Visually seductive gambling and pornography, for example, are certain matches to these phones' capabilities.

8   Like them or not, these applications are coming.

9   The new wireless systems introduce a range of other complex issues. Even older cell phones could easily be used as audio bugs, often without any modifications.

10   Wireless networks provide the perfect infrastructure for feeding audio—and now video—back to parties located anywhere on the planet. Wireless spy-cams could be planted anywhere, to be used for good or ill. Whistleblowers, voyeurs and spies are headed for a bonanza.

11   News gathering is also likely to change. The ability for virtually anyone to capture photos of ongoing events, such as accidents, disasters or crimes in progress, and almost instantly send them back to a website, news bureau or other globally accessible source, has vast implications.

12   When images can be transmitted so easily and rapidly in real time, a common technique for trying to prevent the publication of undesirable photos—grabbing the camera and smashing it—will no longer be effective.

13   The wireless carriers are likely to encourage all of these applications to the greatest extent possible. After all, they're in the business of selling air time.

14   It's not just about audio and video, either.

15   The increasing accuracy of the location-tracking systems implemented in wireless phones and their supporting networks should also raise a red flag.

Nobody would argue the value of using location data to find a person 16 buried in a snowdrift, or having a map pop up on a phone's screen to help someone locate an unfamiliar destination.

But while we're typically assured that location data would only be used 17 commercially with our permission, the mere ability to gather that information suggests the possibility of vast databases tracking the movements of virtually every wireless phone user, even retrospectively over long periods.

Law enforcement and intelligence agencies will view this as a treasure 18 trove. Given the new surveillance powers recently ceded to the government, it's unclear if court orders or even subpoenas would be necessary for government to use wireless location data for a range of purposes, with obvious risks for abuse.

The potential for individuals to abuse this tracking technology is very real. 19 In one recent case, a man was arrested for stalking after using a GPS/cellular system planted under the hood of his ex-girlfriend's car. The location-tracking capabilities of the brand-new phones could make this sort of antisocial behavior even easier.

The impact of new technologies is about to blindside society yet again. We 20 must update our thinking—and in some cases our laws—to take into account the ways in which wireless is very literally changing our world.

QUESTIONS FOR READING

1. What is Weinstein's subject? (Do not say "cell phones"; be more precise.)
2. What capabilities of cell phones are stressed in commercials for them? What is the author's reaction to those commercials?
3. What are the capabilities that will significantly affect society, in the author's view?

QUESTIONS FOR REASONING AND ANALYSIS

1. List both the advantages of wireless phones and the potential problems, as discussed by Weinstein.
2. What is Weinstein's purpose in writing? What *type* of argument is this? What is the author's thesis?
3. Find passages that reveal Weinstein's attitude toward the newest wireless phone capabilities.

QUESTIONS FOR REFLECTING AND WRITING

1. Evaluate Weinstein's argument. Has he convinced you of the potential privacy problems with cell phone components? Why or why not?
2. Weinstein focuses more on specific problems than specific solutions. What general solutions does he recommend? What more specific solutions would you recommend? Be prepared to defend your proposed solutions—or the position that no solutions are needed because there is no problem.

CHAPTER 21

Marriage and Family in the New Century

Six articles compose this chapter, providing you with much to learn about, reflect on, and debate over with regard to marriage and family. No topic is more closely tied to all of us than the topic of family, for we are all members of a family—for better or worse. (Those who choose to leave a family circle are, of course, being shaped by their alienation from that family, so family still influences much of their lives.)

This chapter's writers look at the incredible changes that the twentieth century brought to the institutions of marriage and family. Some approach these changes—and their effects on our lives—from the social science perspective; others take a more jocular or satiric approach. Some write from the perspective of research data; others develop their arguments from emotion or a religious persuasion. Some express strongly held views; others seek common ground. All, however, consider the changes of the past thirty years to have had a profound influence on our lives, an influence that we are not always recognizing or considering when trying to make sense of our world.

PREREADING QUESTIONS

1. Do you expect to have a career? To have a spouse and children? Should society support both men and women having these choices? If so, how?
2. How can the business world, the government, and the community enrich family life for all? What role, if any, should they have in defining marriage?
3. What has been meant by the "traditional family"? How has the traditional family changed in the past thirty years?
4. Do you have a position on gay marriage? If so, what is it, and what is its source?
5. Is there anything that you can learn from arguments presenting opposing views on gay rights and/or acceptance of gay marriages? Why or why not?

Websites Relevant to This Chapter's Topic

Same-Sex Marriage and Domestic Partnerships

http://fullcoverage.yahoo.com/fc/us/same_sex_marriage

This Yahoo! Full Coverage site contains news, opinions, and useful links.

American Psychological Association: Family and Relationships

http://helping.apa.org/family/index.html

This URL takes you directly to the index of articles on marriage and family made available on the APA's information-packed website.

NOT MUCH SENSE IN THOSE CENSUS STORIES	STEPHANIE COONTZ

A professor of history at Evergreen State College in Olympia, Washington, Stephanie Coontz (b. 1944) is the author of numerous articles and books, including *The Way We Never Were: American Families and the Nostalgia Trap* (1992) and *The Way We Really Are* (1997). Coontz is also national cochair of the Council on Contemporary Families (www.contemporaryfamilies.org); it is in this capacity that she is frequently contacted by media personnel working on stories about families. The following article was published July 15, 2001, in the *Washington Post*.

PREREADING QUESTIONS Why does the author get calls from media people asking for explanations of recent census figures on families? What accounts for most of the growth in "single" motherhood?

Nearly every week, the U.S. Census Bureau releases a new set of figures on   1
American families and the living arrangements they have been creating in the past decade. And each time, as the media liaison for a national association of

family researchers, I'm bombarded with telephone calls from radio and television producers seeking a talking head to confirm the wildly differing—and usually wrong—conclusions they've jumped to about what those figures say about the evolving nature of family life in America.

2   In April, for example, Census officials announced that 56 percent of American children were living in "traditional" nuclear families in 1996, up from 51 percent in 1991. Several prime time television shows excitedly reported this "good news" about the American family, and I heard one radio commentator declare that young couples were finally rejecting the "divorce culture" of their parents' generation.

3   But this supposedly dramatic reversal of a 30-year trend was based on a peculiarly narrow definition of a traditional family: a two-parent household with children under 18 and no other relatives in the home. If a grandchild, grandparent or other relative were living in the house, the family was "nontraditional." (There's an obvious irony here, given that nothing is quite so traditional as an extended nuclear family that includes a grandparent!)

4   Evidently, the definition itself was largely responsible for this "trend": Enough such relatives moved to separate households during the first half of the 1990s to increase the proportion of "traditional families," even though the percentage of children living with both biological parents had stayed steady at about 62 percent, and the percentage of married couples had continued its 30-year slide. In other words, the initial reports of a resurgence in traditional families were the result of wishful thinking and a misunderstanding of the terms being used by the census.

5   But hope springs eternal among talk show producers desperate for a new angle. In mid-May, expanding on its earlier study, the Census Bureau reported that the absolute numbers of married couples with children at home had grown in 2000 after falling in two previous head counts (although the proportion of such families in the total population was still shrinking). TV producers jumped on the story, apparently ready to trumpet the return of the "Ozzie and Harriet" family of the '50s. I soon heard from several talk show hosts in the West who, state-by-state printouts in hand, were agog about the exceptionally large increase of such families in *their* regions. They wanted me to find them an expert to comment on the heartening return to traditional values.

6   Their enthusiasm dimmed, however, when I told them that this regional increase in married-couple households with children was due largely to the well-reported influx of Asian and Hispanic immigrants. Their interest evaporated entirely when I reminded them that, as immigrants assimilate, their family patterns tend to match those of the preexisting population.

7   A week later, the Census Bureau reported that the number of unmarried women with children had increased by 25 percent, dwarfing the 7 percent growth in married-couple families. This time we moved into the "bad news" cycle: Media pundits called to confirm their worse fears, looking for more figures to prove that the explosion of single motherhood was creating an ever-deepening social and cultural crisis in the land.

In fact, most of the growth in "single" motherhood during the 1990s was 8
due to an increase in births to women who, while not married, were living with
the child's father. So, much of the recent increase in single motherhood simply
reflected the 71 percent increase in cohabitation between 1990 and 2000. But
the fact that many "single mother" families actually had fathers present didn't
faze the talk show hosts who called seeking confirmation that the sky was
falling because of the "collapse of marriage." This time around, they weren't
the least bit interested in any good news—such as the figures, also released in
May, that showed a 20 percent drop in births to teenagers over the decade.

Then, last month, the Census Bureau reported that the number of house- 9
holds headed by single fathers had increased fivefold, from 393,000 in 1970 to
2 million in 2000. I got two calls from TV producers that day, each rushing to
air a show on this new trend. One asked me to explain how this reflected the
increasing equality of men and women in their commitment to parenting, while
the other wanted someone to tell her viewers why it represented a backlash
against working mothers, who were obviously losing custody to unwed and divorced fathers.

Both producers were crushed when I told them our researchers couldn't 10
confirm either claim, and that we have no way of even knowing how many of
these so-called single fathers are in fact living with the mother of their child outside of marriage, and how many are divorced dads who simply happened to
have their children with them for the weekend on the day they filled out the
form. When I called a Census Bureau researcher to see if he could help
straighten this out, he said my guess was as good as his.

It's not that the census researchers are doing a bad job. The problem is that 11
they're asked to compress America's increasingly fluid family arrangements
into one-dimensional categories that were established at a time when most
single-parent households were created by death rather than by divorce, and
when most people made things easy for data collectors by lying rather than
admitting to "living in sin."

People's new candor about their lifestyles, combined with the undeniable 12
changes in family arrangements that have occurred over the past 40 years,
makes it increasingly hard to capture new family realities in old census categories. And using such categories to talk about families has consequences.

Labeling people single parents, for example, when they may in fact be co- 13
parenting—either with an unmarried other parent in the home or with an
exspouse in a joint custody situation—sitgmatizes their children as the products
of "single parenthood" and makes the uncounted parent invisible to society.
This can lead teachers, school officials, neighbors and other family members to
exclude the uncounted parents from activities and interactions into which they
might otherwise be drawn. In fear of such marginalization, some separated parents find it hard to agree on a custody arrangement that's in the best interests
of the child, because each wants to be the socially recognized parent.

In the past, many "intact" families had fathers who were AWOL from their 14
children's lives. Today, conversely, many "broken" families have fathers who

remain active parents. Harvard fellow Constance Ahorns, who has conducted a 20-year study of post-divorce families and their children, has certainly seen plenty of cases where the nonresident parent, usually the father, stops doing any parenting. But she has found many instances where nonresidential fathers became *more* active in their children's lives after divorce than they were during the marriage. These men need to be recognized for their support, rather than relegated to the same state of nonbeing as the deadbeat dad.

15   It's not only parents who are marginalized by outdated household categories. When I speak on work-family issues to audiences around the country, some of the biggest complaints I hear come from individuals who are described by the census as living in "non-family households." They resent the fact that their family responsibilities literally don't "count," either for society or for their employers. There is no category, for instance, for individuals who spend several days a week caring for an aging parent in the parent's separate residence. Yet one in four households in America today is providing substantial time and care to an aging relative, and more than half of all households say they expect to do so within the next 10 years.

16   It's time for our discussion of family trends to better reflect the complexities of today's family commitments. Perhaps, as Larry McCallum, a therapist who directs the family life program at Augustana College in Rock Island, Ill., suggests, we should do for parents what we have begun to do with racial categories in the census—provide several alternative ways for people to express their overlapping identities. At the very least, we need to drop the idea that we can predict how a family functions solely by its form.

17   The place where we keep our clothes isn't always the only place where we keep our commitments.

QUESTIONS FOR READING

1. Why does Coontz find the Census Bureau's definition of traditional family "ironic"?

2. What number continues a thirty-year decline? That is, what important change in American families continues?

3. Why did western states show an increase in "married-with-children" households?

4. What are the several consequences of using the old census categories to describe today's families?

QUESTIONS FOR REASONING AND ANALYSIS

1. What is Coontz's claim? You may need more than one sentence to present her several interconnected key ideas.

2. In paragraph 2, Coontz puts "traditional" and "good news" in quotation marks. Why? What does she want to communicate with the quotation marks?

3. What attitude toward the media does the author have—and invite readers to have? How do you know?

4. The author's final paragraph is one sentence. What makes it effective? What key words are connected by sound?

QUESTIONS FOR REFLECTING AND WRITING

1. While showing the problems in using the Census Bureau's old categories, Coontz also provides readers with some interesting statistics. What data are most surprising to you? Why?

2. Have you thought about the consequences of stigmatizing and marginalizing the nonlegal father or the divorced parent without primary custody, as Coontz suggests that we do with the old categories? Does this make sense to you? Do you see this as a problem we need to address?

3. What makes a family? Do we need to broaden our definition? If so, how? Reflect on these questions.

4. Why is it so difficult to get rid of old ideas, old ways of seeing or arranging or explaining the world? Make a list of what you see as the primary reasons for the difficulties many people have "thinking outside the envelope."

SOCIAL SCIENCE FINDS: "MARRIAGE MATTERS" | LINDA J. WAITE

A former senior sociologist at the Rand Corporation, Linda Waite (b. 1947) is currently a professor at the University of Chicago. She has coauthored several books, including *Teenage Motherhood* (1979) and *New Families, No Families?* (1991). In this article, published in *The Responsive Community* in 1996, Waite pulls together various studies to explore the effects that marriage has on married people.

PREREADING QUESTIONS Although marriage has declined, what has taken its place? How important is marriage to you? Why?

As we are all too aware, the last few decades have witnessed a decline in   1
the popularity of marriage. This trend has not escaped the notice of politicians and pundits. But when critics point to the high social costs and taxpayer burden imposed by disintegrating "family values," they overlook the fact that individuals do not simply make the decisions that lead to unwed parenthood, marriage, or divorce on the basis of what is good for society. Individuals weigh the costs and benefits of each of these choices to themselves—and sometimes their children. But how much is truly known about these costs and benefits, either by the individuals making the choices or demographers like myself who study them? Put differently, what are the implications, for individuals, of the current increases in nonmarriage? If we think of marriage as an insurance policy—which it is, in some respects—does it matter if more people are uninsured, or are insured with a term rather than a whole-life policy? I shall argue

that it does matter, because marriage typically provides important and substantial benefits, benefits not enjoyed by those who live alone or cohabit.

2   A quick look at marriage patterns today compared to, say, 1950 shows the extent of recent changes. Figures from the Census Bureau show that in 1950, at the height of the baby boom, about a third of white men and women were not married. Some were waiting to marry for the first time, some were divorced or widowed and not remarried. But virtually everyone married at least once at some point in their lives, generally in their early twenties.

3   In 1950 the proportion of black men and women not married was approximately equal to the proportion unmarried among whites, but since that time the marriage behavior of blacks and whites has diverged dramatically. By 1993, 61 percent of black women and 58 percent of black men were not married, compared to 38 percent of white men and 41 percent of white women. So, in contrast to 1950 when only a little over one black adult in three was not married, now a majority of black adults are unmarried. Insofar as marriage "matters," black men and women are much less likely than whites to share in the benefits, and much less likely today than they were a generation ago.

4   The decline in marriage is directly connected to the rise in cohabitation—living with someone in a sexual relationship without being married. Although Americans are less likely to be married today than they were several decades ago, if we count both marriage and cohabitation, they are about as likely to be "coupled." If cohabitation provides the same benefits to individuals as marriage does, then we do not need to be concerned about this shift. But we may be replacing a valuable social institution with one that demands and offers less.

5   Perhaps the most disturbing change in marriage appears in its relationship to parenthood. Today a third of all births occur to women who are not married, with huge but shrinking differences between blacks and whites in this behavior. One in five births to white mothers and two-thirds of births to black mothers currently take place outside marriage. Although about a quarter of the white unmarried mothers are living with someone when they give birth, so that their children are born into two-parent—if unmarried—families, very few black children born to unmarried mothers live with fathers too.

6   I believe that these changes in marriage behavior are a cause for concern, because in a number of important ways married men and women do better than those who are unmarried. And I believe that the evidence suggests that they do better because they are married.

MARRIAGE AND HEALTH

7   The case for marriage is quite strong. Consider the issues of longevity and health. With economist Lee Lillard, I used a large national survey to follow men and women over a 20-year period. We watched them get married, get divorced, and remarry. We observed the death of spouses and of the individuals themselves. And we compared deaths of married men and women to those who were not married. We found that once we took other factors into account, married men and women faced lower risks of dying at any point than those who have never married or whose previous marriage has ended. Widowed women

were much better off than divorced women or those who had never married, although they were still disadvantaged when compared with married women. But all men who were not currently married faced significantly higher risks of dying than married men, regardless of their marital history. Other scholars have found disadvantages in death rates for unmarried adults in a number of countries besides the United States.

How does marriage lengthen life? First, marriage appears to reduce risky 8 and unhealthy behaviors. For example, according to University of Texas sociologist Debra Umberson, married men show much lower rates of problem drinking than unmarried men. Umberson also found that both married men and women are less likely to take risks that could lead to injury than are the unmarried. Second, as we will see below, marriage increases material well-being—income, assets, and wealth. These can be used to purchase better medical care, better diet, and safer surroundings, which lengthen life. This material improvement seems to be especially important for women.

Third, marriage provides individuals—especially men—with someone who 9 monitors their health and health-related behaviors and who encourages them to drink and smoke less, to eat a healthier diet, to get enough sleep and to generally take care of their health. In addition, husbands and wives offer each other moral support that helps in dealing with stressful situations. Married men especially seem to be motivated to avoid risky behaviors and to take care of their health by the sense of meaning that marriage gives to their lives and the sense of obligation to others that it brings.

MORE WEALTH, BETTER WAGES—FOR MOST

Married individuals also seem to fare better when it comes to wealth. One 10 comprehensive measure to financial well-being—household wealth—includes pension and Social Security wealth, real and financial assets, and the value of the primary residence. According to economist James Smith, in 1992 married men and women ages 51–60 had median wealth of about $66,000 per spouse, compared to $42,000 for the widowed, $35,000 for those who had never married, $34,000 among those who were divorced, and only $7,600 for those who were separated. Although married couples have higher incomes than others, this fact accounts for only about a quarter of their greater wealth.

How does marriage increase wealth? Married couples can share many 11 household goods and services, such as a TV and heat, so the cost to each individual is lower than if each one purchased and used the same items individually. So the married spend less than the same individuals would for the same style of life if they lived separately. Second, married people produce more than the same individuals would if single. Each spouse can develop some skills and neglect others, because each can count on the other to take responsibility for some of the household work. The resulting specialization increases efficiency. We see below that this specialization leads to higher wages for men. Married couples also seem to save more at the same level of income than do single people.

The impact of marriage is again beneficial—although in this case not for all 12 involved—when one looks at labor market outcomes. According to recent research by economist Kermit Daniel, both black and white men receive a wage premium if they are married: 4.5 percent for black men and 6.3 percent for white men. Black women receive a marriage premium of almost 3 percent. White women, however, pay a marriage *penalty*, in hourly wages, of over 4 percent. In addition, men appear to receive some of the benefit of marriage if they cohabit, but women do not.

13   Why should marriage increase men's wages? Some researchers think that marriage makes men more productive at work, leading to higher wages. Wives may assist husbands directly with their work, offer advice or support, or take over household tasks, freeing husbands' time and energy for work. Also, as I mentioned earlier, being married reduces drinking, substance abuse, and other unhealthy behaviors that may affect men's job performance. Finally, marriage increases men's incentives to perform well at work, in order to meet obligations to family members.

14   For women, Daniel finds that marriage and presence of children together seem to affect wages, and the effects depend on the woman's race. Childless black women earn substantially more money if they are married but the "marriage premium" drops with each child they have. Among white women only the childless receive a marriage premium. Once white women become mothers, marriage decreases their earnings compared to remaining single (with children), with very large negative effects of marriage on women's earnings for those with two children or more. White married women often choose to reduce hours of work when they have children. They also make less per hour than either unmarried mothers or childless wives.

15   Up to this point, all the consequences of marriage for the individuals involved have been unambiguously positive—better health, longer life, more wealth, and higher earnings. But the effects of marriage and children on white women's wages are mixed, at best. Marriage and cohabitation increase women's time spent on housework; married motherhood reduces their time in the labor force and lowers their wages. Although the family as a whole might be better off with this allocation of women's time, women generally share their husbands' market earnings only when they are married. Financial well-being declines dramatically for women and their children after divorce and widowhood; women whose marriages have ended are often quite disadvantaged financially by their investment in their husbands and children rather than in their own earning power. Recent changes in divorce law—the rise in no-fault divorce and the move away from alimony—seem to have exacerbated this situation, even while increases in women's education and work experience have moderated it.

IMPROVED INTIMACY

16   Another benefit of married life is an improved sex life. Married men and women report very active sex lives—as do those who are cohabiting. But the married appear to be more satisfied with sex than others. More married men say that they find sex with their wives to be extremely physically pleasurable

than do cohabiting men or single men say the same about sex with their partners. The high levels of married men's physical satisfaction with their sex lives contradicts the popular view that sexual novelty or variety improves sex for men. Physical satisfaction with sex is about the same for married women, cohabiting women, and single women with sex partners.

In addition to reporting more active and more physically fulfilling sex lives 17 than the unmarried, married men and women say that they are more emotionally satisfied with their sex lives than do those who are single or cohabiting. Although cohabitants report levels of sexual activity as high as the married, both cohabiting men and women report lower levels of emotional satisfaction with their sex lives. And those who are sexually active but single report the lowest emotional satisfaction with it.

How does marriage improve one's sex life? Marriage and cohabitation pro- 18 vide individuals with a readily available sexual partner with whom they have an established, ongoing sexual relationship. This reduces the costs—in some sense—of any particular sexual contact, and leads to higher levels of sexual activity. Since married couples expect to carry on their sex lives for many years, and since the vast majority of married couples are monogamous, husbands and wives have strong incentives to learn what pleases their partner in bed and to become good at it. But I would argue that more than "skills" are at issue here. The long-term contract implicit in marriage—which is not implicit in cohabitation—facilitates emotional investment in the relationship, which should affect both frequency of and satisfaction with sex. So the wife or husband who knows what the spouse wants is also highly motivated to provide it, both because sexual satisfaction in one's partner brings similar rewards to oneself and because the emotional commitment to the partner makes satisfying him or her important in itself.

To this point we have focused on the consequences of marriage for 19 adults—the men and women who choose to marry (and stay married) or not. But such choices have consequences for the children born to these adults. Sociologists Sarah McLanahan and Gary Sandefur compare children raised in intact, two-parent families with those raised in one-parent families, which could result either from disruption of a marriage or from unmarried childbearing. They find that approximately twice as many children raised in one-parent families than children from two-parent families drop out of high school without finishing. Children raised in one-parent families are also more likely to have a birth themselves while teenagers, and to be "idle"—both out of school and out of the labor force—as young adults.

Not surprisingly, children living outside an intact marriage are also more 20 likely to be poor. McLanahan and Sandefur calculated poverty rates for children in two-parent families—including stepfamilies—and for single-parent families. They found very high rates of poverty for single-parent families, especially among blacks. Donald Hernandez, chief of marriage and family statistics at the Census Bureau, claims that the rise in mother-only families since 1959 is an important cause of increases in poverty among children.

21   Clearly poverty, in and of itself, is a bad outcome for children. In addition, however, McLanahan and Sandefur estimate that the lower incomes of single-parent families account for only half of the negative impact for children in these families. The other half comes from children's access—or lack of access—to the time and attention of two adults in two-parent families. Children in one-parent families spend less time with their fathers (this is not surprising given that they do not live with them), but they also spend less time with their mothers than children in two-parent families. Single-parent families and step-families also move much more frequently than two-parent families, disrupting children's social and academic environments. Finally, children who spend part of their childhood in a single-parent family report substantially lower quality relationships with their parents as adults and have less frequent contact with them, according to demographer Diane Lye.

CORRELATION VERSUS CAUSALITY

22   The obvious question, when one looks at all these "benefits" of marriage, is whether marriage is responsible for these differences. If all, or almost all, of the benefits of marriage arise because those who enjoy better health, live longer lives, or earn higher wages anyway are more likely to marry, then marriage is not "causing" any changes in these outcomes. In such a case, we as a society and we as individuals could remain neutral about each person's decision to marry or not, to divorce or remain married. But scholars from many fields who have examined the issues have come to the opposite conclusion. Daniel found that only half of the higher wages that married men enjoy could be explained by selectivity; he thus concluded that the other half is causal. In the area of mental health, social psychologist Catherine Ross—summarizing her own research and that of other social scientists—wrote, "The positive effect of marriage on well-being is strong and consistent, and the selection of the psychologically healthy into marriage or the psychologically unhealthy out of marriage cannot explain the effect." Thus marriage itself can be assumed to have independent positive effects on its participants.

23   So, we must ask, what is it about marriage that causes these benefits? I think that four factors are key. First, the institution of marriage involves a long-term contract—"'til death do us part." This contract allows the partners to make choices that carry immediate costs but eventually bring benefits. The time horizon implied by marriage makes it sensible—a rational choice is at work here—for individuals to develop some skills and to neglect others because they count on their spouse to fill in where they are weak. The institution of marriage helps individuals honor this long-term contract by providing social support for the couple as a couple and by imposing social and economic costs on those who dissolve their union.

24   Second, marriage assumes a sharing of economic and social resources and what we can think of as co-insurance. Spouses act as a sort of small insurance pool against life's uncertainties, reducing their need to protect themselves—by themselves—from unexpected events.

Third, married couples benefit—as do cohabiting couples—from econo- 25
mies of scale.

Fourth, marriage connects people to other individuals, to their social 26
groups (such as in-laws), and to other social institutions (such as churches and
synagogues) which are themselves a source of benefits. These connections
provide individuals with a sense of obligation to others, which gives life meaning beyond oneself.

Cohabitation has some but not all of the characteristics of marriage and so 27
carries some but not all of the benefits. Cohabitation does not generally imply
a lifetime commitment to stay together; a significant number of cohabiting
couples disagree on the future of their relationship. Frances Goldscheider and
Gail Kaufman believe that the shift to cohabitation from marriage signals "declining commitment within unions, of men and women to each other and to
their relationship as an enduring unit, in exchange for more freedom, primarily
for men." Perhaps as a result, many view cohabitation as an especially poor
bargain for women.

The uncertainty that accompanies cohabitation makes both investment in 28
the relationship and specialization with this partner much riskier than in marriage and so reduces them. Cohabitants are much less likely than married couples to pool financial resources and more likely to assume that each partner is
responsible for supporting himself or herself financially. And whereas marriage
connects individuals to other important social institutions, cohabitation seems
to distance them from these institutions.

Of course, all observations concern only the average benefits of marriage. 29
Clearly, some marriages produce substantially higher benefits for those involved. Some marriages produce no benefits and even cause harm to the men,
women, and children involved. That fact needs to be recognized.

REVERSING THE TREND

Having stated this qualification, we must still ask, if the average marriage 30
produces all of these benefits for individuals, why has it declined? Although this
issue remains a subject of much research and speculation, a number of factors
have been mentioned as contributing. For one, because of increases in women's
employment, there is less specialization by spouses now than in the past; this
reduces the benefits of marriage. Clearly, employed wives have less time and
energy to focus on their husbands, and are less financially and emotionally dependent on marriage than wives who work only in the home. In addition, high
divorce rates decrease people's certainty about the long-run stability of their
marriage, and this may reduce their willingness to invest in it, which in turn increases the chance they divorce—a sort of self-fulfilling prophecy. Also, changes
in divorce laws have shifted much of the financial burden for the breakup of the
marriage to women, making investment within the marriage (such as supporting a husband in medical school) a riskier proposition for them.

Men, in turn, may find marriage and parenthood a less attractive option 31
when they know that divorce is common, because they may face the loss

of contact with their children if their marriage dissolves. Further, women's increased earnings and young men's declining financial well-being may have made women less dependent on men's financial support and made young men less able to provide it. Finally, public policies that support single mothers and changing attitudes toward sex outside of marriage, toward unmarried child-bearing, and toward divorce have all been implicated in the decline in marriage. This brief list does not exhaust the possibilities, but merely mentions some of them.

32   So how can this trend be reversed? First, as evidence accumulates and is communicated to individuals, some people will change their behavior as a result. Some will do so simply because of their new understanding of the costs and benefits, to them, of the choices involved. In addition, we have seen that attitudes frequently change toward behaviors that have been shown to have negative consequences. The attitude change then raises the social cost of the newly stigmatized behavior.

33   In addition, though, we as a society can pull some policy levers to encourage or discourage behaviors. Public policies that include asset tests (Medicaid is a good example) act to exclude the married, as do AFDC programs in most states. The "marriage penalty" in the tax code is another example. These and other policies reinforce or undermine the institution of marriage. If, as I have argued, marriage produces individuals who drink less, smoke less, abuse substances less, live longer, earn more, are wealthier, and have children who do better, we need to give more thought and effort to supporting this valuable social institution.

QUESTIONS FOR READING

1. What is Waite's subject?
2. What groups are healthiest and live the longest? What three reasons does Waite list to explain these health facts?
3. In what ways can marriage increase wealth? Who, when married, loses in hourly wages?
4. What may be the causes of increased productivity for married men?
5. What are some effects of single-parent families on children?
6. If marriage has such benefits, why are fewer people getting married and more getting divorced?

QUESTIONS FOR REASONING AND ANALYSIS

1. What is Waite's claim? Where does she state it?
2. How does the author help readers move through and see the parts of her argument?
3. How does the author defend her causal argument—that marriage itself is a cause of the financial, health, and contentment effects found in married people? Do you find her argument convincing? Why or why not?

4. What kind of evidence, primarily, does Wait provide? Is this evidence persuasive? Why or why not?

QUESTIONS FOR REFLECTING AND WRITING

1. Which statistic most surprises you? Why?

2. What can be done to increase marriage benefits for women, the ones who have least benefited?

3. Should the evidence Waite provides encourage people to choose marriage over divorce, cohabitation, or the single life? If so, why? If no, why not? (Do you have a sense that most adults know—or do not know—the data that Waite provides?)

4. What can be done to change the movement away from marriage? What are Waite's suggestions? What are yours?

THE CONSERVATIVE CASE FOR GAY MARRIAGE | ANDREW SULLIVAN

A native of England with a Ph.D. in political science from Harvard, Andrew Sullivan is editor of Andrewsullivan.com, an online source of commentary on current issues, a *Time* magazine essayist, and a columnist for the *Sunday Times of London*. While editor-in-chief of the *New Republic*, he was named Editor of the Year. He lectures widely and appears frequently on both radio and television programs. The following is a *Time* essay from June 30, 2003.

PREREADING QUESTIONS What does the word *conservative* in the title suggest to you about the author's position and/or approach to the issue of gay marriage? Why might it be useful to present a *conservative* argument on this topic?

A long time ago, the *New Republic* ran a contest to discover the most boring headline ever written. Entrants had to beat the following snoozer, which had inspired the event: WORTHWHILE CANADIAN INITIATIVE. Little did the contest organizers realize that one day such a headline would be far from boring and, in its own small way, a social watershed. 1

Canada's federal government decided last week not to contest the rulings of three provincial courts that had all come to the conclusion that denying homosexuals the right to marry violated Canada's constitutional commitment to civic equality. What that means is that gay marriage has now arrived in the western hemisphere. And this isn't some euphemism. It isn't the quasi-marriage now celebrated in Vermont, whose "civil unions" approximate marriage but don't go by that name. It's just marriage—for all. Canada now follows the Netherlands and Belgium with full-fledged marital rights for gays and lesbians. 2

Could it happen in the U.S.? The next few weeks will give us many clues. The U.S. Supreme Court is due to rule any day now on whether it's legal for Texas and other states to prosecute sodomy among gays but not straights. More critical, Massachusetts' highest court is due to rule very soon on whether the denial of marriage to gays is illicit discrimination against a minority. If Massachusetts rules 3 that it is, then gay couples across America will be able to marry not only in Canada (where there are no residency or nationality requirements for marriage) but also in a bona fide American state. There will be a long process of litigation as various married couples try hard to keep their marriages legally intact from one state to another.

4   This move seems an eminently conservative one—in fact, almost an emblem of "compassionate conservatism." Conservatives have long rightly argued for the vital importance of the institution of marriage for fostering responsibility, commitment and the domestication of unruly men. Bringing gay men and women into this institution will surely change the gay subculture in subtle but profoundly conservative ways. When I grew up and realized I was gay, I had no concept of what my own future could be like. Like most other homosexuals, I grew up in a heterosexual family and tried to imagine how I too could one day be a full part of the family I loved. But I figured then that I had no such future. I could never have a marriage, never have a family, never be a full and equal part of the weddings and relationships and holidays that give families structure and meaning. When I looked forward, I saw nothing but emptiness and loneliness. No wonder it was hard to connect sex with love and commitment. No wonder it was hard to feel at home in what was, in fact, my home.

5   For today's generation of gay kids, all that changes. From the beginning, they will be able to see their future as part of family life—not in conflict with it. Their "coming out" will also allow them a "coming home." And as they date in adolescence and early adulthood, there will be some future anchor in their mind-set, some ultimate structure with which to give their relationships stability and social support. Many heterosexuals, I suspect, simply don't realize how big a deal this is. They have never doubted that one day they could marry the person they love. So they find it hard to conceive how deep a psychic and social wound the exclusion from marriage and family can be. But the polls suggest this is changing fast: the majority of people 30 and younger see gay marriage as inevitable and understandable. Many young straight couples simply don't see married gay peers next door as some sort of threat to their own lives. They can get along in peace.

6   As for religious objections, it's important to remember that the issue here is not religious. It's civil. Various religious groups can choose to endorse same-sex marriage or not as they see fit. Their freedom of conscience is as vital as gays' freedom to be treated equally under the civil law. And there's no real reason that the two cannot coexist. The Roman Catholic Church, for example, opposes remarriage after divorce. But it doesn't seek to make civil divorce and remarriage illegal for everyone. Similarly, churches can well decide this matter in their own time and on their own terms while allowing the government to be neutral between competing visions of the good life. We can live and let live.

7   And after all, isn't that what this really is about? We needn't all agree on the issue of homosexuality to believe that the government should treat every citizen alike. If that means living next door to someone of whom we disapprove, so be it. But disapproval needn't mean disrespect. And if the love of two

people, committing themselves to each other exclusively for the rest of their lives, is not worthy of respect, then what is?

QUESTIONS FOR READING

1. What important decision has Canada's government recently made?
2. What decision did the Supreme Court make on the Texas sodomy case, after Sullivan's essay was published?
3. Why should these rulings be viewed as conservative?
4. What view toward gay marriage is held by the majority of people thirty and younger?

QUESTIONS FOR REASONING AND ANALYSIS

1. What is Sullivan's claim?
2. In paragraph 4, Sullivan puts the term "compassionate conservatism" in quotation marks. Why? What is he suggesting in the sentence?
3. Sullivan includes his own feelings about feeling excluded from family because he is gay. How does this discussion in paragraph 4 aid his argument?
4. How does he rebut the presumed counterargument of religious objections? What analogy does he draw in paragraph 6? Is his rebuttal convincing? Why or why not?
5. How would you describe the tone of this argument? How is the author seeking to use tone to reach readers who might disagree with him?

QUESTIONS FOR REFLECTING AND WRITING

1. Were you aware that the Netherlands, Belgium, and Canada all allow gay marriages? If you did not know this, does this new knowledge affect your thinking about gay marriage in any way? If so, how? If not, why not?
2. What, in your view, is the strongest part of Sullivan's argument? Why?
3. Sullivan is asking readers to support civil equality even though they may have religious objections to gay marriages. Can you separate church and state on this issue? Why or why not?

GAY MARRIAGE, AN OXYMORON | LISA SCHIFFREN

A speech writer for former vice president Dan Quayle, Lisa Schiffren began her career at the *Detroit News*. She now writes on public policy and social issues in popular magazines and newspapers. Her article on gay marriage was published in the *New York Times* on March 23, 1996—before Hawaii decided not to sanction gay marriages.

PREREADING QUESTIONS What does the term *oxymoron* mean? What view of gay marriage does the author's title convey?

1   As study after study and victim after victim testify to the social devastation of the sexual revolution, easy divorce, and out-of-wedlock motherhood, marriage is fashionable again. And parenthood has transformed many baby boomers into advocates of bourgeois norms.

2   Indeed, we have come so far that the surprise issue of the political season is whether homosexual "marriage" should be legalized. The Hawaii courts will likely rule that gay marriage is legal, and other states will be required to accept those marriages as valid.

3   Considering what a momentous change this would be—a radical redefinition of society's most fundamental institution—there has been almost no real debate. This is because the premise is unimaginable to many, and the forces of political correctness have descended on the discussion, raising the cost of opposition. But one may feel the same affection for one's homosexual friends and relatives as for any other and be genuinely pleased for the happiness they derive from relationships while opposing gay marriage for principled reasons.

4   "Same-sex marriage" is inherently incompatible with our culture's understanding of the institution. Marriage is essentially a lifelong compact between a man and woman committed to sexual exclusivity and the creation and nurture of offspring. For most Americans, the marital union—as distinguished from other sexual relationships and legal and economic partnerships—is imbued with an aspect of holiness. Though many of us are uncomfortable using religious language to discuss social and political issues, Judeo-Christian morality informs our view of family life.

5   Though it is not polite to mention it, what the Judeo-Christian tradition has to say about homosexual unions could not be clearer. In a diverse, open society such as ours, tolerance of homosexuality is a necessity. But for many, its practice depends on a trick of cognitive dissonance that allows people to believe in the Judeo-Christian moral order while accepting, often with genuine regard, the different lives of homosexual acquaintances. That is why, though homosexuals may believe that they are merely seeking a small expansion of the definition of marriage, the majority of Americans perceive this change as a radical deconstruction of the institution.

6   Some make the conservative argument that making marriage a civil right will bring stability, an end to promiscuity, and a sense of fairness to gay men and women. But they miss the point. Society cares about stability in heterosexual unions because it is critical for raising healthy children and transmitting the values that are the basis of our culture.

7   Whether homosexual relationships endure is of little concern to society. That is also true of most childless marriages, harsh as it is to say. Society has wisely chosen not to differentiate between marriages, because it would require meddling into the motives and desires of everyone who applies for a license.

8   In traditional marriage, the tie that really binds for life is shared responsibility for the children. (A small fraction of gay couples may choose to raise children together, but such children are offspring of one partner and an outside contributor.) What will keep gay marriages together when individuals tire of each other?

Similarly, the argument that legal marriage will check promiscuity by gay 9
males raises the question of how a "piece of paper" will do what the threat of
AIDS has not. Lesbians seem to have little problem with monogamy or the rest
of what constitutes "domestication," despite the absence of official status.

Finally, there is the so-called fairness argument. The government gives tax 10
benefits, inheritance rights, and employee benefits only to the married. Again,
these financial benefits exist to help couples raise children. Tax reform is an
effective way to remove distinctions among earners.

If the American people are interested in a radical experiment with same- 11
sex marriages, then subjecting it to the political process is the right route. For
a court in Hawaii to assume that it has the power to radically redefine marriage
is a stunning abuse of power. To present homosexual marriage as a fait ac-
compli, without national debate, is a serious political error. A society struggling to recover from thirty years of weakened norms and broken families is
not likely to respond gently to having an institution central to most people's
lives altered.

QUESTIONS FOR READING

1. What is Schiffren's topic?
2. What is Schiffren's definition of marriage? What is the source of our society's
   ideas about marriage?
3. What does the Judeo-Christian tradition say about homosexual unions?
4. If same-sex marriages are to be approved, by what process should this occur,
   in the author's view?

QUESTIONS FOR REASONING AND ANALYSIS

1. What is the author's claim? Where does she state it?
2. How does Schiffren organize her argument? Briefly summarize the main points
   of her argument.
3. How does the author use conciliatory strategies in her argument? Are they
   effective?

QUESTIONS FOR REFLECTING AND WRITING

1. The author asserts that "marriage is fashionable again." Does she provide any
   evidence to support this assertion? Has the number of marriages in the United
   States increased in recent years? (How might you obtain such information?)
2. How does the author explain why there has been no debate about same-sex marriages? Does her explanation match your experience? Has the debate of this topic
   increased since Schiffren wrote in 1996?
3. Schiffren asserts that society does not care about stability in gay relationships,
   only in marriages with children. Does she offer evidence that this is how most
   citizens feel? Or are we to believe that she is speaking in a legal sense—the state's

interest? Should society—we—care about the stability of all relationships? Why or why not? Since "society's" concern has not kept the divorce rate from being slightly more than 50 percent, is this a meaningful argument? Why or why not?

4. Schiffren also asserts that gay males are promiscuous, presumably more so than both lesbians and heterosexuals. Is there evidence for this assertion? Do Schiffren's unsupported assertions affect the quality of her argument? Why or why not?

WILL WOMEN STILL NEED MEN? | BARBARA EHRENREICH

Barbara Ehrenreich (b. 1940), whose focus is women's studies and social commentary, publishes frequently in popular magazines and is the author of several books, including *Nickel and Dimed: On (Not) Getting By in America* (2002), *Blood Rites: Origins and History of the Passions of War* (1997), and *Talking about a Revolution* (1998). Her provocative essay on relations between the sexes in the future was published in *Time* on February 21, 2000.

PREREADING QUESTIONS What is your initial reaction to Ehrenreich's title? Are you surprised? Shocked? Amused? Something else? Would you like to see the sexes go their separate ways?

1   This could be the century when the sexes go their separate ways. Sure, we've hung in there together for about a thousand millenniums so far— through hunting-gathering, agriculture and heavy industry—but what choice did we have? For most of human existence, if you want to make a living, raise children or even have a roaring good time now and then, you had to get the cooperation of the other sex.

2   What's new about the future, and potentially more challenging to our species than Martian colonization or silicon brain implants, is that the partnership between the sexes is becoming entirely voluntary. We can decide to stick together—or we can finally say, "Sayonara, other sex!" For the first time in human history and prehistory combined, the choice will be ours.

3   I predict three possible scenarios, starting with the Big Divorce. Somewhere around 2025, people will pick a gender equivalent of the Mason-Dixon Line and sort themselves out accordingly. In Guy Land the men will be free to spend their evenings staging belching contests and watching old Howard Stern tapes. In Gal Land the women will all be fat and happy, and no one will bother to shave her legs. Aside from a few initial border clashes, the separation will for the most part be amicable. At least the "battle of the sexes," insofar as anyone can remember it, will be removed from the kitchens and bedrooms of America and into the U.N.

4   And why not? If the monosexual way of life were counter to human nature, men wouldn't have spent so much of the past millennium dodging women by enlisting in armies, monasteries and all-male guilds and professions. Up until the past half-century, women only fantasized about their version of the same: a utopia like the one described by 19th century feminist Charlotte Perkins

Gilman, where women would lead placidly sexless lives and reproduce by parthenogenesis. But a real separation began to look feasible about 50 years ago. With the invention of TV dinners and drip-dry shirts, for the first time the average man became capable of feeding and dressing himself. Sensing their increasing dispensability on the home front, and tired of picking up dropped socks, women rushed into the work force. They haven't achieved full economic independence by any means (women still earn only 75% of what men do), but more and more of them are realizing that ancient female dream—a room, or better yet, a condo of their own.

The truly species-shaking change is coming from the new technologies of reproduction. Up until now, if you wanted to reproduce, you not only had to fraternize with a member of the other sex for at least a few minutes, but you also ran a 50% risk that any resulting baby would turn out be a member of the foreign sex. No more. Thanks to in vitro fertilization, we can have babies without having sex. And with the latest techniques of sex selection, we can have babies of whatever sex we want.

Obviously women, with their built-in baby incubators, will have the advantage in a monosexual future. They just have to pack up a good supply of frozen semen, a truckload of turkey basters and go their own way. But men will be catching up. For one thing, until now, frozen-and-thawed ova have been tricky to fertilize because their outer membrane gets too hard. But a new technique called intracytoplasmic sperm injection makes frozen ova fully fertilizable, and so now Guy Land can have its ovum banks. As for the incubation problem, a few years ago feminist writer Gena Corea offered the seemingly paranoid suggestion that men might eventually keep just a few women around in "reproductive brothels," gestating on demand. A guy will pick an ovum for attractive qualities like smart, tall and allergy-free, then have it inserted into some faceless surrogate mother employed as a reproductive slave.

What about sex, though, meaning the experience, not the category? Chances are, we will be having sex with machines, mostly computers. Even today you can buy interactive CD-ROMS like Virtual Valerie, and there's talk of full-body, virtual-reality sex in which the pleasure seeker wears a specially fitted suit—very specially fitted—allowing for tactile as well as audiovisual sensation. If that sounds farfetched, consider the fact that cyber-innovation is currently in the hands of social skills–challenged geeks who couldn't hope to get a date without flashing their Internet stock options.

Still, there's a reason why the Big Divorce scenario isn't likely to work out, even by Y3K: we love each other, we males and females—madly, sporadically, intermittently, to be sure—but at least enough to keep us pair bonding furiously, even when there's no obvious hardheaded reason to do so. Hence, despite predictions of the imminent "breakdown of the family," the divorce rate leveled off in the 1990s, and the average couple is still hopeful or deluded enough to invest about $20,000 in their first wedding. True, fewer people are marrying: 88% of Americans have married at least once, down from 94% in 1988. But the difference is largely made up by couples who set up housekeeping without the blessing of the state. And an astounding 16% of the population has been married three times—which shows a remarkable commitment to, if nothing else, the institution of marriage.

9   The question for the new century is, Do we love each other *enough*—enough, that is, to sustain the old pair-bonded way of life? Many experts see the glass half empty: cohabitation may be replacing marriage, but it's even less likely to last. Hearts are routinely broken and children's lives disrupted as we churn, ever starry-eyed, from one relationship to the next. Even liberal icons like Hillary Rodham Clinton and Harvard Afro-American studies professor Cornel West have been heard muttering about the need to limit the ease and accessibility of divorce.

10   Hence, perhaps, Scenario B: seeing that the old economic and biological pressures to marry don't work anymore, people will decide to replace them with new forms of coercion. Divorce will be outlawed, along with abortion and possibly contraception. Extramarital hanky-panky will be punishable with shunning or, in the more hard-line jurisdictions, stoning. There will still be sex, and probably plenty of it inside marriage, thanks to what will be known as Chemically Assisted Monogamy: Viagra for men and Viagra-like drugs for women, such as apomorphine and Estratest (both are being tested right now), to reignite the spark long after familiarity has threatened to extinguish it. Naturally, prescriptions will be available only upon presentation of a valid marriage license.

11   It couldn't happen here, even in a thousand years? Already, a growing "marriage movement," including groups like the Promise Keepers, is working to make divorce lawyers as rare as elevator operators. Since 1997, Louisiana and Arizona have been offering ultratight "covenant marriages," which can be dissolved only in the case of infidelity, abuse or felony conviction, and similar measures have been introduced in 17 other states. As for the age-old problem of premarital fooling around, some extremely conservative Christian activists have launched a movement to halt the dangerous practice of dating and replace it with parent-supervised betrothals leading swiftly and ineluctably to the altar.

12   But Scenario B has a lot going against it too. The 1998 impeachment fiasco showed just how hard it will be to restigmatize extramarital sex. Sure, we think adultery is a bad thing, just not bad enough to disqualify anyone from ruling the world. Meanwhile, there have been few takers for covenant marriages, showing that most people like to keep their options open. Tulane University sociologist Laura Sanchez speculates that the ultimate effect of covenant marriages may be to open up the subversive possibility of diversifying the institution of marriage—with different types for different folks, including, perhaps someday, even gay folks.

13   Which brings us to the third big scenario. This is the diversity option, arising from the realization that the one-size-fits-all model of marriage may have been one of the biggest sources of tension between the sexes all along—based as it is on the wildly unrealistic expectation that a single spouse can meet one's needs for a lover, friend, co-parent, financial partner, reliably, 24-7. Instead there will be renewable marriages, which get re-evaluated every five to seven years, after which they can be revised, recelebrated or dissolved with no,

or at least fewer, hard feelings. There will be unions between people who don't live together full-time but do want to share a home base. And of course there will always be plenty of people who live together but don't want to make a big deal out of it. Already, thanks to the gay-rights movement, more than 600 corporations and other employers offer domestic-partner benefits, a 60-fold increase since 1990.

And the children? The real paradigm shift will come when we stop trying   14 to base our entire society on the wavering sexual connection between individuals. Romantic love ebbs and surges unaccountably; it's the bond between parents and children that has to remain rocklike year after year. Putting children first would mean that adults would make a contract—not to live together or sleep together but to take joint responsibility for a child or an elderly adult. Some of these arrangements will look very much like today's marriages, with a heterosexual couple undertaking the care of their biological children. Others will look like nothing we've seen before, at least not in suburban America, especially since there's no natural limit on the number of contracting caretakers. A group of people—male, female, gay, straight—will unite in their responsibility for the children they bear or acquire through the local Artificial Reproduction Center. Heather may routinely have two mommies, or at least a whole bunch of resident aunts—which is, of course, more or less how things have been for eons in such distinctly unbohemian settings as the tribal village.

So how will things play out this century and beyond? Just so you will be   15 prepared, here's my timeline:

Between 2000 and 2339: geographical diversity prevails. The Southeast   16 and a large swath of the Rockies will go for Scenario B (early marriage, no divorce). Oregon, California and New York will offer renewable marriages, and a few states will go monosexual, as in Scenario A. But because of the 1996 Defense of Marriage Act, each state is entitled to recognize only the kinds of "marriages" it approves of, so you will need a "marriage visa" to travel across the country, at least if you intend to share a motel room.

Between 2340 and 2387: NATO will be forced to intervene in the Custody   17 Wars that break out between the Polygamous Republic of Utah and the Free Love Zone of the Central Southwest. A huge refugee crisis will develop when singles are ethnically cleansed from the Christian Nation of Idaho. Florida will be partitioned into divorce-free and marriage-free zones.

In 2786: the new President's Inauguration will be attended by all five mem-   18 bers of the mixed-sex, multiracial commune that raised her. She will establish sizable tax reductions for couples or groups of any size that create stable households for their children and other dependents. Peace will break out.

And in 2999: a scholar of ancient history will discover these words penned   19 by a gay writer named Fenton Johnson back in 1996: "The mystery of love and life and death is really grander and more glorious than human beings can grasp, much less legislate." He will put this sentence onto a bumper sticker. The message will spread. We will realize that the sexes can't live without each other, but neither can they be joined at the hip. We will grow up.

QUESTIONS FOR READING

1. What is Ehrenreich's subject?
2. What changes about 50 years ago began to make a separation of the sexes a possibility? What current technologies will really let men and women go their separate ways?
3. In spite of new technologies, what may keep men and women together? What evidence does the author provide?

QUESTIONS FOR REASONING AND ANALYSIS

1. What is the author's claim? Where does she state it?
2. What is Ehrenreich's "Scenario B"? What evidence suggests that this plan will not materialize?
3. What is the third possibility? What is critical to this scenario?
4. Summarize the author's "timeline" for change. How serious is she regarding this timeline? (Examine her word choice and think about her tone.)

QUESTIONS FOR REFLECTING AND WRITING

1. What, for you, is the most startling idea in Ehrenreich's scenarios for the next few centuries? Why? Be prepared to discuss your choice with classmates.
2. What, for you, is the most startling new fact or example (including new technologies) mentioned in this essay? Why? Be prepared to discuss your choice with classmates.
3. Which scenario is most appealing to you? Which most unappealing? Why?
4. The author hopes that eventually we will "grow up." What elements are a part of her idea of growing up with regard to marriage/partnerships/children? Do you agree with her views of growing up? If not, how would you define growing up with regard to gender issues?

ABOLISH MARRIAGE | MICHAEL KINSLEY

A member of the bar with a law degree from Harvard, Michael Kinsley is a former editor of both *Harper's* and the *New Republic*. He is the founding editor (1996) of *Slate*, the online magazine, has been a cohost of CNN's *Crossfire*, and currently writes a weekly column for the *Washington Post*. The following column appeared in the *Post*, July 3, 2003.

PREREADING QUESTIONS What are the key issues in the debate over gay marriage? What are gay marriage proponents seeking? What are social conservatives seeking?

1   Critics and enthusiasts of *Lawrence v. Texas*, last week's Supreme Court decision invalidating state anti-sodomy laws, agree on one thing: The next argument is going to be about gay marriage. As Justice Antonin Scalia noted in his tart dissent, it follows from the logic of *Lawrence*. Mutually consenting sex with the person of your choice in the privacy of your own home is now a basic right

of American citizenship under the Constitution. This does not mean that the government must supply it or guarantee it. But the government cannot forbid it, and the government also should not discriminate against you for choosing to exercise a basic right of citizenship. Offering an institution as important as marriage to male-female couples only is exactly this kind of discrimination. Or so the gay rights movement will now argue. Persuasively, I think.

Opponents of gay rights will resist mightily, although they have been in re- 2 treat for a couple of decades. General anti-gay sentiments are now considered a serious breach of civic etiquette, even in anti-gay circles. The current line of defense, which probably won't hold either, is between social toleration of homosexuals and social approval of homosexuality. Or between accepting the reality that people are gay, even accepting that gays are people, and endorsing something called "the gay agenda." Gay marriage, the opponents will argue, would cross this line. It would make homosexuality respectable and, worse, normal. Gays are welcome to exist all they want, and to do their inexplicable thing if they must, but they shouldn't expect a government stamp of approval.

It's going to get ugly. And then it's going to get boring. So we have two 3 options here. We can add gay marriage to the short list of controversies— abortion, affirmative action, the death penalty—that are so frozen and ritualistic that debates about them are more like kabuki performances than intellectual exercises. Or we can think outside the box. There is a solution that ought to satisfy both camps, and may not be a bad idea even apart from the gay marriage controversy.

That solution is to end the institution of marriage. Or rather (he hastens to 4 clarify, dear) the solution is to end the institution of government-sanctioned marriage. Or, framed to appeal to conservatives: End the government monopoly on marriage. Wait, I've got it: Privatize marriage. These slogans all mean the same thing. Let churches and other religious institutions continue to offer marriage ceremonies. Let department stores and casinos get into the act if they want. Let each organization decide for itself what kinds of couples it wants to offer marriage to. Let couples celebrate their union in any way they choose and consider themselves married whenever they want. Let others be free to consider them not married, under rules these others may prefer. And, yes, if three people want to get married, or one person wants to marry herself, and someone else wants to conduct a ceremony and declare them married, let 'em. If you and your government aren't implicated, what do you care?

In fact, there is nothing to stop any of this from happening now. And a lot 5 of it does happen. But only certain marriages get certified by the government. So, in the United States we are about to find ourselves in a strange situation where the principal demand of a liberation movement is to be included in the red tape of a government bureaucracy. Having just gotten state governments out of their bedrooms, gays now want these governments back in. Meanwhile, social-conservative anti-gays, many of them southerners, are calling on the government in Washington to trample states' rights and nationalize the rules of marriage, if necessary, to prevent gays from getting what they want. The Senate majority leader, Bill Frist of Tennessee, responded to the Supreme

Court's *Lawrence* decision by endorsing a constitutional amendment, no less, against gay marriage.

6   If marriage were an entirely private affair, all the disputes over gay marriage would become irrelevant. Gay marriage would not have the official sanction of government, but neither would straight marriage. There would be official equality between the two, which is the essence of what gays want and are entitled to. And if the other side is sincere in saying that its concern is not what people do in private but government endorsement of a gay "lifestyle" or "agenda," that problem goes away too.

7   Yes, yes, marriage is about more than sleeping arrangements. There are children, there are finances, there are spousal job benefits such as health insurance and pensions. In all of these areas, marriage is used as a substitute for other factors that are harder to measure, such as financial dependence or devotion to offspring. It would be possible to write rules that measure the real factors at stake and leave marriage out of the matter. Regarding children and finances, people can set their own rules, as many already do. None of this would be easy. Marriage functions as what lawyers call a "bright line," which saves the trouble of trying to measure a lot of amorphous factors. You're either married or you're not. Once marriage itself becomes amorphous, who-gets-the-kids and who-gets-health-care become trickier questions.

8   So, sure, there are some legitimate objections to the idea of privatizing marriage. But they don't add up to a fatal objection. Especially when you consider that the alternative is arguing about gay marriage until death do us part.

QUESTIONS FOR READING

1. What will the next argument be about? What ruling will bring on this argument? What about the ruling invites the argument?

2. Who will win the argument, in Kinsley's view?

3. According to the author, where are we in the "tug-of-war" over gay rights? Where would allowing gay marriage put us in the battle?

4. What is the author's solution to end the argument?

5. What is ironic about gays fighting for the right to marry? What is ironic about conservatives seeking a constitutional amendment against gay marriage?

6. What problems would emerge if governments stopped sanctioning marriage altogether? Are these problems insurmountable, in the author's view?

QUESTIONS FOR REASONING AND ANALYSIS

1. What is Kinsley's claim? Where does he state it?

2. When Kinsley writes that the argument over gay marriage will "get boring," what does he mean? How does his comparison to kabuki performances or to debates over abortion or the death penalty illustrate his point here?

3. How does Kinsley seek to convince both sides of the argument that his solution should please them?

4. The author anticipates counterarguments in his last two paragraphs. How effective is his rebuttal?

5. Analyze the essay's tone. How serious do you think Kinsley is in presenting his solution to the argument over gay marriage? If he does not think his solution is viable, then why is he proposing it? What is his purpose in writing?

QUESTIONS FOR REFLECTING AND WRITING

1. What is your reaction to Kinsley's proposal? Is the best solution to get government out of certifying marriage? If we wanted to "think outside the box," could we solve the other problems—of finances, child custody, and so forth—if we wanted to? How would you support the proposal or challenge it?

2. Is there any hope of finding common ground on this issue, or are we doomed to live with another issue that generates only ritualistic "debates"? Do you have any new suggestions for thinking outside the box on social issues that are currently so divisive?

3. How does Kinsley's proposal compare with Barbara Ehrenreich's scenarios? Who has the most realistic vision of the future? Who has the vision you prefer? Why?

CHAPTER 22

Bioethics: A Brave New World?

Undoubtedly changes in computer technology will dramatically change our lives in this twenty-first century. Just as assuredly will our concepts of the family dramatically alter the way we live. But for many people the most dramatic—perhaps the most fearful—changes will come from medical research or biotechnology, most particularly from stem-cell research and cloning. Will medical research take us truly into a utopia, into a world of longevity without most of the disagreeable elements of aging, into a world freed from genetically transmitted disease? Or will biotechnology deliver us into a nightmarish universe of genetically "enhanced" humans who at some point truly cease to be human? These are tough questions. It is difficult to stop scientific study, should we want to, and it is difficult to want to stem the tide of advancements against Parkinson's disease or infertility, to name only two of the many medical problems we would like to solve. The following writers debate the issues that we compile under the term bioethics. The chapter includes writers of differing views and positions on the direction of biotechnology. They follow one of the most important documents on this topic, the executive summary of the President's Council on Bioethics. Although longish, it is worth your careful study and attention as it clearly presents the issues of the debate, as well as explains the Council's recommendations to the president.

PREREADING QUESTIONS

1. How well do you understand stem-cell research and what is referred to as cloning? How important is it to understand the science involved in order to have a position on this research and activity?
2. Do you have a position on stem-cell research and cloning? If so, what are the primary sources on which you base your position? Family? Friends? Biology class? Religious leaders?
3. If you don't have a position, do you think it's important to understand this issue, the points of debate, and then move toward an informed decision? Why or why not? At what point in the research and experimentation into cloning do you think it's imperative to have a position?
4. What can/should individuals do to join in the bioethics debate?

Websites Relevant to This Chapter's Issues
The President's Council on Bioethics

> http://www.bioethics.gov/
>
> In addition to containing the executive summary, this site offers a variety of resources and links on the issue of bioethics.

Bioethics Resources on the Web—NIH

> http://www.nih.gov/sigs/bioethics/
>
> As its name indicates, there are lots of resources at this site.

Center for Bioethics and Human Dignity

> http://www.cbhd.org
>
> Lots of information, but from a perspective of Christian values.

HUMAN CLONING AND HUMAN DIGNITY: AN ETHICAL INQUIRY | PRESIDENT'S COUNCIL ON BIOETHICS

The following work is the executive summary of the report prepared by the President's Council on Bioethics. The Council's task was to study the ethics of human cloning and make a recommendation to the president. The summary reprinted here has been cut slightly for purposes of length only, and the excluded passages have been indicated with ellipses. The full text of the report is available at the council's website. The chair of the Council is Leon R. Kass, the Hertog Fellow at the American Enterprise Institute. (Names of other members of the Council can be found on the website.)

PREREADING QUESTIONS What does the title of the report suggest to you about its approach? About the issues it will examine with regard to human cloning?

1   For the past five years, the prospect of human cloning has been the subject of considerable public attention and sharp moral debate, both in the United States and around the world. Since the announcement in February 1997 of the first successful cloning of a mammal (Dolly the sheep), several other species of mammals have been cloned. Although a cloned human child has yet to be born, and although the animal experiments have had low rates of success, the production of functioning mammalian cloned offspring suggests that the eventual cloning of humans must be considered a serious possibility.

2   In November 2001, American researchers claimed to have produced the first cloned human embryos, though they reportedly reached only a six-cell stage before they stopped dividing and died. In addition, several fertility specialists, both here and abroad, have announced their intention to clone human beings. The United States Congress has twice taken up the matter, in 1998 and again in 2001–2002, with the House of Representatives in July 2001 passing a strict ban on all human cloning, including the production of cloned human embryos. As of this writing, several cloning-related bills are under consideration in the Senate. Many other nations have banned human cloning, and the United Nations is considering an international convention on the subject. . . .

3   The debate over human cloning became further complicated in 1998 when researchers were able, for the first time, to isolate human embryonic stem cells. Many scientists believe that these versatile cells, capable of becoming any type of cell in the body, hold great promise for understanding and treating many chronic diseases and conditions. Some scientists also believe that stem cells derived from cloned human embryos, produced explicitly for such research, might prove uniquely useful for studying many genetic diseases and devising novel therapies. Public reaction to the prospect of cloning-for-biomedical-research has been mixed: some Americans support it for its medical promise; others oppose it because it requires the exploitation and destruction of nascent human life, which would be created solely for research purposes. . . .

THE INQUIRY: OUR POINT OF DEPARTURE

4   As Members of the President's Council on Bioethics, we have taken up the larger ethical and social inquiry called for in the NBAC [National Bioethics Advisory Commission] and NAS [National Academy of Sciences] reports, with the aim of advancing public understanding and informing public policy on the matter. We have attempted to consider human cloning (both for producing children and for biomedical research) within its larger human, technological, and ethical contexts, rather than to view it as an isolated technical development. We focus first on the broad human goods that it may serve as well as threaten, rather than on the immediate impact of the technique itself. By our broad approach, our

starting on the plane of human goods, and our open spirit of inquiry, we hope to contribute to a richer and deeper understanding of what human cloning means, how we should think about it, and what we should do about it.

On some matters discussed in this report, Members of the Council are not 5 of one mind. Rather than bury these differences in search of a spurious consensus, we have sought to present all views fully and fairly, while recording our agreements as well as our genuine diversity of perspectives, including our differences on the final recommendations to be made. By this means, we hope to help policymakers and the general public appreciate more thoroughly the difficulty of the issues and the competing goods that are at stake.

FAIR AND ACCURATE TERMINOLOGY

On the basis of (1) a careful analysis of the act of cloning, and its relation 6 to the means by which it is accomplished and the purposes it may serve, and (2) an extensive critical examination of alternative terminologies, the Council has adopted the following definitions for the most important terms in the matter of human cloning:

- *Cloning:* A form of reproduction in which offspring result not from the chance union of egg and sperm (sexual reproduction) but from the deliberate replication of the genetic makeup of another single individual (asexual reproduction).
- *Human cloning:* The asexual production of a new human organism that is, at all stages of development, genetically virtually identical to a currently existing or previously existing human being. It would be accomplished by introducing the nuclear material of a human somatic cell (donor) into an oocyte (egg) whose own nucleus has been removed or inactivated, yielding a product that has a human genetic constitution virtually identical to the donor of the somatic cell. (This procedure is known as "somatic cell nuclear transfer," or SCNT.) We have declined to use the terms "reproductive cloning" and "therapeutic cloning." We have chosen instead to use the following designations:
- *Cloning-to-produce-children:* Production of a cloned human embryo, formed for the (proximate) purpose of initiating a pregnancy, with the (ultimate) goal of producing a child who will be genetically virtually identical to a currently existing or previously existing individual.
- *Cloning-for-biomedical-research:* Production of a cloned human embryo, formed for the (proximate) purpose of using it in research or for extracting its stem cells, with the (ultimate) goals of gaining scientific knowledge of normal and abnormal development and of developing cures for human diseases.
- *Cloned human embryo:* (a) A human embryo resulting from the nuclear transfer process (as contrasted with a human embryo arising from the union of egg and sperm). (b) The immediate (and developing) product of the initial act of cloning, accomplished by successful SCNT, whether used subsequently in attempts to produce children or in biomedical research. . . .

THE ETHICS OF CLONING-TO-PRODUCE-CHILDREN

7   Two separate national-level reports on human cloning (NBAC, 1997; NAS, 2002) concluded that attempts to clone a human being would be unethical at this time due to safety concerns and the likelihood of harm to those involved. The Council concurs in this conclusion. But we have extended the work of these distinguished bodies by undertaking a broad ethical examination of the merits of, and difficulties with, cloning-to-produce-children.

8   Cloning-to-produce-children might serve several purposes. It might allow infertile couples or others to have genetically-related children; permit couples at risk of conceiving a child with a genetic disease to avoid having an afflicted child; allow the bearing of a child who could become an ideal transplant donor for a particular patient in need; enable a parent to keep a living connection with a dead or dying child or spouse; or enable individuals or society to try to "replicate" individuals of great talent or beauty. These purposes have been defended by appeals to the goods of freedom, existence (as opposed to nonexistence), and well-being—all vitally important ideals.

9   A major weakness in these arguments supporting cloning-to-produce-children is that they overemphasize the freedom, desires, and control of parents, and pay insufficient attention to the well-being of the cloned child-to-be. The Council holds that, once the child-to-be is carefully considered, these arguments are not sufficient to overcome the powerful case against engaging in cloning-to-produce-children.

10   First, cloning-to-produce-children would violate the principles of the ethics of human research. Given the high rates of morbidity and mortality in the cloning of other mammals, we believe that cloning-to-produce-children would be extremely unsafe, and that attempts to produce a cloned child would be highly unethical. Indeed, our moral analysis of this matter leads us to conclude that this is not, as is sometimes implied, a merely temporary objection, easily removed by the improvement of technique. We offer reasons for believing that the safety risks might be enduring, and offer arguments in support of a strong conclusion: that conducting experiments in an effort to make cloning-to-produce-children less dangerous would itself be an unacceptable violation of the norms of research ethics. There seems to be no ethical way to try to discover whether cloning-to-produce-children can become safe, now or in the future.

11   If carefully considered, the concerns about safety also begin to reveal the ethical principles that should guide a broader assessment of cloning-to-produce-children: the principles of freedom, equality, and human dignity. To appreciate the broader human significance of cloning-to-produce-children, one needs first to reflect on the meaning of having children; the meaning of asexual, as opposed to sexual, reproduction; the importance of origins and genetic endowment for identity and sense of self; the meaning of exercising greater human control over the processes and "products" of human reproduction; and the difference between begetting and making. Reflecting on these topics, the Council has identified five categories of concern regarding cloning-to-produce-children. . . .

- *Problems of identity and individuality.* Cloned children may experience serious problems of identity both because each will be genetically virtually identical to a human being who has already lived and because the expectations for their lives may be shadowed by constant comparisons to the life of the "original."
- *Concerns regarding manufacture.* Cloned children would be the first human beings whose entire genetic makeup is selected in advance. They might come to be considered more like products of a designed manufacturing process than "gifts" whom their parents are prepared to accept as they are. Such an attitude toward children could also contribute to increased commercialization and industrialization of human procreation.
- *The prospect of a new eugenics.* Cloning, if successful, might serve the ends of privately pursued eugenic enhancement, either by avoiding the genetic defects that may arise when human reproduction is left to chance, or by preserving and perpetuating outstanding genetic traits, including the possibility, someday in the future, of using cloning to perpetuate genetically engineered enhancements.
- *Troubled family relations.* By confounding and transgressing the natural boundaries between generations, cloning could strain the social ties between them. Fathers could become "twin brothers" to their "sons"; mothers could give birth to their genetic twins; and grandparents would also be the "genetic parents" of their grandchildren. Genetic relation to only one parent might produce special difficulties for family life.
- *Effects on society.* Cloning-to-produce-children would affect not only the direct participants but also the entire society that allows or supports this activity. Even if practiced on a small scale, it could affect the way society looks at children and set a precedent for future nontherapeutic interventions into the human genetic endowment or novel forms of control by one generation over the next. In the absence of wisdom regarding these matters, prudence dictates caution and restraint.

Conclusion: For some or all of these reasons, the Council is in full agreement that cloning-to-produce-children is not only unsafe but also morally unacceptable, and ought not to be attempted.

THE ETHICS OF CLONING-FOR-BIOMEDICAL-RESEARCH

Ethical assessment of cloning-for-biomedical-research is far more vexing. 12
On the one hand, such research could lead to important knowledge about human embryological development and gene action, both normal and abnormal, ultimately resulting in treatments and cures for many dreaded illnesses and disabilities. On the other hand, the research is morally controversial because it involves the deliberate production, use, and ultimate destruction of cloned human embryos, and because the cloned embryos produced for research are no different from those that could be implanted in attempts to produce cloned children. The difficulty is compounded by what are, for now, unanswerable questions as to whether the research will in fact yield the benefits hoped for,

and whether other promising and morally nonproblematic approaches might yield comparable benefits. The Council, reflecting the differences of opinion in American society, is divided regarding the ethics of research involving (cloned) embryos.

13   To make clear to all what is at stake in the decision, Council Members have presented, as strongly as possible, the competing ethical cases for and against cloning-for-biomedical-research in the form of first-person attempts at moral suasion. Each case has tried to address what is owed to suffering humanity, to the human embryo, and to the broader society. Within each case, supporters of the position in question speak only for themselves, and not for the Council as a whole.

A. THE MORAL CASE FOR CLONING-FOR-BIOMEDICAL-RESEARCH

14   The moral case for cloning-for-biomedical-research rests on our obligation to try to relieve human suffering, an obligation that falls most powerfully on medical practitioners and biomedical researchers. We who support cloning-for-biomedical-research all agree that it may offer uniquely useful ways of investigating and possibly treating many chronic debilitating diseases and disabilities, providing aid and relief to millions. We also believe that the moral objections to this research are outweighed by the great good that may come from it. Up to this point, we who support this research all agree. But we differ among ourselves regarding the weight of the moral objections, owing to differences about the moral status of the cloned embryo. These differences of opinion are sufficient to warrant distinguishing two different moral positions within the moral case for cloning-for-biomedical-research:

15   *Position Number One.* Most Council Members who favor cloning-for-biomedical-research do so with serious moral concerns. Speaking only for ourselves, we acknowledge the following difficulties, but think that they can be addressed by setting proper boundaries.

- *Intermediate moral status.* While we take seriously concerns about the treatment of nascent human life, we believe there are sound moral reasons for not regarding the embryo in its earliest stages as the moral equivalent of a human person. We believe the embryo has a developing and intermediate moral worth that commands our special respect, but that it is morally permissible to use early-stage cloned human embryos in important research under strict regulation.
- *Deliberate creation for use.* We believe that concerns over the problem of deliberate creation of cloned embryos for use in research have merit, but when properly understood should not preclude cloning-for-biomedical-research. These embryos would not be "created for destruction," but for use in the service of life and medicine. They would be destroyed in the service of a great good, and this should not be obscured.
- *Going too far.* We acknowledge the concern that some researchers might seek to develop cloned embryos beyond the blastocyst stage, and for those of us who believe that the cloned embryo has a develop-

ing and intermediate moral status, this is a very real worry. We approve, therefore, only of research on cloned embryos that is strictly limited to the first fourteen days of development—a point near when the primitive streak is formed and before organ differentiation occurs.

- *Other moral hazards.* We believe that concerns about the exploitation of women and about the risk that cloning-for-biomedical-research could lead to cloning-to-produce-children can be adequately addressed by appropriate rules and regulations. These concerns need not frighten us into abandoning an important avenue of research.

Position Number Two. A few Council Members who favor cloning-for- 16 biomedical-research do not share all the ethical qualms expressed above. Speaking only for ourselves, we hold that this research, at least for the purposes presently contemplated, presents no special moral problems, and therefore should be endorsed with enthusiasm as a potential new means of gaining knowledge to serve humankind. Because we accord no special moral status to the early-stage cloned embryo and believe it should be treated essentially like all other human cells, we believe that the moral issues involved in this research are no different from those that accompany any biomedical research. What is required is the usual commitment to high standards for the quality of research, scientific integrity, and the need to obtain informed consent from donors of the eggs and somatic cells used in nuclear transfer.

B. THE MORAL CASE AGAINST CLONING-FOR-BIOMEDICAL-RESEARCH

The moral case against cloning-for-biomedical-research acknowledges the 17 possibility—though purely speculative at the moment—that medical benefits might come from this particular avenue of experimentation. But we believe it is morally wrong to exploit and destroy developing human life, even for good reasons, and that it is unwise to open the door to the many undesirable consequences that are likely to result from this research. We find it disquieting, even somewhat ignoble, to treat what are in fact seeds of the next generation as mere raw material for satisfying the needs of our own. Only for very serious reasons should progress toward increased knowledge and medical advances be slowed. But we believe that in this case such reasons are apparent.

- *Moral status of the cloned embryo.* We hold that the case for treating the early-stage embryo as simply the moral equivalent of all other human cells (Position Number Two, above) is simply mistaken: it denies the continuous history of human individuals from the embryonic to fetal to infant stages of existence; it misunderstands the meaning of potentiality; and it ignores the hazardous moral precedent that the routinized creation, use, and destruction of nascent human life would establish. We hold that the case for according the human embryo "intermediate and developing moral status" (Position Number One, above) is also unconvincing, for reasons both biological and moral. Attempts to ground the limited measure of respect owed to a maturing embryo in certain of its developmental features do not succeed, and the invoking of a "special

respect" owed to nascent human life seems to have little or no operative meaning if cloned embryos may be created in bulk and used routinely with impunity. If from one perspective the view that the embryo
seems to amount to little may invite a weakening of our respect, from
another perspective its seeming insignificance should awaken in us a
sense of shared humanity and a special obligation to protect it.

- *The exploitation of developing human life.* To engage in cloning-for-
biomedical-research requires the irreversible crossing of a very significant moral boundary: the creation of human life expressly and
exclusively for the purpose of its use in research, research that necessarily involves its deliberate destruction. If we permit this research to
proceed, we will effectively be endorsing the complete transformation
of nascent human life into nothing more than a resource or a tool. Doing so would coarsen our moral sensibilities and make us a different
society: one less humble toward that which we cannot fully understand,
less willing to extend the boundaries of human respect ever outward,
and more willing to transgress moral boundaries once it appears to be
in our own interests to do so.

- *Moral harm to society.* Even those who are uncertain about the precise
moral status of the human embryo have sound ethical-prudential reasons to oppose cloning-for-biomedical-research. Giving moral approval
to such research risks significant moral harm to our society by (1) crossing the boundary from sexual to asexual reproduction, thus approving
in principle the genetic manipulation and control of nascent human
life; (2) opening the door to other moral hazards, such as cloning-to-
produce-children or research on later-stage human embryos and fetuses; and (3) potentially putting the federal government in the novel
and unsavory position of mandating the destruction of nascent human
life. Because we are concerned not only with the fate of the cloned embryos but also with where this research will lead our society, we think
prudence requires us not to engage in this research.

- *What we owe the suffering.* We are certainly not deaf to the voices of
suffering patients; after all, each of us already shares or will share in the
hardships of mortal life. We and our loved ones are all patients or potential patients. But we are not only patients, and easing suffering is not
our only moral obligation. As much as we wish to alleviate suffering now
and to leave our children a world where suffering can be more effectively relieved, we also want to leave them a world in which we and they
want to live—a world that honors moral limits, that respects all life
whether strong or weak, and that refuses to secure the good of some
human beings by sacrificing the lives of others.

PUBLIC POLICY OPTIONS

18   The Council recognizes the challenges and risks of moving from moral assessment to public policy. Reflections on the "social contract" between science
and society highlight both the importance of scientific freedom and the need

for boundaries. We recognize the special difficulty in formulating sound public policy in this area, given that the two ethically distinct matters—cloning-to-produce-children and cloning-for-biomedical-research—will be mutually affected or implicated in any attempts to legislate about either. Nevertheless, our ethical and policy analysis leads us to the conclusion that some deliberate public policy at the federal level is needed in the area of human cloning.

We reviewed the following seven possible policy options and considered their relative strengths and weaknesses: (1) Professional self-regulation but no federal legislative action ("self-regulation"); (2) A ban on cloning-to-produce-children, with neither endorsement nor restriction of cloning-for-biomedical-research ("ban plus silence"); (3) A ban on cloning-to-produce-children, with regulation of the use of cloned embryos for biomedical research ("ban plus regulation"); (4) Governmental regulation, with no legislative prohibitions ("regulation of both"); (5) A ban on all human cloning, whether to produce children or for biomedical research ("ban on both"); (6) A ban on cloning-to-produce-children, with a moratorium or temporary ban on cloning-for-biomedical- research ("ban plus moratorium"); or (7) A moratorium or temporary ban on all human cloning, whether to produce children or for biomedical research ("moratorium on both"). 19

THE COUNCIL'S POLICY RECOMMENDATIONS

Having considered the benefits and drawbacks of each of these options, and taken into account our discussions and reflections throughout this report, the Council recommends two possible policy alternatives, each supported by a portion of the Members. 20

Majority Recommendation: Ten Members of the Council recommend *a ban on cloning-to-produce-children combined with a four-year moratorium on cloning-for-biomedical-research. We also call for a federal review of current and projected practices of human embryo research, preimplantation genetic diagnosis, genetic modification of human embryos and gametes, and related matters, with a view to recommending and shaping ethically sound policies for the entire field.* Speaking only for ourselves, those of us who support this recommendation do so for some or all of the following reasons: 21

- By permanently banning cloning-to-produce-children, this policy gives force to the strong ethical verdict against cloning-to-produce-children, unanimous in this council (and in Congress) and widely supported by the American people. And by enacting a four-year moratorium on the creation of cloned embryos, it establishes an additional safeguard not afforded by policies that would allow the production of cloned embryos to proceed without delay.
- It calls for and provides time for further democratic deliberation about cloning-for-biomedical research, a subject about which the nation is divided and where there remains great uncertainty. A national discourse on this subject has not yet taken place in full, and a moratorium, by making it impossible for either side to cling to the status-quo, would force

both to make their full case before the public. By banning all cloning for a time, it allows us to seek moral consensus on whether or not we should cross a major moral boundary (creating nascent cloned human life solely for research) and prevents our crossing it without deliberate decision. It would afford time for scientific evidence, now sorely lacking, to be gathered—from animal models and other avenues of human research—that might give us a better sense of whether cloning-for-biomedical-research would work as promised, and whether other morally nonproblematic approaches might be available. It would promote a fuller and better-informed public debate. And it would show respect for the deep moral concerns of the large number of Americans who have serious ethical objections to this research.

- Some of us hold that cloning-for-biomedical-research can never be ethically pursued, and endorse a moratorium to enable us to continue to make our case in a democratic way. Others of us support the moratorium because it would provide the time and incentive required to develop a system of national regulation that might come into use if, at the end of the four-year period, the moratorium were not reinstated or made permanent. Such a system could not be developed overnight, and therefore even those who support the research but want it regulated should see that at the very least a pause is required. In the absence of a moratorium, few proponents of the research would have much incentive to institute an effective regulatory system. Moreover, the very process of proposing such regulations would clarify the moral and prudential judgments involved in deciding whether and how to proceed with this research.

- A moratorium on cloning-for-biomedical-research would enable us to consider this activity in the larger context of research and technology in the areas of developmental biology, embryo research, and genetics, and to pursue a more comprehensive federal regulatory system for setting and executing policy in the entire area.

- Finally, we believe that a moratorium, rather than a lasting ban, signals a high regard for the value of biomedical research and an enduring concern for patients and families whose suffering such research may help alleviate. It would reaffirm the principle that science can progress while upholding the community's moral norms, and would therefore reaffirm the community's moral support for science and biomedical technology.

22   The decision before us is of great importance. Creating cloned embryos for *any* purpose requires crossing a major moral boundary, with grave risks and likely harms, and once we cross it there will be no turning back. Our society should take the time to make a judgment that is well-informed and morally sound, respectful of strongly held views, and representative of the priorities and principles of the American people. We believe this ban-plus-moratorium proposal offers the best means of achieving these goals. . . .

Minority Recommendation: Seven Members of the Council recommend 23
*a ban on cloning-to-produce-children, with regulation of the use of cloned
embryos for biomedical research.* Speaking only for ourselves, those of
us who support this recommendation do so for some or all of the following
reasons:

- By permanently banning cloning-to-produce-children, this policy gives
  force to the strong ethical verdict against cloning-to-produce-children,
  unanimous in this Council (and in Congress) and widely supported by
  the American people. We believe that a ban on the transfer of cloned
  embryos to a woman's uterus would be a sufficient and effective legal
  safeguard against the practice.
- *It approves cloning-for-biomedical-research and permits it to proceed
  without substantial delay.* This is the most important advantage of this
  proposal. The research shows great promise, and its actual value can
  only be determined by allowing it to go forward now. Regardless of how
  much time we allow it, no amount of experimentation with animal models can provide the needed understanding of human diseases. The special benefits from working with stem cells from cloned human embryos
  cannot be obtained using embryos obtained by IVF. We believe this research could provide relief to millions of Americans, and that the government should therefore support it, within sensible limits imposed by
  regulation.
- It would establish, *as a condition of proceeding,* the necessary regulatory protections to avoid abuses and misuses of cloned embryos. These
  regulations might touch on the secure handling of embryos, licensing
  and prior review of research projects, the protection of egg donors, and
  the provision of equal access to benefits.
- Some of us also believe that mechanisms to regulate cloning-for-
  biomedical-research should be part of a larger regulatory program
  governing all research involving human embryos, and that the federal
  government should initiate a review of present and projected practices
  of human embryo research, with the aim of establishing reasonable policies on the matter.

Permitting cloning-for-biomedical-research now, while governing it 24
through a prudent and sensible regulatory regime, is the most appropriate
way to allow important research to proceed while insuring that abuses are
prevented. We believe that the legitimate concerns about human cloning
expressed throughout this report are sufficiently addressed by this ban-plus-
regulation proposal, and that the nation should affirm and support the responsible effort to find treatments and cures that might help many who are
suffering.

QUESTIONS FOR READING

1. What are the two purposes of human cloning?
2. Sum up in your own words the process for human cloning. Sum up the process used in cloning-for-biomedical-research.
3. What is the Council's position on cloning-to-produce-children? What are the possible merits of such action? What are the possible disadvantages?
4. How does the Council rebut the possible merits of cloning-to-produce-children? What are the problems, both practical and ethical, in the Council's view?
5. What are the possible benefits of cloning-for-biomedical-research? What are the possible disadvantages? What is the Council's position on cloning for research?
6. Of those who favor cloning-for-biomedical-research, how do they differ on the moral issues surrounding this research?
7. What are the moral arguments of those who oppose cloning-for-biomedical-research?
8. What is the majority public-policy recommendation of the Council? What are their arguments in support of their recommendation?
9. What is the minority public-policy recommendation of the Council? What are their arguments in support of their recommendation?

QUESTIONS FOR REASONING AND ANALYSIS

1. Examine, first, the arguments against cloning for children. Does the Council make a convincing argument? Much of their argument turns on the repeated statement of the "virtual" identity of the cloned child and the original donor. Is it accurate to see the cloned child as a reproduction of the original donor? Why or why not? To what extent, if any, do these subtle but important distinctions affect your view of their argument on this particular point? Explain.
2. Examine the argument supporting cloning for research. This argument turns on the assertion that the embryo in the first fourteen days does not have the same moral significance as it does after those first fourteen days—as well as on the relief of suffering that may result from such research. Does the Council make a convincing argument? How much does the relief of suffering count in your evaluation? How much does the use of embryos only in the earliest stages count in your evaluation? Explain.

QUESTIONS FOR REFLECTING AND WRITING

1. What, in your opinion, is the most critical issue in deciding for or against cloning-for-biomedical-research? Why?
2. One issue is the moral one, but another is the practical public policy issue. Will a four-year moratorium on cloning-for-biomedical-research enlighten the debate meaningfully? Why or why not? Can a moratorium, in practical terms, be implemented? If so, how? If not, why not?
3. If one allows cloning-for-biomedical-research, will it be possible to control cloning-to-produce-children? Should it be? Where do you stand on these parts of the debate?

THE HORROR | JOSEPH BOTTUM

A graduate of Georgetown University and Boston College (with a Ph.D. in philosophy), Joseph Bottum is books and arts editor of the *Weekly Standard*. His essays, reviews, and poetry have been published in many journals and magazines, and he also hosts *Book Talk*, a syndicated radio program. His collection of poems is *The Fall and Other Poems* (2001). His contribution to a debate on bioethics in *Public Interest* appeared in the Winter 2003 issue.

PREREADING QUESTIONS   What does Bottum's title suggest to you about his position in the bioethics debate? What did the Council vote to ban? What did they vote just a moratorium on?

There are three directions in which we might take a discussion of the report of the President's Council on Bioethics. We might first talk about the issue of cloning itself. Then again, we might turn to the deliberations of the President's Council, as presented in this . . . [chapter], and talk about the divisions and insights of the council's members. Finally, we might take this discussion to be about politics—which is to say, the impact and the importance, in the real world, of the policy recommendations made by the President's Council. About all three of these, I have enormous amounts to say—more than could ever be fit into the time we have. But here are a few first thoughts.

Among the finest features of the report is the perfect civility of its thoughtful deliberations. And yet, that civility comes at a cost, which I am not sure we have fully reckoned. While I applaud nearly all of its work, the council's report does not, for example, sufficiently express the horror and repugnance that the idea of cloning arouses in me.

Perhaps an analogy will help make that feeling clear. I once tried to write a poem about an attractive young woman I had seen walking along the street. I suppose she was not beautiful, per se, but then I have reached the age at which youth itself begins to seem beautiful. Those of you who are still young may not understand what I am talking about. But for those of us growing old, there is a lure in youthfulness—the tautness of it, the glow.

And there is also a crime: to act upon that lure, to seek one's own youth restored by leeching on the youthfulness of others. This is the mockable widower seeking a young bride in Molière's comedies; it is the sexual sickness expressed by Charles Dickens in *Nicholas Nickleby* when the aged Arthur Gride drools over the young Madeleine after using her father's debts to force her into his power.

But I have in mind something more than putting an armful of warm girl in an old man's cold bed. Behind this stands the fantasy of age, that would sacrifice the young to buy its way back from the aches and diseases that age is prone to. There is, for instance, the old witch who wants to fatten up Hansel and Gretel before she bakes them in her oven and devours their youth. And then there is Elizabeth Bathory—the seventeenth-century Hungarian countess and perhaps the most famous figure to come out of Transylvania since Vlad the

Impaler. Her trial records estimate that she slaughtered 600 young virgins in a decade, in order to bathe in their youth-restoring blood.

6   Let me bring this analogy home. It seems to me that the proponents of much of the biotech revolution—the supporters and enablers of the Brave New World of eugenic biotechnology—are forced into the uncomfortable position of insisting that the Countess Bathory was absolutely right, at least about her goals. She merely chose the wrong means.

7   I mean that not quite in the provocative sense in which I phrased it. She was obviously wrong about the effects of virgins' blood, and she lacked the help of Advanced Cell Technology's laboratories in Massachusetts. But she also chose the wrong means when she used living, conscious human beings. The proponents of cloning-for-biomedical-research insist that the objects upon which modern laboratories work are not living human beings but cells—or biological accidents, or bits of human beings—which, because of ancient prejudices, must be spoken of in reverential ways, but which need not be treated any differently than a fingernail clipping or, in that great euphemism of abortionists, "the product of conception."

8   But I want to think about this in terms of human motivation. Indeed, when the President's Council distinguishes "cloning-for-biomedical-research" from "cloning-to-produce-children," it invites us to notice that the primary distinction between them is, in fact, a matter of human motivation—namely, the purpose for which the biotechnologist created the clone.

9   Much has been made, by Francis Fukuyama and others, about the recent efforts of scientists to complete the Baconian project—the great vision of Francis Bacon that science will finally ameliorate the human condition, so that we will all be happy, diseaseless, and nigh on immortal. I think it is right to notice this impending fulfillment of the promise that Bacon made centuries ago. But there is something else to notice as well—namely, that Bacon required for his dream that we dismiss all notion of purpose and goal for the objects of science. Indeed, Bacon's *New Organon* is filled with attacks upon the Aristotelian idea of final causation, a natural purpose or aim for things.

10   But goals don't actually go away just because we want them to. In the space opened up by the dismissal of final cause from science, there entered the malleability of things to the human will. We give things their purpose; we give them their final cause. The human act is conceived to be the only thing in the universe that has motive, purpose, goal, or aim—and those motives will eventually eat up the reality of everything else.

11   In fact, they have already eaten up reality. There are serious political questions that might be raised about the council's report. But think about this: The council was unanimous in wanting to prohibit forever cloning-to-produce-children, and could only by the barest majority reach the compromise of a temporary moratorium on cloning-for-biomedical-research. This seems to me exactly backwards. However much cloning-to-produce-children proceeds along defective means, it still aims at the natural cause of procreation. It wants to make babies.

Cloning-for-biomedical-research, on the other hand, has abandoned the 12 goal. Embryos, fetuses, blastocysts, activated eggs, products of SCNT, whatever euphemism is floating around this week—cloning-for-biomedical-research takes those objects and makes them plastic playthings for the human will. What is worse, it is the human will traveling down a line of motivation that is inherently suspect—if we remember Molière and Dickens, and the old, old stories. We are becoming the people that, once upon a time, our ancestors used fairy tales to warn their children against.

Now, Francis Bacon's scientific vision of modernity is not the only one. 13 There is also a literary vision of modernity. And from Mary Shelley's *Frankenstein* to Aldous Huxley's *Brave New World,* the literary imagination has not pictured the prospect of manufactured human beings with much joy. From Robert Louis Stevenson's *Dr. Jekyll and Mr. Hyde* to H. G. Wells' *The Island of Dr. Moreau,* the literary imagination has not been much taken with scientists who manipulate the deep things of life just because they can.

The truth is, after reading these authors, I worry about people who reach 14 into the stuff of life and twist it to their will. I worry about people who act simply because they can. If they lived in crumbling castles—their hair standing up on end and their voices howling in maniacal laughter—we'd know them to be mad scientists. But they wear nice white lab coats, and their pleasant-looking chief executive appears on television to assure us that they are really acting for the best of medical motives and, besides, there is a great deal of money to be made in biotech and pharmaceutical stocks.

Sometimes the disingenousness is unbearable. Evading the regulations in 15 France, the French company Clonaid recently opened a laboratory in Ivory Coast, and its spokeswoman announced that they had done so in response to the great demand for cloning in sub-Saharan Africa. Ah, yes, my wife suggested: Those poor, starving Africans, desperate for food, drinking water, and the latest fads in biotechnology.

But Clonaid's move to Africa seems to me a final proof of the dangerous- 16 ness of unlimited human will. The people who say that this technology can be regulated are simply ignorant of human nature. If you were to put up a lever with a sign that said, "Don't touch or the world will be destroyed," the paint wouldn't even be dry before someone's last words were, "I just wanted to see what would happen."

We have to applaud the seriousness that Leon Kass has brought to Wash- 17 ington, the tone and tenor of the deliberations, and the report that issued from the President's Council on Bioethics. But I think we must also raise questions about the civility that is the report's finest feature.

QUESTIONS FOR READING

1. What is Bottum's subject?
2. What is his view of the aging trying to regain their youth through the use of others?

3. What is the difference, in the author's view, between cloning-for-biomedical-research and cloning-to-produce-children?

4. What was Francis Bacon's vision of science? What was necessary, in Bacon's eyes, for the achievement of his vision?

5. What is, according to Bottum, backward about the Council's decisions?

6. What dangerous element are we ignoring?

QUESTIONS FOR REASONING AND ANALYSIS

1. What is Bottum's claim? Why does he take exception to the Council's positions?

2. What is his primary reason for disagreeing with the Council's views?

3. What evidence does he offer in support of his primary reason?

4. How would you describe the author's tone? How might his tone help his argument?

QUESTIONS FOR REFLECTING AND WRITING

1. Do you agree that "unlimited human will" is dangerous? Why or why not?

2. If you agree that "unlimited human will" is dangerous, do you agree that this is a good and sufficient reason to ban all research into or using cloning of human cells? Why or why not?

3. Huxley's novel *Brave New World* is repeatedly referred to in debates on bioethics. Have you read the novel? If so, how would you explain its connection to the bioethics debate to someone who has not read the novel? If not, do you think that you should read the novel as part of your research in understanding the issues surrounding bioethics? Why or why not?

THE VIRTUAL CHILD | LEE M. SILVER

Holding a Harvard University Ph.D. in biophysics, Lee Silver is a professor in the Department of Molecular Biology at Princeton University and in the Woodrow Wilson School of Public and International Affairs. He is the author of many articles and books, including *The Last Taboo, Genetics: From Genes to Genomes,* and *Remaking Eden: Cloning and Beyond in a Brave New World* (1977). The following is from a chapter in *Remaking Eden.*

PREREADING QUESTIONS What does the term *eugenics* mean to you? What connotation does the word have for you? What might be the advantages of selecting and/or rejecting particular genes before they are transmitted to one's children?

1   There are some people who equate the early embryo with a human being that is deserving of the same respect as a child or adult, based on the idea that each human embryo contains a human spirit, deposited within it at the time of fertilization. These people are generally opposed to the destruction of any embryos at any time, whether it is through the normal practice of IVF or in response to embryo selection. A scientific critique of this viewpoint was

presented earlier and will not be considered further here. Instead, I will focus on ethical concerns raised by people who are willing to accept the traditional practice of IVF—where embryos are chosen randomly for introduction into a woman's uterus—but are troubled specifically by genetic selection.

Once people reject the notion that an early human embryo is equivalent 2 to a human being, the reasons for opposing embryo selection are varied, but they can all be classified under the rubric of eugenics. *Eugenics.* The word causes people to shudder. But what exactly is eugenics and why is it considered so bad? We must answer these questions before it is possible to continue our discussion.

Unfortunately, answers are not that easy to come by. As the political sci- 3 entist Diane Paul writes, "'Eugenics' is a word with nasty connotations but an indeterminate meaning. Indeed, it often reveals more about its users' attitudes than it does about the policies, practices, intentions, or consequences labeled. . . . The superficiality of public debate on eugenics is partly a reflection of these diverse, sometimes contradictory meanings, which result in arguments that often fail to engage."

In its original connotation, eugenics referred to the idea that a society 4 might be able to improve its gene pool by exerting control over the breeding practices of its citizens. In America, early twentieth-century attempts to put this idea into practice brought about the forced sterilization of people deemed genetically inferior because of (supposed) reduced intelligence, minor physical disabilities, or possession of a (supposed) criminal character. And further "protection of the American gene pool" was endeavored by congressional enactment of harsh immigration policies aimed at restricting the influx of people from Eastern and Southern Europe—regions seen as harboring populations (which included all four grandparents of the author . . .) with undesirable genes. Two decades later, Nazi Germany used an even more drastic approach in its attempt to eliminate—in a single generation—those who carried undesirable genes. In the aftermath of World War II, all of these misguided attempts to practice eugenics were rightly repudiated as discriminatory, murderous, and infringing upon the natural right of human beings to reproductive liberty. *Eugenics* was now clearly a dirty word.

While eugenics was defined originally in terms of a lofty *outcome*—the 5 improvement of a society's gene pool—its contemporary usage has fallen to the level of a *process*. In its new meaning, eugenics is the notion of human beings exerting control over the genes that are transmitted from one generation to the next—irrespective of whether the action itself could have any effect on the gene pool, and irrespective of whether it's society as a whole or an individual family that exerts the control. According to this definition, the practice of embryo screening is clearly eugenics. Since eugenics is horrible, it follows logically that embryo screening is horrible.

Although the fallacy in this logic is transparent, it is remarkable how often 6 it is used by contemporary commentators to criticize reprogenetic technologies. A recent book entitled *The Quest for Perfection: The Drive to Breed*

Better Human Beings uses this theme over and over again to castigate one reproductive practice after another. But simply placing a eugenics label on something does not make it wrong. The Nazi eugenics program was wrong not only because it was mass murder, but also because it was an attempt at genocide. The forced sterilizations in America were wrong because they restricted the reproductive liberties of innocent people. And restrictive immigration policies directed against particular regions of the world are still wrong because they are designed to discriminate directly against particular ethnic groups. Clearly, none of these wrongs can be applied to the voluntary practice of embryo screening by a pair of potential parents.

7   Once we remove ourselves from the eugenics trap, it becomes possible to consider the ethical concerns that surround embryo screening in the absence of anxiety-producing labels. Again, I want to emphasize my intent to consider only those concerns related to genetic selection rather than the random disposal of embryos during the normal process of IVF. I will start out with five general concerns based on concepts of morality and naturalness. I will move on to concerns about the negative impact that embryo screening could have on society. . . .

IT IS IMMORAL TO CHOOSE ONE CHILD OVER ANOTHER

8   When embryo selection is equated with choosing children, there is a palpable sense of revulsion. It is not hard to understand this feeling. Often in the past, and in some places still, genetic choice is exercised through infanticide. The particular choice made most often in some Third World countries is boy babies over girl babies, who are suffocated or drowned soon after birth. In other societies, it is infants with physical disabilities that are most often killed.

9   But the analogy of embryo screening to infanticide is a false one. What embryo screening provides is the ability to select genotypes, not children. Today, parents can use the technology to make sure that their *one* child—whom they had always planned on bringing into the world—is not afflicted with Tay-Sachs.

10   Even in the future, when it becomes possible to draw computer images based on genetic profiles, embryos will still not be *real* children. Virtual children exist only in one's mind, and the consummation of an actual fertilization event is not even a prerequisite for their creation. Once genetic profiles have been obtained for any man and any woman, it becomes possible to determine the virtual gametes that each might produce. Each combination of a virtual male gamete and a virtual female gamete will produce a virtual child. And each one of the trillions upon trillions of virtual children made possible by virtual intercourse between a single man and woman (who may never have met) could be associated with a computer-generated profile as extensive and detailed as those presented for the virtual Alices at the start of this chapter. At the end of the story, however, only one real Alice emerged. And what her parents chose for her were the alleles that she received from each of them.

IT IS WRONG TO TAMPER WITH THE NATURAL ORDER

11   This concern is expressed by many who are not particularly religious in the traditional sense. Still, they feel that there is some predetermined goal for the

evolution of humankind, and that this goal can only be achieved by the current *random* process through which our genes are transmitted to our children. However, unfettered evolution is never predetermined, and not necessarily associated with progress—it is simply a response to unpredictable environmental changes. If the asteroid that hit our planet 60 million years ago had flown past instead, there would never have been any human beings at all. And whatever the natural order might be, it is not necessarily good. The smallpox virus was part of the natural order until it was forced into extinction by human intervention. I doubt that anyone mourns its demise.

EMBRYO SELECTION FOR ADVANTAGEOUS TRAITS IS A MISUSE OF MEDICINE

The purpose of medicine is to prevent suffering and heal those with disease. Based on this definition, it is clear that embryo selection could be put to uses that lie far outside this scope. But medical doctors have used their knowledge and skills to work in other nonmedical areas such as nontherapeutic cosmetic surgery. If we accept the right of medical doctors to enter into nonmedical business practices, we have to accept their right to develop private programs of embryo selection as well. 12

One could argue that since the embryo screening technology was developed with the use of government funds, it should only be used for societally approved purposes. But government funds have been used in the development of nearly all forms of modern technology, both medical and nonmedical. This association has never been viewed as a reason for restricting the use of any other technology in private profit-making ventures. 13

EMBRYO SELECTION TAKES THE NATURAL WONDER AWAY FROM THE BIRTH OF A CHILD

Many prospective parents choose not to learn the sex of their child before birth, even when it is known to their physician through prenatal testing. There is the feeling that this choice allows the moment of birth to be one of parental discovery. If a child's characteristics were pre-determined in many more ways than just sex, many fear that the sense of awe associated with birth would disappear. For some, this may be true. But this is a personal concern that could play a role in whether an individual couple chooses embryo selection for themselves. It can't be used as a rationale to stop others whose feelings are different. 14

WHETHER INTENTIONAL OR NOT, EMBRYO SELECTION COULD AFFECT THE GENE POOL

If embryo selection were available to all people in the world and there was general acceptance of its use, then the gene pool might indeed be affected very quickly. The first result would be the almost-complete elimination of a whole host of common alleles with lethal consequences such as Tay-Sachs, sickle cell anemia, and cystic fibrosis. 15

There are some who argue that it would be wrong to eliminate these alleles, or others, because they might provide *a hidden advantage to the gene* 16 *pool.* This is another version of the "natural order" argument, based here on the idea that even alleles with deleterious effects in isolated individuals exist because they provide some benefit to the species as a whole. Those who make this argument believe that all members of a species somehow function together in genetic terms.

17   This point of view has no basis in reality. It results from a misunderstanding of what the gene pool is, and why we should, or should not, care about it. The concept of the gene pool was invented as a tool for developing mathematical models by biologists who study populations of animals or plants. It is calculated as the frequencies with which particular alleles at particular genes occur across all of the members of a population that interbreed with each other.

18   Most healthy individuals are not carriers of the Tay-Sachs or cystic fibrosis alleles, and if given the choice, I doubt if anyone would want to have his or her genome changed to become a carrier. So on what basis can we insist that others receive a genotype that we've rejected? There is none. Genes do not function in human populations (except in a virtual sense imagined by biologists), they function within individuals. And there is no species-wide knowledge or storage of particular alleles for use in future generations.

19   In fact, there is not even a tendency or rationale for a species to preserve itself at all. At each stage throughout the evolution of our ancestors—from rodentlike mammals to apelike primates to *Australopithecus* to *Homo habilis* to *Homo erectus* and, finally, *Homo sapiens*—small groups of individuals gained genetic advantages that allowed them to survive even as they participated in the death of the species from which they arose! Survival and evolution operate at the level of the individual, not the species.

20   There are some who are not concerned about abstract concepts like the gene pool and evolution so much as they are worried that the genetic elimination of mental illness (an unlikely possibility) would prevent the birth of future Ernest Hemingways and Edgar Allan Poes. This worry is based on the demonstrated association between manic depression (also known as bipolar affective disorder) and creative genius.

21   This could indeed be a future loss for society. But once again, how can we insist that others be inflicted with a predisposition to mental disease (one we wouldn't want ourselves) on the chance that a brilliant work of art would emerge? And if particular aberrant mental states are deemed beneficial to society, the use of hallucinogenic or other types of psychoactive drugs that could achieve the same effect—in timed doses—would seem preferable to mutant genes. It is also important to point out that the perceived loss of mad genius from future society is virtual, not real. If the manic depressive Edgar Allan Poe were never born, we wouldn't miss *The Raven.* Likewise, we don't miss all of the additional piano concertos that Mozart would have composed if he hadn't died at the age of thirty-four.

EMBRYO SELECTION WILL BRING ABOUT DISCRIMINATION

22   With the use of embryo selection, prospective parents will be able to ensure that their children are born without a variety of non-life-threatening

disabilities. These will include a wide range of physical impediments, as well as physiological disabilities (such as deafness or blindness) and learning disabilities.

Many people with hereditary disabilities have overcome adversity to live 23 long and fruitful lives. These people are concerned that the widespread acceptance of embryo selection against their disabilities could reinforce the attitude that they are not full-fledged members of society, and not deserving of love and attention.

Of course, disabilities can result from either genetic or environmental factors. And one common environmental cause of disability in the past was the polio virus, which resulted in paralysis, muscular atrophy, and often physical deformity. Inoculation of children with the polio vaccine was not generally seen as discriminatory against those who were already disabled. Why should genetic inoculation against disability be viewed any differently?

One difference could be in the access of society's members to the inoculation. The polio vaccine was provided to all children, regardless of class or socioeconomic status, while embryo selection may only be available to those families who can afford it. The philosopher Philip Kitcher suggests that as a consequence, "the genetic conditions the affluent are concerned to avoid will be far more common among the poor—they will become 'lower-class' diseases, other people's problems. Interest in finding methods of treatment or for providing supportive environments for those born with the diseases may well wane."

This is a serious concern. But it is important to point out that the privileged 26 class already reduces the likelihood of childhood disabilities through their superior ability to control the environment within which a fetus and child develops. People who argue that embryo selection should *not* be used to prevent serious childhood disabilities because it's unfair to those families who are unable to afford the technology should logically want to ban access of the privileged class to environmental advantages provided to their children as well. Political systems based on this premise have not fared well at the end of the twentieth century.

The alternative method for preventing inequality is referred to as "utopian 27 eugenics" by Kitcher and is based on the vision of George Bernard Shaw of a society in which all citizens have free and equal access to the same disease-preventing technologies (and environments). Although discrimination would not be based on class differences in this utopian society, it could still be aggravated by the overall reduction in the number of disabled persons.

It's important to understand the nature of the relationship that might exist 28 between embryo selection and discrimination against the disabled. Embryo selection will not itself be the cause of discrimination, just as the polio vaccine could not be blamed for discrimination against those afflicted with polio. All it could do, perhaps, is change people's attitudes toward those less fortunate than themselves. An enlightened society would not allow this to happen. Is it proper to blame a technology in advance for the projected moral shortcomings of an unenlightened, future society?

EMBRYO SELECTION WILL BE COERCIVE

29   I distinguished embryo selection from abhorrent eugenic policies of the past with the claim that embryo selection would be freely employed in Western society by prospective parents who were not beholden to the will of the state. As a consequence, the use of the technology would not be associated with any restrictions on reproductive liberty.

30   There are social science critics who say that this claim is naive. They fear that societal acceptance of embryo selection will lead inevitably to its use in a coercive manner. Coercion can be both subtle and direct. Subtle pressures will exist in the form of societal norms that discourage the birth of children deemed unfit in some way. More direct pressures will come from insurance companies or state regulations that limit health coverage only to children who were embryonically screened for the absence of particular disease and predisposition genotypes.

31   How coercion of this type is viewed depends on the political sensibilities of the viewer. Civil libertarians tend to see any type of coercion as an infringement on reproductive rights. And liberal libertarians would be strongly opposed to policies that discriminated against those born with avoidable medical conditions.

32   Communitarians, however, may view the refusal to preselect against such medical conditions as inherently selfish. According to this point of view, such refusal would—by necessity—force society to help the unfortunate children through the expenditure of large amounts of resources and money that would otherwise be available to promote the welfare of many more people.

33   The communitarian viewpoint is considered shocking to many in America today because, as Diane Paul says, "the notion that individual desires should sometimes be subordinated to a larger social good has itself gone out of fashion, to be replaced by an ethic of radical individualism."

EMBRYO SELECTION COULD HAVE A DRAMATIC LONG-TERM EFFECT ON SOCIETY

34   Embryo selection is currently used by a tiny fraction of prospective parents to screen for a tiny number of disease genotypes. For the moment, its influence on society is nonexistent. In fact, there are many critics who think that far too much attention is devoted to a biomedical "novelty item" with no relevance as a solution to any of the problems faced by the world. But with each coming year, the power of the technology will expand, and its application will become more efficient. Slowly but surely, embryo selection will be incorporated into American culture, just as other reproductive technologies have been in the past. And sooner or later, people will be forced to consider its impact on the society within which they live.

35   The nature of that impact will depend as much on the political *status quo* and social norms of the future as they do on the power of the technology itself. In a utopian society of the kind imagined by George Bernard Shaw, all citizens would have access to the technology, all would have the chance to benefit from it, but none would be forced to use it. In this vision of utopia, embryo selection

would take an entire society down the same path, wherever it might lead. Unfortunately, if future protocols of embryo selection remain in any way similar to those used now, the technology will remain prohibitively expensive, and utopian access would bankrupt a country.

A different scenario emerges if Americans hold fast to the overriding importance of personal liberty and personal fortune in guiding what individuals are allowed and able to do. The first effects on society will be small. Affluent parents will have children who are less prone to disease, and even more likely to succeed (on average) than they might have been otherwise as a simple consequence of the affluent environment within which they are raised. But with each generation, the fruits of selection will accumulate. . . . [I]n every subsequent generation, selection could become more and more refined. 36

It is impossible to predict the cumulative outcome of generation upon generation of embryo selection, but some things seem likely. The already wide gap between the rich and the poor could grow even larger as well-off parents provide their children not only with the best education that money can buy, and the best overall environment that money can buy, but the "best cumulative set of genes" as well. Emotional stability, long-term happiness, inborn talents, increased creativity, and healthy bodies—these could be the starting points chosen for the children of the rich. Obesity, heart disease, hypertension, alcoholism, mental illness, and predispositions to cancer—these will be the diseases left to drift randomly among the families of the underclass. 37

But before we rush to ban the use of embryo selection by the privileged, we must carefully consider the grounds on which such a ban would be based. Is this future scenario different—in more than degree—from a present in which embryo selection plays no role at all? If it is within the rights of parents to spend $100,000 for an exclusive private school education, why is it not also within their rights to spend the same amount of money to make sure that a child inherits a particular set of their genes? Environment and genes stand side by side. Both contribute to a child's chances for achievement and success in life, although neither guarantees it. If we allow money to buy an advantage in one, the claim for stopping the other is hard to make, especially in a society that gives women the right to abort for any reason at all. 38

These logical arguments have been tossed aside in some countries like Germany, Norway, Austria, and Switzerland, as well as states like Louisiana, Maine, Minnesota, New Hampshire, and Pennsylvania, where recently passed laws seem to prohibit the use of embryo selection for any purpose whatsoever. In these countries and states, no distinction is made between the prevention of Tay-Sachs disease and selection in favor of so-called positive traits. 39

But if the short history of surrogacy is any guide, all such attempts to limit this technology will be doomed to failure. Many Tay-Sachs-carrying parents will surely feel that it is their "God-given" right to have access to a technology that allowed earlier couples to have nonafflicted children, and just as surely, there will always be a clinic in some open state or country that will accommodate their wishes. And if the technology is available for this one purpose, it will also be available for others. 40

41   It certainly does seem that embryo selection will be with us forever—whether we like it or not—as a powerful tool to be used by more and more parents to choose which of their genes to give to their children. But . . . the power of this tool pales in comparison to what becomes possible when people gain the ability to choose not only from among their own genes, but from any gene that one can imagine, whether or not it already exists.

QUESTIONS FOR READING

1. What does IVF stand for?
2. What is the source of the negative connotation of the word *eugenics*?
3. Why should eugenics in its negative connotation not apply to embryo screening?
4. Why is embryo screening not choosing one child over another?
5. How does Silver defend embryo screening as within the purview of medicine?
6. In what sense is concern for the gene pool another version of the "natural order" argument? Why is it not a valid argument for rejecting embryo screening?
7. Why is the possible discrimination against the disabled not a good reason for rejecting embryo selection? What advantages do the affluent already have that the poor do not have?
8. What types of coercion to use embryo selection might develop? What is the communitarian response to this anxiety?
9. How will embryo selection affect future generations? Why should the effects not lead us to reject this technological advance?

QUESTIONS FOR REASONING AND ANALYSIS

1. What is Silver's implied claim? What does his reasoning support?
2. Why is defining and discussing eugenics a necessary first step in Silver's argument?
3. Examine the structure of Silver's argument; how is it organized?
4. What *type* of argument can this be classified as? What is Silver "doing" with each of his eight points or concerns about embryo selection?

QUESTIONS FOR REFLECTING AND WRITING

1. What is the most important new idea or new fact in this essay for you? Why did you select that idea or fact?
2. Has Silver responded to each of the ethical concerns in a convincing way? Why or why not? Are some issues more troubling to you than others? If so, which ones and why? Are some rebuttals of Silver more convincing than others? If so, which sections of his argument are, in your view, weakest?
3. If you had the opportunity to remove disease-carrying genes and select genes for health or looks or intelligence for your future child, would you do so? If so, why? If not, why not?

OF HEADLESS MICE . . . AND MEN[1] | CHARLES KRAUTHAMMER

A graduate of Harvard Medical School and board certified in psychiatry, Charles Krauthammer (b. 1950) is a syndicated columnist and a regular on the political talk show *Inside Washington*. He has won a Pulitzer Prize for political commentary. He has also served on the President's Council on Bioethics, but he wrote the following essay for *Time* magazine in 1998, before the Council was instituted.

PREREADING QUESTIONS   Who is "Dolly"? Why is she significant in the debate on bioethics?

Last year Dolly the cloned sheep was received with wonder, titters and 1 some vague apprehension. Last week the announcement by a Chicago physicist that he is assembling a team to produce the first human clone occasioned yet another wave of Brave New World anxiety. But the scariest news of all—and largely overlooked—comes from two obscure labs, at the University of Texas and at the University of Bath. During the past four years, one group created headless mice; the other, headless tadpoles.

For sheer Frankenstein wattage, the purposeful creation of these animal 2 monsters has no equal. Take the mice. Researchers found the gene that tells the embryo to produce the head. They deleted it. They did this in a thousand mice embryos, four of which were born. I use the term loosely. Having no way to breathe, the mice died instantly.

Why then create them? The Texas researchers want to learn how genes de- 3 termine embryo development. But you don't have to be a genius to see the true utility of manufacturing headless creatures: for their organs—fully formed, perfectly useful, ripe for plundering.

Why should you be panicked? Because humans are next. "It would almost 4 certainly be possible to produce human bodies without a forebrain," Princeton biologist Lee Silver told the London *Sunday Times*. "These human bodies without any semblance of consciousness would not be considered persons, and thus it would be perfectly legal to keep them 'alive' as a future source of organs."

"Alive." Never have a pair of quotation marks loomed so ominously. Take 5 the mouse-frog technology, apply it to humans, combine it with cloning, and you become a god: with a single cell taken from, say, your finger, you produce a headless replica of yourself, a mutant twin, arguably lifeless, that becomes your own personal, precisely tissue-matched organ farm.

There are, of course, technical hurdles along the way. Suppressing the 6 equivalent "head" gene in man. Incubating tiny infant organs to grow into larger ones that adults could use. And creating artificial wombs (as per Aldous Huxley), given that it might be difficult to recruit sane women to carry headless fetuses to their birth/death.

It won't be long, however, before these technical barriers are breached. 7 The ethical barriers are already cracking. Lewis Wolpert, professor of biology at University College, London, finds producing headless humans "personally

---

[1]Play on the title of a John Steinbeck novella, *Of Mice and Men.* —Ed.

distasteful" but, given the shortage of organs, does not think distaste is sufficient reason not to go ahead with something that would save lives. And Professor Silver not only sees "nothing wrong, philosophically or rationally," with producing headless humans for organ harvesting, he wants to convince a skeptical public that it is perfectly O.K.

8   When prominent scientists are prepared to acquiesce in—or indeed encourage—the deliberate creation of deformed and dying quasi-human life, you know we are facing a bioethical abyss. Human beings are ends, not means. There is no grosser corruption of biotechnology than creating a human mutant and disemboweling it at our pleasure for spare parts.

9   The prospect of headless human clones should put the whole debate about "normal" cloning in a new light. Normal cloning is less a treatment for infertility than a treatment for vanity. It is a way to produce an exact genetic replica of yourself that will walk the earth years after you're gone.

10   But there is a problem with a clone. It is not really you. It is but a twin, a perfect John Doe Jr., but still a junior. With its own independent consciousness, it is, alas, just a facsimile of you.

11   The headless clone solves the facsimile problem. It is a gateway to the ultimate vanity: immortality. If you create a real clone, you cannot transfer your consciousness into it to truly live on. But if you create a headless clone of just your body, you have created a ready source of replacement parts to keep you—your consciousness—going indefinitely.

12   Which is why one form of cloning will inevitably lead to the other. Cloning is the technology of narcissism, and nothing satisfies narcissism like immortality. Headlessness will be cloning's crowning achievement.

13   The time to put a stop to this is now. Dolly moved President Clinton to create a commission that recommended a temporary ban on human cloning. But with physicist Richard Seed threatening to clone humans, and with headless animals already here, we are past the time for toothless commissions and meaningless bans.

14   Clinton banned federal funding of human-cloning research, of which there is none anyway. He then proposed a five-year ban on cloning. This is not enough. Congress should ban human cloning now. Totally. And regarding one particular form, it should be draconian: the deliberate creation of headless humans must be made a crime, indeed a capital crime. If we flinch in the face of this high-tech barbarity, we'll deserve to live in the hell it heralds.

QUESTIONS FOR READING

1. What is the occasion for Krauthammer's essay?

2. Why create headless mice? What can this research be a basis for?

3. What are some of the problems to creating headless humans? Does the author think these problems are insurmountable?

4. How, in the author's view, should headless cloning influence the discussion of normal human cloning?

5. In what way is a clone not really you? How can a headless clone of you solve the problem? What would it give you, essentially?

QUESTIONS FOR REASONING AND ANALYSIS

1. What is Krauthammer's claim? Where does he state it? What does he gain by this placement?

2. Krauthammer uses some clever wording. Find some examples, explain the idea in each, and explain how each obtains its power.

3. Note the references to *Brave New World,* Aldous Huxley, and Frankenstein, references that appear repeatedly in discussions of biomedical technology. Explain each reference's significance in Krauthammer's essay.

4. What are the author's grounds, the support for his claim? Evaluate his argument.

QUESTIONS FOR REFLECTING AND WRITING

1. Do you agree that the "deliberate creation of headless humans" should be a capital crime? If yes, why? If not, how would you rebut Krauthammer's argument?

2. Do you agree that human cloning should be banned "totally" by Congress? Why or why not?

3. Is it possible to shut down scientific investigation? What might happen if we ban cloning research in the United States? What are the dangers, if any, of a society seeking to prohibit scientific study? Should scientists be answerable to the elected officials of a society? Reflect on these interconnected questions and be prepared to debate these issues.

A NEW LOOK, AN OLD BATTLE: STEM-CELL RESEARCH MAY CURE DIABETES. IT MAY TEACH US HOW TO THINK ABOUT ABORTION, TOO | ANNA QUINDLEN

Anna Quindlen (b. 1953) is a syndicated columnist connected with the *New York Times.* She has won the Pulitzer Prize for commentary and has published several volumes of her columns. She has also written several novels, including *Black and Blue* (1998) and, most recently, *Blessings* (2002). Her following "Last Word" *Newsweek* column was published April 9, 2001.

PREREADING QUESTIONS What are the potential benefits to stem-cell research? What is needed to do stem-cell research? What is the source of conflict over this research?

Public personification has always been the struggle on both sides of the 1 abortion battle lines. That is why the people outside clinics on Saturday mornings carry signs with photographs of infants rather than of zygotes, why they wear lapel pins fashioned in the image of tiny feet and shout, "Don't kill your baby," rather than, more accurately, "Don't destroy your embryo." Those who support the legal right to an abortion have always been somewhat at a loss in the face of all this. From time to time women have come forward to speak about their decision to have an abortion, but when they are prominent, it seems a bit like grandstanding, and when they are not, it seems a terrible invasion of privacy when privacy is the point in the first place. Easier to marshal the act of presumptive ventriloquism practiced by the opponents, pretending to speak for those unborn unknown to them by circumstance or story.

2   But the battle of personification will assume a different and more sympathetic visage in the years to come. Perhaps the change in the weather was best illustrated when conservative Senator Strom Thurmond invoked his own daughter to explain a position opposed by the anti-abortion forces. The senator's daughter has diabetes. The actor Michael J. Fox has Parkinson's disease. Christopher Reeve is in a wheelchair because of a spinal-cord injury. Ronald Reagan is locked in his own devolving mind by Alzheimer's.[1] In the faces of the publicly and personally beloved lies enormous danger for the life-begins-at-conception lobby.

3   The catalytic issue is research on stem cells. These are versatile building blocks that may be coaxed into becoming any other cell type; they could therefore hold the key to endless mysteries of human biology, as well as someday help provide a cure for ailments as diverse as diabetes, Parkinson's, spinal-cord degeneration, and Alzheimer's. By some estimates, more than 100 million Americans have diseases that scientists suspect could be affected by research on stem cells. Scientists hope that the astonishing potential of this research will persuade the federal government to help fund it and allow the National Institutes of Health to help oversee it. This is not political, researchers insist. It is about science, not abortion.

4   And they are correct. Stem-cell research is typically done by using frozen embryos left over from in vitro fertilization. If these embryos were placed in the womb, they might eventually implant, become a fetus, then a child. Unused, they are the earliest undifferentiated collection of cells made by the joining of the egg and sperm, no larger than the period at the end of this sentence. One of the oft-used slogans of the anti-abortion movement is "abortion stops a beating heart." There is no heart in this pre-implantation embryo, but there are stem cells that, in the hands of scientists, might lead to extraordinary work affecting everything from cancer to heart disease.

5   All of which leaves the anti-abortion movement trying desperately to hold its hard line, and failing. Judie Brown of the American Life League can refer to these embryos as "the tiniest person," and the National Right to Life organization can publish papers that refer to stem-cell research as the "destruction of life." But ordinary people with family members losing their mobility or their grasp on reality will be able to be more thoughtful and reasonable about the issues involved.

6   The anti-abortion activists know this, because they have already seen the defections. Some senators have abandoned them to support fetal-tissue

---

[1] Until his death June 5, 2004.—Ed.

research, less promising than stem-cell work but still with significant potential for treating various ailments. Elected officials who had voted against abortion rights found themselves able to support procedures that used tissue from aborted fetuses; perhaps they were men who had fathers with heart disease, who had mothers with arthritis and whose hearts resonated with the possibilities for alleviating pain and prolonging life. Senator Thurmond was one, Senator McCain another. Former senator Connie Mack of Florida recently sent a letter to the president, who must decide the future role of the federal government in this area, describing himself "as a conservative pro-life now former member" of Congress, and adding that there "were those of us identified as such who supported embryonic stem-cell research."

When a recent test of fetal tissue in patients with Parkinson's had disastrous   7
side effects, the National Right to Life Web site ran an almost gloating report: "horrific," "rips to shreds," "media cheerleaders," "defy description." The tone is a reflection of fear. It's the fear that the use of fetal tissue to produce cures for debilitating ailments might somehow launder the process of terminating a pregnancy, a positive result from what many people still see as a negative act. And it's the fear that thinking—really thinking—about the use of the earliest embryo for life-saving research might bring a certain long-overdue relativism to discussions of abortion across the board.

The majority of Americans have always been able to apply that relativism   8
to these issues. They are more likely to accept early abortions than later ones. They are more tolerant of a single abortion under exigent circumstances than multiple abortions. Some who disapprove of abortion in theory have discovered that they can accept it in fact if a daughter or a girlfriend is pregnant.

And some who believe that life begins at conception may look into the va-   9
cant eyes of an adored parent with Alzheimer's or picture a paralyzed child walking again, and take a closer look at what an embryo really is, at what stem-cell research really does, and then consider the true cost of a cure. That is what Senator Thurmond obviously did when he looked at his daughter and broke ranks with the true believers. It may be an oversimplification to say that real live loved ones trump the imagined unborn, that a cluster of undifferentiated cells due to be discarded anyway is a small price to pay for the health and welfare of millions. Or perhaps it is only a simple commonsensical truth.

QUESTIONS FOR READING

1. What distinction does Quindlen make between babies and embryos? Why do the anti-abortion forces not make this distinction? What do they accomplish?

2. How will pro-choice voices be able to use the anti-abortion strategy of personification in the "new" battle? What is the new conflict over?

3. In the face of the medical promise of stem-cell research, what has been happening to the ranks of anti-abortion activists?

4. What, in the view of the author, do the anti-abortion activists fear about fetal-tissue and stem-cell research? What might accepting this research lead to?

QUESTIONS FOR REASONING AND ANALYSIS

1. What is Quindlen's claim?

2. Analyze Quindlen's argument. What kinds of support does she use?

3. When the author asserts that the majority of Americans have always thought in relative terms about abortion, what does she expect readers to know? That is, why is this assertion not a fallacy of overgeneralization?

4. When the author writes that "real live loved ones trump the imagined unborn," what does she mean? To what is Quindlen appealing in paragraph 9?

5. Consider the author's tone. What does she seek to accomplish by her choice of tone?

QUESTIONS FOR REFLECTING AND WRITING

1. Evaluate Quindlen's argument. Does she make a case for stem-cell research? For a less absolute position on abortion? If yes, why? If no, how would you rebut her argument?

2. Do you have a position on abortion? If so, is it "relative" or "absolute"? Defend your answer.

3. Should stem-cell research be permitted? Why or why not?

THINK BABY LOUISE, AND DON'T BE AFRAID | ROBIN MARANTZ HENIG

A science writer who lives in New York City, Robin Henig has published nine books, including *The Monk in the Garden: The Lost and Found Genius of Gregor Mendel, the Father of Genetics* (2001) and *Pandora's Baby: How the First Test Tube Babies Sparked the Reproductive Revolution* (2004). The following essay, drawn from her work on *Pandora's Baby*, appeared in the *Washington Post* on July 13, 2003.

PREREADING QUESTIONS What is the author referring to in her title *Pandora's Baby*? (If you don't know the story, look it up.) Who is she referring to in the article's title when she writes "Baby Louise"? What can you anticipate that her essay will be about?

1   The world's first test tube baby turns 25 this month. You might know her name—Louise Brown—and that the pair of doctors responsible for her birth sounded vaguely like an old vaudeville team. You might know that those doctors, Steptoe and Edwards, were from Britain; if you were alive at the time, you might even remember that the city where they did their experiments, and where Louise was born, was Oldham.

2   But what you probably don't know, or don't remember, is how frightening it was to wait for that landmark birth. Most of those who were paying attention, from scientists to church officials to editorial writers, were sure that the world's first test tube baby would be abnormal: genetically deformed, less-than-human, monstrous, at the very least a freak of nature who would have to grow up with the eyes of the world charting its every move.

Amazingly, Louise was pink and perfect, normal in every way. When she 3
arrived just before midnight on July 25, 1978, with 10 fingers, 10 toes and a
lovely, lusty cry, she was graphic evidence that lab manipulations didn't have to
harm the embryo. The age of assisted reproduction had begun.

The fears that preceded Louise's birth are similar to the fears today about 4
other reproductive technologies. Some of the voices currently raised in opposition to the thorniest interventions—cloning and designer babies in particular—
are the very same voices raised a generation ago in opposition to in vitro
fertilization (IVF). And some of these voices are saying the very same things
now that they were saying in the 1970s. But even if the players and the rhetoric
are the same, the situation is not. We are, it seems, on the verge of learning the
wrong lessons from the IVF experience, bending too far in the direction of over-
regulating reproductive research because we have seen the unfortunate results
of under-regulation.

Listen, for example, to Leon Kass, a bioethics professor at the University of 5
Chicago whose voice has been part of this debate for 25 years. "More is at
stake [with IVF research] than in ordinary biomedical research or in experi-
menting with human subjects at risk of bodily harm," Kass testified before
the federal government's Ethics Advisory Board shortly after Louise Brown's
birth. "At stake is the idea of the humanness of our human life and the meaning of our embodiment, our sexual being, and our relation to ancestors and
descendants."

Kass is now President Bush's leading bioethics advisor, and when he talks 6
about cloning he uses many of the same words he used in 1978. He sees moral
ruin and calamity in the petri dishes where human embryos grow. Now as then,
his concerns can be expressed in a simple shorthand: He worries about the
so-called slippery slope.

The term implies a certain inevitability to scientific progress, an inability to 7
put a stop to increasingly more loathsome applications of knowledge once
we achieve that knowledge. If the slope of progress is indeed slippery, then
any first step—even if it is not objectionable when considered in isolation—
becomes objectionable because it could lead to some sort of abuse.

The slippery slope argument emerges often in scientific history, whenever 8
a powerful new development might have dreadful ramifications. People talked
about the slippery slope since the first artificial insemination was publicized in
1909, conjuring images of selective breeding and a race of illegitimate souls.
They talked about it after the first heart transplant in 1967, after the first animal-
to-human transplant in 1984, and, in 2002, after the first transplanted uterus.
Early cases of assisted suicide stimulated talk about a slippery slope that would
lead to wholesale killing of the aged or infirm; early attempts at amniocentesis
begat fears about a slippery slope toward the elimination of fetuses that were
imperfect in some way—or that were simply the "wrong" sex.

To be sure, some of these first steps have led to brutal applications— 9
abortions of female fetuses in China and India, for example, and shameful experiences with eugenics around the world—but fear of such horrors should
not cause us to prohibit procedures that are in themselves innocuous, and

that might easily lead to enhancement of our collective fate rather than to devastation.

10   If IVF was the first step down a slippery slope of its own, then it seems to have landed us in exactly the spot that Kass and others said it would. Earlier this month, two reports from the annual meeting of the European Society of Human Reproduction and Embryology made it seem that fun-with-embryos had gotten a little out of hand. An American scientist, Norbert Gleicher, announced that he and his colleagues had successfully inserted cells from a male embryo into an early-stage female embryo, creating a mixed-gender chimera that some journalists called a "she-male." Another team, from Israel and the Netherlands, described a trick that was even more bizarre: harvesting eggs from aborted fetuses and culturing them so they could be used in IVF, thereby creating a baby with a biological mother who had never been born.

11   No one would be talking about "she-male" embryos or fetal mothers if the techniques of IVF hadn't been perfected over the past quarter-century. These newer maneuvers, as well as all the others that most frighten people, begin with the same steps used for IVF: extraction of the eggs and sperm, fertilization in a petri dish, culture of the embryo until it reaches a certain stage and, finally, implantation into a receptive uterus. Of the scenarios that are now causing so much anxiety—cloning, pre-implantation genetic diagnosis, genetic engineering of sex cells, the creation of human/animal hybrids, the culturing of human embryos as a source of replacement parts—none is possible without the techniques of basic IVF: laboratory fertilization and embryo transfer.

12   Even if a slippery slope exists, it cannot be allowed to dictate science policy. Regulating something that can be done now on the basis of fears about what *might* be done later is a mistake. And it can result in some unintended and paradoxical effects. For all the railing against IVF in the '70s, the protests led to less control over IVF rather than more. Early on, opponents thought the best way to stop troublesome science was to keep the federal government from financing it, and they fought against using taxpayer money for research involving fetuses or embryos—which by extension, included IVF. One by one, a succession of bioethics commissions were formed to review these bans; one by one, the commissions recommended that the bans be lifted.

13   But politicians, some of whom were afraid of alienating a vocal anti-abortion lobby opposed to the experimental use of fetuses and embryos, generally did not want to hear that they should underwrite such controversial research. As a result, a pattern developed for the bioethicists' role in the regulatory minuet: sit on a commission, hold meetings, attend public hearings, write a report that says the research is ethically acceptable, have the report ignored, watch the next president or Congress convene a new commission, and repeat.

14   Even after the fetal research ban was lifted, and then the embryo research ban, the government still refused to sponsor IVF research. But the lack of federal support for IVF didn't stop scientists from working on it—it just led them to carry on beneath the radar, out of the reach of the main mechanism for oversight, which was (and still is) the federal research grant and the standards it imposes on its recipients. If no one was getting government grants for IVF,

then no one was being required to adhere to any standards. Entrepreneurial scientists were doing IVF anyway, bolstered by private money from infertile couples desperate for babies. Most of these scientists were honorable men and women with solid reputations and the loftiest of goals. A few, however, were motivated by the things that drive so many innovators, scientists included—ego, curiosity, ambition, even greed. They were free agents who essentially did whatever they wanted and whatever the market would bear. Their efforts turned some of the fertility industry into a cowboy science driven by supply and demand.

Cloning is in many respects the contemporary version of cowboy science; 15 cloners are today's daredevils and rogues, making claims of success that they have yet to document with genetic proof or even an actual baby. This is why so many politicians, here and elsewhere, have been trying so hard to put cloning in its place—not by refusing to fund it, as happened to ill effect with IVF, but through legislation to ban it, whether the cloning takes place for research or for the sake of creating a cloned person.

They want to keep human cloning from going the way of IVF, which became 16 part of the ordinary landscape simply because it was easier to ignore a controversial new technology than to regulate it. But they might be learning the wrong lesson—and we all might be the poorer for it.

What legislators should learn from the IVF experience is that unfunded re- 17 search will take place anyway, but in a less open and less coherent direction than might have occurred with government support. What they should be doing is not outlawing cloning, especially therapeutic cloning, but embracing it— to encourage research that might lead to cures for dozens of degenerative diseases and to keep it from dangerously veering off down the slope that is so famously slippery.

As the world's first test tube baby turns 25, half a million others born 18 through assisted reproductive technology can raise a glass in celebration of the new treatments for infertility that have subsequently developed. The agony of childlessness, for a couple that wants children, has been greatly eased because of the path blazed by Louise Brown's doctors, and her parents, too, who didn't even realize at first that they were involved in an enterprise that had never worked before. And look at all that has followed. Much of it might have been troublesome, but much more of it has been miraculous.

Happy birthday, Louise. 19

QUESTIONS FOR READING

1. What are the fears that were raised twenty-six years ago about IVF? How are they similar to the fears expressed today about cloning?

2. What is the slippery slope argument as it is applied to scientific progress?

3. What are some negative examples of the misuse of reproductive research?

4. In what way is IVF at the base of current issues such as cloning and genetic engineering?

5. What has been the government's relationship to reproductive research in all its stages? Why is this, in the author's view, a problem?

6. What should legislators learn from the last twenty-six years of research?

QUESTIONS FOR REASONING AND ANALYSIS

1. What is Henig's claim? What does she want to see happen? Think of her claim in terms of a problem/solution argument.

2. Henig refers to Leon Kass, Chair of the Council on Bioethics. Analyze her argument as a rebuttal to his position on cloning.

3. The author mentions some negative consequences of reproductive research and asserts that some have "turned some of the fertility industry into a cowboy science." Why does she include examples and comments that could be counter-arguments to her position? What does she gain by this move?

4. Look at Henig's opening and conclusion. How does she use Baby Louise effectively to frame her argument?

QUESTIONS FOR REFLECTING AND WRITING

1. Henig demonstrates that government studies and regulations have done little to control research. Is this good or bad? How much control should government place on research? And what is the best way to place that control? Henig makes some suggestions. Start with her ideas and then develop your own position on this issue. Remember that you will have to speak to the issue of feasibility.

2. Who in your view has the better argument: Kass or Henig? Should research into cloning for therapeutic goals be prohibited in the United States? Or, should it be funded and controlled by government oversight? Why?

CHAPTER 23

Some Classic Arguments

This final chapter presents seven of the many well-known arguments worthy of your study. Your instructor may also recommend Niccolo Machiavelli's *The Prince* or George Orwell's "Politics and the English Language," or any of the *Federalist Papers.* All of these arguments illustrate excellent persuasive strategies; they also continue to influence the debates of enduring issues. As you read, observe how these authors use language, sentence patterns, metaphors, irony, and other strategies to drive home their claims.

A MODEST PROPOSAL | JONATHAN SWIFT

For Preventing the Children of Poor People in Ireland from Being a Burden to Their Parents or Country, and for Making Them Beneficial to the Public

Born in Dublin, Jonathan Swift (1667–1745) was ordained in the Anglican Church and spent many years as dean of St. Patrick's in Dublin. Swift was also involved in the political and social life of London for some years, and throughout his life he kept busy writing. His most famous imaginative work is *Gulliver's Travels* (1726). Almost as well known is the essay that follows, published in 1729. Here you will find Swift's usual biting satire but also his concern to improve humanity.

PREREADING QUESTIONS Swift was a minister, but he writes this essay as if he were in a different job. What "voice" or persona do you hear? Does Swift agree with the views of this persona?

1   It is a melancholy object to those who walk through this great town[1] or travel in the country, whey they see the streets, the roads, and cabin doors crowded with beggars of the female sex, followed by three, four, or six children, all in rags, and importuning every passenger for an alms. These mothers, instead of being able to work for their honest livelihood, are forced to employ all their time in strolling to beg sustenance for their helpless infants, who, as they grow up, either turn thieves for want of work, or leave their dear native country to fight for the pretender[2] in Spain or sell themselves to the Barbados.

2   I think it is agreed by all parties that this prodigious number of children in the arms, or on the backs, or at the heels of their mothers, and frequently of their fathers, is in the present deplorable state of the kingdom a very great additional grievance; and therefore, whoever could find out a fair, cheap, and easy method of making these children sound and useful members of the commonwealth would deserve so well of the public as to have his statue set up for a preserver of the nation.

3   But my intention is very far from being confined to provide only for the children of professed beggars; it is of a much greater extent, and shall take in the whole number of infants at a certain age who are born of parents in effect as little able to support them as those who demand our charity in the streets.

4   As to my own part, having turned my thoughts for many years upon this important subject, and maturely weighed the several schemes of other projectors,[3] I have always found them grossly mistaken in the computation. It is true a child just dropped from its dam may be supported by her milk for a solar year with little other nourishment; at most not above the value of two shillings, which the mother may certainly get, or the value in scraps, by her lawful occupation of begging; and, it is exactly at one year that I propose to provide for them in such a manner as instead of being a charge upon their parents or the parish, or

---

[1] Dublin.—Ed.

[2] James Stuart, claimant to the British throne lost by his father, James II, in 1688.—Ed.

[3] Planners.—Ed.

wanting food and raiment for the rest of their lives, they shall on the contrary contribute to the feeding, and partly to the clothing, of many thousands.

There is likewise another great advantage in my scheme, that it will prevent those voluntary abortions, and that horrid practice of women murdering their bastard children, alas, too frequent among us, sacrificing the poor innocent babes, I doubt, more to avoid the expense than the shame, which would move tears and pity in the most savage and inhuman breast. 5

The number of souls in this kingdom being usually reckoned one million and a half, of these I calculate there may be about two hundred thousand couples whose wives are breeders; from which number I subtract thirty thousand couples who are able to maintain their own children, although I apprehend there cannot be so many, under the present distress of the kingdom; but this being granted, there will remain a hundred and seventy thousand breeders. I again subtract fifty thousand for those women who miscarry, or whose children die by accident or disease within the year. There only remain a hundred and twenty thousand children of poor parents annually born. The question therefore is, how this number shall be reared and provided for, which, as I have already said, under the present situation of affairs, is utterly impossible by all the methods hereto proposed. For we can neither employ them in handicraft or agriculture; we neither build houses (I mean in the country) nor cultivate land. They can very seldom pick up a livelihood by stealing until they arrive at six years old, except where they are of towardly parts[4]; although I confess they learn the rudiments much earlier, during which time they can, however, be properly looked upon only as probationers, as I have been informed by a principal gentleman in the country of Cavan, who protested to me that he never knew above one or two instances under the age of six, even in the part of the kingdom renowned for the quickest proficiency in that art. 6

I am assured by our merchants that a boy or girl before twelve years old is no saleable commodity; and even when they come to this age they will not yield above three pounds, or three pounds and a half a crown at most, on the exchange; which cannot turn to account either to the parents or the kingdom, the charge of nutriment and rags having been at least four times that value. 7

I shall now therefore humbly propose my own thoughts, which I hope will not be liable to the least objection. 8

I have been assured by a very knowing American of my acquaintance in London that a young healthy child well nursed is at a year old a most delicious, nourishing, and wholesome food, whether stewed, roasted, baked, or boiled; and I make no doubt that it will equally serve in a fricassee or ragout. 9

I do therefore humbly offer it to public consideration that of the hundred and twenty-thousand children, already computed, twenty thousand may be reserved for breed, whereof only one fourth part to be males, which is more than we allow to sheep, black cattle, or swine; and my reason is that these children are seldom the fruits of marriage, a circumstance not much regarded by our 10

---

[4] Innate abilities.—Ed.

savages, therefore one male will be sufficient to serve four females. That the remaining hundred thousand may at a year old be offered in sale to the persons of quality and fortune, through the kingdom, always advising the mother to let them suck plentifully in the last month, so as to render them plump and fat for the table. A child will make two dishes at an entertainment for friends; and when the family dines alone, the fore or hind quarter will make a reasonable dish, and seasoned with a little pepper or salt will be very good boiled on the fourth day, especially in winter.

11   I have reckoned upon a medium that a child just born will weigh twelve pounds, and in a solar year if tolerably nursed increaseth to twenty-eight pounds.

12   I grant this food will be somewhat dear, and therefore very proper for landlords, who, as they have already devoured most of the parents, seem to have the best title to the children.

13   Infant's flesh will be in season throughout the year, but more plentiful in March, and a little before and after. For we are told by a grave author, an eminent French physician,[5] that fish being a prolific diet, there are more children born in Roman Catholic countries about nine months after Lent than at any other season; therefore reckoning a year after Lent, the markets will be more gutted than usual, because the number of popish infants is at least three to one in this kingdom; and therefore it will have one other collateral advantage, by lessening the number of Papists among us.

14   I have already computed the charge of nursing a beggar's child (in which list I reckon all cottagers, laborers, and four-fifths of the farmers) to be about two shillings per annum, rags included; and I believe no gentleman would repine to give ten shillings for the carcass of a good fat child, which, as I have said, will make four dishes of excellent nutritive meat, when he hath only some particular friend or his own family to dine with him. Thus the squire will learn to be a good landlord, and grow popular among his tenants; the mother will have eight shillings net profit, and be fit for work until she produces another child.

15   Those who are more thrifty (as I must confess the times require) may flay the carcass; the skin of which artificially dressed will make admirable gloves for ladies and summer boots for fine gentlemen.

16   As to our city of Dublin, shambles[6] may be appointed for this purpose, in the most convenient parts of it, and butchers we may be assured will not be wanting; although I rather recommend buying the children alive, and dressing them hot from the knife as we do roasting pigs.

16   A very worthy person, a true lover of his country, and whose virtues I highly esteem, was lately pleased in discoursing on this matter to offer a refinement upon my scheme. He said that many gentlemen of this kingdom, having of late destroyed their deer, he conceived that the want of venison might be well supplied by the bodies of young lads and maidens, not exceeding fourteen years of age nor under twelve, so great a number of both sexes in every county

---

[5] Francois Rabelais.—Ed.

[6] Butcher shops.—Ed.

being now ready to starve for want of work and service; and these to be disposed of by their parents, if alive, or otherwise by their nearest relations. But with due deference to so excellent a friend and so deserving a patriot, I cannot be altogether in his sentiments. For as to the males, my American acquaintance assured me from frequent experience that their flesh was generally tough and lean, like that of our school-boys, by continual exercise, and their taste disagreeable; and to fatten them would not answer the charge. Then as to the females, it would, I think with humble submission, be a loss to the public, because they soon would become breeders themselves; and besides, it is not probable that some scrupulous people might be apt to censure such a practice (although indeed very unjustly) as a little bordering upon cruelty; which, I confess, hath always been with me the strongest objection against any project, how wellsoever intended.

But in order to justify my friend, he confessed that this expedient was put 18 into his head by the famous Psalmanazar,[7] a native of the island Formosa who came from thence to London above twenty years ago, and in conversation told my friend that in his country when any young person happened to be put to death, the executioner sold the carcass to persons of quality as a prime dainty; and that in his time the body of a plump girl of fifteen, who was crucified for an attempt to poison the emperor, was sold to his Imperial Majesty's prime minister of state, and other great mandarins of the court, in joints from the gibbet, at four hundred crowns. Neither indeed can I deny that if the same use were made of several plump young girls in this town, who without one single groat to their fortunes cannot stir abroad without a chair, and appear at the playhouse and assemblies in foreign fineries which they never will pay for, the kingdom would not be the worse.

Some persons of a desponding spirit are in great concern about that vast 19 number of poor people who are aged, diseased, or maimed, and I have been desired to employ my thoughts what course may be taken to ease the nation of so grievous an incumbrance. But I am not in the least pain upon that matter, because it is very well known that they are every day dying and rotting by cold and famine, and filth and vermin, as fast as can be reasonably expected. And as to the younger laborers, they are now in almost as hopeful a condition. They cannot get work, and consequently pine away for want of nourishment to a degree that if at any time they are accidentally hired to common labor, they have not strength to perform it; and thus the country and themselves are in a fair way of being soon delivered from the evils to come.

I have too long digressed, and therefore shall return to my subject. I think 20 the advantages by the proposal which I have made are obvious and many, as well as of the highest importance.

For, first, as I have already observed, it would greatly lessen the number of 21 Papists, with whom we are yearly overrun, being the principal breeders of the nation as well as our most dangerous enemies; and who stay at home on purpose with a design to deliver the kingdom to the pretender, hoping to take

---

[7] A known imposter who was French, not Formosan as he claimed.—Ed.

their advantage by the absence of so many good Protestants, who have chosen rather to leave their country than stay at home and pay tithes against their conscience to an idolatrous Episcopal curate.

22   Secondly, the poorer tenants will have something valuable of their own, which by law may be made liable to distress,[8] and help their landlord's rent; their corn and cattle being already seized, and money a thing unknown.

23   Thirdly, whereas the maintenance of a hundred thousand children, from two years old upwards, cannot be computed at less than ten shillings a piece per annum, the nation's stock will be thereby increased fifty thousand pounds per annum, besides the profit of a new dish introduced to the tables of all gentlemen of fortune in the kingdom who have any refinement in taste. And the money will circulate among ourselves, the goods being entirely of our own growth and manufacture.

24   Fourthly, the constant breeders, besides the gain of eight shillings sterling per annum by the sale of their children, will be rid of the charge of maintaining them after the first year.

25   Fifthly, this food would likewise bring great custom to taverns, where the vintners will certainly be so prudent as to procure the best receipts for dressing it to perfection, and consequently have their houses frequented by all the fine gentlemen, who justly value themselves upon their knowledge in good eating; and a skillful cook, who understands how to oblige his guests, will contrive to make it as expensive as they please.

26   Sixthly, this would be a great inducement to marriage, which all wise nations have either encouraged by rewards or enforced by laws and penalties. It would increase the care and tenderness of mothers towards their children, when they were sure of a settlement for life to the poor babes, provided in some sort by the public; to their annual profit instead of expense. We should soon see an honest emulation among the married women, which of them could bring the fattest child to the market. Men would become as fond of their wives during the time of their pregnancy as they are now of their mares in foal, their cows in calf, or sows when they are ready to farrow; nor offer to beat or kick them (as it is too frequent a practice) for fear of a miscarriage.

27   Many other advantages might be enumerated. For instance, the addition of some thousand carcasses in our exportation of barrelled beef, the propagation of swine's flesh, and improvement in the art of making good bacon, so much wanted among us by the great destruction of pigs, too frequent at our tables, which are no way comparable in taste or magnificence to a well-grown fat, yearling child, which roasted whole will make a considerable figure at a lord mayor's feast or any other public entertainment. But this and many others I omit, being studious of brevity.

28   Supposing that one thousand families in this city would be constant customers for infants' flesh, besides others who might have it at merry meetings, particularly weddings and christenings, I compute that Dublin would take off annually about twenty thousand carcasses, and the rest of the kingdom

---

[8] Can be seized by lenders.—Ed.

(where probably they will be sold somewhat cheaper) the remaining eighty thousand.

I can think of no one objection that will possibly be raised against this pro- 29 posal, unless it should be urged that the number of people will be thereby much lessened in the kingdom. This I freely own, and it was indeed one principal design in offering it to the world. I desire the reader will observe that I calculate my remedy for this one individual kingdom of Ireland and for no other that ever was, is, or I think ever can be upon earth. Therefore let no man talk to me of other expedients: of taxing our absentees at five shillings a pound: of using neither clothes nor household furniture except what is of our own growth and manufacture: of utterly rejecting the materials and instruments that promote foreign luxury: of curing the expensiveness or pride, vanity, idleness, and gaming in our women: of introducing a vein of parsimony, prudence and temperance: of learning to love our country, wherein we differ even from Laplanders and the inhabitants of Topinamboo[9]: of quitting our animosities and factions, nor act any longer like the Jews, who were murdering one another at the very moment their city was taken[10]: of being a little cautious not to sell our country and consciences for nothing: of teaching landlords to have at least one degree of mercy towards their tenants. Lastly, of putting a spirit of honesty, industry, and skill into our shopkeepers; who, if a resolution could now be taken to buy only our native goods, would immediately unite to cheat and exact upon us in the price, the measure, and the goodness, nor could ever yet be brought to make one fair proposal of just dealing, though often and earnestly invited to it.

Therefore I repeat, let no man talk to me of these and the like expedients, 30 till he hath at least a glimpse of hope that there will ever be some hearty and sincere attempt to put them in practice.

But as to myself, having been wearied out for many years with offering 31 vain, idle, visionary thoughts, and at length utterly despairing of success, I fortunately fell upon this proposal, which, as it is wholly new, so it hath something solid and real, of no expense and little trouble, full in our own power, and whereby we can incur no danger in disobliging England. For this kind of commodity will not bear exportation, the flesh being of too tender a consistence to admit a long continuance in salt, although perhaps I could name a country which would be glad to eat up our whole nation without it.

After all, I am not so violently bent upon my own opinion as to reject any 32 offer proposed by wise men, which shall be found equally innocent, cheap, easy, and effectual. But before something of that kind shall be advanced in contradiction to my scheme, and offering a better, I desire the author, or authors, will be pleased maturely to consider two points. First, as things now stand, how they will be able to find food and raiment for a hundred thousand useless mouths and backs. And secondly, there being a round million of creatures in human figure throughout this kingdom, whose whole subsistence put into a

---

[9] An area in Brazil.—Ed.

[10] Some Jews were accused of helping the Romans and were executed during the Roman siege of Jerusalem in 70 A.D.—Ed.

common stock would leave them in debt two million of pounds sterling, adding those who are beggars by profession to the bulk of farmers, cottagers, and laborers, with their wives and children who are beggars, in effect; I desire those politicians who dislike my overture, and may perhaps be so bold to attempt an answer, that they will first ask the parents of these mortals whether they would not at this day think it a great happiness to have been sold for food at a year old in the manner I prescribe, and thereby have avoided such a perpetual scene of misfortunes as they have since gone through by the oppression of landlords, the impossibility of paying rent without money or trade, the want of common sustenance, with neither house nor clothes to cover them from the inclemencies of weather, and the most inevitable prospect of entailing the like or greater miseries upon their breed forever.

33   I profess, in the sincerity of my heart, that I have not the least personal interest in endeavoring to promote this necessary work, having no other motive than the public good of my country, by advancing our trade, providing for infants, relieving the poor, and giving some pleasure to the rich. I have no children by which I can propose to get a single penny, the youngest being nine years old, and my wife past childbearing.

QUESTIONS FOR READING

1. How is the argument organized? What is accomplished in paragraphs 1–7? In paragraphs 8–16? In paragraphs 17–19? In paragraphs 20–28? In paragraphs 29–33?

2. What specific advantages does the writer offer in defense of his proposal?

QUESTIONS FOR REASONING AND ANALYSIS

1. What specific passages and connotative words make us aware that this is a satirical piece using irony as its chief device?

2. After noting Swift's use of irony, what do you conclude to be his purpose in writing?

3. What can you conclude to be some of the problems in eighteenth-century Ireland? Where does Swift offer direct condemnation of existing conditions in Ireland and attitudes of the English toward the Irish?

4. What actual reforms would Swift like to see?

QUESTIONS FOR REFLECTING AND WRITING

1. What are some of the advantages of using irony? What does Swift gain by this approach? What are possible disadvantages in using irony? Reflect on irony as a persuasive strategy.

2. What are some current problems that might be addressed by the use of irony? Make a list. Then select one and think about what "voice" or persona you might use to bring attention to that problem. Plan your argument with irony as a strategy.

CIVIL DISOBEDIENCE | HENRY DAVID THOREAU

Naturalist, essayist, poet, transcendentalist, Thoreau (1817–1862) was a man of wide interests. His two most famous works—*Walden* (1854) and the essay "Civil Disobedience" (delivered as a lecture in 1848 and published in 1849)—have influenced many readers who have shared his search for "higher laws."

PREREADING QUESTION What should be our response to unjust laws?

I heartily accept the motto,—"That government is best which governs 1 least;"[1] and I should like to see it acted up to more rapidly and systematically. Carried out, it finally amounts to this, which also I believe,—"That government is best which governs not at all;" and when men are prepared for it, that will be the kind of government which they will have. Government is at best but an expedient; but most governments are usually, and all governments are sometimes, inexpedient. The objections which have been brought against a standing army, and they are many and weighty, and deserve to prevail, may also at last be brought against a standing government. The standing army is only an arm of the standing government. The government itself, which is only the mode which the people have chosen to execute their will, is equally liable to be abused and perverted before the people can act through it. Witness the present Mexican war,[2] the work of comparatively a few individuals using the standing government as their tool; for, in the outset, the people would not have consented to this measure.

This American government,—what is it but a tradition, though a recent 2 one, endeavoring to transmit itself unimpaired to posterity, but each instant losing some of its integrity? It has not the vitality and force of a single living man; for a single man can bend it to his will. It is a sort of wooden gun to the people themselves; and, if ever they should use it in earnest as a real one against each other, it will surely split. But it is not the less necessary for this; for the people must have some complicated machinery or other, and hear its din, to satisfy that idea of government which they have. Governments show thus how successfully men can be imposed on, even impose on themselves, for their own advantage. It is excellent, we must all allow; yet this government never of itself furthered any enterprise, but by the alacrity with which it got out of its way. *It* does not keep the country free. *It* does not settle the West. *It* does not educate. The character inherent in the American people has done all that has been accomplished; and it would have done somewhat more, if the government had not sometimes got in its way. For government is an expedient by which men would fain succeed in letting one another alone; and, as has been said, when it is most expedient, the governed are most let alone by it. Trade and commerce, if they were not made of India rubber, would never manage to bounce over the obstacles which legislators are continually putting in their way; and, if one were to judge these men wholly by the effects of their actions, and

---

[1] Motto of the monthly journal *United States Monthly Magazine and Democratic Review.*—Ed.

[2] From 1846 to 1848.—Ed.

not partly by their intentions, they would deserve to be classed and punished with those mischievous persons who put obstructions on the railroads.

3   But, to speak practically and as a citizen, unlike those who call themselves no-government men, I ask for, not at once no government, but *at once* a better government. Let every man make known what kind of government would command his respect, and that will be one step toward obtaining it.

4   After all, the practical reason why, when the power is once in the hands of the people, a majority are permitted, and for a long period continue, to rule, is not because they are most likely to be in the right, nor because this seems fairest to the minority, but because they are physically the strongest. But a government in which the majority rule in all cases cannot be based on justice, even as far as men understand it. Can there not be a government in which majorities do not virtually decide right and wrong, but conscience?—in which majorities decide only those questions to which the rule of expediency is applicable? Must the citizen ever for a moment, or in the least degree, resign his conscience to the legislator? Why has every man a conscience, then? I think that we should be men first, and subjects afterward. It is not desirable to cultivate a respect for the law, so much as for the right. The only obligation which I have a right to assume, is to do at any time what I think right. It is truly enough said, that a corporation has no conscience; but a corporation of conscientious men is a corporation *with* a conscience. Law never made men a whit more just; and, by means of their respect for it, even the well-disposed are daily made the agents of injustice. A common and natural result of an undue respect for law is, that you may see a file of soldiers, colonel, captain, corporal, privates, powder-monkeys and all, marching in admirable order over hill and dale to the wars, against their wills, aye, against their common sense and consciences, which makes it very steep marching indeed, and produces a palpitation of the heart. They have no doubt that it is a damnable business in which they are concerned; they are all peaceably inclined. Now, what are they? Men at all? or small moveable forts and magazines, at the service of some unscrupulous man in power? Visit the Navy Yard, and behold a marine, such a man as an American government can make, or such as it can make a man with its black arts, a mere shadow and reminiscence of humanity, a man laid out alive and standing, and already, as one may say, buried under arms with funeral accompaniments, though it may be

> "Not a drum was heard, nor a funeral note,
> As his corse to the ramparts we hurried;
> Not a soldier discharged his farewell shot
> O'er the grave where our hero we buried."[3]

5   The mass of men serve the State thus, not as men mainly, but as machines, with their bodies. They are the standing army, and the militia, jailers, constables, *posse comitatus,* &c. In most cases there is no free exercise whatever of the judgment or of the moral sense; but they put themselves on a level with

---

[3] By Charles Wolfe, 1791–1823.—Ed.

wood and earth and stones; and wooden men can perhaps be manufactured that will serve the purpose as well. Such command no more respect than men of straw, or a lump of dirt. They have the same sort of worth only as horses and dogs. Yet such as these even are commonly esteemed good citizens. Others, as most legislators, politicians, lawyers, ministers, and office-holders, serve the State chiefly with their heads; and, as they rarely make any moral distinctions, they are as likely to serve the devil, without intending it, as God. A very few, as heroes, patriots, martyrs, reformers in the great sense, and *men,* serve the State with their consciences also, and so necessarily resist it for the most part; and they are commonly treated by it as enemies. A wise man will only be useful as a man, and will not submit to be "clay," and "stop a hole to keep the wind away,"[4] but leave that office to his dust at least:—

> "I am too high-born to be propertied,
> To be a secondary at control,
> Or useful serving-man and instrument
> To any sovereign state throughout the world."[5]

He who gives himself entirely to his fellow-men appears to them useless and selfish; but he who gives himself partially to them is pronounced a benefactor and philanthropist.   6

How does it become a man to behave toward this American government to-day? I answer that he cannot without disgrace be associated with it. I cannot for an instant recognize that political organization as *my* government which is the *slave's* government also.   7

All men recognize the right of revolution; that is, the right to refuse allegiance to and to resist the government, when its tyranny or its inefficiency are great and unendurable. But almost all say that such is not the case now. But such was the case, they think, in the Revolution of '75. If one were to tell me that this was a bad government because it taxed certain foreign commodities brought to its ports, it is most probable that I should not make an ado about it, for I can do without them: all machines have their friction; and possibly this does enough good to counterbalance the evil. At any rate, it is a great evil to make a stir about it. But when the friction comes to have its machine, and oppression and robbery are organized, I say, let us not have such a machine any longer. In other words, when a sixth of the population of a nation which has undertaken to be the refuge of liberty are slaves, and a whole country is unjustly overrun and conquered by a foreign army, and subjected to military law, I think that it is not too soon for honest men to rebel and revolutionize. What makes this duty the more urgent is the fact, that the country so overrun is not our own, but ours is the invading army.   8

Paley,[6] a common authority with many on moral questions, in his chapter on the "Duty of Submission to Civil Government," resolves all civil obligation   9

---

[4] Shakespeare, *Hamlet,* V.i. 236–37.—Ed.

[5] Shakespeare, *King John,* V.i.i. 79–82.—Ed.

[6] British philosopher, William Paley.—Ed.

into expediency; and he proceeds to say, "that so long as the interest of the whole society requires it, that is, so long as the established government cannot be resisted or changed without public inconveniency, it is the will of God that the established government be obeyed, and no longer."—"This principle being admitted, the justice of every particular case of resistance is reduced to a computation of the quantity of the danger and grievance on the one side, and of the probability and expense of redressing it on the other." Of this, he says, every man shall judge for himself. But Paley appears never to have contemplated those cases to which the rule of expediency does not apply, in which a people, as well as an individual, must do justice, cost what it may. If I have unjustly wrested a plank from a drowning man, I must restore it to him though I drown myself. This, according to Paley, would be inconvenient. But he that would save his life, in such a case, shall lose it. This people must cease to hold slaves, and to make war on Mexico, though it cost them their existence as a people.

10   In their practice, nations agree with Paley; but does any one think that Massachusetts does exactly what is right at the present crisis?

> "A drab of state, a cloth-o'-silver slut,
> To have her train borne up, and her soul trail in the dirt."[7]

Practically speaking, the opponents to a reform in Massachusetts are not a hundred thousand politicians at the South, but a hundred thousand merchants and farmers here, who are more interested in commerce and agriculture than they are in humanity, and are not prepared to do justice to the slave and to Mexico, *cost what it may*. I quarrel not with far-off foes, but with those who, near at home, co-operate with, and do the bidding of those far away, and without whom the latter would be harmless. We are accustomed to say, that the mass of men are unprepared; but improvement is slow, because the few are not materially wiser or better than the many. It is not so important that many should be as good as you, as that there be some absolute goodness somewhere; for that will leaven the whole lump. There are thousands who are *in opinion* opposed to slavery and to the war, who yet in effect do nothing to put an end to them; who, esteeming themselves children of Washington and Franklin, sit down with their hands in their pockets, and say that they know not what to do, and do nothing; who even postpone the question of freedom to the question of free-trade, and quietly read the prices-current along with the latest advices from Mexico, after dinner, and, it may be, fall asleep over them both. What is the price-current of an honest man and patriot to-day? They hesitate, and they regret, and sometimes they petition; but they do nothing in earnest and with effect. They will wait, well disposed, for others to remedy the evil, that they may no longer have it to regret. At most, they give only a cheap vote, and a feeble countenance and God-speed, to the right, as it goes by them. There are nine hundred and ninety-nine patrons of virtue to one virtuous man; but it is easier to deal with the real possessor of a thing than with the temporary guardian of it.

---

[7] Tourneur, *The Revengers Tragadie,* IV.iv.—Ed.

All voting is a sort of gaming, like chequers or backgammon, with a slight 11
moral tinge to it, a playing with right and wrong, with moral questions; and
betting naturally accompanies it. The character of the voters is not staked. I
cast my vote, perchance, as I think right; but I am not vitally concerned that
that right should prevail. I am willing to leave it to the majority. Its obligation,
therefore, never exceeds that of expediency. Even voting *for the right* is *doing*
nothing for it. It is only expressing to men feebly your desire that it should prevail. A wise man will not leave the right to the mercy of chance, nor wish it to
prevail through the power of the majority. There is but little virtue in the
action of masses of men. When the majority shall at length vote for the abolition of slavery, it will be because they are indifferent to slavery, or because
there is but little slavery left to be abolished by their vote. *They* will then be
the only slaves. Only *his* vote can hasten the abolition of slavery who asserts
his own freedom by his vote.

I hear of a convention to be held at Baltimore, or elsewhere, for the selec- 12
tion of a candidate for the Presidency, made up chiefly of editors, and men who
are politicians by profession; but I think, what is it to any independent, intelligent, and respectable man what decision they may come to, shall we not have
the advantage of his wisdom and honesty, nevertheless? Can we not count
upon some independent votes? Are there not many individuals in the country
who do not attend conventions? But no: I find that the respectable man, so
called, has immediately drifted from his position, and despairs of his country,
when his country has more reason to despair of him. He forthwith adopts one
of the candidates thus selected as the only *available* one, thus proving that he
is himself *available* for any purposes of the demagogue. His vote is of no more
worth than that of any unprincipled foreigner or hireling native, who may have
been bought. Oh for a man who is a *man,* and, as my neighbor says, has a bone
in his back which you cannot pass your hand through! Our statistics are at fault:
the population has been returned too large. How many *men* are there to a
square thousand miles in this country? Hardly one. Does not America offer any
inducement for men to settle here? The American has dwindled into an Odd
Fellow,—one who may be known by the development of his organ of gregari-
ousness, and a manifest lack of intellect and cheerful self-reliance; whose first
and chief concern, on coming into the world, is to see that the alms-houses are
in good repair; and, before yet he has lawfully donned the virile garb, to collect a fund for the support of the widows and orphans that may be; who, in
short, ventures to live only by the aid of the mutual insurance company, which
has promised to bury him decently.

It is not a man's duty, as a matter of course, to devote himself to the erad- 13
ication of any, even the most enormous wrong; he may still properly have other
concerns to engage him; but it is his duty, at least, to wash his hands of it, and,
if he gives it no thought longer, not to give it practically his support. If I devote
myself to other pursuits and contemplations, I must first see, at least, that I do
not pursue them sitting upon another man's shoulders. I must get off him first,
that he may pursue his contemplations too. See what gross inconsistency is
tolerated. I have heard some of my townsmen say, "I should like to have them

order me out to help put down an insurrection of the slaves, or to march to Mexico,—see if I would go;" and yet these very men have each, directly by their allegiance, and so indirectly, at least, by their money, furnished a substitute. The soldier is applauded who refuses to serve in an unjust war by those who do not refuse to sustain the unjust government which makes the war; is applauded by those whose own act and authority he disregards and sets at nought; as if the State were penitent to that degree that it hired one to scourge it while it sinned, but not to that degree that it left off sinning for a moment. Thus, under the name of order and civil government, we are all made at last to pay homage to and support our own meanness. After the first blush of sin, comes its indifference; and from immoral it becomes, as it were, *unmoral*, and not quite unnecessary to that life which we have made.

14   The broadest and most prevalent error requires the most disinterested virtue to sustain it. The slight reproach to which the virtue of patriotism is commonly liable, the noble are most likely to incur. Those who, while they disapprove of the character and measures of a government, yield to it their allegiance and support, are undoubtedly its most conscientious supporters, and so frequently the most serious obstacles to reform. Some are petitioning the State to dissolve the Union, to disregard the requisitions of the President. Why do they not dissolve it themselves,—the union between themselves and the State,—and refuse to pay their quota into its treasury? Do not they stand in the same relation to the State, that the State does to the Union? And have not the same reasons prevented the State from resisting the Union, which have prevented them from resisting the State?

15   How can a man be satisfied to entertain an opinion merely, and enjoy *it*? Is there any enjoyment in it, if his opinion is that he is aggrieved? If you are cheated out of a single dollar by your neighbor, you do not rest satisfied with knowing that you are cheated, or with saying that you are cheated, or even with petitioning him to pay you your due; but you take effectual steps at once to obtain the full amount, and see that you are never cheated again. Action from principle,—the perception and the performance of right,—changes things and relations; it is essentially revolutionary, and does not consist wholly with any thing which was. It not only divides states and churches, it divides families; aye, it divides the *individual*, separating the diabolical in him from the divine.

16   Unjust laws exist: shall we be content to obey them, or shall we endeavor to amend them, and obey them until we have succeeded, or shall we transgress them at once? Men generally, under such a government as this, think that they ought to wait until they have persuaded the majority to alter them. They think that, if they should resist, the remedy would be worse than the evil. But it is the fault of the government itself that the remedy *is* worse than the evil. *It* makes it worse. Why is it not more apt to anticipate and provide for reform? Why does it not cherish its wise minority? Why does it not cry and resist before it is hurt? Why does it not encourage its citizens to be on the alert to point out its faults, and *do* better than it would have them? Why does it always crucify Christ, and excommunicate Copernicus and Luther, and pronounce Washington and Franklin rebels?

One would think, that a deliberate and practical denial of its authority was   17
the only offence never contemplated by government; else, why has it not assigned its definite, its suitable and proportionate penalty? If a man who has no
property refuses but once to earn nine shillings for the State, he is put in prison
for a period unlimited by any law that I know, and determined only by the discretion of those who placed him there; but if he should steal ninety times nine
shillings from the State, he is soon permitted to go at large again.

If the injustice is part of the necessary friction of the machine of govern-   18
ment, let it go, let it go: perchance it will wear smooth,—certainly the machine
will wear out. If the injustice has a spring, or a pulley, or a rope, or a crank, exclusively for itself, then perhaps you may consider whether the remedy will not
be worse than the evil; but if it is of such a nature that it requires you to be the
agent of injustice to another, then, I say, break the law. Let your life be a counter
friction to stop the machine. What I have to do is to see, at any rate, that I do
not lend myself to the wrong which I condemn.

As for adopting the ways which the State has provided for remedying the   19
evil, I know not of such ways. They take too much time, and a man's life will be
gone. I have other affairs to attend to. I came into this world, not chiefly to
make this a good place to live in, but to live in it, be it good or bad. A man
has not every thing to do, but something; and because he cannot do *every
thing*, it is not necessary that he should do *something* wrong. It is not my business to be petitioning the governor or the legislature any more than it is theirs
to petition me; and, if they should not hear my petition, what should I do then?
But in this case the State has provided no way: its very Constitution is the evil.
This may seem to be harsh and stubborn and unconciliatory; but it is to treat
with the utmost kindness and consideration the only spirit that can appreciate
or deserves it. So is all change for the better, like birth and death which con-
vulse the body.

I do not hesitate to say, that those who call themselves abolitionists should   20
at once effectually withdraw their support, both in person and property, from the
government of Massachusetts, and not wait till they constitute a majority of one,
before they suffer the right to prevail through them. I think that it is enough if
they have God on their side, without waiting for that other one. Moreover, any
man more right than his neighbors, constitutes a majority of one already.

I meet this American government, or its representative the State govern-   21
ment, directly, and face to face, once a year, no more, in the person of its tax-
gatherer; this is the only mode in which a man situated as I am necessarily
meets it; and it then says distinctly, Recognize me; and the simplest, the most
effectual, and, in the present posture of affairs, the indispensablest mode of
treating with it on this head, of expressing your little satisfaction with and love
for it, is to deny it then. My civil neighbor, the tax-gatherer, is the very man I
have to deal with,—for it is, after all, with men and not with parchment that I
quarrel,—and he has voluntarily chosen to be an agent of the government.
How shall he ever know well what he is and does as an officer of the government, or as a man, until he is obliged to consider whether he shall treat me, his
neighbor, for whom he has respect, as a neighbor and well-disposed man, or

as a maniac and disturber of the peace, and see if he can get over this obstruction to his neighborliness without a ruder and more impetuous thought or speech corresponding with his action? I know this well, that if one thousand, if one hundred, if ten men whom I could name,—if ten *honest* men only,—aye, if *one* HONEST man, in this State of Massachusetts, *ceasing to hold slaves*, were actually to withdraw from this copartnership, and be locked up in the county jail therefor, it would be the abolition of slavery in America. For it matters not how small the beginning may seem to be: what is once well done is done for ever. But we love better to talk about it: that we say is our mission. Reform keeps many scores of newspapers in its service, but not one man. If my esteemed neighbor, the State's ambassador,[8] who will devote his days to the settlement of the question of human rights in the Council Chamber, instead of being threatened with the prisons of Carolina, were to sit down the prisoner of Massachusetts, that State which is so anxious to foist the sin of slavery upon her sister,—though at present she can discover only an act of inhospitality to be the ground of a quarrel with her,—the Legislature would not wholly waive the subject the following winter.

22   Under a government which imprisons any unjustly, the true place for a just man is also a prison. The proper place to-day, the only place which Massachusetts has provided for her freer and less desponding spirits, is in her prisons, to be put out and locked out of the State by her own act, as they have already put themselves out by their principles. It is there that the fugitive slave, and the Mexican prisoner on parole, and the Indian come to plead the wrongs of his race, should find them; on that separate, but more free and honorable ground, where the State places those who are not *with* her but *against* her,—the only house in a slave-state in which a free man can abide with honor. If any think that their influence would be lost there, and their voices no longer afflict the ear of the State, that they would not be as an enemy within its walls, they do not know by how much truth is stronger than error, nor how much more eloquently and effectively he can combat injustice who has experienced a little in his own person. Cast your whole vote, not a strip of paper merely, but your whole influence. A minority is powerless while it conforms to the majority; it is not even a minority then; but it is irresistible when it clogs by its whole weight. If the alternative is to keep all just men in prison, or give up war and slavery, the State will not hesitate which to choose. If a thousand men were not to pay their tax-bills this year, that would not be a violent and bloody measure, as it would be to pay them, and enable the State to commit violence and shed innocent blood. This is, in fact, the definition of a peaceable revolution, if any such is possible. If the tax-gatherer, or any other public officer, asks me, as one has done, "But what shall I do?" my answer is, "If you really wish to do any thing, resign your office." When the subject has refused allegiance, and the officer has resigned his office, then the revolution is accomplished. But even suppose blood should flow. Is there not a sort of blood shed when the conscience is wounded?

---

[8] Samuel Hoar (1778–1856) went from Concord to the South Carolina legislature to protest treatment of black seamen.

Through this wound a man's real manhood and immortality flow out, and he bleeds to an everlasting death. I see this blood flowing now.

I have contemplated the imprisonment of the offender, rather than the seizure of his goods,—though both will serve the same purpose,—because they who assert the purest right, and consequently are most dangerous to a corrupt State, commonly have not spent much time in accumulating property. To such the State renders comparatively small service, and a slight tax is wont to appear exorbitant, particularly if they are obliged to earn it by special labor with their hands. If there were one who lived wholly without the use of money, the State itself would hesitate to demand it of him. But the rich man—not to make any invidious comparison—is always sold to the institution which makes him rich. Absolutely speaking, the more money, the less virtue; for money comes between a man and his objects, and obtains them for him; and it was certainly no great virtue to obtain it. It puts to rest many questions which he would otherwise be taxed to answer; while the only new question which it puts is the hard but superfluous one, how to spend it. Thus his moral ground is taken from under his feet. The opportunities of living are diminished in proportion as what are called the "means" are increased. The best thing a man can do for his culture when he is rich is to endeavour to carry out those schemes which he entertained when he was poor. Christ answered the Herodians according to their condition. "Show me the tribute-money," said he;—and one took a penny out of his pocket;—If you use money which has the image of Caesar on it, and which he has made current and valuable, that is, *if you are men of the State,* and gladly enjoy the advantages of Caesar's government, then pay him back some of his own when he demands it; "Render therefore to Caesar that which is Caesar's, and to God those things which are God's,"—leaving them no wiser than before as to which was which; for they did not wish to know. **23**

When I converse with the freest of my neighbors, I perceive that, whatever they may say about the magnitude and seriousness of the question, and their regard for the public tranquility, the long and the short of the matter is, that they cannot spare the protection of the existing government, and they dread the consequences of disobedience to it to their property and families. For my own part, I should not like to think that I ever rely on the protection of the State. But, if I deny the authority of the State when it presents its tax-bill, it will soon take and waste all my property, and so harass me and my children without end. This is hard. This makes it impossible for a man to live honestly and at the same time comfortably in outward respects. It will not be worth the while to accumulate property; that would be sure to go again. You must hire or squat somewhere, and raise but a small crop, and eat that soon. You must live within yourself, and depend upon yourself, always tucked up and ready for a start, and not have many affairs. A man may grow rich in Turkey even, if he will be in all respects a good subject of the Turkish government. Confucius said,—"If a State is governed by the principles of reason, poverty and misery are subjects of shame; if a State is not governed by the principles of reason, riches and honors are the subjects of shame." No: until I want the protection of Massachusetts to be extended to me in some distant southern port, where my liberty is **24** endangered, or until I am bent solely on building up an estate at home by peaceful enterprise, I can afford to refuse allegiance to Massachusetts, and her right to my property and life. It costs me less in every sense to incur the penalty of disobedience to the State, than it would to obey. I should feel as if I were worth less in that case.

25 Some years ago, the State met me in behalf of the church, and commanded me to pay a certain sum toward the support of a clergyman whose preaching my father attended, but never I myself. "Pay it," it said, "or be locked up in the jail." I declined to pay. But, unfortunately, another man saw fit to pay it. I did not see why the schoolmaster should be taxed to support the priest, and not the priest the schoolmaster; for I was not the State's schoolmaster, but I supported myself by voluntary subscription. I did not see why the lyceum should not present its tax-bill, and have the State to back its demand, as well as the church. However, at the request of the selectmen, I condescended to make some such statement as this in writing:—"Know all men by these presents, that I, Henry Thoreau, do not wish to be regarded as a member of any incorporated society which I have not joined." This I gave to the town-clerk; and he has it. The State, having thus learned that I did not wish to be regarded as a member of that church, has never made a like demand on me since; though it said that it must adhere to its original presumption that time. If I had known how to name them, I should then have signed off in detail from all the societies which I never signed on to; but I did not know where to find a complete list.

26 I have paid no poll-tax for six years. I was put into a jail once on this account, for one night; and, as I stood considering the walls of solid stone, two or three feet thick, the door of wood and iron, a foot thick, and the iron grating which strained the light, I could not help being struck with the foolishness of that institution which treated me as if I were mere flesh and blood and bones, to be locked up. I wondered that it should have concluded at length that this was the best use it could put me to, and had never thought to avail itself of my services in some way. I saw that, if there was a wall of stone between me and my towns-men, there was a still more difficult one to climb or break through, before they could get to be as free as I was. I did not for a moment feel confined, and the walls seemed a great waste of stone and mortar. I felt as if I alone of all my towns-men had paid my tax. They plainly did not know how to treat me, but behaved like persons who are underbred. In every threat and in every compliment there was a blunder; for they thought that my chief desire was to stand the other side of that stone wall. I could not but smile to see how industriously they locked the door on my meditations, which followed them out again without let or hinderance, and *they* were really all that was dangerous. As they could not reach me, they had resolved to punish my body; just as boys, if they cannot come at some person against whom they have a spite, will abuse his dog. I saw that the State was half-witted, that it was timid as a lone woman with her silver spoons, and that it did not know its friends from its foes, and I lost all my remaining respect for it, and pitied it.

Thus the State never intentionally confronts a man's sense, intellectual or 27
moral, but only his body, his senses. It is not armed with superior wit or honesty, but with superior physical strength. I was not born to be forced. I will
breathe after my own fashion. Let us see who is the strongest. What force has
a multitude? They only can force me who obey a higher law than I. They force
me to become like themselves. I do not hear of *men* being *forced* to live this
way or that by masses of men. What sort of life were that to live? When I meet
a government which says to me, "Your money or your life," why should I be in
haste to give it my money? It may be in a great strait, and not know what to do:
I cannot help that. It must help itself; do as I do. It is not worth the while to
snivel about it. I am not responsible for the successful working of the machinery of society. I am not the son of the engineer. I perceive that, when an acorn
and a chestnut fall side by side, the one does not remain inert to make way for
the other, but both obey their own laws, and spring and grow and flourish as
best they can, till one, perchance, overshadows and destroys the other. If a
plant cannot live according to its nature, it dies; and so a man.

The night in prison was novel and interesting enough. The prisoners in their 28
shirt-sleeves were enjoying a chat and the evening air in the door-way, when I
entered. But the jailer said, "Come, boys, it is time to lock up;" and so they dis-
persed, and I heard the sound of their steps returning into the hollow apart-
ments. My room-mate was introduced to me by the jailer, as "a first-rate fellow
and a clever man." When the door was locked, he showed me where to hang
my hat, and how he managed matters there. The rooms were whitewashed
once a month; and this one, at least, was the whitest, most simply furnished,
and probably the neatest apartment in the town. He naturally wanted to know
where I came from, and what brought me there; and, when I had told him, I
asked him in my turn how he came there, presuming him to be an honest man,
of course; and, as the world goes, I believe he was. "Why," said he, "they accuse me of burning a barn; but I never did it." As near as I could discover, he
had probably gone to bed in a barn when drunk, and smoked his pipe there;
and so a barn was burnt. He had the reputation of being a clever man, had
been there some three months waiting for his trial to come on, and would have
to wait as much longer; but he was quite domesticated and contented, since
he got his board for nothing, and thought that he was well treated.

He occupied one window, and I the other; and I saw, that if one stayed 29
there long, his principal business would be to look out the window. I had
soon read all the tracts that were left there, and examined where former prisoners had broken out, and where a grate had been sawed off, and heard the
history of the various occupants of that room; for I found that even here
there was a history and a gossip which never circulated beyond the walls of
the jail. Probably this is the only house in the town where verses are composed, which are afterward printed in a circular form, but not published. I
was shown quite a long list of verses which were composed by some young
men who had been detected in an attempt to escape, who avenged themselves by singing them.

30   I pumped my fellow-prisoner as dry as I could, for fear I should never see him again; but at length he showed me which was my bed, and left me to blow out the lamp.

31   It was like travelling into a far country, such as I had never expected to behold, to lie there for one night. It seemed to me that I never had heard the town-clock strike before, nor the evening sounds of the village; for we slept with the windows open, which were inside the grating. It was to see my native village in the light of the middle ages, and our Concord was turned into a Rhine stream, and visions of knights and castles passed before me. They were the voices of old burghers that I heard in the streets. I was an involuntary spectator and auditor of whatever was done and said in the kitchen of the adjacent village-inn,—a wholly new and rare experience to me. It was a closer view of my native town. I was fairly inside of it. I never had seen its institutions before. This is one of its peculiar institutions; for it is a shire town. I began to comprehend what its inhabitants were about.

32   In the morning, our breakfasts were put through the hole in the door, in small oblong-square tin pans, made to fit, and holding a pint of chocolate, with brown bread, and an iron spoon. When they called for the vessels again, I was green enough to return what bread I had left; but my comrade seized it, and said that I should lay that up for lunch or dinner. Soon after, he was let out to work at haying in a neighboring field, whither he went every day, and would not be back till noon; so he bade me good-day, saying that he doubted if he should see me again.

33   When I came out of prison,—for some one[9] interfered, and paid the tax,—I did not perceive that great changes had taken place on the common, such as he observed who went in a youth, and emerged a tottering and gray-headed man; and yet a change had to my eyes come over the scene,—the town, and State, and country,—greater than any that mere time could effect. I saw yet more distinctly the State in which I lived. I saw to what extent the people among whom I lived could be trusted as good neighbors and friends; that their friendship was for summer weather only; that they did not greatly purpose to do right; that they were a distinct race from me by their prejudices and superstitions, as the Chinamen and Malays are; that, in their sacrifices to humanity, they ran no risks, not even to their property; that, after all, they were not so noble but they treated the thief as he had treated them, and hoped, by a certain outward observance and a few prayers, and by walking in a particular straight though useless path from time to time, to save their souls. This may be to judge my neighbors harshly; for I believe that most of them are not aware that they have such an institution as the jail in their village.

34   It was formerly the custom in our village, when a poor debtor came out of jail, for his acquaintances to salute him, looking through their fingers, which were crossed to represent the grating of a jail window, "How do ye do?" My neighbors did not thus salute me, but first looked at me, and then at one another, as if I had returned from a long journey. I was put into jail as I was going

---

[9] Probably Maria Thoreau, his aunt.—Ed.

to the shoemaker's to get a shoe which was mended. When I was let out the next morning, I proceeded to finish my errand, and, having put on my mended shoe, joined a huckleberry party, who were impatient to put themselves under my conduct; and in half an hour,—for the horse was soon tackled,[10]—was in the midst of a huckleberry field, on one of our highest hills, two miles off; and then the State was nowhere to be seen.

This is the whole history of "My Prisons."[11]   35

I have never declined paying the highway tax, because I am as desirous of   36 being a good neighbor as I am of being a bad subject; and, as for supporting schools, I am doing my part to educate my fellow-countrymen now. It is for no particular item in the tax-bill that I refuse to pay it. I simply wish to refuse allegiance to the State, to withdraw and stand aloof from it effectually. I do not care to trace the course of my dollar, if I could, till it buys a man, or a musket to shoot one with,—the dollar is innocent,—but I am concerned to trace the effects of my allegiance. In fact, I quietly declare war with the State, after my fashion, though I will still make what use and get what advantage of her I can, as is usual in such cases.

If others pay the tax which is demanded of me, from a sympathy with the   37 State, they do but what they have already done in their own case, or rather they abet injustice to a greater extent than the State requires. If they pay the tax from a mistaken interest in the individual taxed, to save his property or prevent his going to jail, it is because they have not considered wisely how far they let their private feelings interfere with the public good.

This, then, is my position at present. But one cannot be too much on his   38 guard in such a case, lest his action be biassed by obstinacy, or an undue regard for the opinions of men. Let him see that he does only what belongs to himself and to the hour.

I think sometimes, Why, this people mean well; they are only ignorant;   39 they would do better if they knew how: why give your neighbors this pain to treat you as they are not inclined to? But I think, again, this is no reason why I should do as they do, or permit others to suffer much greater pain of a different kind. Again, I sometimes say to myself, When many millions of men, without heat, without ill-will, without personal feeling of any kind, demand of you a few shillings only, without the possibility, such is their constitution, of retracting or altering their present demand, and without the possibility, on your side, of appeal to any other millions, why expose yourself to this overwhelming brute force? You do not resist cold and hunger, the winds and the waves, thus obstinately; you quietly submit to a thousand similar necessities. You do not put your head into the fire. But just in proportion as I regard this as not wholly a brute force, but partly a human force, and consider that I have relations to those millions as to so many millions of men, and not of mere brute or inanimate things, I see that appeal is possible, first and instantaneously, from them to the Maker of them, and, secondly, from them to themselves. But,

---

[10] Harnessed.—Ed.

[11] Reference to memoirs of Italian patriot Silvio Pellico.—Ed.

if I put my head deliberately into the fire, there is no appeal to fire or to the Maker of fire, and I have only myself to blame. If I could convince myself that I have any right to be satisfied with men as they are, and to treat them accordingly, and not according, in some respects, to my requisitions and expectations of what they and I ought to be, then, like a good Mussulman[12] and fatalist, I should endeavor to be satisfied with things as they are, and say it is the will of God. And, above all, there is this difference between resisting this and a purely brute or natural force, that I can resist this with some effect; but I cannot expect, like Orpheus, to change the nature of the rocks and trees and beasts.

40   I do not wish to quarrel with any man or nation. I do not wish to split hairs, to make fine distinctions, or set myself up as better than my neighbors. I seek rather, I may say, even an excuse for conforming to the laws of the land. I am but too ready to conform to them. Indeed I have reason to suspect myself on this head; and each year, as the tax-gatherer comes round, I find myself disposed to review the acts and position of the general and state governments, and the spirit of the people, to discover a pretext for conformity. I believe that the State will soon be able to take all my work of this sort out of my hands, and then I shall be no better a patriot than my fellow-countrymen. Seen from a lower point of view, the Constitution, with all its faults, is very good; the law and the courts are very respectable; even this State and this American government are, in many respects, very admirable and rare things, to be thankful for, such as a great many have described them; but seen from a point of view a little higher, they are what I have described them; seen from a higher still, and the highest, who shall say what they are, or that they are worth looking at or thinking of at all?

41   However, the government does not concern me much, and I shall bestow the fewest possible thoughts on it. It is not many moments that I live under a government, even in this world. If a man is thought-free, fancy-free, imagination-free, that which *is not* never for a long time appearing *to be* to him, unwise rulers or reformers cannot fatally interrupt him.

42   I know that most men think differently from myself; but those whose lives are by profession devoted to the study of these or kindred subjects, content me as little as any. Statesmen and legislators, standing so completely within the institution, never distinctly and nakedly behold it. They speak of moving society, but have no resting-place without it. They may be men of a certain experience and discrimination, and have no doubt invented ingenious and even useful systems, for which we sincerely thank them; but all their wit and usefulness lie within certain not very wide limits. They are wont to forget that the world is not governed by policy and expediency. Webster never goes behind government, and so cannot speak with authority about it. His words are wisdom to those legislators who contemplate no essential reform in the existing government; but for thinkers, and those who legislate for all time, he never once glances at the subject. I know of those whose serene and wise speculations on this theme would soon reveal the limits of his mind's range and hospitality. Yet, compared

---

[12] A Moslem.—Ed.

with the cheap professions of most reformers, and the still cheaper wisdom and eloquence of politicians in general, his are almost the only sensible and valuable words, and we thank Heaven for him. Comparatively, he is always strong, original, and, above all, practical. Still his quality is not wisdom, but prudence. The lawyer's truth is not Truth, but consistency, or a consistent expediency. Truth is always in harmony with herself, and is not concerned chiefly to reveal the justice that may consist with wrong-doing. He well deserves to be called, as he has been called, the Defender of the Constitution. There are really no blows to be given by him but defensive ones. He is not a leader, but a follower. His leaders are the men of '87. "I have never made an effort," he says, "and never propose to make an effort; I have never countenanced an effort, and never mean to countenance an effort, to disturb the arrangement as originally made, by which the various States came into the Union." Still thinking of the sanction which the Constitution gives to slavery, he says, "Because it was a part of the original compact,—let it stand." Notwithstanding his special acuteness and ability, he is unable to take a fact out of its merely political relations, and behold it as it lies absolutely to be disposed of by the intellect,—what, for instance, it behoves a man to do here in America to-day with regard to slavery, but ventures, or is driven, to make some such desperate answer as the following, while professing to speak absolutely, and as a private man,—from which what new and singular code of social duties might be inferred?—"The manner," says he, "in which the government of those States where slavery exists are to regulate it, is for their own consideration, under their responsibility to their constituents, to the general laws of propriety, humanity, and justice, and to God. Associations formed elsewhere, springing from a feeling of humanity, or any other cause, have nothing whatever to do with it. They have never received any encouragement from me, and they never will."[13]

They who know of no purer sources of truth, who have traced up its stream 43 no higher, stand, and wisely stand, by the Bible and the Constitution, and drink at it there with reverence and humility; but they who behold where it comes trickling into this lake or that pool, gird up their loins once more, and continue their pilgrimage toward its fountain-head.

No man with a genius for legislation has appeared in America. They are 44 rare in the history of the world. There are orators, politicians, and eloquent men, by the thousand; but the speaker has not yet opened his mouth to speak, who is capable of settling the much-vexed questions of the day. We love eloquence for its own sake, and not for any truth which it may utter, or any heroism it may inspire. Our legislators have not yet learned the comparative value of free-trade and of freedom, of union, and of rectitude, to a nation. They have no genius or talent for comparatively humble questions of taxation and finance, commerce and manufactures and agriculture. If we were left solely to the wordy wit of legislators in Congress for our guidance, uncorrected by the seasonable experience and the effectual complaints of the people, America would

---

[13] Quotations are from a speech of Webster's in the Senate. Thoreau notes that these quotations were added for the printed version of the essay.—Ed.

not long retain her rank among the nations. For eighteen hundred years, though perchance I have no right to say it, the New Testament, has been written; yet where is the legislator who has wisdom and practical talent enough to avail himself of the light which it sheds on the science of legislation?

45   The authority of government, even such as I am willing to submit to,—for I will cheerfully obey those who know and can do better than I, and in many things even those who neither know nor can do so well,—is still an impure one: to be strictly just, it must have the sanction and consent of the governed. It can have no pure right over my person and property but what I concede to it. The progress from an absolute to a limited monarchy, from a limited monarchy to a democracy, is a progress toward a true respect for the individual. Is a democracy, such as we know it, the last improvement possible in government? Is it not possible to take a step further towards recognizing and organizing the rights of man? There will never be a really free and enlightened State, until the State comes to recognize the individual as a higher and independent power, from which all its own power and authority are derived, and treats him accordingly. I please myself with imagining a State at last which can afford to be just to all men, and to treat the individual with respect as a neighbor; which even would not think it inconsistent with its own repose, if a few were to live aloof from it, not meddling with it, nor embraced by it, who fulfilled all the duties of neighbors and fellow-men. A State which bore this kind of fruit, and suffered it to drop off as fast as it ripened, would prepare the way for a still more perfect and glorious State, which also I have imagined, but not yet anywhere seen.

QUESTIONS FOR READING

1. Thoreau begins by expressing a desire for less government. After stating these views, he calls for what kind of government?

2. What, according to Thoreau, is everyone's obligation? What is not our obligation, with regard to the law or the government?

3. What does Thoreau want Americans of his time to think about their government? What are his two specific complaints about the government in 1848?

4. How did Thoreau feel about his night in jail?

5. Where does he offer a conciliatory passage? What common ground does he find?

6. In paragraph 42, Thoreau asserts that "the lawyer's truth is not Truth." What does he mean by this statement?

QUESTIONS FOR REASONING AND ANALYSIS

1. What is the central claim of Thoreau's argument?

2. Do you agree with Thoreau that you must be responsible for your conscience before being responsible to the government and the law? Why or why not?

3. Do you agree that unjust laws must be disobeyed as the vehicle for change? Why or why not?

QUESTIONS FOR REFLECTING AND WRITING

1. What is one statement of Thoreau's that has most surprised or interested you? Why did you select that statement?

2. Would you demonstrate against an unjust law, risking jail time for your cause? Why or why not? Develop an argument in support of or against action of civil disobedience.

DECLARATION OF SENTIMENTS | ELIZABETH CADY STANTON

Elizabeth Cady Stanton (1815–1902) was one of the most important leaders of the women's rights movement. Educated at the Emma Willard Seminary in Troy, New York, Stanton studied law with her father before her marriage. At the Seneca Falls Convention in 1848 (the first women's rights convention), Stanton gave the opening speech and read her "Declaration of Sentiments." She founded and became president of the National Women's Suffrage Association in 1869.

PREREADING QUESTION As you read, think about the similarities and differences between this document and the "Declaration of Independence." What significant differences in wording and content do you find?

When, in the course of human events, it becomes necessary for one por- 1 tion of the family of man to assume among the people of the earth a position different from that which they have hitherto occupied, but one to which the laws of nature and of nature's God entitle them, a decent respect to the opinions of mankind requires that they should declare the causes that impel them to such a course.

We hold these truths to be self-evident: that all men and women are cre- 2 ated equal; that they are endowed by their Creator with certain inalienable rights; that among these are life, liberty, and the pursuit of happiness; that to secure these rights governments are instituted, deriving their just powers from the consent of the governed. Whenever any form of government becomes destructive of these ends, it is the right of those who suffer from it to refuse allegiance to it, and to insist upon the institution of a new government, laying its foundation on such principles, and organizing its powers in such form, as to them shall seem most likely to effect their safety and happiness. Prudence, indeed, will dictate that governments long established should not be changed for light and transient causes; and accordingly all experience hath shown that mankind are more disposed to suffer, while evils are sufferable, than to right themselves by abolishing the forms to which they were accustomed. But when a long train of abuses and usurpations, pursuing invariably the same object evinces a design to reduce them under absolute despotism, it is their duty to throw off such government, and to provide new guards for their future security. Such has been the patient sufferance of the women under this government, and such is now the necessity which constrains them to demand the equal station to which they are entitled.

3 The history of mankind is a history of repeated injuries and usurpations on the part of man toward woman, having in direct object the establishment of an absolute tyranny over her. To prove this, let facts be submitted to a candid world.

4 He has never permitted her to exercise her inalienable right to the elective franchise.

5 He has compelled her to submit to laws, in the formation of which she had no voice.

6 He has withheld from her rights which are given to the most ignorant and degraded men—both natives and foreigners.

7 Having deprived her of this first right of a citizen, the elective franchise, thereby leaving her without representation in the halls of legislation, he has oppressed her on all sides.

8 He has made her, if married, in the eye of the law, civilly dead.

9 He has taken from her all right in property, even to the wages she earns.

10 He has made her, morally, an irresponsible being, as she can commit many crimes with impunity, provided they be done in the presence of her husband. In the covenant of marriage, she is compelled to promise obedience to her husband, he becoming, to all intents and purposes, her master—the law giving him power to deprive her of her liberty, and to administer chastisement.

11 He has so framed the laws of divorce, as to what shall be the proper causes, and in case of separation, to whom the guardianship of the children shall be given, as to be wholly regardless of the happiness of women—the law, in all cases, going upon a false supposition of the supremacy of man, and giving all power into his hands.

12 After depriving her of all rights as a married woman, if single, and the owner of property, he has taxed her to support a government which recognizes her only when her property can be made profitable to it.

13 He has monopolized nearly all the profitable employments, and from those she is permitted to follow, she receives but a scanty remuneration. He closes against her all the avenues to wealth and distinction which he considers most honorable to himself. As a teacher of theology, medicine, or law, she is not known.

14 He has denied her the facilities for obtaining a thorough education, all colleges being closed against her.

15 He allows her in Church, as well as State, but a subordinate position, claiming Apostolic authority for her exclusion from the ministry, and, with some exceptions, from any public participation in the affairs of the Church.

16 He has created a false public sentiment by giving to the world a different code of morals for men and women, by which moral delinquencies which exclude women from society, are not only tolerated, but deemed of little account in man.

17 He has usurped the prerogative of Jehovah himself, claiming it as his right to assign for her a sphere of action, when that belongs to her conscience and to her God.

He has endeavored, in every way that he could, to destroy her confidence   18
in her own powers, to lessen her self-respect, and to make her willing to lead
a dependent and abject life.

Now in view of this entire disfranchisement of one-half the people of this   19
country, their social and religious degradation—in view of the unjust laws
above mentioned, and because women do feel themselves aggrieved, oppressed, and fraudulently deprived of their most sacred rights, we insist that
they have immediate admission to all the rights and privileges which belong to
them as citizens of the United States.

In entering upon the great work before us, we anticipate no small amount   20
of misconception, misrepresentation, and ridicule; but we shall use every in-
strumentality within our power to effect our object. We shall employ agents,
circulate tracts, petition the State and National legislatures, and endeavor to
enlist the pulpit and the press in our behalf. We hope this Convention will be
followed by a series of Conventions embracing every part of the country.

QUESTIONS FOR READING

1. Summarize the ideas of paragraphs 1 and 2. Be sure to use your own words.
2. What are the first three facts given by Stanton? Why are they presented first?
3. How have women been restricted by law if married or owning property? How have they been restricted in education and work? How have they been restricted psychologically?
4. What, according to Stanton, do women demand? How will they seek their goals?

QUESTIONS FOR REASONING AND ANALYSIS

1. What is Stanton's claim? With what does she charge men?
2. Most—but not all—of Stanton's charges have been redressed, however slowly. Which continue to be legitimate complaints, in whole or in part?

QUESTIONS FOR REFLECTING AND WRITING

1. Do we need a new declaration of sentiments for women? If so, what specific charges would you list? If not, why not?
2. Do we need a declaration of sentiments for other groups—children, minorities, the elderly, animals? If so, what specific charges should be listed? Select one group (that concerns you) and prepare a declaration of sentiments for that group. If you do not think any group needs a declaration, explain why.

ON LIBERTY | JOHN STUART MILL

John Stuart Mill (1806–1873) rose to be an important official in the East India
Company. He is now known as one of the world's most influential philosophers. Some
of his important works include: A System of Logic (1843), Principles of Political

Economy (1848), *The Subjection of Women* (1869), and *On Liberty* (1859), from which the following passages have been taken. In his essay Mill explores the issue of individual freedom in the context of individual good versus social good.

PREREADING QUESTIONS In what two ways can the tyranny of the majority operate in society? Which way may be the most worrisome? Why?

INTRODUCTORY

1   The subject of this Essay is . . . Civil, or Social Liberty: the nature and limits of the power which can be legitimately exercised by society over the individual. A question seldom stated, and hardly ever discussed, in general terms, but which profoundly influences the practical controversies of the age by its latent presence, and is likely soon to make itself recognized as the vital question of the future. It is so far from being new, that, in a certain sense, it has divided mankind, almost from the remotest ages, but in the stage of progress into which the more civilized portions of the species have now entered, it presents itself under new conditions, and requires a different and more fundamental treatment. . . .

2   In political and philosophical theories, as well as in persons, success discloses faults and infirmities which failure might have concealed from observation. The notion, that the people have no need to limit their power over themselves, might seem axiomatic, when popular government was a thing only dreamed about, or read of as having existed at some distant period of the past. Neither was that notion necessarily disturbed by such temporary aberrations as those of the French Revolution, the worst of which were the work of an usurping few, and which, in any case, belonged, not to the permanent working of popular institutions, but to a sudden and convulsive outbreak against monarchical and aristocratic despotism. In time, however, a democratic republic came to occupy a large portion of the earth's surface, and made itself felt as one of the most powerful members of the community of nations; and elective and responsible government became subject to the observations and criticisms which wait upon a great existing fact. It was now perceived that such phrases as "self-government," and "the power of the people over themselves," do not express the true state of the case. The "people" who exercise the power, are not always the same people with those over whom it is exercised, and the "self-government" spoken of, is not the government of each by himself, but of each by all the rest. The will of the people, moreover, practically means, the will of the most numerous or the most active *part* of the people; the majority, or those who succeed in making themselves accepted as the majority: the people, consequently, *may* desire to oppress a part of their number; and precautions are as much needed against this, as against any other abuse of power. The limitation, therefore, of the power of government over individuals, loses none of its importance when the holders of power are regularly accountable to the community, that is, to the strongest party therein. This view of things, recommending itself equally to the intelligence of thinkers and to the inclination of those important classes in European society to whose real or supposed interests democracy is adverse, has

had no difficulty in establishing itself; and in political speculations "the tyranny of the majority" is now generally included among the evils against which society requires to be on its guard.

Like other tyrannies, the tyranny of the majority was at first, and is still vul-   3
garly, held in dread, chiefly as operating through the acts of the public authorities. But reflecting persons perceived that when society is itself the tyrant—society collectively, over the separate individuals who compose it—its means of tyrannizing are not restricted to the acts which it may do by the hands of its political functionaries. Society can and does execute its own mandates: and if it issues wrong mandates instead of right, or any mandates at all in things with which it ought not to meddle, it practises a social tyranny more formidable than many kinds of political oppression, since, though not usually upheld by such extreme penalties, it leaves fewer means of escape, penetrating much more deeply into the details of life, and enslaving the soul itself. Protection, therefore, against the tyranny of the magistrate is not enough; there needs protection also against the tyranny of the prevailing opinion and feeling; against the tendency of society to impose, by other means than civil penalties, its own ideas and practices as rules of conduct on those who dissent from them; to fetter the development, and, if possible, prevent the formation, of any individuality not in harmony with its ways, and compel all characters to fashion themselves upon the model of its own. There is a limit to the legitimate interference of collective opinion with individual independence; and to find that limit, and maintain it against encroachment, is as indispensable to a good condition of human affairs, as protection against political despotism.

But though this proposition is not likely to be contested in general terms,   4
the practical question, where to place the limit—how to make the fitting adjustment between individual independence and social control—is a subject on which nearly everything remains to be done. All that makes existence valuable to any one, depends on the enforcement of restraints upon the actions of other people. Some rules of conduct, therefore, must be imposed, by law in the first place, and by opinion on many things which are not fit subjects for the operation of law. What these rules should be, is the principal question in human affairs; but if we except a few of the most obvious cases, it is one of those which least progress has been made in resolving. No two ages, and scarcely any two countries, have decided it alike; and the decision of one age or country is a wonder to another. Yet the people of any given age and country no more suspect any difficulty in it, than if it were a subject on which mankind had always been agreed. The rules which obtain among themselves appear to them self-evident and self-justifying. This all but universal illusion is one of the examples of the magical influence of custom, which is not only, as the proverb says, a second nature, but is continually mistaken for the first. The effect of custom, in preventing any misgiving respecting the rules of conduct which mankind impose on one another, is all the more complete because the subject is one on which it is not generally considered necessary that reasons should be given, either by one person to others, or by each to himself. People are

accustomed to believe and have been encouraged in the belief by some who aspire to the character of philosophers, that their feelings, on subjects of this nature, are better than reasons, and render reasons unnecessary. The practical principle which guides them to their opinions on the regulation of human conduct, is the feeling in each person's mind that everybody should be required to act as he, and those with whom he sympathizes, would like them to act. No one, indeed, acknowledges to himself that his standard of judgment is his own liking; but an opinion on a point of conduct, not supported by reasons, can only count as one person's preference; and if the reasons, when given, are a mere appeal to a similar preference felt by other people, it is still only many people's liking instead of one. To an ordinary man, however, his own preference, thus supported, is not only a perfectly satisfactory reason, but the only one he generally has for any of his notions of morality, taste, or propriety, which are not expressly written in his religious creed; and his chief guide in the interpretation even of that. Men's opinions, accordingly, on what is laudable or blamable, are affected by all the multifarious causes which influence their wishes in regard to the conduct of others, and which are as numerous as those which determine their wishes on any other subject. Sometimes their reason—at other times their prejudices or superstitions: often their social affections, not seldom their anti-social ones, their envy or jealousy, their arrogance or contemptuousness: but most commonly, their desires or fears for themselves—their legitimate or illegitimate self-interest. Wherever there is an ascendant class, a large portion of the morality of the country emanates from its class interests, and its feelings of class superiority. The morality between Spartans and Helots, between planters and negroes, between princes and subjects, between nobles and roturiers, between men and women, has been for the most part the creation of these class interests and feelings: and the sentiments thus generated, react in turn upon the moral feelings of the members of the ascendant class, in their relations among themselves. Where, on the other hand, a class, formerly ascendant, has lost its ascendency, or where its ascendency is unpopular, the prevailing moral sentiments frequently bear the impress of an impatient dislike of superiority. Another grand determining principle of the rules of conduct, both in act and forbearance which have been enforced by law or opinion, has been the servility of mankind towards the supposed preferences or aversions of their temporal masters, or of their gods. This servility though essentially selfish, is not hypocrisy; it gives rise to perfectly genuine sentiments of abhorrence; it made men burn magicians and heretics. Among so many baser influences, the general and obvious interests of society have of course had a share, and a large one, in the direction of the moral sentiments: less, however, as a matter of reason, and on their own account, than as a consequence of the sympathies and antipathies which grew out of them: and sympathies and antipathies which had little or nothing to do with the interests of society, have made themselves felt in the establishment of moralities with quite as great force. . . .

5   The object of this Essay is to assert one very simple principle, as entitled to govern absolutely the dealings of society with the individual in the way of

compulsion and control, whether the means used be physical force in the form of legal penalties, or the moral coercion of public opinion. That principle is, that the sole end for which mankind are warranted, individually or collectively in interfering with the liberty of action of any of their number, is self-protection. That the only purpose for which power can be rightfully exercised over any member of a civilized community, against his will, is to prevent harm to others. His own good, either physical or moral, is not a sufficient warrant. He cannot rightfully be compelled to do or forbear because it will be better for him to do so, because it will make him happier, because, in the opinions of others, to do so would be wise, or even right. These are good reasons for remonstrating with him, or reasoning with him, or persuading him, or entreating him, but not for compelling him, or visiting him with any evil, in case he do otherwise. To justify that, the conduct from which it is desired to deter him must be calculated to produce evil to some one else. The only part of the conduct of any one, for which he is amenable to society, is that which concerns others. In the part which merely concerns himself, his independence is, of right, absolute. Over himself, over his own body and mind, the individual is sovereign.

It is, perhaps, hardly necessary to say that this doctrine is meant to apply   6 only to human beings in the maturity of their faculties. We are not speaking of children, or of young persons below the age which the law may fix as that of manhood or womanhood. Those who are still in a state to require being taken care of by others, must be protected against their own actions as well as against external injury. . . .

It is proper to state that I forego any advantage which could be derived to   7 my argument from the idea of abstract right as a thing independent of utility. I regard utility as the ultimate appeal on all ethical questions; but it must be utility in the largest sense, grounded on the permanent interests of man as a progressive being. Those interests, I contend, authorize the subjection of individual spontaneity to external control, only in respect to those actions of each, which concern the interest of other people. If any one does an act hurtful to others, there is a *prima facie* case for punishing him, by law, or, where legal penalties are not safely applicable, by general disapprobation. There are also many positive acts for the benefit of others, which he may rightfully be compelled to perform; such as, to give evidence in a court of justice; to bear his fair share in the common defence, or in any other joint work necessary to the interest of the society of which he enjoys the protection; and to perform certain acts of individual beneficence, such as saving a fellow-creature's life, or interposing to protect the defenceless against ill-usage, things which whenever it is obviously a man's duty to do, he may rightfully be made responsible to society for not doing. A person may cause evil to others not only by his actions but by his inaction, and in neither case he is justly accountable to them for the injury. The latter case, it is true, requires a much more cautious exercise of compulsion than the former. To make any one answerable for doing evil to others, is the rule; to make him answerable for not preventing evil, is, comparatively speaking, the exception. Yet there are many cases clear enough and grave enough to justify that exception. In all things which regard the external relations of the individual, he is *de jure* amenable to those whose interests are concerned, and if need be, to society as their protector. There are often good reasons for not holding him to the responsibility; but these reasons must arise from the special expediencies of the case: either because it is a kind of case in which he is on the whole likely to act better, when left to his own discretion, than when controlled in any way in which society have it in their power to control him. . . .

8   There is a sphere of action in which society, as distinguished from the individual, has, if any, only an indirect interest; comprehending all that portion of a person's life and conduct which affects only himself, or, if it also affects others, only with their free, voluntary, and undeceived consent and participation. When I say only himself, I mean directly, and in the first instance: for whatever affects himself, may affect others *through* himself; and the objection which may be grounded on this contingency, will receive consideration in the sequel. This, then, is the appropriate region of human liberty. It comprises, first, the inward domain of consciousness; demanding liberty of conscience, in the most comprehensive sense; liberty of thought and feeling; absolute freedom of opinion and sentiment on all subjects, practical or speculative, scientific, moral, or theological. The liberty of expressing and publishing opinions may seem to fall under a different principle, since it belongs to that part of the conduct of an individual which concerns other people; but, being almost of as much importance as the liberty of thought itself, and resting in great part on the same reasons, is practically inseparable from it. Secondly, the principle requires liberty of tastes and pursuits; of framing the plan of our life to suit our own character; of doing as we like, subject to such consequences as may follow; without impediment from our fellow-creatures, so long as what we do does not harm them even though they should think our conduct foolish, perverse, or wrong. Thirdly, from this liberty of each individual, follows the liberty, within the same limits, of combination among individuals; freedom to unite, for any purpose not involving harm to others: the persons combining being supposed to be of full age, and not forced or deceived.

9   No society in which these liberties are not, on the whole, respected, is free, whatever may be its form of government; and none is completely free in which they do not exist absolute and unqualified. The only freedom which deserves the name, is that of pursuing our own good in our own way, so long as we do not attempt to deprive others of theirs, or impede their efforts to obtain it. Each is the proper guardian of his own health, whether bodily, or mental or spiritual. Mankind are greater gainers by suffering each other to live as seems good to themselves, than by compelling each to live as seems good to the rest. . . .

OF THE LIBERTY OF THOUGHT AND DISCUSSION

10   The time, it is to be hoped, is gone by when any defense would be necessary of the "liberty of the press" as one of the securities against corrupt or tyrannical government. No argument, we may suppose, can now be needed against permitting a legislature or an executive, not identified in interest with

the people, to prescribe opinions to them and determine what doctrines or what arguments they shall be allowed to hear. This aspect of the question, besides, has been so often and so triumphantly enforced by preceding writers that it need not be specially insisted on in this place. Though the law of England, on the subject of the press, is as servile to this day as it was in the time of the Tudors, there is little danger of its being actually put in force against political discussion except during some temporary panic when fear of insurrection drives ministers and judges from their propriety; and, speaking generally, it is not, in constitutional countries, to be apprehended that the government, whether completely responsible to the people or not, will often attempt to control the expression of opinion, except when in doing so it makes itself the organ of the general intolerance of the public. Let us suppose, therefore, that the government is entirely at one with the people, and never thinks of exerting any power of coercion unless in agreement with what it conceives to be their voice. But I deny the right of the people to exercise such coercion, either by themselves or by their government. The power itself is illegitimate. The best government has no more title to it than the worst. It is as noxious, or more noxious, when exerted in accordance with public opinion than when in opposition to it. If all mankind minus one were of one opinion, mankind would be no more justified in silencing that one person than he, if he had the power, would be justified in silencing mankind. Were an opinion a personal possession of no value except to the owner, if to be obstructed in the enjoyment of it were simply a private injury, it would make some difference whether the injury was inflicted only on a few persons or on many. But the peculiar evil of silencing the expression of an opinion is that it is robbing the human race, posterity as well as the existing generation—those who dissent from the opinion, still more than those who hold it. If the opinion is right, they are deprived of the opportunity of exchanging error for truth; if wrong, they lose, what is almost as great a benefit, the clearer perception and livelier impression of truth produced by its collision with error. . . .

We have now recognized the necessity to the mental well-being of mankind (on which all their other well-being depends) of freedom of opinion, and freedom of the expression of opinion, on four distinct grounds, which we will now briefly recapitulate: 11

First, if any opinion is compelled to silence, that opinion may, for aught we can certainly know, be true. To deny this is to assume our own infallibility. 12

Secondly, though the silenced opinion be an error, it may, and very commonly does, contain a portion of truth; and since the general or prevailing opinion on any subject is rarely or never the whole truth, it is only by the collision of adverse opinions that the remainder of the truth has any chance of being supplied. 13

Thirdly, even if the received opinion be not only true, but the whole truth: unless it is suffered to be, and actually is, vigorously and earnestly contested, it will, by most of those who receive it, be held in the manner of a prejudice, with little comprehension or feeling of its rational grounds. And not only this, but, fourthly, the meaning of the doctrine itself will be in danger of being lost 14 or enfeebled, and deprived of its vital effect on the character and conduct: the dogma becoming a mere formal profession, inefficacious for good, but cumbering the ground and preventing the growth of any real and heartfelt conviction from reason or personal experience.

QUESTIONS FOR READING

1. Explain the concept of "the tyranny of the majority." Under what kind of government is this potentially an issue?

2. In paragraph 3, Mill writes: "There is a limit to the legitimate interference of collective opinion with individual independence; and to find that limit . . . is as indispensable . . . as protection against political despotism." This statement establishes two principles; what are they? What is asserted and what is implied in the statement?

3. Why, in Mill's view, are limits on individual behavior necessary in a society?

4. In what two ways does a society impose "rules of conduct" on citizens? How difficult do most people think these are? How do most people arrive at their views?

5. What is the one principle that should be the basis for deciding what constraints on individuals are appropriate? What is not a sufficient reason to restrict an individual?

6. What group is excluded from the principle referred to in question 5? Why?

7. What does freedom of the press provide a society?

8. Summarize Mill's four reasons for protecting freedom of expression of opinion.

QUESTIONS FOR REASONING AND ANALYSIS

1. What is Mill's claim?

2. Mill's study of individual liberty is necessarily abstract because his goal is to establish a universal principle. Given his purpose's influence on his writing, has he written persuasively? Why or why not?

3. Mill says that "a person may cause evil to others not only by his actions but by his inaction" and should be held accountable for both kinds of injuries. Apply this idea to a specific case: Should we have a "Good Samaritan" law that would require motorists to stop to aid a motorist in trouble? (Germany has such a law.) What would Mill say? What would you say? Why?

4. What part of his argument would Mill use to justify prohibiting child pornography? Do you agree with Mill? Why or why not?

QUESTIONS FOR REFLECTING AND WRITING

1. Cigarette advertising is currently banned from television. Should all cigarette advertising be banned? What would Mill say? What do you say? Why?

2. Should individuals be free to act in ways that are "harmful" (in someone else's view) to themselves, so long as they are not harming others? Or should society

seek to legislate on issues of personal morality or personal health? Defend your position.

3. What one of Mill's reasons for not repressing freedom of expression is, in your view, the most persuasive? Why?

A HANGING | GEORGE ORWELL

George Orwell (1903–1950), the pseudonym of Eric Arthur Blair, was a British essayist and novelist best known for his political satires *Animal Farm* (1945) and *1984* (1949). He is also well known for his essay "Politics and the English Language," the essay that set the standard for the analysis of doublespeak in political language. In the following essay, published in *Shooting an Elephant and Other Essays* (1950), Orwell captures the telling details of a brief scene he witnessed.

PREREADING QUESTIONS Why might a writer choose to tell the story of a hanging? What kinds of issues might emerge from such a story?

It was in Burma, a sodden morning of the rains. A sickly light, like yellow tinfoil, was slanting over the high walls into the jail yard. We were waiting outside the condemned cells, a row of sheds fronted with double bars, like small animal cages. Each cell measured about ten feet by ten and was quite bare within except for a plank bed and a pot of drinking water. In some of them brown silent men were squatting at the inner bars, with their blankets draped round them. These were the condemned men, due to be hanged within the next week or two.

One prisoner had been brought out of his cell. He was a Hindu, a puny wisp of a man, with a shaven head and vague liquid eyes. He had a thick, sprouting moustache, absurdly too big for his body, rather like a moustache of a comic man on the films. Six tall Indian warders were guarding him and getting him ready for the gallows. Two of them stood by with rifles and fixed bayonets, while the others handcuffed him, passed a chain through his handcuffs and fixed it to their belts, and lashed his arms tight to his sides. They crowded very close about him, with their hands always on him in a careful, caressing grip, as though all the while feeling him to make sure he was there. It was like men handling a fish which is still alive and may jump back into the water. But he stood quite unresisting, yielding his arms limply to the ropes, as though he hardly noticed what was happening.

Eight o'clock struck and a bugle call, desolately thin in the wet air, floated from the distant barracks. The superintendent of the jail, who was standing apart from the rest of us, moodily prodding the gravel with his stick, raised his head at the sound. He was an army doctor, with a grey toothbrush moustache and a gruff voice. "For God's sake hurry up, Francis," he said irritably. "The man ought to have been dead by this time. Aren't you ready yet?"

Francis, the head jailer, a fat Dravidian in a white drill suit and gold spectacles, waved his black hand. "Yes sir, yes sir," he bubbled. "All iss satisfactorily prepared. The hangman iss waiting. We shall proceed."

5   "Well, quick march, then. The prisoners can't get their breakfast till this job's over."

6   We set out for the gallows. Two warders marched on either side of the prisoner, with their rifles at the slope; two others marched close against him, gripping him by arm and shoulder, as though at once pushing and supporting him. The rest of us, magistrates and the like, followed behind. Suddenly, when we had gone ten yards, the procession stopped short without any order or warning. A dreadful thing had happened—a dog, come goodness knows whence, had appeared in the yard. It came bounding among us with a loud volley of barks, and leapt round us wagging its whole body, wild with glee at finding so many human beings together. It was a large woolly dog, half Airedale, half pariah. For a moment it pranced round us, and then, before anyone could stop it, it had made a dash for the prisoner, and jumping up tried to lick his face. Everyone stood aghast, too taken aback even to grab at the dog.

7   "Who let that bloody brute in here?" said the superintendent angrily. "Catch it, someone!"

8   A warder, detached from the escort, charged clumsily after the dog, but it danced and gambolled just out of his reach, taking everything as part of the game. A young Eurasian jailer picked up a handful of gravel and tried to stone the dog away, but it dodged the stones and came after us again. Its yaps echoed from the jail walls. The prisoner, in the grasp of the two warders looked on incuriously, as though this was another formality of the hanging. It was several minutes before someone managed to catch the dog. Then we put my handkerchief through its collar and moved off once more, with the dog still straining and whimpering.

9   It was about forty yards to the gallows. I watched the bare brown back of the prisoner marching in front of me. He walked clumsily with his bound arms, but quite steadily, with that bobbing gait of the Indian who never straightens his knees. At each step his muscles slid neatly into place, the lock of hair on his scalp danced up and down, his feet printed themselves on the wet gravel. And once, in spite of the men who gripped him by each shoulder, he stepped slightly aside to avoid a puddle on the path.

10   It is curious, but till that moment I had never realised what it means to destroy a healthy, conscious man. When I saw the prisoner step aside to avoid the puddle, I saw the mystery, the unspeakable wrongness, of cutting a life short when it is in full tide. This man was not dying, he was alive just as we were alive. All the organs of his body were working—bowels digesting food, skin renewing itself, nails growing, tissues forming—all toiling away in solemn foolery. His nails would still be growing when he stood on the drop, when he was falling through the air with a tenth of a second to live. His eyes saw the yellow gravel and the grey walls, and his brain still remembered, foresaw, reasoned—reasoned even about puddles. He and we were a party of men walking together, seeing, hearing, feeling, understanding the same world; and in two minutes, with a sudden snap, one of us would be gone—one mind less, one world less.

11   The gallows stood in a small yard, separate from the main grounds of the prison, and overgrown with tall prickly weeds. It was a brick erection like three

sides of a shed, with planking on top, and above that two beams and a cross-bar with the rope dangling. The hangman, a grey-haired convict in the white uniform of the prison, was waiting beside his machine. He greeted us with a servile crouch as we entered. At a word from Francis the two warders, gripping the prisoner more closely than ever, half led, half pushed him to the gallows and helped him clumsily up the ladder. Then the hangman climbed up and fixed the rope round the prisoner's neck.

We stood waiting, five yards away. The warders had formed in a rough 12 circle round the gallows. And then, when the noose was fixed, the prisoner began crying out on his god. It was a high, reiterated cry of "Ram! Ram! Ram! Ram!", not urgent and fearful like a prayer or a cry for help, but steady, rhythmical, almost like the tolling of a bell. The dog answered the sound with a whine. The hangman, still standing on the gallows, produced a small cotton bag like a flour bag and drew it down over the prisoner's face. But the sound, muffled by the cloth, still persisted, over and over again: "Ram! Ram! Ram! Ram! Ram!"

The hangman climbed down and stood ready, holding the lever. Minutes 13 seemed to pass. The steady, muffled crying from the prisoner went on and on, "Ram! Ram! Ram!" never faltering for an instant. The superintendent, his head on his chest, was slowly poking the ground with his stick; perhaps he was counting the cries, allowing the prisoner a fixed number—fifty, perhaps, or a hundred. Everyone had changed colour. The Indians had gone grey like bad coffee, and one or two of the bayonets were wavering. We looked at the lashed, hooded man on the drop, and listened to his cries—each cry another second of life; the same thought was in all our minds: oh, kill him quickly, get it over, stop that abominable noise!

Suddenly the superintendent made up his mind. Throwing up his head he 14 made a swift motion with his stick. "Chalo!" he shouted almost fiercely.

There was a clanking noise, and then dead silence. The prisoner had van- 15 ished, and the rope was twisting on itself. I let go of the dog, and it galloped immediately to the back of the gallows; but when it got there it stopped short, barked, and then retreated into a corner of the yard, where it stood among the weeds, looking timorously out at us. We went round the gallows to inspect the prisoner's body. He was dangling with his toes pointed straight downwards, very slowly revolving, as dead as a stone.

The superintendent reached out with his stick and poked the bare body; it 16 oscillated, slightly. "*He's* all right," said the superintendent. He backed out from under the gallows, and blew out a deep breath. The moody look had gone out of his face quite suddenly. He glanced at his wrist-watch. "Eight minutes past eight. Well, that's all for this morning, thank God."

The warders unfixed bayonets and marched away. The dog, sobered and 17 conscious of having misbehaved itself, slipped after them. We walked out of the gallows yard, past the condemned cells with their waiting prisoners, into the big central yard of the prison. The convicts, under the commend of warders armed with lathis, were already receiving their breakfast. They squatted in long rows, each man holding a tin pannikin, while two warders with buckets marched round ladling out rice; it seemed quite a homely, jolly scene, after the hanging. An enormous relief had come upon us now that the job was done. One felt an impulse to sing, to break into a run, to snigger. All at once everyone began chattering gaily.

18   The Eurasian boy walking beside me nodded towards the way we had come, with a knowing smile: "Do you know, sir, our friend (he meant the dead man), when he heard his appeal had been dismissed, he pissed on the floor of his cell. From fright.—Kindly take one of my cigarettes, sir. Do you not admire my new silver case, sir? From the boxwallah, two rupees eight annas. Classy European style."

19   Several people laughed—at what, nobody seemed certain.

20   Francis was walking by the superintendent, talking garrulously: "Well, sir, all hass passed off with the utmost satisfactoriness. It wass all finished—flick! like that. It iss not always so—oah, no! I have known cases where the doctor wass obliged to go beneath the gallows and pull the prisoner's legs to ensure decease. Most disagreeable!"

21   "Wriggling about, eh? That's bad," said the superintendent.

22   "Ach, sir, it iss worse when they become refractory! One man, I recall, clung to the bars of hiss cage when we went to take him out. You will scarcely credit, sir, that it took six warders to dislodge him, three pulling at each leg. We reasoned with him. 'My dear fellow,' we said, 'think of all the pain and trouble you are causing to me!' But no, he would not listen! Ach, he wass very troublesome!"

23   I found that I was laughing quite loudly. Everyone was laughing. Even the superintendent grinned in a tolerant way. "You'd better all come out and have a drink," he said quite genially. "I've got a bottle of whisky in the car. We could do with it."

24   We went through the big double gates of the prison, into the road. "Pulling at his legs!" exclaimed a Burmese magistrate suddenly, and burst into a loud chuckling. We all began laughing again. At this moment Francis's anecdote seemed extraordinarily funny. We all had a drink together, native and European alike, quite amicably. The dead man was a hundred yards away.

QUESTIONS FOR READING

1. How did Orwell come to witness this hanging? What was his connection?
2. What action by the prisoner made Orwell reflect on what the group was doing?
3. What is the reaction of those watching to the prisoner's cries when he is standing on the gallows?
4. What is the most common reaction as the witnesses leave the gallows and walk back through the main prison yard?

QUESTIONS FOR REASONING AND ANALYSIS

1. What does Orwell accomplish by opening with a description of the row of condemned cells?

2. Study the description of the prisoner and his guards in paragraph 2. What seems ironic about the picture Orwell draws? How does this help to suggest his attitude toward the hanging?

3. What is the significance of the dog? Why does Orwell describe this incident as a "dreadful thing" that happened? How is this scene ironic?

4. Orwell has only one brief passage of general comments; almost all of the essay is narration. What inferences are we encouraged to draw from the details of the event? How would you state Orwell's subject? His thesis? What details from the essay support your assertion of Orwell's thesis?

QUESTIONS FOR REFLECTING AND WRITING

1. What is your emotional reaction to the essay? Has Orwell moved you in any way? Why or why not?

2. Is this essay just about capital punishment? What is Orwell suggesting about being human—and inhuman?

3. Have you had occasion to be distressed or embarrassed by a particular event? If so, what was your reaction? Did you laugh? Or want a drink? Or try to stop what was happening that was upsetting to you? Can you explain why we react to distress by laughter?

AN INQUIRY INTO THE PERSISTENCE OF UNWISDOM IN GOVERNMENT | BARBARA W. TUCHMAN

A native New Yorker, Barbara Wertheim Tuchman (1912–1989), a graduate of Radcliffe College, began her career with the *Nation* magazine, held other journalistic positions, and was awarded many visiting lectureships. But she is most famous for her historical studies. Two of her books, *The Guns of August* (1962) and *Stilwell and the American Experience in China* (1971) won Pulitzer Prizes. Other studies include *The Zimmermann Telegram* (1958), *A Distant Mirror: The Calamitous Fourteenth Century* (1978), and *The March of Folly* (1984). The following essay, first published in *Esquire* in May 1980, in an expanded form serves as the first chapter of *The March of Folly*.

PREREADING QUESTIONS What are Tuchman's purposes in writing? What is her primary purpose?

A problem that strikes one in the study of history, regardless of period, is why man makes a poorer performance of government than of almost any other human activity. In this sphere, wisdom—meaning judgment acting on experience, common sense, available knowledge, and a decent appreciation of probability—is less operative and more frustrated than it should be. Why do men in high office so often act contrary to the way that reason points and enlightened self-interest suggests? Why does intelligent mental process so often seem to be paralyzed?

Why, to begin at the beginning, did the Trojan authorities drag that suspicious-looking wooden horse inside their gates? Why did successive ministries of George III—that "bundle of imbecility," as Dr. Johnson[1] called them collectively—insist on coercing rather than conciliating the Colonies though strongly advised otherwise by many counselors? Why did Napoleon and Hitler invade Russia? Why did the kaiser's[2] government resume unrestricted submarine warfare in 1917 although explicitly warned that this would bring in the United States and that American belligerency would mean Germany's defeat? Why did Chiang Kai-shek[3] refuse to heed any voice of reform or alarm until he woke up to find that his country had slid from under him? Why did Lyndon Johnson, seconded by the best and the brightest, progressively involve this nation in a war both ruinous and halfhearted and from which nothing but bad for our side resulted? Why does the present Administration[4] continue to avoid introducing effective measures to reduce the wasteful consumption of oil while members of OPEC follow a price policy that must bankrupt their customers? How is it possible that the Central Intelligence Agency, whose function it is to provide, at taxpayers' expense, the information necessary to conduct a realistic foreign policy, could remain unaware that discontent in a country crucial to our interests was boiling up to the point of insurrection and overthrow of the ruler upon whom our policy rested? It has been reported that the CIA was ordered *not* to investigate the opposition to the shah of Iran in order to spare him any indication that we took it seriously, but since this sounds more like the theater of the absurd than like responsible government, I cannot bring myself to believe it.

3   There was a king of Spain once, Philip III, who is said to have died of a fever he contracted from sitting too long near a hot brazier, helplessly overheating himself because the functionary whose duty it was to remove the brazier when summoned could not be found. In the late twentieth century, it begins to appear as if mankind may be approaching a similar stage of suicidal incompetence. The Italians have been sitting in Philip III's hot seat for some time. The British trade unions, in a lunatic spectacle, seem periodically bent on dragging their country toward paralysis, apparently under the impression that they are separate from the whole. Taiwan was thrown into a state of shock by the United States' recognition of the People's Republic of China because, according to one report, in the seven years since the Shanghai Communiqué, the Kuomintang rulers of Taiwan had "refused to accept the new trend as a reality."

4   Wooden-headedness is a factor that plays a remarkably large role in government. Wooden-headedness consists of assessing a situation in terms of preconceived, fixed notions while ignoring or rejecting any contrary signs. It is acting according to wish while not allowing oneself to be confused by the facts.

5   A classic case was the French war plan of 1914, which concentrated everything on a French offensive to the Rhine, leaving the French left flank from Belgium to the Channel virtually unguarded. This strategy was based on the

---

[1]An eighteenth-century British writer.—Ed.

[2]Kaiser Wilhelm (1859–1941), emperor of Germany.—Ed.

[3]A Chinese general and political leader (1886?–1975), president of China from 1948 until the Mao revolution in 1949, president of "Nationalist China" (Taiwan) from 1950 to 1975.—Ed.

[4]The Carter administration.—Ed.

belief that the Germans would not use reserves in the front line and, without them, could not deploy enough manpower to extend their invasion through the French left. Reports by intelligence agents in 1913 to the effect that the Germans were indeed preparing their reserves for the front line in case of war were resolutely ignored because the governing spirits in France, dreaming only of their own offensive, did not want to believe in any signals that would require them to strengthen their left at the expense of their march to the Rhine. In the event, the Germans could and did extend themselves around the French left with results that determined a long war and its fearful consequences for our century.

Wooden-headedness is also the refusal to learn from experience, a form in which fourteenth-century rulers were supreme. No matter how often and obviously devaluation of the currency disrupted the economy and angered the people, French monarchs continued to resort to it whenever they were desperate for cash until they provoked insurrection among the bourgeoisie. No matter how often a campaign that depended on living off a hostile country ran into want and even starvation, campaigns for which this fate was inevitable were regularly undertaken.   6

Still another form is identification of self with the state, as currently exhibited by the ayatollah Khomeini. No wooden-headedness is so impenetrable as that of a religious zealot. Because he is connected with a private wire to the Almighty, no idea coming in on a lesser channel can reach him, which leaves him ill equipped to guide his country in its own best interests.   7

Philosophers of government ever since Plato[5] have devoted their thinking to the major issues of ethics, sovereignty, the social contract, the rights of man, the corruption of power, the balance between freedom and order. Few—except Machiavelli,[6] who was concerned with government as it is, not as it should be—bothered with mere folly, although this has been a chronic and pervasive problem. "Know, my son," said a dying Swedish statesman in the seventeenth century, "with how little wisdom the world is governed." More recently, Woodrow Wilson warned, "In public affairs, stupidity is more dangerous than knavery."   8

Stupidity is not related to type of regime; monarchy, oligarchy, and democracy produce it equally. Nor is it peculiar to nation or class. The working class as represented by the Communist governments functions no more rationally or effectively in power than the aristocracy or the bourgeoisie, as has notably been demonstrated in recent history. Mao Tse-tung may be admired for many things, but the Great Leap Forward, with a steel plant in every backyard, and the Cultural Revolution were exercises in unwisdom that greatly damaged China's progress and stability, not to mention the chairman's reputation. The record of the Russian proletariat in power can hardly be called enlightened, although after sixty years of control it must be accorded a kind of brutal success.   9

---

[5]A Greek philosopher (427–347 B.C.).—Ed.

[6]An Italian statesman and philosopher (1469–1527); author of *The Prince.*—Ed.

If the majority of Russians are better off now than before, the cost in cruelty and tyranny has been no less and probably greater than under the czars.

10   After the French Revolution, the new order was rescued only by Bonaparte's military campaigns, which brought the spoils of foreign wars to fill the treasury, and subsequently by his competence as an executive. He chose officials not on the basis of origin or ideology but on the principle of "*la carrière ouverte aux talents*"[7]—the said talents being intelligence, energy, industry, and obedience. That worked until the day of his own fatal mistake.

11   I do not wish to give the impression that men in office are incapable of governing wisely and well. Occasionally, the exception appears, rising in heroic size above the rest, a tower visible down the centuries. Greece had her Pericles,[8] who ruled with authority, moderation, sound judgment, and a certain nobility that imposes natural dominion over others. Rome had Caesar, a man of remarkable governing talents, although it must be said that a ruler who arouses opponents to resort to assassination is probably not as smart as he ought to be. Later, under Marcus Aurelius and the other Antonines,[9] Roman citizens enjoyed good government, prosperity, and respect for about a century. Charlemagne was able to impose order upon a mass of contending elements, to foster the arts of civilization no less than those of war, and to earn a prestige supreme in the Middle Ages—probably not equaled in the eyes of contemporaries until the appearance of George Washington.

12   Possessor of an inner strength and perseverance that enabled him to prevail over a sea of obstacles, Washington was one of those critical figures but for whom history might well have taken a different course. He made possible the physical victory of American independence, while around him, in extraordinary fertility, political talent bloomed as if touched by some tropical sun. For all their flaws and quarrels, the Founding Fathers, who established our form of government, were, in the words of Arthur Schlesinger, Sr., "the most remarkable generation of public men in the history of the United States or perhaps of any other nation." It is worth noting the qualities Schlesinger ascribes to them: They were fearless, high-principled, deeply versed in ancient and modern political thought, astute and pragmatic, unafraid of experiment, and—this is significant—"convinced of man's power to improve his condition through the use of intelligence." That was the mark of the Age of Reason that formed them, and though the eighteenth century had a tendency to regard men as more rational than they in fact were, it evoked the best in government from these men.

13   For our purposes, it would be invaluable if we could know what produced this burst of talent from a base of only two million inhabitants. Schlesinger suggests some contributing factors: wide diffusion of education, challenging economic opportunities, social mobility, training in self-government—all these encouraged citizens to cultivate their political aptitudes to the utmost. Also, he

---

[7]A French expression meaning "tools to those who can handle them."—Ed.

[8]An Athenian statesman of the fifth century B.C.—Ed.

[9]Second-century A.D. Roman emperors.—Ed.

adds, with the Church declining in prestige and with business, science, and art not yet offering competing fields of endeavor, statecraft remained almost the only outlet for men of energy and purpose. Perhaps the need of the moment—the opportunity to create a new political system—is what brought out the best.

Not before or since, I believe has so much careful and reasonable thinking 14 been invested in the creation of a new political system. In the French, Russian, and Chinese revolutions, too much class hatred and bloodshed were involved to allow for fair results or permanent constitutions. The American experience was unique, and the system so far has always managed to right itself under pressure. In spite of accelerating incompetence, it still works better than most. We haven't had to discard the system and try another after every crisis, as have Italy and Germany, Spain and France. The founders of the United States are a phenomenon to keep in mind to encourage our estimate of human possibilities, but their example, as a political scientist has pointed out, is "too infrequent to be taken as a basis for normal expectations."

The English are considered to have enjoyed reasonably benign govern- 15 ment during the eighteenth and nineteenth centuries, except for their Irish subjects, debtors, child laborers, and other unfortunates in various pockets of oppression. The folly that lost the American colonies reappeared now and then, notably in the treatment of the Irish and the Boers,[10] but a social system can survive a good deal of folly when circumstances are historically favorable or when it is cushioned by large resources, as in the heyday of the British Empire, or absorbed by sheer size, as in this country during our period of expansion. Today there are no more cushions, which makes folly less affordable.

Elsewhere than in government, man has accomplished marvels: invented 16 the means in our time to leave the world and voyage to the moon; in the past, harnessed wind and electricity, raised earthbound stone into soaring cathedrals, woven silk brocades out of the spinnings of a worm, composed the music of Mozart and the dramas of Shakespeare, classified the forms of nature, penetrated the mysteries of genetics. Why is he so much less accomplished in government? What frustrates, in that sphere, the operation of the intellect? Isaac Bashevis Singer,[11] discoursing as a Nobel laureate on mankind, offers the opinion that God had been frugal in bestowing intellect but lavish with passions and emotions. "He gave us," Singer says, "so many emotions and such strong ones that every human being, even if he is an idiot, is a millionaire in emotions."

I think Singer has made a point that applies to our inquiry. What frustrates 17 the workings of intellect is the passions and the emotions: ambition, greed, fear, face-saving, the instinct to dominate, the needs of the ego, the whole bundle of personal vanities and anxieties.

---

[10]South Africans of Dutch extraction, whom the British fought for control of South Africa 1899–1902.—Ed.

[11]A Jewish-American novelist and short-story writer (1904–1991); winner of the Nobel Prize in Literature in 1978.—Ed.

18   Reason is crushed by these forces. If the Athenians out of pride and over-confidence had not set out to crush Sparta for good but had been content with moderate victory, their ultimate fall might have been averted. If fourteenth-century knights had not been obsessed by the idea of glory and personal prowess, they might have defeated the Turks at Nicopolis with incalculable consequence for all of Eastern Europe. If the English, 200 years ago, had heeded Chatham's[12] knocking on the door of what he called "this sleeping and confounded Ministry" and his urgent advice to repeal the Coercive Acts[13] and withdraw the troops before the "inexpiable drop of blood is shed in an impious war with a people contending in the great cause of publick liberty" or, given a last chance, if they had heeded Edmund Burke's[14] celebrated plea for conciliation and his warning that it would prove impossible to coerce a "fierce people" of their own pedigree, we might still be a united people bridging the Atlantic, with incalculable consequence for the history of the West. It did not happen that way, because king and Parliament felt it imperative to affirm sovereignty over arrogant colonials. The alternative choice, as in Athens and medieval Europe, was close to psychologically impossible.

19   In the case we know best—the American engagement in Vietnam—fixed notions, preconceptions, wooden-headed thinking, and emotions accumulated into a monumental mistake and classic humiliation. The original idea was that the lesson of the failure to halt fascist aggression during the appeasement era[15] dictated the necessity of halting the so-called aggression by North Vietnam, conceived to be the spearhead of international communism. This was applying the wrong model to the wrong facts, which would have been obvious if our policy makers had taken into consideration the history of the people on the spot instead of charging forward wearing the blinders of the cold war.

20   The reality of Vietnamese nationalism, of which Ho Chi Minh had been the standard-bearer since long before the war, was certainly no secret. Indeed, Franklin Roosevelt had insisted that the French should not be allowed to return after the war, a policy that we instantly abandoned the moment the Japanese were out. Ignoring the Vietnamese demand for self-government, we first assisted the return of the French, and then, when, incredibly, they had been put to rout by the native forces, we took their place, as if Dien Bien Phu[16] had no significance whatever. Policy founded upon error multiplies, never retreats. The pretense that North versus South Vietnam represented foreign aggression was intensified. If Asian specialists with knowledge of the situation suggested a reassessment, they were not persuasive. As a Communist aggressor, Hanoi was

---

[12]William Pitt, first earl of Chatham (1708–1788), opposed British treatment of the American colonies.—Ed.

[13]Laws passed in Britain in 1774 designed to close the port of Boston after the Boston Tea Party.—Ed.

[14]An eighteenth-century British statesman and writer.—Ed.

[15]The period before World War II, when German aggression was ignored in the desire for peace.—Ed.

[16]The town in North Vietnam where French forces were defeated in 1954.—Ed.

presumed to be a threat to the United States, yet the vital national interest at stake, which alone may have justified belligerency, was never clear enough to sustain a declaration of war.

A further, more fundamental error confounded our policy. This was the 21 nature of the client. In war, as any military treatise or any soldier who has seen active service will tell you, it is essential to know the nature—that is, the capabilities *and* intentions—of the enemy and no less so of an ally who is the primary belligerent. We fatally underestimated the one and foolishly overestimated the other. Placing reliance on, or hope in, South Vietnam was an advanced case of wooden-headedness. Improving on the Bourbons,[17] who forgot nothing and learned nothing, our policy makers forgot everything and learned nothing. The oldest lesson in history is the futility and, often, fatality of foreign interference to maintain in power a government unwanted or hated at home. As far back as 500 B.C., Confucious stated, "Without the confidence of the people, no government can stand," and political philosophers have echoed him down through the ages. What else was the lesson of our vain support of Chiang Kai-shek, within such recent experience? A corrupt or oppressive government may be maintained by despotic means but not for long, as the English occupiers of France learned in the fifteenth century. The human spirit protests and generates a Joan of Arc, for people will not passively endure a government that is in fact unendurable.

The deeper we became involved in Vietnam during the Johnson era, the 22 greater grew the self-deception, the lies, the false body counts, the cheating on Tonkin Gulf, the military mess, domestic dissent, and all those defensive emotions in which, as a result, our leaders became fixed. Their concern for personal ego, public image, and government status determined policy. Johnson was not going to be the first President to preside over defeat; generals could not admit failure nor civilian advisers risk their jobs by giving unpalatable advice.

Males, who so far in history have managed government, are obsessed with 23 potency, which is the reason, I suspect, why it is difficult for them to admit error. I have rarely known a man who, with a smile and a shrug, could easily acknowledge being wrong. Why not? *I* can, without any damage to self-respect. I can only suppose the difference is that deep in their psyches, men somehow equate being wrong with being impotent. For a Chief of State, it is almost out of the question, and especially so for Johnson and Nixon, who both seem to me to have had shaky self-images. Johnson's showed in his deliberate coarseness and compulsion to humiliate others in crude physical ways. No self-confident man would have needed to do that. Nixon was a bundle of inferiorities and sense of persecution. I do not pretend to be a psychohistorian, but in pursuit of this inquiry, the psychological factors must be taken into account. Having no special knowledge of Johnson and Nixon, I will not pursue the question other than to say that it was our misfortune during the Vietnam

---

[17]The last royal family to rule in France before the French Revolution in 1792.—Ed.

period to have had two Presidents who lacked the self-confidence for a change of course, much less for a grand withdrawal. "Magnanimity in politics," said Edmund Burke, "is not seldom the truest wisdom, and a great Empire and little minds go ill together."

24　　An essential component of that "truest wisdom" is the self-confidence to reassess. Congressman Morris Udall made this point in the first few days after the nuclear accident at Three Mile Island. Cautioning against a hasty decision on the future of nuclear power, he said, "We have to go back and reassess. There is nothing wrong about being optimistic or making a mistake. The thing that is wrong, as in Vietnam, is *persisting* in a mistake when you see you are going down the wrong road and are caught in a bad situation."

25　　The test comes in recognizing when persistence has become a fatal error. A prince, says Machiavelli, ought always to be a great asker and a patient hearer of truth about those things of which he has inquired, and he should be angry if he finds that anyone has scruples about telling him the truth. Johnson and Nixon, as far as an outsider can tell, were not great askers; they did not want to hear the truth or to face it. Chiang Kai-shek knew virtually nothing of real conditions in his domain because he lived a headquarters life amid an entourage all of whom were afraid to be messengers of ill report. When, in World War I, a general of the headquarters staff visited for the first time the ghastly landscape of the Somme,[18] he broke into tears, saying, "If I had known we sent men to fight in that, I could not have done it." Evidently he was no great asker either.

26　　Neither, we now know, was the shah of Iran. Like Chiang Kai-shek, he was isolated from actual conditions. He was educated abroad, took his vacations abroad, and toured his country, if at all, by helicopter.

27　　Why is it that the major clients of the United States, a country founded on the principle that government derives its just powers from the consent of the governed, tend to be unpopular autocrats? A certain schizophrenia between our philosophy and our practice afflicts American policy, and this split will always make the policy based on it fall apart. On the day the shah left Iran, an article summarizing his reign said that "except for the generals, he has few friends or allies at home." How useful to us is a ruler without friends or allies at home? He is a kind of luftmensch,[19] no matter how rich or how golden a customer for American business. To attach American foreign policy to a ruler who does not have the acceptance of his countrymen is hardly intelligent. By now, it seems to me, we might have learned that. We must understand conditions—and by conditions, I mean people and history—on the spot. Wise policy can only be made on the basis of *informed*, not automatic, judgments.

28　　When it has become evident to those associated with it that a course of policy is pointed toward disaster, why does no one resign in protest or at least for the peace of his own soul? They never do. In 1917, the German chancellor Bethmann-Hollweg pleaded desperately against the proposed resumption

---

[18]A muddy marshland area of northern France near the English Channel.—Ed.

[19]German for "airhead."—Ed.

of unrestricted submarine warfare, since, by bringing in the United States, it would revive the Allies' resources, their confidence in victory, and their will to endure. When he was overruled by the military, he told a friend who found him sunk in despair that the decision meant *"finis Germaniae."* When the friend said simply, "You should resign," Bethmann said he could not, for that would sow dissension at home and let the world know he believed Germany would fail.

This is always the refuge. The officeholder tells himself he can do more 		29 from within and that he must not reveal division at the top to the public. In fact if there is to be any hope of change in a democratic society, that is exactly what he must do. No one of major influence in Johnson's circle resigned over our Vietnam policy, although several, hoping to play it both ways, hinted their disagreement. Humphrey, waiting for the nod, never challenged the President's policy, although he campaigned afterward as an opponent of the war. Since then, I've always thought the adulation given to him misplaced.

Basically, what keeps officeholders attached to a policy they believe to be 		30 wrong is nothing more nor less, I believe, than the lure of the office, or Potomac fever. It is the same whether the locus is the Thames or the Rhine or, no doubt, the Nile. When Herbert Lehman ran for a second term as senator from New York after previously serving four terms as governor, his brother asked him why on earth he wanted it. "Arthur," replied the senator, "after you have once ridden behind a motorcycle escort, you are never the same again."

Here is a clue to the question of why our performance in government is 		31 worse than in other activities: because government offers power, excites that lust for power, which is subject to emotional drives—to narcissism, fantasies of omnipotence, and other sources of folly. The lust for power, according to Tacitus,[20] "is the most flagrant of all the passions" and cannot really be satisfied except by power over others. Business offers a kind of power but only to the very successful at the very top, and even they, in our day, have to play it down. Fords and Du Ponts, Hearsts and Pulitzers nowadays are subdued, and the Rockefeller who most conspicuously wanted power sought it in government. Other activities—in sports, science, the professions, and the creative and performing arts—offer various satisfactions but not the opportunity for power. They may appeal to status seeking and, in the form of celebrity, offer crowd worship and limousines and recognition by headwaiters, but these are the trappings of power, not the essence. Of course, mistakes and stupidities occur in nongovernmental activities too, but since these affect fewer people, they are less noticeable than they are in public affairs. Government remains the paramount field of unwisdom because it is there that men seek power over others— and lose it over themselves.

There are, of course, other factors that lower competence in public affairs, 		32 among them the pressure of overwork and overscheduling; bureaucracy, especially big bureaucracy; the contest for votes that gives exaggerated influence

---

[20]A Roman historian (C.A.D. 55–c.120).—Ed.

to special interests and an absurd tyranny to public opinion polls. Any hope of intelligent government would require that the persons entrusted with high office should formulate and execute policy according to their best judgment and the best knowledge available, not according to every breeze of public opinion. But reelection is on their minds, and that becomes the criterion. Moreover, given schedules broken down into fifteen-minute appointments and staffs numbering in the hundreds and briefing memos of never less than thirty pages, policy makers never have time to *think.* This leaves a rather important vacuum. Meanwhile, bureaucracy rolls on, impervious to any individual or cry for change, like some vast computer that when once penetrated by error goes on pumping it out forever.

33   Under the circumstances, what are the chances of improving the conduct of government? The idea of a class of professionals trained for the task has been around ever since Plato's *Republic.* Something of the sort animates, I imagine, the new Kennedy School of Government at Harvard. According to Plato, the ruling class in a just society should be men apprenticed to the art of ruling, drawn from the rational and the wise. Since he acknowledged that in natural distribution these are few, he believed they would have to be eugenically bred and nurtured. Government, he said, was a special art in which competence, as in any other profession, could be acquired only by study of the discipline and could not be acquired otherwise.

34   Without reference to Plato, the Mandarins of China were trained, if not bred, for the governing function. They had to pass through years of study and apprenticeship and weeding out by successive examinations, but they do not seem to have developed a form of government much superior to any other, and in the end, they petered out in decadence and incompetence.

35   In seventeenth-century Europe, after the devastation of the Thirty Years' War, the electors of Brandenburg, soon to be combined with Prussia, determined to create a strong state by means of a disciplined army and a trained civil service. Applicants for the civil positions, drawn from commoners in order to offset the nobles' control of the military, had to complete a course of study covering political theory, law and legal philosophy, economics, history, penology, and statutes. Only after passing through various stages of examination and probationary terms of office did they receive definitive appointments and tenure and opportunity for advancement. The higher civil service was a separate branch, not open to promotion from the middle and lower levels.

36   The Prussian system proved so effective that the state was able to survive both military defeat by Napoleon in 1807 and the revolutionary surge of 1848. By then it had begun to congeal, losing many of its most progressive citizens in emigration to America; nevertheless, Prussian energies succeeded in 1871 in uniting the German states in an empire under Prussian hegemony. Its very success contained the seed of ruin, for it nourished the arrogance and power hunger that from 1914 through 1918 was to bring it down.

37   In England, instead of responding in reactionary panic to the thunders from the Continent in 1848, as might have been expected, the authorities, with commendable enterprise, ordered an investigation of their own

government practices, which were then the virtually private preserve of the propertied class. The result was a report on the need for a permanent civil service to be based on training and specialized skills and designed to provide continuity and maintenance of the long view as against transient issues and political passions. Though heavily resisted, the system was adopted in 1870. It has produced distinguished civil servants but also Burgess, Maclean, Philby, and the fourth man.[21] The history of British government in the last 100 years suggests that factors other than the quality of its civil service determine a country's fate.

In the United States, civil service was established chiefly as a barrier to pa-   38 tronage and the pork barrel rather than in search of excellence. By 1937, a presidential commission, finding the system inadequate, urged the development of a "real career service . . . requiring personnel of the highest order, competent, highly trained, loyal, skilled in their duties by reason of long experience, and assured of continuity." After much effort and some progress, that goal is still not reached, but even if it were, it would not take care of elected officials and high appointments—that is, of government at the top.

I do not know if the prognosis is hopeful or, given the underlying emotional   39 drives, whether professionalism is the cure. In the Age of Enlightenment, John Locke[22] thought the emotions should be controlled by intellectual judgment and that it was the distinction and glory of man to be able to control them. As witnesses of the twentieth century's record, comparable to the worst in history, we have less confidence in our species. Although professionalism can help, I tend to think that fitness of character is what government chiefly requires. How that can be discovered, encouraged, and brought into office is the problem that besets us.

No society has yet managed to implement Plato's design. Now, with   40 money and image-making manipulating our elective process, the chances are reduced. We are asked to choose by the packaging, yet the candidate seen in a studio-filmed spot, sincerely voicing lines from the TelePrompTer, is not the person who will have to meet the unrelenting problems and crucial decisions of the Oval Office. It might be a good idea if, without violating the First Amendment, we could ban all paid political commercials and require candidates (who accept federal subsidy for their campaigns) to be televised live only.

That is only a start. More profound change must come if we are to bring   41 into office the kind of person our form of government needs if it is to survive the challenges of this era. Perhaps rather than educating officials according to Plato's design, we should concentrate on educating the electorate—that is, ourselves—to look for, recognize, and reward character in our representatives and to reject the ersatz.

---

[21]British civil servants who were exposed in the 1970s as Russian spies.—Ed.

[22]A seventeenth-century English philosopher.—Ed.

QUESTIONS FOR READING

1. How does Tuchman define unwisdom or wooden-headedness?

2. From Tuchman's examples of unwisdom in paragraphs 2–7, what do you conclude to be the characteristics of governmental folly that she is most interested in?

3. What question does the author raise in paragraph 16? What is one answer to that question?

4. Why, according to Tuchman, do male leaders have particular difficulty admitting to error and then changing their policy? What American presidents illustrate her point?

5. What should leaders opposed to a government's policy do? Why do few office holders act as they should when their government perpetuates folly?

6. Tuchman asserts that emotions in general drown reason and lead to folly. What particular emotion or drive leads to the enormous display of unwisdom in government?

QUESTIONS FOR REASONING AND ANALYSIS

1. Using Tuchman's summaries of events and your knowledge of history, do you basically agree with her examples of unwisdom? Why or why not?

2. Why does the author include the discussion in paragraphs 11 through 14? What point does she want to establish in this section?

3. If you believe that women have as much difficulty as men do in admitting to error, do you agree with Tuchman that self-confidence is an important trait for leaders of both genders? If so, how do we "test" for this trait in candidates for office? Any suggestions?

QUESTIONS FOR REFLECTING AND WRITING

1. Reflect on Tuchman's suggestions for reducing unwisdom in government. Do you think these are useful strategies for change? Why or why not?

2. What solutions do you have to offer?

3. Today many more women are in elected positions, especially at the local and state levels of government. Select any local or state female elected official and learn about her personality and politics. Then decide: Would she be an example of unwisdom or wisdom? Why? (Note for your research: Most state and local governments have websites. Those are good places to start if you do not know any official to study. Once you have the name of someone to study, you can do a Google search; she probably also has a website.)

I HAVE A DREAM | MARTIN LUTHER KING, JR.

Martin Luther King, Jr. (1929–1968), Baptist minister, civil rights leader dedicated to nonviolence, president of the Southern Christian Leadership Conference, Nobel Peace Prize winner in 1964, was assassinated in 1968. He was an important figure in the August 1963 poor people's march on Washington, where he delivered his speech from the steps of the Lincoln Memorial.

King's plea for equality, echoing the language and cadences of both the Bible and "The Gettysburg Address," has become a model of effective oratory.

PREREADING QUESTION What is the purpose or what are the purposes of King's speech?

Five score years ago, a great American, in whose symbolic shadow we 1 stand, signed the Emancipation Proclamation. This momentous decree came as a great beacon light of hope to millions of Negro slaves who had been seared in the flames of withering injustice. It came as a joyous daybreak to end the long night of captivity.

But one hundred years later, we must face the tragic fact that the Negro is 2 still not free. One hundred years later, the life of the Negro is still sadly crippled by the manacles of segregation and the chains of discrimination. One hundred years later, the Negro lives on a lonely island of poverty in the midst of a vast ocean of material prosperity. One hundred years later, the Negro is still languished in the corners of American society and finds himself an exile in his own land. So we have come here today to dramatize an appalling condition.

In a sense we have come to our nation's Capital to cash a check. When the 3 architects of our republic wrote the magnificent words of the Constitution and the Declaration of Independence, they were signing a promissory note to which every American was to fall heir. This note was a promise that all men would be guaranteed the unalienable rights of life, liberty, and the pursuit of happiness.

It is obvious today that America has defaulted on this promissory note in- 4 sofar as her citizens of color are concerned. Instead of honoring this sacred obligation, America has given the Negro people a bad check which has come back marked "insufficient funds." But we refuse to believe that the bank of justice is bankrupt. We refuse to believe that there are insufficient funds in the great vaults of opportunity of this nation. So we have come to cash this check— a check that will give us upon demand the riches of freedom and the security of justice. We have also come to this hallowed spot to remind America of the fierce urgency of *now*. This is no time to engage in the luxury of cooling off or to take the tranquilizing drug of gradualism. *Now* is the time to make real the promises of Democracy. *Now* is the time to rise from the dark and desolate valley of segregation to the sunlit path of racial justice. *Now* is the time to open the doors of opportunity to all of God's children. *Now* is the time to lift our nation from the quicksands of racial injustice to the solid rock of brotherhood.

It would be fatal for the nation to overlook the urgency of the moment and 5 to underestimate the determination of the Negro. This sweltering summer of the Negro's legitimate discontent will not pass until there is an invigorating autumn of freedom and equality. 1963 is not an end, but a beginning. Those who hope that the Negro needed to blow off steam and will now be content will have a rude awakening if the nation returns to business as usual. There will be neither rest nor tranquility in America until the Negro is granted his citizenship rights. The whirlwinds of revolt will continue to shake the foundations of our nation until the bright day of justice emerges.

6   But there is something that I must say to my people who stand on the warm threshold which leads into the palace of justice. In the process of gaining our right place we must not be guilty of wrongful deeds. Let us not seek to satisfy our thirst for freedom by drinking from the cup of bitterness and hatred. We must forever conduct our struggle on the high plane of dignity and discipline. We must not allow our creative protest to degenerate into physical violence. Again and again we must rise to the majestic heights of meeting physical force with soul force. The marvelous new militancy which has engulfed the Negro community must not lead us to a distrust of all white people, for many of our white brothers, as evidenced by their presence here today, have come to realize that their destiny is tied up with our destiny and their freedom is inextricably bound to our freedom. We cannot walk alone.

7   And as we walk, we must make the pledge that we shall march ahead. We cannot turn back. There are those who are asking the devotees of civil rights, "When will you be satisfied?" We can never be satisfied as long as the Negro is the victim of the unspeakable horrors of police brutality. We can never be satisfied as long as our bodies, heavy with the fatigue of travel, cannot gain lodging in the motels of the highways and the hotels of the cities. We cannot be satisfied as long as the Negro's basic mobility is from a smaller ghetto to a larger one. We can never be satisfied as long as a Negro in Mississippi cannot vote and a Negro in New York believes he has nothing for which to vote. No, no, we are not satisfied, and we will not be satisfied until justice rolls down like waters and righteousness like a mighty stream.

8   I am not unmindful that some of you have come here out of great trials and tribulations. Some of you have come fresh from narrow jail cells. Some of you have come from areas where your quest for freedom left you battered by the storms of persecution and staggered by the winds of police brutality. You have been the veterans of creative suffering. Continue to work with the faith that unearned suffering is redemptive.

9   Go back to Mississippi, go back to Alabama, go back to South Carolina, go back to Georgia, go back to Louisiana, go back to the slums and ghettos of our northern cities, knowing that somehow this situation can and will be changed. Let us not wallow in the valley of despair.

10   I say to you today, my friends, that in spite of the difficulties and frustrations of the moment I still have a dream. It is a dream deeply rooted in the American dream.

11   I have a dream that one day this nation will rise up and live out the true meaning of its creed: "We hold these truths to be self-evident; that all men are created equal."

12   I have a dream that one day on the red hills of Georgia the sons of former slaves and the sons of former slaveowners will be able to sit down together at the table of brotherhood.

13   I have a dream that one day even the state of Mississippi, a desert state sweltering with the heat of injustice and oppression, will be transformed into an oasis of freedom and justice.

I have a dream that my four little children will one day live in a nation where 14
they will not be judged by the color of their skin but by the content of their
character.

I have a dream today. 15

I have a dream that one day the state of Alabama, whose governor's lips 16
are presently dripping with the words of interposition and nullification, will be
transformed into a situation where little black boys and black girls will be able
to join hands with little white boys and white girls and walk together as sisters
and brothers.

I have a dream today. 17

I have a dream that one day every valley shall be exalted, every hill and 18
mountain shall be made low, the rough places will be made plain, and the
crooked places will be made straight, and the glory of the Lord shall be revealed, and all flesh shall see it together.

This is our hope. This is the faith with which I return to the South. With this 19
faith we will be able to hew out of the mountain of despair a stone of hope.
With this faith we will be able to transform the jangling discords of our nation
into a beautiful symphony of brotherhood. With this faith we will be able to
work together, to pray together, to struggle together, to go to jail together, to
stand up for freedom together, knowing that we will be free one day.

This will be the day when all of God's children will be able to sing with new 20
meaning

My country, 'tis of thee,
Sweet land of liberty,
    Of thee I sing;
Land where my fathers died,
Land of the pilgrims' pride,
From every mountain-side
    Let freedom ring.

And if America is to be a great nation this must become true. So let free- 21
dom ring from the prodigious hilltops of New Hampshire. Let freedom ring
from the mighty mountains of New York. Let freedom ring from the heighten-
ing Alleghenies of Pennsylvania!

Let freedom ring from the snowcapped Rockies of Colorado! 22

Let freedom ring from the curvaceous peaks of California! 23

But not only that; let freedom ring from Stone Mountain of Georgia! 24

Let freedom ring from Lookout Mountain of Tennessee! 25

Let freedom ring from every hill and molehill of Mississippi. From every 26
mountainside, let freedom ring.

When we let freedom ring, when we let it ring from every village and every 27
hamlet, from every state and every city, we will be able to speed up that day
when all of God's children, black men and white men, Jews and Gentiles,
Protestants and Catholics, will be able to join hands and sing in the words of
the old Negro spiritual, "Free at last! thank God almighty, we are free at last!"

QUESTIONS FOR READING

1. King is directly addressing those participants in the poor people's march who are at the Lincoln Memorial. What other audience did he have as well?

2. How does the language of the speech reflect King's vocation as a Christian minister? How does it reflect his sense of his place in history?

QUESTIONS FOR REASONING AND ANALYSIS

1. List all the elements of style discussed in Chapter 2 that King uses. What elements of style dominate?

2. What stylistic techniques do Lincoln and King share?

3. Find one sentence that you think is especially effective and explain why you picked it. Is the effect achieved in part by the way the sentence is structured?

4. Explain each metaphor in paragraph 2.

5. State the claim of King's argument.

QUESTIONS FOR REFLECTING AND WRITING

1. Which, in your view, is King's most vivid and powerful metaphor? Why do you find it effective?

2. If King were alive today, would he would want to see another march on Washington? If so, what would be the theme, or purpose, of the march? If not, why not?

3. Would King have supported the Million Man March? The rally of the Promise Keepers? Why or why not? (If necessary, do some research on these two events.)

Understanding Literature

The same process of reading nonfiction can be used to understand literature—fiction, poetry, and drama. You still need to read what is on the page, looking up unfamiliar words and tracking down references you don't understand. You still need to examine the context, to think about who is writing to whom, under what circumstances, and in what literary format. And, to respond fully to the words, you need to analyze the writer's techniques for developing ideas and expressing attitudes.

Although it seems logical that the reading process should be much the same regardless of the work, not all readers of literature are willing to accept that logic. Some readers want a work of literature to mean whatever they think it means. But what happened to the writer's desire to communicate? If you decide that a Robert Frost poem, for example, should mean whatever you are feeling when you read it, you might as well skip the reading of Frost and just commune with your feelings. Presumably you read Frost to gain some new insight from him, to get beyond just your vision and see something of human experience and emotion from a new vantage point.

Other readers of literature hesitate over the concept of *literary analysis,* or at least over the word *analysis.* These readers complain that analysis will "tear the work apart" and "ruin it." If you are inclined to share this attitude, stop for a minute and think about the last sports event you watched. Do you remember thinking, "Davenport's going to serve wide and come in; she has to against Hingis." Or perhaps a friend explained: "North Carolina is so good at stalling to use up the clock; Duke will have to foul to get the ball and have a chance to tie the game." Both games are being analyzed! And that analysis makes each event more fully experienced by those who understand at least some of the elements of tennis or basketball.

The analogy is clear. You, too, can be a fan of literature. You can enjoy reading and discussing your reading once you learn to use your active reading and analytic skills to open up a poem or story, and once you sharpen your knowledge of literary terms and concepts so that you can "speak the language" of literary criticism with the same confidence with which you discuss the merits of a full court press or a drop volley.

GETTING THE FACTS: ACTIVE READING, SUMMARY, AND PARAPHRASE

Let's begin with the following poem by Paul Dunbar. As you read, make marginal notes, circling a phrase you fancy, putting a question mark next to a difficult line, underscoring words you need to look up. Note, too, your emotional reactions as you read.

PROMISE | PAUL LAWRENCE DUNBAR

Born of former slave parents, Dunbar (1872–1906) was educated in Dayton, Ohio. After a first booklet of poems, *Oak and Ivy,* was printed in 1893, several friends helped Dunbar get a second collection, *Majors and Minors,* published in 1895. A copy was given to author and editor William Dean Howells, who reviewed the book favorably, increasing sales and Dunbar's reputation. This led to a national publisher issuing *Lyrics of Lowly Life* in 1896, the collection that secured Dunbar's fame.

I grew a rose within a garden fair,
And, tending it with more than loving care,
I thought how, with the glory of its bloom,
I should the darkness of my life illume;
And, watching, ever smiled to see the lusty bud   5
Drink freely in the summer sun to tint its blood.

My rose began to open, and its hue
Was sweet to me as to it sun and dew;
I watched it taking on its ruddy flame
Until the day of perfect blooming came,   10
Then hasted I with smiles to find it blushing red—
Too late! Some thoughtless child had plucked my rose and fled!

"Promise" should not have been especially difficult to read, although you may have paused a moment over "illume" before connecting it to "illuminate," and you may have to check the dictionary for a definition of "tinct." Test your knowledge of content by listing all the facts of the poem. Pay attention to the poem's basic situation. Who is speaking? What is happening, or what thoughts is the speaker sharing? In this poem, the "I" is not further identified, so you will have to refer to him or her as the *speaker*. You should not call the speaker "Dunbar," however, because you do not know if Dunbar ever grew a rose.

In "Promise" the speaker is describing an event that has taken place. The speaker grew a rose, tended to it with care, and watched it begin to bloom; then, when the rose was in full bloom, some child picked the rose and took it away. The situation is fairly simple, isn't it? Too simple, unfortunately, for some readers who decide that the speaker never grew a rose at all. But when anyone writes, "I grew a rose within a garden fair," it is wise to assume that the writer means just that. People do grow roses, most often in gardens, and then the gardens are made "fair" or beautiful by the flowers growing there. Read first for the facts; try not to jump too quickly to broad generalizations.

As with nonfiction, one of the best ways to make certain you have understood a literary work is to write a summary or paraphrase. Since a summary condenses, you are most likely to write a summary of a story, novel, or play, whereas a paraphrase is usually reserved for poems or complex short passages. When you paraphrase a difficult poem, you are likely to end up with more words than in the original because your purpose is to turn cryptic lines into more ordinary sentences with normal word order. For example, Dunbar's "Then hasted I with smiles" can be paraphrased to read: "Then, full of smiles, I hurried."

When summarizing a literary work, remember to use your own words, draw no conclusions, giving only the facts, but focus your summary on the key events in the story. (Of course the selecting you do to write a summary represents preliminary analysis; you are making some choices about what is important in the work. The "steps" of observation, analysis, and interpretation do overlap.) Read the following short story by Langston Hughes and then write your own summary. Finally, compare yours to the summary that follows the story.

EARLY AUTUMN | LANGSTON HUGHES

Like many American writers, Langston Hughes (1902–1967) moved from the Middle West to New York City, lived and worked in France, and then returned to the United States to a career in writing. He was a journalist, fiction writer, and poet, the author of more than 60 books. The success of his novel *Not Without Laughter* (1930) secured his reputation and enabled him to become the first black American to support himself as a professional writer. Known as "the bard of Harlem," Hughes was an important public figure and voice for black writers. "Early Autumn" is reprinted from the collection *Something in Common* (1963).

When Bill was very young, they had been in love. Many nights they had spent walking, talking together. Then something not very important had come between them, and they didn't speak. Impulsively, she had married a man she thought she loved. Bill went away, bitter about women.

Yesterday, walking across Washington Square, she saw him for the first time in years.

"Bill Walker," she said.

He stopped. At first he did not recognize her, to him she looked so old.

"Mary! Where did you come from?"

Unconsciously, she lifted her face as though wanting a kiss, but he held out his hand. She took it.

"I live in New York now," she said.

"Oh"—smiling politely. Then a little frown came quickly between his eyes.

"Always wondered what happened to you, Bill."

"I'm a lawyer. Nice firm, way downtown."

"Married yet?"

"Sure. Two kids."

"Oh," she said.

A great many people went past them through the park. People they didn't know. It was late afternoon. Nearly sunset. Cold.

"And your husband?" he asked her.

"We have three children. I work in the bursar's office at Columbia."

"You're looking very . . ." (he wanted to say *old*) ". . . well," he said.

She understood. Under the trees in Washington Square, she found herself desperately reaching back into the past. She had been older than he then in Ohio. Now she was not young at all. Bill was still young.

"We live on Central Park West," she said. "Come and see us sometime."

"Sure," he replied. "You and your husband must have dinner with my family some night. Any night. Lucille and I'd love to have you."

The leaves fell slowly from the trees in the Square. Fell without wind. Autumn dusk. She felt a little sick.

"We'd love it," she answered.

"You ought to see my kids." He grinned.

Suddenly the lights came on up the whole length of Fifth Avenue, chains of misty brilliance in the blue air.

"There's my bus," she said.

He held out his hand. "Good-by."

"When . . ." she wanted to say, but the bus was ready to pull off. The lights on the avenue blurred, twinkled, blurred. And she was afraid to open her mouth as she entered the bus. Afraid it would be impossible to utter a word.

Suddenly she shrieked very loudly, "Good-by!" But the bus door had closed.

The bus started. People came between them outside, people crossing the street, people they didn't know. Space and people. She lost sight of Bill. Then she remembered she had forgotten to give him her address—or to ask him for his—or tell him that her youngest boy was named Bill, too.

Summary of "Early Autumn"

Langston Hughes's short story "Early Autumn" is about two people, Mary and Bill, who were in love once but broke up and did not speak to each other. Mary married someone else "impulsively" and does not see Bill again until one late afternoon, years later, in New York City's Washington Square. When Mary speaks, Bill does not at first recognize her. They discuss their jobs, their marriages, their children. When Mary invites Bill to visit, he says "Sure" and that she should have dinner with his family sometime. When Mary's bus arrives and she gets on, she has trouble speaking. She realizes that they have not set a date or exchanged addresses. She has also forgotten to tell him that her youngest son is named Bill.

Note that the summary is written in the present tense to recount the events that take place during the time of the story. Brevity is achieved by condensing several lines of dialogue into a statement such as "they discuss their jobs." Notice, too, that the summary is not the same as the original; the emotions of the characters, conveyed through what is said—and not said—are missing.

Now for a paraphrase. Read the following sonnet by Shakespeare, looking up unfamiliar words and making notes. Remember to read to the end of a unit of thought, not just to the end of a line. Some sentences continue through several lines; if you pause before you reach punctuation, you will be confused. Write your own paraphrase, not looking ahead in the text, and then compare yours with the one that follows the poem.

SONNET 116 | WILLIAM SHAKESPEARE

Surely the best-known name in literature, William Shakespeare (1564–1616) is famous as both a dramatist and a poet. Rural Warwickshire and the market town of Stratford-on-Avon, where he grew up, showed him many of the character types who were to enliven his plays, as did the bustling life of a young actor in London. Apparently his sonnets were intended to be circulated only among his friends, but they were published nonetheless in 1609. His thirty-seven plays were first published together in 1623. Shakespeare's 154 sonnets vary, some focusing on separation and world-weariness, others on the endurance of love.

> Let me not to the marriage of true minds
> Admit impediments. Love is not love
> Which alters when it alteration finds,
> Or bends with the remover to remove.
> O, no! it is an ever-fixed mark   5
> That looks on tempests and is never shaken;
> It is the star to every wand'ring bark,
> Whose worth's unknown, although his height be taken.
> Love's not Time's fool, though rosy lips and cheeks
> Within his bending sickle's compass come;   10
> Love alters not with his brief hours and weeks,

> But bears it out even to the edge of doom.
>   If this be error and upon me proved,
>   I never writ, nor no man ever loved.

Paraphrase of "Sonnet 116"

I cannot accept barriers to the union of steadfast spirits. We cannot call love love if it changes because it discovers change or if it disappears during absence. On the contrary, love is a steady guide that, in spite of difficulties, remains unwavering. Love can define the inherent value in all who lack self-knowledge, though superficially they know who they are. Love does not lessen with time, though signs of physical beauty may fade. Love endures, changeless, eternally. If anyone can show me to be wrong in this position, I am no writer and no man can be said to have loved.

We have examined the facts of a literary work, what we can call the internal situation. But, as we noted in Chapter 2, there is also the external situation or context of any piece of writing. For many literary works, the context is not as essential to understanding as it is with nonfiction. You can read "Early Autumn," for instance, without knowing much about Langston Hughes, or the circumstances in which he wrote the story, although such information would enrich your reading experience. There is a body of information, however, that is very important, what we can call the external literary situation. Literary externals are those basic elements of a work that readers should take note of before they begin to read.

> REMEMBER: Active reading includes looking over a work first and predicting what will come next. Do not just start reading words without first understanding what kind of work you are about to read.

Let's review some of these essentials.

- First, don't make the mistake of calling every work a "story." When you read—and then later discuss—literature, make clear distinctions among stories, novels, plays, and poems.
- Poems can be further divided into narrative, dramatic, and lyric poems.
- A *narrative poem,* such as Homer's *The Iliad,* tells a story in verse. A *dramatic poem* records the speech of at least one character.
- A poem in which only one figure speaks—but clearly addresses words to someone who is present in a particular situation—is called a *dramatic monologue.*
- *Lyric poems,* Dunbar's "Promise," for example, may place the speaker in a situation or may express a thought or feeling with few, if any, situational details, but lyric poems have in common the convention that we as readers are listening in on someone's thoughts, not listening to words directed to a sec-

ond, created figure. These distinctions make us aware of how the words of the poem are coming to us. Are we hearing a storyteller or someone speaking? Or, are we overhearing someone's thoughts?

Lyric poems can be further divided into many subcategories or types. Most instructors will expect you to be able to recognize some of these types. You should be able to distinguish between a poem in *free verse* (no prevailing metrical pattern) and one in *blank verse* (continuous unrhymed lines of iambic pentameter.) (Note: A metrical line will contain a particular number—pentameter is five—of one kind of metrical "foot." The iambic foot consists of one unstressed syllable followed by one stressed syllable.) You should also be able to tell if a poem is written in some type of *stanza* form (repeated units with the same number of lines, same metrical pattern, and same rhyme scheme), or if it is a *sonnet* (always 14 lines of iambic pentameter with one of two complex rhyme schemes labeled either English or Italian). You want to make it a habit to observe these external elements before you read. To sharpen your observation, complete the following exercise.

EXERCISE: Observing Literary Types and Using Literary Terms

1. After surveying this appendix, make a list of all the works of literature by primary type: short story, poem, play.

2. For each work on your list, add two additional pieces of information: whether the author is American or British, and in what century the work was written. Why should you be aware of the writer's dates and nationality as you read?

3. Further divide the poems into narrative, dramatic, or lyric, as appropriate.

4. List as many of the details of type or form as you can for each poem. For example, if the poem is written in stanzas, describe the stanza form used: the number of lines, the meter, the rhyme scheme. If the poem is a sonnet, determine the rhyme scheme. (Note: Rhyme scheme is indicated by using letters, assigning "a" to the first sound and using a new letter for each new sound. Thus, if two consecutive lines rhyme, the scheme is *aa, bb, cc, dd,* and so on.)

SEEING CONNECTIONS: ANALYSIS

Although we read first for the facts and an initial emotional response, we do not stop there, because as humans we seek meaning. Surely there is more to "Early Autumn" than the summary suggests; emotionally we know this to be true. As with nonfiction, one of the best places to start analysis is with a work's organization or structure. Lyric poems will be shaped by many of the same structures found in essays: chronological, spatial, general to particular, particular to general, a list of particulars with an unstated general point, and so forth.

In "Promise," Dunbar gives one illustration, recounted chronologically, to make a point that is left unstated. "Sonnet 116" contains a list of characteristics of love underscored in the conclusion by the speaker's conviction that he is right.

Analysis of Narrative Structure

In stories (and plays and narrative poems) we are given a series of events, in time sequence, involving one or more characters. In some stories, episodes are only loosely connected but are unified around a central character (Mark Twain's *Adventures of Huckleberry Finn,* for example). Most stories present events that are at least to some extent related causally; that is, action A by the main character leads to event B, which requires action C by the main character. This kind of plot structure can be diagrammed, as in Figure 1.

Figure 1 introduces some terms and concepts useful in analyzing and discussing narratives. The story's *exposition* refers to the background details needed to get the story started, including the time and place of the story and relationships of the characters. In "Early Autumn" Hughes begins by telling us that the action will take place in lower Manhattan, late in the afternoon, between a man and a woman who had once loved each other. The *complication* refers to an event; something happens to produce tension or conflict. In "Early Autumn" the meeting of Mary and Bill, after many years, could be an occasion for joy but seems to cause a complication instead. Mary expects to be kissed but Bill merely offers his hand; Bill smiles "politely" and then frowns. The meeting becomes a complication for both characters because it generates a *conflict* within each character. Bill's conflict seems the more manageable; he turns on his polite behavior to get through the unexpected encounter. Mary is more upset; seeing Bill makes her feel old, and she is hardly able to speak when she boards the bus. A key question arises: Why is Mary so upset?

Although some stories present one major complication leading to a climactic moment of decision or insight for the main character, many actually repeat the pattern, presenting several complications—each with an attempted resolution that generates yet another complication—until we reach the high point of tension, the *climax.* The climax then generates the story's *resolution* and ending. These terms are useful even though some stories end abruptly without having

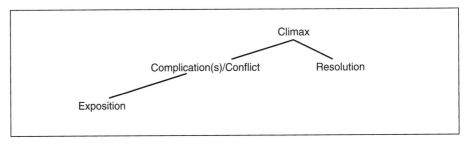

FIGURE 1 Plot Structure

much resolution. An abbreviated resolution is part of the modern writer's view of reality, that life goes on, with problems remaining unresolved. The climax in "Early Autumn" comes when Mary boards her bus and then realizes that she will once again be separated from Bill. This story's climax is muted and merges quickly into the resolution of the last line. The ending offers little genuine resolution; our recognizing this fact helps us better understand the story.

Analysis of Character

An analysis of plot structure has shown that Mary is the more troubled character. You should recognize that Mary is not in conflict *with* Bill but rather is in conflict *over* him, or over her feelings for him, still strong in spite of years of a life without him. Note the close connection between complication (event) and conflict (what the characters are feeling). Fiction requires both plot and character, events and players in those events. In serious literature the greater emphasis is usually on character, on what we learn about human life through the interplay of character and incident.

As we shift attention from the plot of "Early Autumn" to the characters, it helps to consider how writers present character. Writers have several techniques for conveying character:

- Descriptive details. (Bill's polite smile followed by a frown.)
- Dramatic scenes. (Instead of telling us, they show us. Most of "Early Autumn" consists of dialogue between Mary and Bill.)
- Contrast among characters. (We have already observed that Mary and Bill react differently to their encounter.)
- Other elements in the work. (Names can be significant, or characters can become associated with objects, or details of setting can become symbolic.)

Understanding character is always a challenge because we must infer from a few words, gestures, and actions. Looking at all of a writer's options for presenting character will keep us from overlooking important details.

Analysis of Elements of Style and Tone

Important elements in "Early Autumn" include the time of day and the title. How are they connected? What do they suggest about the characters? All the elements, discussed in Chapter 2, that shape a writer's style and create tone can be found in literary works as well and need to be considered as a part of your analysis. Hughes's title is actually a metaphor and, reinforced by the late-in-the-day meeting, suggests that this meeting comes too late for Mary to regain what she has lost—her youth and her youthful love. Shakespeare's "Sonnet 116" develops the speaker's ideas about love through a series of metaphors. The rose in Dunbar's "Promise," is not a metaphor, though, because it is not part of a comparison. Yet, as we read "Promise" we sense that the poem is about something more serious than the nurturing and stealing of one flower, no matter how beautiful. Again, this work's title gives us a clue that the rose stands for something more than itself; it is a symbol. Traditionally the red rose is a symbol of love. To tie the poem together, we will have to see how the title, the usual symbolic value of the rose, and the specifics of the poem connect.

DRAWING CONCLUSIONS: INTERPRETATION

We have studied the facts of several works and analyzed their structures and other key elements. To reach some conclusions from this information and shape it into an organized form is to offer an interpretation of the work. At this point, readers can be expected to disagree somewhat, but if we have all read carefully and applied our knowledge of literature, differences should, most of the time, be ones of focus or emphasis. Presumably no one is prepared to argue that "Promise" is about pink elephants or "Early Autumn" about the Queen of England, because neither work contains any facts to support those conclusions.

What conclusions can we reach about "Promise"? A beautiful flower has been nurtured into bloom by a speaker who expects it to brighten his or her life. The title lets us know that the rose represents great promise. Has a rival stolen the speaker's loved one, represented symbolically by the rose? A thoughtless child would not be an appropriate rival for an adult speaker, so in the context of this poem, the rose represents, more generally, something that the speaker cherishes in anticipation of the pleasure it will bring.

In "Early Autumn" the pain that Mary feels when she meets Bill in Washington Square comes from her awareness that she still loves Bill and that he is lost to her. Bill has gone on to a happy life in which she has no part. The lights blur because Mary's eyes are filled with tears as the conversation makes her aware that Bill has given her little thought over the years, whereas Mary, to keep some part of Bill in her life, has named her youngest son Bill. The details of the story, an analysis of plot and character conflict, and the story's metaphors support these conclusions.

WRITING ABOUT LITERATURE

When you are assigned a literary essay, you will usually be asked to write either an explication or an analysis. An *explication* presents a reading of a complex poem. It will combine paraphrase and explanation to clarify the poem's meaning. A *literary analysis* can take many forms. You may be asked to analyze one element in a work: character conflict, the use of setting, the tone of a poem. Or you could be asked to contrast two works. Usually an analytic assignment requires you to connect analysis to interpretation, for we analyze the parts to better understand the whole. If you are asked to examine the metaphors in a Shakespeare sonnet, for example, you will want to show how understanding the metaphors contributes to an understanding of the entire poem. In short, literary analysis is much the same as a style analysis of an essay, and thus the guidelines for writing about style discussed in Chapter 2 apply here as well.* Successful analyses are based on accurate reading, reflection on the work's emotional impact, and the use of details from the work to support conclusions.

Literary analyses can also incorporate material beyond the particular work. We can analyze a work in the light of biographical information or from a particular political ideology. Or, we can study the social-cultural context of the work, or relate it to a literary tradition. These are only a few of the many approaches to the study of literature, and they depend on the application of knowledge outside the work itself. For undergraduates, topics based on these approaches usually require research. The second student research essay in Section 3 (see pp. 331–35) is a literary analysis. Alan examines Faulkner's *Intruder in the Dust* as an initiation novel. He connects his analysis to works by Hawthorne and Arthur Miller. What is taken from his research is documented and helps develop and support his own conclusions about the story.

To practice close reading, analysis, and interpretation of literature, read the following works. Use the questions after each work to aid your analysis of and responses to the literature.

SONNET 73 | WILLIAM SHAKESPEARE

See p. 683 for information about Shakespeare.

> That time of year thou mayst in me behold
> When yellow leaves, or none, or few, do hang
> Upon those boughs which shake against the cold,
> Bare ruined choirs where late the sweet birds sang.
> In me thou see'st the twilight of such day   5
> As after sunset fadeth in the west,
> Which by and by black night doth take away,
> Death's second self, that seals up all in rest.
> In me thou see'st the glowing of such fire
> That on the ashes of his youth doth lie,   10
> As the deathbed whereon it must expire,
> Consumed with that which it was nourished by.
>   This thou perceivest, which makes thy love more strong,
>   To love that well which thou must leave ere long.

QUESTIONS FOR READING, REASONING, AND REFLECTING

1. Paraphrase the poem.
2. Using letters to mark the pattern, determine the poem's rhyme scheme.
3. What structure, or grouping by lines, is suggested by the rhyme scheme? How does Shakespeare use this structure?

---

*Remember: The guidelines for referring to authors, titles, and direct quotations—presented in Chapter 1—also apply.

4. To what does the speaker compare himself in each quatrain (set of four lines)? What do the three comparisons have in common?

5. What is the emotional impact of each metaphor? Is the feeling more positive in some than in others? What does the poet gain by the order of the metaphors?

6. What attitude toward growing old does the speaker convey through the selection and ordering of the metaphors?

TO HIS COY MISTRESS | ANDREW MARVELL

One of the last poets of the English Renaissance, Andrew Marvell (1621–1678) graduated from Cambridge University, spent much of his young life as a tutor, and was elected to Parliament in 1659. He continued in public service until his death. Most of his best-loved lyric poems come from his years as a tutor. "To His Coy Mistress" was published in 1681.

Had we but world enough, and time,
This coyness, lady, were no crime.
We would sit down, and think which way
To walk, and pass our long love's day.
Thou by the Indian Ganges' side   5
Shouldst rubies find; I by the tide
Of Humber would complain. I would
Love you ten years before the Flood,
And you should, if you please, refuse
Till the conversion of the Jews.   10
My vegetable° love should grow   *slowly vegetative*
Vaster than empires, and more slow;
An hundred years should go to praise
Thine eyes, and on thy forehead gaze;
Two hundred to adore each breast,   15
But thirty thousand to the rest;
An age at least to every part,
And the last age should show your heart.
For, lady, you deserve this state,
Nor would I love at lower rate.   20
   But at my back I always hear
Time's wingèd chariot hurrying near;
And yonder all before us lie
Deserts of vast eternity.
Thy beauty shall no more be found,   25
Nor in thy marble vault shall sound
My echoing song; then worms shall try
That long preserved virginity,
And your quaint honor turn to dust,
And into ashes all my lust.   30
The grave's a fine and private place,
But none, I think, do there embrace.
   Now therefore, while the youthful hue
Sits on thy skin like morning dew,

And while thy willing soul transpires   35
At every pore with instant fires,
Now let us sport us while we may,
And now, like amorous birds of prey,
Rather at once our time devour
Than languish in his slow-chapped power.   40
Let us roll all our strength and all
Our sweetness up into one ball,
And tear our pleasures with rough strife
Thorough° the iron gates of life.   *through*   45
Thus, though we cannot make our sun
Stand still, yet we will make him run.

QUESTIONS FOR READING, REASONING, AND REFLECTING

1. Describe the poem's external form.
2. How are the words coming to us? That is, is this a narrative, dramatic, or lyric poem?
3. Summarize the speaker's argument, using the structures *if, but,* and *therefore*.
4. What figure of speech do we find throughout the first verse paragraph? What is its effect on the speaker's tone?
5. Find examples of irony and understatement in the second verse paragraph.
6. How does the tone shift in the second section?
7. Explain the personification in line 22.
8. Explain the metaphors in lines 30 and 45.
9. What is the paradox of the last two lines? How can it be explained?
10. What is the idea of this poem? What does the writer want us to reflect on?

THE PASSIONATE SHEPHERD TO HIS LOVE | CHRISTOPHER MARLOWE

Cambridge graduate, Renaissance dramatist second only to Shakespeare, Christopher Marlowe (1564–1593) may be best known for this lyric poem. Not only is it widely anthologized, it has also spawned a number of responses by such significant writers as the seventeenth-century poet John Donne and the twentieth-century humorous poet Ogden Nash. For the Renaissance Period the shepherd was a standard figure of the lover.

Come live with me and be my love,
And we will all the pleasures prove
That valleys, groves, hills, and fields,
Woods, or steepy mountain yields.

And we will sit upon the rocks,
Seeing the shepherds feed their flocks,   5
By shallow rivers to whose falls
Melodious birds sing madrigals.

And I will make thee beds of roses
And a thousand fragrant posies,   10
A cap of flowers, and a kirtle
Embroidered all with leaves of myrtle;

A gown made of the finest wool
Which from our pretty lambs we pull;
Fair lined slippers for the cold,   15
With buckles of the purest gold;

A belt of straw and ivy buds,
With coral clasps and amber studs:
And if these pleasures may thee move,
Come live with me, and be my love.   20

The shepherds' swains shall dance and sing
For thy delight each May morning:
If these delights thy mind may move,
Then live with me and be my love.

QUESTIONS FOR READING, REASONING, AND REFLECTING

1. Describe the poem's external structure.

2. What is the speaker's subject? What does he want to accomplish?

3. Summarize his "argument." How does he seek to convince his love?

4. What do the details of his argument have in common—that is, what kind of world or life does the speaker describe? Is there anything missing from the shepherd's world?

5. Would you like to be courted in this way? Would you say yes to the shepherd? If not, why?

THE NYMPH'S REPLY TO THE SHEPHERD | SIR WALTER RALEIGH

The renowned Elizabethan courtier, Sir Walter Raleigh (1552–1618) led a varied life as both a favorite of Queen Elizabeth and out of favor at court, as a colonizer and writer, and as one of many to be imprisoned in the Tower of London. In the following poem, Raleigh offers a response to Marlowe, using the nymph as the voice of the female lover.

If all the world and love were young,
And truth in every shepherd's tongue,
These pretty pleasures might me move
To live with thee and be thy love.

Time drives the flocks from field to fold   5
When rivers rage and rocks grow cold,
And Philomel becometh dumb;
The rest complains of cares to come.

The flowers do fade, and wanton fields
To wayward winter reckoning yields;   10
A honey tongue, a heart of gall,
Is fancy's spring, but sorrow's fall.

Thy gowns, thy shoes, thy beds of roses,
Thy cap, thy kirtle, and thy posies
Soon break, soon wither, soon forgotten,—   15
In folly ripe, in reason rotten.

Thy belt of straw and ivy buds,
Thy coral clasps and amber studs,
All these in me no means can move
To come to thee and be thy love.   20

But could youth last and love still breed,
Had joys no date nor age no need,
Then these delights my mind might move
To live with thee and be thy love.

QUESTIONS FOR READING, REASONING, AND REFLECTING

1. Describe the poem's external structure.
2. What is the context of the poem, the reason the speaker offers her words?
3. Analyze the speaker's argument, using *if* and *but* as your basic structure—and then the concluding, qualifying *but*.
4. What evidence does the speaker provide to support her argument?
5. Who has the more convincing argument: Marlowe's shepherd or Raleigh's nymph? Why?

TAXI | AMY LOWELL

Educated at private schools and widely traveled, American Amy Lowell (1874–1925) was both a poet and a critic. Lowell frequently read her poetry and lectured on poetic techniques, defending her verse and that of other modern poets.

When I go away from you
The world beats dead
Like a slackened drum.
I call out for you against the jutted stars
And shout into the ridges of the wind.   5
Streets coming fast,
One after the other,
Wedge you away from me,
And the lamps of the city prick my eyes
So that I can no longer see your face.   10
Why should I leave you,
To wound myself upon the sharp edges of the night?

QUESTIONS FOR READING, REASONING, AND REFLECTING

1. Classify the poem according to its external structure.
2. Is this a narrative, dramatic, or lyric poem?
3. Explain the simile in the opening three lines and the metaphor in the last line of the poem.
4. What is the poem's subject? What seems to be the situation in which we find the speaker?
5. How would you describe the tone of the poem? How do the details and the emotional impact of the metaphors help to create tone?
6. What is the poem's meaning or theme? In other words, what does the poet want us to understand from reading her poem?

THE STORY OF AN HOUR | KATE CHOPIN

Now a highly acclaimed short-story writer, Kate Chopin (1851–1904) enjoyed a decade of publication and popularity from 1890 to 1900 and then critical condemnation followed by 60 years of neglect. Chopin began her writing career after her husband's death, having returned to her home in St. Louis with her six children. She saw two collections of her stories published—*Bayou Folk* in 1894 and *A Night in Acadie* in 1897—before losing her popularity with the publication of her short novel *The Awakening* in 1899, the story of a woman struggling to free herself from years of repression and subservience.

Knowing that Mrs. Mallard was afflicted with a heart trouble, great care was taken to break to her as gently as possible the news of her husband's death.

It was her sister Josephine who told her, in broken sentences; veiled hints that revealed in half concealing. Her husband's friend Richards was there, too, near her. It was he who had been in the newspaper office when intelligence of the railroad disaster was received, with Brently Mallard's name leading the list of "killed." He had only taken the time to assure himself of its truth by a second telegram, and had hastened to forestall any less careful, less tender friend in bearing the sad message.

She did not hear the story as many women have heard the same, with a paralyzed inability to accept its significance. She wept at once, with sudden, wild abandonment, in her sister's arms. When the storm of grief had spent itself she went away to her room alone. She would have no one follow her.

There stood, facing the open window, a comfortable, roomy armchair. Into this she sank, pressed down by a physical exhaustion that haunted her body and seemed to reach into her soul.

She could see in the open square before her house the tops of trees that were all aquiver with the new spring life. The delicious breath of rain was in the air. In the street below a peddler was crying his wares. The notes of a distant song which some one was singing reached her faintly, and countless sparrows were twittering in the eaves.

There were patches of blue sky showing here and there through the clouds that had met and piled one above the other in the west facing her window.

She sat with her head thrown back upon the cushion of the chair, quite motionless, except when a sob came up into her throat and shook her, as a child who has cried itself to sleep continues to sob in its dreams.

She was young, with a fair, calm face, whose lines bespoke repression and even a certain strength. But now there was a dull stare in her eyes, whose gaze was fixed away off yonder on one of those patches of blue sky. It was not a glance of reflection, but rather indicated a suspension of intelligent thought.

There was something coming to her and she was waiting for it, fearfully. What was it? She did not know; it was too subtle and elusive to name. But she felt it, creeping out of the sky, reaching toward her through the sounds, the scents, the color that filled the air.

Now her bosom rose and fell tumultuously. She was beginning to recognize this thing that was approaching to possess her, and she was striving to beat it back with her will—as powerless as her two white slender hands would have been.

When she abandoned herself a little whispered word escaped her slightly parted lips. She said it over and over under her breath: "free, free, free!" The vacant stare and the look of terror that had followed it went from her eyes. They stayed keen and bright. Her pulses beat fast, and the coursing blood warmed and relaxed every inch of her body.

She did not stop to ask if it were or were not a monstrous joy that held her. A clear and exalted perception enabled her to dismiss the suggestion as trivial.

She knew that she would weep again when she saw the kind, tender hands folded in death; the face that had never looked save with love upon her, fixed and gray and dead. But she saw beyond that bitter moment a long procession of years to come that would belong to her absolutely. And she opened and spread her arms out to them in welcome.

There would be no one to live for her during those coming years; she would live for herself. There would be no powerful will bending hers in that blind persistence with which men and women believe they have a right to impose a private will upon a fellow-creature. A kind intention or a cruel intention made the act seem no less a crime as she looked upon it in that brief moment of illumination.

And yet she had loved him—sometimes. Often she had not. What did it matter! What could love, the unsolved mystery, count for in face of this possession of self-assertion which she suddenly recognized as the strongest impulse of her being!

"Free! Body and soul free!" she kept whispering.

Josephine was kneeling before the closed door with her lips to the keyhole, imploring for admission. "Louise, open the door! I beg; open the door—you will make yourself ill. What are you doing, Louise? For heaven's sake open the door."

"Go away. I am not making myself ill." No; she was drinking in a very elixir of life through that open window.

Her fancy was running riot along those days ahead of her. Spring days, and summer days, and all sorts of days that would be her own. She breathed a quick prayer that life might be long. It was only yesterday she had thought with a shudder that life might be long.

She arose at length and opened the door to her sister's importunities. There was a feverish triumph in her eyes, and she carried herself unwittingly like a goddess of Victory. She clasped her sister's waist, and together they descended the stairs. Richards stood waiting for them at the bottom.

Someone was opening the front door with a latchkey. It was Brently Mallard who entered, a little travel-stained, composedly carrying his grip-sack and umbrella. He had been far from the scene of accident, and did not even know there had been one. He stood amazed at Josephine's piercing cry; at Richards' quick motion to screen him from the view of his wife.

But Richards was too late.

When the doctors came they said she had died of heart disease—of joy that kills.

QUESTIONS FOR READING, REASONING, AND REFLECTING

1. Analyze the story's plot structure, using the terms presented in Figure 1 (p. 686).
2. What is Mrs. Mallard's conflict? Explain the opposing elements of her conflict as precisely as you can.
3. When Mrs. Mallard goes to her room, she gazes out the window. Consider the details of the scene; what do these details have in common? How do the details help us understand what Mrs. Mallard experiences?
4. Why is it inaccurate to say that Mrs. Mallard does not love her husband? Cite evidence from the story.
5. The author James Joyce has described a character's moment of insight or intuition as an "epiphany." What is Mrs. Mallard's epiphany?
6. Are we to agree with the doctor's explanation for Mrs. Mallard's death? What term is appropriate to describe the story's conclusion?

THE ONES WHO WALK AWAY FROM OMELAS | URSULA K. LE GUIN

A graduate of Radcliffe College and Columbia University, Ursula K. Le Guin (b. 1929) is the author of more than 20 novels and juvenile books, several volumes of poetry, and numerous stories and essays published in science fiction, scholarly, and popular journals. Her fiction stretches the categories of science fiction or fantasy and challenges a reader's moral understanding. First published in 1973, the following story, according to Le Guin, was inspired by a passage in William James's "The Moral Philosopher and the Moral Life" in which he asserts that we could not tolerate a situation in which the happiness of many people was purchased by the "lonely torment" of one "lost soul."

With a clamor of bells that set the swallows soaring, the Festival of Summer 1 came to the city Omelas, bright-towered by the sea. The rigging of the boats in harbor sparkled with flags. In the streets between houses with red roofs and painted walls, between the old moss-grown gardens and under avenues of trees, past great parks and public buildings, processions moved. Some were decorous: old people in long stiff robes of mauve and gray, grave master work-men, quiet, merry women carrying their babies and chatting as they walked. In other streets the music beat faster, a shimmering of gong and tambourine, and the people went dancing, the procession was a dance. Children dodged in and out, their high calls rising like the swallows' crossing flights over the music and the singing. All the processions wound towards the north side of the city, where on the great water-meadow called the Green Fields boys and girls, naked in the bright air, with mudstained feet and ankles and long, lithe arms, exercised their restive horses before the race. The horses wore no gear at all but a halter with-out bit. Their manes were braided with streamers of silver, gold, and green. They flared their nostrils and pranced and boasted to one another; they were vastly excited, the horse being the only animal who has adopted our cere-monies as his own. Far off to the north and west the mountains stood up half circling Omelas on her bay. The air of morning was so clear that the snow still crowning the Eighteen Peaks burned with white-gold fire across the miles of sunlit air, under the dark blue of the sky. There was just enough wind to make the banners that marked the racecourse snap and flutter now and then. In the silence of the broad green meadows one could hear the music winding through the city streets, farther and nearer and ever approaching, a cheerful faint sweet-ness of the air that from time to time trembled and gathered together and broke out into the great joyous clanging of the bells.

Joyous! How is one to tell about joy? How describe the citizens of Omelas? 2

They were not simple folk, you see, though they were happy. But we do 3 not say the words of cheer much any more. All smiles have become archaic. Given a description such as this one tends to make certain assumptions. Given a description such as this one tends to look next for the King, mounted on a splendid stallion and surrounded by his noble knights, or perhaps in a golden litter borne by great-muscled slaves. But there was no king. They did not use swords, or keep slaves. They were not barbarians. I do not know the rules and laws of their society, but I suspect that they were singularly few. As they did without monarchy and slavery, so they also got on without the stock exchange, the advertisement, the secret police, and the bomb. Yet I repeat that these were not simple folk, not dulcet shepherds, noble savages, bland utopians. They were not less complex than us. The trouble is that we have a bad habit, encouraged by pedants and sophisticates, of considering happiness as some-thing rather stupid. Only pain is intellectual, only evil interesting. This is the treason of the artist: a refusal to admit the banality of evil and the terrible bore-dom of pain. If you can't lick 'em, join 'em. If it hurts, repeat it. But to praise despair is to condemn delight, to embrace violence is to lose hold of everything else. We have almost lost hold, we can no longer describe a happy man, nor make any celebration of joy. How can I tell you about the people of Omelas? They were not naïve and happy children—though their children were, in fact, happy. They were mature, intelligent, passionate adults whose lives were not wretched. O miracle! But I wish I could describe it better. I wish I could convince you. Omelas sounds in my words like a city in a fairy tale, long ago and far away, once upon a time. Perhaps it would be best if you imagined it as your own fancy bids, assuming it will rise to the occasion, for certainly I cannot suit you all. For instance, how about technology? I think that there would be no cars or helicopters in and above the streets; this follows from the fact that the people of Omelas are happy people. Happiness is based on a just discrimination of what is necessary, what is neither necessary nor destructive, and what is destructive. In the middle category, however—that of the unnecessary but undestructive, that of comfort, luxury, exuberance, etc.—they could perfectly well have central heating, subway trains, washing machines, and all kinds of marvelous devises not yet invented here, floating light-sources, fuelless power, a cure for the common cold. Or they could have none of that: it doesn't matter. As you like it. I incline to think that people from towns up and down the coast have been coming in to Omelas during the last days before the Festival on very fast trains and double-decked trams, and that the train station of Omelas is actually the handsomest building in town, though plainer than the magnificent Farmers' Market. But even granted trains, I fear that Omelas so far strikes some of you as goody-goody. Smiles, bells, parades, horses, bleh. If so, please add an orgy. If an orgy would help, don't hesitate. Let us not, however, have temples from which issue beautiful nude priests and priestesses already half in ecstasy and ready to copulate with any man or woman, lover or stranger, who desires union with the deep godhead of the blood, although that was my first idea. But really it would be better not to have any temples in Omelas—at least, not manned temples. Religion yes, clergy no. Surely the beautiful nudes can just wander about, offering themselves like divine soufflés to the hunger of the needy and the rapture of the flesh. Let them join the processions. Let tambourines be struck above the copulations, and the glory of desire be proclaimed upon the gongs, and (a not unimportant point) let the offspring of these delightful rituals be beloved and looked after by all. One thing I know there is none of in Omelas is guilt. But what else should there be? I thought that first there were no drugs, but that is puritanical. For those who like it, the faint insistent sweetness of *drooz* may perfume the ways of the city, *drooz* which first brings a great lightness and brilliance to the mind and limbs, and then after some hours a dreamy languor, and wonderful visions at last of the very arcana and inmost secrets of the Universe, as well as exciting the pleasure of sex beyond all belief; and it is not habit-forming. For more modest tastes I think there ought to be beer. What else, what else belongs in the joyous city? The sense of victory, surely, the celebration of courage. But as we did without clergy, let us do without soldiers. The joy built upon successful slaughter is not the right kind of joy; it will not do; it is fearful and it is trivial. A boundless and generous contentment, a magnanimous triumph felt not against some outer enemy but in communion with the finest and fairest in the souls of all men everywhere and the splendor of the world's summer; this is what swells the hearts of the people of Omelas, and the victory they celebrate is that of life. I really don't think many of them need to take *drooz*.

4   Most of the processions have reached the Green Fields by now. A marvelous smell of cooking goes forth from the red and blue tents of the provisioners. The faces of small children are amiably sticky; in the benign grey beard of a man a couple of crumbs of rich pastry are entangled. The youths and girls have mounted their horses and are beginning to group around the starting line of the course. An old woman, small, fat, and laughing, is passing out flowers from a basket, and tall young men wear her flowers in their shining hair. A child of nine or ten sits at the edge of the crowd, alone, playing on a wooden flute. People pause to listen, and they smile, but they do not speak to him, for he never ceases playing and never sees them, his dark eyes wholly rapt in the sweet, thin magic of the tune.

5   He finishes, and slowly lowers his hands holding the wooden flute.

6   As if that little private silence were the signal, all at once a trumpet sounds from the pavilion near the starting line: imperious, melancholy, piercing. The horses rear on their slender legs, and some of them neigh in answer. Soberfaced, the young riders stroke the horses' necks and soothe them, whispering, "Quiet, quiet, there my beauty, my hope." They begin to form in rank along the starting line. The crowds along the racecourse are like a field of grass and flowers in the wind. The Festival of Summer has begun.

7   Do you believe? Do you accept the festival, the city, the joy? No? Then let me describe this one more thing.

8   In a basement under one of the beautiful public buildings of Omelas, or perhaps in the cellar of one of its spacious private homes, there is a room. It has one locked door, and no window. A little light seeps in dustily between cracks in the boards, secondhand from the cobwebbed window somewhere across the cellar. In one corner of the little room a couple of mops, with stiff, clotted, foul-smelling heads, stand near a rusty bucket. The floor is dirt, a little damp to the touch, as cellar dirt usually is. The room is about three paces long and two wide: a mere broom closet or disused tool room. In the room a child is sitting. It could be a boy or a girl. It looks about six, but actually is nearly ten. It is feeble-minded. Perhaps it was born defective, or perhaps it has become imbecile through fear, malnutrition, and neglect. It picks its nose and occasionally fumbles vaguely with its toes or genitals, as it sits hunched in the corner farthest from the bucket and the two mops. It is afraid of the mops. It finds them horrible. It shuts its eyes, but it knows the mops are still standing there; and the door is locked; and nobody will come. The door is always locked; and nobody ever comes, except that sometimes—the child has no understanding of time or interval—sometimes the door rattles terribly and opens, and a person, or several people, are there. One of them may come in and kick the child to make it stand up. The others never come close, but peer in at it with frightened, disgusted eyes. The food bowl and the water jug are hastily filled, the

door is locked, the eyes disappear. The people at the door never say anything, but the child, who has not always lived in the tool room, and can remember sunlight and its mother's voice, sometimes speaks. "I will be good," it says. "Please let me out. I will be good!" They never answer. The child used to scream for help at night, and cry a good deal, but now it only makes a kind of whining, "eh-haa-eh-haa," and it speaks less and less often. It is so thin there are no calves to its legs; its belly protrudes; it lives on a half-bowl of corn meal and grease a day. It is naked. Its buttocks and thighs are a mass of festered sores, as it sits in its own excrement continually.

9   They all know it is there, all the people of Omelas. Some of them have come to see it, others are content merely to know it is there. They all know that it has to be there. Some of them understand why, and some do not, but they all understand that their happiness, the beauty of their city, the tenderness of their friendships, the health of their children, the wisdom of their scholars, the skill of their makers, even the abundance of their harvest and the kindly weathers of their skies, depend wholly upon this child's abominable misery.

10   This is usually explained to children when they are between eight and twelve, whenever they seem capable of understanding; and most of those who come to see the child are young people, though often enough an adult comes, or comes back, to see the child. No matter how well the matter has been explained to them, these young spectators are always shocked and sickened at the sight. They feel disgust, which they had thought themselves superior to. They feel anger, outrage, impotence, despite all the explanations. They would like to do something for the child. But there is nothing they can do. If the child were brought up into the sunlight out of that vile place, if it were cleaned and fed and comforted, that would be a good thing, indeed; but if it were done, in that day and hour all the prosperity and beauty and delight of Omelas would wither and be destroyed. Those are the terms. To exchange all the goodness and grace of every life in Omelas for that single, small improvement: to throw away the happiness of thousands for the chance of the happiness of one: that would be to let guilt within the walls indeed.

11   The terms are strict and absolute; there may not even be a kind word spoken to the child.

12   Often the young people go home in tears, or in a tearless rage, when they have seen the child and faced this terrible paradox. They may brood over it for weeks or years. But as time goes on they begin to realize that even if the child could be released, it would not get much good of its freedom: a little vague pleasure of warmth and food, no doubt, but little more. It is too degraded and imbecile to know any real joy. It has been afraid too long ever to be free of fear. Its habits are too uncouth for it to respond to humane treatment. Indeed, after so long it would probably be wretched without walls about it to protect it, and darkness for its eyes, and its own excrement to sit in. Their tears at the bitter injustice dry when they begin to perceive the terrible justice of reality, and to accept it. Yet it is their tears and anger, the trying of their generosity and the acceptance of their helplessness, which are perhaps the true source of the splendor of their lives. Theirs is no vapid, irresponsible happiness. They know

that they, like the child, are not free. They know compassion. It is the existence of the child, and their knowledge of its existence, that makes possible the mobility of their architecture, the poignancy of their music, the profundity of their science. It is because of the child that they are so gentle with children. They know that if the wretched one were not there snivelling in the dark, the other one, the flute-player, could make no joyful music as the young riders line up in their beauty for the race in the sunlight of the first morning of summer.

Now do you believe in them? Are they not more credible? But there is one 13 more thing to tell, and this is quite incredible.

At times one of the adolescent girls or boys who go to see the child, does 14 not go home to weep or rage, does not, in fact, go home at all. Sometimes also a man or woman much older falls silent for a day or two, and then leaves home. These people go out into the street, and walk down the street alone. They keep walking, and walk straight out of the city of Omelas, through the beautiful gates. They keep walking across the farmlands of Omelas. Each one goes alone, youth or girl, man or woman. Night falls; the traveler must pass down village streets, between the houses with yellow-lit windows, and on out into the darkness of the fields. Each alone, they go west or north, towards the mountains. They go on. They leave Omelas, they walk ahead into the darkness, and they do not come back. The place they go towards is a place even less imaginable to most of us than the city of happiness. I cannot describe it at all. It is possible that it does not exist. But they seem to know where they are going, the ones who walk away from Omelas.

QUESTIONS FOR READING, REASONING, AND REFLECTING

1. What is the general impression you get of the city of Omelas from the opening paragraph? To what senses does the author appeal?
2. Describe the people of Omelas. Are they happy? Do they have technology? Guilt? Religion? Soldiers? Drugs?
3. What shocking detail emerges about Omelas? On what does this ideal community thrive?
4. How do the children and teens respond to the locked-up child at first? How do they reconcile themselves to the situation? What do some residents do?
5. Can you understand the reason most residents accept the situation? Can you understand those who walk away? With which group do you most identify? Why?
6. On what does Le Guin want us to reflect? How would you state the story's theme?

TRIFLES | SUSAN GLASPELL

Born in Iowa, Susan Glaspell (1882?–1948) attended Drake University and then began her writing career as a reporter with the *Des Moines Daily News.* She also started writing and selling short stories; her first collection, *Lifted Masks,* was published in 1912. She completed several novels before moving to Provincetown with her husband, who started the Provincetown Players in 1915. Glaspell wrote seven short plays and four long plays for this group, including *Trifles* (1916). The well-known "Jury of Her Peers" (1917) is a short-story version of the play *Trifles*. Glaspell must have recognized that the plot of *Trifles* was a gem worth working with in more than one literary form.

Characters

George Henderson, County Attorney
Henry Peters, Sheriff
Lewis Hale, A Neighboring Farmer
Mrs. Peters
Mrs. Hale

SCENE: *The kitchen in the now abandoned farmhouse of* JOHN WRIGHT, *a gloomy kitchen, and left without having been put in order—unwashed pans under the sink, a loaf of bread outside the bread-box, a dish-towel on the table—other signs of incompleted work. At the rear, the outer door opens and the* SHERIFF *comes in followed by the* COUNTY ATTORNEY *and* HALE. *The* SHERIFF *and* HALE *are men in middle life; the* COUNTY ATTORNEY *is a young man; all are much bundled up and go at once to the stove. They are followed by the two women—the* SHERIFF'*s wife first; she is a slight wiry woman, a thin nervous face.* MRS. HALE *is larger and would ordinarily be called more comfortable looking, but she is disturbed now and looks fearfully about as she enters. The women have come in slowly, and stand close together near the door.*

COUNTY ATTORNEY

[*Rubbing his hands.*] This feels good. Come up to the fire, ladies.

MRS. PETERS

[*After taking a step forward.*] I'm not—cold.

SHERIFF

[*Unbuttoning his overcoat and stepping away from the stove as if to mark the beginning of official business.*] Now, Mr. Hale, before we move things about, you explain to Mr. Henderson just what you saw when you came here yesterday morning.

COUNTY ATTORNEY

By the way, has anything been moved? Are things just as you left them yesterday?

SHERIFF

[*Looking about.*] It's just the same. When it dropped below zero last night I thought I'd better send Frank out this morning to make a fire for us—no use getting pneumonia with a big case on, but I told him not to touch anything except the stove—and you know Frank.

COUNTY ATTORNEY
Somebody should have been left here yesterday.

SHERIFF
Oh—yesterday. When I had to send Frank to Morris Center for that man who went crazy—I want you to know I had my hands full yesterday. I knew you could get back from Omaha by today and as long as I went over everything here myself—

COUNTY ATTORNEY
Well, Mr. Hale, tell just what happened when you came here yesterday morning.

HALE
Harry and I had started to town with a load of potatoes. We came along the road from my place and as I got here I said, "I'm going to see if I can't get John Wright to go in with me on a party telephone." I spoke to Wright about it once before and he put me off, saying folks talked too much anyway, and all he asked was peace and quiet—I guess you know about how much he talked himself; but I thought maybe if I went to the house and talked about it before his wife, though I said to Harry that I didn't know as what his wife wanted made much difference to John—

COUNTY ATTORNEY
Let's talk about that later, Mr. Hale. I do want to talk about that, but tell now just what happened when you got to the house.

HALE
I didn't hear or see anything; I knocked at the door, and still it was all quiet inside. I knew they must be up, it was past eight o'clock. So I knocked again, and I thought I heard somebody say, "Come in." I wasn't sure, I'm not sure yet, but I opened the door—this door [*indicating the door by which the two women are still standing*] and there in that rocker—[*pointing to it*] sat Mrs. Wright.
[*They all look at the rocker.*]

COUNTY ATTORNEY
What—was she doing?

HALE
She was rockin' back and forth. She had her apron in her hand and was kind of—pleating it.

COUNTY ATTORNEY
And how did she—look?

HALE

Well, she looked queer.

COUNTY ATTORNEY

How do you mean—queer?

HALE

Well, as if she didn't know what she was going to do next. And kind of done up.

COUNTY ATTORNEY

How did she seem to feel about your coming?

HALE

Why, I don't think she minded—one way or other. She didn't pay much attention. I said, "How do, Mrs. Wright, it's cold, ain't it?" And she said, "Is it?"—and went on kind of pleating at her apron. Well, I was surprised; she didn't ask me to come up to the stove, or to set down, but just sat there, not even looking at me, so I said, "I want to see John." And then she—laughed. I guess you would call it a laugh. I thought of Harry and the team outside, so I said a little sharp: "Can't I see John?" "No," she says, kind o' dull like. "Ain't he home?" says I. "Yes," says she, "he's home." "Then why can't I see him?" I asked her, out of patience. " 'Cause he's dead," says she. "*Dead?*" says I. She just nodded her head, not getting a bit excited, but rockin' back and forth. "Why—where is he?" says I, not knowing what to say. She just pointed upstairs—like that [*himself pointing to the room above*]. I got up, with the idea of going up there. I walked from there to here—then I says, "Why, what did he die of?" "He died of a rope around his neck," says she, and just went on pleatin' at her apron. Well, I went out and called Harry. I thought I might—need help. We went upstairs and there he was lyin'—

COUNTY ATTORNEY

I think I'd rather have you go into that upstairs, where you can point it all out. Just go on now with the rest of the story.

HALE

Well, my first thought was to get that rope off. It looked . . . [*Stops, his face twitches*] . . . but Harry, he went up to him, and he said, "No, he's dead all right, and we'd better not touch anything." So we went back downstairs. She was still sitting that same way. "Has anybody been notified?" said Harry. He said it business-like—and she stopped pleatin' of her apron. "I don't know," she says. "You don't *know?*" says Harry. "No," says she. "Weren't you sleepin' in the bed with him?" says Harry. "Yes," says she, "but I was on the inside." "Somebody slipped a rope round his neck and strangled him and you didn't wake up?" says Harry. "I didn't wake up," she said after him. We must'a looked as if we didn't see how that could be, for after a minute she said, "I sleep sound." Harry was going to ask her more questions but I said maybe we ought to let her tell her story first to the coroner, or the sheriff, so Harry went fast as he could to Rivers' place, where there's a telephone.

COUNTY ATTORNEY
And what did Mrs. Wright do when she knew that you had gone for the coroner?

HALE
She moved from that chair to this one over here [*Pointing to a small chair in the corner*] and just sat there with her hands held together and looking down. I got a feeling that I ought to make some conversation, so I said I had come in to see if John wanted to put in a telephone, and at that she started to laugh, and then she stopped and looked at me—scared. [*The* County Attorney, *who has had his notebook out, makes a note.*] I dunno, maybe it wasn't scared. I wouldn't like to say it was. Soon Harry got back, and then Dr. Lloyd came, and you, Mr. Peters, and so I guess that's all I know that you don't.

COUNTY ATTORNEY
[*Looking around.*] I guess we'll go upstairs first—and then out to the barn and around there. [*To the* Sheriff.] You're convinced that there was nothing important here—nothing that would point to any motive.

SHERIFF
Nothing here but kitchen things.
[*The* County Attorney, *after again looking around the kitchen, opens the door of a cupboard closet. He gets up on a chair and looks on a shelf. Pulls his hand away, sticky.*]

COUNTY ATTORNEY
Here's a nice mess.
[*The women draw nearer.*]

MRS. PETERS
[*To the other woman.*] Oh, her fruit; it did freeze. [*To the* Lawyer.] She worried about that when it turned so cold. She said the fire'd go out and her jars would break.

SHERIFF
Well, can you beat the woman! Held for murder and worryin' about her preserves.

COUNTY ATTORNEY
I guess before we're through she may have something more serious than preserves to worry about.

HALE
Well, women are used to worrying over trifles.
[*The two women move a little closer together.*]

COUNTY ATTORNEY
[*With the gallantry of a young politician.*] And yet, for all their worries, what would we do without the ladies? [*The women do not unbend. He goes to the sink, takes a dipperful of water from the pail and pouring it into a basin, washes his hands. Starts to wipe them on the roller-towel, turns it for a cleaner place.*] Dirty towels! [*Kicks his foot against the pans under the sink.*] Not much of a housekeeper, would you say, ladies?

MRS. HALE
[*Stiffly.*] There's a great deal of work to be done on a farm.

COUNTY ATTORNEY
To be sure. And yet [*with a little bow to her*] I know there are some Dickson County farmhouses which do not have such roller towels.
[*He gives it a pull to expose its full length again.*]

MRS. HALE
Those towels get dirty awful quick. Men's hands aren't always as clean as they might be.

COUNTY ATTORNEY
Ah, loyal to your sex, I see. But you and Mrs. Wright were neighbors. I suppose you were friends, too.

MRS. HALE
[*Shaking her head.*] I've not seen much of her of late years. I've not been in this house—it's more than a year.

COUNTY ATTORNEY
And why was that? You didn't like her?

MRS. HALE
I liked her all well enough. Farmers' wives have their hands full, Mr. Henderson. And then—

COUNTY ATTORNEY
Yes—?

MRS. HALE
[*Looking about.*] It never seemed a very cheerful place.

COUNTY ATTORNEY
No—it's not cheerful. I shouldn't say she had the homemaking instinct.

MRS. HALE
Well, I don't know as Wright had, either.

COUNTY ATTORNEY
You mean that they didn't get on very well?

MRS. HALE
No, I don't mean anything. But I don't think a place'd be any cheerfuller for John Wright's being in it.

COUNTY ATTORNEY
I'd like to talk more of that a little later. I want to get the lay of things upstairs now.
[*He goes to the left, where three steps lead to a stair door.*]

SHERIFF
I suppose anything Mrs. Peters does'll be all right. She was to take in some clothes for her, you know, and a few little things. We left in such a hurry yesterday.

COUNTY ATTORNEY
Yes, but I would like to see what you take, Mrs. Peters, and keep an eye out for anything that might be of use to us.

MRS. PETERS
Yes, Mr. Henderson.
[*The women listen to the men's steps on the stairs, then look about the kitchen.*]

MRS. HALE
I'd hate to have men coming into my kitchen, snooping around and criticizing.
[*She arranges the pans under the sink which the* Lawyer *had shoved out of place.*]

MRS. PETERS
Of course it's no more than their duty.

MRS. HALE
Duty's all right, but I guess that deputy sheriff that came out to make the fire might have got a little of this on. [*Gives the roller towel a pull.*] Wish I'd thought of that sooner. Seems mean to talk about her for not having things slicked up when she had to come away in such a hurry.

MRS. PETERS

[*Who has gone to a small table in the left corner of the room, and lifted one end of a towel that covers a pan.*] She had bread set.
[*Stands still.*]

MRS. HALE

[*Eyes fixed on a loaf of bread beside the breadbox, which is on a low shelf at the other side of the room. Moves slowly toward it.*] She was going to put this in there. [*Picks up loaf, then abruptly drops it. In a manner of returning to familiar things.*] It's a shame about her fruit. I wonder if it's all gone. [*Gets up on the chair and looks.*] I think there's some here that's all right, Mrs. Peters. Yes—here; [*holding it toward the window*] this is cherries, too. [*Looking again.*] I declare I believe that's the only one. [*Gets down, bottle in her hand. Goes to the sink and wipes it off on the outside.*] She'll feel awful bad after all her hard work in the hot weather. I remember the afternoon I put up my cherries last summer.
[*She puts the bottle on the big kitchen table, center of the room. With a sigh, is about to sit down in the rocking-chair. Before she is seated realizes what chair it is; with a slow look at it, steps back. The chair which she has touched rocks back and forth.*]

MRS. PETERS

Well, I must get those things from the front room closet. [*She goes to the door at the right, but after looking into the other room, steps back.*] You coming with me, Mrs. Hale? You could help me carry them.
[*They go in the other room; reappear,* Mrs. Peters *carrying a dress and skirt,* Mrs. Hale *following with a pair of shoes.*]

MRS. PETERS

My, it's cold in there.
[*She puts the clothes on the big table, and hurries to the stove.*]

MRS. HALE

[*Examining the skirt.*] Wright was close. I think maybe that's why she kept so much to herself. She didn't even belong to the Ladies Aid. I suppose she felt she couldn't do her part, and then you don't enjoy things when you feel shabby. She used to wear pretty clothes and be lively, when she was Minnie Foster, one of the town girls singing in the choir. But that—oh, that was thirty years ago. This all you was to take in?

MRS. PETERS

She said she wanted an apron. Funny thing to want, for there isn't much to get you dirty in jail, goodness knows. But I suppose just to make her feel more natural. She said they was in the top drawer in this cupboard. Yes, here. And then her little shawl that always hung behind the door. [*Opens stair door and looks.*] Yes, here it is.
[*Quickly shuts door leading upstairs.*]

MRS. HALE

[*Abruptly moving toward her.*] Mrs. Peters?

MRS. PETERS

Yes, Mrs. Hale?

MRS. HALE

Do you think she did it?

MRS. PETERS

[*In a frightened voice.*] Oh, I don't know.

MRS. HALE

Well, I don't think she did. Asking for an apron and her little shawl. Worrying about her fruit.

MRS. PETERS

[*Starts to speak, glances up, where footsteps are heard in the room above. In a low voice.*] Mr. Peters says it looks bad for her. Mr. Henderson is awful sarcastic in a speech and he'll make fun of her sayin' she didn't wake up.

MRS. HALE

Well, I guess John Wright didn't wake when they was slipping that rope under his neck.

MRS. PETERS

No, it's strange. It must have been done awful crafty and still. They say it was such a—funny way to kill a man, rigging it all up like that.

MRS. HALE

That's just what Mr. Hale said. There was a gun in the house. He says that's what he can't understand.

MRS. PETERS

Mr. Henderson said coming out that what was needed for the case was a motive; something to show anger, or—sudden feeling.

MRS. HALE

[*Who is standing by the table.*] Well, I don't see any signs of anger around here. [*She puts her hand on the dish towel which lies on the table, stands looking down at table, one half of which is clean, the other half messy.*] It's wiped to here. [*Makes a move as if to finish work, then turns and looks at loaf of bread outside the breadbox. Drops towel. In that voice of coming-back to familiar things.*] Wonder how they are finding things upstairs. I hope she had it a little more red-up up there. You know, it seems kind of *sneaking*. Locking her up in town and then coming out here and trying to get her own house to turn against her!

MRS. PETERS

But Mrs. Hale, the law is the law.

MRS. HALE

I s'pose 'tis. [*Unbuttoning her coat.*] Better loosen up your things, Mrs. Peters. You won't feel them when you go out.

[Mrs. Peters *takes off her fur tippet, goes to hang it on hook at back of room, stands looking at the under part of the small corner table.*]

MRS. PETERS

She was piecing a quilt.

[*She brings the large sewing basket and they look at the bright pieces.*]

MRS. HALE

It's log cabin pattern. Pretty, isn't it? I wonder if she was goin' to quilt it or just knot it? [*Footsteps have been heard coming down the stairs. The* Sheriff *enters followed by* Hale *and the* City Attorney.]

SHERIFF

They wonder if she was going to quilt it or just knot it!

[*The men laugh, the women look abashed.*]

COUNTY ATTORNEY

[*Rubbing his hands over the stove.*] Frank's fire didn't do much up there, did it? Well, let's go out to the barn and get that cleared up.

[*The men go outside.*]

MRS. HALE

[*Resentfully.*] I don't know as there's anything so strange, our takin' up our time with little things while we're waiting for them to get the evidence. [*She sits down at the big table smoothing out a block with decision.*] I don't see as it's anything to laugh about.

MRS. PETERS

[*Apologetically.*] Of course they've got awful important things on their minds. [*Pulls up a chair and joins* Mrs. Hale *at the table.*]

MRS. HALE

[*Examining another block.*] Mrs. Peters, look at this one. Here, this is the one she was working on, and look at the sewing! All the rest of it has been so nice and even. And look at this! It's all over the place! Why, it looks as if she didn't know what she was about!

[*After she has said this they look at each other, then start to glance back at the door. After an instant* Mrs. Hale *has pulled at a knot and ripped the sewing.*]

MRS. PETERS

Oh, what are you doing, Mrs. Hale?

MRS. HALE

[*Mildly.*] Just pulling out a stitch or two that's not sewed very good. [*Threading a needle.*] Bad sewing always made me fidgety.

MRS. PETERS

[*Nervously.*] I don't think we ought to touch things.

MRS. HALE

I'll just finish up this end. [*Suddenly stopping and leaning forward.*] Mrs. Peters?

MRS. PETERS

Yes, Mrs. Hale?

MRS. HALE

What do you suppose she was so nervous about?

MRS. PETERS

Oh—I don't know. I don't know as she was nervous. I sometimes sew awful queer when I'm just tired. [Mrs. Hale *starts to say something, looks at* Mrs. Peters, *then goes on sewing.*] Well I must get these things wrapped up. They may be through sooner than we think. [*Putting apron and other things together.*] I wonder where I can find a piece of paper, and string.

MRS. HALE

In that cupboard, maybe.

MRS. PETERS

[*Looking in cupboard.*] Why, here's a bird-cage. [*Holds it up.*] Did she have a bird, Mrs. Hale?

MRS. HALE

Why, I don't know whether she did or not—I've not been here for so long. There was a man around last year selling canaries cheap, but I don't know as she took one; maybe she did. She used to sing real pretty herself.

MRS. PETERS

[*Glancing around.*] Seems funny to think of a bird here. But she must have had one, or why would she have a cage? I wonder what happened to it.

MRS. HALE

I s'pose maybe the cat got it.

MRS. PETERS

No, she didn't have a cat. She's got that feeling some people have about cats—being afraid of them. My cat got in her room and she was real upset and asked me to take it out.

MRS. HALE

My sister Bessie was like that. Queer, ain't it?

MRS. PETERS

[*Examining the cage.*] Why, look at this door. It's broke. One hinge is pulled apart.

MRS. HALE

[*Looking too.*] Looks as if someone must have been rough with it.

MRS. PETERS

Why, yes.
[*She brings the cage forward and puts it on the table.*]

MRS. HALE

I wish if they're going to find any evidence they'd be about it. I don't like this place.

MRS. PETERS

But I'm awful glad you came with me, Mrs. Hale. It would be lonesome for me sitting here alone.

MRS. HALE

It would, wouldn't it? [*Dropping her sewing.*] But I tell you what I do wish, Mrs. Peters. I wish I had come over sometimes when *she* was here. I—[*looking around the room*]—wish I had.

MRS. PETERS

But of course you were awful busy, Mrs. Hale—your house and your children.

MRS. HALE

I could've come. I stayed away because it weren't cheerful—and that's why I ought to have come. I—I've never liked this place. Maybe because it's down in a hollow and you don't see the road. I dunno what it is, but it's a lonesome place and always was. I wish I had come over to see Minnie Foster sometimes. I can see now—
[*Shakes her head.*]

MRS. PETERS

Well, you mustn't reproach yourself, Mrs. Hale. Somehow we just don't see how it is with other folks until—something comes up.

MRS. HALE

Not having children makes less work—but it makes a quiet house, and Wright out to work all day, and no company when he did come in. Did you know John Wright, Mrs. Peters?

MRS. PETERS

Not to know him; I've seen him in town. They say he was a good man.

MRS. HALE

Yes—good; he didn't drink, and kept his word as well as most, I guess, and paid his debts. But he was a hard man, Mrs. Peters. Just to pass the time of day with him—[*Shivers.*] Like a raw wind that gets to the bone. [*Pauses, her eye falling on the cage.*] I should think she would'a wanted a bird. But what do you suppose went with it?

MRS. PETERS

I don't know, unless it got sick and died.
[*She reaches over and swings the broken door, swings it again, both women watch it.*]

MRS. HALE

You weren't raised round here, were you? [Mrs. Peters *shakes her head.*] You didn't know—her?

MRS. PETERS

Not till they brought her yesterday.

MRS. HALE

She—come to think of it, she was kind of like a bird herself—real sweet and pretty, but kind of timid and—fluttery. How—she—did—change. [*Silence; then as if struck by a happy thought and relieved to get back to everyday things.*] Tell you what, Mrs. Peters, why don't you take the quilt in with you? It might take up her mind.

MRS. PETERS

Why, I think that's a real nice idea, Mrs. Hale. There couldn't possibly be any objection to it, could there? Now, just what would I take? I wonder if her patches are in here—and her things.
[*They look in the sewing basket.*]

MRS. HALE

Here's some red. I expect this has got sewing things in it. [*Brings out a fancy box.*] What a pretty box. Looks like something somebody would give you. Maybe her scissors are in here. [*Opens box. Suddenly puts her hand to her* nose.] Why—[Mrs. Peters *bends nearer, then turns her face away.*] There's something wrapped up in this piece of silk.

MRS. PETERS

Why, this isn't her scissors.

MRS. HALE

[*Lifting the silk.*] Oh, Mrs. Peters—it's—
[Mrs. Peters *bends closer.*]

MRS. PETERS

It's the bird.

MRS. HALE

[*Jumping up.*] But, Mrs. Peters—look at it! Its neck! Look at its neck! It's all—other side *to.*

MRS. PETERS

Somebody—wrung—its—neck.
[*Their eyes meet. A look of growing comprehension, or horror. Steps are heard outside. Mrs. Hale slips box under quilt pieces, and sinks into her chair. Enter Sheriff and County Attorney. Mrs. Peters rises.*]

COUNTY ATTORNEY

[*As one turning from serious things to little pleasantries.*] Well ladies, have you decided whether she was going to quilt it or knot it?

MRS. PETERS

We think she was going to—knot it.

COUNTY ATTORNEY

Well, that's interesting, I'm sure. [*Seeing the bird-cage.*] Has the bird flown?

MRS. HALE

[*Putting more quilt pieces over the box.*] We think the—cat got it.

COUNTY ATTORNEY

[*Preoccupied.*] Is there a cat?
[Mrs. Hale *glances in a quick covert way at* Mrs. Peters.]

MRS. PETERS

Well, not *now.* They're superstitious, you know. They leave.

COUNTY ATTORNEY

[*To* Sheriff Peters, *continuing an interrupted conversation.*] No sign at all of anyone having come from the outside. Their own rope. Now let's go up again and go over it piece by piece. [*They start upstairs.*] It would have to have been someone who knew just the—

[Mrs. Peters *sits down. The two women sit there not looking at one another, but as if peering into something and at the same time holding back. When they talk now it is in the manner of feeling their way over strange ground, as if afraid of what they are saying, but as if they can not help saying it.*]

MRS. HALE

She liked the bird. She was going to bury it in that pretty box.

MRS. PETERS

[*In a whisper.*] When I was a girl—my kitten—there was a boy took a hatchet, and before my eyes—and before I could get there—[*Covers her face an instant.*] If they hadn't held me back I would have—[*Catches herself, looks upstairs where steps are heard, falters weakly*]—hurt him.

MRS. HALE

[*With a slow look around her.*] I wonder how it would seem never to have had any children around. [*Pause.*] No, Wright wouldn't like the bird—a thing that sang. She used to sing. He killed that, too.

MRS. PETERS

[*Moving uneasily.*] We don't know who killed the bird.

MRS. HALE

I knew John Wright.

MRS. PETERS

It was an awful thing was done in this house that night, Mrs. Hale. Killing a man while he slept, slipping a rope around his neck that choked the life out of him.

MRS. HALE

His neck. Choked the life out of him.
[*Her hand goes out and rests on the bird-cage.*]

MRS. PETERS

We don't know who killed him. We don't *know.*

MRS. HALE

[*Her own feeling not interrupted.*] If there'd been years and years of nothing, then a bird to sing to you, it would be awful—still, after the bird was still.

MRS. PETERS

[*Something within her speaking.*] I know what stillness is. When we homesteaded in Dakota, and my first baby died—after he was two years old, and me with no other then—

MRS. HALE

[*Moving.*] How soon do you suppose they'll be through, looking for the evidence?

MRS. PETERS

I know what stillness is. [*Pulling herself back.*] The law has got to punish crime, Mrs. Hale.

MRS. HALE

[*Not as if answering that.*] I wish you'd seen Minnie Foster when she wore a white dress with blue ribbons and stood up there in the choir and sang. [*A look around the room.*] Oh, I *wish* I'd come over here once in a while! That was a crime! That was a crime! Who's going to punish that?

MRS. PETERS

[*Looking upstairs.*] We mustn't—take on.

MRS. HALE

I might have known she needed help! I know how things can be—for women. I tell you, it's queer, Mrs. Peters. We live close together and we live far apart. We all go through the same things—it's all just a different kind of the same thing. [*Brushes her eyes, noticing the bottle of fruit, reaches out for it.*] If I was you I wouldn't tell her her fruit was gone. Tell her it *ain't*. Tell her it's all right. Take this in to prove it to her. She—she may never know whether it was broke or not.

MRS. PETERS

[*Takes the bottle, looks about for something to wrap it in; takes petticoat from the clothes brought from the other room, very nervously begins winding this around the bottle. In a false voice.*] My, it's a good thing the men couldn't hear us. Wouldn't they just laugh! Getting all stirred up over a little thing like a—dead canary. As if that could have anything to do with—with—wouldn't they *laugh!*

[*The men are heard coming downstairs.*]

MRS. HALE

[*Under her breath.*] Maybe they would—maybe they wouldn't.

COUNTY ATTORNEY

No, Peters, it's all perfectly clear except a reason for doing it. But you know juries when it comes to women. If there was some definite thing. Something to show—something to make a story about—a thing that would connect up with this strange way of doing it—

[*The women's eyes meet for an instant. Enter* Hale *from outer door.*]

HALE

Well, I've got the team around. Pretty cold out there.

COUNTY ATTORNEY

I'm going to stay here awhile by myself. [*To the* Sheriff.] You can send Frank out for me, can't you? I want to go over everything. I'm not satisfied that we can't do better.

SHERIFF

Do you want to see what Mrs. Peters is going to take in?

[*The* Lawyer *goes to the table, picks up the apron, laughs.*]

COUNTY ATTORNEY

Oh, I guess they're not very dangerous things the ladies have picked out. [*Moves a few things about, disturbing the quilt pieces which cover the box. Steps back.*] No, Mrs. Peters doesn't need supervising. For that matter, a sheriff's wife is married to the law. Ever think of it that way, Mrs. Peters?

MRS. PETERS

Not—just that way.

SHERIFF

[*Chuckling.*] Married to the law. [*Moves toward the other room.*] I just want you to come in here a minute, George. We ought to take a look at these windows.

COUNTY ATTORNEY

[*Scoffingly.*] Oh, windows!

SHERIFF

We'll be right out, Mr. Hale.

[Hale *goes outside. The* Sheriff *follows the* County Attorney *into the other room. Then* Mrs. Hale *rises, hands tight together, looking intensely at* Mrs. Peters, *whose eyes make a slow turn, finally meeting* Mrs. Hale's. *A moment* Mrs. Hale *holds her, then her own eyes point the way to where the box is concealed. Suddenly* Mrs. Peters *throws back quilt pieces and tries to put the box in the bag she is wearing. It is too big. She opens box, starts to take bird out, cannot touch it, goes to pieces, stands there helpless. Sound of a knob turning in the other room. Mrs. Hale snatches the box and puts it in the pocket of her big coat. Enter County Attorney and Sheriff.*]

COUNTY ATTORNEY

[*Facetiously.*] Well, Henry, at least we found out that she was not going to quilt it. She was going to—what is it you call it, ladies?

MRS. HALE

[*Her hand against her pocket.*] We call it—knot it, Mr. Henderson.

QUESTIONS FOR READING, REASONING, AND REFLECTING

1. Explain the situation as the play begins.
2. Examine the dialogue of the men. What attitudes about themselves—their work, their abilities, their importance—are revealed? What is their collective opinion of women?
3. When Mrs. Hale and Mrs. Peters discover the dead bird, what do they begin to understand?
4. What other "trifles" in the kitchen provide additional evidence as to what has happened?
5. What trifles can be seen as symbols? What do they reveal about Mrs. Wright's life and character?
6. What is the play about primarily? Is it a murder mystery? Does it speak for feminist values? Is it about not seeing—not really knowing—others? In a few sentences, state what you consider to be the play's dominant theme. Then list the evidence you would use to support your conclusion.
7. Is there any sense in which one could argue that Mrs. Wright had a right to kill her husband? If you were a lawyer, how would you plan her defense? If you were on the jury, what sentence would you recommend?

1. Prepare an explication of either Amy Lowell's "Taxi" or Sir Walter Raleigh's "The Nymph's Reply to the Shepherd." You will need to explain both what the poem says and what it means—or what it accomplishes.

2. Analyze William Shakespeare's selection and ordering of metaphors in "Sonnet 73." What attitude toward death is developed through that selection and arrangement?

3. Analyze Mrs. Mallard's conflict, and decision about that conflict, as the basis for your understanding of the dominant theme in "The Story of an Hour."

4. You are Mrs. Wright's attorney (see *Trifles,* p. 701). Write your closing argument in her defense, explaining why only a light sentence is warranted for Mrs. Wright. Select details from the play to support your assertions about Mrs. Wright's character and motivation.

5. Explain what you think are the most important ideas about community in Ursula K. Le Guin's "The Ones Who Walk Away from Omelas."

6. John Donne in "The Bait" and Ogden Nash in "Love Under the Republicans (or Democrats)" also have responses to Marlowe's "The Passionate Shepherd to His Love." Select one of these poems, read and analyze it, and then evaluate its argument as a response to Marlowe's shepherd.

Credits

Applebaum, Anne. "Parallel Universes." *The Washington Post*, July 22, 2003. Reprinted by permission.

Barry, Dave. "Remote Control." Copyright © 2003 Tribune Media Services, Inc. All rights reserved. Reprinted by permission.

Bedau, Hugo Adam. *Death Is Different: Studies in the Morality, Law, and Politics of Capital Punishment.* Copyright © 1987 by Hugo Adam Bedau. Reprinted with the permission of Northeastern University Press.

Bernstein, Joseph. "Animal Rights vs. Animal Research: A Modest Proposal." 1996, v. 22. BMJ Publishing Group. Reprinted by permission.

Borjas, George J. "Heaven's Door." Copyright © 1999 by Princeton University Press. Reprinted by Bork, Robert H. "Addicted to Health." *The National Review.* Copyright © 1997 by National Review, Inc., 215 Lexington Avenue, New York, NY 10016. Reprinted by permission.

Boswell, Thomas. "Very Familar, Largely Unknown." *The Washington Post*, July 24, 2003. Reprinted by permission.

Bottum, J. "The Horror." Reprinted with permission of the author. Copyright © National Affairs Inc., *The Public Interest*, No. 150, Winter 2003, Washington D.C.

Brady, Sarah. "Gun Registration: It's Common Sense." *The Washington Post*, June 11, 1999. Reprinted by permission.

Brahmstedt, Christian. "Help Those Who Help, Not Hurt, Themselves" by Christian Brahmstedt, Letter to the Editor, *The Washington Post*, January 2, 1989. Copyright © *The Washington Post*.

Brzezinski, Zbigniew. "War and Football." *The Washington Post*, January 7, 2000. Reprinted by permission.

Califano, Joseph A., Jr. "Don't Make Teen Drinking Easier." *The Washington Post*, May 11, 2003. Reprinted by permission.

Carlson, Margaret. "A Case for National Id." Copyright © 2002 Time Inc. Reprinted by permission.

Catton, Bruce. Excerpts from "Grant and Lee: A Study in Contrasts" by Bruce Catton in *The American Story.* Copyright © U.S. Capital Historical Society, all rights reserved.

Centerwall, Brandon. "Television and Violent Crime" by Brandon Centerwall, reprinted from *The Public Interest*, No. 111 (Spring 1993), pp. 56-70. Copyright © 1993 by National Affairs.

Cohen, Richard. "Alone Together" by Richard Cohen, *Sunday Washington Post Magazine*, June 8, 1997. Copyright © 1997 Washington Post Writers Group. Reprinted by permission.

Cohen, Richard. "Kids Who Kill Are Still Kids." *The Washington Post*, August 3, 2001. Reprinted by permission.

Collier, Linda J. "Adult Crime: Adult Time." *The Washington Post*, 1998. Reprinted by permission.

Coontz, Stephanie. "Not Much Sense in Those Census Figures." *The Washington Post*, July 15, 2001. Reprinted by permission.

Cowan, Jonathan. "False Choices on Gun Safety." *The Washington Post*, October 10, 2002. Reprinted by permission.

Davis, Mark. "A Little Civility, Please." *The Fort Worth Star-Telegram*, March 5, 2003. Reprinted by permission.

Deford, Frank. "Solving the Title IX Problem." CNNSI; posted June 19, 2002. Reprinted courtesy of the author.

Dionne, E.J., Jr. "The Tucker Execution" by E.J. Dionne Jr. *The Washington Post*, February 10, 1998. Copyright © 1998, Washington Post Writers Group. Reprinted with permission.

Dionne, E.J., Jr. "Choose Your Utopia" by E.J. Dionne, Jr. *The Washington Post*, April 22, 1997. Copyright © 1997, Washington Post Writers Group. Reprinted with permission.

Ehrenreich, Barbara. "Will Women Still Need Men?" Copyright © 2002 Time Inc. Reprinted by permission.

Epstein, Richard. "The Next Rights Revolution." *The National Review.* Copyright © 1999 by National Review, Inc., 215 Lexington Avenue, New York, Ny 10016. Reprinted by permission.

Fields, Suzanne. "Bad Raps: Music Rebels in Their Thug Life." Reprinted with permission of *Insight*. Copyright © 2003 News World Communications, Inc. All rights reserved.

Folkerts, Jean and Stephen Lacy. "Box: TV Land Versus Real Life" from *The Media in Your Life: An Introduction to Mass Communication*, 2e. Published by Allyn and Bacon, Boston, MA. Copyright © 2001 by Pearson Education. Reprinted by permission of the publisher.

Fraser, Ronald. "Let the Going Get Tough—We Have Our SUVs." *The Washington Post*, Feb. 7, 2000. Reprinted by permission.

Fuentes, Annette. "Won't You Be My Neighbor?" from *American Demographics*. Copyright © 2000, Primedia Business Magazines and Media Inc. All rights reserved.

Fukuyama, Francis. "Neuropharmacology and the Control of Behavior" from *Our Posthuman Future*. Copyright © 2002 by Francis Fukuyama. Reprinted by permission of Farrar, Strauss, and Giroux, LLC.

Garfinkel, Simson. "Privacy Under Attack." *Database Nation*, 2000/2001. Reprinted by permission.

Gavora, Jessica. "Title IX Quota Creep" fr. *National Review*. On-line, June 11, 2002. Reprinted courtesy of United Feature Syndicate, Inc.

Gee, Chancellor. "My Plan to Put the College Back in College Sports." *The Washington Post*, September 21, 2003. Reprinted by permission.

Goodman, Ellen. "Fat Environment." *The Washington Post*, July 26, 2003. Reprinted by permission.

Goodman, Ellen. "Choosing Families." *The Washington Post*, November 24, 1998. Reprinted by permission.

Grebb, Michael. "Feds vs. First Amendment." *Cablevision* magazine, June 28, 1999. Reprinted from *Cablevision* magazine copyright © 1999 by Cahners Business Information. Used by permission.

Griswold, Daniel T. "Confronting the Problem of Illegal Mexican Migration to the U.S." *USA Today*, March 2003. Reprinted by permission.

Henig, Robin Marantz. "Think Baby Louise, and Don't Be Afraid." *The Washington Post*, July 13, 2003. Reprinted by permission.

Henninger, Daniel. "Doing the Numbers on Public Schools Adds Up to Zero." Reprinted with permission of *The Wall Street Journal*, copyright © June 26, 2003. Dow Jones & Company, Inc. All rights reserved.

Henslin, J. *Sociology: A Down to Earth Approach*, 5/e. Published by Allyn and Bacon, Boston, MA. Copyright © 2001 by Pearson Education. Reprinted by permission of the publisher.

Hentoff, Nat. "Expelling *Huck Finn*." *The Washington Post*, November 27, 1999. Reprinted by permission.

Hughes, Langston. "Early Autumn" from *Short Stories* by Langston Hughes. Copyright © 1996 by Ramona Bass and Arnold Rampersad. Reprinted by permission of Hill and Wang, a division of Farrar, Straus and Girioux, LLC.

Jeffrey, Nancy Ann. "A Rude Awakening." *The Wall Street Journal*, May 12, 2000. Reprinted by permission.

"Journalism and the Larger Truth." *Time*, July 2, 1984. Reprinted by permission.

Kahlenberg, Richard D. "Affirmative Action: There's a Third Way." *The Washington Post*, March 31, 2003. Reprinted by permission.

Kilbourne, Jean. "Deadly Persuasion: Why Women and Girls Must Fight the Addictive Power of Advertising." Reprinted with the permission of The Free Press, a division of Simon & Schuster Adult Publishing Group, from *Deadly Persuasion: Why Women and Girls Must Fight the Addictive Power of Advertising*. Copyright © 1999 by Jean Kilbourne. All rights reserved.

Kim, Jungwon. "The New Campus Raids." Reprinted with permission from the June 2, 2003 issue of *The Nation*.

Kimel, Martin. "Justice Filmed is Justice Distorted." *The Washington Post*, 2002. Reprinted by permission.

King, Martin Luther Jr. "I Have a Dream." Reprinted by arrangement with the Estate of Martin Luther King Jr., c/o Writers House as agents for the proprietor New York, NY. Copyright © 1963 Dr. Martin Luther King Jr., copyright renewed 1991 Coretta Scott King.

Kinsley, Michael. "Abolish Marriage." *The Washington Post*, July 3, 2003. Reprinted by permission.

Krauthammer, Charles. "Of Headless Mice . . . and Men." Copyright © 2002 Time Inc. Reprinted by permission.

Krauthammer, Charles. "The Greatness Gap." Copyright © 2002 Time Inc. Reprinted by permission.

Lawrence, Charles R. "Extending the Reach of Affirmative Action" by Charles R. Lawrence III and Mari J. Matsuda from *We Won't Go Back: Making the Case for Affirmative Action*. Copyright © 1997 by Charles R. Lawrence III and Mari J. Matsuda. Reprinted by permission of Houghton Mifflin Co. All rights reserved.

LeGuin, Ursula. "The Ones Who Walk Away from Omelas." Copyright © 1973 by Ursula K. LeGuin; first appeared in *New Dimensions 3*. Reprinted by permission of the author and the author's agent, Virginia Kidd.

Levine, Suzanne Braun. "Caution: Children Watching." Originally published in *Ms.* magazine, July/August 1994, reprinted by permission of the author.

Malkin, Michelle. "Parental Neglect Leads Teenagers to Be Seduced on the Internet." Reprinted with permission of *Insight*. Copyright © 2003 News World Communications, Inc. All rights reserved.

Mathabane, Mark. "If You Assign My Book, Don't Censor It." *The Washington Post*, November 28, 1999. Reprinted by permission.

Mitchell, Josh. "No American Foreign Policy and the King George Syndrome." *The Washington Post*, Aug. 10, 2003. Reprinted by permission.

Silver, Lee M. "Remaking Eden." Copyright © 1998 by Lee M. Silver. Reprinted by permisson of HarperCollins Publishers Inc. Avon Books.

Singer, P.A. and M. Siegler. "Euthanasia—A Critique." Copyright © 1990 Massachussetts Medial Society. All rights reserved.

Sprigge, Timothy. "A Reply to Joseph Bernstein." 1996, v. 22. BMJ Publishing Group. Reprinted by permission.

"Springing a Radioactive Leak." *Time*, February 8, 1982. Copyright © 1982 by Time, Inc. Reprinted by permission.

Steele, Shelby. "A Victory for White Guilt." Reprinted from *The Wall Street Journal*, Copyright © June 26, 2003. Dow Jones & Company, Inc. All rights reserved.

Steinberg, Mark. " 'Numbed Down' in America." Copyright © *The Washington Post*, June 17, 2000. Reprinted by permission.

Steinem, Gloria. "Supremacy Crimes," Aug/Sep 1999. Reprinted by permission.

Sullivan, Andrew. "The Conservative Case for Gay Marriage." *Time*, June 30, 2003. Reprinted by permission.

Tackett, Michael. "President Sidesteps Exit Strategy Issue." *The Chicago Tribune*, Sept. 8, 2003. Reprinted by permission.

Thurow, Lester C. "Why Women Are Paid Less Than Men." *The New York Times*, March 8, 1981. Copyright © 1981 by The New York Times Company. Reprinted by permission.

Tuchman, Barbara W. "The Persistence of Unwisdom in Government." Reprinted by the permission of Russell & Volkening as agents for the author. Copyright © 1980 by Barbara Tuchman, renewed in 1998 by Lester Tuchman.

van den Haag, Ernest. From "The Ultimate Punishment: A Defense" by Ernest van den Haag, *Harvard Law Review*, May 7, 1986. Copyright © 1986 by the Harvard Law Association. Reprinted by permission of the author.

Waite, Linda J. "Social Science Finds: Marriage Matters." From *The Responsive Community*, Vol. 6, issue 3, Summer 1996. Copyright © 1996 by *The Responsive Community*. Reprinted with permission.

Wattenberg, Ben, "Don't Wobble on Immigration." Reprinted by permission.

Weinstein. "Tiny Cell Phone or Big Brother?" Reprinted from *Wired News*, www. wired.com. Copyright © 2003 Wired Digital Inc., a Lycos Network Company. All rights reserved.

Wilkins, Julia. "Protecting Our Children from Internet Smut: Moral Duty or Moral Panic? " by Julia Wilkins, *The Humanist*, Sept./Oct 1997. Reprinted by permission of Julia Wilkins, a special education teacher in Buffalo, NY.

Will, George F. "Tobacco Road" by George F. Will, *The Washington Post,* February 16, 1992, Washington Post Writers Group. Reprinted with permission.

Wilson, James. "A New Strategy in the War on Drugs." *The Wall Street Journal*, April 13, 2000. Reprinted from *The Wall Street Journal*. Copyright © 2000. Dow Jones & Company, Inc. All rights reserved.

Winn, Marie. "Verbal and Nonverbal Thought" from *The Plug-In Drug*, revised edition by Marie Winn. Copyright © 1977, 1985 by Marie Winn Miller. Used by permission of Viking Penguin, a division of Penguin Putnam, Inc.

Wright, Karen. "Guns, Lies, and Video." *Discover*, April 2003. Copyright © 2003 Karen Wright. This article first appeared in *Discover* magazine.

Wyszomierski, Teressa. "The Case for Letting Cameras into the Sacred Jury Room." The *Chicago Tribune*. Copyright © 2003 Chicago Tribune Company. All rights reserved. Used with permission.

Index